# Census Substitutes & State Census Records

♦ ♦ 3rd Edition ♦ ♦

## Volume 2

## Southeastern States

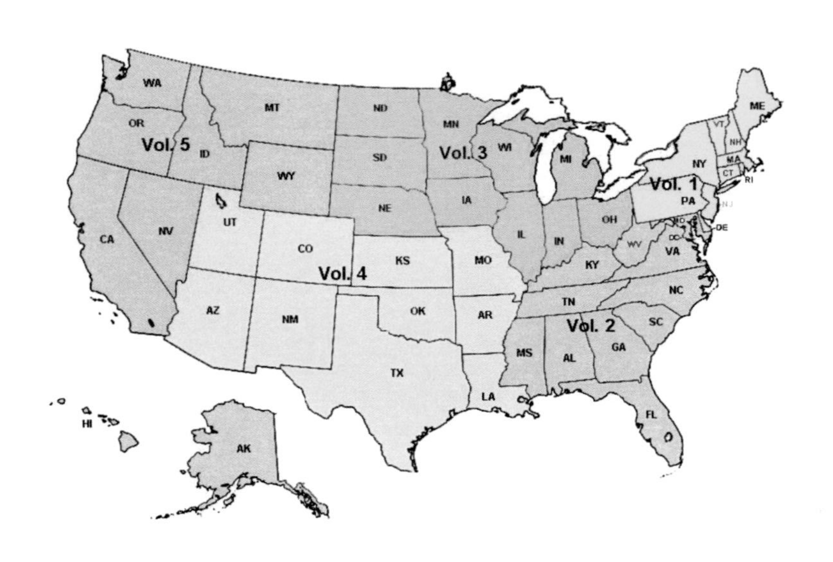


by


**William Dollarhide**

Published by Family Roots Publishing Co., LLC
PO Box 1682
Orting, WA 98360-1682
**www.familyrootspublishing.com**

Library of Congress Control Number: 2020934867

ISBN (Paperback): 978-1-62859-286-3
ISBN (eBook): 978-62859-287-0

Recommended Citation:
***Census Substitutes & State Census Records, 3rd Edition,***
***Volume Two – Southeastern States,*** by William Dollarhide,
publ. Family Roots Publishing Co., LLC, Orting, WA, 2020, 303 pages.

*Printed in the United States of America*

# Contents – Vol. 2

## Southeastern States

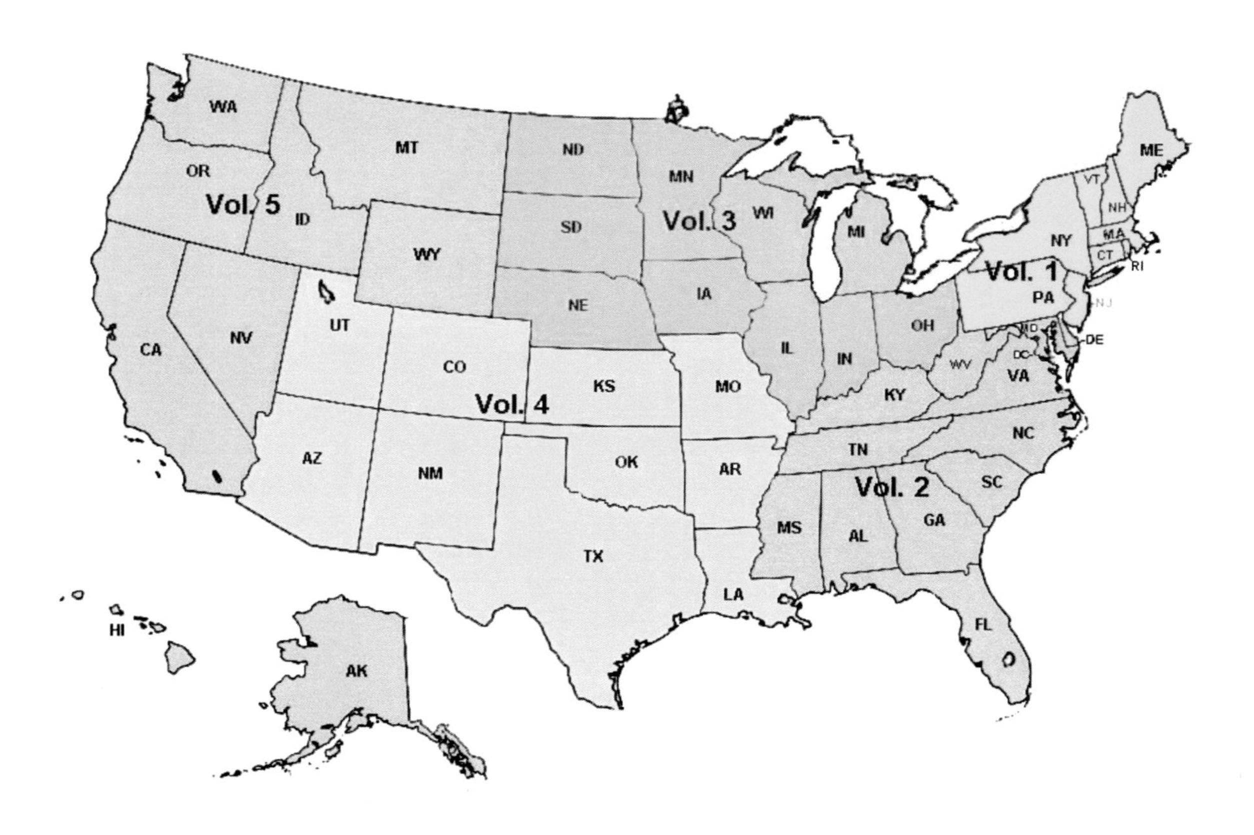


## State Finder, Vols. 1-5

# Foreword

## by Leland K. Meitzler

In late 2003 Bill Dollarhide came by my office and asked if I had any ideas for *Genealogy Bulletin* articles. As it turned out, I had just finished organizing materials for a lecture on state and territorial census records and had a file folder full of data I had collected over the years on my desk. I suggested he put something together on that subject and gave him the file to review. After looking through my file, Bill decided that we needed to identify the many substitutes to censuses (statewide tax lists, voter registration lists, and such), as he quickly noted that a number of states did not take any state or territorial censuses at all. Bill began compiling a bibliography of not only extant state and territorial censuses, but substitute lists as well.

Researched and compiled by region, he added timelines of historical references to show the jurisdictions in place at the time of each census. Compiling the material by region was a logical way to go, as we quickly realized that in most cases, it would have been difficult to write about one state without writing about those surrounding it. So, if you start with Maine, for example, the adjoining state of New Hampshire would be the next chapter, then Vermont, Massachusetts, and so on.

Much of the data found in the two-volume First Edition (2008) was initially published in serial form in the old *Genealogy Bulletin (1983-2006).* That said, the District of Columbia, for which there are many excellent sources, was never published. Also never published was The Oregon Country chapter. However, both chapters were included in the First Edition.

In the three-volume Second Edition (2016), numerous online sources were added, reflecting the ongoing efforts of both public and private companies to digitize relevant records.

In this new five-volume Third Edition (2020), the Northeastern States (Volume 1) adds seven (7) U.S. Territories for the first time. In addition, the *Western & Pacific States (V*olume 5) has an all-new *Maps, Descriptions, and Internet Access for the U.S. Federal Censuses, 1790-1950;* followed by an updated *U.S. Census Substitutes* chapter. Each of the 50 states & DC in this 3rd Edition has many more citations for newly added online databases and recently digitized microfilm collections – in just three years, the number went from 3,865 to 8,067 hyperlinks.

Bill also spent countless hours compiling tabulated charts that may be worth the cost of this book all by themselves. The first, found on page 13, is a chart for the non-state census states. There happens to be 13 of them (including the District of Columbia). This chart lists the states and the years covered by census substitutes. The second chart, found on pages 14-15, lists the 38 states that have extant colonial, pre-statehood, territorial, and state censuses, complete with the census year, and an indication if the census is available online as of the date of publication. The third chart, found on page 16, shows in graphic form the states that had censuses taken in common years – "on the fives." Census dates for some states are within a range. The fourth chart, on page 17, shows the availability of federal censuses for all states, 1790-1950.

Note that the title of this series of volumes is *Census Substitutes & State Census Records,* which reflects the fact that the volumes really contain a list of census substitutes, with state censuses turning out to be in the minority. Substitutes outnumber censuses by a factor of ten to one! However, the state censuses identified in this series are by far the most complete lists of Colonial, Territorial, or State Censuses published to date.

State and Territorial Censuses have long fascinated me. Many were taken in order to get congress to allow statehood. Some territories would take censuses on a nearly annual basis, in the attempt to show that they had the population base necessary to justify statehood.

Other states, like New York, had authorization of non-federal censuses written into their state constitutions. New York was one of the most prolific when it came to state censuses, as it produced numerous schedules, most falling on the ubiquitous "fives." Today we have extant New York censuses for 1825, 1835, 1845, 1855, 1865, 1875, 1892, 1905, 1915, and 1925. Some of the early years are not complete, but what is available is certainly useful. The 1925 New York census was taken as well as any other, and the population returns are largely legible and complete. However, the census was wrought with scandal, leaving New Yorkers with a taste of bitterness for such things. To make a long story short, it seems that the New York Secretary of State, a former Dean of Home Economics at Syracuse University, Florence Elizabeth Smith Knapp, took nepotism to a whole new level. As the state official in charge of the 1925 census, she put family and friends on the payroll, and while this was not illegal, most of these folks did little or nothing to earn their salaries. Even her 74-year old mother, Ella Smith, enjoyed a non-working stint as an assistant supervisor. Florence's stepdaughter, Clara Blanche Knapp, a professor at Middlebury College in Vermont, was on the payroll for over $5,000 in income, while never leaving the state of Vermont. Moreover, checks written to both Ella and Blanche seemed to have been endorsed into Florence E.S. Knapp's bank account. Numerous other family members and friends were paid substantial sums for non-work. In 1928, Mrs. Knapp finally went on trial for her misdeeds, and found guilty of first-degree grand larceny for misappropriation of state funds. She served 30 days in the Albany Jail. She could have gotten 10 years. So ended the brief political career of the first woman ever to be elected to state-wide office in New York. So also ended the state censuses of New York State.

Iowa, Kansas, Rhode Island, Florida, North Dakota, and South Dakota also took censuses up through 1925. South Dakota and Florida even took censuses in 1935 and 1945! The real value of state censuses is found in the numerous schedules enumerated in the mid-nineteenth century. Thirty-eight states took non-federal censuses that are still extant today.

And then there are the substitutes. They are of prime importance, since 12 states, as well as the District of Columbia, took no state censuses at all. And even if your ancestors lived in a state where censuses were taken "on the fives," census substitutes are helpful, especially if the family was on the move.

Although Mr. Dollarhide has used all kinds of substitutes throughout this volume, more attention has been given to tax lists, voter registration rolls, vital records, directories, statewide probate indexes, land records, and even military censuses, than most others. These records are often easily accessible and using this guide, you will be able to quickly find them for your own use. You are in for a treat, so sit back and look up the states of your ancestors. You will find information on records you never knew existed. Then… go get the records, and happy hunting!

- Leland K. Meitzler
Publisher

# Introduction

## Census Substitutes & State Census Records

Census Substitutes are those name lists derived from tax lists, directories, military lists, land ownership lists, voter registrations, and other compilations of names of residents for an entire state, or part of a state. A census substitute can be used to determine the names of residents in a given area when a federal or state census is missing. Moreover, a census substitute can be used as an alternative name list; confirming, contradicting, or adding to information found in a federal or state census.

This book identifies at least ten times the number of Census Substitute titles than any previous work ever published. All states are represented with significant alternative name lists – name lists that stop time for a certain year and place and name the residents of a certain place. Since all of these name lists are specific to a certain year, they are listed within each state category in chronological order. Incorporated into the lists are any State Census titles – a reference to a state census taken for a specific year.

### Federal vs. State Censuses

Federal Censuses have their origins in the constitutional provision for apportionment of the U.S. House of Representatives. The first federal census was taken in 1790, and beginning about the same time, state censuses were conducted for the same reason, that is, apportionment of the various state legislatures.

Although the primary purpose of all censuses was to simply count the population, beginning with the first federal census of 1790, more information than a simple tally was added. This included the name and age of a person and progressively more details about a household for each subsequent census year. State censuses followed this same pattern.

State censuses usually add even more information than the federal censuses, and as a result, they are premier genealogical resources. Except in cases where a federal census is lost, state census records are not substitutes for the federal censuses – state censuses were almost always taken between federal census years, and usually add unique information and details about a household not found in a federal census. If a state census exists between federal census years, it may add marginally to the knowledge one gains about a family. But, more often, it will add critical information, such as more exact dates of birth, marriages, deaths; plus, additional children, different residences, other relatives living with a family; and more.

### Non-State Census States

Thirteen (13) states (including DC) have never conducted a state-sponsored census. For these Non-State Census States, this review attempts to identify as many census substitutes as possible. In some cases, the census substitutes are for a single county within a state, and by listing multiple county name lists for about the same time period, regional coverage is achieved.

For an overview of the Non-State Census States, see Table 1 (page 13) showing the years for which census substitutes exist. More detail for each census substitute year indicated on the table is covered in the bibliographic sections.

## State Census States

Thirty-eight (38) states have conducted censuses separate from the federal censuses. The number of censuses taken by each of the State Census States ranges from one (1) census year, e.g., the 1852 California; to twenty-four (24) census years, e.g., the 1792-1866 Mississippi territorial/state censuses. For this review, all of the state-sponsored censuses are identified, plus, to a lesser degree than the non-state census states, census substitutes available. See Table 2 (pages 14-15) for an overview of the State Census States, the year for each surviving census for a state; and an indication of which specific years are now available online as digitized databases.

## Locating the Extant State Census Records

Generally, state censuses were conducted from the time of territorial status or early statehood up until about 1905, but a few continued until 1925, 1935, or 1945. The last state censuses taken by any of the states was in 1945 (Florida and South Dakota). Due to budget restraints, the Depression Era of the 1930s was a contributing factor to states ending their census-taking endeavors. Eventually, all states of the Union stopped using the population figures from state censuses and began using the federal census figures for apportionment of their state legislatures.

While the surviving federal census manuscripts are all located mostly in one repository (the National Archives), state census manuscripts are spread across the country in the various state archives or local repositories. The accessibility of state censuses may be just as good as federal censuses – but one needs to know where they are located first.

Beginning in 1941, the U.S. Bureau of the Census issued a bibliographic report attempting to identify all known state censuses, those undertaken by the various states separate from the federal censuses since 1790.[1] Prepared by Henry J. Dubester of the Library of Congress, the report was the first known attempt to research all of the state constitutions and subsequent laws related to state censuses for all of the states. The Dubester report sought, first, to identify what state censuses had ever been authorized by a state constitution or legislature; and second, to identify what census manuscripts still survive. The identification of extant state censuses was very incomplete, due to the war and under-funding of the project.

However, Dubester's review of each state's constitutional provisions for taking state censuses still stands as the best overview of what state censuses were ever authorized. The report cites the specific articles of the state constitutions or the actual state laws relating to censuses for all states.

Unfortunately, the fact that a state legislature authorized a state census does not mean one was actually taken. For example, the State Constitution of California of 1849 authorized a census in the years 1852 and 1855 and each ten years thereafter, all for the purpose of apportionment of its state legislature. Yet, only one was ever taken, that for 1852. Later, the California Constitution of 1879 provided that the decennial national census serve as the basis for legislative apportionment.[2]

This was fairly typical of all states. Even in those states for which several decades of state censuses now survive, they eventually got out of the census business, turning to the federal decennial censuses to determine apportionment. For example, New York took state censuses from 1825 and every ten years thereafter until 1925, yet, in 1938, New York decided to use the federal decennial censuses thereafter.[3]

Since the Dubester report, there have been several attempts to list all known state censuses, where they are located, and the contents of the census name lists. All of these attempts differ dramatically, because some of the lists rely on the Dubester report, which may have been accurate in identifying which state censuses were ever authorized but was not nearly complete in identifying the extant manuscripts of state census records. For example, Table 4-8 of *The Source,*[4] seems to use the census years cited in the Dubester report for "authorized state censuses" rather than those actually extant. There are lists of state censuses for each state in *The Red Book*,[5] but are only a slight improvement over those found in *The Source*. And, several Internet sites offer lists of state censuses, all of which seem to take data previously published in the *Source* or *The Red Book*, and similar publications.

Based on survey results from all states, the Family History Library prepared a two-volume publication, *U.S. State and Special Census Register: A Listing of Family History Library Microfilm Numbers,* compiled by G. Eileen Buckway and Fred Adams, a revised edition published by the FHL in 1992 (FHL book 973 X2 v. 1 & 2, and fiche #6104851 (vol. 1) and #6104852 (vol. 2). This is a particularly good guide to military censuses, school censuses, and special censuses of American Indian tribes. As a guide to state censuses, however, the list is incomplete. Since the results of the surveys from each of the states were only partially successful, there are many omissions.

Clearly, the best list of state censuses to date is Ann S. Lainhart, *State Census Records*, published by Genealogical Publishing Co., Inc., Baltimore, in 1992. The book identifies state censuses in 43 states, including 5 states without state censuses (but have major state-wide census substitutes available). For the 38 state census states, the lists generally do not include colonial or pre-territorial censuses. With a few exceptions, census substitutes such as those compiled from tax lists, voter registration lists, military lists, or other name sources, are also not included. Still, Lainhart's book stands as the most complete list ever done.

At the time when most of the previous state census lists were put together, there were some research tools unavailable to the authors. Today, the Internet as a resource for finding place-specific records is overwhelming. And, special tools such as the Periodical Source Index (PERSI)[6] which indexes articles in over 11,000 different genealogical periodicals (by subject, place, and surname) gives a big boost to the task of finding references to relevant articles using keywords such as "state census," "territorial census," or "tax list." In addition, the State Archives and/or State Libraries where obscure census originals and substitute name lists reside often have a website with an online searchable catalog.

For any genealogical research project, it helps to be close to the Family History Library (FHL) in Salt Lake City. But from any place where a researcher has access to the Internet, the FamilySearch™ online catalog as a genealogical research tool has no equal. Searching for published state censuses and census substitutes in the FHL catalog will not bring up every extant resource, but it is more complete than any other library in the world.

## The Evolution of Regional Chapters to State Chapters

In the 2008 First Edition of this work, the two volumes had chapters for six (6) Eastern Regions and five (5) Western Regions of the United States.

For the 2016 Second Edition, the three volumes included an Eastern volume with five (5) regions; the Central Volume had three (3) regions; and the Western volume had four (4) regions; plus, an all-new Nationwide Chapter was added to the Western volume. A timeline for each region was prepared to put the area into a historical perspective from a genealogist's point of view.

This 2020 Third Edition was expanded to five volumes, each volume a region of the United States. Therefore, the content of each state's review now includes much of the content that was done at the regional level in the earlier editions, e.g., there is now a Timeline specific to each state.

The organization of the state bibliographic lists has changed as well. The Second Edition had several category listings for bibliographic entries, including State Resource Centers, Ancestry.com, Family-Search.org, and others. This Third Edition has just one (1) listing where all databases from any provider are presented in chronological order.

## About PERSI

PERSI (PERiodical Source Index) is a digitized database project of the Allen County Public Library (ACPL), Fort Wayne, IN. Since 1986, the PERSI extractors have indexed article titles, places, and surnames from over 11,000 genealogical & historical periodicals. The PERSI database is currently available online through the FindMyPast.com subscription website.

A number of printed articles found in periodicals were included in the state bibliography listings that follow. The Fort Wayne library has an online order form for requesting a printed copy of any article indexed in the PERSI database, see **http://genealogycenter.org/docs/default-source/resources/articlerequest.pdf?sfvrsn=2**.

## Federal Censuses

Since the Second Edition was published in 2016, the digital images of all federal censuses 1790-1940 became accessible to the public via the Family History Library online catalog. It is now possible to view the digital images for any state's federal censuses separate from the various indexed databases at FamilySearch.org, Ancestry.com, My Heritage.com, et al. This meant adding the URL link for each state's digitized federal censuses in this Third Edition.

The Nationwide Chapter (Vol. 5) was completely reorganized into Part 1: *Maps, Descriptions, and Internet Access for the U.S. Federal Censuses, 1790-1950;* and Part 2: *U.S. Census Substitutes.* To review the federal censuses in more detail, refer to *The Census Book*[7] for each census year. The new 2019 *Census Book* has a detailed review of published federal censuses online, 1790-1950.

The maps of the changing county boundaries for all of the states shown in *Map Guide to the U.S. Federal Census, 1790-1920*[8] should also be helpful for reviewing substitute or state census years between federal census years.

- bill$hide

---

**Notes:**

1. *State Censuses: An Annotated Bibliography of Censuses of Population Taken After the Year 1790 by States and Territories of the United States*, prepared by Henry J. Dubester, Chief, Census Library Project, Library of Congress, published Washington, DC, by United States Department of Commerce, Bureau of the Census, 1941, rev. 1948.

2. Dubester, *State Censuses*, p. 3.

3. Dubester, *State Censuses*, p. 50.

4. *The Source: A Guidebook of American Genealogy*, first edition, edited by Arlene Eakle and Johni Cerny, published by Ancestry, Inc., Salt Lake City, 1984.

5. *The Red Book: American State, County & Town Sources*, edited by Alice Eichholz, rev. ed., published by Ancestry, Inc., Salt Lake City, UT, 1992.

6. Allen County Public Library, *Periodical Source Index (PERSI)*, updated semi-annually. [database online at various contracted websites] Original data: Allen County Public Library. Periodical Source Index, Fort Wayne, IN: Allen County Public Library Foundation, 1985- .

7. *The Census Book: Facts, Schedules & Worksheets for the U.S Federal Censuses,* by William Dollarhide, publ. Family Roots Publishing Co., Orting, WA, 2019, 245 pages. See **www.familyrootspublishing.com/store/product_view.php?id=3643.**

8. *Map Guide to the U.S. Federal Censuses, 1790-1920,* by William Thorndale and William Dollarhide, published by Genealogical Publishing Co., Inc., Baltimore, 1987-2016, 445 pages. See **www.familyrootspublishing.com/store/product_view.php?id=67.**

**Table 1 – Non-State Census States.** The following 13 states (including DC) have never conducted a state-sponsored census (or no state census survives). Census Substitutes for each state are shown for a range of years. Refer to the bibliographic listings for details about each.

| State | Terr. | State | Years for which Census Substitutes are Available |
|---|---|---|---|
| **Alaska** | 1912 | 1959 | 1870, 1873, 1878, 1885, 1887, 1890-1895, 1902-1912, 1905, 1908-1914, 1910- 1929, 1913-1916, 1917-1918, 1947, 1950, 1959-1986, and 1960-1985. |
| **Delaware** | — | 1787 | 1609-1888, 1646-1679, 1680-1934, 1682-1759, 1684-1693, 1726, 1755, 1759, 1779, 1782, 1785, 1790, 1800, 1807, 1850-1860, and 1862-1872. |
| **District* of Columbia** | 1801 | 1871* | 1803, 1807, 1818, 1867, 1878, 1885, 1888, 1894, 1897, 1905-1909, 1912-1913, 1915, 1917, 1919, and 1925. |
| **Idaho** | 1863 | 1890 | 1863, 1865-1874, 1871-1881, 1880, 1890, 1911-1937, 1911-1950, and 1930. |
| **Kentucky** | — | 1792 | 1773-1780, 1774-1796, 1780-1909, 1781-1839, 1782-1787, 1782-1875, 1787, 1787-1811, 1787-1875, 1788-1875, 1789-1882, 1792-1830, 1792-1913, 1792-1796, 1793-1836, 1794-1805, 1794-1817, 1795, 1796-1808, 1797-1866, 1800, 1820-1900, 1851-1900, 1859-1860, 1860-1936, 1861-1865, 1862-1866, and 1895- 1896. |
| **Montana** | 1864 | 1889 | 1860, 1856-1993, 1864-1872, 1868-1869, 1868-1929, 1870, 1880, 1870-1957, 1872- 1900, 1879-1880, 1881-1928, 1881-2000, 1891-1929, 1894, 1913, 1906- 1917, 1909- 1910, 1917-1918, 1921, and 1930-1975. |
| **New Hampshire** | — | 1788 | 1648, 1709. 1723, 1736, 1740, 1763, 1767, 1775, 1776, 1779, 1789, 1795-1816, 1797, 1802, 1803, 1821, 1826, 1833, 1836, 1838, 1849, 1855 & 1865 MA, 1860, 1862-1866, 1903, and 1902-1921 |
| **Ohio** | 1787 | 1803 | 1787-1840, 1787-1871, 1788-1799, 1788-1820, 1790, 1800-1803, 1801-1814, 1801-1824, 1802, 1803-1827, 1804, 1807, 1810, 1812, 1816-1838, 1816-1838, 1825, 1827, 1832-1850, 1833-1994, 1835, 1846-1880, 1851-1900, 1851-1907, and 1907. |
| **Pennsylvania** | — | 1787 | 1682-1950, 1759, 1680-1938, 1680s-1900s, 1760s-1790s, 1700s, 1780, 1798, 1740- 1900, 1887-1893, and 1870. |
| **Texas** | — | 1845 | 1736-1838, 1700s-1800s, 1756-1830s, 1782-1836, 1809-1836, 1814-1909, 1821-1846, 1826, 1826-1835, 1820s-1846, 1820-1829, 1826-1836, 1829-1836, 1830-1839, 1835, 1835-1846, 1836, 1836-1935, 1837-1859, 1840-1849, 1840, 1846, 1837-1910, 1851-1900, 1858, 1861-1865, 1863, 1865-1866, 1867, 1874, 1882-1895, 1884, 1889-1894, 1890, 1914, 1917-1918, 1896-1948, and 1964-1968. |
| **Vermont** | — | 1791 | 1770s-1780s, 1700s-1800s, 1654-1800, 1710-1753, 1721-1800, 1770-1832, 1771, 1782, 1788, 1793, 1796-1959, 1800s-1870, 1807, 1813, 1815, 1816, 1827-1833, 1828, 1832, 1843, 1852-1959, 1855-1860, 1861-1866, 1865, 1869, 1871-1908, 1874, 1880-1881, 1881-1882, 1882-1883, 1883-1884, 1884, 1887-1888, 1888, 1889, and 1895-1924. |
| **Virginia** | — | 1788 | 1600s-1700s, 1600s, 1619-1930, 1623-1990, 1623-1800, 1632-1800, 1654-1800, 1704-1705, 1720, 1736-1820, 1740, 1744-1890, 1760, 1769-1800, 1779, 1779-1978, 1779-1860, 1782-1785, 1785, 1787, 1809-1848, 1810, 1815, 1828-1938, 1835, 1835-1941, 1840, 1861, 1861-1865, 1852, 1853-1896, and 1889-1890. |
| **West Virginia** | — | 1863 | 1600s-1900s, 1777-1850, 1787, 1782-1907, 1782-1850, 1782-1860, 1782, 1783-1900, 1783-1850, 1785-1850, 1787,1850, 1789-1850, 1792-1850, 1797-1899, 1797-1851, 1799-1850, 1800, 1801-1850, 1810, 1811-1850, 1862-1866, 1863-1900, and 1899-1900. |

From ***Census Substitutes & State Census Records*** by William Dollarhide, publ. Family Roots Publishing Co., Orting WA

### Table 2 – State Census States – Alabama to Michigan

The following 38 states have state-sponsored censuses available:

| State | Year a Terr. | Year a State | Years for which State Censuses are available (underlined year = an online database is available) | Notes |
|---|---|---|---|---|
| Alabama | 1817 | 1819 | **Colony:** 1706 1721 1764 1785 1786-1803 **AL Territory:** 1801* 1808* 1809* 1810* 1816* 1818 **State:** 1820** 1821 1823 1832 1838 1844 1850** 1855 1866. | * as part of MS Terr. ** separate from federal. |
| Arizona | 1863 | 1912 | **AZ Territory:** 1831 1864 1866 1867* 1869* 1874* 1876* 1882* | *1-2 counties only |
| Arkansas | 1819 | 1836 | **Colony:** 1686-1791 **AR Territory:** 1814* 1823 1827 1829 1833 1835 **State:** 1838 1854 1865 | * as part of MO Terr. |
| California | — | 1850 | **Colony:** 1790 1790-1796 1822 1834 1836 1837 **State:** 1852 only | |
| Colorado | 1861 | 1876 | **CO Territory:** 1861 1866* **State:** 1885 | * 2 counties only |
| Connecticut | -- | 1788 | **Colony:** 1762 **State:** 1917* | * Military census, males over 16 |
| Florida | 1822 | 1845 | **Colony:** 1759 1763-1779 1783-1814 **FL Territory:** 1825 1838 **State:** 1845** 1855 1864* 1867 1875 1885 1895 1935 1945 | * Military census ** Statehood census |
| Georgia | — | 1788 | 1800 federal* **State:** Partial lists only: 1827 1838 1845 1852 1859 1879 1890 federal** 1890 (statewide reconstruction). | * Oglethorpe Co only ** Washington Co only |
| Hawaii | 1900 | 1959 | **Kingdom of Hawaii:** 1840-1866 1878 1890 1896 | |
| Illinois | 1809 | 1818 | **IL Territory:** 1810 **State:** 1818 1820* 1825 1830* 1835 1840* 1845 1855 1865. | * separate from federal |
| Indiana | 1800 | 1816 | **IN Territory:** 1807. **State:** A few townships only: 1857 1871 1877 1883 1889 1901 1913 1919 1931 | |
| Iowa | 1838 | 1846 | As part of **WI Territory:** 1836 **IA Territory:** 1838 **State:** 1844 1845 1847 1849 1851 1852 1853 1854 1856 1859 1873 1875 1885 1888 1893 1895 1896 1897 1905 1915 1925 | |
| Kansas | 1854 | 1861 | **KS Territory:** 1855 1856 1857 1858 1859 **State:** 1865 1875 1885 1895 1905 1915 1925 | |
| Louisiana | 1809 | 1812 | **Orleans District:** 1804 **State:** 1833 1837 1890 federal* | *Ascension Parish only |
| Maine | — | 1820 | 1837 only. | |
| Maryland | — | 1788 | 1776 1778 1783* | * Tax list |
| Massachusetts | — | 1788 | 1855 1865 | |
| Michigan | 1805 | 1837 | **MI Territory:** 1827 1834 **State:** 1837 1845 1854 1864 1874 1884 1894 | |

From *Census Substitutes & State Census Records* by William Dollarhide, publ. Family Roots Publishing Co., Orting WA

## Table 2 – State Census States – Minnesota to Wyoming

Continuation of states with state-sponsored censuses available:

| State | Year a Terr. | Year a State | Years for which State Censuses are available (underlined year = an online database is available) | Notes |
|---|---|---|---|---|
| Minnesota | 1849 | 1858 | **MN Territory:** 1849 1853 1855 1857* **State:** 1865 1875 1885 1895 1905 | * special federal |
| Mississippi | 1798 | 1817 | **Colony:** 1792** **MS Territory:** 1801 1805 1809 1810 1813 1815 1816 1817 **State:** 1818 1820* 1822 1823 1824 1825 1830* 1837 1840* 1841 1845 1850* 1853 1857 1866 | * separate from federal<br>** Natchez District only |
| Missouri | 1805 | 1821 | **Colony:** 1752 1791 1797 **MO Territory:** 1817 1818 1819 **State:** 1844* 1845* 1846* 1852* 1856* 1864* 1868* 1876** | * 1-2 counties only<br>** 28 counties |
| Nebraska | 1854 | 1867 | **NE Territory**: 1854 1855 1856 1865 **State:** Lancaster & Cass Co Only: 1874 1875 1876 1877 1878 1881 1882 1883 1884 1885 | |
| Nevada | 1861 | 1864 | **NV Territory:** 1861 1862 1863 **State:** 1864 1875 | |
| New Jersey | — | 1787 | 1855 1865 1875* 1885 1895 1905 1915 | * a few townships only |
| New Mexico | 1850 | 1912 | **Colony:** 1600 1750 1790 **Territory:** 1885 | |
| New York | — | 1788 | 1825 1835 1845 1855 1865 1875 1892 1905 1915 1925 | |
| North Carolina | — | 1789 | **Pre-statehood:** 1784 -1787. | |
| North Dakota | 1861* | 1889 | **Dakota Territory:** 1885 **State:** 1905 (statistics only) 1915 1925 | * Dakota Territory |
| Oklahoma | 1890 | 1907 | **OK Territory**: 1890* **State:** 1907 federal (Seminole Co. only) | * separate from federal |
| Oregon | 1848 | 1859 | **OR Provisional Territory:** 1842 1843 1845 1846 **OR Territory:** 1849 1853 1854 1855 1856 1857 1858 1859 **State:** 1865* 1875* 1885* 1895* 1905 | * indexes for a few counties only |
| Rhode Island | — | 1790 | 1865 1875 1885 1905 1915 1925 1935 | |
| South Carolina | — | 1788 | 1829 1839 1869 1875 | |
| South Dakota | 1861* | 1889 | **Dakota Territory:** 1885 **State:** 1895 1905 1915 1925 1935 1945 | * Dakota Territory |
| Tennessee | 1790* | 1796 | **Southwest Territory:** 1790 (Reconstructed) **State:** 1891 (partial) | |
| Utah | 1850 | 1896 | **UT Territory:** 1856 only. | |
| Washington | 1853 | 1889 | **WA Territory:** 1851* 1856 1857 1858 1859 1861 1871 1879 1881 1883 1885 1887 **State:** 1891 1892 1894 1898 | * As part of Oregon Territory. |
| Wisconsin | 1836 | 1848 | **WI Territory:** 1836 1838 1842 1846 1847 **State:** 1855 1865 1875 1885 1895 1905 | |
| Wyoming | 1868 | 1890 | **WY Territory:** 1869 1885* . | *1 county only |

From ***Census Substitutes & State Census Records*** by William Dollarhide, publ. Family Roots Publishing Co., Orting, WA

**Table 3 – State Censuses Taken in Common Years.** As a means of comparing state censuses taken by the 38 state census states, this table shows the common years for which many states conducted a state census. Many were done in years ending in "5." Census dates for some states are within a range, e.g., within 3 years of 1825, are indicated in the 1825 column.

| | 1815 | 1825 | 1835 | 1845 | 1855 | 1865 | 1875 | 1885 | 1895 | 1905 | 1915 | 1925 | 1935 | 1945 |
|---|---|---|---|---|---|---|---|---|---|---|---|---|---|---|
| **Alabama** | ● | ● | ● | ● | ● | ● | | | | | | | | |
| **Arizona** | | | | | | ● | | | | | | | | |
| **Arkansas** | ● | ● | ● | | ● | ● | | | | | | | | |
| **California** | | | | | ● | | | | | | | | | |
| **Colorado** | | | | | | ● | | ● | | | | | | |
| **Connecticut** | | | | | | | | | | | ● | | | |
| **Florida** | | ● | | | ● | | ● | ● | ● | | | ● | ● | ● |
| **Georgia** | | ● | ● | ● | ● | | ● | | | | | | | |
| **Hawaii** | | | | ● | | ● | ● | | ● | | | | | |
| **Illinois** | | ● | ● | ● | ● | | | | | | | | | |
| **Indiana** | | | | | ● | | | ● | ● | | ● | | | |
| **Iowa** | | | ● | ● | ● | | ● | ● | ● | ● | ● | ● | | |
| **Kansas** | | | | | ● | ● | ● | ● | ● | ● | ● | ● | | |
| **Louisiana** | | | ● | | | | | | | | | | | |
| **Maine** | | | ● | | | | | | | | | | | |
| **Maryland** | | | | | | | | | | | | | | |
| **Massachusetts** | | | | | ● | ● | | | | | | | | |
| **Michigan** | | | ● | ● | ● | ● | ● | ● | ● | | | | | |
| **Minnesota** | | | | ● | ● | ● | ● | ● | ● | ● | | | | |
| **Mississippi** | ● | ● | ● | ● | ● | ● | | | | | | | | |
| **Missouri** | | | | ● | ● | ● | ● | | | | | | | |
| **Nebraska** | | | | | ● | ● | ● | ● | | | | | | |
| **Nevada** | | | | | | ● | ● | | | | | | | |
| **New Jersey** | | | | | ● | ● | ● | ● | ● | ● | ● | | | |
| **New Mexico** | | | | | | | | ● | | | | | | |
| **New York** | | ● | ● | ● | ● | ● | ● | | ● | ● | ● | ● | | |
| **No. Carolina** | | | | | | | | | | | | | | |
| **No. Dakota** | | | | | | | | ● | | ● | ● | ● | | |
| **Oklahoma** | | | | | | | | | ● | ● | | | | |
| **Oregon** | | | | ● | ● | ● | ● | ● | ● | ● | | | | |
| **Rhode Island** | | | | | | ● | ● | ● | ● | ● | ● | ● | ● | |
| **So. Carolina** | | ● | ● | | | ● | ● | | | | | | | |
| **So. Dakota** | | | | | | | | ● | ● | ● | ● | ● | ● | ● |
| **Tennessee** | | | | | | | | | ● | | | | | |
| **Utah** | | | | | ● | | | | | | | | | |
| **Washington** | | | | | ● | | ● | ● | ● | | | | | |
| **Wisconsin** | | | ● | | ● | ● | ● | ● | ● | ● | | | | |
| **Wyoming** | | | | | | ● | | | | | | | | |
| *No. of States:* | 3 | 8 | 12 | 11 | 21 | 20 | 17 | 16 | 16 | 11 | 9 | 7 | 3 | 2 |

From ***Census Substitutes & State Census Records*** by William Dollarhide, publ. Family Roots Publishing Co., Orting WA

| State | Year a Terr | Year a State | Federal Census Years | | | | | | | | | | | | | | | | |
|---|---|---|---|---|---|---|---|---|---|---|---|---|---|---|---|---|---|---|---|
| | | | 1790 | 1800 | 1810 | 1820 | 1830 | 1840 | 1850 | 1860 | 1870 | 1880 | 1890 | 1900 | 1910 | 1920 | 1930 | 1940 | 1950 |
| **Alabama** | 1817 | 1819 | | | | lost | ● | ● | ● | ● | ● | ● | lost | ● | ● | ● | ● | ● | ● |
| **Alaska** (to US 1867) | 1912 | 1959 | No census taken, District of Alaska, 1870, 1880, or 1890 → | | | | | | | | -- | -- | -- | ● | ● | ● | ● | ● | ● |
| **Arizona** | 1863 | 1912 | | | | | | | | | ● | ● | lost | ● | ● | ● | ● | ● | ● |
| **Arkansas** | 1819 | 1836 | | | | lost | ● | ● | ● | ● | ● | ● | lost | ● | ● | ● | ● | ● | ● |
| **California** (to US 1848) | — | 1850 | | | | | | | ● | ● | ● | ● | lost | ● | ● | ● | ● | ● | ● |
| **Colorado** | 1861 | 1876 | | | | | | | | | | ● | lost | ● | ● | ● | ● | ● | ● |
| **Connecticut** | — | 1788 | ● | ● | ● | ● | ● | ● | ● | ● | ● | ● | lost | ● | ● | ● | ● | ● | ● |
| **Delaware** | — | 1787 | ● | ● | ● | ● | ● | ● | ● | ● | ● | ● | lost | ● | ● | ● | ● | ● | ● |
| **Distr. of Columbia** | 1801 | — | | ● | ● | ● | ● | ● | ● | ● | ● | ● | lost | ● | ● | ● | ● | ● | ● |
| **Florida** | 1822 | 1845 | | | | | | | ● | ● | ● | ● | lost | ● | ● | ● | ● | ● | ● |
| **Georgia** | — | 1788 | lost | lost | lost | ● | ● | ● | ● | ● | ● | ● | lost | ● | ● | ● | ● | ● | ● |
| **Hawaii** (to US 1898) | 1900 | 1959 | | | | | | | | | | | | ● | ● | ● | ● | ● | ● |
| **Idaho** | 1863 | 1890 | | | | | | | | | ● | ● | lost | ● | ● | ● | ● | ● | ● |
| **Illinois** | 1809 | 1818 | | | part | ● | ● | ● | ● | ● | ● | ● | lost | ● | ● | ● | ● | ● | ● |
| **Indiana** | 1800 | 1816 | | lost | lost | ● | ● | ● | ● | ● | ● | ● | lost | ● | ● | ● | ● | ● | ● |
| **Iowa** (* part of WI Terr.) | 1838 | 1846 | | | | | | ●* | ● | ● | ● | ● | lost | ● | ● | ● | ● | ● | ● |
| **Kansas** | 1854 | 1861 | | | | | | | | ● | ● | ● | lost | ● | ● | ● | ● | ● | ● |
| **Kentucky** (*Distr. of VA) | — | 1791 | lost* | lost | ● | ● | ● | ● | ● | ● | ● | ● | lost | ● | ● | ● | ● | ● | ● |
| **Louisiana** (*OrleansTer) | 1809 | 1812 | | | ●* | ● | ● | ● | ● | ● | ● | ● | lost | ● | ● | ● | ● | ● | ● |
| **Maine** (*Distr. of MA) | — | 1820 | ●* | ●* | ●* | ● | ● | ● | ● | ● | ● | ● | lost | ● | ● | ● | ● | ● | ● |
| **Maryland** | — | 1788 | ● | ● | ● | ● | ● | ● | ● | ● | ● | ● | lost | ● | ● | ● | ● | ● | ● |
| **Massachusetts** | — | 1788 | ● | ● | ● | ● | ● | ● | ● | ● | ● | ● | lost | ● | ● | ● | ● | ● | ● |
| **Michigan** | 1805 | 1837 | | | lost | ● | ● | ● | ● | ● | ● | ● | lost | ● | ● | ● | ● | ● | ● |
| **Minnesota** | 1849 | 1858 | MN Terr. had a special federal census in 1857 → | | | | | | ● | ● | ● | ● | lost | ● | ● | ● | ● | ● | ● |
| **Mississippi** | 1798 | 1817 | | lost | lost | ● | ● | ● | ● | ● | ● | ● | lost | ● | ● | ● | ● | ● | ● |
| **Missouri** | 1805 | 1821 | | | lost | lost | ● | ● | ● | ● | ● | ● | lost | ● | ● | ● | ● | ● | ● |
| **Montana** | 1864 | 1889 | | | | | | | | | ● | ● | lost | ● | ● | ● | ● | ● | ● |
| **Nebraska** | 1854 | 1867 | | | | | | | | ● | ● | ● | lost | ● | ● | ● | ● | ● | ● |
| **Nevada** | 1861 | 1864 | | | | | | | | | ● | ● | lost | ● | ● | ● | ● | ● | ● |
| **New Hampshire** | — | 1788 | ● | ● | ● | ● | ● | ● | ● | ● | ● | ● | lost | ● | ● | ● | ● | ● | ● |
| **New Jersey** | — | 1787 | lost | lost | lost | lost | ● | ● | ● | ● | ● | ● | lost | ● | ● | ● | ● | ● | ● |
| **New Mexico** | 1850 | 1912 | | | | | | | ● | ● | ● | ● | lost | ● | ● | ● | ● | ● | ● |
| **New York** | — | 1788 | ● | ● | ● | ● | ● | ● | ● | ● | ● | ● | lost | ● | ● | ● | ● | ● | ● |
| **North Carolina** | — | 1789 | ● | ● | ● | ● | ● | ● | ● | ● | ● | ● | lost | ● | ● | ● | ● | ● | ● |
| **North Dakota*** | 1861 | 1889 | *1860, 1870, 1880 as part of Dakota Territory → | | | | | | | ● | ● | ● | lost | ● | ● | ● | ● | ● | ● |
| **Ohio** (*NW Terr.) | 1787 | 1803 | | * lost | lost | ● | ● | ● | ● | ● | ● | ● | lost | ● | ● | ● | ● | ● | ● |
| **Oklahoma** | 1890 | 1907 | 1 month prior to statehood in 1907, Oklahoma Territory had a special federal census | | | | | | | | | | lost | ● | ● | ● | ● | ● | ● |
| **Oregon** | 1848 | 1859 | | | | | | | ● | ● | ● | ● | lost | ● | ● | ● | ● | ● | ● |
| **Pennsylvania** | — | 1787 | ● | ● | ● | ● | ● | ● | ● | ● | ● | ● | lost | ● | ● | ● | ● | ● | ● |
| **Rhode Island** | — | 1790 | ● | ● | ● | ● | ● | ● | ● | ● | ● | ● | lost | ● | ● | ● | ● | ● | ● |
| **South Carolina** | — | 1788 | ● | ● | ● | ● | ● | ● | ● | ● | ● | ● | lost | ● | ● | ● | ● | ● | ● |
| **South Dakota*** | 1861 | 1889 | *1860, 1870, 1880 as part of Dakota Territory → | | | | | | | ● | ● | ● | lost | ● | ● | ● | ● | ● | ● |
| **Tennessee** (*SW Terr) | 1790 | 1796 | *** tally** | lost | lost | **part** | ● | ● | ● | ● | ● | ● | lost | ● | ● | ● | ● | ● | ● |
| **Texas** (to US 1845) | — | 1845 | | | | | | | ● | ● | ● | ● | lost | ● | ● | ● | ● | ● | ● |
| **Utah** | 1850 | 1896 | | | | | | | ● | ● | ● | ● | lost | ● | ● | ● | ● | ● | ● |
| **Vermont** | — | 1791 | ● | ● | ● | ● | ● | ● | ● | ● | ● | ● | lost | ● | ● | ● | ● | ● | ● |
| **Virginia** | — | 1788 | lost | lost | ● | ● | ● | ● | ● | ● | ● | ● | lost | ● | ● | ● | ● | ● | ● |
| **Washington** | 1853 | 1889 | | | | | | | | ● | ● | ● | lost | ● | ● | ● | ● | ● | ● |
| **West Virginia** | — | 1863 | Part of Virginia, 1790-1860 | | | | | | | | ● | ● | lost | ● | ● | ● | ● | ● | ● |
| **Wisconsin** | 1836 | 1848 | | | | | | ● | ● | ● | ● | ● | lost | ● | ● | ● | ● | ● | ● |
| **Wyoming** | 1868 | 1890 | | | | | | | | | ● | ● | lost | ● | ● | ● | ● | ● | ● |

From *Census Substitutes & State Census Records* by William Dollarhide, publ. Family Roots Publishing Co., Orting WA

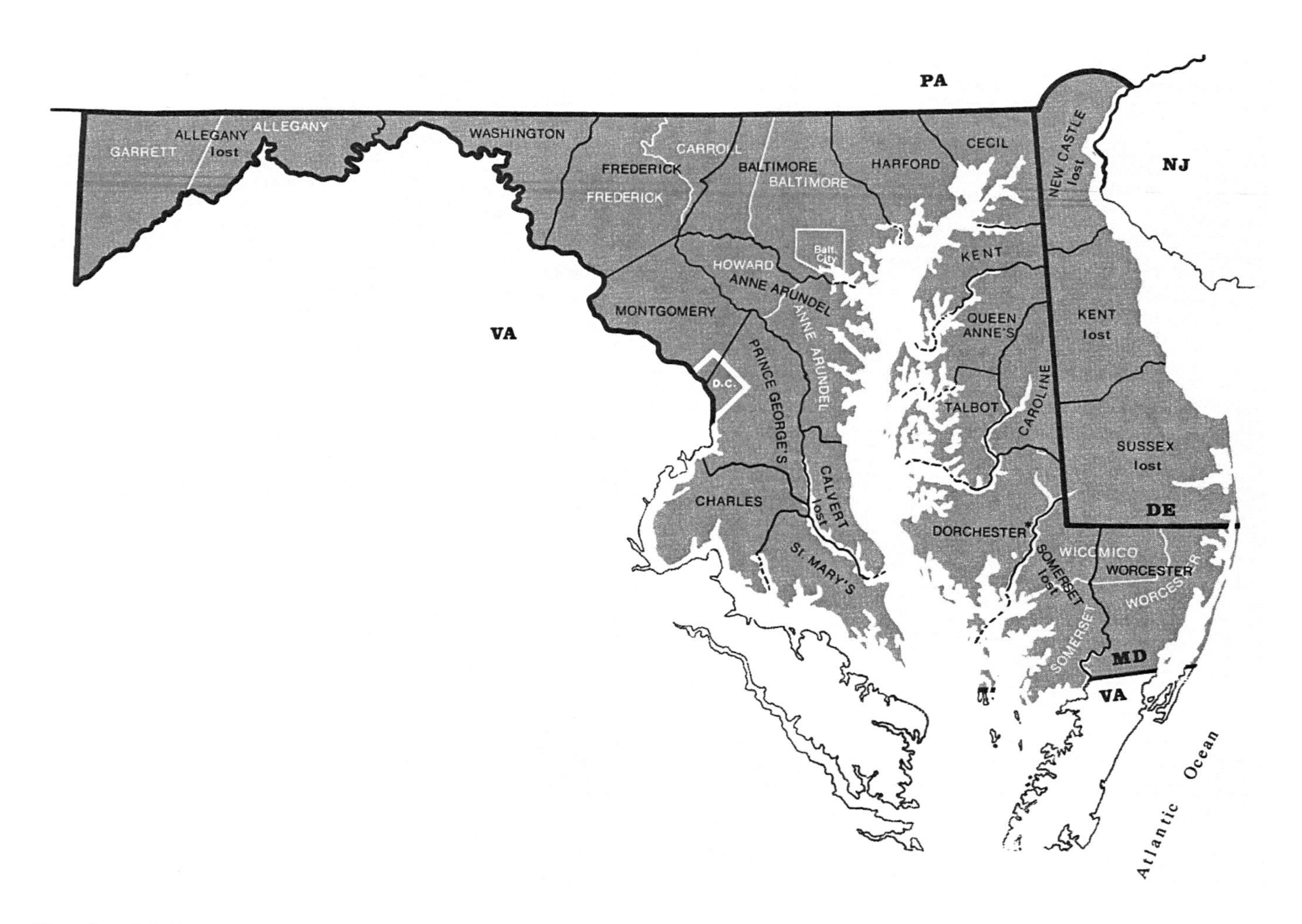


**Maryland & Delaware • 1790.** Shown in black are the nineteen counties of Maryland and the three counties of Delaware at the time of the August 1790 federal census. The current county boundaries, where different, are shown in white. Adding the independent city of Baltimore, the state of Maryland currently has 24 county-equivalents. The original 1790 census manuscripts for all three Delaware counties were lost. Maryland's lost 1790 censuses were for Allegany, Calvert, and Somerset counties, shown as "lost" on the map. The 1790 census revealed the population of Maryland as 319,728 people, including 103,036 slaves. The boundary of the modern District of Columbia is shown in white. In July 1790, the new capital district was authorized but the land was not finally ceded, purchased, and surveyed by the federal government until September 1791. The town of Georgetown was enumerated as part of Maryland (census extant); and the town of Alexandria was enumerated as part of Virginia (census lost). **Map Source:** Page 152, ***Map Guide to the U.S. Federal Censuses, 1790-1920***, by William Thorndale and William Dollarhide.

# Maryland

## Censuses & Substitute Name Lists

### Historical Timeline for Maryland, 1497-1790

**1497-1498.** Italian explorer Giovanni Caboto (John Cabot) was commissioned by the English King Henry VII to explore North America. He landed in 1497 on the island of Newfoundland. In 1498, he visited the coast of present New Jersey, Delaware, Maryland, Virginia, North Carolina, South Carolina, and Georgia.

**1524.** Giovanni da Verrazano, an Italian sailing for King Francis I of France, sailed past Chesapeake Bay and Delaware Bay. He kept moving north to visit present New York, Connecticut, Rhode Island, Massachusetts, and Maine.

**1558.** Elizabeth I became Queen of England. The first explorations of North America took place during her 45-year reign, the Elizabethan Era, or "Golden Age." When Elizabeth I was crowned, England was nearly bankrupt, but during her reign, the English Empire expanded and thrived, and English culture flourished in Literature, Theatre, Music, and Architecture.

**1603-1606. England**. In 1603, James I (James VI of Scotland since 1566), became King of England, the first monarch to rule both England and Scotland. James I declared that he ruled with the "divine right of kings," meaning he was not subject to the will of the people, but only to the will of God. James I may have been most remembered for commissioning a Bible translation. Perhaps more memorable for Americans was that James I chartered two joint stock companies for the purpose of settlement in North America. In 1606, the *Virginia Company of London* and the *Virginia Company of Plymouth* were granted territory from present North Carolina to Maine, with the Long Island Sound as the approximate dividing line.

**1607**. May. **Jamestown.** The first permanent English settlement in North America was founded on the James River, a few miles from its mouth on Chesapeake Bay. The Jamestown colony was established by the London Company. It was followed in August 1607 by the Sagadahoc Colony, founded by the Plymouth Company at the mouth of the Kennebec River in present Maine. Also called the Popham Colony, it lasted only a year.

**1610. Delaware Bay and River.** Samuel Argall, an English sea captain who led a supply mission to Jamestown, named the bay and river after Thomas West, the 3rd Baron De La Warr, and the first governor of the Virginia Colony.

**1620-1623.** A new Royal Charter was issued by King James I to the Plymouth Council for New England (formerly the Virginia Company of Plymouth) to establish colonial settlements in New England. In that same year, the *Mayflower* dropped anchor off Cape Cod, and Plymouth Colony was founded by a small group of Separatists/Pilgrims, who had fled England for Holland a few years earlier.

**1625. England.** Charles I became King of England, Scotland, and Ireland. Like his father, James I, Charles believed in the "divine right of kings," and held that the actions of Parliament were less important than his own, which of course, were inspired by God, not man. Charles was immediately under suspicion of being soft on Catholics, mainly because of his marriage to Henrietta Maria of France, a Roman Catholic. Groups of radical Protestants in England began to form an opposition to the new king. In response, along with his Archbishop, William Laud, the king began a campaign to purge his church of the largest group of non-conformists, the so-called Puritans, a militant Calvinist religious sect attempting to purify the Church of England. Unfortunately, Charles I took on a job that led to civil war in England as well as the loss of his head. But, his campaign can be credited as the main cause for the founding of the Massachusetts Bay Colony in New England.

**1628.** The **Massachusetts Bay Company** was granted a royal charter for an English colony to be established in North America within the bounds of the Plymouth Council of New England. It is said that King Charles I was misled as to the religious leanings of the Massachusetts Bay Company leaders, all prominent Puritans, not Pilgrims, as he had surmised.

**1629. The Great Migration** to New England began. As a result of the king's campaign to purge non-conformists from the Church of England, large groups of people were disenfranchised. Charles I disbanded Parliament and ruled England alone for eleven years. The Puritans referred to this era as "the eleven years of tyranny." It was during these eleven years that about 80,000 Puritans felt compelled to leave England. About a fourth of them moved to Holland; another fourth of them to Ireland; a fourth to the West Indies, particularly the islands of Barbados, Nevis, and St. Kitts; and the final group, some 21,000 Puritan immigrants, established the Massachusetts Bay Colony of North America.

**1629. George Calvert,** 1st Baron Baltimore, founder of the Avalon Colony of Newfoundland, arrived in Virginia. Calvert was a former Secretary of State in the government of King James I. He was not well received in Virginia, partly because of his Catholic beliefs, but also because of his known desire to start a colony in an area north of Jamestown claimed by the Virginia Company. George Calvert had been raised a Catholic, but during his political career, held several offices that required loyalty oaths to the Church of England. He resigned all of his government duties in 1625, publicly declared his Catholic faith, and began planning for an English colony in North America that could be a haven for the persecuted Catholics of England.

**1631. Claiborne Colony.** William Claiborne was a successful planter, trader, and prominent leader of the Virginia Colony. He was a rival of George Calvert for obtaining rights for a colony north of Jamestown on Chesapeake Bay. Claiborne was a councilor and received backing by the Virginia council for a trading post on Chesapeake Bay. On a trip to London, Claiborne received a royal trading commission from King Charles I that essentially granted him rights to settle any part of North America not previously granted. In 1631, Claiborne recruited a group of indentured servants in London and established a small plantation on Kent Island (present Kent County, Eastern Shore of Maryland).

**1632. Province of Maryland.** George Calvert was successful in petitioning King Charles I for a royal charter but died five weeks before the charter was signed. The Maryland Proprietorship was granted to his son and heir, Cecilius (Cecil) Calvert, 2nd Lord Baltimore. The colony was named Maryland after Henrietta Maria of France, the Catholic Queen Consort of Protestant English King Charles I. Cecil Calvert managed the Province of Maryland from his home, Kiplin Hall, in North Yorkshire, England. The area of the royal charter included most of the Chesapeake peninsula (now Delmarva Peninsula), including all of present Delaware, and extended north from the Potomac River to the 40th Parallel.

**1633.** William Claiborne's claims that the Virginia colony still had jurisdiction over his Kent Island settlement went to the Privy Council in London. The Council ruled against Claiborne, and he lost jurisdiction of the settlement to the new Maryland colony.

**1634.** ***The Ark*** and ***The Dove*** were hired by Cecil Calvert to transport the first settlers to the Province of Maryland. In early 1634, the two ships carrying over 120 settlers arrived at the mouth of the Chesapeake Bay. After exploring the area of the Potomac River, on March 25, 1634 the settlers went ashore on St. Clement's Island. Soon after, they purchased land from the Indians and established the first settlement of St. Mary's City. One of the passengers was 28-year old Leonard Calvert, who was named the colonial governor of the colony by his older brother, the Proprietor Governor, Cecil Calvert, 2nd Baron Baltimore. About half of the first settlers were known to be Roman Catholics. The Province of Maryland, led by the Catholic Calvert family, allowed religious freedom for all who came. The uniqueness of the Maryland freedoms might be compared with the Massachusetts Bay Colony, which had a law against being a Catholic (or the wrong kind of Protestant). The penalty in 1634 Massachusetts for being a Quaker or a Catholic was a death sentence. Regardless of their religious beliefs, the first settlers to the Maryland colony discovered some of the world's most perfect soil and climate for raising bumper crops of tobacco. Because of that fact, the colony was successful immediately.

**1635. General Assembly.** The first session of the General Assembly of the Province of Maryland was held at St. Mary's City. Patterned after the House of Commons of England, the legislators were freemen (land owners) selected from the parishes and hundreds prior to the formation of counties. Lord Baltimore, as the proprietor and original owner of all land in the colony, had the right to appoint any number of delegates.

**1635. Headright System and Indentured Servants.** As a proprietary colony, all land within the Province of Maryland was owned outright by the Lords Baltimore. Although Cecil Calvert actually issued a number of Maryland land grants as early as 1633 from his base in England, the first land grants issued in Maryland began in 1635, undertaken personally by Leonard Calvert, the colonial governor. The land grant system employed was identical to the Virginia system, often called the Headright System. The granting of land was based on the number of persons transported into the colony. A man transporting himself received land, and if he added others in the transportation, he would receive a certain number of acres of land "per head." The key element in the Headright System was that all persons (including convicts) transported to the colony were also entitled to receive land grants. But, if the transported person could not repay the one who paid for his passage, he would be compelled to serve a period of servitude for a number of years to repay the debt, after which he could receive his land grant. The contract between the Master and the Servant was done on a single sheet of parchment, written twice, then torn in half with copies given to each party. The manner of tearing the paper was to use jagged edges, or in Latin, *dentils*, so rejoining the two halves would have to be an exact fit. The document, copied into the county court records, became known as an *Indenture,* and the person going into servitude became known as an *Indentured Servant*. The Headright system was the main method of obtaining workers for the tobacco plantations of Maryland until the use of slave labor eventually replaced the Headright system in the early 1700s.

**1637.** Saint Mary's County was formed, the first county in the Province of Maryland. The original area included present Saint Mary's, Anne Arundel, and Howard counties. The county seat and first capital of the Province of Maryland was at St. Mary's City.

**1642.** Kent County was established, encompassing William Claiborne's original Kent Island settlement of 1631, as well as the area of present Kent and Talbot counties. The first county seat was at New Yarmouth, later moved to Chestertown. The first settlers in the county were mostly Puritans.

**1642. English Civil War.** Since taking the throne in 1625, King Charles I had purged most of the Puritans from the Church of England. To deal with a Parliament opposing his every move, in 1629, Charles disbanded Parliament and ruled England on his own. That action canceled over 400 years of liberties gained by Parliament since the Magna Carta. When Parliament was restored in 1640, it quickly became dominated by the same Puritans who Charles had removed from the Church of England. Beginning in 1642, Royalist supporters were forced to fight the armies of the Puritan Parliament in the English Civil War. The supporters of Charles I did not fare well against them.

**1645. Maryland.** Captain Richard Ingle, an English privateer and supporter of the Puritan side in England, led a revolt against the Catholic-led government of Maryland. He joined with William Claiborne, another Puritan/Parliamentarian, who was looking for any opportunity to take back Kent Island. With a single ship, Captain Ingle attacked the Maryland capital St. Mary's City in the name of Parliament. He imprisoned leaders of the colony, but Governor Leonard Calvert escaped to Virginia. Calvert returned with an armed force and took back his colony in August 1646. Though most of his men were granted amnesty, Ingle was specifically exempted from it and executed. Claiborne continued to fight the Calverts in any way he could.

**1645. England.** After his defeat and capture in 1645, Charles I refused to accept his captors' demands for a constitutional monarchy, and briefly escaped captivity in 1647. While recaptured, his teenage son, Prince Charles, was able to marshal Scottish forces for the king. However, by 1648, Oliver Cromwell had consolidated the English opposition. King Charles I was tried, convicted, and beheaded for high treason in January 1649. Charles, Jr. was soon after crowned the king of Scotland. The Civil War continued until 1651.

**1647-1648. Maryland.** In June 1647, Leonard Calvert was stricken with a sudden illness and died at the age of 41 years. On his death bed he appointed Thomas Greene as the 2nd Colonial Governor of Maryland. Greene was a Royalist and Roman Catholic, like Leonard Calvert. In 1648, Cecil Calvert replaced him with William Stone, a Protestant and supporter of Parliament. The Province of Maryland had a large number of Catholics, but they were now slightly outnumbered by Protestants, and Cecil Calvert may have tried to appease the Protestants with his appointment of William Stone. Meanwhile, Calvert's nemesis, William Claiborne, tried to get the Puritan-controlled Parliament to revoke the Maryland charter from the Calverts, saying they could not be trusted. Parliament disagreed, and the Calverts retained their Maryland charter. Claiborne did manage to get Parliament to grant him a commission to suppress any Royalist uprisings in the Chesapeake region.

**1649. Maryland.** The English colonies were still divided between the Puritans/Parliamentarians and the Royalists/Cavaliers. The New England colonies were probably 85-90% Puritan, and the Virginia colony was probably 60-65% Royalist. The Maryland colony was about 55% Puritan. In 1649, Maryland's Governor, William Stone, invited any Puritans of Virginia to settle in Maryland. Also in that year, all Maryland settlers were granted religious freedom by the official Maryland Act of Religious Toleration.

**1650. Anne Arundel County.** The third county in the Province of Maryland was Providence County, established in 1650. The earliest settlers were mostly Puritans from Virginia who had been lured to Maryland with land grants offered by Governor William Stone. In 1658, Providence was renamed Anne Arundel to honor the wife of Cecil Calvert (she had died in 1649). The original county area was taken from the bounds of Saint Mary's County, and included present Howard County.

**1651-1658. Commonwealth of England.** Charles, Jr. had lived in exile after the execution of his father, Charles I. In 1649, the Scots had proclaimed 19-year-old Charles the King of Scotland. But, the Puritan leader, Oliver Cromwell, defeated his army in 1651, and Charles fled to France. Cromwell was to become the Lord Protectorate of the Commonwealth of England, with a puritan-controlled Parliament. During this time, William Claiborne made attempts to have the Kent Island settlement restored to the Virginia Colony. Again, Claiborne's request was denied by Parliament. But taking on a role as a leader of the Puritan revolt, Claiborne led several armed attacks against the Maryland Colony, including the burning down of all the original Catholic churches of southern Maryland. After Cromwell died in 1658, the English people became dissatisfied with the government that he had established.

**1660. England.** In 1660, a new Parliament invited Charles to return and declared him king. Charles II was restored to the throne as King of England, Scotland, and Ireland. He was a strong and effective supporter of the fledgling English colonies. During his 25-year reign, the English colonials forced out the remaining pockets of Atlantic settlements made earlier by the Dutch, Swedes, and Danes. Charles II saw the Atlantic colonies as a source of trade and commerce, supported development, and granted several more charters for settlement. All of the English colonies thrived as a result. He was the first monarch to recognize the potential for the North American colonies to become a contiguous, viable commonwealth. He encouraged the development of post roads, and a regular communication between the Governors. Charles II was responsible for setting the tone of self-government, religious tolerance, and individual freedoms in the English colonies that were to become American institutions.

**1661.** Charles Calvert arrived in St. Mary's City as the new Deputy Governor of the Maryland colony. He was the 24-year old son and heir of Cecil Calvert, the proprietor of the Maryland colony.

**1664-1665. New York and New Jersey.** After English forces relieved the Dutch of their colony of New Netherlands in 1664, King Charles II granted to his brother, James, the Duke of York (in England) and the Duke of Albany (in Scotland), all of the territory between the Delaware and Connecticut Rivers. James immediately renamed the area as the Province of New York. In 1665, James granted to Sir George Carteret and Lord Berkley of Stratton, a part of the New York colony between the Hudson River and the Delaware River. Carteret's portion was named West New Jersey, Berkley's portion was named East New Jersey. The two Proprietors appointed a governor for the combined Province of New Jersey, with land sales by both East New Jersey and West New Jersey.

**1674. Chesapeake Peninsula.** After a couple of exchanges back and forth, the original settlements of the Swedes and Dutch on Delaware Bay were finally taken over by the English, under the direction of James, the Duke of York, who added the areas to his New York colony. Soon after, the dividing line between present Delaware and Maryland on the Chesapeake Peninsula was established. (The general use of the term *Delmarva Peninsula* did not began until the 1920s). At first, there was little opposition by Maryland to the new line, even though it encroached on the original Maryland charter by a large area.

**1675.** Cecil Calvert, 2nd Baron Baltimore, died at the age of 70 years at his home, Kiplin Hall, in North Yorkshire. He was succeeded by his son, Charles Calvert, who was living in Maryland at the time.

**1681. Pennsylvania.** King Charles II granted to William Penn a land charter to repay a debt owed to the Penn family. This was the largest English land grant to an individual, and William Penn became the sole owner and proprietor, with allegiance to the king of England. Penn's charter specified that the colony was bounded on the "...South by a Circle drawn at twelve miles distance from New Castle ... unto the beginning of the fortieth degree of Northern Latitude..." Later surveys revealed that the town of New Castle in fact lay several miles south of the 40th Parallel. Maryland's 1632 charter had specified that their northern boundary was the 40th parallel, and after Penn's grant in 1681, a 25-mile strip of land from the Delaware River to the Appalachian Mountains was claimed by both colonies. Neither Pennsylvania nor Maryland had settlements in the cross-claimed area until many years later, and the boundary remained in dispute for nearly 80 years.

**1682. Delaware.** The area of present Delaware was transferred from the Duke of York, proprietor of New York to William Penn, proprietor of Pennsylvania. The area became known as the "Lower Counties on Delaware."

**1684.** Charles Calvert, the 3rd Baron Baltimore, left Maryland and arrived at his Kiplin Hall home in England. He was never to return to Maryland. A few years after his return to England, he saw the loss of his family's title to Maryland: the end of the Calvert proprietorship; and the establishment of the replacement Royal Colony of Maryland.

**1685. England.** After the death of King Charles II, who died without issue, his brother, the Duke of York, became King James II. Parliament was suspicious of his religious beliefs, and thought he was too tolerant with Catholics. In 1686, James II was successful in establishing the *Dominion of New England*, an administrative union of colonies, encompassing the area from the Delaware River to the Penobscot River. The Dominion installed religious tolerance in the colonies of New Jersey, New York, Connecticut, New Haven, Rhode Island, New Hampshire and Massachusetts Bay, but the reforms were short-lived.

**1688. King James II Deposed.** After James II had declared his Catholic beliefs, he was deposed in 1688. His Protestant daughter, Mary, was declared the legal heir to the throne. She had married her cousin, William of Orange, the Stadtholder/Ruler of Holland, and Europe's most staunch Protestant leader. Because of William's stature as the leader of the Protestant insurrection which had overthrown the Catholic James II, Parliament asked both William and Mary to rule England jointly. The Protestant/Whig-controlled Parliament considered the skirmish a holy war, and later gave the insurrection the name of *Glorious Revolution*. The Dominion of New England was dissolved in 1689, and the concept of religious tolerance reverted back to the prohibition of Catholics to hold public office in all of the English colonies. James was exiled to France, where he died in 1701.

**1689. Maryland.** The Protestant Revolution of 1689, sometimes called "Coode's Rebellion" after one of its leaders, John Coode, took place in the Province of Maryland when Puritans, by then a majority in the colony, revolted against the proprietary government, led by the Roman Catholic Charles Calvert, 3rd Baron Baltimore. The rebellion followed the "Glorious Revolution" in England of 1688, which saw the Protestant Monarchs William and Mary replace the Catholic King James II. In Maryland, the Lords Baltimore lost control of their proprietary colony and for the next 25 years Maryland would be ruled directly by the English Crown. The Protestant Revolution also saw the effective end of Maryland's early experiments with religious toleration, as Catholicism was outlawed, and Roman Catholics forbidden from holding public office. Religious toleration would not be restored in Maryland until after the American Revolution.

**1689. The Jacobites.** After the English Revolution of 1688, a political party of supporters of deposed King James II was established in England They became known as Jacobites (derived from Jacobus, Latin for James). Parliament, however, was under control of the political party called the Whigs who saw the Jacobites as their mortal enemy and fought them in battle during and after the 1688 Revolution. In the first armed *Jacobite Rising* of 1689, they were quickly defeated; but they continued to oppose the Whigs for decades after the Revolution. The Whigs dominated Parliament from the 1680s to the 1760s. They were made up of Puritans, Non-conformists, and other anti-Catholic sects. The Jacobites were Roman Catholics or liberal Protestants. At the hands of the Whigs, the Jacobites experienced forced evacuations from Scotland and England as part of the Whigs penal policies. After the second *Jacobite Rising* of 1715, many of the expelled Jacobites were transported to the Province of Maryland.

**1692.** William III and Mary II declared Maryland to be a royal colony. The first official royal governor appointed was Sir Lionel Copley.

**1695.** The capital of the Province of Maryland was moved from mostly Catholic St. Mary's City to mostly Protestant Annapolis.

**1707.** During the reign of Queen Anne, the **United Kingdom of Great Britain** was established after the Union with Scotland Act passed the English Parliament in 1706; and the Union with England Act passed the Parliament of Scotland in 1707. The English Colonies were now the British Colonies.

**1715.** After the death of Charles Calvert, 3rd Baron Baltimore, his 36-year old son, Benedict Calvert became the 4th Baron Baltimore. Benedict had spent most of his adult life trying to get the king to restore the Maryland Proprietorship to the Calvert family, but after he attained his title, he died two months later, making his son, Charles Calvert, the 5th Baron Baltimore at the age of fifteen years. Young Charles benefited from the petitions of his father, who had assured the king that he was willing to convert to the Anglican faith. After declaring a sworn oath that he was renouncing Roman Catholicism and joining the Church of England, young Charles Calvert was granted the restored proprietorship of the Province of Maryland by King George I. Charles Calvert came of age in 1721 and then assumed personal control of Maryland, now a proprietary colony again with the Church of England as its official church.

**1729.** The City of Baltimore was founded. Due to its natural harbor, Baltimore became an important port for the importation of sugar cane from the Caribbean colonies, and the exportation of tobacco to England. In 1851, Baltimore began keeping separate records from Baltimore County, and is today the largest independent city in the U.S. Baltimore City is classified as a "county-equivalent" by the U.S. Census Bureau.

**1730-1732. Cresap's War.** In the royal grants of both colonies, the 40th Parallel was mentioned as the northern boundary of 1632 Maryland and the southern boundary of 1681 Pennsylvania. But Pennsylvania's grant language incorrectly placed the headwaters of the Chesapeake Bay as the assumed position of the 40th Parallel, which was actually 25 miles further north. Maryland maintained its claim to the 40th Parallel, even though their claim would have put the city of Philadelphia in Maryland, not Pennsylvania.

Palatine Germans (Pennsylvania Dutch), and Scots-Irish immigrants were the first to settle in the Lancaster area. By 1725, both groups reached the Susquehanna River, which became a barrier to further western settlement. In that year, the Maryland colony issued a land grant to Thomas Johnson, who operated a ferry at Peach Bottom. In 1730, Wight's Ferry and a land office was established by the Pennsylvania colony to facilitate settlement across the river. When the colony of Maryland heard of Wight's Ferry, Lord Baltimore authorized Thomas Cresap of Maryland to open a ferry and land office at Blue Rock. Fights broke out between workers of the competing ferries. The battles of the "war" were mostly in court, and in 1732, Charles Calvert, 5th Baron Baltimore, signed a provisional agreement with William Penn's sons, which drew a compromise line between the Pennsylvania claim and the original Maryland claim. He later reneged, saying the document he signed was not correct. The Maryland and Pennsylvania settlers continued to battle each other over jurisdiction in areas of present Harford Co MD and York Co PA. The compromise line was not finally agreed to until 1760, when King George III ordered Lord Baltimore (the 6th) to formally accept the 1732 agreement of his father. The new line was not surveyed and marked on the ground until 1767, when it became known as the Mason-Dixon Line.

**1767. Mason-Dixon Line.** In 1764, the two proprietary colonies of Maryland and Pennsylvania joined in the appointment of surveyors Charles Mason and Jeremiah Dixon. They were given the job to mark the boundary between the Maryland colony and the Pennsylvania colony. Pennsylvania included the *Lower Counties on Delaware*, which was part of the survey. Along the length of the Mason-Dixon Line, stone monuments were erected every five miles, each with the engraved coat of arms of the Penn Family on the PA/DE side, the arms of the Calvert family on the MD side. The survey was completed and approved by both colonies in 1767. The Mason-Dixon Line became the unofficial dividing line between the southern and northern colonies/states.

**1775. Delaware.** The three *Lower Counties on Delaware* broke away from Pennsylvania. They adopted a constitution and became the "Delaware State," the first of all the colonies to call themselves a state, and one of the thirteen to sign the Declaration of Independence.

**1776. Maryland.** Four Marylanders signed the Declaration of Independence. About the same time the Maryland Convention declared independence from Great Britain, and the first State Constitution of Maryland was adopted.

**1788.** April 28th. Upon adoption of the Constitution of the United States, Maryland became the 7th state in the Union.

**1790.** July. **Residence Act.** The U.S. Congress approved the creation of a permanent national capital district to be located at a site selected by the President. Later that year, President George Washington, a former surveyor, sketched a ten-mile square that crossed the Potomac River, encompassing the existing towns of Georgetown on the Maryland side, and Alexandria on the Virginia side. The land was acquired in 1791, after cessions by Virginia and Maryland.

**1790.** August 2. The first **Federal Census** was taken in the 13 original states, plus the 14th state of Vermont.

---

## Things a Genealogist Needs to Know About Maryland

**Maryland's Counties.** In its first session of 1635, the Maryland General Assembly established a provision for a county as the default unit of government. Managed by a board of commissioners, the county organization remains unchanged today. County governments in Maryland provide services normally rendered at the municipal level in other states, and there is little incentive for a community to incorporate. For example, the largest county, Montgomery (over one million people), has only three incorporated municipalities, with a combined population of about 125,000). Some of the largest communities in Maryland, such as Bethesda, Silver Spring, Columbia, and Towson are unincorporated and receive their municipal services from the county.

**Maryland's Hundreds & Parishes.** The earliest censuses and tax lists of Maryland are often divided by several hundreds within a county. The term *hundred* to describe a subdivision of a county dates back to the time of the Roman occupation of Britain. Back then, a hundred was an area encompassing at least 100 male residents of the right age to go to war. Roman troops were divided into units of 100 men, each commanded by a Centurion. In early Maryland, a hundred described an area with at least 100 households and this was the jurisdiction used for recording the names of taxpayers.

The parish system was installed in Maryland after the Church of England was adopted as the official church by the Royal Colony of Maryland in 1692. Thereafter, in some Maryland counties, the term hundred and parish may describe the same area. But usually, the term hundred died out, eventually replaced by the term parish.

## Maryland State Archives

The first archives building in Maryland dates back to 1935, when the Hall of Records was first opened in Annapolis. Renamed the Maryland State Archives, in 1986 a new Archives building was opened. Since then, the MSA has been acknowledged as the premier state archival facility in the U.S. and is frequently visited by archivists from all over the world as the model to follow elsewhere. It is well known for the size and completeness of its historical collections and for the many outstanding indexes to original records.

**Genealogy Resources.** The MSA is without equal as a resource for genealogical research in Maryland. Visit the MSA's ***Family Historians*** webpage. See **http://msa.maryland.gov/msa/homepage/html/family.html.** This webpage describes the following:

- **How to Order Copies.** Records, Photographs & Maps, Art, and Publications.
- **Search Online Databases.** List of available online searchable databases.
- **Beginner's Guide to Research.** Things you should know before searching the Archives site.

• **Guide to Family History Research.** Helps the family history researcher with orderly procedures to attack problems, links to online sources, and references to some of the helpful books available.
• **Find Specific Records.** Lists of records and how to find within the Guide to Government Records.
• **Online Genealogy Workshops.** Introduces family history researchers to research methods and resources presented at the Archives' in-house workshops.
• **Topical Genealogy Index.** Specific topics discussed in the Guide.

## Bibliography

### Maryland Censuses & Substitutes

This bibliography identifies Censuses and Substitute Name Lists for the Province of Maryland beginning in 1633, followed by those of the State of Maryland from 1788. For a sense of the political environment at the time of each name list, see the Historical Timeline for the events taking place.
- Maryland took a census of its entire population in 1776 and again in 1778; as well as an every-county tax list in 1783.
- After statehood in 1788, no state-sponsored censuses were ever conducted in Maryland.
- A complete 1797 Federal Direct Tax name list survives for all counties.
- Federal censuses open to the public are generally complete for all Maryland counties, except for a few communities in 1790, and the entire 1890, lost due to a fire in the 1920s. Each of the federal censuses, 1790 through 1940 are noted, but the following list is comprised mostly of substitute name lists within the categories of Court Records, City Directories, Histories, State Militia Lists, Tax Lists, Vital Records, and Voter Lists – all identified below in chronological order:

♦ ♦ ♦ ♦ ♦

**1633-1680.** ***The Early Settlers of Maryland: An Index to Names of Immigrants Compiled From Records of Land Patent, in the Hall of Records, Annapolis, Maryland*** **[Printed Book],** compiled by Gust Skordas. This was the first list of the founders of Maryland compiled from original land records at the MD state archives, publ. Genealogical Publishing Co., Baltimore, 1968, 536 pages, FHL book 975.2 W2s.xi.

- See also ***A Supplement to "The Early Settlers of Maryland" Comprising 8,680 Entries Correcting Omissions and Errors in Gust Skordas, The Early Settlers of Maryland*** **[Printed Book & Digital Version],** by Carson Gibb, publ. Maryland State Archives, 1997. FHL Book 975.2 W2s supp. A searchable digitized version of this work is available at the Maryland State Archives website, with the title ***The New Early Settlers of Maryland.*** See **http://msa.maryland.gov/msa/speccol/sc4300/sc4341/html/search.html.**
- **NOTE:** from the Maryland State Archives webpage entitled, *Introduction to New Early Settlers of Maryland:* "During the first years of his Province of Maryland, 1634-1681, Lord Baltimore rewarded people who transported themselves or others with rights to land, usually called Headrights. For most of the period, the reward was a right to 50 acres of land per person transported. To enter and exercise his rights, a person had to give the names of those, including himself, whom he had transported. Therefore, the records of these transactions include the names of the settlers. From these records, lists of settlers have been made since early in the nineteenth century. But only in 1968 was one published. This was Gust Skordas's *The Early Settlers of Maryland*, immediately a cornerstone of genealogy. In 1997 A Supplement corrected and enlarged *The Early Settlers.* Now *The New Early Settlers of Maryland*, a complete revision, replaces Skordas's work. In 1975 Russell Menard wrote that the 'best estimate' of immigration to Maryland between 1634 and 1681 is 32,000 (*Economy and Society in Early Colonial Maryland*, 1975, pp. 175-6). *The New Early Settlers* has about 34,000 entries, which, allowing for duplications, is close to Menard's estimate."
- See also ***Various Indexes of Early Settlers of Maryland, 1633-1680*** **[Microfilm & Digital Capture],** by the Daughters of the American Revolution, Baltimore Chapter, filmed by the Genealogical Society of Utah, 1949, 1 roll, FHL #13158. To access the digital images, see the online FHL catalog page: **www.familysearch.org/search/catalog/304529.**

**1633-1900.** ***General Index of Wills of St. Mary's County, Maryland*** **[Online Database],** digitized and OCR indexed at the Ancestry.com website. Source: Book, same title, by Margaret Roberts Hodges, 1920s. **https://search.ancestry.com/search/db.aspx?dbid=25471.**

**1634-1999.** ***Maryland Register of Wills Records* [Online Database],** digitized at FamilySearch.org. Source: Prerogative Court, Hall of Records, Annapolis, MD. This is an image-only database of probate records from court record collections from the Register of Wills in Maryland counties. Probate records often include wills, and other records dealing with the administration of estates including bonds, inventories, guardianships, real estate, and various indexes to the records. Includes the following counties: Allegany, Anne Arundel, Calvert, Caroline, Carroll, Cecil, Charles, Frederick, Garrett, Harford, Howard, Kent, Montgomery, Prince George's, Queen Anne's, Somerset, St. Mary's, Talbot, Washington, and Worcester. Also includes records from Baltimore City. Browse through 1,933,787 images, organized by County, then Volume Title, and Year. See
**www.familysearch.org/search/collection/1803986.**

**1634.** ***The Ark and The Dove Adventurers* [Printed Book],** by the society of The Ark and The Dove, edited by George Ely Russell and Donna Valley Russell. In November 1633 the 358-ton Ark and the 26-ton Dove sailed from the Isle of Wight in England, transporting some 125 colonists to settle the Proprietary Province of Maryland. *The Ark and The Dove Adventurers* is the first comprehensive account of these original Maryland colonists, and it contains compiled genealogies of their descendants to the fifth generation when possible, much like the five-generation project of the Mayflower Society or the six-generation project of the Order of First Families of Virginia. Publ. Genealogical Publishing Co, Baltimore, 2005, 296 pages, FHL book 975.2 D2.

**1634.** ***Passenger List of The Ark and The Dove* [Online Database],** a list containing the names of 122 persons was originally listed at the website for The Society of The Ark and The Dove. For an archived database, see
**https://web.archive.org/web/20160909181156/www.thearkandthedove.com/passengers.html.**

**1634-1654.** ***The flowering of the Maryland Palatinate: An Intimate and Objective History of the Province of Maryland to the Overthrow of Proprietary Rule . . .* [Printed Book & Online Database],** by Harry Wright Newman, publ. Washington, DC, 1961, Reprint GPC, Baltimore, 2008, 359 pages, FHL book 975.2 H2nh. To access a digital version of the 1961 book, visit the online FHL catalog page for this title. See **https://familysearch.org/search/catalog/231258.**

**1634-1718.** ***Maryland Marriage Evidences* [Printed Book],** by Robert W. Barnes. From intro: "The present volume contains marriage records taken from religious and civil sources and, in addition, marriage references taken from land, court, and probate records." Includes index. Publ. Genealogical Publishing Co, Baltimore, 2005, 486 pages, FHL book 975.2 V28b.

**1634-1734.** ***Colonial Maryland Soldiers and Sailors* [Printed Book],** by Henry C. Peden, Jr., publ. Willow Bend Books, Westminster, MD, 2001, 398 pages, FHL book 975.2 M2ph.

**1634-1777.** ***Maryland, Compiled Marriage Index* [Printed Book & Online Database],** compiled by Robert Barnes, publ. Genealogical Publishing Co., 1975, 1978, 233 pages, FHL book 975.2 K2bar. This is the first of three books of marriages compiled by Robert Barnes, covering 1634-1777; 1778-1800; and 1801-1820. A searchable digital version of this book is available at the Ancestry.com website. This database has 23,319 records. See
**http://search.ancestry.com/search/db.aspx?dbid=4738.**

**1634-1777.** ***Index of Maryland Colonial Wills: at Land Office, Annapolis, Maryland* [Printed Book],** compiled by James M. Magruder, Jr. An index to the Maryland colonial wills as contained in the Prerogative Court records as Wills, Libers 1-41 in the Hall of Records in Annapolis. Publ. Genealogical Publishing Co, Baltimore, 1967, 543 pages, FHL book 975.2 P22m 1967.

**1634-1848.** ***History of Maryland: From its First Settlement in 1634, to the year 1848* [Online Database],** digitized by the Genealogical Society of Utah, 2013, from the book by James McSherry, publ. Baltimore, 1849, 405 pages. To view a digital version of this book, see the online FHL catalog page for this title. See
**https://familysearch.org/search/catalog/2213021.**

**1634-1900.** ***General Index of Wills of St. Mary's County, Maryland* [Printed Book & Online Database],** compiled by Margaret Roberts Hodges. Publ. by the Carter Braxton Chapter, DAR, 1938, 135 pages, FHL book 975.241 S2h. Also on microfilm, FHL film #441447. To access a digital version of this book, visit the online FHL catalog page for this title:
**https://familysearch.org/search/catalog/253802.**

**1634-1935.** ***Register of Maryland's Heraldic Families: Period From 1634-1935*** **[Printed Book & Online Database],** by Alice Norris Parran, publ. National Society of the Colonial Dames of America, 1935-1937, Baltimore, 2 vols., FHL book 975. 2 D2pa v.1-2. To access a digital version of Vol. 1 and Vol. 2, visit the online FHL catalog page for this title. See **https://familysearch.org/search/catalog/176229.**

**1634-1999.** ***Maryland Register of Wills Records*** **[Online Database],** indexed at the FamilySearch.org website. This is an image-only database with probate records from court record collections from the Register of Wills in Maryland counties. Probate records often include wills, and other records dealing with the administration of estates including bonds, inventories, guardianships, real estate, and various indexes to the records. Includes the following counties: Allegany, Anne Arundel, Calvert, Caroline, Carroll, Cecil, Charles, Frederick, Garrett, Harford, Howard, Kent, Montgomery, Prince George's, Queen Anne's, Somerset, St. Mary's, Talbot, Washington, and Worcester. Also includes records from Baltimore City. This database has 1,933,787 records. See **www.familysearch.org/search/collection/1803986.**

**1634-1976.** ***Maryland Genealogies: A Consolidation of Articles from the Maryland Historical Magazine. In Two Volumes. With an Introduction by Robert Barnes*** **[Printed Book],** Excerpted and reprinted from the Maryland Historical Magazine with added introduction, contents, and indexes. Publ. Genealogical Publishing Co, Baltimore, 1980, reprinted 2008, 2 vols., 549 pp & 548 pp. See FHL book 975.2 D2m.

**1634–2000s.** ***Maryland – Collection Catalog at MyHeritage*** **[Online Database],** over 180 databases can be searched here. Databases include censuses, directories, family histories, town histories, military rosters, college/school year books, and more. This is a subscription site, but all initial searches are free. A free search can be done for a name, place, year, or keyword. See **www.myheritage.com/records/Maryland/all-records.**

**1635-1777.** ***The Maryland Calendar of Wills*** **[Printed Volumes & Online Database],** compiled by Jan Baldwin Cotton, F. Edward Wright, and Annie Walker Burns, originally published Kohn & Pollock, Baltimore, 1904-1928, reprinted Genealogical Publishing Co, Baltimore, 1968, 16 vols. Contents: Vol. 1: Wills from 1635, earliest probated to 1685; Vol. 2 : Wills from 1685 to 1702; Vol. 3: Wills from 1703 to 1713; Vol. 4: Wills form 1713 to 1720; Vol. 5: Wills from 1720 to 1726; Vol. 6: Wills from 1726 to 1732; Vol. 7: Wills from 1732 to 1738; Vol. 8: Wills from 1738 to 1743; Vol. 9: Wills from 1744 to 1749; Vol. 10: Wills from 1748 to 1753; Vol. 11: Wills from 1753 to 1760 ; Vol. 12: Wills from 1759 to 1764; Vol. 13: Wills from 1764 to 1767; vol. 14: Wills from 1767 to 1772; Vol. 15: Wills from 1772 to 1774; and Vol. 16: Wills from 1774 to 1777. See FHL book 975.2 P28c 1968. Volumes 1-8 (1635-1743) were digitized and indexed at the Ancestry.com website. See **http://search.ancestry.com/search/db.aspx?dbid=3250.**

**1635-1777.** ***Maryland State Archives – Prerogative Court (Wills)*** **[Online Database],** digitized images of the handwritten wills are grouped by years. Use the Maryland Calendar of Wills to find the year, names, and file numbers, then access the original images here: **http://guide.mdsa.net/series.cfm?action=viewSeries&ID=s538.**

- **NOTE:** This is the first of six online databases, ***Maryland State Archives - Prerogative Court of Maryland:*** 1) 1635-1777 (Will Books); 2) 1657-1777 (Testamentary Proceedings); 3) 1674-1777 (Inventories & Accounts); 4) 1718-1777 (Inventories); 5) 1718-1777 (Accounts); and 6) 1751-1777 (Balance Books).

**1635-1775.** ***The Complete Book of Emigrants in Bondage*** **[Printed Book & Digital Version],** by Peter Wilson Coldham. Between 1614 and 1775 some 50,000 English men, women, and children were sentenced by judicial process to be sent to the American colonies for a variety of crimes. Most were transported to Virginia or Maryland. The earliest in Maryland came in 1635, a year after the formation of the colony. The data on these involuntary colonists came from a variety of official records which the author of this work spent over fifteen years studying. Among those covered were minutes of eleven Courts of Assize and Jail Delivery and of twenty-eight Courts of Quarter Session, as well as Treasury Papers, Money Books, Patent Rolls, State Papers, and Sessions Papers. The names of those deported are printed in alphabetical order and form what can be considered the largest passenger list of its kind ever published. The data presented in this volume is highly condensed, but most entries include some or all of the following information: parish of origin, sentencing court, nature of the offense, date of sentence, date and ship on which transported, date and place landed in America, and the English county in

which the sentence was passed. Publ. Genealogical Publishing Co, Baltimore, 1988-1992, 920 pages, FHL book 973 W2c 1988. To access the digital images, see the online FHL catalog page:
**www.ancestry.com/search/collections/61074.**
- See also ***More Emigrants in Bondage*** [Printed Book], by Peter Wilson Coldham, Publ. GPC, Baltimore, 2002, FHL book 973 W2c 2002.
- See also ***The King's Passengers to Maryland and Virginia*** **[Printed Book],** by Peter Wilson Coldham, publ. Family Line Pub., Westminster, MD, 1997, 450 pages, FHL book 975.2 W3wi.

**1635-1777.** ***Maryland, Wills and Probate Records*** **[Online Database],** digitized and indexed at the Ancestry.com website. Source: Ancestry extractions from MD County, District and Probate Courts. May include Wills, Letters of Administration, Inventories, Distributions and Accounting, Bonds, or Guardianships. Each record may include: Name, Probate Place, Inferred Death Place, and Item Description. This database has 24,012 records. See
**https://search.ancestry.com/search/db.aspx?dbid=9068.**

**1635-1789.** ***A Biographical Dictionary of the Maryland Legislature*** **[Printed Book],** by Edward C. Papenfuse, et al, 2 vols., publ. John Hopkins University Press, 1979, 1985. Included are biographical sketches of every legislator in Maryland for the first 150 years of the colony. The biographies are genealogical treasures. See FHL book 975.2 N2p v.1-2.

**1635-1800.** ***Maryland Prisoners Languishing in Gaol*** **[Printed Book],** by Henry C. Peden. Contents: Vol. 1: 1635-1765; Vol. 2: 1766-1800. Includes indexes. Publ. Colonial Roots, Lewes, DE, 2013, 2 vols., FHL book 975.2 J6p v.1-2.

**1635-1800.** ***British Roots of Maryland Families*** **[Printed Book],** by Robert W. Barnes. In general, families are traced back two or more generations in England and brought forward two or more generations in Maryland. Vol. 1 identifies 500 families. followed by a 140-page index containing the names of 20,000 individuals. Vol. 2 adds another 200 families, plus another 120 settlers in other colonies that came to light after the first volume was published. Publ. Genealogical Publishing Co, Baltimore, 2 vols., 1999-2002, 646 pages + 345 pages, FHL book 975.2 D2ba v. 1-2.

**1635-1830.** ***Scots in the Mid-Atlantic Colonies*** **[Printed Book],** by David Dobson, publ. Genealogical Publishing Co, Baltimore, 2002, 139 pages, FHL book 974F2dds.
- See also ***Scots in the Mid-Atlantic States, 1783-1883*** **[Printed Book],** by David Dobson, publ. Genealogical Publishing Co, Baltimore, 2002, 142 pages, FHL Book 974 F2dd.
- See also, ***Scots on the Chesapeake, 1607-1830*** **[Printed Book & Online Database],** by David Dobson, publ. Genealogical Publishing Co, Baltimore, 1992, 169 pages, FHL book 973 W2dda. All three books name over 3,000 Scots immigrants to the mid-Atlantic region (NY, NJ, PA, DE, MD, & VA), before and after the Revolutionary War. The books provide a series of sketches conveying such information as the immigrant's place and date of birth and death, occupation, date of arrival and place of settlement in the U.S., and names of spouse and children. The third Dobson book, *Scots on the Chesapeake, 1607-1830,* is available online at the Ancestry.com website. See
**http://search.ancestry.com/search/db.aspx?dbid=48519.**

**1635-1982.** ***Maryland Biographical Sketch Index*** **[Printed Book],** compiled by Samuel M. Andrusko. Includes an index to over 10,500 biographical sketches contained in 33 Maryland histories. Publ. Silver Spring, MD, 1983, FHL book 975.2 D3a.

**1635-1990.** ***An Historical List of Public Officials of Maryland: Governors, Legislators, and other Principal Officers of Government*** **[Printed Book],** by Edward C. Papenfuse, et al, publ. Maryland State Archives, 1990, 542 pages, FHL book 975.2 B4m.

**1636-2013.** ***Archives of Maryland*** **[Printed Volumes & Online Database].** In 1883, the state of Maryland began publishing the *Archives of Maryland*, a serial that publishes historical documents that form the constitutional, legal, legislative, judicial, and administrative basis of Maryland's government from the 17th century through the present day. It is published by the Maryland State Archives. The first volume of the *Archives* came out in 1883, covering proceedings and acts of the General Assembly starting in 1637. These legislative session minutes often mention the names of persons petitioning the Assembly, and the index of names is like a census of Maryland during the colonial period. As of June 2020, there were 865 volumes in the series, covering proceedings of various sorts from 1636-2016. More volumes are still being issued, at irregular intervals.

To see the titles and contents of the online volumes, go to the main Maryland State Archives Web site at **http://aomol.msa.maryland.gov/html/index.html.**

**1637-1787.** ***Inhabitants of Kent County, Maryland*** **[Printed Book],** by Henry C. Peden, Jr. Includes index, publ. Family Line Publications, Westminster, MD, 1994, 272 pages, FHL book 975.236 D2p.

**1637-1999. Maryland, Register of Will Records [Online Database],** digitized at the FamilySearch.org website. Includes images of probate records from court record collections from the Register of Wills in Maryland counties. Probate records often include wills, and other records dealing with the administration of estates including bonds, inventories, guardianships, real estate, and various indexes to the records. Includes the following counties: Allegany, Anne Arundel, Calvert, Caroline, Carroll, Cecil, Charles, Frederick, Garrett, Harford, Howard, Kent, Montgomery, Prince George's, Queen Anne's, Somerset, St. Mary's, Talbot, Washington, and Worcester. Also includes records from Baltimore City. This collection is being published as images become available. NOTE: The date 1629 is impossible, since the first county (St. Mary's) was created in 1637. See **https://familysearch.org/search/collection/1803986.**

**1639-1724.** ***Index, Rent Roll, St. Mary's County, Maryland*** **[Printed Book],** by Annie Walker Burns, c1940, 34 pages, FHL book 975.241 R22b.

**1642-1875.** ***Old Kent: The Eastern Shore of Maryland; Notes Illustrative of the Most Ancient Records of Kent County Maryland, and of the Parishes of St. Paul's, Shrewsbury and I. U. and Genealogical Histories of Land and Distinguished Families of Maryland, and their Connections by Marriage, etc., with an Introduction*** **[Printed Book & Online Database],** by George A. Hanson. Includes index. Originally published by J.P. Des Forges, Baltimore, 1876; reprinted GPC, Baltimore, 1967, 383 pages, FHL book 975.21 D2h 1967. To access a digital version of this book, visit the online FHL catalog page: **https://familysearch.org/search/catalog/73277.**

**1642-1960. Index to the Wills of Maryland: Howard County, 1840-1950 & Kent County [Printed Book],** edited by Joan Hume. The index is arranged chronologically under each letter of the alphabet and gives the name of the testator, date of the will, and the liber and folio where the original may be found. The index for Kent County includes references to a number of colonial wills that may have been omitted from the Magruder index. Publ. Genealogical Publishing Co, Baltimore, 1970, 213 pages, FHL book 975.2 P22hh.

**1648-1790.** ***Land Records, Kent County, Maryland*** **[Microfilm & Digital Capture],** from the originals at the Hall of Records (now Maryland State Archives). The MSA has an index on microfilm for the years 1648-1955. Records for the years 1686 to 1691 are lost. An Index is included with most volumes. Filmed by the Genealogical Society of Utah, 1947-1948, 9 rolls, beginning with FHL film #14148 (Liber K 1677-1685 +). To access the digital images, see the online FHL catalog page: **https://familysearch.org/search/catalog/41185.**

**1648-1825. Maryland Eastern Shore Vital Records [Printed Book],** compiled by F. Edward Wright. Includes indexes. Contents: Vol. 1: 1648-1725; Vol. 2: 1726-1750; Vol. 3: 1751-1775; Vol. 4: 1776-1800; and Vol. 5: 1801-1825. Publ. Family Line Publications, Silver Spring, MD, 1982-1986, 5 vols., FHL 975.21 K2wf v.1-5.

**1649-1658.** ***First Families of Anne Arundel County, Maryland*** **[Printed Book & Digital Version],** by Donna Valley Russell, publ. Catoctin Press, New Market, MD, 1999-2002, 2 vols., xxxii, 154pp; xxxi, 191pp, FHL book 975.255 D3r v.1-2. To access a digital version of Vol. 1, visit the online FHL catalog page : **https://familysearch.org/search/catalog/960083.**

**1649-1800.** ***Inhabitants of Cecil County, Maryland*** **[Printed Book],** by Henry C. Peden. Names were taken from church, civil, and military records. Contents: Vol. 1: 1649-1774; Vol. 2: 1774-1800. Publ. Colonial Roots, 2006, 2 vols., FHL book 975.238 X38p v.1-2

**1650-1772. Queen Anne's County, Maryland, Land Office, Rent Rolls [Printed Book],** abstracted by Leslie and Neil Keddle. Volumes include surname indexes. From intro: "Contains the rent rolls which were documents listing all patents for the purpose of collecting the quit-rents due to the province's proprietor, the Lords Baltimore. Quit rents were a form of land tax that were collected on an annual basis by the Proprietary government. The rolls were a means of maintaining a record of lands that had been surveyed, assigned, and possessed." Contents: Vol. 1: 1650-1679: Vol. 2: 1681-1704: Vol. 3: 1708-1772; Vol. 4: 1681-1702: Vol. 5: tracts, additional rent rolls. FHL has vols. 1, 2 and 3 bound together into one volume, and vols. 4 and 5 bound together into one volume. See FHL book 975.234 R28k v.1-3 & 975.234 R28k v.4-5.

**1650-1875.** ***The founders of Anne Arundel and Howard Counties, Maryland: A Genealogical and Biographical Review from Wills, Deeds and Church Records*** **[Microfilm & Online Database],** from a book by J.D. Warfield, publ. Baltimore, 1905. Filmed by the Genealogical Society of Utah, 1978, 1 roll, FHL film #1036676. To access a digital version of this book, visit the online FHL catalog page for this title. See **https://familysearch.org/search/catalog/180894.**

**1650-1879.** ***The History of Montgomery County, Maryland, From its Earliest Settlement in 1650 to 1879*** **[Printed Book & Digital Version],** by Thomas H.S. Boyd. This is an historical, biographical, and genealogical work on Montgomery County, Maryland, with chapters on the founding and early settlement of the county and biographical sketches of prominent men. It was reprinted with an added index of names. Originally printed 1879, reprinted by Genealogical Publishing Co, Baltimore, 1968, 187 pages, FHL book 975.284 H2b. To access a digital version of this book, visit the online FHL catalog page for this title. See **https://familysearch.org/search/catalog/247048.**

**1650-1995.** ***Maryland, Births and Christenings*** **[Online Database],** indexed at the FamilySearch.org website. This name index to births, baptisms, and Christenings came from the microfilm of the Genealogical Society of Utah originally filmed on site at various Maryland counties. This database has 199,433 records. See **https://familysearch.org/search/collection/1674912.**

**1654-1685.** ***Bristol and America, a Record of the First Settlers in the Colonies of North America 1654-1685: Including the Names With Places of Origin of More than 10,000 Servants to Foreign Plantations Who Sailed From the Port of Bristol to Virginia, Maryland, and Other Parts of the Atlantic coast, and Also to the West Indies From 1654 to 1685*** **[Printed Book],** compiled by W. Dodgson Bowman, N. Dermott Harding, and R. Hargreaves-Mawdsley, this list was compiled and published from records of the Corporation of the City of Bristol, England, originally published in London: [R.S. Glover], 1929, 1931, reprinted by Genealogical Publishing Co., Inc., Baltimore, 1970, 210 pages. Includes an index that was originally issued in a separate volume. See FHL book 973 W3b.

**1654-1695.** ***Births, Charles County, Maryland*** **[Typescript],** by Minnie Mickley, 26 pages, FHL book 975.247 V2 A1 No. 8.

**1655-1850.** ***Maryland, Compiled Marriages*** **[Online Database],** indexed at the Ancestry.com website. Compiled by Jordan Dodd, Liahona Research, acquired by Ancestry, 2004. Original data: Most of the records in this index may be found at the Maryland Historical Society or the Family History Library. More specific source information is listed with each entry. Original marriage licenses should be located at the county clerk's office. This database has over 250,000 individuals (brides & grooms). See **http://search.ancestry.com/search/db.aspx?dbid=7846.**

**1656-1662.** ***Index to Kent County, Md. Court Records*** **[Microfilm & Digital Capture],** from a manuscript at the Maryland Historical Society, Baltimore. Filmed by the Genealogical Society of Utah, 1949, 1 roll, FHL film #14206. To access the digital images, see the online FHL catalog page: **www.familysearch.org/search/catalog/46091.**

**1657-1777.** ***Maryland State Archives – Prerogative Court (Testamentary Proceedings)*** **[Online Database],** digitized images of the handwritten probate records are grouped by years: **http://guide.mdsa.net/series.cfm?action=viewSeries&ID=SM15.**

**1658.** ***Residents of Charles Co., Md in 1658: Their Immigration/Transportation Records*** **[Printed Book & Online Database],** by Ralph D. Smith. This is an extraction of names from a variety of sources. Charles County was created in 1658, taken from the bounds of St. Mary's County. Publ. R.D. Smith, Port Orange, FL, 2009, 6 vols, FHL book 975.247 W2s .1-6. To access a digital version (all 6 vols.) of this book, visit the online FHL catalog page for this title: **https://familysearch.org/search/catalog/1648834.**

**1658-1677.** ***The Women of Charles Co., MD*** **[Printed Book & Digital Version],** by Ralph D. Smith, publ. Port Orange, FL, 2011, 287 pages, FHL book 975.247 D3. To access the digital version, see the online FHL catalog page: **www.familysearch.org/search/catalog/1887698.**

**1658-1713.** ***Charles County Gentry: A Genealogical History of Six Emigrants: Thomas Dent, John Dent, Richard Edelen, John Hanson, George Newman, Humphrey Warren: All Scions of Armorial Families of old England who settled in Charles County, Maryland, and their Descendants.*** **[Printed Book & Online Database],** by Harry Wright Newman, publ. Washington, DC, 1940, 321 pages, FHL book 975.247 D2n. To access a digital version of this book, visit the online FHL catalog page for this title. See **https://familysearch.org/search/catalog/255279.**

**1658-1722.** ***Index to Rent Roll (Land Records) of Talbot County, Maryland*** **[Printed Book],** by Annie Walker Burns. Publ. A.B. Burns, c1945, 51 pages, FHL book 975.232 R22b. Also on microfiche, FHL fiche #6050102.

**1658-1940.** ***Maryland County Marriages*** **[Online Database],** indexed at the FamilySearch.org website. Source: FamilySearch extractions from Clerks of Circuit Court from Baltimore, Charles, Dorchester, Frederick, Harford, Prince George's, Somerset, and St. Mary's counties. This database has 106,686 records. See **www.familysearch.org/search/collection/2523377.**

**1658-1967.** ***Maryland, St. Mary's County, Probate General Index*** **[Online Database],** digitized by the Genealogical Society of Utah, 2011. Contains indexes from the Orphans' Court and the Register of Wills, St. Mary's County, Maryland. To view the digital images, access the online FHL catalog page for this title. See **https://familysearch.org/search/catalog/1986549.**

**1659-1723.** ***Index, Rent Roll, Dorchester County, Maryland*** **[ Microfilm & Digital Capture],** from a book compiled by Annie Walker Burns, publ. Baltimore, c1940, 64 pages. Filmed by the Library of Congress Photoduplication Service, 1987, 1 roll, FHL film #1550153. To access the digital images, see the online FHL catalog page: **www.familysearch.org/search/catalog/514269.**

**1659-1750.** ***Citizens of the Eastern Shore of Maryland*** **[Printed Book],** compiled by F. Edward Wright, published by Family Line Publications, Silver Spring, MD, 1986. Includes index. Contents: Listings of taxables, petitioners, bounty recipients, overseers of roads, militiamen, cattle mark registrants, charity cases, persons reimbursed by the court and persons fined. See FHL book 975.21 D2w.

**1659-1759. Baltimore County Families [Printed Book],** by Robert W. Barnes. Baltimore County originally embraced all or parts of present-day Anne Arundel, Carroll, Harford, and Cecil counties, and this is a book that provides comprehensive genealogical data on the hundreds of families and thousands of individuals who settled in the parent county during the first hundred years of its existence. Most of the immigrants were either migrants from Southern Maryland, Virginia's Eastern Shore, and Pennsylvania or immigrants from the British Isles whose ranks included servants, convicts, and Jacobite rebels. Publ. Genealogical Publishing Co, Baltimore, 1989, 924 pages, FHL book 975.271 D2b.

**1659-1800.** ***Baltimore County Marriage Evidences and Family Relationships*** **[Printed Book],** by Robert W. Barnes. For this companion volume to *Baltimore County Families*, Mr. Barnes has unearthed over 10,000 marriages from indirect sources. Arranged alphabetically by the surname of the groom (in most cases), the entries provide the names of the bride and groom, date of marriage, and the source. In many instances we also learn the name of persons related to the spouses, name of the officiating minister, or other information. Publ. Genealogical Publishing Co, Baltimore, 2014, 566 pages, FHL book 975.271 K2b.

**1659-1850.** ***Index of Baltimore County Wills*** **[Printed Book],** compiled by Bettie S. Carothers and Robert W. Barnes. Publ. Carothers, Lutherville, MD, 1979, 79 pages, FHL book 975.271 P22c.

**1660-1777.** ***Index to Baltimore County Wills*** **[Printed Book],** by Raymond B. Clark, publ. Clark, Arlington, VA, 1982, 21 pages, FHL book 975.2 P22c No. 7.

**1662-1745.** ***Judgement Records of Dorchester, Queen Anne's, and Talbot Counties, Maryland*** **[Printed Book],** by F. Edward Wright. These judgment records basically cover (with a few gaps) the following date spans: Dorchester County, 1690-1745; Queen Anne's County, 1709-1716; and, Talbot County, 1662-1717. Publ. Delmarva Roots, Lewes, DE, 2001, 217 pages, FHL book 975.2 P28w.

**1662-1777.** ***Index to Talbot County, Maryland Wills*** **[printed Book],** by Raymond B. Clark. Names in this index were taken from the *Maryland Calendar of Wills*, and James M. Magruder's *Index of Maryland Colonial*

*Wills 1634-1777*, and *Talbot County Will Libers,* publ. R.B. Clark, Arlington, VA, 1982, 23 pages, FHL book 975.2 P22c.

**1662-1911. *Maryland, Births and Christenings Index* [Online Database],** indexed at the Ancestry.com website. Source: FamilySearch extractions. Details in the index entries vary depending on the original record, but they may include: Name, Gender, Race, Birthplace, Birth Date, Christening Place, Christening Date, Death Date, Age at death; Father's name, age, birthplace; Mother's name, age, birthplace; Paternal Grandparents, Maternal Grandparents, and FHL film number. This database has 176,875 records. See **https://search.ancestry.com/search/db.aspx?dbid=2565.**

**1662-1960. *Maryland: Index to the Wills of St. Mary's County, 1662-1960 and Somerset County, 1664-1955* [Printed Book],** edited by Joan Hume. The index to St. Mary's County wills is arranged alphabetically by the name of the testator and gives the date and source of the original will. The Somerset index is arranged chronologically and thereunder alphabetically. Altogether, about 5,000 wills for St. Mary's County and 7,500 wills for Somerset County, many of them dated prior to 1800, are indexed. Publ. Genealogical publishing Co, Baltimore, 1970, reprinted 2003, 277 pages, FHL 975.2 P22hs.

**1665-1687. *Baltimore County Land Records: from the Maryland Historical Magazine* [Printed Book],** by Louis Dow Sisco, with a new introduction and index by Robert Barnes. Publ. Clearfield, Baltimore, 1992, 113 pages, FHL book 975.271 R28s. For a searchable digital version of this book, visit the Ancestry.com website. See **http://search.ancestry.com/search/db.aspx?dbid=49034.**

**1666-1720. *Index to Somerset County, Maryland, Births, Marriages, Deaths* [Printed Book],** by Annie Walker Burns, 79 pages, FHL book 975.223 V22b.

**1666-1970. *Maryland, Marriages* [Online Database],** indexed at the FamilySearch.org website. This name index to marriages came from the microfilm of the Genealogical Society of Utah, originally filmed on site at various Maryland counties. This database has 256,134 records. See **https://familysearch.org/search/collection/1675199.**

**1667-1899. *Maryland, Compiled Marriages* [Online Database],** indexed at the Ancestry.com website, from a database compiled by Jordan Dodd, Liahona Research, 2000. The first publication contained county marriages for Harford, Kent, Allegany, Carroll, Frederick, Montgomery, Prince George's, Washington, Cecil, Somerset, Queen Anne's, Worcester, Caroline, Anne Arundel, and Talbot counties. An update now includes marriages from Dorchester and Frederick counties. This database has 84,761 records. See **http://search.ancestry.com/search/db.aspx?dbid=4729.**

**1668-1995. *Maryland, Church Records* [Online Database],** indexed at the FamilySearch.org website. Source: FamilySearch index to records of various libraries, churches, historical and national societies, private, and public records. This database has 115,481 records. See **www.familysearch.org/search/collection/2385204.**

**1674-1718. *Maryland State Archives – Prerogative Court (Inventories and Accounts)* [Online Database],** digitized images of the handwritten probate records are grouped by years. See **http://guide.mdsa.net/series.cfm?action=viewSeries&ID=SM13.**

***1678 Maryland Tax List* [Online Database],** extracted from the Maryland Archives, Proceedings and Acts of the General Assembly of Maryland, Oct 1678-Nov 1683. A name list by county is at the USGenWeb site for Maryland. See **http://files.usgwarchives.net/md/statewide/taxlists/1678-tax-list.txt.**

**1679-1783. *Settlers of Maryland* [Printed Book & Online Database],** by Peter Coldham Wilson. This five-volume series is a continuation of the work started by Gust Skordas and Carson Gibb. It may include county, name of tract, acreage, date, and references. In the early 1680s, the headright system was replaced by cash sales of proprietary lands. 5 vols., publ. Genealogical Publishing Co, Baltimore, 1995-1996, FHL Book 975.2 R28c. An online version of the five volumes was digitized and indexed at the Ancestry.com website with the title, ***Settlers of Maryland, 1679-1783. Consolidated Edition* [Online Database].** See **http://search.ancestry.com/search/db.aspx?dbid=49058.**

- The five volumes of this same publication were also digitized and indexed online at the Ancestry.com website as five separate databases, see

1) ***Settlers of Maryland, 1679-1700.***
**http://search.ancestry.com/search/db.aspx?dbid=49355.**

2) ***Settlers of Maryland, 1701-1730.***

http://search.ancestry.com/search/db.aspx?dbid=49059.
3) *Settlers of Maryland, 1731-1750.*
http://search.ancestry.com/search/db.aspx?dbid=49356.
4) *Settlers of Maryland, 1751-1765.*
http://search.ancestry.com/search/db.aspx?dbid=49357.
5) *Settlers of Maryland, 1766-1783.*
http://search.ancestry.com/search/db.aspx?dbid=49358.

***1681 (Sept) Maryland Tax List* [Online Database],** extracted from the Maryland Archives, Proceedings and Acts of the General Assembly of Maryland, Oct 1678-Nov 1683. An alpha name list is at the USGenWeb site for Maryland. See
http://files.usgwarchives.net/md/statewide/taxlists/1681-sep-tax-list.txt.

***1681 (Nov) Maryland Tax List* [Online Database],** extracted from the Maryland Archives, Proceedings and Acts of the General Assembly of Maryland, Oct 1678-Nov 1683. An alpha name list is at the USGenWeb site for Maryland. See
http://files.usgwarchives.net/md/statewide/taxlists/1681-nov-tax-list.txt.

**1681-1994. *A Record of Interments at the Friends Burial Ground, Baltimore, Maryland (est. 1681)* [Printed Book & Online Database].** Compiled by E. Erick Hoopes, publ. Clearfield, Baltimore, 1995, 66 pages, FHL book 975.26 V38h. For a digital version of this book, see the Ancestry.com website. See
http://search.ancestry.com/search/db.aspx?dbid=48186.

***1682 Maryland Tax List* [Online Database],** extracted from the Maryland Archives, Proceedings and Acts of the General Assembly of Maryland, Oct 1678-Nov 1683. A name list is at the USGenWeb site for Maryland. See
http://files.usgwarchives.net/md/statewide/taxlists/1682-tax-list.txt.

**"1689 Public Levy in Colonial Maryland" [Printed Article],** in *Maryland Historical Magazine,* Vol. 53, No. 3 (Sep 1958).

**"1689 Somerset County, Maryland Inhabitants" [Printed Article],** in *Southeast Alabama Genealogical Society Quarterly*, Vol. 16, No. 4 (Apr 2000).

**1689-1780s. *To Maryland From Overseas: A Complete Digest of the Jacobite Loyalists Sold into White Slavery in Maryland, and the British and Continental Background of Approximately 1,400 Maryland Settlers from 1634 to the Early Federal Period with Source Documentation.* [Printed Book & Online Database],** by Harry Wright Newman, originally publ. H.W. Newman, Annapolis, MD, 1982, reprinted by Genealogical Publishing Co, Baltimore, 2002, 196 pages, FHL book 975.2 W2n. A digital version of this book is located at the Ancestry.com website. See
http://search.ancestry.com/search/db.aspx?dbid=49382.

**"1692 Tax List, Baltimore County, Maryland" [Printed Article],** in *Notebook of the Baltimore County Genealogical Society,* Vol. 13, No. 3 (Sep 1997).

**1692-1763. *Inhabitants of Baltimore County* [Printed Book],** compiled by F. Edward Wright, publ. Family Line Publications, Silver Spring, MD, 1987, 117 pages, FHL book 975.271 D2w.

**"1693 List of Taxables, Northside Patapsco Hundred, Baltimore County, Maryland" [Printed Article],** in *Notebook of the Baltimore County Genealogical Society,* Vol. 13, No. 4 (Dec 1997).

**1693. *The 1693 Census of the Swedes on the Delaware: Family Histories of the Swedish Lutheran Church Members Residing in Pennsylvania, Delaware, West New Jersey and Cecil County, Md.,* [Printed Book],** by Peter Stebbins Craig, publ. SAG Publications, Winter Park, FL, 1993, FHL book 973 X4c. To access a digital version of this book, visit the online FHL catalog page for this title. See
https://familysearch.org/search/catalog/633634.

**"1699 List of Taxables, Baltimore County, Maryland" [Printed Article],** in *Maryland Historical Magazine*, Vol. 12, No. 1 (Mar 1917); and in Maryland and Delaware Genealogist, Vol. 1, No. 2 (Dec 1959).

**1699-1706. *Baltimore County, Maryland, Tax List* [Printed Book],** compiled by Raymond B. Clark, Jr. & Sara Seth Clark, publ. 1964, 78 pages, FHL book 975.271 R4c.

**"1700 List of Taxables, Baltimore County, Maryland" [Printed Article],** in *Maryland and Delaware Genealogist,* Vol. 1, No. 3 (Mar 1960) and Vol. 1, No. 4 (Jun 1960).

**1700-1724. *Maryland Rent Rolls: Baltimore and Anne Arundel Counties, 1700-17076, 1705-1724, a Consolidation of Articles from the Maryland Historical Magazine* [Printed Book],** originally prepared in articles by the Maryland Historical Society, 1924-1931, this consolidation identifies the Rent Rolls that the Proprietors of Maryland assembled at various times to keep account of land grants and landowners from whom quit rent was due. The quit rents, an early form of property tax, were paid to the Proprietors throughout the Colonial Period. Publ. Genealogical Publishing Co, Baltimore, reprinted 2012, 282 pages, FHL book 975.2 R2m.

**1700s-1800s.** ***Maryland Settlers and Soldiers*** **[CD-ROM].** Includes records ranging from newspaper abstracts and marriage licenses to military diaries and cemetery transcriptions, this Family Archive compilation identifies approximately 313,000 of Maryland's settlers and soldiers. Publ. Genealogical Publishing Co for Family Tree Maker's family archives, FHL CD No. 521.

**"1701 List of Taxables, Baltimore County, Maryland" [Printed Article],** in *Maryland and Delaware Genealogist*, Vol. 2, No. 1 (Fall 1960, through Vol. 3, No. 3 (Mar 1962).

**"1702 List of Taxables, Baltimore County, Maryland" [Printed Article],** in *Maryland and Delaware Genealogist*, Vol. 4, No. 1 (Jan 1963) through Vol. 4, No. 4 (Oct 1963).

**1715-1745.** ***Jacobites of 1715 and 1745. North East Scotland*** **[Printed Book],** by Frances McDonnell. Includes an index to names, many of whom were transported to Virginia or Maryland. Publ. Genealogical Publishing Co, Baltimore, 1996, 2008, 2 Vols., FHL book 941 H2mcf.

**1716.** ***Jacobite Rebellion Ships*** **[Online Database],** an index to the manifests of ten ships to America with expelled Jacobites on board. The lists were prepared by the Immigrant Ships Transcription Guild (ISTG). See **http://immigrantships.net/jacobite/indexjacobite.html.**

**1718-1775.** ***Bound for America: The Transportation of British Convicts to the Colonies*** **[Printed Book],** by A. Roger Ekirch. Includes indexes to convicts, primarily to Virginia and Maryland. The Maryland group undoubtedly included a number of Jacobites. Publ. Clarendon Press, Oxford, England, 1987, 277 pages, FHL book 975 W2e.

**1718-1777.** See ***Maryland State Archives – Prerogative Court (Inventories)*** **[Online Database],** digitized images of the handwritten probate records are grouped by years. See **http://guide.mdsa.net/series.cfm?action=viewSeries&ID=SM11.**

**1718-1777.** ***Maryland State Archives – Prerogative Court (Accounts)*** **[Online Database],** digitized images of the handwritten probate records are grouped by years. See **http://guide.mdsa.net/series.cfm?action=viewSeries&ID=SM7.**

**"1718 Tax Assessment List, Baltimore County, Maryland" [Printed Article],** in *History Trails,* Vol. 30, No. 1-2 (1995).

**"1719 Anglican Inhabitants, Prince George's County, Maryland" [Printed Article],** in *Prince George's County Genealogical Society Bulletin*, Vol. 10, No. 6 (Feb 1979).

**"1724 Tax Lists, Somerset County, Maryland" [Printed Article],** in *National Genealogical Society Quarterly,* Vol. 61, No. 3 (Sep 1973) through Vol. 61, No. 4 (Dec 1973).

**"1725 Taxables, Annamessex Hundred, Somerset County, Maryland"[Printed Article],** in *Maryland Genealogical Society Bulletin,* Vol. 31, No. 2 (Spring 1990).

**"1725 Tax List, Somerset County, Maryland" [Printed Article],** in *Maryland Connections Queries,* Vol. 10, No. 2 (Jan 2000) through Vol. 11, No. 5 (Jul 2001).

**1725-1900.** ***Maryland and Virginia Convict Runaways: A Survey of English Sources*** **[Printed Book],** by Peter Wilson Coldham, publ. Genealogical Publishing Co, Baltimore, 2012, 105 pages, FHL book 975.5 P2cp.

**1727-1839.** ***Marriages and Deaths from the Maryland Gazette*** **[Printed Book],** by Robert Barnes, publ. Genealogical Publishing Co, Baltimore, 1972, 234 pages, FHL book 975.2 V2b. For a digital version of this book, see the Ancestry.com website. See **http://search.ancestry.com/search/db.aspx?dbid=48542.**

**1727-1882.** ***History of Western Maryland: Being a History of Frederick, Montgomery, Carroll, Washington, Allegany, and Garrett Counties from the Earliest Period to the Present Day; Including Biographical Sketches of their Representative Men*** **[Printed Book],** by J. Thomas Scharf, originally published Philadelphia, 1882; reprinted Genealogical Publishing Co, Baltimore, 1968, 2 vols., FHL book 975.2 H2s v.1-2. To access a digital version of vol. 1 and vol. 2, visit the online FHL catalog page: **https://familysearch.org/search/catalog/231288.**

- See also, ***Index to Scharf's History of Western Maryland: Volumes I and II*** **[Printed Book],** by Helen Long, publ. Family Line Publications, Westminster, MD, 1995, 369 pages, FHL book 975.2 H2 index.

**1727-1882.** ***Western Maryland Pioneers: Marriages, Early Settlers, Births and Deaths With Location, arranged and alphabetized by Hilda Chance*** **[Microfilm & Digital Version],** original published Liberty, PA, H. Chance, c1965, 2 vols., filmed by the Genealogical Society of Utah, 1968. Contents, Vol. 1: Frederick County Marriages Before 1830; Wills of Frederick County Before 1800; Frederick County Early Settlers, Land Grants, Land Purchasers, Some of These Were Local Officials. Frederick County Births and Deaths; Births and deaths of Early Washington County From Cemetery and Newspaper Obits. Early Marriages of Hagerstown, Washington County. Contents, Vol. 2: Early marriages of Allegany County; Early Marriages of Garrett County; Early Marriages of Montgomery County; Early Settlers, Montgomery County; Land Grants and Purchases, Births and Deaths of Montgomery County; Births and Deaths of Carroll County; Early Marriages of Carroll County; First Settlers of Carroll County from 1727; First Wills of Carroll County. From preface: "This is not a history of Maryland but lists, alphabetically arranged, of 8,000 early settlers, marriages, births and deaths, with dates, from cemeteries and newspapers, land grants and early wills index. These are taken from two large volumes of Thomas Scharf, 1882." See FHL film #560192. To access a digital version of volumes 1 & 2, visit the online FHL catalog page for this title. See **https://familysearch.org/search/catalog/180298.**

**1728-1922. Maryland Newspaper Archives [Online Database],** digitized and indexed newspapers at the GenealogyBank website for the following cities: Annapolis, Baltimore, Bel Air, Cambridge, Chestertown, Cumberland, Easton, Elkton, Frankfort, Frederick, Frostburg, Greenbelt, Hagers-Town, Hagerstown, Halifax, Jackson, La Plata, Leonardtown, Pocomoke City, Port Tobacco, Rising Sun, Rockville, Snow Hill, Thurmont, Towson, Uniontown, Upper Marlboro, and Westminster, see **www.genealogybank.com/gbnk/newspapers/explore/USA/Maryland.**

**1730-1825.** ***Cecil County, Maryland, Nottingham Quaker Meeting Records, 1730-1825*** **[Online Database],** indexed at the Ancestry.com website. Source: Ancestry extractions from Nottingham Monthly Meetings, Cecil Co MD. Includes birth, marriage and deaths. See **https://search.ancestry.com/search/db.aspx?dbid=5025.**

**"1732-1733 Taxables, St. Mary's County, Maryland" [Printed Article],** in *Calvert County Maryland Genealogy Newsletter,* Vol. 3, No. 12 (Mar 1989).

**"1732-1733 Tax Lists, Calvert County, Maryland" [Printed Article],** in *Maryland and Delaware Genealogist,* Vol. 30, No. 3 (Summer 1989); Vol. 30, No. 4 (Fall 1989) and Vol. 31, No. 2 (Spring 1990).

**"1732-1733 Tax Lists, St. Leonard's Creek Hundred, Calvert County, Maryland" [Printed Article],** in *Maryland and Delaware Genealogist,* Vol. 31, No. 1 (Winter 1990).

**"1733 Eltonhead Hundred Taxables, Calvert County, Maryland" [Printed Article],** in *Calvert County Maryland Genealogy Newsletter,* Vol. 8, No. 4 (Jul 1993).

***1733 Tax List, Charles County, Maryland*** **[Online Database],** indexed at the USGenWeb site for Charles Co MD. See **http://files.usgwarchives.net/md/charles/taxlists/ch1733tax.txt.**

**"1733 Taxables, Prince George's County, Maryland" [Printed Article],** in *Western Maryland Genealogy,* Vol. 3, No. 3 (Jul 1987).

**"1733 List of Taxables, Monocracy Hundred, Frederick County, Maryland" [Printed Article],** in *Maryland's Colonial Families Newsletter,* Vol. 3, No. 1 (Spring 1994).

***1734 Tax List (Partial), Charles County, Maryland*** **[Online Database],** indexed at the USGenWeb site for Charles Co MD. See **http://files.usgwarchives.net/md/charles/taxlists/ch1734tax.txt**

**1736-1737**. ***Maryland Death Records as taken from Maryland Account Book No. 15, dated 1736 to 1737*** **[Online Database],** compiled by Annie Walker Burns, 1955, 63 pages, publ. Washington, DC. To access a digital version, visit the online FHL catalog page for this title. See
**https://familysearch.org/search/catalog/1949934.**
- This database is also available at the Ancestry.com website. See
**https://search.ancestry.com/search/db.aspx?dbid=24896.**

**"1740 Tax List, Anne Arundel County, Maryland" [Printed Article],** in *Maryland Genealogical Society Bulletin,* Vol. 18, No. 1 (Winter 1977).

**1742-1868.** See ***Land Records, Worcester County, Maryland, 1742-1850; Indexes 1742-1868*** **[Microfilm & Digital Capture],** from originals at the Maryland State Archives and the Worcester County Courthouse in Snow Hill, MD. Filmed by the Genealogical Society of Utah, 1948, 34 rolls, beginning with FHL film #14565 (Grantee Index 1742-1844; Grantor Index, 1742-1844). To access the digital images, see the online FHL catalog page:
**https://familysearch.org/search/catalog/65266.**

**1748-1765**. ***This Was the Life, Excerpts from the Judgement Records of Frederick County, Maryland*** **[Printed Book & Online Database],** transcribed and edited by Millard Milburn Rice. Publ. Monocacy Book Co, 1979, 308 pages, FHL book 975.287 P2r. For a digital version of this book, visit the Ancestry.com website. See
**http://search.ancestry.com/search/db.aspx?dbid=49379.**

**1748-1972.** ***Names in Stone: 75,000 Cemetery Inscriptions From Frederick County, Maryland*** **[Printed Book & Online Database],** by Jacob Mehrling Holdcraft. Reprinted with *More Names in Stone* (1972), adding another 3,300 inscriptions. Arranged in alpha order. Publ. Genealogical Publishing Co, Baltimore, 1985, 2 vols., 1,371 pages, FHL book 975.287 V3h 1985 v.1-2. For a digital version of Names in Stone, vol. 1 & 2, see the Ancestry.com website.
- For Vol. 1, see
**http://search.ancestry.com/search/db.aspx?dbid=49053.**
- For Vol. 2, see
**http://search.ancestry.com/search/db.aspx?dbid=49265.**

**1751-1776.** ***Maryland State Archives – Prerogative Court (Balance Book)*** **[Online Database],** digitized images of the handwritten probate records are grouped by years. See
**http://guide.mdsa.net/series.cfm?action=viewSeries&ID=SM9.**

**1752-1930.** ***Baltimore City Directories*** **[Microfiche & Microfilm],** originals by various publishers, filmed by Research Publications, Woodbridge, CT, 1980-1984. Most of these directories include suburban areas surrounding Baltimore city. FHL has microfiche for 1752, 1796, 1799-1804, 1807-1808, 1810, 1812, 1814-1819, 1822-1824, 1827, 1829, 1831, 1833, 1835-1838, 1840-1843, 1845, 1847-1851, and 1853-1860; and microfilm for 1863 through 1930. The microfiche series begins with FHL fiche #6043563 (1752 Baltimore); the microfilm series begins with FHL film #1376528 (1863-1864 Baltimore City Directory). For a complete list of all 95 fiche and roll numbers, see the online FHL catalog page for this title. See
**https://familysearch.org/search/catalog/528824.**

**1753-1851.** ***Maryland, Catholic Families*** **[Online Database],** indexed at the Ancestry.com website. Original data: 1) O'Rourke, Timothy J. *Catholic Families of Southern Maryland: Records of Catholic Residents of St. Mary's County in the Eighteenth Century.* Baltimore, MD, USA: Genealogical Publishing Co., 2003. 2) Koch, Richard T. *Western Maryland Catholics, 1819-1851.* Baltimore, MD, USA: Genealogical Publishing Co., 2000. This database has 13,595 records. See
**https://search.ancestry.com/search/db.aspx?dbid=61446.**

***1754 Tax List, Charles County, Maryland*** **[Online Database],** extracted at the USGenWeb site for Charles Co MD. See
**http://files.usgwarchives.net/md/charles/taxlists/ch1754tax.txt.**

**"1756 & 1757 Tax on Bachelors, Harford County, Maryland" [Printed Article],** in *Harford County Historical Society Newsletter,* (Jan 2001).

**"1756-1762 Tax on Bachelors, Baltimore County, Maryland" [Printed Article],** in Maryland Connections Queries, Vol. 2, No. 2 (Dec 1991).

**1756-1763.** See ***Marylanders and Delawareans in the French and Indian War, 1756-1763*** **[Printed Book],** by Henry C. Peden, Jr., publ. Colonial Roots, Lewes, DE, 2004, 364 pages, FHL book 975.M2pe.

***1758 Tax List Index, Charles County, Maryland*** **[Online Database],** indexed at the USGenWeb site for Charles Co MD. See
**http://files.usgwarchives.net/md/charles/taxlists/ch1758txi.txt.**

**"1760-1761 Rent Rolls, Frederick County, Maryland" [Printed Article],** in *Western Maryland Genealogy,* Vol. 2, No. 3 (Jul 1986).

**"1761 Taxables in Old Town and Sugarland Hundred, Frederick County, Maryland" [Printed Article],** in *Western Maryland Genealogy,* Vol. 6, No. 3 (Jul 1990).

**"1763 Taxables, Soldiers Delight Hundred, Baltimore County, Maryland" [Printed Article],** in *Maryland Connections Queries,* Vol. 10, No. 2 (Jan 2000) through Vol. 10, No. 6 (Aug 2000).

**"1763 Census of Acadians in Maryland" [Printed Article],** in Louisiana Genealogical Register, Vol. 21, No. 4 (Dec 1974).

**1763-1769.** ***"When Drunk is Very Bold." White Maryland Runaways, 1763-1769*** **[Printed Book],** by Joseph Lee Boyle. The roughly 750 runaway notices in "When Drunk Is Very Bold" name upwards of 2,500 people in all. The transcriber has gathered this otherwise inaccessible data by combing through twenty colonial newspapers, including the *Maryland Gazette.* The majority of the runaways named were from Maryland. Includes an introductory history of the convict trade and indentured servitude in Maryland, as well as an extensive bibliography and a comprehensive name index. Publ. Genealogical Publishing Co, Baltimore, 2011, 382 pages, available at the publisher's website: **www.genealogical.com.**

**1766.** ***Miscellaneous Lists of Taxables in 1766, Cecil County, Maryland*** **[Online Database],** name list at the USGenWeb site for Maryland. See **http://files.usgwarchives.net/md/cecil/taxlists/tax1766.txt.**

***1766 Tax Levy of Worcester County, Maryland*** **[Online Database],** indexed at the RootsWeb site for Worcester Co MD. See **http://freepages.genealogy.rootsweb.ancestry.com/~fassitt /levy1.html.**

**1767-1790.** ***Catholic Families of Southern Maryland: Records of Catholic Residents of St. Mary's County in the Eighteenth Century*** **[Printed Book],** by Timothy J. O'Rourke. Contains the marriages and baptisms from the Jesuit parishes of St. Francis Xavier and St. Inigoes, which, in the case of baptisms (1767-1794), give the names of children, parents, and godparents, and the date of baptism; and in the case of marriages (1767-1784), the names of the married partners and the date of marriage. Other records include congregation lists (1768-1769), rent rolls (various dates), births (various dates), subscribers to the Oath of Allegiance (1778), militia lists (1794), and voters' lists (1789-1790). Publ. Genealogical Publishing Co, Baltimore, 2008, 143 pages, FHL book 975.241 F2o.

**"1768 St. Inigoes Census, St. Mary's County, Maryland" [Printed Article],** name list in *Maryland Connections Queries,* Vol. 5, No. 3 (Feb 1995) through Vol. 9, No. 2 (Jan 1999).

**"1769 St. Inigoes Census, St. Mary's County, Maryland" [Printed Article],** in *Maryland Connections Queries,* Vol. 8, No. 5 (Jul 1998).

**1772-1777.** ***Magruder's Maryland Colonial Abstracts: Wills, Accounts and Inventories, 5 vols. in 1.*** **[Printed Book],** by James M. Magruder, Jr. These abstracts of about 1,500 Maryland wills, accounts, and inventories are completely indexed and cover the period 1772 through 1777. The information consists of the names of testators; dates of drawings and probates of wills, accounts, and inventories; places of residence; names and residence of wives, children, and legatees; amount and kind of property; and the names of overseers and witnesses, with references to the exact sources for the abstracts. Originally published Annapolis, 1934-1999, 5 vols., reprinted in 1 vol. by Genealogical Publishing Co, Baltimore, 1968, 682 pages total, FHL book 975.2 S2mj 1968. See also the FHL's set of 5 vols, FHL book 975.2 S2mj. To access a digital version of Vol. 2 (1774-1777), visit the online FHL catalog for the 1934-1939 publication. See **https://familysearch.org/search/catalog/231899.**

**1772-1890.** ***Maryland, Compiled Census and Census Substitutes Index*** **[Online Database].** Indexed at the Ancestry.com website. The census indexes were originally compiled by Accelerated Indexing Systems, Salt Lake City, UT and acquired by Ancestry in 1999, with these Maryland lists: 1790 Federal Census Index; 1800 Federal Census Index; 1810 Federal Census Index; 1820 Federal Census Index; 1830 Federal Census Index; 1840 Federal Census Index; 1840 Pensioners List; 1850 Federal Census Index; 1850 Slave Schedules; 1860 Federal Census Index; 1860 Slave Schedules; 1890 Naval Veterans; Early Census Index. This database has 332,937 records. For more detailed descriptions of each database, see **http://search.ancestry.com/search/db.aspx?dbid=3552.**

**1774-1778.** ***Charles County, Maryland, Court Records, An Every-Name Index*** **[Printed Book & Online Database],** by T.L.C. Genealogy, Miami Beach, FL, 1995, 124 pages, FHL book 975.247 P22t. See also, ***Index to Court Records, Charles County, Maryland*** **[Printed Book],** compiled by Annie Walker Burns, 1939, 2 vols. Contents: Vol. 1: A to F; Vol. 2: G to W. A searchable digital version is available at the Ancestry.com website. See
**http://search.ancestry.com/search/db.aspx?dbid=25712.**

**1774-1815.** ***Book of Marriage Licenses of Caroline County, Maryland*** **[Microfilm & Online Database],** from a book compiled by H.D. Cranor. Filmed by the Genealogical Society of Utah, 1948, 1 roll, FHL film #20438. For a digital version of this book, see the Ancestry.com website. See
**http://search.ancestry.com/search/db.aspx?dbid=48196.**
- See also ***Carolina County, Maryland Marriages, 1774-1815*** **[Online Database],** indexed at the Ancestry.com website. Original data: Cranor, Henry Downes. Marriage Licenses of Caroline County, Maryland, 1774-1815. Philadelphia, PA, USA: Henry Downes Cranor, 1904. See
**https://search.ancestry.com/search/db.aspx?dbid=4707.**

**1774-1919.** ***History of Caroline County, Maryland*** **[Printed Book & Online Database],** by Laura C. Cochrane, et al. It begins with Caroline's founding in 1774 from Dorchester and Queen Anne's counties to 1919. Throughout the text are many biographical sketches of leading citizens (e.g. Col. William Whitely, Mathew Drive, William Frazier, and Thomas Culbreth) and their families, which establish their contribution to the county and the state. There are also lists of soldiers from Caroline County who served in the various wars from the Revolution through World War I. Originally publ. J.W. Stowell, Federalsburg, MD, 1920, 348 pages, FHL book 975.231 H2h. To access a digital version of the 1920 edition, visit the online FHL catalog page for this title:
**https://familysearch.org/search/catalog/255391.**
- See also, ***History of Caroline County*** **[Printed Book],** a reprint by Genealogical Publishing Co, Baltimore, 1994, 359 pages, with an added index of over 1,700 names. Available at the publisher's website: **www.genealogical.com.**

**1774-1949.** ***American Biographical Library*** **[Online Database],** indexed at the Ancestry.com website. Containing over 75,000 full-text biographies, the American Biographical Library is comprised of the following works: *Biographical Directory of the American Congress, 1774-1949*; *Biographical Cyclopedia of American Women.* 2 vols; *Daughters of America (Women of the Century); Historical Register of Officers of the Continental Army During the War of the Revolution*; *Herringshaw's Encyclopedia of American Biography of the Nineteenth Century*; *American Biographical Notes: Being Short Notices of Deceased Persons, Chiefly Those Not Included in Allen's or Drake's Biographical Dictionary*; *Plymouth Colony*; and *The Twentieth Century Biographical Dictionary of Notable Americans*. Search the combined index for Maryland entries. See
**http://search.ancestry.com/search/db.aspx?dbid=2016.**

**"1775-1778 Census, Charles County, Maryland" [Printed Article],** name list in *Southern States Courier,* Vol. 3, No. 1 (Jan 1986).

**1775-1783.** ***Maryland Revolutionary Records: Data Obtained from 3,050 Pension Claims and Bounty Land Applications, Including 1,000 Marriages of Maryland Soldiers and a List of 1,200 Proved Services of Soldiers and Patriots of Other States*** **[Printed Book],** by Harry Wright Newman, originally printed 1938, H.W. Newman, reprinted Genealogical Publishing Co, Baltimore, 1980, 155 pages, FHL book 975.2 M2n. A digitized version of this book is available online at the Ancestry.com website. See
**http://search.ancestry.com/search/db.aspx?dbid=24897.**

**1775-1783.** ***Muster Rolls and Other Records of Service of Maryland Troops in the American Revolution*** **[Printed Book & Online Database],** originally published as Volume XVIII of the Archives of Maryland by the Maryland Historical Society, 1900. Reprinted Clearfield/Genealogical Publishing Co, Baltimore, 1996, 736 pages, FHL book 975.2 B4m v.18. This book was digitized and indexed at the Ancesstry.com website. See
**http://search.ancestry.com/search/db.aspx?dbid=48594.**

**1775-1783.** ***Maryland Militia in the Revolutionary War*** **[Printed Book],** by S. Eugene Clements and F. Edward Wright, publ. Family Line Publications, Westminster, MD, 1987, 351 pages, FHL book 975.2 M28c.

**1775-1783.** ***Maryland Revolutionary Records: Data Obtained from 3,050 Pension Claims and Bounty Land Applications, Including 1,000 Marriages of Maryland Soldiers and a List of 1,200 Proved Services of Soldiers and Patriots of Other States*** **[Printed Book & Online Database],** by Harry Wright Newman, publ.

Genealogical Publishing Co, Baltimore, 1980, 155 pages, FHL book 975.2 M2n 1980. For a digital version of this book, see
**https://search.ancestry.com/search/db.aspx?dbid=4260.**
- See also, ***Revolutionary Records of Maryland* [Online Database],** (from the 1924 book by Gaius Marcus Brumbaugh and Margaret Roberts Hodges), digitized and OCR indexed at the Ancestry.com website. **Table of Contents:** Title Page, Preface, Montgomery County, Maryland, 1778; Washington County, Maryland, 1778; Frederick County, Maryland, 1778; Prince George's County, Maryland, 1775-1783; and Index to This Book. See
**https://search.ancestry.com/search/db.aspx?dbid=48222.**

***1776 Census of Maryland*** [Printed Index & Online Database], compiled by Bettie Stirling Carothers, publ. Lutherville, MD, 1975, 212 pages, FHL 975.2 X2p 1776. To access a digital version of this book, see the FHL catalog page for this title. See
**https://familysearch.org/search/catalog/253505.** Or visit the Ancestry.com website for the title, ***Maryland, Colonial Census, 1776.*** See
**http://search.ancestry.com/search/db.aspx?dbid=4247.**

***1776 Census of Frederick County, Maryland*** {Printed Book & Digital Version], by John Miller, no publ. data. To access the digital images, see the online FHL catalog page: To access the digital version, see the online FHL catalog page:
**www.familysearch.org/search/catalog/2144817.**

**"Baltimore Residents Before 1776" [Printed Article],** in *Maryland Historical Magazine,* Vol. 42, No. 1 (Mar 1947).

**"1776 Provincial Maryland Census, Deptford Hundred, Fells Point" [Printed Article],** in *Maryland Historical Magazine*, Vol. 25, No. 3 (Sep 1930).

**"1776 Straight Hundred, Dorchester County, Maryland" [Printed Article],** name list in *Dorchester County Genealogical Magazine,* Vol. 3, No. 4 (Nov 1983).

**"1776 Naticoke Hundred, Dorchester County, Maryland" [Printed Article],** name list in *Dorchester County Genealogical Magazine,* Vol. 3, No. 1 (May 1983).

**"1776 Census, Harford County, Maryland" [Printed Article],** in *Genealogy,* Vol. 6, No. 12 (Dec 1916).

**"1776 Tax List, Transquakin Hundred, Dorchester County, Maryland" [Printed Article],** name list published serially in *Dorchester County Genealogical Magazine,* Vol. 3, No. 5 (Jan 1984) through No. 6 (Mar 1984).

**"1776 Taxables, Carroll County, Maryland" [Printed Article],** in *Carrolltonian,* Vol. 9, No. 4 (Jun 1990).

***1776 & 1778 Provincial Maryland Censuses* [Original Documents & Online Database].** Originals at the Maryland State Archives in Annapolis. The 1776 name lists are extant for Anne Arundel, Baltimore, Caroline, Dorchester, Frederick, Harford, Prince George's, Queen Anne, and Talbot Counties. The 1778 name lists are extant for Caroline, Charles, and Queen Anne's Counties only. The 1776 & 1778 colonial name lists are included in a larger census database accessible online at the MSA census indexes website. See
**http://census.msa.maryland.gov.**

**1776-1783. *Maryland Revolutionary War Records* [Online Database],** digitized and indexed at Ancestry.com, compiled from records at the Maryland State Archives by Harry W. Newman, 1938. This database is a collection of pension and bounty land claims on the state for military service in the war. Most records provide the soldier's name, birth date, rank, spouse, marriage date, and location of marriage. Many entries also contain unit information, location of service, number of acres awarded, and issue date. It contains over 3,000 pension and bounty applications along with nearly 1,000 marriages of Maryland soldiers and a list of 1,200 proved services of soldiers and patriots from other states. This database has 5,838 records, see
**www.ancestry.com/search/collections/4260.**

***1776, 1790 Dorchester; 1790 Worcester Census of Maryland* [Printed Book],** by Jody Powell, publ. J. Powell, Roanoke, TX, 1991, 58 pages, FHL book 975.2 A1 N. 187.

**1776-1864. *Maryland Records: Colonial, Revolutionary, County and Church* [Microfilm & Online Database],** from a book of original sources compiled by Gaius Marcus Brumbaugh. The FHL has microfilm of the original 2-vol. book published Baltimore: Williams & Wilkins, 1915, and Lancaster, PA, Lancaster Press, 1928. Includes index. Contents: **Vol. I:** Provincial census of August 31, 1776, Prince

George's county: Marriage licenses issued at Upper Marlborough, Prince George's county, 1777-1800: Two muster rolls, militia, Prince George's county: French war, 1799: Provincial census of 1776, Frederick County; Earliest records of marriages and births of All Saints' parish, Frederick, MD (1727-1781); Tombstone inscriptions from the old cemetery of All Saints' parish. Frederick, MD; Poll list of presidential election, November 9-12, 1796, Frederick County, MD; Constable's census of Charles County, 1775-1778; Marriage licenses of St. Mary's County, 1794-1864; and the Provincial census of 1776, Anne Arundel County. **Vol. II:** State of his Lordship's manor, 1776, 1767, 1768; Census of 1776; Oaths of fidelity and support; Early Maryland Naturalizations; Kilty's Laws; Revolutionary war pensions; some original commissions, etc.; and marriage records. It should be noted that Brumbaugh's 1915 extraction of the 1776 Maryland Census differs from the Carothers 1977 extraction, in that Brumbaugh chose to group some family names together, even though they may not have appeared together in the census lists. Carothers' lists are as they appeared on the originals, and an index to the names can be used to find the original arrangement. The Brumbaugh book is available on FHL film #1033832. To access the digital versions (Vol. I & Vol. II) visit the online FHL catalog page for this title. See **https://familysearch.org/search/catalog/155413.**

- The 2-vol. Brumbaugh work is also a Maryland online census source at Ancestry.com. for Vol. I, see **http://search.ancestry.com/search/db.aspx?dbid=6161.**
- For Vol. 2, see **http://search.ancestry.com/search/db.aspx?dbid=48204.**

**1776-1882.** ***Western Maryland Pioneers: Marriages, Early Settlers, Births and Deaths with Location*** [Printed Book, Microfilm & Digital Version], compiled by Hilda Chance, Liberty, PA, 1965, 2 vols. From the FHL catalog: "This is not a history of Maryland but lists, alphabetically arranged, of 8,000 early settlers, marriages, births and deaths, with dates, from cemeteries and newspapers, land grants and early wills index. These are taken from two large volumes of Thomas Scharf, 1882." **Contents: Vol. 1:** Frederick County marriage before 1830. Wills of Frederick County before 1800. Frederick County early settlers, land grants, land purchasers, some of these were local officials. Frederick County births and deaths. Births and deaths of early Washington County from cemetery and newspaper obits. Early marriages of Hagerstown, Washington County. **Vol. 2:** Early marriages of Allegany County. Early marriages of Garrett County. Early marriages of Montgomery County. Early settler, Montgomery County, Md., land grants and purchases. Births and deaths of Montgomery County. Births and deaths of Carroll County. Early marriages of Carroll County. First settlers of Carroll County from 1727. First wills of Carroll County. FHL film #560192. To access the digital version, see the online FHL catalog page: **www.familysearch.org/search/catalog/180298.**

**1776-1932.** ***Washington County, Maryland, Surname List of Deeds*** **[Printed Book],** by Dale Walton Morrow and Deborah Jensen Morrow. Publ. Traces, Center, MD, 1982, 48 pages, FHL book 975.291 R22m.

**"1777 Tax List, Montgomery County, Maryland" [Printed Article],** in *Maryland Connections Queries,* Vol. 6, No. 5 (Jun 1966), through Vol. 10, No. 1 (Nov 1999).

**1777-1783.** ***Montgomery County (Maryland) Tax Lists*** **[Microfilm & Digital Capture],** from the originals at the Montgomery County Historical Society, Rockville, MD. Filmed by the Genealogical Society of Utah, 1975, 1 roll, FHL film #1001813. To access the digital images, see the online FHL catalog page: **www.familysearch.org/search/catalog/49833.**

**1777-1804.** ***Index to the Record of Maryland Marriages*** **[Microfilm & Digital Capture],** from a typescript at the Maryland Historical Society, Baltimore. Filmed by the Genealogical Society of Utah, 1949, 1 roll, FHL film #13148. To access the digital images, see the online FHL catalog page: **www.familysearch.org/search/catalog/300779.**

**1777-1836.** ***Marriage Records, Prince Georges Co., Maryland*** **[Online Database],** digitized and OCR indexed at the Ancestry.com website. Original data: Greene, Sylvia Gorman.. *Marriage records, Prince Georges Co., Maryland, 1777 to 1836.* Mt. Rainier, Md.: unknown, 1941. See **https://search.ancestry.com/search/db.aspx?dbid=25573.**

**1777-1840.** ***Cecil County, Maryland Marriage Licenses*** **[Printed Book],** compiled by the Captain Jeremiah Baker Chapter, DAR. Contains a list of approximately 4,000 marriages. The entries give the precise date of the marriage, the full name of the groom, full maiden name of the bride, and the names of officiating ministers. Arranged alphabetically by the surname of the groom. Includes an index to brides. Originally published 1928, reprinted by Genealogical Publishing Co, Baltimore, 1974, 105 pages, FHL book 975.238 V28c.

**1777-1886.** ***Index of Marriage Licenses, Prince George's County, Maryland*** **[Printed Book & Online Database],** by Helen W. Brown. This work consists of an alphabetical list of nearly 14,000 names (male and female) with dates of marriage licenses. Includes names, dates, and any supplementary information, such as the name of a minister or place of residence or occupation. Publ. Genealogical Publishing Co, Baltimore, 1971, 249 pages, FHL book 975.251 V25b. For a digital version of this book, see the Ancestry.com website. See
**http://search.ancestry.com/search/db.aspx?dbid=48197.**

**1777-1917.** ***General Index of Wills of Anne Arundel County, Maryland*** **[Online Database],** digitized and OCR indexed at the Ancestry.com website. Source: Book, same title, by Margaret Roberts Hodges, 1922:
**https://search.ancestry.com/search/db.aspx?dbid=26147.**

**"1778 Tax List, Harford County, Maryland" [Printed Article],** in *Maryland Genealogical Society Bulletin,* Vol. 18, No. 1 (Winter 1977).

**1778. Orderly Book of the Maryland Loyalists Regiment, June 18, 1778, to October 12, 1778 [Online Database],** digitized and indexed at the Ancestry.com website. See
**http://search.ancestry.com/search/db.aspx?dbid=48189.**

**1778-1800.** ***Maryland Marriages*** **[Printed Book & Online Database],** compiled by Robert Barnes, publ. Genealogical Publishing Co., 1978, 300 pages, FHL book 975.2 K2ba. A searchable digital version of this book is available at the Ancestry.com website. See
**http://search.ancestry.com/search/db.aspx?dbid=48201.**

**1780.** ***Somerset County, Maryland Militia, Revolutionary War 1780 Princess Anne Battalion, Monie Company*** **[Online Database],** name list at the USGenWeb site for Somerset Co MD. See
**http://files.usgwarchives.net/md/somerset/military/sompabat.txt.**

**1780-1855.** ***Dorchester County Maryland, Marriage License Records*** **[Printed Book & Online Database],** by Katherine H. Palmer, publ. Cambridge, MD, c1930, at the Clayton Library, Houston, TX; digitized by the Genealogical Society of Utah, 2013. To access a digital version this book, visit the online FHL catalog page for this title. See
**https://familysearch.org/search/catalog/2226518.**

**1780-1865.** ***Complete List of Marriage Records in Dorchester County, from May 24, 1780 to July 1865*** **[Microfilm & Online Database],** from a book compiled by Katherine H. Palmer, publ. Cambridge, MD, 1930, 116 pages; filmed by the Library of Congress Photoduplication Service, 1987, FHL film #1490397. To access a digital version of this book, visit the online FHL catalog page for this title. See
**https://familysearch.org/search/catalog/514582.**

**"1781 Assessment Records, Choptank Hundred, Caroline County, Maryland" [Printed Article],** in *Maryland Genealogical Society Bulletin,* Vol. 35, No. 4 (Fall 1994).

**"1781-1782 Residents Who Paid Taxes, Somerset County, Maryland" [Printed Article],** in *More From the Shore,* Vol. 3, No. 1 (Spring 1984).

**"1782 Tax List, Frederick County, Maryland" [Printed Article],** in *Western Maryland Genealogy,* Vol. 15, No. 1 (Jan 1999).

***1783 Tax List of Maryland*** **[Printed Book & Online Database],** compiled by Bettie Stirling Carothers. Includes names extracted from the originals of the Provincial Maryland Tax List of 1783 at the Maryland State Archives. Publ. Lutherville, MD, 1977, indexed. FHL has Vol. 1: Cecil, Talbot, Harford, and Calvert Counties only. FHL book 975.2 R4c. A digital version is available at the Maryland State Archives website, see
**http://msa.maryland.gov/msa/stagser/s1400/s1437/html/ssi1437e.html.**

***1783 Tax List of Maryland, Index, Anne Arundel County*** **[Online Database],** indexed at the Maryland State Archives website. See
**http://msa.maryland.gov/msa/stagser/s1400/s1437/html/1437aa.html.**

**"1783 Patapsco Hundred Tax List, Anne Arundel County, Maryland" [Printed Article],** in *Anne Arundel Readings,* Vol. 2, No. 1 (Jan 1999).

***1783 Tax List of Maryland, Index, Baltimore County*** **[Online Database],** indexed at the Maryland State Archives website. See
**http://msa.maryland.gov/msa/stagser/s1400/s1437/html/1437ba.html.**

***1783 Tax List of Baltimore County, Maryland* [Printed Book & Digital Version],** abstracted by Robert W. Barnes & Bettie Stirling Carothers; maps by George J. Horvath, Jr., publ. by Carothers, Lutherville, MD, 1978, 117 pages, FHL book 975.271 R48b. To access a digital version of this book, visit the online FHL catalog page for this title. See **https://familysearch.org/search/catalog/656633.**

***1783 Tax List of Maryland, Index, Calvert County* [Online Database],** indexed at the Maryland State Archives website. See **http://msa.maryland.gov/msa/stagser/s1400/s1437/html/1437cv.html.**

***1783 Tax List of Maryland, Index, Caroline County* [Online Database],** indexed at the Maryland State Archives website. See **http://msa.maryland.gov/msa/stagser/s1400/s1437/html/1437ca.html.**

***1783 Tax List of Maryland (Cecil, Talbot, Harford & Calvert Counties)* [Printed Book],** by Bettie Carothers, publ. Carothers, Lutherville, MD, 1977, FHL book 975.2 R4. To access a digital version of this book, visit the online FHL catalog page for this title. See **https://familysearch.org/search/catalog/172221.**

***1783 Tax List of Maryland, Index, Cecil County* [Online Database],** indexed at the Maryland State Archives website. See **http://msa.maryland.gov/msa/stagser/s1400/s1437/html/1437ce.html.**

***1783 Tax List of Maryland, Index, Charles County* [Online Database],** indexed at the Maryland State Archives website. See **http://msa.maryland.gov/msa/stagser/s1400/s1437/html/1437ch.html.**

***1783 Tax List of Maryland, Index, Dorchester County* [Online Database],** indexed at the Maryland State Archives website. See **http://msa.maryland.gov/msa/stagser/s1400/s1437/html/1437do.html.**

**"1783 Tax List, Dorchester County, Maryland" [Printed Article],** in *Dorchester County Genealogical Magazine,* Vol. 9, No. 3 (Sep 1989).

**"1783 Tax list, Herring Point-Hog Range, Dorchester County, Maryland" [Printed Article],** in *Dorchester County Genealogical Magazine,* Vol. 9, No. 1 (May 1989).

**"1783 Tax List, Dorchester County, Maryland" [Printed Article],** in *Dorchester County Genealogical Magazine,* Vol. 3, No. 2 (Jul 1983) through Vol. 12, No. 5 (Jan 1993).

**"1783 Tax Records, Dorchester County, Maryland" [Printed Article],** in *Dorchester County Genealogical Magazine,* Vol. 4, No. 2 (Jul 1984).

***1783 Tax List of Maryland, Index, Harford County* [Online Database],** indexed at the Maryland State Archives website. See **http://msa.maryland.gov/msa/stagser/s1400/s1437/html/1437ha.html.**

***1783 Tax List of Maryland, Index, Kent County* [Online Database],** indexed at the Maryland State Archives website. See **http://msa.maryland.gov/msa/stagser/s1400/s1437/html/1437ke.html.**

***1783 Tax List of Maryland, Index, Montgomery County* [Online Database],** indexed at the Maryland State Archives website. See **http://msa.maryland.gov/msa/stagser/s1400/s1437/html/1437mo.html.**

***1783 Tax List of Maryland, Index, Queen Anne's County* [Online Database],** indexed at the Maryland State Archives website. See **http://msa.maryland.gov/msa/stagser/s1400/s1437/html/1437qa.html.**

***1783 Tax List of Maryland, Index, Somerset County* [Online Database],** indexed at the Maryland State Archives website. See **http://msa.maryland.gov/msa/stagser/s1400/s1437/html/1437so.html.**

***1783 Tax Lists for Somerset County and Worcester County, Maryland* [Printed Book & Online Database],** transcribed by Ruth T. Dryden, 110 pages, FHL book 975.221 R49d. Also on microfiche, FHL fiche #6117597. To view a digital version of this book, visit the online FHL catalog page for this title: **https://familysearch.org/search/catalog/455432.**

***1783 Tax List of Maryland, Index, Talbot County* [Online Database],** indexed at the Maryland State Archives website. See **http://msa.maryland.gov/msa/stagser/s1400/s1437/html/1437ta.html.**

***1783 Tax List of Maryland, Index, Washington County*** **[Online Database],** indexed at the Maryland State Archives website. See
**http://msa.maryland.gov/msa/stagser/s1400/s1437/html/1437wa.html.**

***1783 Tax List of Maryland, Index, Worcester County*** **[Online Database],** indexed at the Maryland State Archives website. See
**http://msa.maryland.gov/msa/stagser/s1400/s1437/html/1437wo.html.**

**"1783 Tax List, Harford County, Maryland" [Printed Article],** in *Harford Historical Bulletin,* No. 24 (Spring 1985).

**"1783 Tax Assessment, Washington County, Maryland" [Printed Article],** in *Western Maryland Genealogy,* Vol. 7, No. 2 (Apr 1991) through Vol. 9, No. 3 (Jul 1993).

**"1785 Tax Lists, Carroll County, Maryland" [Printed Article],** in *Carrolltonian,* Vol. 13, No. 2 (Dec 1993).

**1787.** See ***Naturalizations, Washington County, Maryland, January 1787*** **[Online Database],** index at the USGenWeb site for Washington Co MD. See
**http://files.usgwarchives.net/md/washington/history/area/wash87.txt.**

**"1788 Name List, Patapsco Lower, Carroll County, Maryland" [Printed Article],** in *Maryland Genealogical Society Bulletin,* Vol. 7, No. 1 (Feb 1966).

**1790.** ***Heads of Families at the First Census of the United States Taken in the Year 1790, Maryland*** **[Printed Extract/Index & Digital Version],** pub. Census Bureau, Washington, DC, 1907, 189 pages, FHL book 975.2 X2ma 1790. The Census Office of 1850 became the Bureau of the Census in 1905, promoted to a full-time federal agency for the first time. The Census Bureau's first project was to compile an extract and index to the 1790 federal census. Working from the available original manuscripts, the 1790 districtwide census losses included those for Kentucky, Delaware, Georgia, New Jersey, and Virginia. Since Virginia had extant tax lists covering all of its counties for the years immediately preceding 1790, the Census Bureau used these tax lists to reconstruct the 1790 name lists for the entire state of Virginia. A few 1790 counties of other states were also reconstructed from tax lists, including certain counties in North Carolina and Maryland. Therefore, the Maryland 1790 name lists taken from the originals, such as those at FamilySearch, Ancestry, et al, are inferior to the Maryland name lists in this 1907 book. To access a digital version of this book, visit the FHL catalog page:
**https://familysearch.org/search/catalog/2365132.**

**1790-1840.** ***Maryland, 1790 thru 1840 Federal Census: Population Schedules*** **[Microfilm & Digital Capture],** from the National Archives, filmed 1938-1969, 27 rolls. To access the digital images, see the online FHL catalog page:
**www.familysearch.org/search/catalog/745493.**

**1790-1860.** ***U.S. Circuit Court Criminal Case Files*** **[Online Database],** indexed at the Ancestry.com website. This database contains images of criminal case files of the U.S. Circuit Court for the: District of Maryland, 1795-1860; Southern District of New York, 1790-1853; Eastern District of Pennsylvania, 1791-1840; and Eastern District of Louisiana, New Orleans, 1870-1871. Types of documents found in the case files include bills of indictment, presentments, pleas of defendants, recognizances, depositions, affidavits, subpoenas, writs, orders of the court, petitions, warrants, bonds, Presidential orders of pardon from imprisonment, and other papers filed in criminal actions. See
**http://search.ancestry.com/search/db.aspx?dbid=1248.**

**1790-2007.** See ***Web: Washington County, Maryland, Obituary Index*** **[Online Database].** This is a database of the Washington County Free Library, accessible from the Ancestry.com website. See
**http://search.ancestry.com/search/db.aspx?dbid=70013.**

**1790-1943.** See ***Washington County, Maryland Obituary Locator*** **[Printed Book],** by C. William Ridenour. Publ. Willow Bend Books, Westminster, MD, 2000-2001, 580 pages, FHL book 975.291 V42r.

**1791-1865.** See ***Marriage Records, Allegany County, Maryland*** **[Microfilm & Digital Capture],** from the originals at the Allegany County Courthouse, Cumberland, MD. Filmed by the Genealogical Society of Utah, 1948, 1 roll, FHL film #13310. To access the digital images, see the online FHL catalog page:
**www.familysearch.org/search/catalog/388433.**

**"1793 Tax Assessment, Allegany County, Maryland" [Printed Article],** in *Western Maryland*

*Genealogy,* Vol. 6, No. 2 (Apr 1990) through Vol. 6, No. 4 (Oct 1990).
- See also ***1793 Tax Assessment, Allegany County, Maryland*** **[Printed Book],** by MariLee Beatty Hageness, publ. MLH Research, Anniston, Al, 2001, 38 pages, FHL book 975.294 R4h.

**"1793 Tax List, Taylorsville Area, Carroll County, Maryland" [Printed Article],** in *Western Maryland Genealogy,* Vol. 5, No. 4 (Oct 1989).

**"1793 Tax Assessment, Unity and Burnt Woods, Frederick County, Maryland" [Printed Article],** in *Western Maryland Genealogy*, Vol. 13, No. 2 (Apr 1997).

**"1793 Tax Assessment, District 1, Frederick County, Maryland" [Printed Article],** in *Western Maryland Genealogy,* Vol. 13, No. 1 (Jan 1997).

**1793 Tax Assessment, Montgomery County, Maryland" [Printed Article],** in *Western Maryland Genealogy,* Vol. 12, No. 1 (Jan 1996) through Vol. 12, No. 4 (Oct 1996).

**"1795 Inhabitants of Georgetown, Montgomery County, Maryland" [Printed Article],** in *Maryland Genealogical Bulletin,* Vol. 12, No. 2 (Apr 1941).

**1795-1931.** ***Maryland, Federal Naturalization Records*** **[Online Database],** indexed at the Ancestry.com website. Source: National Archives records of District Courts. For each person, the records may include Declarations of Intention to become a Citizen; Petitions for Naturalization, Oaths of Allegiance, Certificates of Naturalization. Records may include a Name, Birth Date, Birth Place, Immigration Year, Place of Residence, Occupation, Date of Departure, Place of Departure, Place of Arrival, Spouse's Name/Birthdate/residence, Number of Children with child's Name, Birthdate, Birthplace, and Residence. This database has 78,347 records. See
**https://search.ancestry.com/search/db.aspx?dbid=61200.**

**1796-1810.** See ***The Marriage Licenses of Talbot County, Maryland*** **[Printed Book & Digital Version],** compiled by the Carter Braxton Chapter, DAR, c1947, 51 pages, FHL book 975.232 V29c. Also on microfilm, see FHL film #14519. For a digital version of this book, visit the online FHL catalog page for this title. See
**https://familysearch.org/search/catalog/293006.**

- Another digital version is at the Ancestry.com website. See
**https://search.ancestry.com/search/db.aspx?dbid=24895.**

**1796-1816. Marriages and Deaths from Baltimore Newspapers [Printed Book],** by Robert Barnes. Compiled from 17 newspapers, includes 7,500 abstracts, naming brides, parents, and relatives. Publ. Genealogical Publishing Co, Baltimore, 1978, 383 pages, FHL book 975.26 V2b.
- See also ***Marriages and Deaths from Baltimore Newspapers, 1796-1816*** **[Online Database],** digitized and OCR indexed at the Ancestry.com website. See
**https://search.ancestry.com/search/db.aspx?dbid=48541.**

**1796-1850.** ***Montgomery County, Maryland Marriages*** **[Printed Book],** by Tressie Nash Bowman, publ. Rockville, MD, 1966, 101 pages, FHL 975.284 V25b.

**1796-1940.** ***Maryland, Probate Estate and Guardianship Files*** **[Online Database],** digitized and indexed at the FamilySearch.org website. Includes name index and images of probate estate files from the Register of Wills office in the county courthouses. Currently, the following counties are represented in this collection: Allegany (1779-1946), Baltimore City (1922-1941), Calvert (1882-1940), Caroline (1838-1940), Cecil (1851-1940), Garrett (1873-1946), Kent (1749-1940), Prince George's (1796-1940), and Queen Anne's (1833-1940), Somerset (1789-1946), Wicomico (1868-1940). This database has 89,727 records. See
**https://familysearch.org/search/collection/1542664.**

**"1797 Tax List, Baltimore County, Maryland" [Printed Article],** in *National Genealogical Society Quarterly,* Vol. 66, No. 3 (Sep 1978).

**"1797 Taxables, Queen Anne's County, Maryland" [Printed Article],** in *Chesapeake Cousins,* Vol. 20, No. 1 (Fall 1993).

**1797-1951**. ***Maryland, Naturalization Indexes*** **[Online Database],** digitized and indexed at the FamilySearch.org website. Collection of six separate alphabetic indexes to naturalization petitions filed in the U.S. Circuit and District courts of Maryland from 1797 to 1951. Each index comprises a specific time period. 1797-1906, Oct 1906-Apr 1915, Apr 1915-Apr 1920, Apr 1920-Oct 1925, Nov 1925-Dec 1951, and the sixth is an index to aliens who joined the U.S. military between May 1918 and Apr 1923. An Index was

provided by Fold3.com. This database has 85,222 records. See
**https://familysearch.org/search/collection/1838829.**

**"1798 Federal Direct Tax-Maryland" [Printed Article],** a name list published in *Maryland Genealogical Society Bulletin*, beginning with Vol. 5, No. 4 (Oct 1934).

**1798. *The Particular Assessment Lists for Baltimore and Carroll Counties, 1798* [Printed Book & Digital Version],** by George J. Horvath, publ. Family Line Publications, Westminster, MD, 178 pages, FHL book 975.2 R28hgv. To access a digital version of this book, visit the online FHL catalog page for this title. See
**https://familysearch.org/search/catalog/2143991.**

**1798 Federal Assessment Rolls, Maryland [Printed Articles].** In addition to the above, several Maryland countywide name lists have been published:

- Allegany County, see **"1798 Property Owners in Assessment Book,"** published in *The Old Pike Post,* Vol. 15, No. 1 (Mar 1998) through Vol. 15, No. 3 (Sep 1998).
- Baltimore County, see **"1798 Tax Assessment List,"** in *Maryland and Delaware Genealogist,* published serially, beginning with Vol. 18, No. 3 (Apr 1977).
- Carroll County, see **"1798 Tax Assessment,"** in *Historical Society of Carroll County, Maryland Newsletter,* Vol. 26, No. 1 (Jan 1976).
- Frederick County, see **"1798 Tax Assessment List",** in *Western Maryland Genealogy*, Vol. 10, No. 2 (Apr 1994) through Vol. 14, No. 4 (Oct 1998); and in *Antietam Ancestors*, Vol. 1, No. 3 (Summer 1984) through Vol. 2. No. 1 (Winter 1985).
- Prince George's County, see **"1798 Tax List, Prince George's County, Maryland,"** in *Prince George's County Genealogical Society Bulletin,* Vol. 5, No. 8 (Oct 1974).

**1798. *Federal Direct Tax of 1798, St. Mary's County, Maryland: Taken as of 1 October 1798* [Printed Book],** transcribed by Wanda M. Schuhart, publ. St. Mary's County Historical Society, 1998, 247 pages, FHL book 975.241 R48s.

**1798-1800 *1798 Federal Assessment Rolls, Maryland & District of Columbia, with some 1790, 1799, and 1800 name lists added* [Microfilm & Digital Capture].** This is basically the contents of the 1798 Federal Direct Tax List for Maryland, but with some added name lists for certain counties for subsequent years. Originals microfilmed by Maryland Hall of Records Commission, 1965. Includes 1798 taxpayer name lists for Ann Arundel Co.; Caroline Co.; Baltimore County & City, District of Columbia (Washington County, DC, the portion formerly in Maryland); Prince Georges Co.; Queen Anne's Co.; and added lists for 1798-1800 Baltimore City; Baltimore County, 1798 (mostly) with some 1799 & 1800; 1798-1800 Charles Co.; 1798-1800 Harford Co.; 1798-1800 St. Mary's Co.; 1798-1800 Somerset Co.; and a 1790 Talbot County list. The FHL has 13 rolls of microfilm, beginning with FHL film #499893 (1798 Anne Arundel Co). To access the digital images, see the online FHL catalog page:
**https://familysearch.org/search/catalog/340141.**

**1798-1808. *A Name Index to the Baltimore City Tax Records of the Baltimore City Archives* [Printed Book & Online Database],** edited by Richard J. Cox, publications of the Baltimore City Archives No. 4. Publ. Baltimore City Archives, 1981, 229 pages, FHL book 975.26 R42n. For a searchable digital version of this book, visit the Ancestry.com website. See
**http://search.ancestry.com/search/db.aspx?dbid=4203.**

**1798-1832. *County Tax Assessment of Talbot County, Maryland* [Printed Book],** by Cynthia V. Schmidt. Includes indexes. Contents: Vol. 1: 1798; Vol. 2: 1817; and Vol. 3: 1832. Publ. C.V. Schmidt, Cordova, MD, 2003, 3 vols., FHL book 975.232 R4s. v.1-3.

**1799-1994. *Maryland Online Historical Newspapers* [Online Database],** links to newspaper sites with images of newspapers published in Baltimore City (1779-1992, Google News Archive & Library of Congress); Dorchester – Cambridge (1856-1857, Google New Archive); and Prince George's – Upper Marlboro (1946-1994, Georgia State University Library). See
**https://sites.google.com/site/onlinenewspapersite/Home/usa/md.**

**1799-1860. *Index to Marriage Records, Washington County, Maryland* [Microfilm & Digital Capture],** from the originals at the Washington County courthouse, Hagerstown, MD. Filmed by the Genealogical Society of Utah, 1948, 1 roll, FHL film 14643. To access the digital images, see the online FHL catalog page:
**www.familysearch.org/search/catalog/121170.**

**1800. *Maryland 1800 Census Index* [Printed Index],** compiled by Ronald Vern Jackson, et al, publ. Accelerated Indexing Systems, 1976, 154 pages, FHL book 975.2 X2p 1800.

**"1800, 1804, Poll Book, Annapolis, Anne Arundel County, Maryland"** [Printed Article], in *Maryland Historical Magazine*, (1991).

**1801-1820.** ***Maryland Marriages*** **[Printed Book & Online Database],** compiled by Robert Barnes, publ. Genealogical Publishing Co., 1993, 260 pages, FHL book 975.2 K2baa. An indexed digital version of this book is available at the Ancestry.com website: **http://search.ancestry.com/search/db.aspx?dbid=48202.**

**1802-1965.** ***Early State Records Online, Newspapers*** **[Online Database],** links to Maryland newspaper images at the Maryland State Archives website. Included are the *American and Commercial Daily Advertiser*, 1802-1807; *Baltimore Clipper*, 1847-1863; *Baltimore Whig*, Jul 1810-Dec 1810; *Cambridge Chronicle*, 1830-1947; *Cecil Whig*, 1870-1874; *Centreville Observer*, 1871-1918; *Easton Gazette*, 1854-1871; *Ellicott City Times*, 1854-1871; *Kent County News*, Jan 1965-Jun 1965; *Maryland Journal*, Jan 1889-Dec 1889), *Maryland News Sheet*, 1861-1862; *Maryland Republican*, Jun 1809-Dec 1809; *Montgomery County Sentinel*, 1860-1872; *Queenstown News*, 1888-1903; *Republican Star/Eastern Shore General Advertiser*, 1802-1803; and *South,* 1861-1862: **http://msa.maryland.gov/megafile/msa/speccol/sc4800/sc4872/html/newspapers.html.**

**1804 Baltimore County Tax Assessment Lists [Printed Articles],** Name lists (by Hundreds) serialized in *Maryland Genealogical Society Bulletin*:

- Unnamed Hundred, in Vol. 41, No. 3 (Summer 2000).
- Patapsco Hundred, in Vol. 42, No. 2 (Spring 2001).
- Mine Run Hundred, in Vol. 41, No. 4 (Fall 2000).
- Soldiers Delight Hundred, in Vol. 42, No. 2 (Spring 2001).
- Middle River Hundred, in Vol. 42, No. 2 (Spring 2001).
- North Hundred, in Vol. 41, No. 2 (Spring 2000).

- See also, ***1804 Tax Assessment: Baltimore County, Maryland*** **[Printed Book],** by Michael A. Ports, publ. Clearfield, Baltimore, 2013, 157 pages, FHL 975.271 R4p.

**"1804-1812 Tax List, Allegany County, Maryland" [Printed Article],** in *Western Maryland Genealogy*, Vol. 16, No. 1 (Jan 2000) through Vol. 16, No. 4 (Oct 2000).

**"1804-1820 Tax Lists, Allegany County, Maryland" [Printed Article],** in *Western Maryland Genealogy*, Vol. 17, No. 1 (Jan 2001) through Vol. 17, No. 4 (Oct 2001).

**1810.** ***Maryland 1810 Census Index, A-Z*** **[Printed Index],** compiled and published by Heritage Quest, Bountiful, UT, 2000, 287 pages, FHL book 975.2 X22m 1810.

***1814-1910 Baltimore City Directories*** **[Online Database],** see the parent web directory for city directories for 1814-1815, 1856, 1858, 1860, 1864, 1873, 1874, 1878, 1879, 1880, 1881, 1883, 1886, 1890, 1891, 1900, and 1910. Indexed at the USGenWeb site for Maryland. See **http://files.usgwarchives.net/md/baltimorecity/directories/.**

**1816-1845.** ***Index to Marriage Records of Anne Arundel County, Maryland*** **[Printed Book],** compiled by Annie Walker Burns, publ. Annapolis, c1949, 60 pages, FHL book 975.255 V22b.

**1817-1819.** ***Biographical Data from Baltimore Newspapers*** **[Printed Book],** by Robert W. Barnes. Refers to more than 7,000 inhabitants whose whereabouts, falling as they do in non-census years, would continue to elude researchers for some time to come. Publ. Genealogical Publishing Co, Baltimore, 2011, 190 pages, FHL book 975.271. B38b.

**1819-1820.** ***Passenger Arrivals, 1819-1820. (Originally published as Letter from the Secretary of State, with a Transcript of the List of Passengers Who Arrived in the United States from the 1st of October 1819, to the 30th of September 1820) With an Added Index*** **[Printed Book],** includes ports in Maryland. This is a reprint of the original publ. U.S. Senate, 1821, reprinted Genealogical Publishing Co, Baltimore, 1971, 342 pages, FHL book 973 W3 1971.

**1819-1851.** ***Western Maryland Catholics*** **[Printed Book],** by Richard T. Koch and Phyllis I. Davidson. This is a collection of birth, baptismal, marriage, and death records for the parishes of St. Ignatius in Mt. Savage, and St. Mary's in Cumberland, Maryland. Includes an index to 12,000 names. Publ. Genealogical Publishing Co, Baltimore, 1998, reprinted 2012, 294 pages, FHL book 975.29 K28k.

**1820.** ***Maryland 1820 Census Index*** **[Printed Book],** edited by Ronald Vern Jackson, et al, publ. Accelerated Indexing Systems, Bountiful, UT, 1977, 123 pages, FHL book 975.2 X2p 1820.

**1820-1872.** ***Baltimore, Passenger and Immigration Lists*** **[Online Database],** indexed at the Ancestry.com website. Source: National Archives microfilm series

M255. Each record may include Name, Gender, Age, Occupation, Place of Origin, Destination, Name of ship, Type of ship, Port of departure, Port of arrival, and Date of arrival, This database has 226,945 records: **https://search.ancestry.com/search/db.aspx?dbid=7480.**

**1820-1897.** ***Maryland, Baltimore Passenger Lists Index*** **[Online Database],** digitized at the FamilySearch.org website, from the National Archives microfilm, series M327. This database has 779,885 images (index cards). See **https://familysearch.org/search/collection/2173933.**

**1820-1948.** ***Maryland, Baltimore Passenger Lists Index*** **[Online Database],** digitized and indexed at the FamilySearch.org website, from the National Archives microfilm, series M255, M596 and T844. This database has 798,916 images (index cards). See **https://familysearch.org/search/collection/2018318.**

**1820-1964.** ***Baltimore, Passenger Lists*** **[Online Database],** indexed at the Ancestry.com website. Original data: Selected Passenger and Crew Lists and Manifests. National Archives, Washington, DC. Each record may include Name, Age, Gender, Ethnicity, nationality or last country of permanent residence; Destination, Arrival Date, Port of Arrival, Port of Departure, Ship name, and Microfilm roll and page. This database has 2,001,537 records. See **https://search.ancestry.com/search/db.aspx?dbid=8679.**

**1823-1826.** ***Marriage Records of Baltimore County, Maryland*** **[Printed Book & Online Database],** compiled by Annie Walker Burns, publ. Washington, DC, c1955, FHL book 975.271 V28b. For a digital version of this book, see the online FHL catalog page for this title:
**https://familysearch.org/search/catalog/488223.**
- This database is also available at the Ancestry.com website: See
**https://search.ancestry.com/search/db.aspx?dbid=25572.**

**"1825 Tax List, Somerset County, Maryland,"** in *Maryland Genealogical Society Bulletin,* Vol. 31, No. 1 (Winter 1990).

**1827-1946.** See ***City Directories, Baltimore, 1827-1857 & City Directories, Baltimore, Coleman Directories, 1913-1946*** **[Online Database],** extracted from the Archives of Maryland, available at the Maryland State Archives website. See
**http://msa.maryland.gov/megafile/msa/speccol/sc2900/sc2908/html/officials.html.**

**1827-1867.** ***Suspicious Deaths in Mid-19th Century Baltimore: A Name Index to Corner Inquest Reports at the Baltimore City Archives; Relating to 4,000 Deaths in 1827, 1835-1860, 1864 and 1867*** **[Printed Book],** prepared by Baltimore City Archives, publ. Family Lines Pub., Silver Spring, MD, 1986, 29 pages, FHL book 975.2 A1 No. 76.

**1830.** ***Maryland 1830 Census Index*** **[Printed Index],** edited by Ronald Vern Jackson, et al, publ. Accelerated Indexing Systems, Bountiful, UT, 1976, 119 pages, FHL book 975.2 X2p 1830.

**"1831 Tax List, Martins District #4, Dorchester County, Maryland" [Printed Article],** in *Dorchester County Genealogical Magazine,* Vol. 5, No. 4 (Nov 1985) and Vol. 5, No. 5 (Jan 1986).

**"1831 Tax List, Hooper Island District No. 6, Dorchester County, Maryland" [Printed Article],** in *Dorchester County Genealogical Magazine,* Vol. 5, No. 3 (Sep 1994) through Vol. 5, No. 6 (Mar 1986).

**"1831-1838 Tax Assessment, Dorchester County (Relationships Shown)" [Printed Article],** in *Dorchester County Genealogical Society Magazine,* Vol. 16, No. 6 (Mar 1997).

**"1832 Tax List, Dorchester County, Maryland" [Printed Article],** in *Dorchester County Genealogical Magazine*, Vol. 6 (Mar 1985).

**"1832 Tax List, Neck District #8, Dorchester County, Maryland" [Printed Article],** in *Dorchester County Genealogical Magazine*, Vol. 5, No. 2 (Jul 1985).

**"1835 Tax List, Somerset County, Maryland" [Printed Article],** in *Maryland Connections Queries*, Vol. 10, No. 5 (Jul 2000).

**"1836 Tax List, Dorchester County, Maryland" [Printed Article],** in Dorchester County Genealogical Magazine, Vol. 4, No. 5 (Jan 1985).

**"1836 Tax Records, Lakes District #5, Dorchester County, Maryland" [Printed Article],** in *Dorchester County Genealogical Magazine,* Vol. 5, No. 1 (May 1985).

**"1837 Tax List, Dorchester County, Maryland" [Printed Article],** in *Dorchester County Genealogical Magazine,* Vol. 6, No. 6 (Mar 1987).

**1837-1850.** ***Index to Marriages and Deaths in the Baltimore Sun*** **[Printed Book & Online Database],** by Thomas W. Hollowak. Part 1 is an alphabetical listing of grooms; part 2 is an index to brides and other names in the entries. About 60,000 persons are listed. Publ. Genealogical Publishing Co, Baltimore, 1978, 787 pages, FHL book 975.26 B38h. A searchable digital version of this index is available at the Ancestry.com website. See
**https://search.ancestry.com/search/db.aspx?dbid=48587**.

**1837-1899.** ***Carroll County, Maryland, Marriage Licenses*** **[Printed Book],** compiled Genealogy Department Volunteers, Carroll County Public Library, publ. by the library, 1987, 268 pages, FHL book 975.277 V28fc.

**1840.** ***Maryland 1840 Census Index*** **[Printed Index],** edited by Ronald Vern Jackson, et al, publ. Accelerated Indexing Systems, Bountiful, UT, 164 pages, FHL book 975.2 X2p 1840.

**1840-1850.** ***License Book, Howard County, Maryland*** **[Microfilm & Digital Capture],** from originals at the Howard County Courthouse, Ellicott City, MD. Contains marriage, retailers, ordinary, stud horse, and theatrical exhibitions licenses, tax on trustees' commissions, hawkers, peddlers and miscellaneous licenses, and taxes on suits. Handwritten copy of the license book containing only marriage, retailers and ordinary licenses. Filmed by the Genealogical Society of Utah, 1949, 1 roll, FHL film #14143. To access the digital images, see the online FHL catalog page:
**www.familysearch.org/search/catalog/37801.**

**1841-1865.** ***Marriage Licenses of Frederick County*** **[Printed Book & Online Database],** by Margaret E. Myers, publ. Willow Bend Books, Westminster, MD, 2000, 265 pages, FHL book 975.287 V28mmea. To view a digital version of this book, visit the online FHL catalog page for this title:
**https://familysearch.org/search/catalog/656646.**

**"1844 Tax List, Dorchester County, Maryland" [Printed Article],** in *Dorchester County Genealogical Magazine,* Vol. 6, No. 3 (Sep 1987) through Vol. 7, No. 6 (Mar 1988).

**1845 Dorchester County Tax Lists [Printed Articles]**, name lists published serially in *Dorchester County Genealogical Magazine,*

- Fork District, in Vol. 5, No. 3 (Sep 1985).
- Neck District, in Vol. 14, No. 1 (May 1994).
- Parson Creek, in Vol. 6, No. 2 (Jul 1986).
- School #10, Parents and Children, in Vol. 26, No. 2 (Spring 2000).

**1846-1848.** ***Maryland and District of Columbia Volunteers in the Mexican War*** **[Printed Book],** by Charles J. Wells, publ. Family Line Publications, Westminster, MD, 1991, 89 pages, FHL book 975.2 M2we.

**1850.** ***Maryland, 1850 Federal Census: Population Schedules*** **[Microfilm & Digital Capture],** from the originals at the National Archives, 26 rolls of film, beginning with FHL film #13194. To access the digital images, see the online FHL catalog page:
**www.familysearch.org/search/catalog/744483.**

**1850.** See ***Maryland 1850 Census Index*** **[Printed Index],** edited by Ronald Vern Jackson, et al, publ. Accelerated Indexing Systems, Bountiful, UT, 1976, 444 pages, FHL book 975.2 X2p 1850.

**1850. Maryland, 1850 Mortality Schedules [Microfilm & Digital Capture],** from the National Archives, 1 roll of film, FHL film #1429789. To access the digital images, see the online FHL catalog page:
**www.familysearch.org/search/catalog/265395.**

**1850-1883.** ***Index of Baltimore City, Maryland, Wills*** **[Printed Book],** compiled by Elaine Obbink Zimmerman and Kenneth Edwin Zimmerman, From intro: "In 1851 Baltimore City and Baltimore County became two separate jurisdictions. The first recorded Baltimore City will is dated 26 November 1851." publ. Heritage Books, Westminster, MD, 2005, 219 pages, FHL book 975.26 P22z.

**1850-1900.** ***The Omega Connections: Obituaries From Eastern Shore of Maryland Newspapers, 1850-1900; over 10,000 Names*** **[Printed Book],** by Irma Sweltzer Harper. Contents: Vol. 1: A-K; Vol. 2: L-Z; Vol. 3: Obituaries and Odds and Ends, 1900-1920. publ. St. Michaels, MD, 1995-2003, 3 vols., FHL book 975.2 V48h v.1-3.

**1851-1919.** ***Index to Baltimore County, Maryland Wills*** **[Printed Book],** compiled by Carol L. Porter, publ. Baltimore County Genealogical Society, Towson, MD, 2007, 133 pages, FHL book 975.271 P22p.

**1851-1860.** ***Index to Marriages in The Baltimore Sun*** **[Printed Book & Online Database],** This book is a sequel to the author's *Index to Marriages and Deaths*

*in The (Baltimore) Sun, 1837-1850*, deals only with marriages, but goes through 1860. Arranged alphabetically by grooms' names, there also is an index of brides and others mentioned in the marriage notices. About 15,000 marriages are recorded, and with the others mentioned, about 35,000 persons are cited in the text. Each entry has the marriage date, and exactly where and when it appeared in the paper. Publ. Genealogical Publishing Co, Baltimore, 1978, reprinted 2007, 292 pages, FHL book 975.26 B38ha. For a digitized version of this book, see the Ancestry.com website:
**http://search.ancestry.com/search/db.aspx?dbid=48588.**

**1853-1986. *Maryland, Baltimore, Loudon Park Cemetery Records* [Online Database],** digitized and indexed at FamilySearch.org. Includes index cards recording interments, deeds, and lots. This database has 356,159 records, see
**www.familysearch.org/search/collection/3021633.**

**1853-1898. *Maryland, Kent County, Voter Registration Records* [Online Database],** from the Kent County register of Wills, Chestertown, MD. This database has 26,797 records, see
**www.familysearch.org/search/collection/2100301.**

**1855-1899. *Genealogical Abstracts, Montgomery County* [Printed Book],** compiled by Mary Gordon Malloy and Marian W. Jacobs. Publ. Rockville, MD, Montgomery County Historical Society, 1986, 488 pages, FHL book 975.284 D28m.

**1859-1936. *Frederick (Maryland) City Directories* [Microfiche & Microfilm],** from various publishers. Filmed by Research Publications, Woodbridge, CT, 1980-1984; FHL has 1859-1860, 1915, 1928-1929, 1931-1932, and 1935-1936, beginning on FHL fiche #6043918 (1859-1860 Frederick directory) and FHL film #2308951 (1915-1935/1936 directories).

**1860. *Maryland, 1860 Federal Census: Population Schedules* [Microfilm & Digital Capture],** filmed by the National Archives, 1967, series M653, 37 rolls, beginning with FHL film #803456 (Allegany Co). To access the digital images, see the online FHL catalog:
**www.familysearch.org/search/catalog/704932.**

**1860. *Maryland 1860 Federal Census Index: Except the City of Baltimore* [Printed Index],** edited by Ronald Vern Jackson, publ. Accelerated Indexing Systems, Salt Lake City, UT, 1988, 493 pages, FHL book 975.2 X28j 1860.

**1860. *Maryland 1860 Mortality Schedules* [Microfilm & Digital Capture],** from the National Archives, 1 roll, FHL film #1429789. To access the digital images, see the online FHL catalog page:
**www.familysearch.org/search/catalog/265410.**

**1861-1865. *History and Roster of Maryland Volunteers, War of 1861-5* [Printed Book, Printed Index & Online Database],** by L. Allison Wilmer, J.H. Jarrett, Geo. W. F. Vernon. Sponsored by the MD General Assembly, this official report includes references to over 36,000 soldiers, sailors or marines who served in Maryland units of the Union Army and Navy. Original 2-vols publ. Guggenheimer, Weil & Co., Baltimore, 1898-1899, reprinted 1987, Family Line Publications, Silver Spring, MD, 2 vols., FHL book 975.2 M2wi v.1-2. See also ***History and Roster of Maryland Volunteers: Index,*** by Martha and Bill Reamy, publ. Family Line Publications, Westminster, MD, 1990, 153 pages, FHL book 975.2 M2wd index. Both volumes are available online at the Ancestry.com website. For vol. 1, see
**http://search.ancestry.com/search/db.aspx?dbid=3087.**
For Vol. 2, see
**http://search.ancestry.com/search/db.aspx?dbid=3088.**

**1861-1865. *Maryland, Civil War Service Records of Confederate Soldiers* [Online Database],** digitized and indexed at the FamilySearch.org website. Includes Confederate service records of soldiers who served in organizations from Maryland. The records typically contain card abstracts of entries relating to the soldier as found in original muster rolls, returns, rosters, payrolls, appointment books, hospital registers, Union prison registers and rolls, parole rolls, inspection reports; and the originals of any papers relating solely to the particular soldier. For each military unit the service records are arranged alphabetically by the soldier's surname. This database has 43,508 records. See **https://familysearch.org/search/collection/1932373.**

**1861-1865. *The Maryland Line in the Confederate Army* [Printed Book],** by W.W. Goldsborough, publ. Olde Soldier Books, Gaithersburg, MD, 1987, 371 pages, FHL book 975.2 M2g.
- See also ***Index to The Maryland Line in the Confederate Army* [Printed Book & Digital Version],** compiled by Mrs. Charles Lee Lewis, United Daughters of the Confederacy, publ. Maryland Hall of Records, 1945, FHL book 975.2 B4ma No. 3. To access a digital version of this index, visit the online FHL catalog page:
**https://familysearch.org/search/catalog/145996.**

**1861-1865.** ***Maryland, Civil War Service Records of Union Soldiers*** **[Online Database],** digitized and indexed at the FamilySearch.org website. Includes the Union service records of soldiers who served in organizations from Maryland. The records include a jacket-envelope for each soldier, labeled with his name, his rank, and the unit in which he served. The records contain card abstracts of entries relating to the soldier as found in original muster rolls, returns, rosters, payrolls, appointment books, hospital registers, prison registers and rolls, parole rolls, inspection reports; and the originals of any papers relating solely to the particular soldier. For each military unit the service records are arranged alphabetically by the soldier's surname. This database has 642,857 records. See **https://familysearch.org/search/collection/1932407.**

**1861-1865.** ***Maryland Soldiers in the Civil War, Vol. 1*** **[Online Database],** indexed at the Ancestry.com website. Original data: L. Allison Wilmer, James H. Jarrett, George W. F. Vernon. *History and Roster of Maryland Volunteers, War of 1861-5, Volume 1.* Press of Guggenheimer, Weil & Company, 1898. Each record includes a Name, Race, Enlistment of Muster In Date, Discharge or Muster Out Date4, and Remarks. This database has 34,350 records. See **https://search.ancestry.com/search/db.aspx?dbid=3087.**

**1861-1865.** ***Maryland Soldiers in the Civil War, Vol. 2*** **[Online Database],** indexed at the Ancestry.com website. Original data: L. Allison Wilmer, James H. Jarrett, George W. F. Vernon. *History and Roster of Maryland Volunteers, War of 1861-5, Volume 1.* Press of Guggenheimer, Weil & Company, 1898. See **https://search.ancestry.com/search/db.aspx?dbid=3088.**

**1861-1949.** ***Washington County, Maryland, Marriage Index*** **[Online Database],** a database of the Washington County Free Library, accessible at the Ancetry.com website. See **http://search.ancestry.com/search/db.aspx?dbid=70012.**

**"1862 Tax Assessment, Maryland" [Printed Article],** name lists extracted in *Chesapeake Cousins*, beginning with Vol. 4, No. 1 (1976).

**1862-1865.** See ***1865 List of Qualified Voters & 1862 Union Draft List, Somerset County, Maryland*** **[Printed Book],** compiled by Rebecca F. Miller. Publ. Miller's Choice, Princess Anne, MD, 1991, 15 pages, FHL book 975.2 A1 No. 188.

**1862-1866.** ***Internal Revenue Assessment Lists for Maryland*** **[Microfilm & Digital Capture],** from the originals at the National Archives, Washington, DC. These are name lists of taxpayers taken during the Civil War in Maryland. A tax was levied for all annual incomes exceeding $600. Legacies and distributive shares of personal property were also taxed. All persons, partnerships, firms, associations, and corporations were to submit a list to the assistant assessor of their division showing the amount of their annual income, articles owned subject to special tax or duty, and the quantity of taxable goods made or sold. The name lists for Maryland are organized as follows: District 1: Caroline, Cecil, Dorchester, Kent, Queen Anne's, Somerset, Talbot and Worcester counties; District 2: Baltimore city (wards 1-7) and Baltimore (districts 5-7, 9-12) and Harford counties; District 3 includes Baltimore city (wards 8-20); District 4: Allegany, Carroll, Frederick and Washington counties; and District 5: Anne Arundel, Baltimore (districts 1-4, 8, 13), Calvert, Charles, Howard, Montgomery, Prince George's and St. Mary's counties. Some records are damaged, some are missing, and some are filed out of order. Most are arranged by year or month, then division of district and then alphabetically. Filmed by the National Archives, series M771, 21 rolls, beginning with FHL roll #1534367 (District 1 – Annual lists, 1862-1864). To access the digital images, see the online FHL catalog page: **https://familysearch.org/search/catalog/88651.**

**1862-1900s.** See ***Civil War Burials in Baltimore's Loudon Park Cemetery*** **[Printed Book & Online Database],** compiled by Anna Miller Watring, publ. Clearfield / Genealogical Pub. Co, Baltimore, 1996. The largest cemetery in Baltimore, Loudon Park Cemetery has the burials of over 2,300 Union soldiers and at least 650 Confederate soldiers. The book was digitized and indexed online at the Ancestry.com website. See **http://search.ancestry.com/search/db.aspx?dbid=48176.**

- See also, ***Baltimore, Maryland, Loudon Park National Cemetery, 1862-2010*** **[Online Database],** indexed at the Ancestry.com website. This database contains digital images of all gravestones in Loudon Park National Cemetery and includes burials through 2010 for more than 6,400 people. See **https://search.ancestry.com/search/db.aspx?dbid=2288.**

**1865-1885.** ***Indices to Cecil County, Maryland Marriage Licenses*** **[Printed Book],** copied by Harry A. Hovermill, publ. Cecil County Genealogical Society, Charlestown, MD, 1982, 106 pages, FHL book 975.238 V22h.

**1865-1872.** ***Maryland and Delaware, Freedman's Bureau Field Office Records*** **[Online Database],** indexed at the FamilySearch.org website. This is an image-only database. The Bureau of Refugees, Freedmen, and Abandoned Lands (often called the Freedmen's Bureau) was created in 1865 at the end of the American Civil War to supervise relief efforts including education, health care, food and clothing, refugee camps, legalization of marriages, employment, labor contracts, and securing back pay, bounty payments and pensions. These records include letters and endorsements sent and received, account books, applications for rations, applications for relief, court records, labor contracts, registers of bounty claimants, registers of complaints, registers of contracts, registers of disbursements, registers of freedmen issued rations, registers of patients, reports, rosters of officers and employees, special and general orders and circulars received, special orders and circulars issued, records relating to claims, court trials, property restoration, and homesteads. This database has 36,376 records. See **www.familysearch.org/search/collection/1989156.**

**1865-1888.** ***Kent County, Maryland Marriages, 1865-1888*** **[Printed Book],** by Jerry M. Hynson, publ. Heritage Books, Westminster, MD, 2007, 632 pages, FHL book 975.236 V22h.

**1865-1894.** ***Baltimore City Birth Records, 1865-1894*** **[Printed Book],** transcribed by Mary K. Meyer, publ. 1997, 2000, Willow Bend Books, Westminster, MD, 34 pages, FHL book 975.2 A1 No. 238.

**1865-1906.** ***Lower Eastern Shore, Maryland, Marriages Including the Counties of Somerset, Worcester, Wicomico*** **[Printed Book],** by Ruth T. Dryden, publ. R.T. Dryden, San Diego, CA, 1991, 537 pages, FHL book 975.22 V28d.

**1866-1894.** ***Index of Obituaries and Marriages in the Baltimore Sun*** **[Printed Book],** by Francis P. O'Neill, published Colonial Roots, Lewes, DE, 2009-2013. 8 vols. Contents: Vol. 1: 1866-1870 (A-J); Vol. 2: 1866-1870 (J-Z); Vol. 3: 1871-1875 (A-J); Vol. 4: 1871-1875 (K-Z)); Vol. 5: 1876-1880; Vol. 6: 1881-1885; Vol. 7: 1886-1890; and Vol. 8: 1891-1891. See FHL book 975.26 B32o 1866-1894.

**1866-2005.** ***Sharpsburg, Maryland, Antietam National Cemetery*** **[Online Database],** indexed at the Ancestry.com website. Source: Ancestry extractions. This database contains digital images of all gravestones in Antietam National Cemetery, located in Sharpsburg, Maryland. Antietam National Cemetery was established in 1866, and this collection includes burials through 2005 for more than 3,100 people. Information on the markers varies. Some may contain only a number of initials; others may include facts such as name, birth date, death date, age, rank, and state of origin. See **https://search.ancestry.com/search/db.aspx?dbid=2285.**

**1866-2009.** ***Annapolis, Maryland, Annapolis National Cemetery*** **[Online Database],** indexed at the Ancestry.com website. Source: Ancestry extractions. This database contains digital images of all gravestones in the Annapolis National Cemetery, located in Annapolis, Maryland. Annapolis National Cemetery was established in 1862, and this collection includes burials through 2009 for more than 2900 people. Cemetery section is provided for each image. Information on the markers varies. Some may contain only a number of initials; others may include facts such as name, birth date, death date, age, rank, and state of origin. See **https://search.ancestry.com/search/db.aspx?dbid=2284.**

***1867 Howard County Voters List*** **[Online Database],** indexed at the USGenWeb site for Howard Co MD. See **http://files.usgwarchives.net/md/howard/history/local/vote1867.txt.**

**1867-1919.** ***Wicomico County, Maryland, Wills*** **[Printed Book],** abstracted by Leslie and Neil Keddle. 4 vols., contents: Vol. 1: Dec. 1867 - Dec. 1879; Vol. 2: Dec. 1880-1897; Vol. 3: Dec. 1897 -1911; Vol. 4: 1912-1919. Publ. Family Tree Workshop, Salisbury, MD, 2001, FHL book 975.225 P28k v.1-4.

**1870.** ***Maryland, 1870 Federal Census: Population Schedules*** **[Microfilm & Digital Capture],** from the National Archives, 46 rolls, beginning with FHL film #552065. To access the digital images, see the online FHL catalog page: **www.familysearch.org/search/catalog/698901.**

**1870.** ***Maryland 1870 Census Index*** **[Printed Index],** edited by Raeone Christensen Steuart, publ. Heritage Quest, Bountiful, UT, 1999, 2 vols. (xviii, 1,590 pages), Contents: Vol. 1: A-K; Vol. 2: L-Z. FHL book 975.2 X22m 1870 v. 1-2.

**1870-1871. "Marriage and Death Notices For Carroll County" [Printed Article & Digital Version],** in the *Carrolltonian*, Vol.. 25, No. 1 (Sep 2005) To access a digital version of this article, visit the online FHL catalog page for this title:
**https://familysearch.org/search/catalog/2369239.**

**1870-1883.** ***Harford County Taxpayers in 1870, 1872 and 1883*** **[Printed Book],** by Henry C. Peden, Jr., Published Aberdeen, MD, Harford County Genealogical Society, 1992, 133 pages, FHL book 975.274 R48p.

**1872-1902.** ***Thirty Years of Garrett County Marriage Records: The Glades Star*** **[Printed Book],** publ. Garrett County Historical Society, Oakland, MD, 2002, FHL book 975.297 V2f.

**1872-1960.** See ***Index to the Wills of Maryland: Garrett County, 1872-1960 & Harford County, 1774-1960*** **[Printed Book],** edited by Joan Hume. The index is arranged chronologically under each letter of the alphabet and gives the name of the testator, date of the will, and the liber and folio where the original may be found. Publ. Genealogical Publishing Co, Baltimore, 1970, 182 pages, FHL book 975.2 P22h.

**"1873 Tax List, Dorchester County, Maryland" [Printed Article],** in *Dorchester County Genealogical Magazine*, Vol. 10, No. 6 (Mar 1991).

**1875-1949.** See ***Maryland State Archives Vital Records, Death Index, Baltimore City, 1875-1880, 1943-1949,*** **[Online Database].** The images of the index cards are available for viewing at the Maryland State Archives webpage. See
**http://vitalrec.msa.maryland.gov/pages/seriesunit.aspx?qu=S&sr=1483&src=cty&it=database.**

**1875-1972.** ***Maryland State Archives Vital Records, Death Index, Baltimore City*** **[Online Database].** The images of the index pages are available for viewing at the Maryland State Archives webpage. See
**http://vitalrec.msa.maryland.gov/pages/seriesunit.aspx?qu=CE&sr=42&src=cty&it=pages.**

**1877-1992.** ***Maryland, Deaths and Burials*** **[Online Database],** indexed at the FamilySearch.org website. This name index to death and burial records came from the microfilm of the Genealogical Society of Utah originally filmed on site at various Maryland counties. This database has 3,709 records. See
**https://familysearch.org/search/collection/1675198.**

**1877-1992.** ***Baltimore, Maryland, Deaths and Burials Index*** **[Online Database],** digitized and indexed at the Ancestry.com website. (Obtained from FamilySearch). This database has 10,373 records. See
**http://search.ancestry.com/search/db.aspx?dbid=2566.**

**1880.** ***Maryland, 1880 Federal Census: Soundex and Population Schedules*** **[Microfilm & Digital Capture],** from the originals at the National Archives, Washington, DC (ca1985). After filming, the originals were transferred to the Maryland State Law Library, Annapolis, MD. Filmed on 73 rolls, beginning with FHL film #447215 (1880 Soundex: A000 thru A536); and FHL film #1254495 (1880 Population Schedules: Allegany Co). To access the digital images (Population Schedules), see the online FHL catalog page:
**https://familysearch.org/search/catalog/673565.**

**1880.** ***The Maryland Directory*** **[Printed Book, Microfilm & Digital Capture],** publ. J. Frank Lewis, 1880, 593 pages, filmed by W.C. Cox & Co., Tucson, AZ, 1974, 1 roll, film #1000059. To access the digital images, see the online FHL catalog page:
**www.familysearch.org/search/catalog/36511.**

**1882-1918.** ***Hagerstown, Washington County, Maryland City Directories, as part of Chambersburg (Pennsylvania) City Directories*** **[Microfilm],** from various publishers, filmed by Research Publications, Woodbridge, CT, 1995, 2 rolls. FHL has 1882-1883, 1884-1885, 1887-1888, and 1918. Full title: *Boyd's General Directory of Chambersburg, Carlisle, Hagerstown, Mechanicsburg and Waynesboro, together with a business directory of the principal towns in the Cumberland Valley, compiled and published by W. Harry Boyd.* See FHL film #2258222 (1882-1887) and FHL film #2310356 (1918).

**1884-1935.** ***Cumberland (Maryland) City Directories*** **[Microfilm],** from various publishers. Includes other Allegany County cities. Filmed by Research Publications, Woodbridge, CT, c1995. FHL has 8 rolls: 1884-1885, 1890, 1895-1897, 1899, 1901, 1903-

1919, 1921-1929, and 1931-1935, beginning with FHL film #2156782 (1884-1885-Cumberland city directory including Frostburg and Lonaconing). For a complete list of roll numbers and contents of each roll, see the online FHL catalog page for this title. See **https://familysearch.org/search/catalog/992512.**

***1890 Special Census of the Civil War Veterans of the State of Maryland* [Printed Book],** compiled by L. Tilden Moore, publ. Willow Bend Books, Westminster, MD, 2002-2005, 7 vols. Includes full name index. Contents: Vol. 1: Garrett, Allegany and Washington counties; Vol. 2: Carroll, Frederick, Montgomery, Prince George's, Calvert, Charles and St. Mary's counties; Vol. 3: Howard, Anne Arundel, Harford, Cecil and Kent counties and the United States Naval Academy; Vol. 4: Caroline, Dorchester, Queen Anne, Somerset, Talbot, Wicomico and Worcester counties; Vol. 7: Baltimore county and Baltimore city institutions. See FHL book 975.2 M2ml v. 1-7.

**1890. *Queen Anne's County, Maryland Register of Voters From the Poll Books of 1890* [Printed Book],** by Trish Surles, publ. Surles, Gambrills, MD, 2002, 79 pages, FHL book 975.234 N4s.

***1896 Tax Assessment for Queen's Anne County, Maryland* [Printed Book],** compiled by Trish Surles, publ. Gambrills, MD, 2003, 7 vols. Contents: Vol. 1: District 1, Dixon District, Sudlersville/Templeville; Vol. 2:. District 2; Vol. 3: District 3, Centreville; Vol. 4: District 4, Kent Island; Vol. 5: District 5, Queenstown area ; Vol. 6: District 6, Ruthsberg area; and Vol. 7: Crumpton area. See FHL book 975.234 R4st v.1-4 and 975.234 R4st v.5-7.

**1898. *Roster of the Soldiers and Sailors Who Served in Organizations from Maryland, During the Spanish-American War* [Printed Book],** compiled under the authority of the House of Delegates of Maryland by Hugh Ridgely Riley and Charles S. Carrington. Originally published by W.J.C. Dulany, Baltimore, 1901; reprinted Family Line Publications, 1990, 72 pages, FHL book 975.2 M2r.

**1898-1951. *Maryland State Archives Vital Records, Death Index* [Online Database].** The images of the original Health Department index cards are available at the Maryland State Archives webpage. See **http://guide.msa.maryland/gov/pages.series.aspz?ID=SM25**

**1898-1919.** See ***Birth Index of St. Mary's, Charles and Calvert Counties, Maryland: 1898 Through 1919* [Printed Book],** compiled by Anne Ascosi Baker, publ. St. Mary's County Historical Society, Leonardtown, MD, 1997, 403 pages, FHL book 975.24 X28b.

**1899. *Baltimore City Directory* [Online Database],** digitized and OCR indexed at the Ancestry.com website. This database has 2,021 records. See **https://search.ancestry.com/search/db.aspx?dbid=25625.**

**1900. *1900 Federal Census: Soundex and Population Schedules* [Microfilm & Digital Capture],** from the originals held by the Bureau of the Census in the 1940s. After microfilming, Congress allowed the Census Bureau to destroy the originals to free up space for WWII-related files. Filmed on 154 rolls, beginning with FHL film #124477 (Soundex: A000 thru A416); and FHL film #1240604 (Population Schedules: Allegany Co). To access the digital images (Population Schedules), see the online FHL catalog page: **https://familysearch.org/search/catalog/655770.**

**"1901-1902 Public School #1 Register, Dorchester County, Maryland" [Printed Article],** in *Dorchester County Genealogical Magazine,* Vol. 15, No. 1 (May 1995).

**1906-1931. *Maryland, Naturalization Petitions* [Online Database],** digitized and indexed at the FamilySearch.org website. Includes about 13,800 Naturalization petitions filed at the U.S. District Court for the district of Maryland. Also includes certificates of arrival, oaths of allegiance, and declarations of intention (to become citizens). National Archives series M1640. Index provided by Fold3.com. See **https://familysearch.org/search/collection/1854313.**

**1910. *Maryland, 1910 Federal Census: Population Schedule*s [Microfilm & Digital Capture],** from originals held by the Bureau of the Census in the 1940s. After microfilming, Congress allowed the Census Bureau to destroy the originals to free up space for WWII-related files. Filmed on 22 rolls, beginning with FHL film #1374562 (Allegany Co). To access the digital images, see the online FHL catalog page: **https://familysearch.org/search/catalog/637202.**

**1910-1951.** ***Maryland State Archives Vital Records, Death Index*** **[Online Database].** The images of the original Health Department index cards are available at the Maryland State Archives webpage. See **http://guide.msa.maryland.gov/pages/series.aspx?ID-S1176**

**1910-1953.** ***Applications for Membership*** **[Microfilm & Digital Capture]**, of original records of The Society of The Ark and The Dove, Baltimore, MD. Arranged by application number. Includes index. See FHL film #2068. To access the digital images, see the online FHL catalog page:
**www.familysearch.org/search/catalog/479311.**

**1910-1954.** ***Maryland, Crew Lists of Vessels and Airplanes*** **[Online Database],** indexed at the Ancestry.com website. Source: National Archives microfilm series A3505. This is an image-only database searchable by microfilm roll number. This database has 226,945 records. See
**https://search.ancestry.com/search/db.aspx?dbid=5324.**

***1911 Directory of Bethesda District, Montgomery County, Maryland; Including Map Showing Country Between Washington City and the Rockville District*** **[Microfilm],** from a book compiled by S.D. Caldwell, pub. L. G. Kelly, 1911, 60 pages. Filmed by the Library of Congress Photoduplication Service, 1 roll, FHL film #1550165.

**1912-1913.** ***Nelson's Suburban Directory of Maryland and Virginia Towns Adjacent to the District of Columbia*** **[Microfilm],** from a book published by J.C. Nelson, Washington, DC, 1912. Filmed by the Library of Congress Photoduplication Service, 1987, 1 roll, FHL film #1491084.

**1912.** ***Baltimore City Directory*** **[Online Database],** digitized and OCR indexed at the Ancestry.com website. This database has 2,660 records. See
**https://search.ancestry.com/search/db.aspx?dbid=27009.**

**1913.** ***Baltimore City Directory*** **[Online Database],** digitized and OCR indexed at the Ancestry.com website. This database has 2,682 records. See
**https://search.ancestry.com/search/db.aspx?dbid=24206.**

**1917-1918.** See ***Maryland Military Men, 1917-18*** **[Online Database],** indexed at the Ancestry.com website. Original data: Maryland in the World War, 1917-1919; Military and Naval Service Records. Vol. I-II. Baltimore, MD, USA: Twentieth Century Press, 1933. The names of over 67,900 men are included in the collection. See
**http://search.ancestry.com/search/db.aspx?dbid=4545.**

**1920.** ***Maryland, 1920 Federal Census: Soundex and Population Schedules*** **[Microfilm & Digital Capture],** from the originals held by the Bureau of the Census in the 1940s. After microfilming, Congress allowed the Census Bureau to destroy the originals to free up space for WWII-related files. Filmed on 153 rolls, beginning with FHL film #1825722 (Soundex: A000 thru A352); and FHL film #1820652 (Population Schedules: Allegany Co). To access the digital images (Population Schedules), see the online FHL catalog page: **https://familysearch.org/search/catalog/571898.**

**1930.** ***Maryland, 1930 Federal Census: Population Schedules*** **[Microfilm & Digital Capture],** from originals held by the Bureau of the Census in the 1940s. After microfilming, Congress allowed the Census Bureau to destroy the originals to free up space for WWII-related files. Filmed on 40 rolls, beginning with FHL film #2340578 (Allegany Co). To access the digital images, see the online FHL catalog page:
**https://familysearch.org/search/catalog/1036357.**

**1931-1932.** ***Frederick, Maryland, City Directory: Rural Routes, also a Buyers' Guide and a Complete Classified Business Directory*** **[Printed Book],** by the R.L. Polk and Co, Baltimore, 1931, FHL book 975.287 E4p 1931-1932.

**1936-2007.** ***Maryland, Baltimore, Lock Funeral Home Records*** **[Online Database],** digitized at the FamilySearch.org website. This is an image-only database provided to FamilySearch by the Lock Funeral Home. This database has 5,863 records. See
**www.familysearch.org/search/collection/2445431.**

**1937.** ***Inventory of the County and Town Archives of Maryland; No. 21, Washington County, Hagerstown*** **[Printed Book & Online Database],** from the original Maryland Historical Records Survey Project (WPA), publ. Baltimore, 1937, 153 pages, FHL book 975.291 A3h. To access a digital version of this book, visit the online FHL catalog page for this title. See
**https://familysearch.org/search/catalog/258251.**

**1938.** ***Inventory of the County and Town Archives of Maryland; No. 11, Garrett County, Oakland*** **[Printed Book & Digital Version],** from the original Maryland Historical Records Survey Project (WPA), publ. Baltimore, 1938, 128 pages, FHL book 975.297 A3h. To access a digital version of this book, visit the online FHL catalog page:
**https://familysearch.org/search/catalog/257485.**

**1939.** ***Inventory of the County and Town Archives of Maryland; No. 15, Montgomery County, Rockville*** **[Printed Book & Digital Version],** from the original Maryland Historical Records Survey Project (WPA), publ. Baltimore, 1939, 319 pages, FHL book 975.284 A3h. To access a digital version of this book, visit the online FHL catalog page:
**https://familysearch.org/search/catalog/257542.**

**1939.** ***Inventory of the County and Town Archives of Maryland; No. 13, Howard County, Ellicott City*** **[Printed Book & Digital Version],** from the original Maryland Historical Records Survey Project (WPA), publ. Baltimore, 1939, 188 pages, FHL book 975.281 A3h. To access a digital version of this book, visit the online FHL catalog page: See
**https://familysearch.org/search/catalog/257576.**

**1940.** ***Maryland, 1940 Federal Census: Population Schedules*** **[Microfilm & Digital Images],** from the original records held by the Bureau of the Census in the 1940s. After microfilming, Congress allowed the Census Bureau to destroy the originals to free up space for WWII-related files. Filmed on 29 rolls, beginning with FHL film #5461060 (Allegany Co). The Family History Library (FHL) has the microfilm archived at their Granite Mountain Record Vault. They are not available for viewing but the entire digital collection is available online at several sites. To access the digital images, see the online FHL catalog page:
**https://familysearch.org/search/catalog/2057760.**

**1940 Federal Census Finding Aids [Online Database].** The National Archives prepared a special website online with a detailed description of the 1940 federal census. Included at the site are descriptions of location finding aids, such as Enumeration District maps, Geographic Descriptions of Census Enumeration Districts, and a list of 1940 City Directories available at the National Archives. The finding aids are all linked to other National Archives sites. The National Archives website also has a link to 1940 Search Engines using Stephen P. Morse's "One-Step" system for finding a 1940 E.D. or street address conversion. See
**www.archives.gov/research/census/1940/general-info.html#questions.**

**1940.** ***Inventory of the County and Town Archives of Maryland; No. 22, Wicomico County, Salisbury*** **[Printed Book & Digital Version],** from the original Maryland Historical Records Survey Project (WPA), publ. Baltimore, 1940, 223 pages, FHL book 975.225 A5h. To access a digital version of this book, visit the online FHL catalog page:
**https://familysearch.org/search/catalog/257646.**

**1940.** ***Inventory of the County and Town Archives of Maryland; No. 6, Carroll County, Westminster*** **[Printed Book & Digital Version],** from the original Maryland Historical Records Survey Project (WPA), publ. Baltimore, 1940, 273 pages, FHL book 975.273 A3h. To access a digital version of this book, visit the online FHL catalog page:
**https://familysearch.org/search/catalog/257599.**

**1940.** ***Inventory of the Church Archives of Maryland: Protestant Episcopal Diocese of Maryland*** **[Printed Book & Digital Version],** from the original Maryland Historical Records Survey Project (WPA), publ. Baltimore, 1940, 310 pages, FHL book 975.2 K2h. To access a digital version of this book, visit the online FHL catalog page
**https://familysearch.org/search/catalog/257659.**

**1940-1945.** ***Maryland, World War II Draft Registration Cards*** **[Online Database],** digitized at FamilySearch.org, from National Archives microfilm, Records of the Selective Service System. The images of the card indexes are arranged in alpha order. This database has 532,405 records, see
**www.familysearch.org/search/collection/2568865.**

**1941.** ***Inventory of the County and Town Archives of Maryland; No. 2, Anne Arundel County, Annapolis*** **[Printed Book & Digital Version],** from the original Maryland Historical Records Survey Project (WPA), publ. Baltimore, 1941, 353 pages, FHL book 975.255 A3. To access a digital version of this book, visit the online FHL catalog page.
**https://familysearch.org/search/catalog/257623.**

**1941-1945.** ***Maryland Selective Service Systems Registration Cards (World War II): Fourth Registration*** **[Microfilm & Digital Capture],** from the originals at the National Archives Regional Branch, Philadelphia, PA. Filmed by the Genealogical Society of Utah, 2000-2001, 64 rolls, beginning with FHL film #2223305 (Aakko, Emil to Andrews, Roy Allen). To access the digital images, see the online FHL catalog page: **https://familysearch.org/search/catalog/985149.**

**1944-2001.** ***Washington County, Maryland Obituary Locator*** **[CD-ROM],** by C. William Ridenour, publ. Heritage Books, Bowie, MD, 2005, FHL CD #1:004-20051006. Note: see 1790-1943 for the first set (in book form).

**1950-1956.** ***Maryland, Piney Point Crew Lists*** **[Online Database],** digitized images at the FamilySearch.org website. This collection contains Crew Lists of Vessels Arriving at Piney Point, Maryland, August 1950-March 1956. The records usually contain the name of the vessel and shipmaster, ports and dates of departure and arrival, and the following information about each crew member: full name, position in ship's company, age, gender, race, and nationality. These records correspond with NARA publication A3436 and were filmed at the National Archives, College Park, MD. The database has 620 images. See
**https://familysearch.org/search/collection/2443336.**

**1954-1955.** ***Polk's Maryland-Washington Suburban (Montgomery and Prince Georges Counties, Md.) Directory*** **[Printed Book],** publ. R. L. Polk & Co, Washington, DC, 1954, FHL book 975.2 E4p.

**1954-1957.** ***Maryland, Baltimore, Passenger and Crew Lists of Vessels and Airplanes*** **[Online Database],** digitized and indexed at the FamilySearch.org website. Source: National Archives microfilm series M1477. Each record may include: Name, Event Type, Event Date, Event Place, and Birthplace. This database has 36,070 images and partial index. See
**https://familysearch.org/search/collection/2072742.**

**1990 - Current.** ***Maryland Recent Newspaper Obituaries*** **[Online Database]**, digitized and indexed newspaper obituaries at the GenealogyBank website, including newspapers from these cities: Annapolis, Glenburnie, Arbutus, Baltimore, Bowie, Cambridge, Catonsville, Centreville, Chestertown, Columbia, Crisfield, Crofton, Cumberland, Denton, Dundalk, Easton, Eldersburg, Elkton, Essex, Frederick, Hagerstown, Lexington Park, Oakland, Owings Mills, Parkville, Carney, Perry Hall, White Marsh, Potomac, Prince Frederick, Salisbury, Stevensville, Towson, Upper Marlboro, Waldorf, and Westminster. See
**www.genealogybank.com/gbnk/obituaries/explore/USA/ Maryland.**

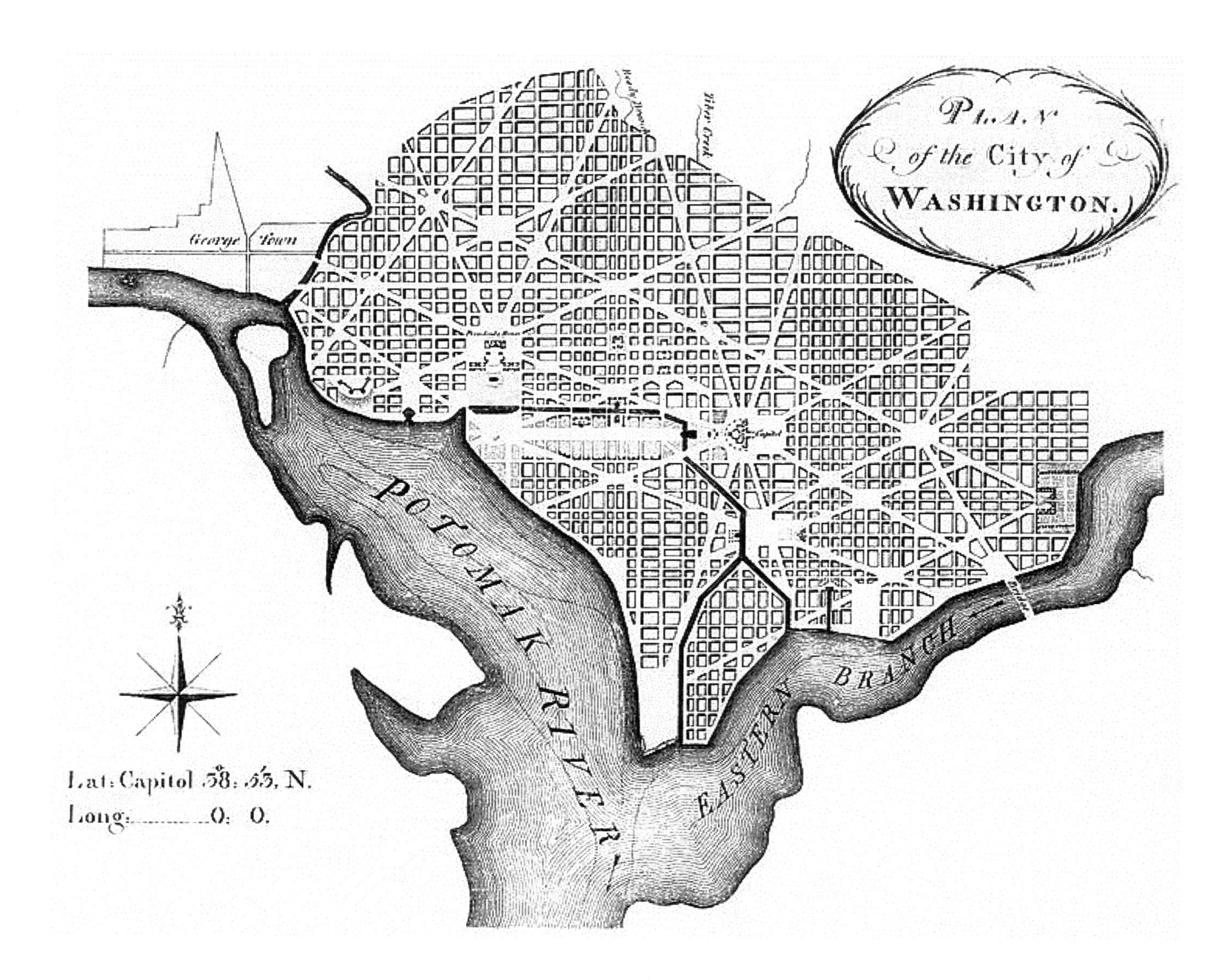


**The L'Enfant Plan for Washington, D.C., as revised by Andrew Ellicott in 1792.** The design for the City of Washington was largely the work of Pierre Charles L'Enfant, a French-born architect, engineer, and city planner who first arrived in the colonies as a military engineer during the American Revolutionary War. In 1791, President Washington commissioned L'Enfant to lay out the design of the new capital based on plans of cities such as Amsterdam, Paris, Frankfurt, Karlsruhe, and Milan brought from Europe by Thomas Jefferson in 1788. L'Enfant's design envisioned a garden-lined "grand avenue" approximately 1 mile in length and 400 feet wide in the area that is now the National Mall. In March 1792, President Washington dismissed L'Enfant due to his insistence on micromanaging the city's planning, which had resulted in conflicts with the three commissioners appointed to supervise the capital's construction. Andrew Ellicott, who had worked with L'Enfant surveying the city, was then commissioned to complete the plans. Though Ellicott revised the original plans, including changes to some street patterns, L'Enfant is still credited with the overall design of the city. The City of Washington was bounded by what is now Florida Avenue to the north, Rock Creek to the west, and the Anacostia River to the east. (Map source: Wikipedia).

# District of Columbia
## Censuses & Substitute Name Lists

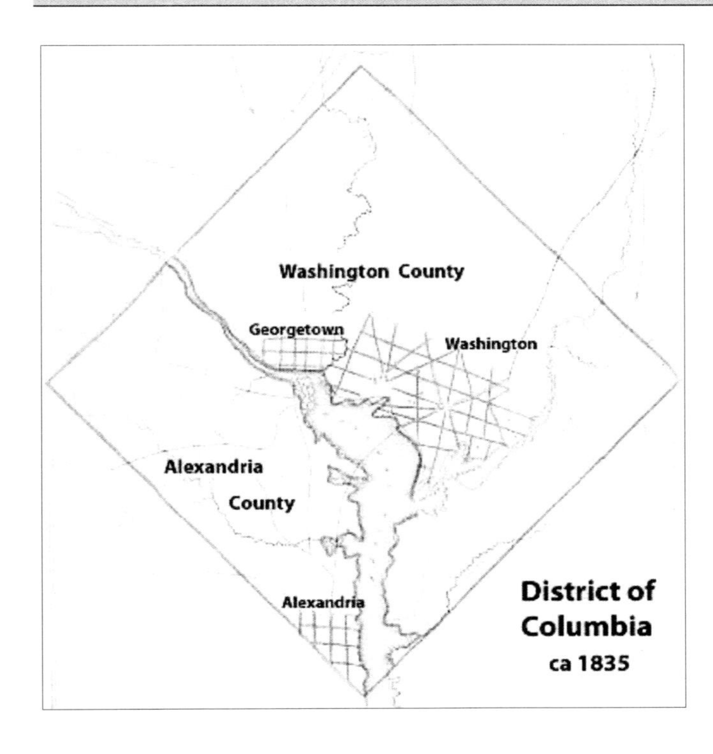


### Historical Timeline for the District of Columbia, 1790-1992

**1790.** July. **Residence Act.** The U.S. Congress approved the creation of a permanent national capital district to be located on the Potomac River. The 1787 U.S. Constitution had called for a "...district, (not exceeding ten miles square)," with the exact site to be selected by the President. In 1790, President George Washington, a former surveyor, sketched a ten-mile square that crossed the Potomac River, encompassing the existing towns of Georgetown on the Maryland side, and Alexandria on the Virginia side.

**1790.** August. **Federal Census.** Within the unsurveyed new capital district, the town of Georgetown was enumerated as part of Maryland (census extant); and the town of Alexandria was enumerated as part of Virginia (census lost).

**1791. The City of Washington** was first surveyed and named in September, as was the name *Columbia*, a poetic name for the United States in use at that time. Georgetown remained the main community in the northern part of the District for several more years.

**1800.** The capital of the United States was officially moved from Philadelphia to Washington in December. The 1800 federal census for the inhabitants of the national capital district was taken as part of the Maryland and Virginia enumerations. The population of the Georgetown/Washington side was 8,144, while the Alexandria side had 5,959 residents.

**1801. Territory of Columbia.** The Organic Act of 1801 established "The Territory called Columbia" as a jurisdiction exclusively under the control of Congress. This Act established a territorial judicial system, provided for a committee in Congress to manage the affairs of the district; and created two counties, Washington County on the northern side of the Potomac, and Alexandria County on the southern side. From 1790-1801, both Virginia and Maryland considered the residents in their ceded areas as citizens, qualified to vote in state and federal elections; and they were included in the federal censuses taken there in 1790 and 1800 as part of Virginia and Maryland. The 1801 Act essentially disenfranchised the District residents, who now had no representation in Congress or home rule.

**1814.** British troops burned the capitol and other federal buildings during the War of 1812. Contrary to popular belief, no original federal censuses were lost in the fires, with the possible exception of the 1810 District of Columbia schedules. None of the federal census name lists had been moved to Washington yet. That did not happen until after an 1830 law asked for the clerks of the district courts in all states to send the original copies to the U.S. Secretary of State's Office in Washington, DC.

**1820.** Congress amended the charter of the city of Washington for the direct election of the mayor by resident voters.

**1846.** Congress passed a law returning the city of Alexandria and Alexandria County to the state of Virginia, an act referred to as a retrocession.

**1848.** Congress adopted a new charter for the City of Washington and expanded the number of elected offices to include a board of assessors, a surveyor, a collector and a registrar.

**1871. District of Columbia**. The elected mayor and council of Washington City and Georgetown, and the County Levy Court were abolished by Congress and replaced by a governor and council appointed by the president. An elected House of Delegates and a non-voting delegate to Congress were created. In this Act, the jurisdiction and territorial government came to be called the *District of Columbia*, combining the governments of Georgetown, the City of Washington and the County of Washington.

**1874.** The territorial government of the District of Columbia was abolished, including the non-voting delegate to Congress. Three temporary commissioners and a subordinate military engineer were thereafter appointed by the president.

**1878.** In the Organic Act of 1878, Congress established the District of Columbia government as a municipal corporation governed by three commissioners appointed by the President. This form of government continued until 1973.

**1895.** No longer a city, the area of Georgetown was officially added to the city of Washington. The boundaries of the City of Washington and the District of Columbia were now the same.

**1961.** The 23rd Amendment to the Constitution gave District residents the right to vote for president.

**1973.** Congress approved the District of Columbia Self-Government and Governmental Reorganization Act, which established an elected mayor and a 13-member council.

**1978**. Congress approved the District of Columbia Voting Rights Amendment, which would have given District residents voting representation in the House and the Senate. However, the proposed constitutional amendment was not ratified by the necessary number of states (38) within the allotted seven years.

**1980.** District electors approved the District of Columbia Statehood Constitutional Convention of 1979, which called for convening a state constitutional convention.

**1982.** After a constitutional convention, a Constitution for the ***State of New Columbia*** was ratified by District voters. But, no action by Congress was taken.

**1983-1993.** Another state constitution was drafted, which again referred to the proposed state as *New Columbia.* Since 1983, more than a dozen statehood bills were introduced in Congress, but only two bills were reported out of the committee of jurisdictions: In 1992, the U.S. House of Representatives approved an enabling act for statehood for Washington, DC, but the U.S. Senate did not approve the measure. The second of these bills made it to the House floor in November 1993 for the debate and vote on D.C. statehood. It was defeated in the House of Representatives by a vote of 277 to 153.

**1994-2013.** For twenty years after the 1993 vote, there were bills introduced each year to grant statehood to the District of Columbia, but there were no congressional hearings, and none were ever brought to a vote.

**2014-2015**. The U.S. Senate Committee on Homeland Security and Government Affairs held a hearing on bill S. 132 which would have created a new state out of the current District of Columbia, similar to the 1993 bill. On Jan 25, 2015, A new bill was introduced by U.S. Sen. Tom Carper (D-Del.), ranking member of the Homeland Security and Governmental Affairs Committee, leading a group of 17 senators in introducing legislation that would grant Washington, D.C. full statehood. Rep. Eleanor Holmes Norton (D-D.C.) introduced companion legislation in the House, H.R. 317, in January.

**2016.** Apr. District Mayor Muriel Bowser called for a city-wide vote on whether the District of Columbia should become a state. A proposed state constitution followed, one that would make the Mayor of the District of Columbia the governor of the proposed state, and the members of the DC City Council would make up the proposed House of Delegates.

**2016.** Nov. The voters of the District of Columbia voted for statehood with an 86% majority in favor.

**2019.** The ***Washington D.C. Admission Act*** was introduced in the U.S. Senate. According to **GovTrack:** "...this bill is in the first stage of the legislative process. It was introduced into Congress on February 28, 2019. It will typically be considered by committee next before it is possibly sent on to the House or Senate as a whole. Rep. Eleanor Holmes Norton (D-D.C.) introduced companion legislation in the House, H.R. 51, January 3, 2019. Prognosis: 3% chance of being enacted according to Skopos Labs."

## District of Columbia Jurisdictions

For genealogists looking for evidence of their DC ancestors, access to records from a territory, county, city, or district jurisdiction may be necessary. The District of Columbia holds a unique status in this country's political system, functioning the same as a state, a county, and a city. Currently, the governments of the district and the city are the same. Some functions are done under the name District of Columbia, others under the name of the City of Washington, DC.

Specific functions usually performed by state–level governments include state courts, driver licensing, liquor control, unemployment compensation, food and drug inspection, and professional licensing, just to name a few. It is the mayor of the city of Washington who administers these state-level functions; plus the mayor manages city-level functions such as police and fire departments.

The "state court" of the District of Columbia is also unique – it is actually a circuit division of the Supreme Court of the United States, and the "state judge" is usually the Chief Justice of the Supreme Court. This current system was preceded by several different governmental structures, jurisdictions and names; and local political control changed often.

Neither the District of Columbia nor the City of Washington have ever taken a census apart from the federal censuses. But, there were numerous name lists generated by the various DC jurisdictions that can serve as substitutes.

# Bibliography
## District of Columbia
## Censuses & Substitutes

The following bibliography is arranged in chronological order, with the earliest name lists from Alexandria and Georgetown prior to the formation of the District of Columbia.

**1600s-1700.** ***Original Patentees of Land at Washington Prior to 1700*** **[Printed Book],** by Bessie Wilmarth Gahn. includes index. Originally published Washington, 1936, reprinted by Genealogical Publishing Co., Baltimore, MD, 1969, 85 pages, FHL book 975.3R21g.

**1600s-2000s.** ***District of Columbia – Collection Catalog*** **[Online Database],** over 100 databases can be searched at the "Search all District of Columbia Collections" search/browse screen at the MyHeritage website. Databases include censuses, family histories, town histories, military rosters, and more. A search can be done for a name, place, year, or keyword. See **www.myheritage.com/records/District-of-Columbia/all-records.**

**1600s-2000s.** ***District of Columbia USGenWeb Archives*** **[Online Databases],** includes Search Engines for Full Name Search, Surname Search, RootsWeb, and Google. Record categories include: Birth Records, Biographies, Cemeteries, Census and Tax Lists, Church Records, City Directories, Court Records, Death Records, Deeds and Real Estate Records, Divorce Records, Historical Records, Marriage Records, Military Records, Newspaper Articles, Obituaries, Photographs, Publications, and Schools. See **http://usgwarchives.net/dc/dcfiles.htm.**

**1600s-2000s.** ***Linkpendium – District of Columbia: Family History & Genealogy, Census, Birth, Marriage, Death Vital Records & More*** **[Online Databases].** Linkpendium is a portal to websites with genealogical information. The District of Columbia section is organized by Location (Number of Sites): Anacostia (11), Brookland (5), Georgetown (75), and Washington City (1,643). See **www.linkpendium.com/dc-genealogy.**

**1700-1900.** ***Genealogical Collection, Daughters of the American Revolution, District of Columbia*** **[Microfilm & Digital Capture],** from the original records at the DAR Library, Washington, DC. Most volumes are indexed. This collection contains over 250 volumes of Bible records, church records, genealogies, lineages, newspaper records, probate records, and vital records on individuals born ca 1700-1900. Filmed by the Genealogical Society of Utah, 1976, 51 rolls, beginning with FHL film #845766 (DC records, vol. 1-3, misc. records). For a complete list of roll numbers, roll contents, and the digital images of each roll, see the online FHL catalog page:
**www.familysearch.org/search/catalog/235353.**

**1747.** ***Assessments for Town and County of Alexandria*** **[Microfilm & Digital Capture],** from the originals at the Arlington County Courthouse, Arlington, Virginia. Contains two lists. Both are arranged alphabetically by the first letter of the surname. The first list gives the name of the land owner, residence, number of lots, property, value of the ground, value of improvements, total of ground and improvements. The second list gives the name of the owner, residence, number of acres, distance and bearing from the Courthouse, location, value of land per acre, including improvements, sum added to land on account of improvements, and remarks. Filmed by the Virginia State Library, 1981, 1 roll, FHL film #1902939. For access to the digital images of this roll, see the online FHL catalog page for this title:
**www.familysearch.org/search/catalog/1052402.**

**1749-1780.** See ***Alexandria, Virginia, Town Lots 1749-1801, Together With Proceedings of the Board of Trustees, 1749-1780*** **[Printed Book[,** compiled by Constance K. Ring and Wesley E. Pippenger. Includes index. Published by Family Line Publications, Westminster, MD, 1995, 218 pages, FHL book 975.5296 R2r.

**1769-1960.** ***District of Columbia, Select Deaths and Burials Index*** **[Online Database],** indexed at the Ancestry.com website. Source: FamilySearch extractions from microfilm at the Family History Library, Salt Lake City. Each index record includes: Name, Gender, Death age, Marital status, Birth date, Death date, Father, Mother, Spouse, FHL film number, and Reference ID. This database has 190,903 records:
**https://search.ancestry.com/search/db.aspx?dbid=60260.**

**1775-1988.** ***Cemetery Records, Rock Creek Cemetery, Washington, DC*** **[Microfilm & Digital Capture],** from original index cards at Rock Creek Cemetery, operated by St. Paul's Episcopal Church, Washington, DC. Cards in alphabetical order by surname of deceased. Filmed by the Genealogical Society of Utah, 1988, 14 rolls, beginning with FHL film #1530545 (Introduction to records, Abajian, Albert – Briscoe, Alice I). For a complete list of roll numbers, roll contents, and the digital images of certain rolls, see the online FHL catalog page for this title:
**www.familysearch.org/search/catalog/77801.**

**1776-1815.** ***Abstracts of Wills in the District of Columbia: Compiled From Records in the Office of the Register of Wills*** **[Printed Book],** compiled by Mrs. Alexander H. Bell, 2 vols., published 1945-1946, Washington, DC, Includes index. FHL book 975.3 S2b v.1-2. Also on microfilm, FHL film #207695 (Vol. 1 only); and also on microfiche, FHL fiche #6051443 (vol. 1) and fiche #6051444 (vol. 2).

**1776-1830s.** ***Revolutionary, War of 1812 & Indian Wars Pensioner List of Washington, D.C. and Alexandria, Virginia*** **[Digital Version],** digitized by FamilySearch International, 2015. To access the digital images, see the online FHL catalog page:
**www.familysearch.org/search/catalog/2564711.**

**1800-1991.** ***Washington, DC Newspaper Archives*** **[Online Database],** digitized and indexed at the GenealogyBank.com website. One search screen for names and keywords in the following Washington, DC newspapers: American Statesman, Battery, Black Networking News, Campaign, Campaign Constitution, Christian Statesman, City of Washington Gazette, Colored American, Columbia, Columbian Star, Constitution Courier, Daily Critic, Daily Evening Advocate, Daily Globe, Daily Madisonian, Daily National Era, Daily National Intelligencer, Daily National Journal, Daily Union, Democratic Expositor, Democratic Expositor and National Crisis, Democratic Flag-Ship, Dollar Globe, Evening Star, Evening Union, Extra Globe, Globe, Grit, Hickory Tree, Huntress Leader, Madisonian for the Country, Monitor, National Chronicle, National Era, National Intelligencer, National Journal, National Radical, New National Era, Paul Pry, People's Advocate, Price-Current, and Commercial Advertiser, Real Estate Record, Reconstructionist Republic, Semi-weekly Union, Signal, Spirit of 'Seventy-Six, States Times, Union Guard, United States Telegraph, United States Telegraph Extra, United States Weekly Telegraph, Universal Gazette, Washington Bee, Washington City Weekly Gazette, Washington Expositor, Washington Gazette, Washington Sentinel, Washington Times, Washington Tribune, Washingtonian, and Farmers, Mechanics and Merchants Gazette, Weekly Globe, Weekly Union, and Woman's Campaign. See **www.genealogybank.com/explore/newspapers/all/usa/district-of-columbia/washington-dc.**

**1783-1801.** ***Alexandria, Virginia Alexandria Hustings Court Deeds*** **[Printed Book],** compiled by James D. Munson, 2 vols. Contents: Vol. 1: 1783-1797, Vol. 2:1797-1801. Volumes cover the time period when Alexandria's first court of record, the Alexandria Hustings Court, began recording deeds in 1782 to 1801 when the town and environs became Alexandria County and were incorporated into the District of Columbia. The court was renamed at this time the Circuit Court of the District of Columbia for the County of Alexandria. Published by Heritage Books, Bowie, MD, 1990-1991, 2 vols., FHL book 975.5926 R2m v.1-2.

**1783-1870 Deeds, Alexandria City/County, Virginia.** See ***Deed Books, 1783-1865; Index, 1793-1870*** **[Microfilm & Digital Capture],** from the original records at the Alexandria City Courthouse in Alexandria, Virginia. Includes a general index. Most volumes are also individually indexed. Alexandria County was formed in 1789 from Fairfax County and included Alexandria City. It was formally established in 1801 as a county in the District of Columbia. In 1846 the county was given back to Virginia and organized in 1847 as a Virginia county. Alexandria County underwent a name change in 1920, becoming Arlington County. The city of Alexandria became an independent city in 1852. The 1783-1801 records were registered with the Hustings Court in the city of Alexandria. From 1801 to 1847 the deeds were recorded in the Circuit Court of the District of Columbia which was held for the county of Alexandria. After 1847 they were recorded with the County Court for the city and county of Alexandria. Filmed by the Genealogical Society of Utah, 1951, 37 rolls, beginning with FHL film #30168. For a complete list of roll numbers, roll contents, and digital images of each roll, see the online FHL catalog page for this title: **www.familysearch.org/search/catalog/10508.**

**1783-1801.** ***Alexandria, Virginia, Alexandria Hustings Court Deeds*** **[Printed Index],** compiled by James D. Munson, published by Heritage Books, Bowie, MD 1991, 2 vols. Includes indexes to grantors and grantees. Contents: vol. 1: 1783-1797; vol. 2: 1797-1801. The deed books cover the time period when Alexandria's first court of record, the Alexandria Hustings Court, began recording deeds in 1782 through 1801. The deeds indexed are those issued prior to Alexandria County becoming part of the District of Columbia in 1801. FHL book 975.5296 R2m v 1-2.

**1787-1800.** ***Personal Property Tax Lists, Alexandria, Virginia*** **[Microfilm & Digital Capture],** from the originals at the Virginia State Library and Archives in Richmond, VA. Arranged in alphabetical order by the first letter of the surname for each year. Lists give name of person taxed or tithed, type and amount of taxable property, amount of tax, and the county statistics. The lists for 1791-1794 and 1797 are missing. Filmed by the Genealogical Society of Utah, 1993, 1 roll, FHL film #1905755. For access to the digital images of this roll, see the online FHL catalog page for this title: **www.familysearch.org/search/catalog/696432.**

**1789-1799.** ***Abstracts of the Newspapers of Georgetown and the Federal City: And some Early Maps of the District of Columbia*** **[Printed Book],** compiled by F. Edward Wright. Includes index. Published by Family Line Publications, Silver Spring, MD, 1986, 109 pages, FHL book 975.3 B38w.

**1790-1854.** ***Georgetown, District of Columbia Newspaper Archives*** **[Online Database],** digitized and indexed at the GenealogyBank.com website. One search screen for names and keywords in the following Georgetown newspapers: Cabinet, Centinel and Country Gazette, Centinel of Liberty, Columbian Chronicle, Federal Republican, Federal Republican for the Country, Georgetown Advocate, Independent American, Messenger, Metropolitan Museum and Washington and George-town Advertiser, National Messenger, Olio, Senator, Spirit of 'Seventy-Six, Times and Patowmack Packet, and Washington Federalist See **www.genealogybank.com/gbnk/newspapers/explore/USA/District_of_Columbia/Georgetown.**

**1791-1800.** ***District of Columbia Original Land Owners, 1791-1800*** **[Printed Book],** compiled by Wesley E. Pippenger, published by W.E. Pippenger, Westminster, MD, 1999, 156 pages. FHL book 975.3 R2p.

**1791-1878.** ***Public Records, Georgetown*** **[Microfilm & Digital Capture],** from the originals at the National Archives, Washington, DC. Georgetown was founded in Maryland in 1751, became part of the Territory of Columbia in 1791, District of Columbia in 1801, and remained an incorporated city until 1871, when it was merged into the city of Washington, DC. These public records include account books, journals, ledgers, daybooks, assessment ledgers, real estate records, printed ordinances, and employee and service accounts. Filmed by the National Archives, 1965, 24 rolls, beginning with FHL film #1024458 (Account book, 1801-1808). For a complete list of roll numbers, roll contents, and the digital images of each roll, see the online FHL catalog page for this title:
**www.familysearch.org/search/catalog/408329.**

**1792-1817.** ***Index to District of Columbia Land Records*** **[Printed Book],** compiled by Wesley E. Pippenger, published by W.E. Pippenger, Tappahannock, VA, 2009, 466 pages, FHL book 975.3 R22p.

**1792-1919.** See ***Land Records; 1792-1886; General Index to Deeds, 1792-1919*** **[Microfilm & Digital Capture],** from the original records at the District of Columbia Courthouse, Washington, DC. Filmed by the Genealogical Society of Utah, 1972, 694 rolls, beginning with FHL film #89525 (General index to deeds v. 1-4 1792-1828). For a complete list of roll numbers, roll contents, and digital images of each roll, see the online FHL catalog page:
**www.familysearch.org/search/catalog/216566.**

**1795-1863 Records of Coffin Sales,** see ***William King's Mortality Books*** **[Printed Book],** transcribed from the originals by Jan Donovan and Carlton Fletcher, published by Heritage Books, Bowie, MD, 2001, 2004, 2 vols. William King was a cabinet maker in Georgetown, and kept careful records of every coffin constructed for Georgetown and Washington families, including the name of the deceased and the person paying for the coffin. FHL book 975.3/G1 V3k vol. 1 (1795-1832) and FHL book 975.3/G1 V3k vol. 2 (1833-1863).

**1798 Federal Direct Tax, District of Columbia.** See ***Federal Assessment, 1790-1805, Maryland, District of Columbia*** **[Microfilm & Digital Capture],** from the original manuscripts (hand and typewritten) held by the Maryland Hall of Records, Annapolis, MD. Filmed by the Hall of Records, 1965, 13 rolls, for all Maryland counties, including "District of Columbia, Maryland," which was mainly a name list of tax payers from Georgetown and environs. The 1798 name list for the District of Columbia is on FHL film #499897. To access the digital images, see the online FHL catalog page: **www.familysearch.org/search/catalog/340141.**

**1799-1837.** See ***Wills, Book IV, dated 1799 to 1837: As Recorded in the Office of Wills, Municipal Court, Washington, D.C.*** **[Microfilm & Digital Capture],** from the original typescript at the DAR Library, Washington, DC, 104 pages. Includes index. Filmed by the Genealogical Society of Utah, 1972, 1 roll, FHL film #907978. To access the digital images, see the online FHL catalog page:
**www.familysearch.org/search/catalog/453935.**

**- 1800 NOTE:** In the 1800 federal census, the two counties of the District were enumerated separately: Washington County, DC was included with Maryland (Montgomery Co and Prince Georges Co, manuscript extant); Alexandria County, DC was included with Virginia (Fairfax Co, manuscript lost).

**1800-1850.** ***Marriage and Death Notices from the National Intelligencer (Washington, DC)*** **[Microfilm],** from a book by George A. Martin and Frank J. Metcalf, Special Publication No. 41, National Genealogical Society. Filmed by the society, 1976, 3 rolls, FHL film #929472 (Index Notices 1800-1834), #929473 (Notices, 1835-1846), and #929474 (Notices 1847-1850).

***1800, 1820, 1830, & 1840 District of Columbia Federal Censuses: Population Schedules*** **[Microfilm & Digital Capture],** from the originals at the National Archives, Washington, DC. Filmed as a series, 1800 and 1820-1840, by the National Archives, 1938-1960, 4 rolls, as follows:

- "District of Columbia, Maryland" (1800), FHL film #6697.
- District of Columbia (1820), FHL Film #6698.
- District of Columbia (1830), FHL film #6699.
- District of Columbia (1840, FHL film #6700.

To access the digital images for each roll, see the online FHL catalog page for this series, 1800-1840:
**www.familysearch.org/search/catalog/745484.**

**1800-1951.** See ***Will books, 1800-1878; Index to Wills, 1800-1951 (Alexandria County, District of Columbia (1801-1846); Arlington County, Virginia (1846-1920); and Alexandria, Virginia, an Independent City, 1920 to date)*** **[Microfilm & Digital Capture],** from the original records at the Alexandria City Courthouse in Alexandria, Virginia and the Arlington County Courthouse in Arlington, Virginia. Includes general index. Most volumes are also individually indexed. Includes accounts, inventories and other related probate matters. Contains probate records 1800-1801 for the Hustings Court and the Corporation Court for Alexandria City. From 1801 to 1846 the court was the Orphans Court for Alexandria County while the county was part of the District of Columbia. In 1846, when Alexandria County was returned to Virginia, the court became the County Court. Alexandria was renamed Arlington County in 1920. Filmed by the Genealogical Society of Utah, 1951, 6 rolls, beginning with FHL film #30499 (Index to wills, 1800-1951). To access the digital images, see the online FHL catalog page: **www.familysearch.org/search/catalog/279393.**

**1800-1879.** See ***Georgetown Property Tax Records, 1800-1820, and 1862-1879*** **[Microfilm & Digital Capture],** from the originals at the National Archives, Washington, DC. From intro: "This microfilm publication reproduces records of the local government of the city of Georgetown, 1800-1879. Georgetown, which was founded in Maryland in 1751, was governed by its own mayor and council until 1871, when Congress revoked its charter. Georgetown retained its name as a topographical designation, however, until 1895, when Congress abolished its existence as a separate city, consolidating it with Washington, D.C." Some volumes are indexed. Filmed by the Archives, series M605, 9 rolls, beginning with FHL film #1024464.(Tax records 1800-1813). To access the digital images, see the online FHL catalog page: **www.familysearch.org/search/catalog/408565.**

**1800-1954.** ***Historical Court Records of Washington, District of Columbia*** **[Online Database],** digitized and OCR indexed at the Ancestry.com website. Source: Book, same title, by Homer A. Walker, 14 vols., 1,442 pages. The records are organized by types, then alphabetical. See **https://search.ancestry.com/search/db.aspx?dbid=25493.**

**1800-1890.** ***District of Columbia, Compiled Census and Census Substitutes Index*** **[Online Database],** indexed at the FamilySearch.org website. Source: Accelerated Indexing Systems, 1999. This collection contains the following indexes: 1800 Federal Census Index; 1810 Federal Census Index; 1820 Federal Census Index; 1830 Federal Census Index; 1840 Federal Census Index; 1840 Pensioners List; 1850 Federal Census Index; 1850 Slave Schedule; 1860 Federal Census Index; 1860 Slave Schedules; 1870 Federal Census Index; 1890 Veterans Schedule; 1890 Naval Veterans. This database has 5,659 records. See **https://search.ancestry.com/search/db.aspx?dbid=3540.**

**1801-1802. Liber A, District of Columbia, Alexandria County [Microfilm & Digital Capture],** from the originals at the Arlington County Courthouse, Arlington, VA. Includes various court proceedings. The first few pages of each book is an index to the parties involved and they type of proceeding. To access the digital images, see the online FHL catalog page: **www.familysearch.org/search/catalog/1128933.**

**1801-1808.** ***Proceedings of the Orphan's Court: Washington County, District of Columbia*** **[Printed Book],** compiled by Wesley E. Pippenger, published by Willow Bend Books, Westminster, MD, 1998, 94 pages. FHL book 975.3 P2p.

**1801-1811.** ***Washington County, D.C., Indentures of Apprenticeship*** **[Online Database],** indexed at the Ancestry.com website. Source: National Archives microfilm M2011. An Indenture of Apprenticeship is a contract where an apprentice is bound to the service of a master for a specific amount of time in order to learn a trade, craft, profession or business. The apprentices ranged in age from 5 to 17 and the contract usually lasted until the age of 21. The original contract was signed in the presence of a notary public and once approved by the Orphans Court was copied into these records by the Register of Wills. The Indentures of Apprenticeship contain: Apprentice name, Apprentice place of residence, Apprentice age, Apprentice date of birth, Apprentice race, Parent/guardian name, and Date of indenture. This database has 400 records. See **https://search.ancestry.com/search/db.aspx?dbid=1937.**

**1801-1818.** ***Alexandria City and County, Virginia, Deed Books Extracts*** **[Printed Book],** compiled by Patrick G. Wardell. Includes index. Published by Heritage Books, Bowie, MD, 1989, 476 pages, FHL book 975.5295 R2w.

**1801-1822.** ***Alexandria County, District of Columbia (now Arlington Co., VA) Marriages Bonds and Minister's Returns*** **[Microfilm & Digital Capture],** from the original typescript at the Dr. Elisha Dick chapter, DAR, Alexandria, VA. Filmed by the Genealogical Society of Utah, 1970, 1 roll, FHL film #850089. To access the digital images, see the online FHL catalog page:
**www.familysearch.org/search/catalog/301565.**

**1801-1825.** ***Washington, D.C. Compiled Marriages*** **[Online Database],** indexed at the Ancestry.com website. Taken from a series of marriage record extracts by Liahona Research. Records are limited to the names of the bride and groom and the date of the marriage. This database has 9,661 records. See **http://search.ancestry.com/search/db.aspx?dbid=2084.**

**1801-1827.** ***Order Book*** **[Microfilm & Digital Capture],** from the originals at the Arlington County Courthouse, Arlington, VA. The Federal Judicial District for the District of Potomac was created February 13, 1801 and covered the counties of Fairfax and Loudoun in Virginia, and Montgomery and part of Prince George County in Maryland. It was held in Alexandria County (now Arlington County). On April 29, 1802 it became the District Court of the United States for the District of Columbia. It was also known as a Court of Admiralty. The early cases pertained mainly to those involving sailing ships. Later cases hardly referred to any ships. Includes index. Filmed by the Virginia State Library, 1 roll, FHL film #1902940. To access the digital images, see the online FHL catalog page:
**www.familysearch.org/search/catalog/1128703.**

**1801-1838.** ***Georgetown, District of Columbia, Marriage and Death Notices*** **[Printed Book],** by Wesley E. Pippenger, published by Heritage Books, Bowie, MD, 2004, 330 pages. Includes index. This compilation of marriage and death notices was taken from nine newspapers that were published in Georgetown during the period 1801-1838. There are some gaps due to missing newspapers. FHL book 975.3/G1 V28p.

**1801-1850.** ***A List of Certificates Returned of the Solemnization of Marriages in the County of Alexandria in the District of Columbia*** **[Microfilm & Digital Capture],** from the original records at the Arlington County Courthouse in Arlington, Virginia. The certificates were returned to the clerk of the U.S. Circuit Court of the District of Columbia, Alexandria County in the State of Virginia. They are also called ministers' returns. Alexandria County became part of the District of Columbia in 1801. The area was returned to Virginia in 1846, and the name changed to Arlington County in 1920. Each record notes the date of marriage, names of parties married, and by whom married. Filmed by the Virginia State Library, 1981, 1 roll, FHL film #1902941. To access the digital images, see the online FHL catalog page:
**www.familysearch.org/search/catalog/1129363.**

**1801-1852.** ***District of Columbia Probate Records: Will Books 1 through 6, and Estate Files*** **[Printed Book],** compiled by Wesley E. Pippenger. Includes a table of contents naming each deceased person and a name index for all associated names. Published by Family Lines Publications, Westminster, MD, 1996, 526 pages, FHL book 975.3 P28p.

***1801-1863 Minutes of the U.S. Circuit Court for the District of Columbia*** **[Microfilm & Digital Capture],** from the originals at the National Archives, Central Plains Region, series M1021, 6 rolls, beginning with FHL film #940130. To access the digital images, see the online FHL catalog page:
**www.familysearch.org/search/catalog/227108.**

**1801-1878.** ***Historical Court Records of Washington, DC – Death Records as taken from Administration of Estates*** **[Online Database],** indexed at the Ancestry.com website. See
**http://search.ancestry.com/search/db.aspx?dbid=25494.**

**1801-1929. Index to District of Columbia Estates [Printed Book],** compiled by Wesley E. Pippenger, published by Heritage Books, Westminster, MD, 2008, 841 pages, FHL book 975.3 P22pwe.

***1801-1930 Probate Records, District of Columbia, Register of Wills*** **[Microfilm & Digital Capture],** from the originals at the Office of Public Records, Washington, DC. Folders are arranged alphabetically by year. These are loose papers. General index is to files by number but by using the date the will was filed or other date it is possible to locate the will. Filmed by the Genealogical Society of Utah, 1996-1997, 133 rolls, beginning with FHL film #2050077 (Index: A – Buchoff, 1801-1929). To access the digital images, see the online FHL catalog page:
**www.familysearch.org/search/catalog/780576.**

**1810-1930.** ***Probate Records (District of Columbia)*** **[Microfilm & Digital Capture],** from the original records at the Office of Public Records, Washington, DC. Filmed by the Genealogical Society of Utah,

1996-1997, 133 rolls, beginning with FHL film #2050077 (Index: A – Buchoff 1801-1929). To access the digital images, see the online FHL catalog page: **www.familysearch.org/search/catalog/780576.**

**1801-1950.** ***Index to District of Columbia Wills*** **[Printed Book],** prepared by Dorothy S. Provine, published by Willow Bend Books, Westminster, MD, 1996, 2 vols. This index provides the name, year, and box number. Contents: Vol. 1: 1801-1920; Vol. 2:1921-1950. FHL book 975.3 P22P v.1-2.

**1801-1952.** ***Washington, D.C., Wills and Probate Records*** **[Online Database],** digitized and indexed at the Ancestry.com website. Source: Washington, D.C. District and Probate Courts. The 1737 date was for a birth of a person (in Baltimore, MD) not a year of probate. Probate records include Wills, Letters of Administration, Inventories, Distributions and Accounting, Bonds, and Guardianships. Each index record includes: Name, Probate date, Probate place, Inferred death place, and Item description. A Table of Contents indicates the type and number of papers. This database has 30,314 records. See **https://search.ancestry.com/search/db.aspx?dbid=9083.**

**1801-1997.** ***Guardianship Cases Index (District of Columbia)*** **[Microfilm & Digital Capture],** from the original records at the District of Columbia Records Center, Washington, DC. This index is by name of minor. There is some misfiling. Filmed by the Genealogical Society of Utah, 1997, 4 rolls, beginning with FHL film #2073131 (Index: Abernathey-Fisher). To access the digital images, see the online FHL catalog page: **www.familysearch.org/search/catalog/677591.**

**1802-1928.** ***District of Columbia Guardianship Index*** **[Printed Book],** compiled by Wesley E. Pippenger, published by Willow Bend Books, 1998, 401 pages. FHL book 975.3 P22pw.

**1802-1909.** ***Index to Naturalization Records of the U.S. Supreme Court for the District of Columbia*** **[Microfilm & Digital Capture],** from the original records located at the National Archives, Washington, DC. Filmed by the Archives, 1999, series M1827, 1 roll. FHL has film #2311054 (Index, 1802-1909). To access the digital images, see the online FHL catalog page: **www.familysearch.org/search/catalog/1130697.**

**- 1810 NOTE:** The 1810 Federal Census for the District of Columbia was lost. It is possible it was destroyed on August 24, 1814; the day British troops burned several buildings in Washington during the War of 1812.

**1810-1953.** ***District of Columbia, Marriage Records*** **[Online Database],** indexed at the Ancestry.com website. Source: Clerk of the Superior Court, Records Office, Washington D.C. This database is an index to marriages. Each index record includes: Name, Gender, Age, Birth date, Marriage date, Marriage place, Spouse, and File number. This database has 863,462 records. See **https://search.ancestry.com/search/db.aspx?dbid=61404.**

**1811-1813.** ***DC Militia Muster Rolls of the War of 1812*** **[Online Database],** indexed at the USGenWeb site for DC. See **http://theusgenweb.org/dcgenweb/records/muster.shtml.**

**1811-1830.** ***Marriage Licenses of Washington, D.C.*** **[Printed Index],** compiled by F. Edward Wright, published by Family Line Publications, Silver Spring, MD, 1988, 159 pages. Arranged in alphabetical order for both males and females. FHL book 975.3 V28w.

**1811-1858.** ***Washington D.C. Marriage Licenses*** **[Online Database],** indexed at the USGenWeb site for DC. See **http://files.usgwarchives.net/dc/vitals/dcmarrdr.txt.**

**1811-1870.** ***District of Columbia Marriage Licenses: Registers*** **[Printed Book],** compiled by Wesley E. Pippenger. Names are alphabetical with an entry for both the bride and groom in vol. 1 and by groom with a bride's index in vol. 2. Published by Family Line Publications, Westminster, MD, 1994, 2 vols., FHL book 975.3 V28p v.1-2.

**1811-1950.** ***District of Columbia Marriages*** **[Online Database],** digitized and indexed at the FamilySearch.org website. Source: Clerk of the Superior Court, Records Office, Washington, D.C. This database has 605,303 records. See **www.familysearch.org/search/collection/1803979.**

**1811-1986.** See ***Marriage Records (District of Columbia), 1811-1950; Indexes, 1811-1986*** **[Microfilm & Digital Capture],** from the originals at the District of Columbia Records Center, Washington, DC. Each volume is indexed. Filmed by the

Genealogical Society of Utah, 1997-2007, 213 rolls, beginning with FHL film #2079172 (Index to marriage records, 1811-1858). To access the digital images, see the online FHL catalog page:
**www.familysearch.org/search/catalog/682872.**

**1818-1864.** ***Selected Final Pension Payment Vouchers District of Columbia*** **[Printed Book],** abstracted by Alycon Trubey Pierce. Arranged alphabetically by name of individual applying with a name index. Published by Willow Bend Books, 1998, 235 pages, FHL book 975.3 M28p.

**1820.** ***Index to the 1820 Census of Maryland and Washington, D.C.*** **[Printed Index],** compiled by Gary W. Parks, published by Genealogical Publishing Co., Baltimore, MD, 1986, 274 pages, FHL book 975 X22p 1820.

**1820.** ***District of Columbia, 1820 Census Index*** **[Printed Index],** edited by Ronald Vern Jackson, et al, published by Accelerated Indexing Systems, Bountiful, UT, 1976, 86 pages, FHL book 975.3 X2p 1820.

**1820-1863.** ***District of Columbia Court and Emancipation Records*** **[Online Database],** digitized at the FamilySearch.org website. Source: National Archives microfilm M520, M433, and M434. From Records of the Board of Commissioners for the Emancipation of Slaves in the district of Columbia, 1862-1863, an image-only database. This database has 12,462 images. See
**www.familysearch.org/search/collection/2515818.**

**1820-1863.** ***Habeas Corpus Case Records*** **[Microfilm & Digital Capture],** from the originals at the National Archives, Microfilm pub. M0434. Filmed by the National Archives, 1963, 2 rolls, FHL #1601546 & #1601547. To access the digital images, see the online FHL catalog page:
**www.familysearch.org/search/catalog/588809.**
- See also, ***Washington, D.C., Habeas Corpus Case Records, 1820-1863*** **[Online Database],** indexed at the Ancestry.com website. National Archives microfilm M434. This database includes writs of habeas corpus from the U.S. Circuit Court of the District of Columbia.. The records include criminal matters, financial disputes and bankruptcy, apprenticeships, family matters, and military cases. Records may include the following details: Names and aliases, Ages, Places of residence, Names of family members and witnesses, Occupations, Reason for confinement, and Outcome. This database has 1,004 records. See
**https://search.ancestry.com/search/db.aspx?dbid=2981.**

**1820-1988.** ***Cemetery Records, Congressional Cemetery Association, Washington, DC*** **[Microfilm & Digital Capture],** from original records at the Congressional Cemetery Association. Includes index. Interspersed with the index are special lists of Civil War burials, famous people card file, Interment journals, range books, and vault book. Filmed by the Genealogical Society of Utah, 1978, 1988, 13 rolls, beginning with FHL film #1530459 (Index: Abbey Mausoleum – Brown, Samuel). To access the digital images, see the online FHL catalog page:
**www.familysearch.org/search/catalog/19606.**

**1822.** ***Washington Directory: Showing the Name, Occupation, and Residence of Each Head of a Family and Person in Business, the Names of the Members of Congress, and Where They Board; Together With Other Useful Information*** **[Microfilm],** from the original book published by W. Duncan, Washington, DC, 1822, 148 pages. Filmed by the Genealogical Society of Utah, 1966, 4 microfiche, FHL fiche #6125565.
- See also ***Washington Directory of 1822*** **[Printed Book],** reprint of original by Family Line Publications, Silver Spring, MD, ca1985, 43 pages. FHL book 975.3 E4w.

**1822-1899.** ***Obituaries Published by the Christian Index*** **[Printed Book],** abstracted and edited by Mary Overby, published by the Georgia Baptist Historical Society, 1975, 1982, 2 vols., FHL book 975.8 V4o. v.1-2.

**1822-1935.** ***Washington D.C. City Directories*** **[Microfiche],** from the originals published by various publishers. Filmed by Research Publications, Woodbridge, CT, 1980-1984, 44 microfiche, beginning with FHL fiche #6044618 (1822: The Washington Directory by William Duncan (3 fiches). 1822 followed by directories for the years 1827, 1843 1846, 1850, 1853, 1855, 1858, 1860, and a complete run of years from 1862 through 1935. For a complete list of fiche numbers and the contents of each, see the online FHL catalog page:
**www.familysearch.org/search/catalog/539257.**

**1826-1850.** ***Washington, D.C. Compiled Marriages*** **[Online Database],** indexed at the Ancestry.com website. Taken from a series of marriage record extracts by Liahona Research, 2000. Records are limited to the names of the bride and groom and the date of the marriage. This database has 9,240 records: **http://search.ancestry.com/search/db.aspx?dbid=5277.**

*1827 City Directory, Washington, DC* **[Online Database],** digitized and indexed at the Ancestry.com website. Taken from the S.A. Elliot Directory of Washington, DC, the database has the names of over 3,000 people, mostly heads of households. See **http://search.ancestry.com/search/db.aspx?dbid=6054.**

**1828-1837.** ***Record, Abstract of Wills, Municipal Court, Washington, DC, Vol. 4*** **[Photocopy of Typescript],** compiled by members of the Daughters of the American Revolution. Includes index. A photocopy of the original is at the Family History Library, Salt lake City, FHL book 975.3 S2d.

**1829-1862.** ***A Complete Guide to the History and Inmates of the U.S. Penitentiary, District of Columbia, 1829-1862*** **[Printed Book],** by Mary C. Thornton. From the Introduction: "Most of my information came from records stored at the National Archives in Washington, D.C. and in College Park, MD. Some information came from old issues of the 'Evening Star,' stored on microfilm in the Washingtonian Division of the Main Library in Washington D.C. . . . "In addition to the names of the convicts, numerous other names appear throughout the text. These include the names of people who were victims, judges, law enforcement personnel, Civil War soldiers, doctors, ministers, etc." Published by Heritage Books, Bowie, MD, 2003, 272 pages, FHL book 975.3 J6t.

**1830.** ***District of Columbia, 1830 Census Index*** **[Printed Index],** edited by Ronald Vern Jackson, et al, published by Accelerated Indexing Systems, Bountiful, UT, 1977, 17 pages, FHL book 975.3 X2p 1830.

**1830-1921.** ***District of Columbia Marriages*** **[Online Database],** digitized and indexed at the FamilySearch.org website. Source: FamilySearch extractions from microfilm at the Family History Library, Salt Lake City. Each index record includes: Name, Birth date, Age, Spouse's name, Spouse's birth date, Spouse's age, Event date, Event place, Race, Marital status, Spouse's race, and Spouse's marital status. This database has 239,999 records. See **www.familysearch.org/search/collection/1674801.** - This database is also available at the Ancestry.com website. See **https://search.ancestry.com/search/db.aspx?dbid=60261.**

**1830-1955.** ***District of Columbia Births and Christenings*** **[Online Database],** digitized and indexed at the FamilySearch.org website, a name index to records from the District of Columbia, originally compiled by the FamilySearch.org site, the database contains 109,908 records. See **www.familysearch.org/search/collection/1674779.** This database is also available at the Ancestry.com website:. See **https://search.ancestry.com/search/db.aspx?dbid=60259.**

**1831-1899.** ***Columbian Harmony Cemetery Records, District of Columbia*** **[Microfilm],** compiled by Paul E. Sluby, Sr., C.G., for The Columbian Harmony Society, Washington, DC. From the Foreword: "The Columbia Harmony Society was established to serve as a mutual aid organization for free Negroes and freed black slaves. Burials which commenced in the harmony Cemetery in 1829 were restricted to the interment of members of that Society. Subsequently, the cemetery received burials from outside of the Society membership." See FHL film #962039.

*1835 Federal Pension List, District of Columbia* **[Online Database],** indexed at the RostersTripod.com site: **http://rosters.tripod.com/index-36.html.**

**1840.** ***District of Columbia, 1840 Census Index*** **[Printed Index],** edited by Ronald Vern Jackson, et al, published by Accelerated Indexing Systems, Bountiful, UT, 1977, 18 pages, FHL book 975.3 X2p 1840.

**1840-1964.** ***District of Columbia Deaths and Burials*** **[Online Database],** digitized and indexed at the FamilySearch.org website, a name index to death and burial records from the District of Columbia. Microfilm copies of these records are available at the Family History Library in Salt Lake City. This database contains 81,744 records. See **www.familysearch.org/search/collection/1674800.**

**1845-1988.** ***Cemetery Records (Oak Hill Cemetery, Washington, DC)*** **[Microfilm & Digital Capture],** from original Interment Indexes and Lot Owner Indexes at the cemetery. Although the cemetery was

created in 1849, there are some reburials from other areas, therefore some death dates earlier than 1849. Filmed by the Genealogical Society of Utah, 1988, 6 rolls, beginning with FHL film #1543685 (Interment Index: Abbaticchio, Ada Rebecca Alexander – Cutts Richard D). To access the digital images, see the online FHL catalog page:
**www.familysearch.org/search/catalog/158291.**

**1847-1938.** ***Register of Burials in District of Columbia Cemeteries*** **[Microfilm & Digital Capture],** from the original records (6 vols.) at the DAR Library, Washington, DC. Includes records of the Joseph F. Birch undertakers. Filmed by the Genealogical Society of Utah, 1971, 1 roll, FHL #887587. For access to the digital images of this roll, see the online FHL catalog page for this title:
**www.familysearch.org/search/catalog/256299.**

**1847-1938.** ***Register of Burials of the Joseph F. Birch Funeral Home: January 1, 1847 - December 31, 1938*** **[Printed Book],** transcribed by Paul E. Sluby, Sr.; Stanton L. Wormley, published by the Columbian Harmony Society, Washington, DC, 1989, 4 vols. Includes copies of the original records of this Georgetown funeral home. Includes surname index for each volume. The funeral home was apparently known by slight variations of the name over a period of time. FHL book 975.3 V39r v. 1-4.

**1850.** ***The Washington Directory, and Congressional and Executive Register*** **[Printed Book & Digital Version],** compiled and published by Edward Waite, digitized by FamilySearch International, 2015. To access the digital images, see the online FHL catalog page: **www.familysearch.org/search/catalog/2504560.**

***1850 District of Columbia Federal Census: Population Schedules & Slave Schedules*** **[Microfilm & Digital Capture],** from the originals at the National Archives, Washington, DC. Filmed by the National Archives, 1964, 2 rolls, FHL film #6702 (DC excluding Washington), and FHL film #6703 (Washington, and Slave Schedules). For access to the digital images for each roll, see the online FHL catalog page for this title:
**www.familysearch.org/search/catalog/744474.**

**1850.** ***District of Columbia 1850 Census Index*** **[Printed Index],** edited by Ronald Vern Jackson, et al, published by Accelerated Indexing Systems, Bountiful, UT 1977, 44 pages, FHL book 975.3 X2p 1850.

**1850.** ***District of Columbia 1850 Mortality Schedule*** **[Printed Index],** edited by Ronald Vern Jackson, et al, published by Accelerated Indexing Systems, Bountiful, UT, 1981, 44 pages, FHL book 975.3 X28j 1850.

**1850 Washington DC Mortality Schedule [Online Database],** indexed at Christine's site. See **http://ccharity.com/dcmortality.**

**1850-1853.** See ***Georgetown District of Columbia 1850 Federal Population Census (Schedule 1) and 1853 Directory of Residents of Georgetown*** **[Printed Book],** by Wesley E. Pippenger. Includes index. Published by Willow Bend Books, Westminster, MD, 1999, 236 pages, FHL book 975.3/G1 X2p.

**1850-1870.** See ***Non-population Census Schedules for the District of Columbia, 1850-1870: Agriculture, Industry, Mortality, and Social Statistics; and Non-population Schedules for Worcester County, Maryland, 1850, Agriculture*** **[Microfilm],** from the originals at the Duke University Library, Durham, NC. Filmed by the National Archives, Washington, DC, 1994, 1 roll, FHL film #2155488.

***1850-1880 District of Columbia Federal Census, Mortality Schedules*** **[Microfilm & Digital Capture],** from the originals at the DAR Library, Washington, DC. Filmed by the National Archives, 1962, series T655, 3 rolls, beginning with FHL film #1549978. Each roll contains the filmed originals of the mortality schedules, and a typescript index to the name lists for each year, 1850-1880, compiled by the DAR. To access the digital images, see the online FHL catalog page:
**www.familysearch.org/search/catalog/783143.**

**1851-1863.** ***Slave Emancipation Records*** **[Online Database],** indexed at the Ancestry.com website. Source: National Archives microfilm M433. From the descriptive brochure: "This microfilm publication reproduces all the records relating to slavery in the District of Columbia that were kept by the U.S. Circuit Court for the District of Columbia. These include emancipation papers, manumission papers, 1857–63, and case papers relating to fugitive slaves, 1851–63." This database has 7,336 records:
**https://search.ancestry.com/search/db.aspx?dbid=2171.**
- See also, ***District of Columbia Court and Emancipation Records, 1820-1863*** **[Online Database],** digitized at FamilySearch. This database has 12,462 images, see
**www.familysearch.org/search/collection/2515818.**

- See also ***Records of the United States District Court for the District of Columbia Relating to Slaves, 1801-1827*** **[Microfilm & Digital Capture],** filmed by the Genealogical Society of Utah, 2 rolls, FHL film #1299307-8. To access the digital images, see the online FHL catalog page:
**www.familysearch.org/search/catalog/132046.**

**1853.** ***The 1853 Washington and Georgetown Directory*** **[Printed Book & Online Database],** from the original compiled and published by Alfred Hunter; revised by Wesley E. Pippenger, originally published by Kirkwood & McGill, 1853. Reprinted by Colonial Roots, Lewes, DE, 2004, 160 pages. FHL book 975.3 E4h. Also online, see the DC USGenWeb for alpha groups:
- 1853 DC Directory, Abbott to Davidson: See **http://files.usgwarchives.net/dc/misc/georgetown1.txt.**
- 1853 DC Directory, Davis to Johnson: See **http://files.usgwarchives.net/dc/misc/georgetown2.txt.**
- 1853 DC Directory, Johnston to Rhodes: See **http://files.usgwarchives.net/dc/misc/georgetown3.txt..**
- 1853 DC Directory, Rodier to Zimmerman: See **http://files.usgwarchives.net/dc/misc/georgetown4.txt.**

**1854-1855.** ***The Daily Globe, Washington, DC*** **[Online Database],** digitized and OCR indexed at the Ancestry.com website. The database is a fully searchable text version of the newspaper. The newspaper can be browsed or searched using a computer-generated index. See
**http://search.ancestry.com/search/db.aspx?dbid=6665.**

**1854-1988.** ***Interment Card File, Glenwood Cemetery, Washington, DC*** **[Microfilm & Digital Capture],** from the original index cards at the cemetery. Filmed by the Genealogical Society of Utah, 1988, 8 rolls, beginning with FHL film #1530876 (Camp, Virginia B – Farley, Lawerence M). To access the digital images, see the online FHL catalog page:
**www.familysearch.org/search/catalog/583089.**
- This microfilm series is also available at FamilySearch.org as an image-only database with the title, ***District of Columbia, Glenwood Cemetery Records, 1854-2013*** **[Online Database],** This database has 52,042 images. See
**www.familysearch.org/search/collection/2170640.**

**1855-1974.** See ***District of Columbia Interments, 1855-1874; Death certificates, 1874-1931; Index to (1) Interments, (2) Death Certificates, (3) "Foreign" Death Certificates, 1855-1949; Stillbirth Certificates, 1874-1964*** **[Microfilm & Digital Capture],** from the original records at the Health Department in Washington, D.C. Certificates are loose papers. This material has some missing or non-readable pages. "Foreign" deaths refers to death certificates for a person who died outside of DC, but the body was brought to DC for burial. Filmed by the Genealogical Society of Utah, 1995, 1998-1999, 130 rolls, beginning with FHL film #1994618 (Index to old register of deaths, 1855-1874; Index, vol. 1-2, 1874-1882). To access the digital images, see the online FHL catalog page: **www.familysearch.org/search/catalog/748603.**

**1855-1870.** ***Daily National Intelligencer, Index to Deaths*** **[Printed Index],** compiled by Wesley E. Pippenger, published by Heritage Books, Westminster, MD, 2004, 137 pages. Arranged in alphabetical order by surname. From preface: "The present work is an index of death notices that appeared primarily under the column heading 'Deaths' as found most often in the earlier years on the front page of each four-page issue. By 1865, notices typically appeared on page three of each issue. Each entry in the present index contains as much information from the death notice that can be inserted on a single line. The compiler did not analyze each issue for death information that might be contained in other articles or editorials. Researchers should consult the newspaper for the complete notice. During the war years, one will find an occasional list of dead as submitted by the Navy Department; not all of these lists were indexed." FHL book 975.3 B32p.

**1855-1874.** ***District of Columbia Interments: Index to Deaths January 1, 1855 to July 31, 1874*** **[Printed Book],** by Wesley E. Pippenger. Published by the author, Westminster, MD, 1999, 409 pages, FHL book 975.3 V32p.

**1856-1897.** ***Presbyterian Cemetery Records, (Georgetown) Washington, DC, 1856-1897*** **[Printed Book],** by Paul E. Sluby, Sr. and Stanton L. Wormley. Includes surname index. Published by Columbian Harmony Society, Washington, DC, 1990, 213 pages, FHL book 975.3 V3spr.

**1858-1988.** ***Cemetery Records (Prospect Hill Cemetery, Washington, DC)*** **[Microfilm & Digital Capture],** from original Interment Files at the cemetery. Includes History of the Prospect Hill Cemetery Society of Washington, DC, by P.G. Gleis. Filmed by the Genealogical Society of Utah, 1988, 5 rolls, beginning with FHL film #1530539 (History of

Prospect Hill Cemetery Society of Washington, DC, 1858-1950, by P.G. Gleis; Interment Index: Abel, Chri – Gott, Mark K.). To access the digital images, see the online FHL catalog page:
**www.familysearch.org/search/catalog/370295.**

**1860.** ***District of Columbia, 1860 Federal Census: Population Schedules*** **[Microfilm & Digital Capture],** from the originals at the National Archives, Washington, DC. Filmed twice by the National Archives, 1950, 1967, 6 rolls total, beginning with FHL film #803101 (2nd filming, DC, Georgetown). To access the digital images, see the online FHL catalog page: **www.familysearch.org/search/catalog/704565.**

**1860. Boyd's Washington and Georgetown Directory [Digital Version].** To access the digital images, see the online FHL catalog page:
**www.familysearch.org/search/catalog/2852434.**

***1860 District of Columbia Census Index: Heads of Households and Other Surnames in Households Index*** **[Printed Index],** compiled by Bryan Lee Dilts, Published by Index Publishing, Salt Lake City, UT, 1984, 109 pages, FHL book 975.3 X22d.

**1860.** ***District of Columbia 1860 Census Index*** **[Printed Index],** edited by Ronald Vern Jackson, et al, published by Accelerated Indexing Systems, Bountiful, UT 1984, 322 pages, FHL book 975.3 X22dc 1860.

**1860.** ***District of Columbia 1860 Mortality Schedule*** **[Printed Index],** edited by Ronald Vern Jackson, et al, published by Accelerated Indexing Systems, Bountiful, UT, 1981, 40 pages, FHL book 975.3 X28j 1860.

**1860-1869 Georgetown Land Transfers.** See ***Real Estate Belonging to the District of Columbia, 1860-1869*** **[Microfilm],** from the original manuscript at the National Archives, Washington, DC. The book contains some transfers of property up to 1873. Filmed by the Archives, series M605, 1965, 1 roll, FHL film #1024477.

**1861-1865.** ***Index to Compiled Service Records of Volunteer Union Soldiers Who Served in Organizations From the District of Columbia*** **[Microfilm & Digital Capture],** from the original records at the National Archives, Washington, DC. Filmed by the Archives, 1964, series M538, 3 rolls, beginning with FHL film #881964 (Index, A-G, 1861-1865). To access the digital images, see the online FHL catalog page:
**www.familysearch.org/search/catalog/314826.**

**1861-1865.** ***Civil War Cemeteries of the District of Columbia Metropolitan Area*** **[Printed Book],** compiled by Paul E. Sluby; edited by Stanton L. Wormley. Published by the Columbian harmony Society, 1982, 128 pages, FHL book 975.3 V3s.

**1861-1918.** ***Death Records, District of Columbia*** **[Online Database],** index to deaths from various sources: Newspapers, WWI deaths from Government Printing Office reports. Indexed at the USGenWeb site for DC. See
**http://usgwarchives.net/dc/recordtocs/deaths.htm.**

**1862-1863.** ***Washington, D.C., Slave Owner Petitions*** **[Online Database],** indexed at the Ancestry.com website. Source: National Archives microfilm M520. In April of 1862 the U.S. government passed an act abolishing slavery in the District of Columbia. Petitions for compensation offered to slave owners whose slaves were emancipated by the act are contained in this database. These descriptions range from meeting minutes to petitions submitted and compensations awarded as well as additional administrative documents. This database has 4,250 records. See
**https://search.ancestry.com/search/db.aspx?dbid=2159.**

**1862.** ***Boyd's Washington and Georgetown Directory*** **[Digital Version].** To access the digital images, see the online FHL catalog page:
**www.familysearch.org/search/catalog/2852437.**

**1862-1960 Washington, DC Directories.** See ***U.S. City Directories*** **[Online Database],** digitized and indexed at the Ancestry.com website. See each directory title page image for the full title and publication information. This collection is one of the largest single databases on the Internet, with a total of 1.56 billion names, all indexed from scanned images of the city directory book pages. All states are represented except Alaska, and there are directories for Washington, DC, 1862-1960. For the complete list of years available, use Ancestry's Browse this Collection feature to choose District of Columbia / Washington / Year. This database has 1,560,284,702 records. See
**https://search.ancestry.com/search/db.aspx?dbid=2469.**

**1862-1866.** ***Internal Revenue Assessment Lists for the District of Columbia*** **[Microfilm & Digital Capture],** from the originals at the National Archives in Washington, DC Records indicate a name and place of residence for each person subject to the tax. (generally, land owners, but occasionally those with personal property only). Value of property had to be more than $500.00. Filmed by the Archives, 1969, series M760, 8 rolls, beginning with FHL film #1578491 (Annual tax lists, divisions 1-8, 1863-1864). To access the digital images, see the online FHL catalog page:
**www.familysearch.org/search/catalog/577966.**

**1863-1872.** ***District of Columbia, Freedmen's Bureau Field Office Records*** **[Online Database],** indexed at the FamilySearch.org website. The Bureau of Refugees, Freedmen, and Abandoned Lands (often called the Freedmen's Bureau) was created in 1865 at the end of the American Civil War to supervise relief efforts including education, health care, food and clothing, refugee camps, legalization of marriages, employment, labor contracts, and securing back pay, bounty payments and pensions. These records include letters and endorsements sent and received, account books, applications for rations, applications for relief, court records, labor contracts, registers of bounty claimants, registers of complaints, registers of contracts, registers of disbursements, registers of freedmen issued rations, registers of patients, reports, rosters of officers and employees, special and general orders and circulars received, special orders and circulars issued, records relating to claims, court trials, property restoration, and homesteads. This database has 90,597 records. See
**www.familysearch.org/search/collection/2333782.**

**1864.** ***Boyd's [1864] Washington and Georgetown Directory*** **[Printed Book & Digital Capture],** compiled by Andrew Boyd, Published by Taylor and Maury, Washington, DC, 1864. A digital image of this directory is available at the FHL catalog page. See **www.familysearch.org/search/catalog/2025427.**

**1864-1936.** ***Washington, District of Columbia, Battleground National Cemetery*** **[Online Database],** indexed at the Ancestry.com website. This database contains digital images of all gravestones in Battleground National Cemetery, located in Washington D.C. Battleground National Cemetery was established in 1864, and this collection includes burials through 1936 for 43 people. See
**https://search.ancestry.com/search/db.aspx?dbid=2292.**

**1865-1874.** ***District of Columbia Interments: Index to Deaths, January 1, 1865 to July 31, 1874*** **[Printed Book],** compiled by Wesley E. Pippenger, published by W.E. Pippenger, Westminster, MD, 1999, 409 pages, FHL book 975.3 V32p.

**1865-1876.** ***The Georgetown Courier Marriage and Death Notices: Georgetown, District of Columbia, November 18, 1865 to May 6, 1876*** **[Printed Book],** compiled by Wesley E. Pippenger, published by Willow Bend Book, Westminster, MD, 1998, 206 pages. FHL book 975.3 V4p.

**1867.** ***Boyd's Washington and Georgetown Directory*** **[Digital Version].** To access the digital images, see the online FHL catalog page:
**www.familysearch.org/search/catalog/2852435.**

**1870.** ***District of Columbia, 1870 Federal Census: Population Schedules*** **[Microfilm & Digital Capture],** from the originals at the National Archives, Washington, DC. Film twice by the National Archives, 1962, 1968, 7 rolls total, beginning with FHL film #545622 (2nd Filming, DC, Wards 1-2). To access the digital images, see the online FHL catalog page: **www.familysearch.org/search/catalog/698891.**

***1870 District of Columbia Census Index: Heads of Households and Other Surnames in Households Index*** **[Printed Index],** compiled by Bryan Lee Dilts, Published by Index Publishing, Salt Lake City, UT, 1985, 180 pages, FHL book 975.3 X22db.

**1870.** ***District of Columbia 1870 Census Index*** **[Printed Index],** edited by Raeone Christensen Steuart. Index line includes name, age, place of birth, for every member of a household. Published by Heritage Quest, Bountiful, UT, 1998, 334 pages, FHL book 975.3 X22s 1870.

**1870.** ***District of Columbia 1870 Census Index*** **[Printed Index],** edited by Ronald Vern Jackson, et al, published by Accelerated Indexing Systems, Bountiful, UT 1986, 614 pages, FHL book 975.3 X22j 1870.

**1870.** ***District of Columbia 1870 Mortality Schedule*** **[Printed Index],** edited by Ronald Vern Jackson, et al, published by Accelerated Indexing Systems, Bountiful, UT, 1981, 45 pages, FHL book 975.3 X28j 1870.

**1871.** ***Boyd's Washington and Georgetown Directory*** **[Digital Version].** To access the digital images, see the online FHL catalog page:
**www.familysearch.org/search/catalog/2852436.**

**1872-1894.** ***Graceland Cemetery Washington, DC: Brief History and Records of Interments 1872-1894*** **[Printed Book],** by Paul E. Sluby, Sr.. Includes index. Published by Comprehensive Research, Temple Hills, MD, 2010, 258 pages, FHL book 975.3 V3spg.

**1874-1879.** ***District of Columbia Death Records, August 1, 1874 to July 31, 1879*** **[Printed Book],** compiled by Wesley E. Pippenger. Records are arranged in alphabetical order. Published by Family Line Publications, Westminster, MD, 1996, 387 pages, FHL book 975.3 V28pd.

**1874-1897.** See ***District of Columbia Birth Records, 1874-1897; Indexes, 1874-1897*** **[Microfilm & Digital Capture],** from the originals at the Health Department, Washington, DC. Includes indexes to certificate numbers. The certificates are loose papers. Filmed by the Genealogical Society of Utah, 1995, 1998, 31 rolls, beginning with FHL film #2020343 (Index, 1874-1889). To access the digital images, see the online FHL catalog page:
**www.familysearch.org/search/catalog/748648.**

**1874-1897.** ***District of Columbia Birth Returns*** **[Online Database],** digitized at the FamilySearch.org website. Includes images of birth returns and birth index registers from the Health Department in Washington, D.C. The birth returns name the parents but do not name the child. Browse through the images, organized by Record Type, Number, and Year Range. This database has 90,550 images. See
**www.familysearch.org/search/collection/2001148.**

**1874-1950.** See ***District of Columbia Marriage Returns, 1874-1902, 1907-1923; Consents, 1896-Dec. 1950*** **[Microfilm & Digital Capture],** from the original records at the District of Columbia Records Center, Washington, DC. Filmed by the Genealogical Society of Utah, 1997, 59 rolls, beginning with FHL film #2070925 (Returns, license No. 1 – 1300, 1874-1876). To access the digital images, see the online FHL catalog page:
**www.familysearch.org/search/catalog/677313.**

**1874-1961** ***District of Columbia Deaths*** **[Online Database],** digitized and indexed at the FamilySearch.org website. Name index and images of death records taken from the FHL microfilm, 111 rolls. This database has 437.136 records. See
**www.familysearch.org/search/collection/1803967.**

**1877-1900.** ***District of Columbia Marriage Records Index*** **[Printed book],** compiled by Wesley E. Pippenger and Dorothy S. Provine, 3 vols., published by W.E. Pippenger, Arlington, VA, 1997, FHL book 975.3 V22pa v.1-3.

**1880.** ***District of Columbia, 1880 Federal Census: Soundex and Population Schedules*** **[Microfilm & Digital Capture],** from the originals at the National Archives, Washington, DC (in 1968), now located at the Historical Society of Washington, Washington, DC. Filmed by the National Archives, 1968, 13 rolls, beginning with FHL film #445528 (Soundex: A000-B650), and FHL film #1254121 (Population schedules: DC and city of Washington, ED 1 – ED 22). To access the digital images, see the online FHL catalog page:
**www.familysearch.org/search/catalog/670381.**

**1880. District of Columbia 1880 Mortality Schedule [Printed Index],** edited by Ronald Vern Jackson, et al, published by Accelerated Indexing Systems, Bountiful, UT, 1981, 67 pages, FHL book 975.3 X28j 1880.

**1887-1902.** See ***Registers of Marriages in the District of Columbia, Feb. 1887-Jan. 1902; Indexes, ca1886-1901*** **[Microfilm & Digital Capture],** from the original records at the District of Columbia Records Center, Washington, DC. Filmed by the Genealogical Society of Utah, 1997, 3 rolls, beginning with FHL film #2079251 (Index to register of marriages, ca1886-1900). To access the digital images, see the online FHL catalog page:
**www.familysearch.org/search/catalog/1130593.**

**1888-1923.** ***District of Columbia Foreign Deaths*** **[Printed Book],** compiled by Wesley E. Pippenger. A "foreign death" was a DC description of a death which occurred outside of DC, but the body was buried in DC. Lists name, number, age, race, date and place of death, and burial place. Published by Heritage Books, Westminster, MD, 2004, 2005, 285 pages, FHL book 975.3 V2pd.

**1888-1965.** ***Foreign Death Certificates*** **[Microfilm & Digital Capture],** from the original records at the District of Columbia Records Center, Washington, DC. These "foreign" certificates are records for deaths

which typically occurred outside of the District of Columbia, but the body was transported to the District of Columbia for burial – most everywhere else except DC, they are called "burial permits." Filmed by the Genealogical Society of Utah, 1997-1999, 52 rolls, beginning with FHL film #2116145 (Foreign certificate Nos. 1-1700, 1888-1895). To access the digital images, see the online FHL catalog page:
**www.familysearch.org/search/catalog/684938.**

**1889-1941.** ***Boyd's District of Columbia Directory*** **[Printed Books & Microfilm],** certain years available in book form at the FHL, with FHL book 975.3 E4b (year); and microfilm of other years, beginning with FHL film #1000737. FHL Library has: 1889 (film only), 1891 (film only),1893 (film only), 1894 (film only), 1897 (film only), 1898 (film only), 1904, 1907-1909, 1910 (film only), 1912 (film only), 1913, 1915-1919, 1921 (film only), 1929, 1930, 1939, and 1941. For a complete list of titles, years, and roll numbers and contents of each, see the online FHL catalog page:
**www.familysearch.org/search/catalog/2832516.**

***1890 Washington, D.C. City Directory*****[Online Database],** indexed at Ancestry.com. Source: R.L. Polk Co., 1890. This database has 176,194 records. See
**www.ancestry.com/search/collections/4583.**

**1890 District of Columbia Federal Census: Surviving Fragments.** See ***Population Schedules of the Eleventh Census of the United States, 1890*** **[Microfilm & Digital Capture],** from the original records at the National Archives. Filmed by the National Archives, series M407, 1962, 6 rolls. Most of the 1890 population schedules were destroyed in a fire in 1921. Only a total of 6,160 names (out of 63 million) could be extracted from the surviving fragments. The households from the District of Columbia were filmed on the second roll in the series, FHL film #926498 (District of Columbia: Dwellings on Q St., R St., S St., 13th St., 14th St., 15th St., Corcoran St., Riggs St., and Johnson Ave.). To access the digital images, see the online FHL catalog page:
**www.familysearch.org/search/catalog/231212.**

***1890 District of Columbia Census Index: Special Schedule… Enumerating Union Veterans of the Civil War*** **[Printed Index],** edited by Ronald Vern Jackson, et al, published by Accelerated Indexing Systems, Salt Lake City, UT, 1983, 9 pages, FHL book 975.3 X22j 1890.

**1892-1922.** ***Washington, D.C., Ex-Slave Pension Correspondence and Case Files*** **[Online Database],** indexed at the Ancestry.com website. Source: National Archives microfilm M2110. This database contains correspondence, petitions, advertisements, membership certificates, reports, depositions, case files, and other documents associated with the pension movement and the government's investigations. Records may include names, dates, residences, and other details about individuals involved in the pension movement. This database has 2,939 records. See
**https://search.ancestry.com/search/db.aspx?dbid=1992.**

**1900.** ***District of Columbia, 1900 Federal Census: Soundex and Population Schedules*** **[Microfilm & Digital Capture],** from the original records held by the Bureau of the Census in the 1940s. After microfilming, Congress allowed the Census Bureau to destroy the originals to free up space for WWII-related files. Filmed on 49 rolls, beginning with FHL film #1242595 (Soundex: A000-A650), and FHL film #1240158 (Population Schedules: EDs 1- 150). To access the digital images, see the online FHL catalog page:
**www.familysearch.org/search/catalog/647892.**

**1904-1924.** ***The Washington Post (Washington, D.C.)*** **[Online Database],** digitized and OCR indexed at the Ancestry.com website. The database is a fully searchable text version of the newspaper. The newspaper can be browsed or searched using a computer-generated index. See
**http://search.ancestry.com/search/db.aspx?dbid=6445.**

**1908-1909.** ***American Biographical Directories, District of Columbia: Concise Biographies of its Prominent and Representative Contemporary Citizens, and Valuable Statistical Data*** **[Microfilm & Digital Capture],** with an historical sketch by Henry B. F. MacFarland, published by Potomac Press, Washington, DC, 1908, 589 pages. Filmed by W. C. Cox Co., Tucson, AZ, 1974. FHL has 1 roll, FHL #1000157. To access the digital images, see the online FHL catalog page:
**www.familysearch.org/search/catalog/42807.**

**1910.** ***District of Columbia, 1910 Federal Census: Population Schedules*** **[Microfilm & Digital Capture],** from the original records held by the Bureau of the Census in the 1940s. After microfilming, Congress allowed the Census Bureau to destroy the originals to free up space for WWII-related files. Filmed on 7 rolls, beginning with FHL

film #1374162 (DC, ED's 1-33). To access the digital images, see the online FHL catalog page:
**www.familysearch.org/search/catalog/647827.**

**1910.** ***District of Columbia 1910 Census Index*** **[Printed Index],** compiled and published by Heritage Quest, North Salt Lake, UT, 2001, 2 vols. FHL book 975.3 X22h 1910 v.1-2.

**1912-1931.** ***Washington, D.C. Suburban Directories*** **[Microfilm],** from the original records located in various libraries and societies. Filmed by Primary Source Microfilm, Woodbridge, CT, ca1995, 4 rolls, beginning with FHL #2310369 (1912-1913) and continuing with directories for 1914, 1915, 1916, 1917, 1918, 1923, 1927-1928, and 1930-1931. For a complete list of roll numbers and contents of each roll, see the online FHL catalog page for this title:
**www.familysearch.org/search/catalog/1128693.**

**1912-1940.** ***Record of Disinterment*** **[Microfilm & Digital Capture],** from the original records at the District of Columbia Records Center, Washington, DC. These are permits to disinter and re-bury bodies. Includes name of deceased, date of death, original burial place and new burial place. Filmed by the Genealogical Society of Utah, 1997, 3 rolls, FHL film #2070922, $2070923, & #2070924. To access the digital images, see the online FHL catalog page:
**www.familysearch.org/search/catalog/682705.**

**1917-1918.** ***District of Columbia, World War I Selective Service System Draft Cards*** **[Microfilm & Digital Capture],** from the original records at the National Archives, East Point, Georgia. The draft cards are arranged alphabetically by the surname of the registrants. Filmed by the National Archives, 1987-1988, 19 rolls, beginning with FHL film #1570933 (A-McPherson). To access the digital images, see the online FHL catalog page:
**www.familysearch.org/search/catalog/746972.**

**1918-1924.** ***Washington, D.C., Military Naturalization Petitions*** **[Online Database],** indexed at the Ancestry.com website. Source: Records of District Courts of the U.S., National Archives. This database contains Petitions for Naturalization filed by former soldiers in Washington, D.C., courts during the years 1918–1924. Petitions may include a wide range of details, such as Name, Current address, Occupation, Birth date and place, Current and former citizenship, Marriage and spouse details, Children, and Emigration details. This database has 6,517 records. See
**https://search.ancestry.com/search/db.aspx?dbid=3034.**

**1920.** ***District of Columbia, 1920 Federal Census: Soundex and Population Schedules*** **[Microfilm & Digital Capture],** from the original records held by the Bureau of the Census in the 1940s. After microfilming, Congress allowed the Census Bureau to destroy the originals to free up space for WWII-related files. Filmed on 56 rolls, beginning with FHL film #1823934 (Soundex: A000-A536), and FHL film #1820205 (Population Schedules: EDs 1-40). To access the digital images, see the online FHL catalog page:
**www.familysearch.org/search/catalog/567641.**

**1930.** ***District of Columbia, 1930 Federal Census: Population Schedules*** **[Digital Capture],** from the original records held by the Bureau of the Census in the 1940s. After microfilming, Congress allowed the Census Bureau to destroy the originals to free up space for WWII-related files. Filmed on 14 rolls, beginning with FHL film #2340027 (DC, ED's 1-34). To access the digital images, see the online FHL catalog page:
**www.familysearch.org/search/catalog/1035333.**

**1940.** ***District of Columbia, 1940 Federal Census: Population Schedules*** **[Digital Capture].** After microfilming in the 1940s, the Census Bureau destroyed the originals to make room for WWII-related files. The microfilm was transferred to the National Archives in 1950 and digitized in 2012 for the opening to the public of the 1940 population schedules. To access the digital images, see the online FHL catalog:
**www.familysearch.org/search/catalog/2057747.**

***1940 Federal Census Finding Aids*** **[Online Database].** The National Archives prepared a special website online with a detailed description of the 1940 federal census. Included at the site are descriptions of location finding aids, such as Enumeration District Maps, Geographic Descriptions of Census Enumeration Districts, and a list of 1940 City Directories available at the National Archives. The finding aids are all linked to other National Archives sites. The National Archives website also has a link to 1940 Search Engines using Stephen P. Morse's "One-Step" system for finding a 1940 E.D. or street address conversion. See
**www.archives.gov/research/census/1940/general-info.html#questions.**

**1940-1947.** ***District of Columbia, World War II Draft Registration Cards*** **[Digital Capture],** from the originals at the National Personnel Records Center, St. Louis, MO. Digitized by the Genealogical Society of Utah, 2016, from 261 rolls of microfilm, beginning with FHL (DGS) #101697609 (Aldridge, Arthur - Allen, Willard James). To access the digital images, see the online FHL catalog page:
**www.familysearch.org/search/catalog/2659399.**
- For an Online Database dd 1940-1945, see **www.familysearch.org/search/collection/2548055.**

**1942-1962.** See ***Washington, D.C., Passenger and Crew Lists, 1942-1962*** **[Online Database],** indexed at the Ancestry.com website. Source: National Archives microfilm. These passenger and crew lists from both ships and aircraft were recorded on a variety of forms that were then turned over to the Immigration and Naturalization Service. Details requested on the forms varied, but they typically include the name of the vessel and arrival date, ports of departure and arrival (as well as future destinations on a ship's itinerary), dates of departure and arrival, shipmaster, full name, age, gender, physical description, military rank (if any), occupation, birthplace, citizen of what country, and residence. For military transports, you may find the next of kin, relationships, and address listed as well. Later manifests may include visa or passport numbers. This database has 156,905 records. See
**https://search.ancestry.com/search/db.aspx?dbid=9112.**

***1958-1964 Safell Funeral Home Register, Washington, DC*** [Printed Book & Digital Version], digitized by FamilySearch International, 2009. To access the digital images, see the online FHL catalog page: **www.familysearch.org/search/catalog/1647877.**

**1990-Current.** See ***District of Columbia Newspaper Obituaries, 1990-Current*** **[Online Database].** Digitized and indexed at the GenealogyBank.com website. One search screen for obituaries published in the following newspapers: Asian Fortune, Catholic Standard, Cox Washington Bureau, InTowner, McClatchy Washington Bureau, Washington Informer, Washington Jewish Week, and Washington Times. See **www.genealogybank.com/gbnk/obituaries/explore/USA/District_of_Columbia/Washington.**

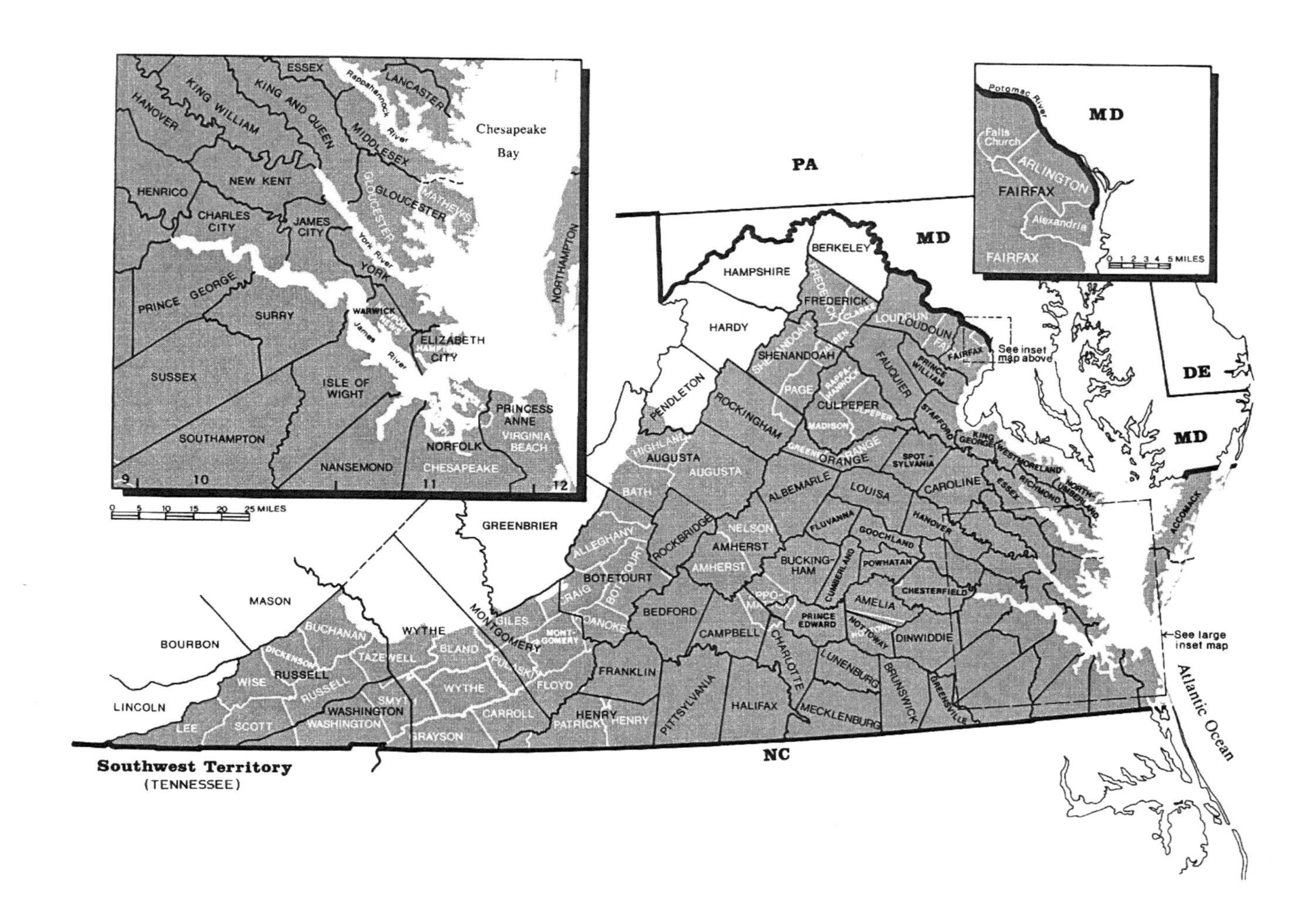


**Virginia • 1790.** The white lines and names show the current counties. Those in black are for 1790. Virginia in 1790 included what are now Kentucky and West Virginia (not shown). The small inset map is for the area that included the District of Columbia (created in 1791). **Map Source:** Page 349, *Map Guide to the U.S. Federal Censuses, 1790-1920*, by William Thorndale and William Dollarhide.

# Virginia

## Censuses & Substitute Name Lists

### Historical Timeline for Virginia, 1497-1788

**1497-1498.** Italian sea captain Giovanni Caboto was commissioned by the English King Henry VII to explore America. He landed in 1497 on the island of Newfoundland. On his second trip in 1498, he visited the coasts of present New Jersey, Delaware, Maryland, Virginia, North Carolina, South Carolina, and Georgia. In honor of the event, the king changed his name to John Cabot.

**1558.** Elizabeth I became Queen of England. The early exploration of North America took place during her 45-year reign, the Elizabethan Era, or "Golden Age." When Elizabeth I was crowned, England was nearly bankrupt, but during her reign, the English Empire expanded and thrived, and English culture flourished in Literature, Theatre, Music, and Architecture.

**1584.** Sir Walter Raleigh claimed and named Virginia for the "Virgin Queen," Elizabeth I, an area from present Chesapeake Bay to Florida, and everything below a northwestern line to the North Pole.

**1584-1590. Roanoke Colony.** In 1584, Queen Elizabeth I granted to Sir Walter Raleigh a charter for the colonization of the entire area of North America. In 1585, the first group of settlers led by Sir Richard Grenville, established a colony at the north end of Roanoke Island (present Dare County, North Carolina). The first group left Roanoke Island after a few months, returning to England with Sir Francis Drake. When a second group brought by Grenville in 1586 found the colony abandoned, the bulk of the second group returned to England as well. The final group, led by Governor John White, arrived in 1587. Soon after, he returned to England to plead for more supplies. White had left 90 men, 17 women, and 11 children, including his grand-daughter, Virginia Dare, the first English birth in America. It took White over three years to return to Roanoke due to several incidents with pirates, the Anglo-Spanish War, and the Spanish Armada. When he did return to Roanoke Island in August 1590, there was no trace of the colonists. There was no sign of a struggle or battle at the site or surrounding areas. To this day, no one is completely sure what happened to "The Lost Colony."

**1603.** James I became King of England, the first monarch to rule both England and Scotland. (He was James VI of Scotland since 1566). During his reign, the first permanent English colonies were established in Virginia and New England. James I was an advocate for the transportation of thousands of clan people living along the Scottish-English border to Ulster Province / Northern Ireland.

**1606.** Two joint stock companies were founded in 1606, both with royal charters issued by King James I for the purpose of establishing colonies in North America. The Virginia Company of London was given a land grant between Latitude 34° (Cape Fear) and Latitude 41° (Long Island Sound). The Virginia Company of Plymouth was founded with a similar land grant between Latitude 38° (Potomac River) and Latitude 45° (St. John River), which included a shared area with the London Company between Latitude 38° and Latitude 41°..

**1607. April 26. Virginia.** Three ships under the command of Capt. Christopher Newport sought shelter in Chesapeake Bay. The forced landing led to the

the founding of Jamestown on the James River, the first permanent English settlement, consisting of 104 men and boys. The Jamestown colony was led by Capt. John Smith and his cousin, Bartholomew Gosnold. A year later, about 100 new settlers arrived, finding only 38 survivors from the first group. In 1610, recently appointed governor of Virginia, Thomas West (Lord De La Warr) arrived at Jamestown to find only 60 settlers alive.

**1609.** The 2nd Virginia Charter of 1609 extended the jurisdiction of the London Company to include former areas of the Plymouth Company. The language of the new charter now included the words, "sea to sea." (James I was assured that the Pacific Ocean was just a bit west of the Appalachian Mountains).

**1624.** Virginia became a royal colony. Governors were now appointed by the Crown, and the colony agreed to make the Church of England the official church of state.

**1625.** Charles I became King of England, Scotland, and Ireland. Soon after taking office, Charles began to note a large number of non-conformists among his subjects. Along with his Archbishop, William Laud, the King began a campaign to purge his church of the largest group of non-conformists, the so-called "Puritans," a militant Calvinist religious group attempting to purify the Church of England.

**1629-1640.** As a result of the Charles I campaign to purge non-conformists from the Church of England, large groups of people were disenfranchised. Charles I disbanded Parliament and ruled England alone for eleven years. The Puritans referred to this era as "the eleven years of tyranny." It was during these eleven years that some 21,000 Puritan immigrants established the Massachusetts Bay Colony of North America.

**1633.** The Middle Plantation of the Virginia Colony was founded. The first settlement after Jamestown, it later became Williamsburg.

**1642. English Civil War.** When Parliament was restored in 1640, it quickly became dominated by the same Puritans who King Charles I had removed from the Church of England. Beginning in 1642, Royalist supporters were forced to fight the armies of the Puritan Parliament in the English Civil War. The English Colonies took sides: the Virginia colony favored the Royalist/Cavalier side, while the New England colonies were in support of the Parliamentarian/Puritan side. The Province of Maryland had earlier allowed all religious persuasions to settle in Maryland. During the English Civil War, Maryland granted free land as refuge to any Puritans from Virginia to settle there. The founding of Annapolis was by former Virginia people.

**1642. Virginia.** Sir William Berkeley was appointed governor by Charles I. He served from 1642 to 1652 and again from 1660 to 1677. His brother Lord John Berkeley, was the first Proprietor of the East New Jersey colony, and both brothers were Lords Proprietors of the Province of Carolina. Governor William Berkeley immediately began offering land grants to the 2nd sons of the English Cavaliers (royalist supporters of the King during the Civil War). Berkeley's plan for Virginia transformed a moribund colony into a culture patterned after the elitist plantation system of southwest England.

**1645-1651. England.** After his defeat and capture in 1645, Charles I refused to accept his captors' demands for a constitutional monarchy, and briefly escaped captivity in 1647. While recaptured, his teenage son, Prince Charles, was able to marshal Scottish forces for the king. However, by 1648, Oliver Cromwell had consolidated the English opposition. King Charles I was tried, convicted, and beheaded for high treason in January 1649. The Civil War continued until 1651, when Oliver Cromwell, a Puritan, became Lord Protectorate, ruling the Commonwealth of England for the next seven years.

**1650.** The first settlements near Albemarle Sound were established by pioneers from tidewater Virginia.

**1658-1660. England.** After Oliver Cromwell died in 1658, his son, Richard, was too weak politically to remain in power. In 1660, a new Parliament offered a restored English throne to the exiled Scottish King, son of Charles I, who accepted to become King Charles II.

**1699. Virginia.** The colonial capital moved from Jamestown to the newly incorporated town of Williamsburg.

**1707.** England and Scotland merged into the **United Kingdom of Great Britain.** The English Colonies now became the British Colonies.

**1717.** The arrival of the first Scots-Irish immigrants to the British Colonies was via Boston, New York City, Philadelphia, Alexandria, New Bern, and Charles Towne. The so-called Scots-Irish (or Ulster Scots) were former border clan people who had lived near the Scottish-English border for centuries. A good number of them had moved into areas of Northern Ireland in the early 1600s, and a mass migration to most of the British colonies of America began in about 1717. By 1775, the

Scots-Irish outnumbered, by three times, all other British migration groups (Puritans, Cavaliers, Quakers). In western Virginia, the "Irish Road" got its name from the Scots-Irish immigrants, who themselves called it, "The Great Valley Road."

**1746. Pioneer's Road.** The first wagon road through the Blue Ridge Mountains of Virginia was constructed in 1746, allowing wagon traffic from Alexandria to Winchester, Virginia. The first travelers on the roadway were almost exclusively Scots-Irish immigrants, who had changed their travel plans to arrive in Alexandria instead of Philadelphia. The trace of the old Pioneer's Road is now US Hwy 50.

**1754-1763. French and Indian War.** In 1754, a 22-year-old Virginian, George Washington, was given a commission as a Lt. Colonel. He led a Virginia Militia unit against the French-backed Indians.
- The 1763 **Treaty of Paris** ended the French and Indian War (in Europe and Canada: the Seven Years War). France ceded virtually all of its North American claims east of the Mississippi to Britain.
- King George III declared the "Proclamation Line of 1763," which established an Indian Reserve that stretched from the Appalachian Mountain Range to the Mississippi River.

**1765. The Stamp Act** was issued by King George III. It was the first direct tax levied against the American colonies without approval of their legislatures. In Boston, the Sons of Liberty was formed as a reactionary force.

**1768. Treaty of Fort Stanwix.** A new "Line of Property" was drawn, separating British Territory from Indian Territory. From Fort Stanwix (present Rome, NY), the division line ran to Fort Pitt (now Pittsburgh) and down the Ohio River to the Tennessee River. The Fort Stanwix treaty line effectively ceded all of present West Virginia and Kentucky to the British Colony of Virginia.

**1769-1772.** The Colony of Virginia saw the Treaty of Fort Stanwix as an opportunity to open up settlement to its western lands. Beginning in 1769, land surveys were conducted in the Kanawha, Kentucky, and Cumberland River valleys In 1772, Fincastle County, Virginia was created, an area that included most of present West Virginia and all of present Kentucky.

**1774. Lord Dunmore's War.** Due to the attacks against British colonists moving into the lands south of the Ohio River, the Governor of Virginia, John Murray, 4th Earl of Dunmore, asked the Virginia House of Burgesses to declare a state of war with the hostile Indian nations. Dunmore said that Virginians needed to defend their legal right based on the 1768 Treaty of Fort Stanwix. The war ended after Dunmore's victory in the Battle of Point Pleasant (mouth of the Kanawha River on the Ohio River) in October 1774. In the resulting treaty, the Indians lost the right to hunt in the area south of the Ohio River. Thus, Dunmore's War opened the way for an all-out effort to bring settlers into the western areas of Virginia.

**1775.** Virginian Patrick Henry, a delegate to the 2nd Virginia Convention gave a memorable speech, ending with "Give me liberty or give me death."

**1776.** Virginian Thomas Jefferson wrote the Declaration of Independence.
- Virginia adopted a new State Constitution and declared its independence from Great Britain.

**1775-1783. The Transylvania Land Company.** In 1775, the Cherokee Indians sold North Carolina Judge Richard Henderson huge quantities of land between the Ohio, Kentucky, and Cumberland rivers for the Transylvania Land Company. Under Henderson's employ, Daniel Boone blazed and cleared the "Wilderness Trail" and established Fort Boonesborough. By 1783, some 60,000 settlers had used the Wilderness Trail to move into present Kentucky. Titles to Henderson's land holdings were not recognized by either Virginia or North Carolina and the company dissolved in 1783.

**1780. Virginia.** The capital of the Virginia Colony was moved from Williamsburg to Richmond. One of the reasons for the move was that the only wagon road to Williamsburg was virtually impassable during the Spring floods. As a result of the move, time stopped in 1780 in Colonial Williamsburg, which remains an authentic remnant of the colonial era of Virginia.

**1781.** At the Siege of Yorktown, British General Charles Cornwallis surrendered to the American forces led by General George Washington.

**1783.** The Treaty of Paris was the official end of the Revolutionary War, and the first recognition of the United States of America as an independent nation.

**1788.** Jun 25. **Virginia** adopted the U.S. Constitution to become the 10th state in the Union, with the state capital at Richmond.

## Online Resources at Virginia State Websites

**The Library of Virginia – Virginia Memory.** The state library/archives has a long list of digital collections, including Photographs, Maps, Confederate Pension Rolls (soldiers and widows), Jamestown 2007 Commemorative Collection, Revolutionary War, War of 1812, Civil War, World War I, WPA Life Histories Collection, and more. See **www.virginiamemory.com/collections/collections_a_to_z.**

**Virginia Military Institute – Digital Exhibits.** Includes Civil War and New Market, Stonewall Jackson, Genealogy & Alumni Photos & Portraits, Letters, Diaries, Manuscripts, Digital Publications, Military Oral History, VMI Archives (historical rosters database, all enrolled students, 1839-1935), and more. See **www.vmi.edu/archives/digital-collections.**

**Virginia Commonwealth University – Digital Collections.** Includes Confederate Military Hospitals, Medical College histories, Medical artifacts collection, Nursing Histories, Slavery in Richmond, Robertson Hospital Register, Civil War historical files, Oral Histories Collection, and more. See **http://dig.library.vcu.edu.**

**Virginia Tech – ImageBase.** Topics include: Agriculture, Appalachia, Civil War, Maps, Southwest Virginia, Historical Photograph collection, and more. See **https://imagebase.lib.vt.edu/browse.php.**

## Bibliography
### Virginia Censuses & Substitutes

The Commonwealth of Virginia has never taken a state census, so to find lists of the names of inhabitants, one must turn to tax lists, land grants, deed indexes, and other substitute name lists.

Virginia's earliest federal censuses do not provide much help to genealogists looking for ancestors there. The entire 1790 federal census was lost; and only two counties are extant for the 1800 federal census. For the 1810 census, about one fourth of its counties were lost. The first statewide census complete for Virginia was the 1820. Thereafter, Virginia's federal censuses through 1940 are complete for all counties and independent cities (except 1890, lost for all states).

In 1908, the Census Bureau published the *Heads of Families* list of names for the lost 1790 Virginia census by using extant county tax lists from 1782-1785. Other substitutes in the bibliography that follows identify many more statewide census substitutes as well as countywide name lists for the period before 1820:

♦ ♦ ♦ ♦ ♦

**1607-1625.** ***Adventurers of Purse and Person, Virginia*** **[Printed Book],** compiled and edited by John Frederick Dorman. From intro: "The purpose of this [3-vol.] set is to document the adventurers who were approximately 900 stockholders mentioned in the 1st, 2nd and 3rd charters of the Virginia colony. There are 109 of these stockholders who qualified as either 'adventurers of purse' or 'adventurers of person.' The 'adventurers of purse' were individuals who either came to Virginia in the period 1607-1624/5 and had descendants or who did not come to Virginia within that period but whose grandchildren were residents there. The 'adventurers of person' were individuals who were immigrants to Virginia and left descendants there. The foundation for this work is the Muster of Jan 1624/25 which had never before been printed in full." – p. xiii, v. 1. Includes bibliographic footnotes and indexes. Contents: Vol. 1: Families A-F; Vol. 2: Families G-P; and Vol. 3: Families R-Z. Publ. Genealogical Publishing Co, 2004-2007, 3 vols, FHL book 975.5 H2j v.1-3.

**1607-1967.** ***Virginia Genealogical Society Quarterly*** **[Online Database],** digitized and indexed at the Ancestry.com website. The first 40 volumes of the *Quarterly* were indexed by every word. This database has 9,866 records. See **http://search.ancestry.com/search/db.aspx?dbid=6131.**

**1607-2000s.** ***Virginia GenWeb Archives*** **[Online Database].** The VAGenWeb site offers free genealogical databases with searchable statewide name lists and for all Virginia counties and independent cities. Databases may include Bibles, Biographies, Cemeteries, Censuses, Court, Death, Deeds, Directories, Histories, Marriages, Military, Newspapers, Obituaries, Photos, Schools, Tax Lists, Wills, and more. See **http://usgwarchives.net/va/vafiles.htm.**

**1607-2000s.** ***Linkpendium – Virginia: Family History & Genealogy, Census, Birth, Marriage, Death Vita Records & More*** **[Online Databases].** Linkpendium is a genealogical portal site with links to state, county, town, and local databases. Currently listed are selected sites for Virginia statewide resources (932), Independent Cities, Renamed Counties, Discontinued Counties (117), Accomack County (605), Albemarle County (641), Alleghany County (234), Amelia County (315), Amherst County (300), and 90 more Virginia counties. See **www.linkpendium.com/va-genealogy.**

**1607-2007.** ***Virginia, Historical Society Papers*** **[Online Database],** digitized and indexed at the FamilySearch.org website. The collection includes bible records, genealogy papers, and miscellaneous records. Some records have been indexed and are searchable as part of this collection. This database has 17,449 records. See
**https://familysearch.org/search/collection/1932510.**

**1619-1930.** ***Virginia Historical Index: In Two Volumes*** **[Printed Book],** by Earl Gregg Swem, originally published Roanoke, Virginia: Stone Printing, 1934-1936, 2 vols. This is often referred to as "Swem's Index," an analysis of the information that relates to Virginians in the following periodicals and books: *The Virginia Magazine of History and Biography,* volumes 1-38, 1893-1930; the *William and Mary College Quarterly Historical Magazine,* first series, ... volumes 1-27, 1892-1919; the *William and Mary College Quarterly Historical Magazine*, second series, volumes 1-10, 1921-1930; *Tyler's Quarterly Historical and Genealogical Magazine*, volumes 1-10, 1919-1929; *Virginia Historical Register and Literary Advertiser,* volumes 1-6, 1848-1853; the *Lower Norfolk County Virginia Antiquary*, volumes 1-5, 1895-1906; *Hening's Statutes at Large, ... 1619-1792*, volumes 1-13; *Calendar of Virginia State Papers and other manuscripts preserved in the Capitol at Richmond, 1652-1869, volumes 1-11.*"--V. 1, pref. Contents: v. 1. A-K -- v. 2. L-Z. FHL book 975.5 H22s v. 1-2 and FHL film #604696.
- See also ***Virginia Historical Index*** **[CD-ROM],** by E. G. Swem, digitized images of reprint published: Gloucester, Mass.: P. Smith, 1965. 2 v., published by Broderbund, 1998, Family Tree Maker's Family Archives, Genealogical Records, CD #202.

**1621.** ***Walloons and French to Virginia, 1621*** **[Online Database],** indexed at the Genealogy Quest website. See **http://genealogy-quest.com/1621-walloons-french-virginia.**

**1623-1666.** ***Virginia Immigrants*** **[Online Database],** indexed at the Ancestry.com website. Source: George Greer's *Early Virginia Immigrants, 1623-1666*, publ. 1912. Compiled from land records stored in Richmond, this collection of immigrants might be called "Indentured Servants of early Virginia." For this time period, the primary land records were part of the Headright system of Virginia. The records give an immigrant's name, arrival date, and port of entry, plus the name of the "sponsor" (the one paying the person's passage, and usually, the one who became the master of the servant). This database has 17,450 records. See
**http://search.ancestry.com/search/db.aspx?dbid=2063.**
- See Also, ***Cavaliers and Pioneers: Abstracts of Virginia Land Patents and Grants, 1623-1666*** **[Online Database]**, indexed at the Ancestry.com website. Publ. 1939, reprinted by GPC, 1963-1991. This is another version of Greer's *Virginia Immigrants*. See
**http://search.ancestry.com/search/db.aspx?dbid=48408.**

**1623-1776.** ***Virginia Colonial Records, 1600s-1700s*** **[CD-ROM],** originally published by Broderbund, 1999, (Family Tree Maker Archives No. 503), See FHL CD-ROM No. 9, pt. 503. Contents:

- *1623-1666, Early Virginia Immigrants*, by George Cabell Greer; Some Emigrants to Virginia, by W. G. Stanard (2nd edition, enlarged).
- *Virginia Colonial Abstracts, vols. I-III*, by Beverley Fleet.
- *Virginia Gleanings in England: Abstracts of 17th and 18th Century Wills and Administrations Relating to Virginia and Virginians,* by Lothrop Withington.
- *Colonial records of Virginia; The Colonial Virginia Register: A List of Governors, Councilors, and Other High Officials, and Also of Members of the House of Burgesses, and the Revolutionary Conventions of the Colony of Virginia,* compiled by William G. and Mary Newton Stanard.
- *English duplicates of Lost Virginia Records,* compiled by Louis de Cognets, Jr.
- *Personal Names in Henings Statutes at Large of Virginia and Shepherd's Continuation,* by Joseph J. Casey.
- *Cavaliers and Pioneers: Abstracts of Virginia land Patents and Grants, 1623-1666,* Abstracted and Indexed by Nell Marion Nugent.
- *The Quit Rents of Virginia, 1704,* compiled by Annie Laurie Wright Smith.
- *List of Colonial Soldiers of Virginia; Virginia County Records, Vol. II: Virginia Colonial Militia, 1671-1776,* edited by William Armstrong Crozier.
- *Virginia's Colonial Soldiers*, by Lloyd DeWitt Bockstruck.

**1623-1800.** ***Cavaliers and Pioneers: A Calendar of Virginia Land Grants*** **[Printed Book & Microfilm],** compiled by Nell M. Nugent, published Dietz Print Co., Richmond, 1929-1931, 272 pages. Often referred to as "Nugent's List," which was his first list of names of the founders of Virginia, based on the earliest land grants. This first edition was filmed by the Genealogical Society of Utah, 1991, 1 roll, FHL film #1320992. Over the years, additional volumes were added to form a seven-volume set. For the full series, see *Cavaliers and Pioneers: Abstracts of Virginia Land Patents and Grants.* The 1963, 1979, and 1983 editions of vol. 1 were published by Genealogical Publishing Company, Inc., Baltimore. Vols. 1-3 were abstracted and indexed by Nell Marion Nugent. Vol. 4 was abstracted by members of the Virginia Genealogical Society and edited by Denis Hudgins, while vols. 5-7 were edited by Dennis Ray Hudgins. Vols. 2-3 published by the Virginia State Library, Richmond. Vols. 4-7 published by the Virginia Genealogical Society, Richmond. Volumes are individually indexed. Contents: vol. 1: 1623-1666; vol. 2: 1666-1695; vol. 3: 1695-1732; vol. 4: 1732-1741; vol. 5: 1741-1749; vol. 6: 1749-1762; and vol. 7: 1762-1776. FHL book 975.5 R2n v. 1-7. Also on microfilm: FHL film #1320779.

**1623-1991.** See ***Index, Land Patents and Grants, 1623-1774, 1779-1991* [Microfilm & Digital Capture],** from the originals at the VA State Library. Arranged by name of patentee (grantee), each card shows the date of patent (grant), the county in which the land was located when granted, the number of acres in each tract, a brief description of the property and the volume and beginning page where the record appears. Filmed by the Genealogical Society of Utah, 1991-1992, 55 rolls, beginning with FHL film #1854108 (ABC Enterprises – Antwerp). To access the digital images, see the online FHL catalog page:
**https://familysearch.org/search/catalog/584567.**

**1624/25. *The Muster of the Inhabitants of the Colledge Land in Virginia taken the 23rd January 1624/25: Transcribed from the Original in the State Paper Office, American & West Inds., vol. 447* [Printed Book & Microfilm],** copied from the original manuscript by Louise Van H. Ingersoll. Contains lists of inhabitants of the "Colledge Land," "Neck-of-Land in the Corporation of Charles Cittie," "West and Sherley hundred, Charles Cittie," "Chaplains choyse and the Trueloves Company, Charles Cittie," "Peirseys hundred," "Pashehays and the Maine, belonging to the Corporation of James Citty," "James Citty," "Neck-of-Land near James Citty," "Hog Island," "Martins Hundred," "Mulbury Island," "Wariscoyack," "Basses Choyce," "Newportes Newes," "Elizabeth Cittie," and the "Easterne Shore over the Baye." Gives the name of the head of household, names of persons in household, ages, the ship they arrived on, and a list of provisions brought by them. Also includes list of deaths with each area. See FHL book 975.5 X2pd. Also on microfilm, FHL film #844901.

**1628-1768. *Irish Immigrants to Virginia* [Online Database],** from a list of names collected by George Cabell Greer from land records in Richmond. Indexed at the USGenWeb site for Virginia. See
**http://files.usgwarchives.net/va/misc/irishva.txt.**

**1632-1800.** See ***Virginia Wills and Administrations: An Index of Wills Recorded in Local Courts of Virginia, 1632-1800, and of Administrations on Estates Shown by Inventories of the Estates of Intestates Recorded in Will (and other) Books of Local Courts, 1632-1800* [Microfilm],** from the book compiled by Clayton Torrence, originally published by William Byrd Press, Richmond, 1932, 483 pages. Filmed by the Genealogical Society of Utah, 1955, 1 roll, FHL film #29274; another filming FHL film #485954.

**1634-1951. *Virginia, Isle of Wight County Records* [Online Database],** digitized at the FamilySearch.org website. Images from original records at the Circuit Court in Isle of Wight, Virginia. Records include marriages, guardianships, military lists, court orders, dockets, bonds, fees, and judgments. Browse the images, organized by type of record. This database has 110,540 records. See
**https://familysearch.org/search/collection/2034267.**

**1639-1850. *Virginia, Land, Marriage, and Probate Records* [Online Database],** indexed at the Ancestry.com website. This data set contains information on approximately 135,000 individuals mentioned in abstracts of deeds, marriages, and wills from Virginia's Augusta, Isle of Wight, Norfolk, and Spotsylvania Counties. This database has 134,392 records. See
**http://search.ancestry.com/search/db.aspx?dbid=7832.**

**1640-1800. *Virginia, Apprentice Index* [Online Database],** indexed at the Ancestry.com website. This compilation of apprentices is part of a larger computer database containing biographical records of nearly 8,000 artisans who worked in Virginia before 1801. It was created as part of a study of the role of artisans in colonial Virginia. Each record includes, when provided, the name, age, sex, and race of the indentured individual, the father's name, the name of the person they are indentured to, the trade to be learned, date indentured, and date of release from the contract. This database has 2,765 records. See
**http://search.ancestry.com/search/db.aspx?dbid=3111.**

**1649-1800.** ***Virginia, Marriages of the Northern Neck of Virginia*** **[Online Database],** indexed at the Ancestry.com website. Source: Robert Headley's *Married Well and Often: Marriages of the Northern Neck of Virginia, 1649–1800,* publ. 2003, Genealogical Publishing Co. Includes the names of husband and wife and the date of marriage. May also contain parents, grandparents, former spouses, children of previous marriages, securities for the groom, guardians, and clergymen. This database has 14,680 records. See **http://search.ancestry.com/search/db.aspx?dbid=5063.**

**1660-1800.** ***Virginia, Compiled Marriages*** **[Online Database],** indexed at the Ancestry.com website. Originally edited by Jordan Dodd, from county records on microfilm at the Family History Library, Salt Lake City. Includes name of bride and groom, date of marriage, and place of marriage. This database has 88,130 records. See **http://search.ancestry.com/search/db.aspx?dbid=3002.**

**1660-1923.** ***Virginia, Extracted Vital Records*** **[Online Database].** This database consists of miscellaneous vital records from Virginia, or records about Virginians, taken from *The Virginia Magazine of History and Biography*, The *William and Mary College Quarterly*, and *Tyler's Quarterly*. Many different types of records and historical information may be found within the database. Indexed information may include primary names and names of family members, as well as birth, marriage, death, and burial information. This database has 22,984 records, see **www.ancestry.com/search/collections/61462.**

**1664-1666.** ***Transported Quakers*** **[Online Database],** narratives of ship passengers leaving England and arriving in Virginia and other destinations. Names and dates listed at the Genealogy Quest website. See **http://genealogy-quest.com/1664-1666-transported-quakers/.**

**1670s-1800s.** ***Encyclopedia of American Quaker Genealogy, Vol. 6: Virginia*** **[Online Database],** indexed at the Ancestry.com website. The Society of Friends (Quakers) were opposed to civil marriage ceremonies, and unless a couple were married within the meeting, they could not continue as members. The huge number of "marriages out of union" are noted in the monthly meeting records, and often give the wife's maiden name as well her new married name, so a genealogical connection can be made to her Quaker parents, grandparents, etc. The recording of births and deaths was also universal, and whole family groups might be listed in the record books. Another important record was when a member of one meeting wanted to move to another meeting. Such transfers were recorded, and the moving persons were given a letter attesting to their membership in good standing, which would be presented to the new meeting house for admission. Thus, it is possible to trace the movements of whole families from one state to another. This database has 1,039 pages. See **http://search.ancestry.com/search/db.aspx?dbid=48135.**

**1690-1740.** ***English Duplicates of Lost Virginia Records*** **[Online Database],** indexed at the Ancestry.com website. Source: Book, same title, by Louis des Cognets, Jr., originally printed 1958, reprinted by Genealogical Publishing Co, 1981, 1990. Includes records of transactions in certain Virginia courts that were transmitted to the English government and residing (1958) at the Public Record Office, London. This database has 387 pages. See **http://search.ancestry.com/search/db.aspx?dbid=48412.**

**1700.** ***French Refugees in Virginia, 1700*** **[Online Database],** "List of the French Refugiez arrived with the Marquis de la Muce in Virginia." Names listed at the Genealogy Quest website. See **http://genealogy-quest.com/1700-french-refugees-virginia.**

**1700-1850.** ***Virginia Tax Records: From the Virginia Magazine of History and Biography, the William and Mary College Quarterly, and Tyler's Quarterly*** **[Printed Book],** with an index by Gary Parks, published by Genealogical Publishing Co., Inc., Baltimore, 1983, 663 pages. Excerpted and reprinted with added publisher's note, contents, and index. FHL book 975.5 R4v.

**1700-1850.** ***Virginia Marriage Records*** **[Online Database],** indexed at the Ancestry.com website. Source: Elizabeth Petty Bentley's *Virginia Marriage Records: From the Virginia Magazine of History and Biography, the William and Mary College Quarterly, and Tyler's Quarterly.* Publ. 1984, Genealogical Publishing Co. This database has 33,706 records. See **http://search.ancestry.com/search/db.aspx?dbid=3143.**

**1700-1850.** ***Virginia Military Records*** **[Online Database],** indexed at the Ancestry.com website. Source: Elizabeth Petty Bentley's *Virginia Military Records: From the Virginia Magazine of History and Biography, the William and Mary College Quarterly, and Tyler's Quarterly.* Publ. 1983, Genealogical Publishing Co. This database has 1,032 pages. See **http://search.ancestry.com/search/db.aspx?dbid=48440.**

**1700-1850.** ***Virginia Will Records*** **[Online Database],** indexed at the Ancestry.com website. Source: Judith McGhan, indexer, *Virginia Will Records: From the Virginia Magazine of History and Biography, the William and Mary College Quarterly, and Tyler's Quarterly.* Publ. 1993, Genealogical Publishing Co. This database has 997 pages. See **http://search.ancestry.com/search/db.aspx?dbid=48444.**

**1700-1850.** ***Virginia Land Records*** **[Online Database],** indexed at the Ancestry.com website. Source: Gary Parks, indexer, *Virginia Land Records:From the Virginia Magazine of History and Biography, the William and Mary College Quarterly, and Tyler's Quarterly.* Publ. 1982, Genealogical Publishing Co. This database has 894 pages. See **http://search.ancestry.com/search/db.aspx?dbid=48438.**

**1700-1850.** ***Virginia Tax Records*** **[Online Database],** indexed at the Ancestry.com website. Source: Gary Parks, indexer, *Virginia Tax Records: From the Virginia Magazine of History and Biography, the William and Mary College Quarterly, and Tyler's Quarterly.* Publ. 1983, Genealogical Publishing Co. This database has 669 pages. See **http://search.ancestry.com/search/db.aspx?dbid=48646.**

**1704.** ***The Quit Rents of Virginia*** **[Online Database],** Source: *The Quit Rents of Virginia, 1704*, compiled by Annie Laurie Wright Smith, publ. 1958; reprinted by Genealogical Publishing Co. 1975, indexed at the Ancestry.com website. This database has 120 pages: **http://search.ancestry.com/search/db.aspx?dbid=48421.**

***1704-1705 Alphabetical Rent Roll of Virginia*** **[Online Database],** extracted from The Planters of Colonial Virginia, by Thomas Wertenbaker. Indexed at the USGenWeb site for Virginia. See **http://files.usgwarchives.net/va/misc/1704va.txt.**

**1720.** ***Virginia in 1720: A Reconstructed Census*** **[Printed Book],** by T.L.C. Genealogy, Miami Beach, FL, 1998, 221 pages. From intro: "This book, which is based on primary records (deeds, wills, tax lists, order books, etc.), is an alphabetical list of Virginia inhabitants, their county of residence, and the source of the information about them." FHL book 975.5 X22t 1720.

**1730-1799.** ***Virginia Wills Before 1799: A Complete Abstract Register of all Names Mentioned in Over Six Hundred Recorded Wills ... copied*** **[Online Database],** indexed at the Ancestry.com website. Source: *Virginia wills before 1799: a complete abstract register of all names mentioned in over six hundred recorded wills ... copied from the court house records of Amherst, Bedford, Campbell, Loudoun, Prince William, and Rockbridge Counties,* by William Montgomery Clemens, publ. 1924. This database has 107 pages. See **http://search.ancestry.com/search/db.aspx?dbid=10611.**

**1732-1774.** ***Colonial Soldiers of the South*** **[Online Database],** indexed at the Ancestry.com website. The records are chiefly muster rolls and pay rolls of the militias of Maryland, Virginia, North and South Carolina, and Georgia, and they identify about 55,000 soldiers by name, rank, date, militia company, and district. Other records provide data on age, height, country of birth, occupation, and date and place of enlistment. Also, there are the recruits who served under Washington's ensign in Virginia, and the ordinary settlers and frontiersmen who did their duty. This database has 1,272 pages. See **http://search.ancestry.com/search/db.aspx?dbid=49108.**

**1735-1950.** ***Virginia, Surry County Marriage Records*** **[Online Database],** indexed at the FamilySearch.org website. Source: Surry Co VA register of deeds. Records include certificates to obtain a marriage license, marriage bonds and consents, marriage licenses, and marriage returns. This database has 18,329 records. See **https://familysearch.org/search/collection/1468642.**

**1736-1820.** ***Abstracts of Marriage and Obituary Notices in Virginia Newspapers Before 1820*** **[Microfilm & Digital Capture],** compiled by Viginius Cornick Hall from original records at the Virginia Historical Society in Richmond, Virginia. Abstracts are on cards which are in alphabetical order by name. Information on the cards varies but gives at least a name, the date of the event or newspaper, and the newspaper's name. Filmed by the Genealogical Society of Utah, 1987, 4 rolls, beginning with FHL film #1508537 (Abbot, Mrs. Josiah to Dean, Samuel), thru FHL film #1508569 (Snell, Ann to Zoll). To access the digital images, see the online FHL catalog page: **www.familysearch.org/search/catalog/474907.**

**1736-1986.** ***Virginia Newspaper Archives*** **[Online Databases],** digitized and indexed newspapers at the GenealogyBank website, for Alexandria, Boydton, Charlottesville, Dumfries, Fincastle, Fredericksburg, Leesburg, Lexington, Lynchburg, Norfolk, Petersburg, Richmond, Staunton, Warrenton, Williamsburg, and Winchester. See
**www.genealogybank.com/explore/newspapers/all/usa/Virginia.**

**1740.** ***Virginia in 1740: A Reconstructed Census*** **[Printed Book],** by T.L.C. Genealogy, Miami Beach, FL, 1992, 308 pages. From intro: "This book, which is based on deeds, wills, tax lists, order books, etc., is an alphabetical list of Virginia inhabitants, their county of residence, and the source of the information about them." FHL book 975.5 X22t 1740 and FHL film #697799.

**1740-1850.** ***Virginia, Compiled Marriages*** **[Online Database],** indexed at the Ancestry.com website. Source: Originally edited by Jordan Dodd, from county records on microfilm at the Family History Library, Salt Lake City. Includes name of bride and groom, date of marriage, and place of marriage. This database has 337,520 records. See
**http://search.ancestry.com/search/db.aspx?dbid=3723.**

**1757-1938.** ***Virginia, Orange County Marriage Records*** **[Online Database],** digitized and indexed at the FamilySearch.org website. This database has 11,823 records. See
**https://familysearch.org/search/collection/1883379.**

**1759-1776.** ***Hopewell, Virginia, Friends Memberships*** **[Online Database],** indexed at the Ancestry.com website. Source: Hopewell Certificates of Membership and Removal, 1759-1776. The Friends (Quakers) held their monthly meetings at Hopewell, Virginia, during which they recorded the names of the members, the date, the location, and if removed from the society, the reason why. This database has 4,211 records. See
**http://search.ancestry.com/search/db.aspx?dbid=3123.**

**1769-1800. Annals of Southwest Virginia [Online Database],** indexed at the Ancestry.com website. Source: Book, same title, by Lewis Preston Summers, publ. 1929. A source for the names of the first settlers of Botetourt, Fincastle, Montgomery, Washington, and Wythe counties, Virginia. This database has 1,795 records. See
**http://search.ancestry.com/search/db.aspx?dbid=10533.**

**1771-1943.** ***Virginia, County Marriage Records*** **[Online Database],** digitized and indexed at FamilySearch.org. This collection includes the following counties: Accomack, Franklin, Giles, Rockingham, and Westmoreland. The content and time period varies. This database has 37,040 records, see **www.familysearch.org/search/collection/2134304.**

**1774-1791.** ***Master Index, Virginia Surveys and Grants (in Kentucky)*** **[Printed Book & Digital Version],** compiled by Joan E Brookes-Smith, publ. Kentucky Historical Society, Frankfort, KY, 1976, 261 pages, FHL book 974.9 R22. Also on microfilm: FHL film #1320833. To access the digital version, see the online FHL catalog page:
**www.familysearch.org/search/catalog/193613.**

**1776-1783.** ***Virginia Militia in the Revolutionary War*** **[Online Database],** indexed at the Ancestry.com website. Source: J.T. McAllister's *Virginia Militia in the Revolutionary War,* publ. 1913. Includes a summary of the Militia's military movements arranged by counties, declarations of Virginia Militia Pensioners, Militia officers appointed in various counties, and pensioners residing in and outside of Virginia in 1835 who received pensions as VA militiamen. This database has 5,756 records. See
**http://search.ancestry.com/search/db.aspx?dbid=3076.**

**1779.** ***A Short Census of Virginia, 1779*** **[Printed Book],** by William H. Dumont, from an article in the National Genealogical Society Quarterly, Vol. 46, No. 4 (Dec 1958), p.163-211. From page 163: "A short census of Virginia for 1779 can be found in one of the old loan records of the United States Treasury. Over 4,200 Virginians turned in their paper money to the Virginia Loan office in 1779 and 1780." Tables 3-4 gives name, county and/or state, entry no., and amount deposited. Tables 1-2 and 5 are statistical. Table 2 also gives the county with its abbreviation. FHL book 975.5 X2p 1779 and FHL film 908198.

**1779-1924.** See ***Surveys, 1779-1878; Index, Land Surveys, 1779-1924*** **[Microfilm & Digital Capture],** from the original records of the Virginia Land Office now at the Virginia State Library, Richmond. Contains recorded plats and descriptions of lands on which grants have been issued since the establishment of the Commonwealth Land Office. The name of the individual for whom the survey was made, the county in which the land was located, the number of acres in the tract, its metes and bounds, the date of the survey, and the names of the chain carriers and the surveyor

are given. Accompanying papers, such as assignments, are recorded along with the survey, but accompanying warrants are not recorded. Filmed by the Virginia State Library, 1949, 92 rolls, beginning with FHL film #29542 (Index to surveys, 1779-1819). To access the digital images, see the online FHL catalog page:
**https://familysearch.org/search/catalog/415347.**

**1779-1860.** ***Bounty Warrants*** **[Microfilm & Digital Capture],** from the original records at the Virginia State Library in Richmond. Contains documentation accepted for proof of military service. Includes typed card index. Filmed by the Genealogical Society of Utah, 1954, 31 rolls, beginning with FHL film #29850 (Index, Aaron, William to Payner, Wm.). To access the digital images, see the online FHL catalog page:
**https://familysearch.org/search/catalog/414179.**

***1782-1785 List of Inhabitants (Virginia)*** **[Microfilm & Digital Capture],** from typescripts and original records at the Virginia State Library in Richmond, VA. This series of original Virginia tax lists was used by the U.S. Census Bureau for its 1908 *Heads of Families* as a substitute for the lost 1790 Virginia federal census. There are lists for thirty-nine counties and the town of Williamsburg, Information found in the lists for 1782 and 1783 include the name of the head of the household, the number of white inhabitants, and the number of slaves, while the lists for 1784 and 1785 include the heads of households, the number of whites, and the numbers of dwelling houses and "outhouses." The original lists were created by Virginia by four acts passed by the General Assembly. The county courts were to appoint justices to make lists of people in their precincts. The county court clerks were to collect the lists and send them to the Governor. The premise for the creation of these lists was taxation but they have been used as a census. Contents: Albemarle 1785; Amelia 1782, 1785; Amherst 1783, 1785; Bedford 1783 (summary only); Charlotte 1782 (summary only), 1783; Chesterfield 1783; Cumberland 1782, 1784; Essex 1783; Fairfax 1782, 1785; Fluvanna 1782; Frederick 1782; Gloucester 1783, 1784; Greenbrier 1783; Greensville 1783, 1785; Halifax 1782, 1784; Hampshire 1782, 1784; Hanover 1782; Harrison 1785; Isle of Wight 1782; Lancaster 1783, 1785; Mecklenburg 1782; Middlesex 1783; Monongalia 1782; Nansemond 1783, 1784, 1785; New Kent 1782, 1784; Norfolk 1782, 1784, 1785; Northumberland 1782, 1784; Orange 1782, 1785; Pittsylvania 1782, 1785; Powhatan 1783; Prince Edward 1783, 1785; Princess Anne 1783, 1785; Richmond 1783; Rockingham 1784; Shenandoah 1783, 1785; Southhampton 1783, 1785; Stafford 1785; Surry 1782, 1784; Sussex 1782; Warwick 1782, 1784; Williamsburg City 1782. Filmed by the Genealogical Society of Utah, 1992, 1 roll, FHL film #1854091. To access the digital images, see the online FHL catalog page:
**www.familysearch.org/search/catalog/386611.**

**1782-1785.** ***Heads of Families at the First Census of the United States Taken in the Year 1790: Records of the State Enumerations, 1782 to 1785 – Virginia*** One volume of the *Heads of Families* (12-vol. series), the first project undertaken by the new U.S. Census Bureau, 1903-1908. A summary appears as follows: "The counties for which the names of the heads of families are returned on the state census lists are 39 in number, and contained in 1790 a population of 370,000; 41 counties with 377,000 population are lacking; this publication covers, therefore, only about one-half of the state." See
**www.familysearch.org/search/catalog/329264.**

**1782-1787.** ***Virginia Tax Payers, Other Than Those Published by the United States Census Bureau*** **[Printed Book & Digital Version],** by Augusta B. Fothergill and John Mark Naugle, publ. 1940, 142 pages. Includes lists from Fayette and Lincoln counties, Kentucky. To access the digital version, see the online FHL catalog page:
**www.familysearch.org/search/catalog/76783.**

**1785.** ***Botetourt County, Virginia, 1785 Enumeration*** **[Printed Book, Microfilm & Digital Version],** copied and indexed by Charles T. Burton, published by mimeograph, Troutville, Virginia, 197?, 11 pages. Includes index. "The area enumerated included all or parts of the present-day counties of Botetourt, Alleghany, Bath, Craig, and Roanoke." Gives name of family, number of white people in family, number of dwellings, and number of other buildings. FHL book 975.583 X2b and FHL film #928249. To access the digital version, see the online FHL catalog page:
**www.familysearch.org/search/catalog/64750.**
- For the Ancestry.com version, see
**www.ancestry.com/search/collections/10615.**

**1785-1940.** ***Virginia Marriages*** **[Online Database],** indexed at the FamilySearch.org website. Name index to marriage records from microfilm at the Family History Library. This database has 1,219,044 records. See **https://familysearch.org/search/collection/1708698.**
- See also, ***Virginia, Select Marriages, 1785-1940*** **[Online Database],** indexed at the Ancestry.com website. Source: FamilySearch extractions from county records on microfilm at the Family History Library. Each record includes a name of a spouse. Many records include a name of a child, father, or mother as well. This database has 6,102,360 records. See **http://search.ancestry.com/search/db.aspx?dbid=60214.**

**1787.** ***The 1787 Census of Virginia: An Accounting of the Name of Every White Male Tithable Over 21 Years, the Number of White Males Between 16 & 21 Years, the Number of Slaves Over 16 & Those Under 16 Years, Together With a Listing of Their Horses, Cattle & Carriages, and Also the Names of all Persons to Whom Ordinary Licenses and Physician's Licenses Were Issued*** **[Printed Book],** compiled by Netti Schreiner-Yantis and Florene Speakman Love. Published by Genealogical Books in Print, Springfield, VA, 1987, 3 vols. Includes records presently in the states of Kentucky and West Virginia. FHL book 975.5 R4sn.

***1790 / 1800 Virginia Tax List Censuses*** **[Online Database],** "Plus the missing counties for the 1810 Census. Reconstructed 1790 and 1800 Federal Censuses using Tax List Microfilm Images with Every Name Indexes." See **www.binnsgenealogy.com/VirginiaTaxListCensuses.**

**1800-1890.** ***Virginia, Compiled Census and Census Substitutes Index*** **[Online Database],** indexed at the Ancestry.com website. Originally edited by Ronald Jackson, publ. Accelerated Indexing Systems, Salt Lake City, acquired by Ancestry in 1999 (Its first census database). This collection contains the following indexes: 1800 Accomack County Federal Census Index; 1810 Federal Census Index; 1820 Federal Census Index; 1830 Federal Census Index; 1840 Federal Census Index; 1840 Pensioners List; 1850 Federal Census Index; 1850 Slave Schedule; 1860 Federal Census Index; 1860 Slave Schedule; 1870 Federal Census Index; 1890 Veterans Schedules; 1890 Naval Veterans Schedule; Early Census Index. This database has 197,777 records. See **http://search.ancestry.com/search/db.aspx?dbid=3578.**

***1809-1848 Burned County Data, as Found in the Virginia Contested Election Files*** **[Printed Book],** compiled by Benjamin B. Weisiger, III, published by the author, Richmond, VA, 1986, 103 pages. The depositions regarding qualifications of the voters are from the counties of Hanover, Buckingham, Charles City, Gloucester, New Kent, James City and Caroline. Contains information about land ownership, age, length of residence in the county, and other information. This other information were proofs of status from attached wills, deeds, marriage data, Bible records, etc. Voter or poll lists were not included in book because they were too lengthy. Includes index. FHL book 975.5 P2w and FHL film #1697900.

***1810 Frederick County, Virginia Census*** **[Online Database],** digitized and indexed at Ancestry.com. From a printed extract by Crickard, Beverly, WV, 1979. see **www.ancestry.com/search/collections/10620.**

***1810 Census of Augusta County, Virginia*** **[Online Database],** digitized and indexed at Ancestry.com. From a printed extract by Crickard, Beverly, WV, 1979. see **www.ancestry.com/search/collections/10616.**

***1810 Census of Bath County, Virginia*** **[Online Database],** digitized and indexed at Ancestry.com. From a printed extract by Crickard, Beverly, WV, 1979. see **www.ancestry.com/search/collections/10617.**

***1810 Census of Botetourt County, Virginia*** **[Online Database],** digitized and indexed at Ancestry.com. From a printed extract by Crickard, Beverly, WV, 1979. see **www.ancestry.com/search/collections/10618.**

***1810 Census of Giles County, Virginia*** **[Online Database],** digitized and indexed at Ancestry.com. From a printed extract by Crickard, Beverly, WV, 1979. see **www.ancestry.com/search/collections/10619.**

***1810 Census of Montgomery County, Virginia*** **[Online Database],** digitized and indexed at Ancestry.com. From a printed extract by Crickard, Beverly, WV, 1979. see **www.ancestry.com/search/collections/10621.**

**1810.** See ***A Supplement to the 1810 Census of Virginia: Tax Lists of the Counties for Which the Census is Missing*** **[Printed Book],** transcribed and edited by Netti Schreiner-Yantis, published by Genealogical Books in Print, Springfield, VA, 1971, 324 pages. FHL book 975.5 R4s.

**1810-1840.** ***Virginia, 1810 Thru 1840 Federal Census: Population Schedules*** **[Microfilm & Digital Capture],** filmed by the National Archives, 1938-1961, 44 rolls, beginning with FHL film #181426. To access the digital images, see the online FHL catalog page: **www.familysearch.org/search/catalog/745508.**

**1812-1814.** ***Virginia Militia in the War of 1812*** **[Online Database],** indexed at the Ancestry.com website. Originally published as *Pay Rolls of Militia Entitled to Land Bounty Under the Act of Congress of Sept. 28, 1850, Copied from the Rolls in the Auditor's Office at Richmond, publ. 1851.* Reprinted by Genealogical Publishing Co, 1999. This database has about 1,600 pages.
- For Vol. 1, see **http://search.ancestry.com/search/db.aspx?dbid=48441.**
- For Vol. 2, see **http://search.ancestry.com/search/db.aspx?dbid=48441.**

***1815 Directory of Virginia Landowners (and Gazetteer)*** **[Printed Book],** abstracted by Roger G. Ward, published by Iberian Publishing Co., Athens, GA, 1997-2000, 6 vols. Arranged in alphabetical order within each county. Contents: Vol. 1: Central region (comprising the counties of Albemarle, Amelia, Amherst, Buckingham, Charles City, Chesterfield, Cumberland, Dinwiddie, Fluvanna, Goochland, Hanover, Henrico, Louisa, Nelson, New Kent, Nottoway, Powhatan, Prince George, & the independent cities of Petersburg and Richmond); Vol. 2: South central region (comprising the counties of Bedford, Brunswick, Campbell, Charlotte, Franklin, Greensville, Halifax, Henry, Lunenburg, Mecklenburg, Patrick, Pittsylvania, Prince Edward, Southampton, and Sussex; Vol. 3: Eastern region (comprising the counties of Accomack, Caroline, Elizabeth City, Essex, Gloucester, Isle of Wight, James City, King and Queen, King George, King William, Lancaster, Mathews, Middlesex, Nansemond, Norfolk, Northampton, Northumberland, Princess Ann, Richmond, Surry, Warwick, Westmoreland, and York, and the independent city of Norfolk); Vol. 4: Northern region (comprising the counties of Alexandria, Culpeper, Fairfax, Fauquier, Frederick, Independent City of Alexandria, Independent City of Fredericksburg, Independent City of Winchester, Loudoun, Madison, Orange, Prince William, Rockingham, Shenandoah, Spotsylvania and Stafford); Vol. 5: Southwest region (comprising the following counties of Augusta, Bath, Botetourt, Giles, Grayson, Greenbrier, Lee, Monroe, Montgomery, Pendleton, Rockbridge, Russell, Scott, Tazewell, Washington, and Wythe, and the independent city of Staunton); and Vol. 6: Northwest region (comprising the counties of Berkeley, Brooke, Cabell, Hampshire, Hardy, Harrison, Jefferson, Kanawha, Mason, Monongalia, Ohio, Pendleton, Randolph, Tyler, and Wood). Includes Given name, personal identifiers (if any); location/place-name of land; and miles/direction from the 1815 courthouse. FHL book 975 E4w, v. 1-6.

**1820.** ***Missing Pages From the 1820 Virginia Census*** **[Online Database],** pages from Accomack, Monongalia, Pittsylvania, Randolph, Shenandoah & Southampton Counties. Indexed at VAGenWeb Archives site. See **www.vagenweb.org/shenandoah/missing1820census.html.**

***1828-1938 Index to Marriage Notices in the Religious Herald*** **[Printed Book],** prepared by the Historical Records Survey of Virginia, Division of Community Service Programs, Works Projects Administration, 1941. Reprinted by Genealogical Pub. Co., 1996, 316 pages. The Religious Herald was published in Richmond, Virginia, as a weekly newspaper since January 1828. FHL book 975.5 V22in.

**1833-2006.** ***Virginia, Danville City Cemetery Records*** **[Online Database],** digitized at the FamilySearch.org website. Source: Danville Public Works Dept. Images only: Cemetery records for several cemeteries in Danville, Virginia. Records include indexes, burial records, deed books, and plot books. Although the collection contains information on individuals buried, 1833-2006, coverage will vary between cemeteries. Browse the collection, organized by the name of the cemetery, then type of cemetery record (plot index, deeds, etc.). This database has 4,093 images. See **https://familysearch.org/search/collection/1386587.**

**1835-1941.** See ***Index to Marriage Notices in the Southern Churchman, 1835-1941*** **[Printed Book],** prepared by the Historical Records Survey of Virginia, Service Division, Work Projects Administration, sponsored by the Virginia Conservation Commission. 1942, 2 vols., Vol. 1: A-K; Vol. 2: L-Z. FHL book 975.5 V22i, v.1&2 and FHL film #908352.

**1850.** ***Virginia, 1850 Federal Census: Population Schedules* [Microfilm & Digital Capture],** filmed by the National Archives, 1964, 62 rolls, beginning with FHL film #29707. To access the digital images, see the online FHL catalog page:
**www.familysearch.org/search/catalog/744503.**

**1850-1880.** ***Virginia, Census Records: Non-Population Schedules* [Microfilm & Digital Capture],** from the originals at the National Archives, Washington, DC. Includes Agriculture, Mortality, and Social Statistics schedules. Filmed by the National Archives, digitized by FamilySearch International. To access the digital images, see the online FHL catalog page: **www.familysearch.org/search/catalog/2822786.**

**1851-1929.** ***Virginia Marriages* [Online Database],** indexed at the Ancestry.com website. Originally edited by Jordan Dodd, from county records on microfilm at the Family History Library, Salt Lake City. Includes name of bride and groom, date of marriage, and place of marriage. This database has 56,743 records. See
**http://search.ancestry.com/search/db.aspx?dbid=4498.**
- **NOTE:** an earlier version of this database has 29,984 records. See
**http://search.ancestry.com/search/db.aspx?dbid=3976.**

***1852 Elliott & Nye's Virginia Directory and Business Register* [Microfiche],** by Elliott & Nye, printers, microfilm of originals published by Research Publications, Woodbridge, CT, 1980-1984, 7 microfiche, FHL fiche #6044617.

**1853-1912.** ***Virginia Deaths and Burials* [Online Database],** indexed at the FamilySearch.org website. Name index to death and burial records from microfilm at the Family History Library. This database has 611,127 records. See
**https://familysearch.org/search/collection/1708697.**

**1853-1917.** ***Virginia Births and Christenings* [Online Database],** indexed at the FamilySearch.org website. Name index to birth, baptism, and christening records from microfilm at the Family History Library, Salt Lake City, UT. This database has 1,991,095 records. See **https://familysearch.org/search/collection/1708660.**

**1853-1917.** ***Virginia, Deaths and Burials Index* [Online Database],** indexed at the Ancestry.com website. Source: FamilySearch extractions from county records on microfilm at the Family History Library, Salt Lake City. A record may include: name, birth date, birthplace, age, occupation, race, gender, residence, street address, spouse, marital status, date of death, place of death, date of burial, place of burial, cemetery, father's name and birth-place, mother's name and birthplace, and FHL film number. This database has 757,683 records. See
**http://search.ancestry.com/search/db.aspx?dbid=2558.**
- The FamilySearch (1853-1912) database has 609,569 records, see
**www.familysearch.org/search/collection/1708697.**

**1853-1866.** ***Virginia, Slave Birth Index* [Online Database],** digitized and indexed from birth registers compiled by the WPA ca1938, now located at the Virginia State Library & Archives, Richmond, VA. This database has 154,885 records, see
**www.familysearch.org/search/collection/3326815.**

**1854-1911.** See ***Virginia Birth Records, 1912-2016, Delayed Birth Records, 1854-1911* [Online Database],** from Ancestry's description: "This database contains an index of birth details extracted from Virginia birth records for the years 1864-2014 as well as images of birth records for the years 1864–1914, which fall outside the 100-year privacy restriction. You'll find basic details such as name, birth date and place, father's name, mother's name, and certificate number." Even though this description does not match the inclusive years of the title, see
**www.ancestry.com/search/collections/9277.**

**1854-2014.** See ***Virginia, Birth Records, 1912-2014, Delayed Birth Records, 1854-1911* [Online Database],** digitized and indexed at the Ancestry.com website. Source: VA Dept of Health. This database contains an index of birth details extracted from Virginia birth records for the years 1864-2014 as well as images of birth records for the years 1864–1913. Details include a name, birth date and place, father's name, mother's name, and certificate number. This database has 8,308,630 records. See
**http://search.ancestry.com/search/db.aspx?dbid=9277.**

**1860.** ***Virginia, 1860 Federal Census: Population Schedules* [Microfilm & Digital Capture],** filmed by the National Archives, 1950, 1967, 81 rolls; digitized by FamilySearch International. To access the digital images, see the online FHL catalog page:
**www.familysearch.org/search/catalog/707241.**

**1861-1865.** ***Virginia, Civil War Service Records of Confederate Soldiers*** **[Online Database]**, indexed at the FamilySearch.org website. Source: National Archives microfilm series M324. Includes card abstracts of entries relating to the soldier as found in original muster rolls, returns, rosters, payrolls, appointment books, hospital registers, Union prison registers and rolls, parole rolls, inspection reports; and the originals of any papers relating solely to the particular soldier. This database has 2,252,877 records. See **https://familysearch.org/search/collection/1932382.**

**1861-1865.** ***Virginia, Civil War Service Records of Union Soldiers*** **[Online Database],** indexed at the FamilySearch.org website. Source: National Archives microfilm series M398. Includes card abstracts of entries relating to the soldier as found in original muster rolls, returns, rosters, payrolls, appointment books, hospital registers, prison registers and rolls, parole rolls, inspection reports; and the originals of any papers relating to the particular soldier. This database has 15,239 records. See
**https://familysearch.org/search/collection/1932427.**

**1865-1866.** ***Internal Revenue Assessment Lists for Virginia*** **[Microfilm & Digital Capture],** from the originals at the National Archives, Washington, DC, Filmed by the National Archives, series M0793, 6 rolls, beginning with FHL film #1578235. To access the digital images, see the online FHL catalog page:
**www.familysearch.org/search/catalog/572851.**

**1870.** ***Virginia, 1870 Federal Census: Population Schedules*** **[Microfilm & Digital Capture],** filmed by the National Archives, 1962, 1968, 67 rolls; digitized by FamilySearch International. To access the digital images, see the online FHL catalog page:
**www.familysearch.org/search/catalog/698924.**

**1870.** ***Virginia Inhabitants County by County in 1870*** **[Microfilm & Digital Capture],** from the originals at the VA State Library, Richmond. It may not be obvious from the title, but this is the State of Virginia's original copy of the 1870 federal census. From this original set (in June 1870), a handwritten copy was made and sent to the Census Office in Washington, DC. The federal copy was microfilmed by the National Archives in the 1960s. In the early 2000s, the federal microfilm set was digitized and indexed by Ancestry, FamilySearch, et al. Using this state copy on microfilm, one can compare the same entries of the digitized federal copy – there are always copying errors made, and it will be possible to see different spellings of names, different ages for people, and different places of birth, etc. Evidence that this was the state copy of the VA 1870 federal census is that the entire series was microfilmed onsite at the Virginia State Library in Richmond, Virginia by the Genealogical Society of Utah in 1954, 21 rolls, beginning with FHL film #29746 (Accomack and Albemarle counties). To access the digital images for certain rolls, see the online FHL catalog page:
**https://familysearch.org/search/catalog/394443.**

**1870.** ***Virginia State Copies of Special Schedules of the 1870 Federal Census*** **[Microfilm].** In addition to Virginia's extant state copy of its 1870 federal population schedules, state original 1870 Non-Population schedules are also extant, all located at the VA State Library in Richmond. The following special schedules are available on microfilm:

- 1870 VA Industry Census, 1 roll, FHL film #29745.
- 1870 VA Agriculture Census, 4 rolls, FHL film #29739-29742.
- 1870 VA Social Statistics, 1 roll, FHL film #29743.
- 1870 VA Mortality Schedules, 1 roll, FHL film #29744 (another copy, FHL film #1421033).

**1870-1912.** ***Virginia, Richmond City Birth Index*** **[Online Database],** indexed at the FamilySearch.org website. Card index to births in the city of Richmond, Virginia, 1870-1912. The cards are generally arranged alphabetically by the surname and given name(s) of the individual. This database has 50,615 records. See
**https://familysearch.org/search/collection/1929534.**

**1880.** ***Virginia, 1880 Federal Census: Soundex and Population Schedules*** **[Microfilm & Digital Capture],** filmed by the National Archives, c1970, 127 rolls; digitized by FamilySearch International. To access the digital images (Population Schedules), see the online FHL catalog page:
**www.familysearch.org/search/catalog/676532.**

**1888-1891 Virginia City Directories [Online Database],** indexed at the Ancestry.com website.
- For **Norfolk,** 1889 & 1891, see
**http://search.ancestry.com/search/db.aspx?dbid=4622.**

**1898-1988.** ***Newport News, Virginia, Daily Press Obituary Index*** **[Online Database],** indexed at the Ancestry.com website. Includes names of the deceased and survivors. This database has records 174,222 records. See
**http://search.ancestry.com/search/db.aspx?dbid=70484.**

**1899-1909.** ***Virginia, Winchester, Evening Star Obituaries*** **[Online Database],** indexed at the FamilySearch.org website. Source: Handley Regional Library, Winchester, VA. Includes Obituaries from the Winchester Evening Star arranged by year then alphabetically by name. This database has 5,819 records. See
**https://familysearch.org/search/collection/1464685.**
- See also, ***Virginia, Winchester, Evening Star Obituaries, 1899-1909*** **[Online Database],** indexed at the Ancestry.com website. Source: FamilySearch database obtained from the Handley Regional Library, Winchester, VA. These records generally contain the following information: Name of deceased, Date and place of death, Residence, Names of family members, Cause of death, Date and place of burial, and Undertaker. This database has 5,819 records. See
**http://search.ancestry.com/search/db.aspx?dbid=60215.**

**1900.** ***Virginia, 1900 Federal Census: Soundex and Population Schedules*** **[Microfilm & Digital Capture],** filmed by the Census Bureau, c1943, 217 rolls; digitized by FamilySearch International. To access the digital images (Population Schedules), see the online FHL catalog page:
**www.familysearch.org/search/catalog/653957.**

**1901-1938.** ***Virginia, Federal Naturalization Records*** **[Online Database],** digitized and indexed at Ancestry.com. Includes Petitions, Declarations, and Naturalization Certificates from various court district of Virginia. This database has 6,839 records, see
**www.ancestry.com/search/collections/61212.**

**1904-1963.** ***Virginia, Passenger and Crew Lists*** **[Online Database],** indexed at the Ancestry.com website. Source: National Archives microfilm. Records include the name age, gender, physical description, occupation, birthplace, citizen of what country, and residence. This database has records 78,986 records:
**http://search.ancestry.com/search/db.aspx?dbid=9128.**

**1906-1929.** ***Virginia Naturalization Petitions*** **[Online Database],** digitized at the FamilySearch.org website. Images only: Naturalization petitions from four U.S. District Courts in Virginia and corresponding to four record series at the National Archives: Naturalization Petitions of the U.S. District Court for the Western District of Virginia (Abingdon), 1914-1929 (M1645), Naturalization Petitions of the U.S. District Court for the Western District of Virginia (Charlottesville), 1910-1929 (M1646), Naturalization Petitions of the U.S. District and Circuit Courts for the Eastern District of Virginia (Richmond), 1906-1929 (M1647), and Naturalization Petitions of the U.S. District Court for the Eastern District of Virginia (Alexandria), 1909-1920 (M1648). This database has 11,999 records. See
**https://familysearch.org/search/collection/1877093.**

**1910.** ***Virginia, 1910 Federal Census: Soundex and Population Schedules*** **[Microfilm & Digital Capture],** filmed by the Census Bureau, c1943, 217 rolls; digitized by FamilySearch International. To access the digital images (Population Schedules), see the online FHL catalog page:
**www.familysearch.org/search/catalog/646880.**

**1912-1913.** ***Virginia Birth Certificates*** **[Online Database],** from Department of Health originals at the Virginia State Library. This database has 31,521 records, see
**www.familysearch.org/search/collection/2388824.**

**1912-1987.** ***Virginia, Death Certificates*** **[Online Database],** digitized and indexed at FamilySearch.org, from original Department of Health records at the Virginia State Library. This database has 2,682,595 records, see
**www.familysearch.org/search/collection/2377565.**

**1912-2014.** ***Virginia, Death Records*** **[Online Database],** digitized and indexed at the Ancestry.com website. Source: VA Dept of Health. This collection contains an index of details extracted from Virginia death records for the years 1988–2014, as well as images of death records for 1912–1987. Many records include an age at death, death date, place of death, death registration date, place of birth, and a death certificate date. Some records may contain birth years, spouse, and parents' names. This database has records 11,182,320 records.
**http://search.ancestry.com/search/db.aspx?dbid=9278.**

**1912-2016.** See ***Virginia Birth Records, 1912-2016, Delayed Birth Records, 1854-1911*** **[Online Database],** from Ancestry's description: "This database contains an index of birth details extracted from Virginia birth records for the years 1864-2014 as well as images of birth records for the years 1864–1914, which fall outside the 100-year privacy restriction. You'll find basic details such as name, birth date and place, father's name, mother's name, and certificate number." This description does not match the inclusive years of the title. This database has 9,080,019 records, see
**www.ancestry.com/search/collections/9277.**

**1918-2014.** ***Virginia, Divorce Records*** **[Online Database],** indexed at the Ancestry.com website. Source: VA Dept of Health. This collection contains an index of details extracted from Virginia divorce records for the years 1989–2014, as well as images for the years 1918–1988. Each record may include names, birthdates, residence, marriage date, divorce date and place, age at time of divorce, gender, race, occupation, spouse's name, birth date, age, gender, race, and occupation. This database has 2,887,687 records. See
**http://search.ancestry.com/search/db.aspx?dbid=9280.**

**1920.** ***Virginia, 1920 Federal Census: Soundex and Population Schedules*** **[Microfilm & Digital Capture],** filmed by the Census Bureau, c1943, 111 rolls; digitized by FamilySearch International. To access the digital images (Population Schedules), see the online FHL catalog page:
**www.familysearch.org/search/catalog/558330.**

**1929-1976.** ***Virginia, Fluvanna County Colbert Funeral Home Records*** **[Online Database],** digitized at the FamilySearch.org website. Source: Colbert Funeral Home, Bremo Bluff, VA. Images only: Colbert Funeral Home records. The funeral home was located in Bremo Bluff and served residents of Fluvanna County and surrounding counties. Each volume is indexed except for the one covering 1973-1976. Browse the images, organized by date ranges. This database has 1,866 records. See
**https://familysearch.org/search/collection/1344895.**

**1930.** ***Virginia, 1930 Federal Census: Soundex and Population Schedules*** **[Microfilm & Digital Capture],** filmed by the Census Bureau, c1970, 178 rolls; digitized by FamilySearch International. To access the digital images (Population Schedules), see the online FHL catalog page:
**www.familysearch.org/search/catalog/1037533.**

**1934-1954.** ***Master File Relocation Card Index for Grave and Cemetery Removal and Relocation*** **[Microfilm & Digital Capture],** from records of the Tennessee Valley Authority, now at the National Archives, East Point, GA. Lists cemetery name and number, deceased, date of birth, date of death, age, type and condition of marker and inscription, nearest living relative or source of information, source's address and relationship to deceased. Filmed by the Genealogical Society of Utah, 1996, 58 rolls, organized by cemeteries in Tennessee, Alabama, Mississippi, North Carolina, Georgia, Kentucky, and Virginia. The Virginia Grave Removal Master Card Index appears on three (3) rolls: FHL #2050202, 2051208, and 2051242. To access the digital images, see the online FHL catalog page:
**www.familysearch.org/search/catalog/778971.**

**1935-2009.** ***Virginia, African-American Funeral Programs*** **[Online Database],** digitized and indexed at the FamilySearch.org website. Images and index of funeral programs from the Middle Peninsula African-American Genealogical and Historical Society of Virginia (MPAAGHS). Programs were donated to MPAAGHS by various individuals within the community. Images are loosely arranged alphabetically by the names of persons collecting and donating the programs and not alphabetically by the names of those in the programs. Some obituaries are included. This database has 20,444 records. See
**https://familysearch.org/search/collection/1880968.**

**1936-1988.** ***Virginia, Marriage Certificates*** **[Online Database],** digitized and indexed at FamilySearch.org, from the original Department of Health records at the Virginia State Library. This database has 2,510,420 records, see
**www.familysearch.org/search/collection/2370234.**

**1936-2014.** ***Virginia, Marriage Records*** **[Online Database],** digitized and indexed at the Ancestry.com website. Source: VA Dept of Health. This collection contains an index of details extracted from Virginia marriage records for the years 1989–2014, as well as images for the years 1936–1988. Each record may include names of bride and groom, race, age at marriage, birth date, gender, mother's name, father's name, marriage date and place, and certificate number. This database has 19,426,036 records. See
**http://search.ancestry.com/search/db.aspx?dbid=9279.**

**1940.** ***Virginia, 1940 Federal Census: Population Schedules*** **[Digital Images],** from the original records held by the Bureau of the Census in the 1940s. After microfilming, Congress allowed the Census Bureau to destroy the originals to free up space for WWII-related files. In 2012, the National Archives digitized the microfilm images for all states and territories. To access the digital images for Virginia only, see the online FHL catalog page:
**https://familysearch.org/search/catalog/2057760.**

**1940 Federal Census Finding Aids [Online Database].** The National Archives prepared a special website online with a detailed description of the 1940 federal census. Included at the site are descriptions of location finding aids, such as Enumeration District maps, Geographic Descriptions of Census Enumeration Districts, and a list of 1940 City Directories available at the National Archives. The finding aids are all linked to other National Archives sites. The National Archives website also has a link to 1940 Search Engines using Stephen P. Morse's "One-Step" system for finding a 1940 E.D. or street address conversion. See **www.archives.gov/research/census/1940/general-info.html#questions.**

**1940-1945.** ***Virginia, World War II Draft Registration Cards*** **[Online Database],** digitized card index, arranged in alpha order. This database has 762,434 records, see **www.familysearch.org/search/collection/2659404.**

**1946-1957.** ***Virginia, Alexandria Passenger and Crew Lists of Vessels*** **[Online Database],** indexed at the FamilySearch.org website. Source: National Archives microfilm series A3435. The records may include full name, age, gender, marital status, occupation, citizenship, race, last permanent residence, birthplace, and final destination. This database has 6,337 records: **https://familysearch.org/search/collection/2376891.**

**1985-Current.** See ***Virginia Recent Newspaper Obituaries)*** **[Online Database],** digitized and indexed newspaper obituaries at the GenealogyBank website, including newspapers from Abingdon, Alexandria, Altavista, Amherst, Appomattox, Arlington, Ashburn Farm, Ashburn Village, Landsdown, Bluemont, Bedford, Big Stone Gap, Bristol, Broadway, Brookneal, Burke, Cascades/Countryside/Potomac Falls/Sterling, Charlottesville, Chase City, Chatham, Clintwood, Culpeper, Danville, Dayton, Drakes Branch, Dumfries/Stafford/Woodbridge, Elkton, Emporia, Fairfax, Fairfax Station, Clifton, Farmville, Floyd, Franklin, Fredericksburg, Front Royal, Galax, Goochland, Great Falls, Harrisonburg, Haymarket., Herndon, Hillsville, Independence, King George, Laurel Hill, Lawrenceville, Leesburg, Lexington, Luray, Lynchburg, Madison, Manassas, Marion, Martinsville, McLean, Mechanicsville, Merrifield, Newport News, Norfolk, Norton, Orange, Petersburg, Powhatan, Reston, Richlands, Richmond, Roanoke, Roanoke, Lynchburg, Rocky Mount, South Hill, Springfield, Stafford, Stanardsville, Strasburg, Suffolk, Victoria, Washington, Waynesboro, Winchester, Wirtz, Woodstock, and Wytheville **www.genealogybank.com/explore/obituaries/all/usa/virginia.**

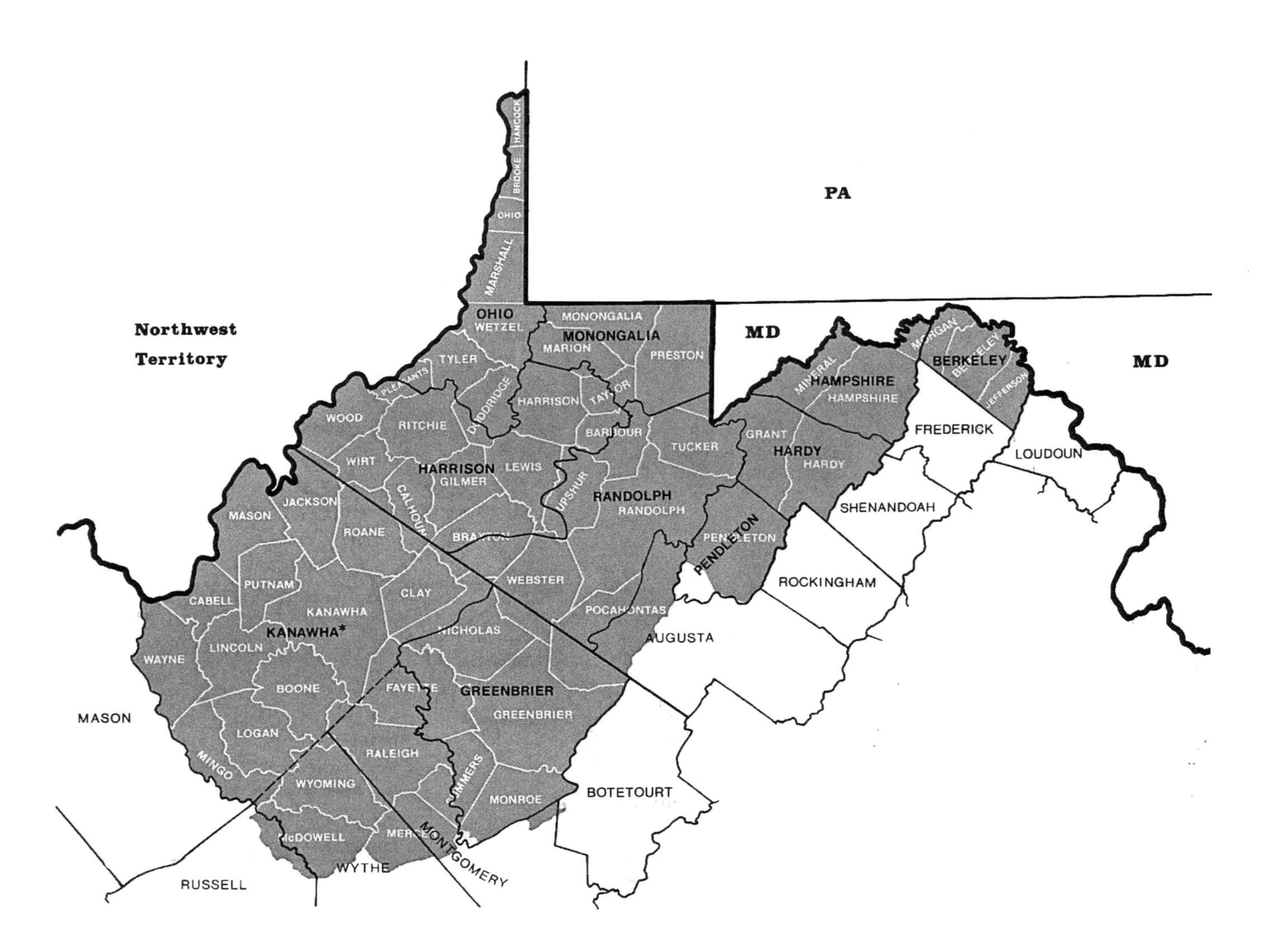


**West Virginia • Aug 1790. (As part of Virginia).** The Virginia counties within the West Virginia area at the time of the 1790 Federal Census are shown in black. The current 55 counties of West Virginia are shown in white. Virginia's population in 1790 was at 691,757 people. Of that total, the West Virginia area was determined to have 55,873 people. Virginia's 1790 census name list was lost. A reconstruction of the names of residents was made using tax lists from all counties, including the counties having areas that became West Virginia. * **Notes:** In 1790, both Kentucky and West Virginia were still part of their parent state of Virginia. Neither progeny state was ever a territory. Kentucky's statehood was in 1792; West Virginia's statehood came in 1863. Kanawha's southeastern boundary was statutorily to run from the Tug Fork of the Sandy River along the *Cumberland Mountains* to the Kanawha River. The ends of this line can be closely identified, but no such connecting continuous ridge exists. **Map Source:** Page 367, *Map Guide to the U.S. Federal Censuses, 1790-1920*, by William Thorndale and William Dollarhide.

# West Virginia

## Censuses & Substitute Name Lists

### Historical Timeline for West Virginia, 1558-1863

**1558.** Elizabeth I became Queen of England. The early exploration of North America took place during her 45-year reign, the Elizabethan Era, or "Golden Age." When Elizabeth I was crowned, England was nearly bankrupt, but during her reign, the English Empire expanded and thrived, and English culture flourished in Literature, Theatre, Music, and Architecture.

**1584. Virginia.** Sir Walter Raleigh claimed and named Virginia for the "Virgin Queen," Elizabeth I, an area from present Chesapeake Bay to Florida, and everything below a northwestern line to the North Pole.

**1603. England.** James I became King of England, the first monarch to rule both England and Scotland. (He was James VI of Scotland since 1566). During his reign, the first permanent English colonies were established in Virginia and New England. James I was an advocate for the transportation of thousands of clan people living along the Scottish-English border to Ulster Province, Northern Ireland.

**1606.** Two joint stock companies were founded in 1606, both with royal charters issued by King James I for the purpose of establishing colonies in North America. The Virginia Company of London was given a land grant between Latitude 34° (Cape Fear) and Latitude 41° (Long Island Sound). The Virginia Company of Plymouth was founded with a similar land grant between Latitude 38° (Potomac River) and Latitude 45° (St. John River), which included a shared area with the London Company between Latitude 38° and Latitude 41°..

**1607. April 26. Virginia.** Three ships under the command of Capt. Christopher Newport sought shelter in Chesapeake Bay. The forced landing led to the founding of Jamestown on the James River, the first permanent English settlement, consisting of 104 men and boys. The Jamestown colony was led by Capt. John Smith and his cousin, Bartholomew Gosnold. A year later, about 100 new settlers arrived, finding only 38 survivors from the first group. In 1610, recently appointed governor of Virginia, Thomas West (Lord De La Warr) arrived at Jamestown to find only 60 settlers alive.

**1609. Virginia.** The 2nd Virginia Charter of 1609 extended the jurisdiction of the London Company to include former areas of the Plymouth Company. The language of the new charter now included the words, "sea to sea." (James I was assured that the Pacific Ocean was just a bit west of the Appalachian Mountains).

**1625. England.** Charles I became King of England, Scotland, and Ireland. Soon after taking office, Charles began to note a large number of non-conformists among his subjects. Along with his Archbishop, William Laud, the King began a campaign to purge his church of the largest group of non-conformists, the so-called "Puritans," a militant Calvinist religious group attempting to purify the Church of England.

**1629-1640.** As a result of the Charles I campaign to purge non-conformists from the Church of England, large groups of people were disenfranchised. Charles I disbanded Parliament and ruled England alone for eleven years. The Puritans referred to this era as "the eleven years of tyranny." It was during these eleven years that some 21,000 Puritan immigrants established the Massachusetts Bay Colony of North America.

**1633. Virginia.** The Middle Plantation of the Virginia Colony was founded. The first major inland settlement after Jamestown, it later became Williamsburg.

**1641. Virginia.** Sir William Berkeley was appointed governor by Charles I. He served from 1642 to 1652 and again from 1660 to 1677. His older brother Lord John Berkeley, was the first Proprietor of the East New Jersey colony, and both brothers were Lords Proprietors of the Province of Carolina. William Berkeley transformed the Virginia colony by emulating the culture of southwest England's plantation system.

**1642. English Civil War.** When Parliament was restored in 1640, it quickly became dominated by the same Puritans who King Charles I had removed from the Church of England. Beginning in 1642, Royalist supporters were forced to fight the armies of the Puritan Parliament in the English Civil War. The English Colonies took sides: the Virginia colony favored the Royalist/Cavalier side, while the New England colonies were in support of the Parliamentarian/Puritan side. The Province of Maryland had earlier allowed all religious persuasions to settle in Maryland. During the English Civil War, Maryland granted free land as refuge to any Puritans from Virginia to settle there. As a result, Annapolis, Maryland was first settled by Puritans from Virginia.

**1645-1651. England.** After his defeat and capture in 1645, Charles I refused to accept his captors' demands for a constitutional monarchy, and briefly escaped captivity in 1647. While recaptured, his teenage son, Prince Charles, was able to marshal Scottish forces for the king. However, by 1648, Oliver Cromwell had consolidated the English opposition. King Charles I was tried, convicted, and beheaded for high treason in January 1649. The Civil War continued until 1651, when Oliver Cromwell, a Puritan, became Lord Protectorate, ruling the Commonwealth of England for the next seven years.

**1651.** Sir William Berkeley, Royal Governor of Virginia, wrote pamphlets directed at the 2nd sons of Southwest England, the men, like himself, who had been left out of their father's estate because of the Primogenitor inheritance practice of that part of England. Berkeley offered the 2nd sons land grants for a small sum, with the promise of regaining the title and prestige of an English gentlemen they were denied in England. The timing of the appeal to the 2nd sons was right after the English Civil War, when a large number of Royalists and Cavaliers (Supporters of King Charles I), were left without power and influence. It was this era of English history that produced the leading families of colonial Virginia.

**1658-1660. England.** After Oliver Cromwell died in 1658, his son, Richard, was too weak politically to remain in power. In 1660, a new Parliament offered a restored English throne to the exiled Scottish King, son of Charles I, who accepted to become King Charles II.

**1699. Virginia.** The colonial capital moved from Jamestown to the newly incorporated town of Williamsburg.

**1707.** England and Scotland merged into the **United Kingdom of Great Britain.** The English Colonies now became the British Colonies.

**1717.** The arrival of the first Scots-Irish immigrants to the British Colonies was via Boston, New York City, Philadelphia, Alexandria, New Bern, and Charles Towne. The so-called Scots-Irish (or Ulster Scots) were former border clan people who had lived near the Scottish-English border for centuries. A good number of them had moved into areas of Northern Ireland in the early 1600s, and a mass migration to most of the British colonies of America began in about 1717.

**1746. Pioneer's Road.** The first wagon road through the Blue Ridge Mountains of Virginia was constructed in 1746, allowing wagon traffic from Alexandria to Winchester, Virginia. The first travelers on the roadway were almost exclusively Scots-Irish immigrants, who had changed their travel plans to arrive in Alexandria instead of Philadelphia. The trace of the old Pioneer's Road is now called US Hwy 50.

**1763.** The **Treaty of Paris** ended the French and Indian War (in Europe and Canada: the Seven Years War). France ceded virtually all of its North American claims to Britain. Soon after, King George III declared the "Proclamation Line of 1763," as a way of rewarding the Indians who had helped Britain against the French. The proclamation established an Indian Reserve that stretched from the Appalachian Mountain Range to the Mississippi River.

**1768. Treaty of Fort Stanwix.** A new "Line of Property" was drawn, separating British Territory from Indian Territory. From Fort Stanwix (present Rome, NY), the division line ran to Fort Pitt (now Pittsburgh) and down the Ohio River to the Tennessee River. The Fort Stanwix treaty line effectively ceded all of present West Virginia and Kentucky to the British Colony of Virginia.

**1769-1772.** The Colony of Virginia saw the Treaty of Fort Stanwix as an opportunity to open up settlement to its western lands. Beginning in 1769, land surveys were conducted in the Kanawha, Kentucky, and Cumberland River valleys In 1772, Fincastle County, Virginia was created, an area that included most of present West Virginia and all of present Kentucky. Due to resistance by the Indians and the impending Revolutionary War, the first settlements were delayed for a few years.

**1774. Lord Dunmore's War.** After several Indian attacks against colonists moving into the lands south of the Ohio River, the Governor of Virginia, John Murray, 4th Earl of Dunmore, asked the Virginia House of Burgesses to declare a state of war with the hostile Indian nations. Dunmore said that Virginians needed to defend their legal right based on the 1768 Treaty of Fort Stanwix. Lord Dunmore's War ended after the Virginia Militia's victory at the Battle of Point Pleasant (mouth of the Kanawha River on the Ohio River) in October 1774. In the resulting treaty, the Indians lost the right to hunt in the area south of the Ohio River.
- The Battle of Point Pleasant, two years before the Declaration of Independence, was later designated as the first battle of the Revolutionary War. Lord Dunmore was a British appointed Royal Governor, but he led a militia force made up of mostly western Virginians against a large group of Indians. Expecting a force of British Army regulars to join them, the Virginians were left on their own. The Americans felt they had been set up by the British, believing the British Army had armed the Indians and then waited for the Americans to be defeated. Instead, Dunmore's victory delivered the Ohio River into the hands of the Virginia militia for the duration of the Revolutionary War.
- In 1774, William Morris was the first permanent settler in the Kanawha country, at a place he named Cedar Grove at the mouth of Kelly's Creek. Soon after, simultaneous migrations got underway into the northern and southern areas of present West Virginia.

**1776.** The name Fincastle was dropped, and the area was divided into three new counties: Kentucky, Washington, and Montgomery County, Virginia. The latter two counties were the jurisdictions of most of the first settlements of present West Virginia.
- Even after being betrayed by the British Army in 1774, Lord Dunmore fought furiously to preserve the British colony of Virginia against the American rebels. He fled Virginia in 1776 after an uprising in Norfolk, and later returned to Britain.

**1776-1783. Revolutionary War.** Much of the western expansion in Virginia was put on hold during the Revolutionary War. Fort Fincastle, at the site of present Wheeling, West Virginia, was under constant attacks by British-supported Indians. Later named Fort Henry, the small community successfully defended itself. This account from Lamb's *History of Wheeling City:* "In 1782, a native army along with British soldiers attempted to take Fort Henry. During this siege, Fort Henry's supply of ammunition was exhausted. The defenders decided to dispatch a man to secure more ammunition from the Zane homestead. Betty Zane volunteered for the dangerous task. During her departing run, she was heckled by both native and British soldiers. After reaching the Zane homestead, she gathered a tablecloth and filled it with gunpowder. During her return, she was fired upon but was uninjured. As a result of her heroism, Fort Henry remained in American control." The Battle of Fort Henry was later referred to as the "last battle of the Revolutionary War."

**1789.** A new wagon road from Winchester was completed to Clarksburg, crossing the Allegheny Mountains of Northern Virginia. The wagon road opened the gates for large numbers of settlers into the Monongahela region. Within a few years, the roadway was extended to the Ohio River (at Parkersburg). This same route was improved in the early 1800s to become the Northwest Turnpike. Today it is known as U.S. Highway 50.

**1790. Federal Census.** the southern area (Greenbrier, Kanawha, Montgomery, and Wythe counties) had a population of about 20,000 people. The northern area (Berkeley, Hampshire, Hardy, Harrison, Monongalia, Ohio, Pendleton, and Randolph counties) had a population of about 35,000 people. Refer to the 1790 map on page 96.

**1818. The National Road** was completed for wagon traffic from Cumberland, Maryland to Wheeling, Virginia. The National Road was the first federally financed interstate highway in America, funded by a portion taken from public land sales in the Ohio country beginning in 1787.

**1829.** In reaction to the new state constitution of Virginia favoring slave-holding counties, public protests against slavery arose in the Virginia counties west of the Allegheny Mountains.

**1830.** The Wheeling Gazette proposed separation of western Virginia from eastern Virginia.

**1852.** The longest railroad in the world, the B & O Railroad from Baltimore to Wheeling was completed. It was 370 miles long.

**1863.** Jun 20. **West Virginia** separated from Virginia and became the 35th state in the Union. The first capital was at Wheeling.
- At the start of the Civil War, two state governments evolved in Virginia, one in support of the Confederate cause, another in support of the Union side. In 1862, votes of the people of the West Virginia region resulted in a majority in favor of joining the Union. In 1863, the state of West Virginia was recognized by the Lincoln Administration and declared a U.S. State by presidential decree.
- West Virginia supplied Confederate soldiers as well as Union soldiers to the war effort. After the Civil War, returning West Virginia Confederate soldiers brought the anti-Union voters even with the Union voters in a few West Virginia counties.
- Two counties (Berkeley and Jefferson) tried to undo their inclusion into West Virginia, but an 1866 act of the U.S. Congress overruled their attempt.
- That ruling was followed by an 1866 lawsuit brought by Virginia against West Virginia to have its former counties returned, asserting that West Virginia's statehood was unconstitutional.
- West Virginia was not officially recognized as a U.S. state until the 1871 *Virginia v. West Virginia* ruling of the U.S. Supreme Court in West Virginia's favor.

## West Virginia Archives & History
### The Genealogy Corner

The Genealogy webpage has links to the following features, guides, programs, publications, and subjects:

**WVA&H Websites:**
- Genealogy Surname Exchange
- Archives and History News
- Birth, Death and Marriage Records
- Cemeteries, West Virginia, Artificial Collection
- County Formations, West Virginia
- Counties of West Virginia
- History of the American Negro
- The Martins' Family History, by Caroline Day Martin (1849-1925)
- Quick Guides to Birth, Death, and Marriage Records
- Researching Your Civil War Ancestor
- Researching Your Revolutionary War Ancestor
- State Archives and Libraries
- Upcoming Events
- Virginia Marriage Laws
- Vital Research Records
- West Virginia Union Militia in the Civil War

See www.wvculture.org/history/genealogy/genealog.html.

## Bibliography
### West Virginia Censuses & Substitutes

Since statehood, West Virginia has never taken a state census. And, the Colony/Commonwealth of Virginia never took a state census before or after statehood. Therefore, tax lists, landowner lists, and other name lists are needed as census substitutes. At the time of Virginia's 1790 federal census, the area that would become West Virginia was within 12 Virginia counties, the jurisdictions where any census substitutes might be found today. Of West Virginia's 55 modern counties, 50 were created as Virginia counties.
- Due to the loss of most of Virginia's 1790 and 1800 federal censuses, substitutes such as tax lists are useful to fill in the names of inhabitants. In the 1810 federal census, Virginia had 17 missing counties, but only four were within the area of present West Virginia (Cabell, Greenbrier, Hardy, and Tazewell). Virginia is complete for every county, 1820 through 1860; and West Virginia is complete from its first census taken in its own name in 1870 through 1940 (with the exception of the 1890, lost for all states).

◆ ◆ ◆ ◆ ◆

**1754-1850. West Virginia Estate Settlements [Online Database],** digitized and indexed at the Ancestry.com website. Source: Ross B. Johnson's *West Virginia Estate Settlements: An Index to Wills, Inventories, Appraisements, Land Grants, and Surveys to 1850,* publ. 1978, Genealogical Publishing Co. This is a digitized version of a book with records abstracted from 13 West Virginia counties as part of a WPA Historical Records Survey project. County records

were organized in this order: Hampshire, Berkeley, Monongalia, Ohio, Greenbrier, Harrison, Randolph, Hardy, Pendleton, Kanawha, Brooke, Wood, and Monroe County. See the description for years of coverage, and types of records for each. This database has 179 pages. See
**http://search.ancestry.com/search/db.aspx?dbid=48446.**

**1754-1899.** ***Sims Index to Land Grants in West Virginia*** **[Online Database],** indexed at the Ancestry.com website. Source: Official published report, by Edgar Sims, WV State Auditor, 1952. The date of 1754 is based on the earliest WV county formation (Hampshire Co VA). There may have been land grants issued earlier than 1754 in areas that were not inhabited yet. The records indicate the present county of West Virginia wherein the land grant was located. Without censuses or tax lists for the early years of settlement, this list of the first landowners of the region is the best substitute available. This database has 867 pages. See
**http://search.ancestry.com/search/db.aspx?dbid=25647.**
- the FamilySearch digital version of *Sims Index* and the *Supplement*, see the FHL catalog page:
**www.familysearch.org/search/catalog/109038.**

**1754-1985.** ***West Virginia, Wills and Probate Records*** **[Online Database],** indexed at the Ancestry.com website. Source: Ancestry extractions from district, county, and probate courts. In most cases, the details found in probates include the names and residences of beneficiaries and their relationship to the decedent. There may also be references to debts, deeds, and other documents related to the settling of the estate. This database has 644,064 records. See
**http://search.ancestry.com/search/db.aspx?dbid=9087.**

**1754-2000s.** ***West Virginia GenWeb Archives*** **[Online Database].** The WVGenWeb site offers free genealogical databases with searchable statewide name lists and for all West Virginia counties. Databases may include Bibles, Biographies, Cemeteries, Censuses, Court, Death, Deeds, Directories, Histories, Marriages, Military, Newspapers, Obituaries, Photos, Schools, Tax Lists, Wills, and more. See
**http://usgwarchives.net/wv/wvfiles.htm.**

**1754-2000s.** ***Linkpendium – West Virginia: Family History & Genealogy, Census, Birth, Marriage, Death Vita Records & More*** **[Online Databases].** Linkpendium is a genealogical portal site with links to state, county, town, and local databases. Currently listed are selected sites for West Virginia statewide resources (371), Barbour County (217), Berkeley County (369), Boone County (155), Braxton County (170), Brooke County (243), and 50 more West Virginia counties. See
**www.linkpendium.com/wv-genealogy/.**

***1756 Hampshire County Public Claims*** **[Online Database],** indexed at the USGenWeb site for Hampshire Co WV. See
**http://files.usgwarchives.net/wv/hampshire/military/public.txt.**

**1756-1971.** ***West Virginia Will Books*** **[Online Database],** digitized (with some indexes) at the FamilySearch.org website. Includes images and some indexes for will books from all 55 counties of West Virginia. The 1756 date comes from the first will book of Hampshire County, formed as a Virginia county in 1754. Will books from all other counties begin after 1772. Browse through 325,731 images, organized by county, then by a date range for the will book volumes. Some counties include index books as part of the series. This database has 76,053 records. See
**https://familysearch.org/search/collection/1909099.**

**1769-1800.** ***Annals of Southwest Virginia*** **[Online Database],** digitized and indexed at the Ancestry.com website. Source: book, same title, by Lewis Preston Summers, publ. 1929. Contains minutes of county courts, land surveys, wills, deeds, marriage licenses, list of forts and soldiers stationed therein, list of Revolutionary soldiers, etc. Covers primarily the earliest counties of Virginia west of the Blue Ridge Mountains: Botetourt, Fincastle, Montgomery, Washington, and Wythe counties, Virginia (From that area came the present-day West Virginia counties of Boone, Cabell, Fayette, Greenbrier, Kanawha, Lincoln, Logan, McDowell, Mason, Mercer, Mingo, Monroe, Putnam, Raleigh, Summers, Wayne, and Wyoming). This database has 1,757 pages. See
**http://search.ancestry.com/search/db.aspx?dbid=49061.**

**1774-1781.** ***Rent Rolls Encompassing the Current Counties of Berkeley, Jefferson and Morgan, West Virginia*** **[Online Database],** an index to the rent rolls of old Berkeley County, 1774, 1775, 1776, 1777, 1778 1779, 1780, and 1781. Indexed at the USGenWeb site for Jefferson Co WV. See
**http://genealogytrails.com/wva/jefferson/rentrolls.html.**

**1774-2003.** ***West Virginia Military Research*** **[Online Databases],** sponsored by the WVGenWeb, this is a portal site to databases specific to West Virginia military rosters, beginning with Lord Dunmore's War, Revolutionary War, War of 1812, Civil War (Union and Confederate units), Indian Wars, World War I, World War II, Korean War, Viet Nam, Gulf War, War on Terror, Iraqi Freedom, and Miscellaneous Military. See **www.wvgenweb.org/wvmilitary/index.html.**

**1776-1783.** ***West Virginians in the American Revolution*** **[Online Database],** indexed at the Ancestry.com website. Source: Reprint of articles first published in *West Virginia History,* 1939-1947, publ. Genealogical Publishing Co, 1977-1998. There are detailed biographical sketches for most veterans, including dates and places of residence and names of relatives. This database has 322 pages. See **http://search.ancestry.com/search/db.aspx?dbid=48445.**

**1777-1850.** ***Historical Records Survey for West Virginia (HRS-WV)*** **[Online Inventory].** The WPA writers project of the late 1930s (to index original county records) was more thorough in West Virginia than any other state. Original records were indexed in virtually all West Virginia county courthouses, as well as many churches and cemeteries. The entire collection was microfilmed, and sets are located at various WV locations as well as the Family History Library in Salt Lake City. An online inventory of the entire collection ( 300+ rolls of microfilm) is available at the website of the West Virginia & Regional History Center of the West Virginia University, Morgantown, WV, see **https://wvrhc.lib.wvu.edu/collections/public-records/historical-records-survey.**

**- NOTE: FamilySearch Digitized Images of the HRS-WV Series:** It is now possible to see the digital images of many of the rolls of microfilm. From over 300 rolls of microfilm, and 1,135 titles, FamilySearch International has digitized many database titles (indexes, abstracts, extracts, etc.). To access the database titles and see which have digital images, see the online FHL catalog (results) page: The FHL catalog results page display starts with an alphabetical listing, based on the first word/character of the title, as follows:

1. [Wills], Cabell County, 1803-1851
2. Abstract of wills recorded in Greenbrier County, West Virginia: numbers 3 and 4, 1844-1861
3. Abstracts from will, birth and death records, 1844-1899
4. Abstracts of County Court record books, Randolph County: 1787-1817
5. Adamsville Cemetery inscriptions, Adamsville, West Virginia
6. Allen Cemetery inscriptions, Harrison County, West Virginia
7. Anderson Cemetery inscriptions, Marion County, West Virginia
8. Anderson Cemetery inscriptions, Marion County, West Virginia

...followed by 1,127 more entries like this...

Conclusion: If a researcher knows the name of the county, and the type of record available (from the WVU Inventory), it may be more practical to search the FHL catalog for the West Virginia county to find a particular title of interest and view the digital images. Go to **www.familysearch.org/search/catalog.** Search by: Place. (name of town or county). Availability: (Online).

**1777-1850.** ***Early West Virginia Wills*** **[Printed Book],** compiled by K. T. H. McFarland, published by Closson Press, Apollo, PA, 1993. Includes surname indexes. Contains abstracts of wills for the northwestern-most section of what is now West Virginia. Shows name of deceased or estate; names of heirs, executors, witnesses; date of will and date probated. Contents: Ohio Co., 1777-1850; Marshall Co., 1835-1850; Tyler Co., 1815-1850; Wetzel Co., 1847-1850; and Doddridge Co., 1849-1850. FHL book 975.4 P28m.

**1777-1912.** ***Dyer's Index to Land Grants in West Virginia*** **[Printed Book & Digital Version],** compiled by M.H. Dyer, WV state auditor in 1896. Contains an alphabetical listing by surname showing name of grantee, number of acres, local description, year of land grant, book, and page numbers in original record. Also contains descriptive notes on each county showing date when formed and description of boundaries. Printed by the state printer, Moses Donnally, Charleston, WV, 1896; facsimile reprinted by Higginson Book Co, 1996, 947 pages, FHL book 975.4 R22d. To access the digital images, see the online FHL catalog page: **www.familysearch.org/search/catalog/2538162.**

- *Dyer's Index* is an index to the manuscripts, ***Land Grants, 1748-1912*** **[Microfilm & Digital Capture],** from the original records at the State Capitol (1967), Charleston, WV. Filmed by the Genealogical Society of Utah, 1967, 56 rolls, beginning with FHL film #521685 (Barbour, Berkeley, 1861). To access the digital images, see the online FHL catalog page: **https://familysearch.org/search/catalog/334356.**

**1780-1785.** ***Public Service Claims Certificates*** **[Microfilm & Digital Capture],** from the originals at the Virginia State Library & Archives, Richmond, VA. These certificates were issued by commissioners to persons whose property was impressed for public use. The front of each certificate includes the date, a description of the item impressed (including weight or quantity), its value, and the name of the person from whom it was taken. Includes certificates issued in these West Virginia counties: Berkeley, Greenbrier, Hampshire, Jefferson, and Ohio. Arranged alphabetically by county and within each county alphabetically by the first letter of the recipient's surname. Filmed by the Genealogical Society of Utah, 1991, 11 rolls, beginning with FHL film #1822808. To access the digital images, see the online FHL catalog page: **www.familysearch.org/search/catalog/85140.**

**1780-1970.** ***West Virginia Marriages*** **[Online Database],** indexed at the FamilySearch.org website. Source: FamilySearch extractions from original county records on microfilm at the Family History Library. This database has 1,504,135 records. See **https://familysearch.org/search/collection/1408729.**

**1781-1940.** ***Early West Virginia Settlers*** **[CD-ROM],** originally published by Broderbund in collaboration with the Genealogical Publishing Co., Inc., Baltimore, 2000, part of Family Tree Maker's Family Archives, CD No. 520. See FHL CD-ROM No. 9 pt. 520. Contents:

- Genealogies of West Virginia Families: From the West Virginia Historical Magazine Quarterly, 1901-1905.
- Cabell County Annals and Families, by George Selden Wallace.
- Capon Valley: Its Pioneers and Their Descendants, to 1940, by Maud Pugh (vols. I-II).
- Genealogy of Some Early Families in Grant and Pleasant Districts, Preston County, West Virginia. Greenbrier Pioneers and Their Homes, by Ruth Woods Dayton.
- Roane County, West Virginia Families, by William H. Bishop.
- Pioneers and Their Homes in the Upper Kanawha, by Ruth Woods Dayton.
- Marriage Records of Berkeley County, Virginia For the Period 1781-1854, Located at Berkeley County Court House, Martinsburg, WV, compiled and edited by Guy L. Keesecker.
- Mason County, West Virginia, Marriages, 1806-1915, compiled and edited by Julie Chapin Hesson, Sherman Gene Hesson, & Jane J. Russell.
- Early Records, Hampshire County, Virginia, now West Virginia, compiled by Clara McCormack Sage and Laura Sage Jones.
- West Virginia Estate Settlements: An Index to Wills, Inventories, Appraisements, Land Grants, and Surveys to 1850, compiled by Ross B. Johnson.
- West Virginia Revolutionary Ancestors: Whose Services Were Non-military, and Whose Names, Therefore, Do Not Appear in Revolutionary Indexes of Soldiers and Sailors, compiled by Anne Waller Ready.
- West Virginians in the American Revolution, compiled by Ross B. Johnson.
- The Soldiery of West Virginia: in the French and Indian War, Lord Dunmore's War, the Revolution, the Later Indian wars, the Whiskey Insurrection, the Second war with England, the War with Mexico, and Addenda Relating to West Virginia in the Civil War, the whole compiled from authentic sources by Virgil Anson Lewis.

***1782 Greenbrier County, (West) Virginia Personal Property Tax List*** **[Online Database],** indexed at the New River Notes website. See **www.newrivernotes.com/neighboring_greenbrier_enumerations_1782_personalpropertytax.htm.**

**1782.** ***The First Census of Hampshire County*** **[Microfilm],** from a booklet prepared by the West Virginia Workers of the Federal Writers' Project, WPA, original published: Romney, WV: School for the Deaf and the Blind, 1937, 68 pages. In 1782, when the first census was taken, Hampshire County included within its boundaries the counties of Hardy, Grant, Mineral and portions of Morgan and Pendleton. Filmed by the Genealogical Society of Utah, 1990, 1 rolls, FHL film #1697283

***1782-1850 Personal Property Tax Lists, Greenbrier County, (now West Virginia)*** **[Microfilm & Digital Capture],** from the original records at the Virginia State Library in Richmond, Virginia. Tax lists give

name of person taxed or tithed, type and amount of taxable property, amount of tax, and the county statistics. Greenbrier County kept taxpayers lists by years, 1782 (1 list), 1783 (5 lists), 1784 (2 lists), 1785-1786 (1 list), 1787-1798 (2 lists), 1799-1800 (1 list). From 1801-1850 they kept two lists each year. Filmed by the Virginia State Library, 1986, 3 rolls, FHL film #2024557 (Tax lists, 1782-1816); FHL film #2024558 (Tax lists, 1817-1838); and FHL film #2024559 (Tax lists, 1839-1850). To access the digital images, see the online FHL catalog page:
**www.familysearch.org/search/catalog/777465.**

**1782-1860.** ***Early Records, Hampshire County, Virginia, now West Virginia: Including at the Start Most of Known VA. Aside From Augusta District*** **[Printed Book & Digital Version],** by Clara McCormack Sage and Laura Elisabeth Sage Jones, printed by the Delavan Republican, Delavan, WI, 1939, 138 pages. Contains a synopsis of wills from originals up to 1860; grantees with acreage-location, wife's name, and witnesses; grantor deeds up to 1800; marriage records 1824-1828 and alphabetical arrangement of state census 1782 and 1784; Revolutionary soldiers pensions residing in the county 1835. FHL book 975.495 R2s. Also on microfilm, see FHL film #833355. For access to a digital version of this book, see the online FHL catalog page for this title, see **https://familysearch.org/search/catalog/56458.**

***1782-1907 Land Book, Berkeley County, West Virginia*** **[Microfilm & Digital Capture],** from the original records at the State Auditor's Office, Charleston, WV. Lists of landowners subject to taxation. Each book organized by surname in loose alphabetical order. Filmed by the Genealogical Society of Utah, 1968, 15 rolls, beginning with FHL film #531232 (Land book, 1782-1803). To access the digital images, see the online FHL catalog page:
**https://familysearch.org/search/catalog/58503.**

***1783-1850 Personal Property Tax Lists, Monongalia County, Virginia (now West Virginia)*** **[Microfilm & Digital Capture],** from the original records at the VA State Library, Richmond, VA. Arranged in alphabetical order by the first letter of the surname within each year. The lists give a name of person taxed or tithed, type and amount of taxable property, amount of tax, and the county statistics. Filmed by the Genealogical Society of Utah, 1992, 3 rolls, FHL film #1854104 (Tax lists, 1783-1821); FHL film #1854105 (Tax lists, 1822-1845); and FHL film #1854106 (Tax lists, 1846-1850). To access the digital images, see the online FHL catalog page:
**www.familysearch.org/search/catalog/638370.**

***1783-1900 Land Tax, Hardy County, Virginia/West Virginia*** **[Microfilm],** from a name index in the W. Guy Tetrick Collection, Clarksburg, West Virginia, original prepared by the Historical Records Survey, WPA, 1940. A typewritten list of names. Filmed by the Genealogical Society of Utah, 1958, 1 roll, FHL film #163718. **Note:** this Land Tax index from Hardy County was filmed on the same roll with the following WPA titles (indexes):

- Marriages, Hardy County: 1792-1899
- Wills and inventories, Hardy County: 1827-1898
- Marriage bonds: 1833-1851
- Wills, Hardy County: 1785-1900
- Inventories, Hardy County: 1786-1899
- Births, Hardy County: 1883-1885

**1784-1799.** ***Land Owners, Berkeley County*** **[Microfilm & Digital Capture],** an index prepared by the Historical Records Survey, WPA, 1940. Includes Berkeley County index to wills, inventories, sale bills, etc., a typewritten list of names only, arranged by year. Filmed by the Genealogical Society of Utah, 1958, 1 roll, FHL film #249959. To access the digital images, see the online FHL catalog page:
**www.familysearch.org/search/catalog/161405.**

***1785-1850 Personal Property Tax lists, Harrison County, Virginia (now West Virginia)*** **[Microfilm & Digital Capture],** from the original records at the VA State Library, Richmond, VA. Tax lists give name of person taxed or tithed, type and amount of taxable property, amount of tax, and the county statistics. Harrison County kept one list of taxpayers per year from 1785 to 1799, they kept two lists from 1800-1850. Filmed by the Virginia State Library, 1986, 4 rolls, FHL film #2024579 (Tax lists, 1785-1808); FHL film #2024580 (Tax lists, 1809-1818); FHL film #2024581 (Tax lists, 1819-1836); and FHL film #2024582 (Tax lists, 1837-1850). To access the digital images, see the online FHL catalog page:
**www.familysearch.org/search/catalog/776151.**

**1785-1971.** ***West Virginia, Marriages Index*** **[Online Database],** indexed at the Ancestry.com website. Source: FamilySearch extracts from county records on microfilm at the Family History Library. Each record includes the name of the bride and groom, date and place of marriage, and other information may be

included. The source (FHL film number) is given. This database has 2,887,474 records:
**http://search.ancestry.com/search/db.aspx?dbid=2538.**

**1787.** ***The 1787 Census of Virginia: An Accounting of the Name of Every White Male Tithable Over 21 Years, the Number of White Males Between 16 & 21 Years, the Number of Slaves Over 16 & Those Under 16 Years, Together With a Listing of Their Horses, Cattle & Carriages, and Also the Names of all Persons to Whom Ordinary Licenses and Physician's Licenses Were Issued*** **[Printed Book],** compiled by Netti Schreiner-Yantis and Florene Speakman Love. Published by Genealogical Books in Print, Springfield, VA, 1987, 3 vols. Includes records presently in the states of Kentucky and West Virginia. FHL book 975.5 R4sn.

***1787-1850 Personal Property Tax Lists, Randolph County, Virginia (now West Virginia)*** **[Microfilm & Digital Capture],** from the original records at the VA State Library, Richmond, VA. Lists 1787-1802 are arranged in alphabetical order by the first letter of the first or given name within each year. Lists 1803-1850 are arranged in alphabetical order by the first letter of the surname within each year. Lists give name of person taxed or tithed, type and amount of taxable property, amount of tax, and the county statistics. Filmed by the Genealogical Society of Utah, 1992, 2 rolls, beginning with FHL film #1905702 (Tax lists 1787-1829); and FHL film #1905703 (Tax lists 1830-1850). To access the digital images, see the online FHL catalog page:
**www.familysearch.org/search/catalog/694612.**

**1788-1802.** ***Hampshire County, Virginia (now West Virginia): Volume I-Minute Book Abstracts*** **[Online Database],** indexed at the Ancestry.com website. Source: Vicki Bidinger Horton's book, same title, publ. 2001. This database has 132 pages. See
**http://search.ancestry.com/search/db.aspx?dbid=49178.**

***1789-1850 Personal Property Tax Lists, Pendleton County, Virginia (now West Virginia)*** **[Microfilm & Digital Capture],** from the original records at the VA State Library, Richmond, VA. Arranged in alphabetical order by the first letter of the surname for each year. Lists give name of person taxed or tithed, type and amount of taxable property, amount of tax, and the county statistics. Filmed by the Genealogical Society of Utah, 1992, 3 rolls, FHL film #1870195 (Tax lists, 1789-1816); FHL film #1870196 (Tax lists, 1817-1845); and FHL film #1870187 (Tax lists, 1846-1850). To access the digital images, see the online FHL catalog page:
**www.familysearch.org/search/catalog/637428.**

**1791.** ***Kanawha County Land Owners in 1791*** **[Online Database],** indexed at the RootsWeb site for Kanawha Co WV. See
**www.rootsweb.ancestry.com/~wvkanawh/1791lnd.htm.**

**1791-1904.** ***West Virginia Newspaper Archives*** **[Online Databases],** digitized and indexed newspapers at the GenealogyBank website, for Charles Town, Charleston, Martinsburg, Shepherdstown, and Wheeling. See
**www.genealogybank.com/explore/newspapers/all/usa/west-virginia**

**1792.** ***Kanawha County Tithables in 1792*** **[Online Database],** list taken from *History of Charleston and Kanawha County West Virginia* (Laidley, 1911). Indexed at the RootsWeb website for Kanawha Co WV. See
**www.rootsweb.ancestry.com/~wvkanawh/1792tith.htm.**

***1793-1801 Tax Lists, Kanawha County, West Virginia*** **[Online Database],** indexed at the GenealogyTrails website.
- For the 1793 tax list, see
**http://genealogytrails.com/wva/kanawha/1793taxlist.html.**
- For the 1796 tax list, see
**http://genealogytrails.com/wva/kanawha/1796taxlist.html.**
- For the 1801 tax list, see
**http://genealogytrails.com/wva/kanawha/1801taxlist.html.**

***1797-1851 Personal Property Tax Lists, Brooke County, Virginia (now West Virginia)*** **[Microfilm & Digital Capture],** from the original records at the VA State Library, Richmond, VA. Tax lists give name of person taxed or tithed, type and amount of taxable property, amount of tax, and the county statistics. Brooke County kept two taxpayer lists per year. Filmed by the Virginia State Library, 1986, 3 rolls, FHL film #2024492 (Tax lists, 1797-1804); FHL film #2024493 (Tax lists, 1805-1829); and FHL film #2024494 (Tax lists, 1830-1851). To access the digital images, see the online FHL catalog page:
**www.familysearch.org/search/catalog/776821.**

***1797-1899 Records, Pendleton County, Virginia/West Virginia*** **[Microfilm & Digital Capture],** from the original typescripts at the Pendleton County Clerk's

Office, Franklin, WV, includes Births, 1853-1862; deaths, 1853-1892; land owners; 1789-1804; voters, 1790-1797; surveys, 1789-1797; marriages, 1843-1899; and wills, etc., 1791-1818, 1825-1899. See FHL film #464975. To access the digital images, see the online FHL catalog page:
**www.familysearch.org/search/catalog/232224.**

***1799-1850 Personal Property Tax Lists, Monroe County, Virginia (now West Virginia)* [Microfilm & Digital Capture],** from the original records at the VA State Library, Richmond, VA. Arranged in alphabetical order by the first letter of the surname within each year. Lists give name of person taxed or tithed, type and amount of taxable property, amount of tax, and the county statistics. Filmed by the Genealogical Society of Utah, 1992, 2 rolls, FHL film #1854107 (Tax lists, 1799-1834); and FHL film #1854482 (Tax list, 1835-1850). To access the digital images, see the online FHL catalog page:
**www.familysearch.org/search/catalog/637416.**

**1800. *Virginians in 1800, Counties of West Virginia* [Printed Book],** by Steven A. Bridges, published by the author, Trumbull, CT, 1987, 167 pages. Includes name lists taken from tax assessment lists of Virginia counties that became West Virginia. See FHL book 975.4 R4b.

**1800-1814. *Hampshire County [West] Virginia Personal Property Tax Lists* [Online Database],** indexed at the Ancestry.com website. Source: Vicki Bidinger Horton's book, same title, publ. 2002. This database has over 20,000 names. See
**http://search.ancestry.com/search/db.aspx?dbid=49177.**

***1801-1850 Personal Property Tax Lists, Wood County, Virginia (now West Virginia)* [Microfilm & Digital Capture],** from the original records at the VA State Library, Richmond, VA. Tax lists give name of person taxed or tithed, type and amount of taxable property, amount of tax, and the county statistics. Wood County kept two taxpayers lists per year. Filmed by the Virginia State Library, 1986, 3 rolls, FHL film #2026409 (Tax lists, 1801-1830); FHL film #2026410 (Tax lists, 1831-1844); and FHL film #2026411 (Tax lists, 1845-1850). To access the digital images, see the online FHL catalog page:
**www.familysearch.org/search/catalog/777222.**

***1804 Muster Roll, Monongalia County* [Online Database],** indexed at the USGenWeb Archives website for Monongalia Co WV. See
**http://files.usgwarchives.net/wv/monongalia/military/1804mil.txt.**

**1804-1938. *West Virginia, Births Index* [Online Database],** indexed at the Ancestry.com website. Source: FamilySearch extracts from county records on microfilm at the Family History Library. Each record includes a name, birth date, and birthplace. Parents names may be included. The source (FHL film number) is given. This database has 3,629,631 records. See
**http://search.ancestry.com/search/db.aspx?dbid=2537.**

**1810. *A Supplement to the 1810 Census of Virginia: Tax Lists of the Counties for Which the Census is Missing* [Printed Book],** transcribed and edited by Netti Schreiner-Yantis, published by Genealogical Books in Print, Springfield, VA, 1971, 324 pages. Includes tax lists for the lost (West Virginia) counties of Cabell, Greenbrier, Hardy, and Tazewell. See FHL book 975.5 R4s.

***1811-1850 Personal Property Tax Lists, Ohio County, Virginia (now West Virginia)* [Microfilm & Digital Capture],** from the original records at the VA State Library, Richmond, VA. Arranged in alphabetical order by the first letter of the surname for each year. Lists give name of person taxed or tithed, type and amount of taxable property, amount of tax, and the county statistics. Some of the census years have two lists, one for the upper district and one for the lower district. Filmed by the Genealogical Society of Utah, 1992, 3 rolls, FHL film #1870185 (Tax lists, 1811-1814); FHL film #1870186 (Tax lists, 1815-1831); and FHL film #1870187 (Tax lists, 1832-1850). To access the digital images, see the online FHL catalog page:
**www.familysearch.org/search/catalog/637425.**

**1814-1991. *West Virginia Naturalization Records* [Online Database],** indexed at the FamilySearch.org website. Source: WV State Archives. The collection consists of a variety of naturalization records for 32 of 55 West Virginia Counties. Records include declarations of intention, petitions, oaths of allegiance, certificates of naturalization, registers of naturalizations granted and/or denied, card files of naturalization, naturalization orders, lists of naturalized citizens, naturalization dockets, etc. Counties included are Barbour, Berkeley, Brooke, Clay, Fayette, Gilmer, Greenbrier, Hampshire, Hancock, Hardy, Harrison, Lewis, Logan, Marion, Mason, McDowell, Mineral, Mingo, Monongalia, Nicholas, Ohio, Pocahontas, Preston, Raleigh, Randolph, Roane, Summers, Tucker, Upshur, Wetzel, Wood, and Wyoming. This database has 64,939 records. See
**https://familysearch.org/search/collection/1909003.**

- See also, ***West Virginia, Naturalization Records, 1814-1991*** **[Online Database],** digitized and indexed at the Ancestry.com website. Source: FamilySearch extractions from county records on microfilm at the Family History Library in Salt Lake City. The collection is organized by county. Each county includes declarations of intention, naturalization certificates, and naturalization petitions. This database has 61,585 records. See
**http://search.ancestry.com/search/db.aspx?dbid=60233.**

***1815 Directory of Virginia Landowners (and Gazetteer)*** **[Printed Book],** abstracted by Roger G. Ward, published by Iberian Publishing Co., Athens, GA, 1997-2000, 6 vols. Arranged in alphabetical order within each county. Contents: vol. 5 & 6 are for areas of present West Virginia: vol. 5: Southwest region and vol. 6: Northwest region Includes given name, personal identifiers (if any); location/place-name of land; and miles/direction from the 1815 courthouse. FHL book 975 E4w, v. 1-6.

**1816-1923.** ***Hampshire County Records, Virginia/West Virginia*** **[Online Database],** indexed at the Ancestry.com website. Source: Vicki Bidinger Horton's book, same title, publ. 2000. This database has 210 pages. See
**http://search.ancestry.com/search/db.aspx?dbid=49176.**

**1817-1823.** ***Hampshire County, Virginia (now, West Virginia): Volume II – Minute Book Abstracts*** **[Online Database],** indexed at the Ancestry.com website. Source: Vicki Bidinger Horton's book, same title, publ. 2001. This database has 106 pages. See
**http://search.ancestry.com/search/db.aspx?dbid=49179.**

**1840.** ***List of Taxable Property in the Lower District of Kanawha County for the Year 1840. William C. Wilson, Commissioner of Revenue in Said District*** **[Online Database],** Includes names of persons chargeable with tax, Slaves 12 years & over, Horses, Mares, Colts, Mules, and Pleasure Carriages, State Coaches, Jersey Wagons, or Carryalls, and Value with Harness. Indexed at the RootsWeb site for Kanawha Co WV.
- For surnames, A-H, see
**www.rootsweb.ancestry.com/~wvkanawh/Tax/1840.html**
- For surnames, J-W, see
**www.rootsweb.ancestry.com/~wvkanawh/Tax/1840p2.html.**

**1844-1875.** ***Naturalization Petitions of the U.S. District Court for the Northern District of West Virginia (Wheeling)*** **[Microfilm & Digital Capture],** from the originals at the National Archives, Philadelphia, PA. Includes index. Filmed by the Genealogical Society of Utah, 1990, 2 rolls, FHL film #1704292-3. To access the digital images, see the online FHL catalog page:
**www.familysearch.org/search/catalog/575516.**

***1848-1850 Personal Property Tax Lists, Putnam County, Virginia (now West Virginia)*** **[Microfilm & Digital Capture],** from the original records at the VA State Library, Richmond, VA. Lists give name of person taxed or tithed, type and amount of taxable property, amount of tax, and the county statistics. Filmed by the Genealogical Society of Utah, 1992, 1 roll, FHL film #1905702. To access the digital images, see the online FHL catalog page:
**www.familysearch.org/search/catalog/694610.**

***1850-1880 Mortality Schedules for Virginia Counties Now in West Virginia*** **[Microfilm & Digital Capture],** from the state copies, 1850, 1860, 1870, & 1880 Mortality Schedules, filmed by WV Archives & History, 1974, 2 rolls, FHL film #944493-4. To access the digital images, see the online FHL catalog page:
**www.familysearch.org/search/catalog/330880.**

**1853-1928.** ***West Virginia Births and Christenings*** **[Online Database],** indexed at the FamilySearch.org website. Name index to birth, baptism, and christening records from microfilm at the Family History Library. This database has 410,186 records. See
**https://familysearch.org/search/collection/1708695.**

**1853-1930.** ***West Virginia Births*** **[Online Database],** indexed at the FamilySearch.org website. Name index to county birth records, extracted by FamilySearch indexers from the original records on microfilm at the Family History Library. This database has 1,289,392 records. See
**https://familysearch.org/search/collection/1417341**

**1853-1970.** ***West Virginia Deaths*** **[Online Database],** indexed at the FamilySearch.org website. FamilySearch Description: "Name index of West Virginia statewide and county death records. The statewide death index covers years 1917-1956 and includes all 55 West Virginia counties. The county deaths index covers years 1853-1970. Data is searchable for all state and county records. However, records within each county may not be available for the full year range." This database has 2,408,098 records. See **https://familysearch.org/search/collection/1417434.**

**1853-1973.** ***West Virginia, Deaths Index*** **[Online Database],** indexed at the Ancestry.com website. Source: FamilySearch extracts from county records on microfilm at the Family History Library. Each record includes the name of the deceased, date and place of death, other information, and the FHL film number. This database has 2,446,976 records. See
**http://search.ancestry.com/search/db.aspx?dbid=2568.**

***1854-1932. West Virginia Marriages*** **[Online Database],** indexed at the FamilySearch.org website. Name index to marriage records from microfilm at the Family History Library. This database has 200,367 records. See
**https://familysearch.org/search/collection/1708701.**

***1854-1932. West Virginia Deaths and Burials*** **[Online Database],** indexed at the FamilySearch.org website. Name index to death and burial records from microfilm at the Family History Library. This database has 48,702 records. See
**https://familysearch.org/search/collection/1708700.**

***1859 Directory of the Monongahela and Youghiogheny Valleys*** **[Microfiche],** filmed by Research Publications, Woodbridge, CT, 1980-1984, FHL fiche #6044147.

**1860-1890.** ***West Virginia, Compiled Census and Census Substitutes Index*** **[Online Database],** indexed at the Ancestry.com website. Originally edited by Ronald Jackson, Accelerated Indexing Systems, Salt Lake City. This collection contains the following indexes: 1860 Federal Census Index; 1870 Federal Census Index; 1890 Veterans Schedules. This database has 111,809 records. See
**http://search.ancestry.com/search/db.aspx?dbid=3580.**

***1861-1865. West Virginia Civil War Service Records of Union Soldiers*** **[Online Database],** indexed at the FamilySearch.org website. Source: National Archives microfilm series M508. Includes card abstracts of entries relating to the soldier as found in original muster rolls, returns, rosters, payrolls, appointment books, hospital registers, prison registers and rolls, parole rolls, inspection reports; and the originals relating solely to the particular soldier. This database has 686,688 records. See
**https://familysearch.org/search/collection/1932429.**

**1862-1865.** ***Register of Persons Who Have Taken and Subscribed to…by an Ordinance for the Reorganization of the State Government*** **[Microfilm & Digital Capture],** from the original records at the Arlington County Courthouse, Arlington, VA. In 1861, representatives from 34 counties in Virginia met in Wheeling, Virginia (now West Virginia) to vote against seceding from the Union. Many people in these counties made oaths of loyalty to the government reaffirming their citizenship in the United States. This register is a list of people who did this, the same people who declared their government the "Restored Government of Virginia" (the opposition to the government which had approved Virginia's seceding from the United States and joining the new Confederate State of American). The seat of the "Restored government" was in Wheeling but was moved in 1863 to the city of Alexandria when Wheeling became part of the state of West Virginia. (Alexandria County was renamed Arlington County in 1920). Filmed by the Virginia State Library, 1 roll, FHL film #1902946. To access the digital images, see the online FHL catalog page: **www.familysearch.org/search/catalog/1129583.**

**1862-1866.** ***Internal Revenue Assessment Lists for West Virginia*** **[Microfilm & Digital Capture],** from the originals at the National Archives. Washington, DC. Includes an index of what counties are included in each district for each year. Contents: DISTRICT 1 - Established 10 Oct. 1862 with Brooke, Hancock, Marion, Marshall, Ohio, Pleasants, Preston, Taylor Tyler & Wetzel counties. Reorganized 3 May 1865 with Brooke, Calhoun, Doddridge, Gilmer, Hancock, Harrison, Marion, Marshall, Ohio, Pleasants, Ritchie, Roane, Tyler, Wetzel & Wirt counties. Louis County transferred to District 1 on 1 Aug. 1865 and Wood County on Mar. 14, 1866. DISTRICT 2 - Established 10 Oct 1862 with Barbour, Braxton, Cabell, Calhoun, Clay, Kanawha, Lewis, Mason, Putnam, Randolph, Ritchie, Roane, Tucker, Upshur, Webster, Wirt & Wood counties. Reorganized 3 May 1865 with Barbour, Berkeley, Hampshire, Hardy, Jefferson, Lewis, Monongalia, Morgan, Pendleton, Pocahontas, Preston, Randolph, Taylor, Tucker, Upshur & Webster counties. Marion County transferred here 1 Aug. 1865. DISTRICT 3 - Established 3 May 1865 with Boone, Braxton, Cabell, Clay, Fayette, Greenbrier, Jackson, Kanawha, Logan, McDowell, Mason, Mercer, Monroe, Nicholas, Putnam, Raleigh, Wayne, Wood and Wyoming counties. Filmed by the National Archives, 1972, series M0795, 4 rolls, beginning with FHL #1578241 (District 1). To access the digital images, see the online FHL catalog page:
**https://familysearch.org/search/catalog/572854.**

**1863-1900.** ***West Virginia Marriage Records*** **[Online Database],** indexed at the Ancestry.com website. Source: Jordan Dodd, compiled from county records on microfilm at the Family History Library in Salt Lake City, UT. This database has 178,740 records. See **http://search.ancestry.com/search/db.aspx?dbid=4484.**

**1864-1865.** ***Annual report of the Adjutant General of the State of West Virginia*** **[Online Database],** indexed at the Ancestry.com website. Source: Report, same title, publ. Wheeling, 1866. Organized by regiments, these are the official rosters of West Virginia units of the Civil War, See **http://search.ancestry.com/search/db.aspx?dbid=31411.**

**1870.** ***West Virginia Federal Census: Population Schedules*** **[Microfilm & Digital Capture],** from the originals at the National Archives, Washington, DC. Filmed by the National Archives, 1962, 1968, 24 rolls, beginning with FHL film #553183. To access the digital images, see the online FHL catalog page: **www.familysearch.org/search/catalog/698926.**

**1880.** ***West Virginia, 1880 Federal Census: Soundex and Population Schedules*** **[Microfilm & Digital Capture],** from the originals at the National Archives, Washington, DC. Filmed by the National Archives, c1969, 50 rolls, beginning with FHL film #1255399. To access the digital images (Population Schedules), see the online FHL catalog page: **www.familysearch.org/search/catalog/676537.**

**1883 History.** See ***History of Monongalia County, West Virginia: From its First Settlement to the Present Time, with Numerous Biographical & Family Sketches*** **[Online Database],** a complete online book at the RootsWeb site for Monongalia Co WV. See **www.rootsweb.ancestry.com/~wvmonong/history/1883ch00.htm.**

**1888-1893.** ***Wheeling, West Virginia Directories*** **[Online Database],** indexed at the Ancestry.com website. Source: W. L. Callin's directories for 1888, 1891, and 1893. This database has 49,846 records. See **http://search.ancestry.com/search/db.aspx?dbid=4698.**

**1900.** ***West Virginia 1900 Federal Census: Soundex and Population Schedules*** **[Microfilm & Digital Capture],** filmed by the Census Bureau, c1943, 115 rolls, beginning with FHL film #1241755. To access the digital images (Population Schedules), see the online FHL catalog page: **www.familysearch.org/search/catalog/655035.**

**1908-1938. Declarations of Intention [Microfilm & Digital Capture],** from Naturalization records of the US District Court, Northern District originals located at the federal building, Elkins, WV. To access the digital images, see the online FHL catalog page: **www.familysearch.org/search/catalog/304943.**

**1910.** ***West Virginia 1910 Federal Census: Soundex and Population Schedules*** **[Microfilm & Digital Capture],** filmed by the Census Bureau, c1943, 132 rolls, beginning with FHL film #1375689. To access the digital images (Population Schedules), see the online FHL catalog page: **www.familysearch.org/search/catalog/646888.**

**1920.** ***West Virginia 1920 Federal Census: Soundex and Population Schedules*** **[Microfilm & Digital Capture],** filmed by the Census Bureau, c1943, 137 rolls, beginning with FHL film #1821947. To access the digital images (Population Schedules), see the online FHL catalog page: **www.familysearch.org/search/catalog/558335.**

**1921-1969.** ***West Virginia, Order Sons of Italy in America, Lodge Records*** **[Online Database],** indexed at the Ancestry.com website.
This database has 3,642 records. See **http://search.ancestry.com/search/db.aspx?dbid=2587.**

**1926-1928.** ***Preliminary Form for Petition for Naturalization (U.S. District Court, West Virginia: Northern District)*** **[Microfilm & Digital Capture],** from originals at the Federal Building, Elkins, WV. Filmed by the Genealogical Society of Utah, 1987, 1 roll, FHL film #1481147. To access the digital images, see the online FHL catalog page: **www.familysearch.org/search/catalog/303833.**

**1929-1957.** ***Petitions Granted (U.S. District Court, West Virginia: Northern District)*** **[Microfilm & Digital Capture],** from originals at the Federal Building, Elkins, WV. Filmed by the Genealogical Society of Utah, 1987, 1 roll, FHL film #1481150. To access the digital images, see the online FHL catalog page: **www.familysearch.org/search/catalog/304954.**

**1930.** ***West Virginia 1930 Federal Census: Soundex and Population Schedules*** **[Microfilm & Digital Capture],** filmed by the Census Bureau, c1943, 73 rolls, beginning with FHL film #2342260.

To access the digital images (Population Schedules), see the online FHL catalog page:
**www.familysearch.org/search/catalog/1037538.**

**1931-1970.** ***West Virginia, Marriage Index*** **[Online Database],** indexed at the Ancestry.com website. Source: various public records sources. Each record includes a name, spouse's name, marriage date and place. This database has 57,528 records. See
**http://search.ancestry.com/search/db.aspx?dbid=61032.**

**1940.** ***West Virginia, 1940 Federal Census: Population Schedules*** **[Digital Capture],** from the original records held by the Bureau of the Census in the 1940s. After microfilming, Congress allowed the Census Bureau to destroy the originals to free up space for WWII-related files. In 2012, the microfilm was digitized by the National Archives. To access the digital images for West Virginia only, see the online FHL catalog page:
**https://familysearch.org/search/catalog/2057760.**

**1940 Federal Census Finding Aids [Online Database].** The National Archives prepared a special website online with a detailed description of the 1940 federal census. Included at the site are descriptions of location finding aids, such as Enumeration District maps, Geographic Descriptions of Census Enumeration Districts, and a list of 1940 City Directories available at the National Archives. The finding aids are all linked to other National Archives sites. The National Archives website also has a link to 1940 Search Engines using Stephen P. Morse's "One-Step" system for finding a 1940 E.D. or street address conversion. See
**www.archives.gov/research/census/1940/general-info.html#questions.**

SERIAL NUMBER 602 | 1. NAME (Print) RAYMOND CARR | ORDER NUMBER 1829
2. ADDRESS (Print) ELKINS, RANDOLPH, W.VA
3. TELEPHONE None | 4. AGE IN YEARS 25 | DATE OF BIRTH Mar. 25, 1915 | 5. PLACE OF BIRTH Nymes, West Virginia | 6. COUNTRY OF CITIZENSHIP U.S.A.
7. NAME OF PERSON WHO WILL ALWAYS KNOW YOUR ADDRESS Mrs Nola Jane Carr | 8. RELATIONSHIP OF THAT PERSON Wife
9. ADDRESS OF THAT PERSON Elkins, Randolph, W. Va.
10. EMPLOYER'S NAME W.P.A. Project
11. PLACE OF EMPLOYMENT OR BUSINESS Romney — Romney, Hampshire, W. Va.
I AFFIRM THAT I HAVE VERIFIED ABOVE ANSWERS AND THAT THEY ARE TRUE.
REGISTRATION CARD D. S. S. Form 1 — Raymond Carr

REGISTRAR'S REPORT
DESCRIPTION OF REGISTRANT

| RACE | | HEIGHT (Approx.) | WEIGHT (Approx.) | COMPLEXION | |
|---|---|---|---|---|---|
| White | V | 5' 11" | 164 | Sallow | |
| | | EYES | HAIR | Light | |
| Negro | | Blue | Blonde | Ruddy | |
| | | Gray | Red | Dark | V |
| Oriental | | Hazel | Brown | Freckled | |
| | | Brown V | Black V | Light brown | |
| Indian | | Black | Gray | Dark brown | |
| | | | Bald | Black | |
| Filipino | | | | | |

Other obvious physical characteristics that will aid in identification Two fingers missing on right hand

I certify that my answers are true; that the person registered has read or has had read to him his own answers; that I have witnessed his signature or mark and that all of his answers of which I have knowledge are true, except as follows:

Mary Margaret Jones (Signature of registrar)
Registrar for 7 Elkins W. Va.
Date of registration Oct 16, 1940

LOCAL BOARD, SELECTIVE SERVICE
OCT 24 1940
RANDOLPH COUNTY, WEST VIRGINIA
(The stamp of the Local Board having jurisdiction of the registrant shall be placed in the above space.)

**1940-1945.** See ***West Virginia, World War II Draft Registration Cards*** **[Digital Capture],** from the originals held by the National Archives facility in St. Louis, MO. The index cards were digitized in alphabetical order. To access the digital images, see the online FHL catalog page:
**www.familysearch.org/search/catalog/2659405.**

**1941.** ***West Virginia Cemetery Readings*** **[Online Database],** indexed at the Ancestry.com website. Source: Historical Records Survey project of the WPA, 1939. Each entry provides the decedent's name, birth date, death date, living relative, and survey date. District and name of cemetery are also included, along with a link to a detailed description of the cemetery. This database has 5,218 records. See
**http://search.ancestry.com/search/db.aspx?dbid=4266.**

**1943-1954.** ***Naturalization Records (U.S. District Court, West Virginia: Northern District)*** **[Microfilm & Digital Capture],** from the originals at the Federal Building, Elkins, WV. Includes index with each volume. These are bound loose papers and not in date order. Includes Petitions, Declarations, and Naturalization Certificates. Filmed by the Genealogical Society of Utah, 1987, 2 rolls, FHL film #1481147-8. To access the digital images, see the online FHL catalog page:
**www.familysearch.org/search/catalog/304919.**

**1999-Current. West** ***Virginia Recent Newspaper Obituaries*** **[Online Database],** digitized and indexed newspaper obituaries at the GenealogyBank website, including newspapers from Berkeley, Berkeley Springs, Bluefield, Charleston, Fairmont, Gilbert, Huntington, Keyser, Logan, Madison, Montgomery, Oak Hill, Pineville, Point Pleasant, Princeton, Ravenswood, Ripley, and Williamson. See
**www.genealogybank.com/explore/obituaries/all/usa/west-virginia.**

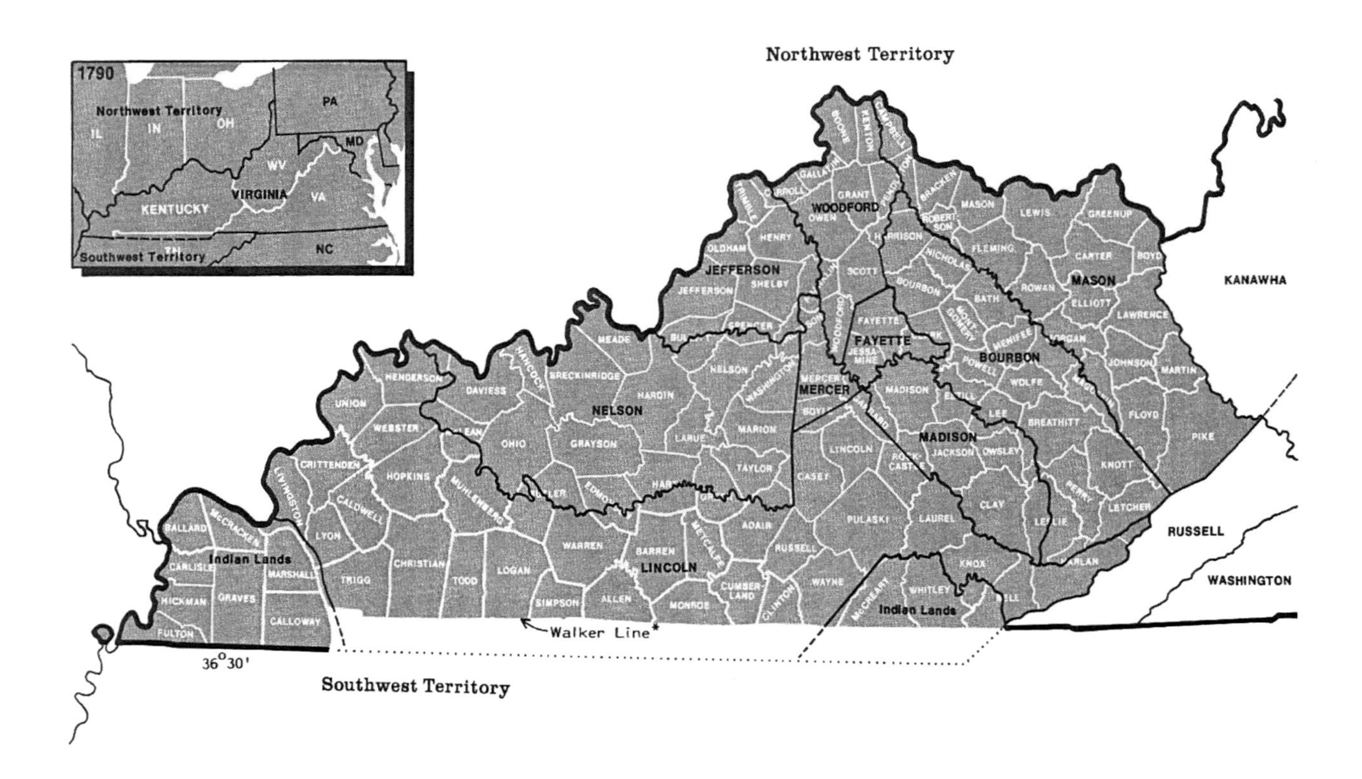


**Kentucky • 1790 (as part of Virginia).** Shown in black are the 1790 Virginia counties comprising the Federal Circuit Court District of Kentucky. Shown in white are the current 120 Kentucky counties. The area labeled as "Indian Lands" on this map was part of the Chickasaw Cession of 1818. For a detailed map showing that Indian Cession, see **http://usgwarchives.net/maps/cessions/ilcmap54.htm.** (Royce Map, Cession No. 100, Map No. 54). ***Notes:** Walker Line: The Kentucky-Tennessee boundary, intended to be Latitude 36°30' North, was run too far north in 1779-1780 by Virginia surveyors. Kentucky finally accepted this erroneous Walker Line in early 1820, but significant parts of the boundary remained uncertain until a resurvey completed in 1859. Some settlers in the disputed strip were unsure in which state they lived. By contrast, the Kentucky-Tennessee line west of the Tennessee River was surveyed in 1819 essentially on 36°30'. The 1790 Federal Census was taken in the 13 original states, plus Vermont (a state in 1791). The 1790 divisions were based on the 16 US Circuit Court boundaries, which matched up with one circuit court for each state except for Massachusetts and Virginia, both having two US Court districts. Massachusetts had a second US Court district with boundaries that matched the area of Maine (a state in 1820). Virginia had a second US Court district with boundaries that matched the area of Kentucky (a state in 1792). **Census losses:** the Kentucky 1790 and 1800 federal censuses were lost. Open to the public are those from 1810-1940 (with the exception of the 1890, lost for all states). The 1950 federal census name lists open to the public in 2022. **Map Source:** Page 122, ***Map Guide to the U.S. Federal Censuses, 1790-1920***, by William Thorndale and William Dollarhide.

# Kentucky

## Censuses & Substitute Name Lists

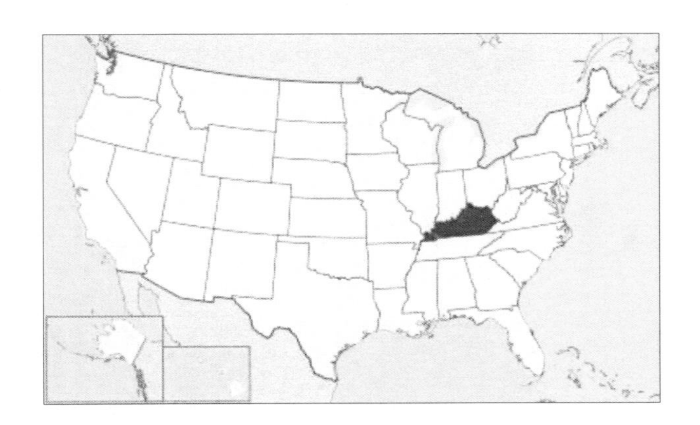

### Historical Timeline for Kentucky, 1541-1934

**1541.** Spanish conquistador Hernando DeSoto visited present Kentucky. Accounts of his expedition described the Indians native to the western region of Kentucky between the Tennessee and Mississippi Rivers. Veterans of the 1532-1535 battles with the Inca Indians of South America, DeSoto and his men were the first Europeans to travel inland within North America. Starting in 1539 from Havana, they landed on the west coast of present Florida, passing through the central areas of Georgia, the Carolinas, Alabama, Tennessee, Kentucky, Mississippi, and Arkansas. Looking for gold and a route to China, his party began with some 620 men, 500 beef cattle, 250 horses and 200 pigs. After three years exploring the area from present Georgia to Arkansas, DeSoto died from fever and was buried in the Mississippi River at a point south of present Memphis. About 300 men of the DeSoto party managed to survive and eventually made their way to Mexico City.

**1739.** Captain Charles de Longueuil was a commander of a French-Canadian military expedition against the Indians along the Ohio River. During the expedition, he discovered the region of Big Bone Lick, now Boone County, Kentucky.

**1750.** Dr. Thomas Walker, a physician from Virginia, explored the Kentucky region via the Cumberland River. His party of five men were the first Englishmen to see the area. They were also the first to erect a cabin in the region.

**1763. Treaty of Paris** ended the French and Indian War (in Europe and Canada: the Seven Years War). France ceded land, including Kentucky, to Britain. Soon after, King George III declared the "Proclamation Line of 1763," as a way of rewarding the Indians who had helped Britain against the French. The proclamation established an Indian Reserve that stretched from the Appalachian Mountain Range to the Mississippi River.

**1768. Treaty of Fort Stanwix.** An adjustment to the Proclamation Line of 1763 was to have a dramatic impact on the area of Kentucky. The British government, led by Sir William Johnson, met with representatives of the Six Nations (the Iroquois) at Fort Stanwix (now Rome, NY). A new "Line of Property" was drawn, separating English Territory from Indian Territory. The new line extended the earlier proclamation line of the Alleghenies much further to the west. From Fort Stanwix, the division line ran to Fort Pitt (now Pittsburgh) and down the Ohio River to the Tennessee River, then into the present Kentucky and Tennessee region. The Fort Stanwix treaty line effectively ceded most of present West Virginia and all of Kentucky to the British Province of Virginia.

**1769-1772.** The Province of Virginia saw the Treaty of Fort Stanwix as an opportunity to open up settlement to its western lands. Beginning in 1769, land surveys were conducted in the Kanawha, Kentucky, and Cumberland River valleys In 1772, Fincastle County, Virginia was created. The area extended from the present western line of Virginia with West Virginia to the Mississippi River. The area included all of the present area of Kentucky. Access to Fincastle county was via the Ohio River, then to one of the tributaries into present West Virginia or Kentucky.

**1774. Lord Dunmore's War.** This was a war between the Virginia militia and the Shawnee and Mingo Indians. Due to the attacks against British colonists moving into the lands south of the Ohio River, the Royal Governor of Virginia, John Murray, 4th Earl of Dunmore, asked the Virginia House of Burgesses to declare a state of war with the hostile Indian nations. Dunmore said that Virginians needed to defend their legal right based on the 1768 Treaty of Fort Stanwix. Militia was drawn from all of Virginia, including the Kentucky region of Fincastle County. The war ended after Dunmore's victory in the Battle of Point Pleasant (mouth of the Kanawha River on the Ohio River) in October 1774. In the resulting treaty, the Indians lost the right to hunt in the area south of the Ohio River. Thus, Dunmore's War opened the way for an all-out effort to bring settlers into the western areas of Virginia.

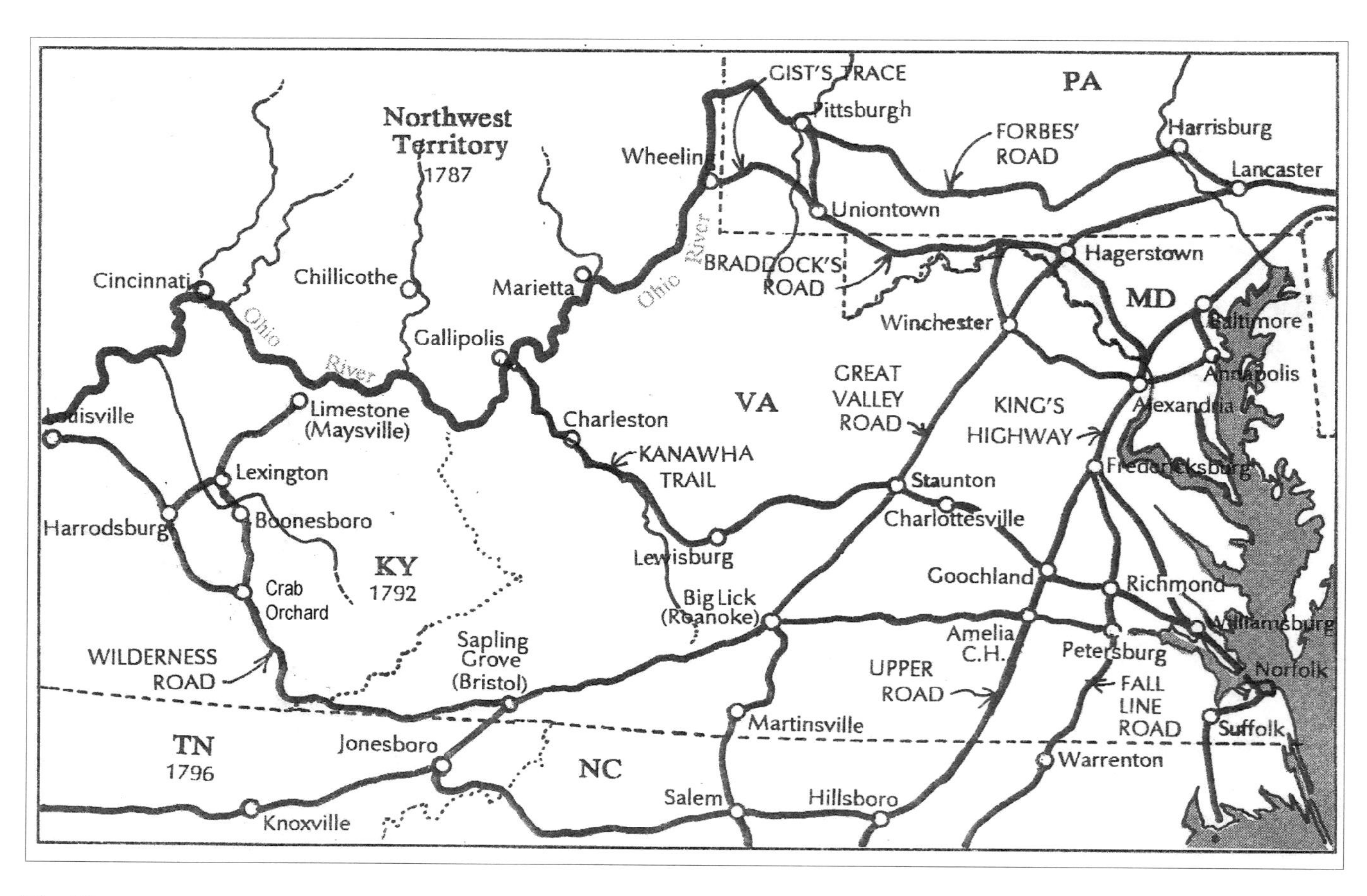


**The Way West, 1774-1796.** Before Lord Dunmore's War in 1774, the settlements of Virginia ended just west of the Great Valley Road. Beginning in 1775, Daniel Boone's Wilderness Trail opened western Virginia to thousands of settlers into present Kentucky. From 1775 to 1795, the Wilderness Trail was a single-file horse path through the mountains and became an extension of the Great Valley Road of Virginia. **Map source:** Page 13, *Map Guide to American Migration Routes, 1735-1815*, by William Dollarhide.

**1774.** Harrodstown (later Harrodsburg) was established as the first settlement in the Kentucky region. Named after James Harrod, who led a group of surveyors into the region, Harrodstown was immediately attacked by Indians and abandoned, but was resettled the following year. The city today is the county seat of Mercer County, Kentucky.

**1775.** Richard Henderson, a North Carolina judge heading up the Transylvania Company, met with three Cherokee Chiefs to purchase lands lying between the Ohio, Kentucky, and Cumberland Rivers—about 20 million acres and about half of the present area of Kentucky. It became known as The Henderson Purchase. Henderson was intent on establishing the Transylvania Colony, with hopes of gaining recognition as a proprietary British colony. However, the Transylvania Company was invalidated by the Virginia Assembly in 1776. Most of the ownership of land in the Kentucky region was reverted back to Virginia until the new state of Kentucky acquired title to any unsold land in 1792.

**1775-1783. Wilderness Trail.** In 1775, a party of 36 men and two women led by pioneer Daniel Boone blazed the Wilderness Trail to establish Fort Boonesborough in present-day Madison County. Boone was hired by Richard Henderson to establish the first settlement of the Transylvania Colony. After the initial trailhead at present Kingsport, Tennessee the trail connected to Shelby's Fort (later Sapling Grove, then Bristol, TN/VA), which became the starting point of the Wilderness Trail. The trail crossed the Cumberland Mountains via the Cumberland Gap. It is estimated that between 1775 and 1783, over 40,000 people migrated into Kentucky using the Wilderness Trail. From 1775 to 1796, the path was passable only by single-file pack teams. Daniel Boone's greatest contribution to America was the settlement of an area west of the Alleghenies. Mainly as a result of the many settlements established in the Kentucky region before the Treaty of Paris of 1783, the entire region west of the Appalachian Mountain Range to the Mississippi River was ceded by the British to the new United States of America.

**First Impressions of Kentucky**

Narrative of Felix Walker, one of Daniel Boone's road cutters on the Wilderness Trail in 1775

"On leaving that river [the Rockcastle], we had to encounter and cut our way through a country of about twenty miles, entirely covered with dead brush, which we found a difficult and laborious task. At the end of which we arrived at the commencement of a cane country, traveled about thirty miles through thick cane and reed, and as the cane ceased, we began to discover the pleasing and rapturous appearance of the plains of Kentucky. A new sky and strange earth seemed to be presented to our view. So rich a soil we had never seen before – covered with clover in full bloom, the woods were abounding with wild game – turkeys so numerous that it might be said they appeared but one flock, universally scattered in the woods...." From *Felix Walker's Narrative*, (Filson Club First Publication Series, Number 16, Louisville, 1901), pp163-64.)

**1776.** December 31st. The name Fincastle was dropped, and the area was divided into three new counties by the Commonwealth of Virginia: Kentucky County, Washington County, and Montgomery County. The boundaries of Kentucky County in 1776 matched the modern boundaries of the state of Kentucky except for the extreme western region still under control of the Chickasaw Indians.

**1780.** June 30th. The name Kentucky was dropped, and the area was carved into Fayette, Jefferson, and Lincoln counties, Virginia. Most of the settlers in those three counties, however, were in sight of the Kentucky River and still referred to their home as "Kentucky."

**1784.** The first of 10 conventions to discuss the separation of the Kentucky region from Virginia was held at Danville, Kentucky. Three main factors contributed to their desire to separate from Virginia: 1) Traveling to the state capital in Richmond was long and dangerous. 2) Any use of the local militia against the Indians required authorization from the Governor of Virginia. And 3), Virginia refused to recognize the importance of trade along the Mississippi and Ohio Rivers to Kentucky's economy.

**1789.** Perhaps a bit of folklore rather than history, Baptist minister Elijah Craig of Kentucky is said to have made the first bourbon whiskey, distilled from corn and aged in charred oak casks. Today, 95 percent of the world's bourbon is distilled and aged in Kentucky. The current population of Kentucky, about 4.5 million people, is exceeded by the 4.9 million barrels of bourbon whiskey being aged in Kentucky rack houses.

**1790.** August 2nd. The first Federal Census showed a population of 73,677 people living in the Kentucky region. African-American slaves comprised 16 percent of Kentucky's population; and slave labor was an integral part of the region, particularly in the central area with its rich farmlands. Although still part of Virginia in 1790, the Kentucky region had its own U.S. Circuit Court, the jurisdiction for all federal censuses, 1790-1870. Kentucky's 1790 circuit court district boundaries matched the present state boundaries. The 1790 census was taken in the name of "Kentucky," even though that name did not become official again until statehood two years later. Kentucky's 1790 census name lists were lost. In 1830, a federal law asked for the return of all original census manuscripts, 1790-1820 to Washington, DC, from each of the U.S. Circuit Court Clerks in the U.S., but apparently, the Kentucky Circuit Court Clerk could not comply. See the map on page 112 for additional 1790 details.

**1792.** June 1. Kentucky became the 15th state admitted to the Union. The population of Kentucky in 1792 was about 90,000 people.

**1796. Wilderness Road.** Soon after statehood the state of Kentucky began planning for the widening and grading of the Wilderness Trail to allow horse-drawn wagons to negotiate the roadway. The first wagons appeared on the road in 1796, and the Wilderness Road immediately became the primary access to the interior of Kentucky. The improved route now had a fork at Crab Orchard. One could angle right to head for Boonesboro on the original Wilderness Trail. From there, the road to Lexington continued to Limestone at the Ohio River. Or, one could angle left at Crab Orchard (on Logan's Trace) and head to Harrodsburg; and then on to Louisville at the Ohio River. By 1810, over 300,000 people had come to Kentucky by way of the Wilderness Road.

**1800.** August 4th . The second Federal Census showed a population of 220,955 people living in Kentucky, three times the 1790 total. Like the 1790, the 1800 census name lists were lost.

**1801.** An estimated 20,000 people attended the great church camp meeting at Cane Ridge (Bourbon County, Kentucky), the single largest event of the Second Great Awakening. What ensued was a period of emotional religious revivals that took place all across the country. The leaders of the revivals – the Methodists and Baptists – grew rapidly. The Christian Church, Church of Christ, and the Disciples of Christ were founded as a direct result of the revivals.

**1810.** August 6th . The third Federal Census showed a population of 406,511 people living in Kentucky, nearly double the number in 1800. The 1810 KY census was the first for which the original name lists have survived.

**1811-1812.** Western Kentucky was heavily damaged by the New Madrid earthquakes, the most intense recorded earthquakes in the contiguous United States. They caused the Mississippi River to change course and created the "Kentucky Bend," an enclave of Fulton County, Kentucky, surrounded on three sides by Missouri, and an interrupted extension of the Kentucky/Tennessee line at Latitude 36°30'.

**1818. The Jackson Purchase.** Under President Andrew Jackson, the U.S. government purchased areas of Kentucky and Tennessee from the Chickasaw Indians in the Treaty of Tuscaloosa. The portion situated in Kentucky was thereafter called "The Jackson Purchase." This was the last Indian Cession in the state of Kentucky.

**1861.** April 12th. The Civil War Began. Kentucky never seceded from the Union and was officially neutral at the beginning of the war. After a failed attempt by Confederate General Leonidas Polk to take the state of Kentucky for the Confederacy, the legislature petitioned the Union for assistance, and thereafter became solidly under Union control. The amount of local support for the North or South was reflected in the number of troops supplied to either side – Kentucky supplied 86,000 troops to the north and 40,000 troops to the south. Ironically, Kentucky was the birthplace of both the Union president, Abraham Lincoln, and the Confederate president, Jefferson Davis.

**1875**. The first Kentucky Derby was held at Churchill Downs in Louisville, Kentucky. The race still occurs annually on the first Saturday in May and is the most attended horse race in North America. The Kentucky Derby later became part of the Triple Crown with the Preakness and Belmont Stakes.

**1878.** The Hatfield-McCoy feud involved two warring families of West Virginia and Kentucky backcountry. The feud began over a pig and escalated into murder, claiming the lives of more than a dozen members of the two families. It becomes headline news around the country and compelled the two states' governors to employ state militias to restore order. The families agreed to stop fighting in 1891.

**1934.** Harland Sanders created a recipe for fried chicken for his Sanders Court & Café in Corbin, Kentucky. The restaurant was so successful that in 1936 Governor Ruby Laffoon granted Sanders the title of honorary "Kentucky Colonel." Sanders then founded Kentucky Fried Chicken in 1952.

---

## Research, Collections & Genealogy Links at the Kentucky Historical Society

The Kentucky Historical Society (KHS) dates back to 1835 and is an agency of the Kentucky state government. The History Campus in downtown Frankfurt includes the Thomas D. Clark Center for Kentucky History, the Kentucky Military History Museum, and the old (1830) State Capitol building. The campus is a mecca for genealogical researchers in Kentucky. The next best thing to visiting the History Campus in person, is to review the KHS resources available online. The primary categories identified for genealogical researchers at the Kentucky Historical Society are listed below, taken from the KHS website. In addition to the collections of the KHS, the other important Kentucky resource centers, databases, and collections are described. At the website, there are hotlinks to their subscription services, as well as links to other genealogy resource centers in Kentucky. See **http://history.ky.gov/research-genealogy/.**

## Search the Collections

• **Kentucky Historical Society Collections Catalog.** The catalog includes descriptions of books, manuscripts, photographs, oral histories, microfilm, and other genealogical resources.

• **KHS Digital Collections.** The Digital Collections is a searchable database of digital images and files from the Kentucky Historical Society's collections.

• **KHS Objects Catalog.** The object collections include everything from fine china to military weaponry. Please be aware that this database does not contain every artifact in the KHS museum collection and that records are updated frequently.

• **Civil Rights Movement in Kentucky Online Digital Media Database** is a comprehensive collection of audio and video interviews and over 10,000 pages of electronic transcripts. All material is full-text searchable and can be sorted by county, subject or by decade.

• **Pass The Word** serves as a centralized database for oral history collections publicly accessible through Kentucky libraries, museums and archives.

## Online Genealogy Resources Available at the Center for Kentucky History

Located on the second floor of the Thomas D. Clark Center for Kentucky History, the Kentucky Historical Society's Martin F. Schmidt Research Library is one stop shopping for over 90,000 published works, over 15,000 reels of microfilm, over 10,000 cubic feet of archival records including genealogical vertical files, manuscripts, photographs, maps and atlases, and over 9,000 oral history interviews. This is the premier genealogical research library in the state of Kentucky. The in-house computers provide access to the following resources:

• **Ancestry Library Edition.** This is a popular genealogy subscription site, with access to a comprehensive and diverse collection of genealogical databases, including U.S. Census images.

• **Louisville Courier Journal Online.** Search articles from the Louisville Courier Journal from 1830-1922. From ProQuest Historical Newspapers.

• **American Periodicals.** Contains periodicals published between 1740 and 1940, including special interest and general magazines, literary and professional journals, children's and women's magazines and many other historically significant periodicals. From ProQuest.

• **Heritage Quest Online.** Digitized from the popular UMI Genealogy and Local History collection on microfiche, this online database is an essential collection of unique material for both genealogical hobbyists and professionals. Includes online census images and over 7.5 million pages from imaged texts. From ProQuest Information and Learning.

• **Kentucky Ancestors Online,** a free publication of the Kentucky Historical Society, features a wide range of article topics and is designed to appeal to family historians of all levels.

• **Encyclopedia Web Edition.** At the Center for Kentucky History, users have online access to the full text of this important reference work. Online subscriptions are currently available only to libraries, schools and other organizations. Users outside the Center for Kentucky History can contact their local public or school librarian for help accessing this service.

• **Kentucky Virtual Library.** Users in the Center for Kentucky History have access to all KYVL databases. Users outside the Center for Kentucky History can contact their local public or school librarian for help accessing this service.

## KHS Recommended Websites

• **Kentucky Department for Libraries and Archives (KDLA)** offers comprehensive services with access to a broad range of information and educational resources. The KDLA catalog includes descriptions and locations for Kentucky official records sets. See **http://kdla.ky.gov/Pages/default.aspx.**

• **Kentucky Land Office,** part of the Kentucky Secretary of State's Office. The website includes several searchable databases and many resources for researching land acquisition in Kentucky. See **www.sos.ky.gov**

• **The FamilySearch Internet Genealogy Service** provides access to extensive genealogical resources gathered by The Church of Jesus Christ of Latter-day Saints. This site also contains their online catalog and information about local LDS Family History Centers. See **https://familysearch.org/.**

• **Kentucky Genealogical Society (KGS).** Review the upcoming events and activities at this new website. See **www.kentuckygenealogicalsociety.org.**

• **Lexington Public Library Kentucky Room and Local History Index.** Visit their Genealogy & Local History page for details. See **www.lexpublib.org/Genealogy-Local-History**

• **Kentucky National Digital Newspaper Program (University of Kentucky Libraries),** includes lists of newspapers available online and those available on microfilm for Interlibrary Loan. See **www.uky.edu/Libraries/NDNP//**

---

## Kentucky Department for Libraries & Archives

**Online Catalog - Search KDLA WorldCat Discovery.** The KDLA Catalog is searchable thru the WorldCat service for all materials at the Kentucky Department for Libraries and Archives. See **https://kdla.ky.gov/common/Pages/WorldCatDiscovery.aspx.**

• **Kentucky Website Archives** – Archived websites of the Governor's Office and the other Constitutional Officers of the Executive Branch, the Legislative Research Commission, and the Administrative Office of the Courts. See **http://kdla.ky.gov/records/e-archives/Pages/KyWebArchive.aspx.**

### Archives Research Room – Kentucky's Historic Public Records

Holdings include Kentucky's city, county and state government records. The following examples reflect many of the valuable public records available for research:

- Birth and Death records for 1852 through 1910: (1852-1862, 1874-1879, 1891-1910)
- Birth and Death City Registers for four Kentucky cities: Covington, Lexington, Louisville, and Newport
- Death certificates for 1911-1960
- Marriage records
- Census and Military records
- Judicial records (Civil, Criminal and Court of Appeals)
- Wills and Deeds
- State Agency records

For further information, you may email the Research Room at **kdla.archives@ky.gov**. If an on-site visit is not possible, submit one of their Records Request forms. See their Professional Researchers list if you want to hire an independent professional researcher to do research for you. See the form and lists at **http://kdla.ky.gov/researchers/Pages/visitingthearchives.aspx.**

---

## Guides to Kentucky Records

***Guide to Kentucky Archival and Manuscript Collections* [Printed Book],** edited by Barbara Teague and Jane A. Minder, 2 vols., published by the Kentucky Department for Libraries and Archives, Public Records Division, 1988, 2 vols, FHL book 976.9 A3g.

***Guide to Selected Manuscripts Housed in the Division of Special Collections and Archives, Margaret I. King Library, University of Kentucky* [Printed Book],** introduction by Thomas D. Clark, compiled by Jeanne Slater Trimble, published by the University of Kentucky, 1987, 124 pages, FHL book 976.9 A3t.

***Guide to Public Vital Statistics Records in Kentucky* [Printed Book & Digital Version],** prepared by the Kentucky Historical Records Survey, Service Division, Work Projects Administration, Louisville, KY, 1942, 257 pages, FHL book 976.9 V2h. To access the digital version, see the online FHL catalog: **www.familysearch.org/search/catalog/86324.**

***Inventory of County Records of Kentucky* [Printed Book & Digital Version],** compiled by Beverly West Hathaway, published by Allstates Research, 1974, 164 pages, FHL book 976.9 A3hba. To access the digital version, see the online FHL catalog: **https://familysearch.org/search/catalog/79676.**

***Bibliography of County Resources* [Printed Book],** by the Kentucky Historical Society, Frankfort, KY, 3 vols. Contents: Vol. 1: Adair-Grayson counties. Vol. 2: Green-Mason counties. Vol. 3: Meade-Woodford counties. These bibliographies are for materials available at the Kentucky Historical Society. See FHL book 976.9 D23b.

***Kentucky: A Guide to the Bluegrass State* [Digitized Book],** by the Federal Writers' Project, WPA, 1939. Part of the American Guide Series, the Kentucky guide was sponsored by the University of Kentucky, published by Hargrove, Brace and Co, New York. During the Great Depression of the 1930s thousands of writers were hired by the Works Progress Administration to create guidebooks on all of the states in the U.S. Only a few states were actually published, and the Kentucky guidebook was probably the best one done for any state. As a primer on Kentucky history, settlement, migration, economy, or just a brush-up historical review for someone with Kentucky ancestors, this is a valuable guide book. For an online digital version of this book, see
**http://search.ancestry.com/search/db.aspx?dbid=28667.**

# Bibliography

## Kentucky Censuses & Substitutes

This bibliography identifies the available Federal Census name lists for Kentucky and adds many census substitute name lists. Together, they include Census Records, County Court Records, Directories, County Histories, State Military Lists, Tax Lists, Vital Records, and Voter Lists.

The earliest name list from the Kentucky region was for residents of Fincastle County, Virginia in 1773. Later, Kentucky County was established in 1776, an area taken from old Fincastle county, and matching the modern boundaries of the State of Kentucky (except for a western tract still under control of the Chickasaws). In 1780, the name Kentucky was dropped, and the area was divided into Fayette, Jefferson and Lincoln counties, Virginia. Any surviving name lists prior to statehood from the first counties are identified in this bibliography.

All of Kentucky's 1790 Federal Census name lists were lost. There were nine counties in the Kentucky region at the time of the 1790 census: Bourbon, Fayette, Jefferson, Lincoln, Madison, Mason, Mercer, Nelson, and Woodford counties. Substitute name lists from each of the nine counties were identified for the period 1785 to 1795, whether published in print, microfilm, or online. After statehood in 1792, all known statewide name lists for Kentucky were identified, and city or countywide name lists were included if the databases were available online.

There have been no state-sponsored censuses taken in Kentucky, but from its first year of statehood in 1792, annual statewide tax lists were authorized, and cover virtually all Kentucky counties. Full microfilm copies, online databases, and printed extracts of many of the name lists have been published. The censuses and substitute name lists begin below in chronological order:

♦ ♦ ♦ ♦ ♦

**1769-1792. *Petitions of Kentucky Inhabitants to the General Assembly of Virginia* [Online Database],** digitized and indexed at the Ancestry.com website. This database was from the work by James R. Robertson, who had gleaned the Kentucky references from the Virginia State Archives in 1914. Although the first petition was dated 1769 it was actually a request for a land grant rather than a communication by someone already an inhabitant of the Kentucky region. The first land grant holders, i.e., the first inhabitants, were listed for 1773. See
**http://search.ancestry.com/search/db.aspx?dbid=6980.**

**1773-1780. *Early Kentucky Land Records* [Printed Book]**, by Neal O. Hammon, published by the Filson Club, Louisville, 1992, 292 pages. Includes general index with names arranged in alphabetical order. FHL book 976.9 R28h.

**1773-1792. *Fincastle & Kentucky County, VA-KY: Records and History* [Printed Book],** by Michael L. Cook and Bettie A. Cummings Cook, Includes name index for each volume. Contents: Fincastle County and Kentucky County: background and history; Acts of the Virginia Legislature pertaining to Fincastle County; Acts of the Virginia Legislature pertaining to Kentucky County, and up to the time that Kentucky became a separate state; land entries from Lincoln and Jefferson counties records pertaining to Kentucky County; Fincastle County, record of surveys; Fincastle County, warrants of officers and soldiers from the Earl of Dunmore, Governor of Virginia; Fincastle County, deed book A, from 1773; Fincastle County, deed and will book B, from 1773; Fincastle County, county court order book no. 1, 1773; Fincastle County, county court order book no. 2, 1774-1776; and marriage records. Published by Cook Pub., Evansville, IN, 1987, 2 vols., FHL Book 976.9 H2cc.

**1773-2000s.** ***Kentucky GenWeb Archives*** **[Online Databases],** name lists are available for all 120 Kentucky counties. Typical county records include Bibles, Biographies, Cemeteries, Censuses, Court, Death, Deeds, Directories, Histories, Marriages, Military, Newspapers, Obituaries, Photos, Schools, Tax Lists, Wills, and more. The KYGenWeb Welcome page has links to a webpage for several categories, see **www.kygenweb.net/.**

***1774-1796 Virginia Land Grant Surveys in Kentucky*** **[Microfilm & Digital Capture],** from the originals and typescript at the Kentucky State Land Office, Frankfort, KY. Filmed by the Genealogical Society of Utah, 1962, 7 rolls, beginning with FHL film #272939 (Index to Virginia Land Grant Surveys). To access the digital images, see the online FHL catalog page: **https://familysearch.org/search/catalog/431250.**

**1774-1791.** ***Master Index, Virginia Surveys and Grants*** **[Printed Book],** compiled by Joan E. Brookes-Smith, published by the Kentucky Historical Society, 1976. This is an index to the VA/KY Land Grant items above. See FHL book 976.9 R22b. Also on microfilm, see FHL film #1320833.

**1775-1815.** ***Calendar of the Kentucky Papers of the Draper Collection of Manuscripts [Online Database],*** indexed at the Ancestry.com website. The Draper Collection resides at the Wisconsin Historical Society in Madison, WI, where Lyman Draper was a librarian and historian who gathered first-account documentation of the "Trans-Allegheny West," an area which included the western Carolinas and Virginia, some portions of Georgia and Alabama, the entire Ohio River valley, and parts of the Mississippi Valley. Draper traveled extensively and corresponded with survivors and relatives of the first settlers, beginning in the 1830s. The Draper Papers are the largest collection of first-hand accounts of the settlement of the region, with an emphasis on the last half of the 18th century. The Kentucky Papers portion of the collection is laden with documents related to Daniel Boone and his contemporaries, and the earliest settlements of the Blue Grass state. See **http://search.ancestry.com/search/db.aspx?dbid=26669.**

**1774-1989.** ***Kentucky, Wills and Probate Records*** **[Online Database],** indexed at the Ancestry.com website. Source: Ancestry extracts from KY County, District, and Probate Courts. The contents of a probate file can vary from case to case, but certain details are found in most probates, most importantly, the names and residences of beneficiaries and their relationship to the decedent. An inventory of the estate assets can reveal personal details about the deceased's occupation and lifestyle. There may also be references to debts, deeds, and other documents related to the settling of the estate. This database has 287,094. See **https://search.ancestry.com/search/db.aspx?dbid=9066.**

**1775-1825.** ***Marylanders to Kentucky*** **[Printed Book],** by Henry C. Peden, Jr., published by Family Line Publications, Westminster, MD, 1991, 202 pages, FHL book 976.9 W2p.

**1775-1860s.** ***Bourbon County, Kentucky, Biographies*** **[Online Database],** span of years derived from the notes that some biographies were for Revolutionary War soldiers, others for Civil War soldiers. Indexed at the Bourbon Co KY Biographies website. See **http://bourboncoky.info/BourbonBiographies.html.**

**1778-1781.** ***Pioneer Soldiers (Extracted from Collins' History of Kentucky)*** **[Online Database],** several name lists were presented at the USGenWeb Archives site. See **http://files.usgwarchives.net/ky/sgorin/military/pioneer/kyr-204.txt.**

**1778-1828.** ***More Marylanders to Kentucky*** **[Printed Book],** by Henry C. Peden, Jr., published by Family Line Publications, Westminster, MD, 1997, 262 pages, FHL book 976.9 W2pe

**1779-1817.** See ***Lincoln and Fayette County Land Entries, 1779-1817; Military Land Entries, 1784-1797; May's Land Entries and Index, 1779-1784*** **[Microfilm & Digital Capture]**, from the originals at the Kentucky State Land Office, Frankfort, KY. Filmed by the Genealogical Society of Utah, 1962, 6 rolls, beginning with FHL film #272974 (Lincoln Co entries 1779-1792). To access the digital images, see the online FHL catalog page: **https://familysearch.org/search/catalog/428127.**

**1780-1799.** ***Lincoln County Deeds and Marriages*** **[Microfilm & Digital Capture],** from a 39-page manuscript (source not noted). Filmed by the Genealogical Society of Utah, 1971, 1 roll, FHL film #855038. To access the digital images, see the online FHL catalog page: **www.familysearch.org/search/catalog/339558.**

**1780-1799.** ***Kentucky: Casey and Lincoln Counties' Pioneer Ancestors Born Before 1800: Featuring a Brief History of the "Cravens Cemetery" – Casey County and its Tie to Fort Boonesborough*** **[Printed Book & Digital Version],** by W.E. Rubarts, published Lexington, KY, 2011, 64 pages, FHL book 976.96 D2r. Also available on CD-ROM, see FHL CD No. 7628. For a link to a digital version of this title, see the online FHL catalog page. See **https://familysearch.org/search/catalog/2102008.**

**1780-1800s.** ***Lincoln County Kentucky, est. 1780*** **[Printed Book],** by the Lincoln Co Historical Society book committee. Includes maps, surname index, and a large family history section. Published by Turner Pub. Co., Paducah, KY, 2002, 295 pages, FHL book 976.9625 D2L.

**1780-1800s.** ***Early Lincoln County, Kentucky History*** **[Microfilm],** from the manuscript compiled and edited by Shirly Dunn, filmed by the Genealogical Society of Utah, 1972, 1 roll, FHL film #874371.

**1780-1800s.** ***Early Kentucky Settlers: The Records of Jefferson County, Kentucky*** **[Printed Book],** from the Filson Club history quarterly, published by Genealogical Publishing Co, Baltimore, MD, 1988, 505 pages. See FHL book 976.944 P28e.

**1780-1800s.** ***Jefferson County, Kentucky, Records*** **[Printed Book],** by Michael L. Cook and Bettie A. Cummings Cook, 5 vols. Includes indexes. Contents: vol. 1- County court minute books, A, 1-3. vol. 2 - County court minute books, 4-9. Vol. 3- Old chancery court case index, Plaintiff's index to case index, Bond & power of attorney books, 1-3. Vol. 4- Will books, 1-3. vol. 5. Deeds books no. 1-7. Published by Cook, Evansville, IN, 1987, FHL book 976.944 P28.

**1780-1800s.** ***Kentucky Court and Other Records: From Original Court Entries – Wills, Deeds, Orders, Suits, Church Minutes, Marriages, Old Bibles and Tombstone Inscriptions; Records from Fayette, Jefferson, and Lincoln (First Three Great Counties), Bath, Bourbon, Bracken, Clark, Fleming, Harrison, Hardin, Jessamine, Mason, Madison, Montgomery, Nicholas, Oldham, Scott, Woodford, and Warren*** **[Printed Book],** compiled by Mrs. William Breckenridge Ardery, originally published by Julia Spencer Ardery, Lexington, KY, 1932, reprinted by Genealogical Publishing Co, 1979, 257 pages, FHL book 976.9 D28awb.

**1780-1800s.** ***Kentucky Pioneer and Court Records, Abstracts of Early Wills, Deeds and Marriages from Court Houses and Records of Old Bible, Churches, Grave Yards, and Cemeteries Copied by American War Mothers, Genealogical Material Collected from Authentic Sources: Records from Anderson, Bourbon, Boyle, Clark, Estill, Fayette, Garrard, Harrison, Jessamine, Lincoln, Madison, Mercer, Montgomery, Nicholas and Woodford Counties*** **[Printed Book, Microfilm & Digital Version],** from the book compiled and published by Mrs. Harry Kennett McAdams, Lexington, KY, 1929, 382 pages, filmed by the Genealogical Society of Utah, 1968, 1 roll, FHL film #459632. For a link to a digital version of this title, see the online FHL catalog page. See **https://familysearch.org/search/catalog/85335.**

**1780-1852.** ***The History of Louisville, From its Earliest Settlement till the Year 1852*** **[Microcard & Digital Version],** by Benjamin Casseday, originally published by Hull and Brother, Louisville, KY, 1852, 255 pages; reprinted as an opaque Microcard by Lost Cause Press, Louisville, KY, 1960, 4 plates, FHL Microcard 976.9 No. 8. To access the digital images, see the online FHL catalog page: **https://familysearch.org/search/catalog/344996.**

**1780-1880.** ***History of Fayette County, Kentucky: With an Outline Sketch of the Blue Grass Region*** **[Printed Book & Digital Version],** by Robert Peter, published O.L. Baskin, Chicago, IL, 1882, 905 pages, FHL book 976.947 H2p. Also on microfilm, FHL film #824109. For a link to a digital version of this title, see the online FHL catalog page: **https://familysearch.org/search/catalog/101400.**

**1780-1901.** ***Court Orders, Minutes (Jefferson County, Kentucky)*** **[Microfilm & Digital Capture],** from the originals at the county court clerk's office, Louisville, KY. Filmed by the Genealogical Society of Utah, 1970, 28 rolls, beginning with FHL film #811569 (Orders, minutes, vol. 1-10, 1780-1813). To access the digital images, see the online FHL catalog page: **https://familysearch.org/search/catalog/128127.**

***1780-1909 Kentucky Deed Books*** **[Microfilm & Digital Capture],** from the original records at the Kentucky Historical Society, Frankfort, KY. Filmed by the society, 1966, 13 rolls, beginning with FHL film #551280 (Index, Deed Books, A-Z, 1796-1798). To access the digital images, see the online FHL catalog page: **https://familysearch.org/search/catalog/135818.**

**1780-1900s.** ***Two Hundred Years at the Falls of the Ohio: A History of Louisville and Jefferson County*** **[Printed Book],** by George H. Yater, published by the Heritage Corporation of Louisville and Jefferson County, 1979, 250 pages, FHL book # 976.944/L1 H2y.

**1781-1839.** ***Kentucky Genealogical Records & Abstracts*** **[Printed Book],** vol. 1, 1781-1839; vol. 2, 1796-1839. compiled by Sherida K. Eddlemon, published by Heritage Books, Bowie, MD, 1997. Includes early Kentucky tax lists. Surname index, each volume. FHL book 976.9 D28e v. 1 & 2.

**1782-1787**. For early tax lists of Fayette and Lincoln counties, Kentucky, see ***Virginia Tax Payers, 1782-1787, Other Than Those Published by the United States Census Bureau*** **[Printed Book],** by Augusta B. Fothergill and John Mark Naugle, published Richmond, 1940, 142 pages. Reprinted Genealogical Publishing Co., Inc., Baltimore, 1978. FHL book 975.5 R4f.

**1782-1792.** ***Virginia Land Grants, 1782-1792*** **[Microfilm & Digital Capture],** from the originals at the Kentucky State Land Office, Frankfort, KY. These are part of the land grants of Virginia transferred to Kentucky when it became a state in 1792. FHL film #1464015. To access the digital images, see the online FHL catalog page:
**www.familysearch.org/search/catalog/490041.**

**1782-1924**. ***The Kentucky Land Grants: A Systematic Index to all of the Land Grants Recorded in the State Land Office at Frankfort, Kentucky*** **[Printed Book & Digital Version]**, by Willard Rouse Jillson, published by the Filson Club, Louisville, KY, 1925, 1,844 pages. See FHL book 976.9V4. This title was digitized online at the Ancestry.com website. See
**http://search.ancestry.com/search/db.aspx?dbid=2073.**

**1782-1900s**. ***Old Kentucky Entries and Deeds: A Complete Index to all of the Earliest Land Entries, Military Warrants, Deeds and Wills of the Commonwealth of Kentucky*** **[Printed Book],** Willard Rouse Jillson, originally published by Filson Club, Louisville, KY, 1926, reprinted 1978, Genealogical Publishing Co, Baltimore, MD, 571 pages, FHL book 976.9 R23jwr.

**1783-1786.** ***First Order Book of the Supreme Court Held for the District of Kentucky*** **[Microfilm & Digital Capture],** from the originals at the University of Kentucky, Lexington, KY. Filmed by the University of KY, 1958, 1 roll, FHL film #156860. To access the digital images, see the online FHL catalog page:
**www.familysearch.org/search/catalog/421899.**

**1783-1822.** ***Circuit Court Common Law Case Files (Jefferson County, Kentucky)*** **[Microfilm & Digital Capture],** from the county court clerk's office, Louisville, KY. Filmed by the Kentucky Dept. of Archives & Libraries, 2004-2005, 27 rolls, beginning with FHL film #2372697 (Case files #54-1151, ca1783-1786). To access the digital images, see the online FHL catalog page:
**https://familysearch.org/search/catalog/1204020.**

**1783-1911.** ***Deeds, Jefferson County, Kentucky*** **[Microfilm & Digital Capture],** from the originals at the County Circuit Court, Louisville, KY. Filmed by the University of Kentucky and the KY Dept. of Archives & Libraries, 1957, 1976, 371 rolls, beginning with FHL film #1490849 ( Grantee Index, 1783-1862). To access the digital images, see the online FHL catalog page:
**https://familysearch.org/search/catalog/236979.**

**1783-1965.** ***Kentucky, County Marriage Records*** **[Online Database],** indexed at the Ancestry.com website. Source: Ancestry extractions, 2016, and certain county courthouse records. Each record may include a Name, Age at marriage, Marriage date, Marriage place, and Parents' names. This database has 2,961,398 records. See
**https://search.ancestry.com/search/db.aspx?dbid=61372.**

**1785-1799.** ***List of Tithables of Nelson County, Kentucky*** **[Microfilm & Digital Version],** from the originals, filmed by the Margaret I. King Library, University of Kentucky, 1954, 1 roll, FHL film #9670. This database was indexed online at the USGenWeb site for Nelson Co KY.
- For part 1, see
**http://files.usgwarchives.net/ky/nelson/taxlists/taxes/nelson2.txt.**
- For part 2, see
**http://files.usgwarchives.net/ky/nelson/taxlists/taxes/nelson3.txt.**

**1785-1800.** ***Kentucky Marriages, Early to 1800: A Research Tool*** **[Printed Book],** compiled, extracted & transcribed by Liahona Research; edited by Jordan R. Dodd, published by Precision Indexing, div. of AGLL, Bountiful, UT, 1990, 242 pages. Names are arranged in alphabetical order. FHL book 976.9 V28k.

**1785-1865.** ***The History of Bourbon County*** **[Printed Book],** by H.E. Everman, published by Bourbon Press, 1977, 29 pages, FHL book 976.9423 H2e.

**1785-1880.** ***Circuit Court Case Files Index (Bourbon County, Kentucky)*** **[Microfilm & Digital Capture],** from the manuscript at the KY Dept. of Libraries & Archives, Frankfort, KY. Filmed by the Genealogical Society of Utah, 2008, 1 roll, FHL film #1708746. To access the digital images, see the online FHL catalog page: **www.familysearch.org/search/catalog/1537484.**

**1785-1882.** ***History of Bourbon, Scott, Harrison and Nicholas Counties, Kentucky*** **[Printed Book],** edited by William Henry Perrin; sketch of Blue Grass region by Robert Peter; index by Ella E. Lee Sheffield, originally published by O.L. Baskin & Co, Chicago, 1882, 815 pages. Reprinted by the Southern Historical Press, Easley, SC, 1979. See FHL book 976.94 H2h.

***1785-1791 Tax List, Nelson County, Kentucky*** **[Online Database],** indexed at the USGenWeb site for Nelson Co KY.
- For 1785-1790 part 1, see **http://files.usgwarchives.net/ky/nelson/taxlists/taxes/nelson2.txt.**
- For 1785-1790 part 2, see **http://files.usgwarchives.net/ky/nelson/taxlists/taxes/nelson3.txt.**
- For 1785-1790 part 3, see **http://files.usgwarchives.net/ky/nelson/taxlists/taxes/nelson4.txt.**
- For 1785-1790 part 4, see **http://files.usgwarchives.net/ky/nelson/taxlists/taxes/nelson1.txt.**
- For 1779, see **http://files.usgwarchives.net/ky/nelson/taxlists/1791tax.txt.**

**1785-1979.** ***Kentucky Marriages, 1785-1979*** **[Online Database],** indexed at FamilySearch.org. This is a name index to marriage records, both brides and grooms, based on data collected by the Genealogical Society of Utah, Salt Lake City. This database has 1,532,533 records. See **https://familysearch.org/search/collection/1674849.**

**1786-1793.** ***Bourbon County, Kentucky Court Orders*** **[Printed Index],** by TLC Genealogy, Miami Beach, FL, 1995, 90 pages, FHL book 976.9423 P22t.

**1786-1802.** See ***Genealogical Abstracts from Bourbon County, Kentucky's "Loose Papers" Microfilms,*** **[Printed Book & Digital Version],** compiled by Dept. of Kentucky Libraries & Archives from various court and marriage records from FHL film #8668, 183075, 183076, and 183077. See FHL book 976.9423 D2g. For a link to a digital version of this book, see the online FHL catalog page for this title: **https://familysearch.org/search/catalog/1908908.**

**1786-1805.** ***Miscellaneous Documents of Bourbon County, Kentucky*** **[Microfilm & Digital Capture],** from the originals at the Bourbon County Courthouse, Paris, KY. Filmed by the Genealogical Society of Utah, 1959, 1 roll, FHL film #183140. To access the digital images, see the online FHL catalog page: **www.familysearch.org/search/catalog/416715.**

**1786-1835.** ***Bourbon County, Kentucky Marriage Bonds*** **[Printed Book],** by Michael L. Cook. Indexed by Glenda K. Trapp. Published by McDowell Publications, Utica, KY, 1980, 82 pages, FHL book 976.9423 V2c.

**1786-1851.** ***Bourbon County, Kentucky Marriage Records*** **[Printed Book],** compiled by Robert E. & Phyllis J. Selby, published by Selby Publishing & Printing, 1982, 93 pages, FHL book 976.9423 V2s.

**1786-1871.** ***Index to Wills, Bourbon County, Kentucky*** **[Microfilm & Digital Capture],** from the originals at the Bourbon County Courthouse, Paris, KY. Filmed by the Genealogical Society of Utah, 1959, 10 rolls, beginning with FHL film #183090 (Index, No. 1-5000, no date). To access the digital images, see the online FHL catalog page: **https://familysearch.org/search/catalog/279820.**

**1786-1905.** ***Deeds, Bourbon County, Kentucky*** **[Microfilm & Digital Capture],** from the manuscripts at the University of Kentucky, Lexington, KY. Filmed by the Genealogical Society of Utah, 1959, 1988-1989, 42 rolls, beginning with FHL film #183100 (Index, A-B & misc.). To access the digital images, see the online FHL catalog page: **https://familysearch.org/search/catalog/431279.**

**1786-1930. Marriage Records, Bourbon County, Kentucky [Microfilm & Digital Capture],** from the manuscript at the Margaret I. King Library, University of Kentucky. Filmed by the library, Lexington, KY, 1954, 1959, 22 rolls, beginning with FHL film #183141 (Index to vol. 1-6 A-F). To access the digital images, see the online FHL catalog page: **https://familysearch.org/search/catalog/437496.**
- This title is also available at the Ancestry.com website: See **http://search.ancestry.com/search/db.aspx?dbid=29469.**

**1786-1990.** ***Kentucky Probate Records*** **[Online Database],** digitized and partially indexed at the FamilySearch website. Probate records include wills, bonds, inventories of estates and other records. Date and record coverage varies by county. This digital collection includes a great number of KY counties (image-only databases). The current index covers only wills from Caldwell, Henry, Hickman, Russell and Trimble counties. Note: The title date of 1727 is impossible – a scan through all of the counties revealed the earliest probate records were from Bourbon Co KY starting in 1786. See
**www.familysearch.org/search/collection/1875188**.

**1787 Tax List**. Kentucky areas included in ***The 1787 Census of Virginia: An Accounting of the Name of Every White Male Tithable Over 21 Years, the Number of White Males Between 16 & 21 Years, the Number of Slaves Over 16 & Those Under 16 Years, Together With a Listing of Their Horses, Cattle & Carriages, and Also the Names of all Persons to Whom Ordinary Licenses and Physician's Licenses Were Issued*** **[Printed Book],** compiled by Netti Schreiner-Yantis and Florene Speakman Love. Includes records of counties presently in the states of Kentucky and West Virginia. FHL book 975.5 R4sn, 3 vols.

**1787 Tax Lists.** ***The Personal Property Tax Lists for the Year 1787: Bourbon, Fayette, Jefferson, Madison, Mercer, Nelson Counties (now Kentucky) and Lincoln County*** **[Printed Book],** by Netti Schreiner Yantis and Florene Speakman Love, published by Genealogical Books in Print, Springfield, VA, 1987, 7 vols, 155 pages. See FHL book 975.5 R4sn.

**1787-1799.** ***Madison County, Kentucky Taxpayers*** **[Printed Book],** by T.L.C. Genealogy, Miami Beach, FL, 1992, 119 pages, FHL book 976.953 R48t.

**1787-1799.** ***Bourbon County, Kentucky Taxpayers*** **[Printed Book],** by T.L.C. Genealogy, Miami Beach, FL, 173 pages, FHL book 976.9423 R48.

**1787-1802.** ***Burnt Records, Fayette County, Kentucky*** **[Microfilm & Digital Capture],** from the originals at the Fayette County Courthouse, Lexington, KY. These are copies, sometime not whole, of materials gathered by 1821. They are not in sequence, so the index must be relied on for locating record types. Filmed by the KY Dept. of Archives & Libraries, 1975, 3 rolls. See FHL film #2111044 (Index, vols. 1-4); FHL film #2111045 (Vols. 4-7); and FHL film #211046 (Vols. 7-8). To access the digital images, see the online FHL catalog page:
**www.familysearch.org/search/catalog/819985.**

**1787-1811 Lincoln County, Kentucky.** ***Early Kentucky Landholders*** **[Printed Book],** compiled by James F. Sutherland, published by Genealogical Publishing Co., Inc., Baltimore, 1986, 376 pages. Compiled from land data contained in Lincoln County, Kentucky tax records. Forty-six of Kentucky's fifty-four counties came out of Lincoln County in this time period and so names disappear from the list over the years. Names of land owners arranged in alphabetical order. FHL book 976.9 R2su.

**1787-1811 Tax Lists**. ***Early Kentucky Householders*** **[Printed Book],** compiled by James F. Sutherland, published by Genealogical Publishing Co., Inc., Baltimore, 1986, 209 pages. Names are arranged in alphabetical order. This book was compiled from annual tax lists used by county tax commissioners. FHL book 976.9625 R4s.

**1787-1852.** ***Indexes to Court Records, Madison County, Kentucky*** **[Microfilm & Digital Capture],** from the originals at the county courthouse, Richmond, KY. Includes indexes for Virginia Supreme Court for the district of Kentucky, 1787-1792; County Court for Madison County, Virginia, 1787-1792; Madison County Court of Quarter Sessions, 1792-1802; Madison County Circuit Court, 1803-1852; and general cross index to civil and criminal case files, 1787-1852. Madison County, Virginia and the Kentucky district were part of Virginia that became Kentucky in 1792 when the state was created. Filmed by the KY Public Records Div., 1981, 1 roll, FHL film #1534019. To access the digital images, see the online FHL catalog page: **www.familysearch.org/search/catalog/473554.**

**1787-1854.** ***Kentucky Obituaries*** **[Printed Book & Online Database],** compiled by G. Glenn Clift, with an index by Anita Comtois, published by Genealogical Publishing Co, Baltimore, MD, 1977, 254 pages, FHL book 976.9 V28c. This book is also available as a digitized version at the Ancestry.com website. See
**http://search.ancestry.com/search/db.aspx?dbid=48036.**

***1787-1875 Tax Books, Lincoln County, Kentucky* [Microfilm & Digital Capture],** from the original records at the Kentucky Historical Society, Frankfort, KY. Filmed by the society, 1952-1953, 5 rolls, beginning with FHL film #8114 (Tax books, 1787-1797). To access the digital images, see the online FHL catalog page:
**https://familysearch.org/search/catalog/156086.**

**1787-1874. *Madison County, Kentucky Tax Books, 1787-1874* [Microfilm & Digital Capture],** from the original at the Kentucky Historical Society, Frankfort, KY. Filmed by the society, 1952-1953, 6 rolls, beginning with FHL film #8126 (Tax books, 1787-1807). To access the digital images, see the online FHL catalog page:
**https://familysearch.org/search/catalog/156105.**

***1787-1878 Bourbon County Tax Books* [Microfilm & Digital Capture],** from the originals at the Kentucky Historical Society. Filmed by the society, 1952-1953, 8 rolls, beginning with FHL film #7879 (Tax books, 1787-1806). To access the digital images, see the online FHL catalog page:
**https://familysearch.org/search/catalog/154761.**

**1788. *Fayette County, Kentucky Tax List*** [Online Database], indexed at the USGenWeb site for Fayette Co KY. See
**http://files.usgwarchives.net/ky/fayette/taxlists/tax1788.txt.**

**1788-1851. *Kentucky Vital Statistics, Record of Wills in Woodford County, Kentucky for the Period of Years 1788 to 1851 Inclusive* [Printed Book],** compiled and published by Annie Walker Burns Bell, 1933, 79 pages, FHL book 976.9465 P26.

***1788-1875 Tax Books, Fayette County, Kentucky* [Microfilm & Digital Capture],** from the original records at the Kentucky Historical Society, Frankfort, KY. Filmed by the society, 1952-19533, 24 rolls, beginning with FHL film #7957 (Tax Books, 1787-1804). For a complete list of roll numbers and the contents of each roll, see the FHL catalog page for this title. See **https://familysearch.org/search/catalog/155158.**

**1788-1792.** See ***Some Pre-1800 Kentucky Tax lists For the Counties of Fayette, 1788; Mason (later Floyd), 1790; Mercer, 1789; Washington, 1792* [Printed Book],** compiled by Levi Todd, et al, published by Borderland Books, Anchorage, KY, 1965, 28 pages. FHL book 976.9 R4t and FHL film #1320548.

**1789-1820.** See ***Mercer County, Kentucky: Census Records, 1789, 1800, 1820, and Tax List, 1795* [Printed Book & Digital Version],** compiled by Betty J. Yenne, published by the Fort Wayne Public Library, Ft. Wayne, KY, 1965, FHL book 976.9485 X2y. For a link to a digital version of this title, see the online FHL catalog page.
**https://familysearch.org/search/catalog/115579.**

***1789-1875 Books, Mercer County, Kentucky* [Microfilm],** from the original records at the Kentucky Historical Society and the Dept. of Libraries and Archives, Frankfort, KY. Filmed by the society, 1952, 1953, 7 rolls, beginning with FHL film #8156 (1789-1812). For a complete list of roll numbers and the contents of each roll, see the FHL catalog page for this title. See
**https://familysearch.org/search/catalog/156196.**

***1789-1892 Tax Books, Jefferson County, Kentucky* [Microfilm & Digital Capture],** from the original records at the Kentucky Historical Society and the Dept. of Libraries and Archives, Frankfort, KY. Filmed by the society, 1952, 1953, 1957, 1958, 1990, 160 rolls, beginning with FHL film #8050 (1789-1801). To access the digital images, see the online FHL catalog page: **https://familysearch.org/search/catalog/156004.**

**1789-1820.** See ***Mercer County, Kentucky: Census Records, 1789, 1800, 1820, and Tax List, 1795* [Printed Book],** compiled by Betty J. Yenne, published by the Fort Wayne Public Library, 1965, FHL book 976.9485 X2y. Also on microfilm, see FHL film #482704.

**1789-1923. *Marriage Bonds & Records, Woodford County, Kentucky* [Microfilm & Digital Capture],** from the originals at the clerk of the county court, Versailles, KY. Filmed by the Genealogical Society of Utah, 1961, 1987, 11 rolls, beginning with FHL film #252320. To access the digital images, see the online FHL catalog page:
**https://familysearch.org/search/catalog/676194.**

**1789-1929. *Order Books, Woodford County, Kentucky* [Microfilm & Digital Capture],** from originals at the Woodford County Courthouse in Versailles, KY. Filmed by the Genealogical Society of Utah, et al, 16 rolls, beginning with FHL film #252314. To access the digital images, see the online FHL catalog page:
**https://familysearch.org/search/catalog/436913.**

**1789-1920s.** ***History of Woodford County*** **[Printed Book & Digital Version],** by Wm. E. Railey, originally published as a series of articles which appeared in the Register of the Kentucky Historical Society, 1920-1929; a book published by the author in 1938; reprint by the Woodford Improvement League, Versailles, KY, 1968, 449 pages, FHL book 976.9465 H2r. For a link to a digital version of this title, see the online FHL catalog page. See
**https://familysearch.org/search/catalog/550558.**

**1790 Tax Lists.** ***First Census of Kentucky, 1790*** **[Printed Book],** compiled by Charles B. Heinemann, published by Genealogical Publishing Co, Baltimore, 1981, 118 pages. This is not the 1790 census but a compilation of tax lists for that year. See FHL book 976.9 X2ph.

**1790.** ***Reconstructed 1790 First Federal Census for Kentucky – Alphabetical*** **[Online Database],** included in Ancestry's "U.S. Census Reconstructed Records, 1660-1820." See
**http://search.ancestry.com/search/db.aspx?dbid=2234.**

**1790-1799.** ***Mason County, Kentucky, Taxpayers*** **[Printed Book],** by T.L.C. Genealogy, Miami Beach, FL, 1993, 159 pages, FHL book 976.9323 R48t.

**1790-1799.** ***Woodford County, Kentucky Taxpayers*** **[Printed Book],** by T.L.C. Genealogy, Miami Beach, FL, 1993, 85 pages, FHL book 976.9465 R48w.

**1790-1808.** ***Fayette County, Kentucky, Acts of the Order Book No. 1*** **[Microfilm & Digital Capture],** from the original typescript at Lexington, KY. Filmed by the Genealogical Society of Utah, 1971, 1 roll, FHL film #855036. To access the digital images, see the online FHL catalog page:
**www.familysearch.org/search/catalog/339351.**

**1790-1974**. ***Fayette County, Kentucky Order Books*** **[Microfilm & Digital Capture],** from the originals at the Fayette County Courthouse, Lexington, KY. Filmed by the Margaret I. King Library, University of Kentucky, 1955, 1975, 42 rolls, beginning with FHL film #1490757 (Indexes, 1790-1936). The order books relate to court decisions from probates, taxation, naturalizations, guardianships, and more. To access the digital images, see the online FHL catalog page:
**https://familysearch.org/search/catalog/430365.**

**1790-1853.** ***Circuit Court Case Files (Woodward County, Kentucky)*** **[Microfilm & Digital Capture],** from the originals filmed by the KY Dept. of Archives & Libraries, Frankfort, KY., 71 rolls, beginning with FHL film #2371377 (Case file, 1790-1825). To access the digital images, see the online FHL catalog page:
**https://familysearch.org/search/catalog/1183956.**

**1790s-1800s.** ***Early Kentucky Tax Records, From the Register of the Kentucky Historical Society*** **[Printed Book],** with an index by Carol Lee Ford. Published by Genealogical Publishing Co., Inc., Baltimore, 1984, 318 pages. Excerpted and reprinted from the Register of the Kentucky Historical Society, with added publisher's note, contents, index. FHL book 976.9 R4e.

**1790s-1800s.** ***Kentucky Historical Society Index to Tax Lists*****, [Printed Book & Microfilm & Digital Version],** prepared by Microfilm Department, Kentucky Historical Society, Lexington, KY, published by the society, 1973, 339 pages. FHL book 976.9 R4k and FHL film #1036831. To access the digital version, see the online FHL catalog page:
**www.familysearch.org/search/catalog/85960.**

**1790s-1900s.** ***The Lawyers and Lawmakers of Kentucky: Full Name Index*** **[Printed Index]**, by Southern Historical Press, Easley, SC, 1982, 30 pages, FHL book 976.9 D3L.

**1790s-1900s.** ***Personal and Family Name Index to the History of Kentucky*** **[Printed Index],** by Albert S. Hunter, published 1970, 50 pages, FHL book 976.9 H2c.

***1791 Tax List, Nelson County, Kentucky*** **[Online Database],** indexed at the USGenWeb site for Nelson Co KY. See
**http://files.usgwarchives.net/ky/nelson/taxlists/1791tax.txt.**

***1792 Tax List, Madison County, Kentucky*** **[Online Database],** indexed at the USGenWeb site for Madison Co KY. See
**http://files.usgwarchives.net/ky/madison/taxlists/1792tax.txt.**

***1792 Tax List, Washington County, Kentucky*** **[Online Database],** indexed at the USGenWeb site for Washington Co KY. See
**http://files.usgwarchives.net/ky/washington/taxlists/tax00001.txt.**

***1792-1794 Residents of Nelson County, Virginia (now Kentucky) Recorded in Tithable and Tax Lists* [Printed Book],** compiled by Margaret Johnson Schroeder and Carl A. Schroeder, published Bardstown, KY, 1988, 4 vols. Old Nelson was definitely in Virginia in 1790, but in 1792, Nelson was one of the original counties of the state, and at that time included more than 15 modern counties of central Kentucky. FHL book 976.9 R48s. Vol. 1-4.

***1792-1830 Index, Old Kentucky Survey and Grants; Index for Tellico Surveys and Grants*, [Printed Book & Microfilm & Digital Capture],** compiled from the original records at the Kentucky Historical Society, Frankfort, KY, Published by the society, 1975, 186 pages. This coordinated index is organized in alphabetical and chronological order, giving the survey number and name surveyed for, acreage, county, watercourse, survey date, original survey book and page, grant date, and original grant book and page for all the Old Kentucky land grants from 1776 to 1838. Tellico claims covered Cherokee lands extending into Southeast Kentucky. FHL book 976.9 R2k and FHL film #1402856. To access the digital images, see the online FHL catalog page:
**www.familysearch.org/search/catalog/286811.**

**1792-1850.** ***Divorces Granted by the Kentucky General Assembly, 1792-1850* [Printed Book],** compiled by Sandra K. Gorin, published Gorin Genealogical Pub., 2010, 73 pages, FHL book 976.9 P2gs.

***1792-1894 Tax Books, Nelson County, Kentucky* [Microfilm & Digital Capture],** from the original records at Frankfort and Lexington, KY. Lists are arranged by district and then alphabetically by the first letter of the surname. Filmed by the Genealogical Society of Utah, 1952-1953, 1957-1958, 1991, 27 rolls, beginning with FHL film #8178 (1811-1826). To access the digital images, see the online FHL catalog page: **https://familysearch.org/search/catalog/156788.**

**1792-1900s.** ***Biographical Directory of the Kentucky General Assembly* [Microfilm & Digital Capture],** from a manuscript at the Kentucky Historical Society, Frankfort, KY, 1964, 1 roll, FHL film #467391. To access the digital images, see the online FHL catalog page: **www.familysearch.org/search/catalog/298581.**

**1792-1900s.** ***Kentucky Genealogy and Biography* [Digitized Book],** by Thomas Westerfield and Samuel McDowell, published by Genealogical Reference, Owensboro, KY, 1969, 5 volumes. For links to the digitized versions of each of the five volumes, see the online FHL catalog page for this title:
**https://familysearch.org/search/catalog/81346**

***1792-1913 Record of Resident and Non-resident Lands Forfeited to the State and Sold for Taxes*, [Microfilm & Digital Capture],** from the original records at the Kentucky State Land Office, Lexington. Filmed by the Genealogical Society of Utah, 1958, 30 rolls, beginning with FHL film #174962 (Index of forfeited resident lands to 1846). To access the digital images, see the online FHL catalog page:
**https://familysearch.org/search/catalog/431145.**

**1793-1802.** ***Case Files, Mason County, Kentucky* [Microfilm & Digital Capture],** from the originals of the Court of Quarter Sessions, Mason County Courthouse, Maysville, KY. Filmed by E & K Microfilming, Morgantown, KY, 1993, 1 roll, FHL film #1943548. To access the digital images, see the online FHL catalog page:
**www.familysearch.org/search/catalog/641856.**

**1793-1836.** ***Early Hardin County, Kentucky Census and Tax Lists* [Printed Book],** compiled by Carolyn Wimp, Mary Sabetti; indexed by Judy Nacke, published by Ancestral Trails, Vine Grove, KY, 1998, 195 pages. Includes every-name index to 1793-1797, 1799-1800, 1805, 1815, 1825, 1836 tax lists; and 1810, 1820, 1830 census lists. From preface: "Includes portions of Kentucky later know as Breckinridge, Daviess, Grayson, Hancock, LaRue, Meade, Ohio, as well as portions of Butler, Edmonson, and Hart Counties, Kentucky." FHL book 976.9845 R4w. A partial list of 1793 Taxpayers is also online at the USGenWeb site for Hardin Co KY:
**http://files.usgwarchives.net/ky/hardin/taxlist/1793tax.txt.**

**1794-1800.** ***Record Book, Bourbon County, Kentucky* [Microfilm & Digital Capture],** from the originals at the Dept. of KY Libraries & Archives, Frankfort, KY. Records include court and land records. Volume includes an index. Filmed by DKLA, 1994, 1 roll, FHL film #2024232. To access the digital images, see the online FHL catalog page:
**www.familysearch.org/search/catalog/758255**

**1794-1804.** ***Fayette County, Kentucky: Deed Book A, 1794-1804, Many Documents Dated Earlier than 1794, Index and Chronological Order of Recordings of Instruments*** **[Printed Book],** compiled by Mary S. Hunt, published Salt Lake City, 19-?, 60 pages. See FHL book 976.947 R2h.

*1794-1805 Nonresident Tax List of Kentucky* **[Microfilm & Digital Capture],** from the originals at Lexington, Kentucky. Filmed by the Genealogical Society of Utah, 1958, 1 roll, FHL film #175004. To access the digital images, see the online FHL catalog page: **www.familysearch.org/search/catalog/408558.**

**1794-1816.** ***Bracken County, KY Wills & Estates (Book A)*** **[Online Database],** an index to the book by Jana Sloan Broglin, from Ye Olde Genealogie Shoppe, Indianapolis. The will abstracts and estate division found in this publication were compiled from Bracken County, Kentucky Will Book 'A'. With approximately 700 surnames indexed, all information regarding heirs, administrators, spouse[s], children, etc. is included. A full text abstraction, only the legal terminology has been dropped. Originally indexed at the Ye Olde Genealogie Shoppe website, now archived: **https://openlibrary.org/publishers/Ye_Olde_Genealogie_Shoppe.**

*1794-1817 Fee Books of the Land Office of Kentucky* **[Microfilm & Digital Capture],** from the originals at Lexington, Kentucky. Name lists of early land buyers, based on records recording fees paid by each. Filmed by the Genealogical Society of Utah, 1958, 1 roll, FHL film #174993. To access the digital images, see the online FHL catalog page:
**www.familysearch.org/search/catalog/427532.**

*1794-1828 Tax Rolls, Harrison County, Kentucky* **[Online Database],** indexed at the RootsWeb site for Harrison Co KY. See
**http://usgenwebsites.org/kyHarrison/Taxrolls1794-1828-1.htm.**

**1794-1984.** ***Kentucky Newspaper Archives*** **[Online Database],** digitized and indexed newspapers at the GenealogyBank website for the following cities: Bardstown, Catlettsburg, Covington, Danville, Frankfort, Georgetown, Harrodsburg, Hickman, Lancaster, Lexington, Louisville, Maysville, Paris, Richmond, Russellville, Washington, and Winchester.
**www.genealogybank.com/gbnk/newspapers/explore/USA/Kentucky/.**

**1794-1954.** ***Deeds, Fayette County, Kentucky*** **[Microfilm & Digital Capture],** from the originals of the county and district courts, Lexington, KY. Filmed by the Margaret I. King Library, University of Kentucky, 1952-1953, 293 rolls, beginning with FHL film #8679 (District Court, Deed Book A). To access the digital images, see the online FHL catalog page:
**https://familysearch.org/search/catalog/436712.**

**1795 Tax Lists.** ***The 1795 Census of Kentucky*** **[Printed Book],** by T.L.C. Genealogy, Miami, FL, 1991, 195 pages. This is not a census, but an alphabetical list of names from the 1795 tax lists. See FHL book 976.9 R48t.

**1795-1810.** ***Fayette County, Kentucky, Marriage Bonds*** **[Printed Book],** compiled by Gwendolyn G. Tipple, published by Kentucky Tee-Search, Lexington, KY, 1986, 16 pages, FHL book 976.947 V2t.

**1795-1814.** ***Marriages, Early Ministers' Reports, Fayette County, Kentucky Records, 1795 to 1814 Inclusive*** **[Microfilm & Digital Capture],** from a manuscript by the DAR, Bryan Station Chapter, Lexington, KY. Filmed by the Genealogical Society of Utah, 1 roll, FHL film #851645. To access the digital images, see the online FHL catalog page:
**www.familysearch.org/search/catalog/313953.**

**1795-1849.** ***Kentucky Will Index*** **[Online Database],** indexed at the Ancestry.com website. This database is an index of wills found in the six southern Kentucky counties of Cumberland, Christian, Russell, Logan, Todd, and Trigg. This update adds the following counties to the database: Fleming, Harrison, and Nicholas. The time span covered by this volume is 1795 through 1849. Each entry lists the book, page number, name of the testator, and date of probate of the original record. See
**http://search.ancestry.com/search/db.aspx?dbid=5661.**

**1795-1850.** ***Northern Kentucky Marriages*** **[Online Database],** digitized and indexed at the Ancestry.com website. Situated across the Ohio river from Cincinnati, Ohio, the three Kentucky counties of Boone, Campbell, and Kenton boasted a total population of over 40,000 in 1850. Information in this database includes the names of bride and groom, marriage date and location. This database has 15,939 records. See
**http://search.ancestry.com/search/db.aspx?dbid=3455.**

***1796-1808 Tax Ledgers (Kentucky State Land Office)* [Microfilm & Digital Capture],** from the originals at Lexington, KY. Filmed by the Genealogical Society of Utah, 1958, 2 rolls, FHL film #174989 (Ledgers, 1796-1798), and #174990 (Ledgers, 1804-1808). To access the digital images, see the online FHL catalog page: **www.familysearch.org/search/catalog/431270.**

**1796-1805. *Woodford County, Kentucky, Will Book B* [Printed Book],** by TLC Genealogy, Miami Beach, FL, 2001, 85 pages, FHL book 976.9465 P28wc.

**1796-1823**. ***Resident Tax List of Kentucky* [Microfilm],** from originals in Lexington, KY, 1 roll, FHL film #174951. To access the digital images, see the online FHL catalog page: **www.familysearch.org/search/catalog/408544.**

***1796-1825 Land Grants South of the Green River* [Microfilm & Digital Capture],** from the originals at the Kentucky Land Office, Frankfort, KY. Filmed by the Genealogical Society of Utah, 1962, 10 rolls, beginning with FHL film #272951 (Index to Grants south of the Green River). To access the digital images, see the online FHL catalog page: **https://familysearch.org/search/catalog/426670.**
- Indexes to Kentucky Land Records are available online at the KY Secretary of State's website. See **https://web.sos.ky.gov/land/.**

***1797 Tax List, Shelby County, Kentucky* [Online Database],** indexed at the RootsWeb site for Shelby Co KY. For Part 1, see **www.rootsweb.ancestry.com/~kybullit/tax_Shelby_1797_1.htm.**

***1797 Tax List, Warren County, Kentucky* [Online Database],** indexed at the Burgoo.com site. See **www.burgoo.com/taxlist1797.html.**

**1797-1865. *Kentucky Marriages* [Printed Book & Digitized Version],** compiled by G. Glenn Clift, published by Genealogical Publishing Co, Baltimore, MD, 1974, 258 pages, FHL book 976.9 V28cg. This book is also available as a digitized version at the Ancestry.com website. See **http://search.ancestry.com/search/db.aspx?dbid=48582.**

**1797-1954**. ***Kentucky County Marriages* [Online Database],** indexed at the FamilySearch.org website. This is a database with images and full index to marriage records created by Kentucky counties. The records include bonds, licenses, certificates, and returns. This database has 184,092 records. See **https://familysearch.org/search/collection/1804888.**

***1799 Tax List, Cumberland County, Kentucky* [Online Database],** indexed at the KYkinfolk website for Cumberland Co KY. See **http://kykinfolk.com/cumberland/1799census.html.**

**1799-1801. *Kentucky, Tax Lists* [Online Database],** indexed at the Ancestry.com website. See **http://search.ancestry.com/search/db.aspx?dbid=3720.**

***1799-1813 Delinquent Tax Lists, Pendleton County, Kentucky* [Online Database],** indexed at the USGenWeb site for Pendleton Co KY. See **http://files.usgwarchives.net/ky/pendleton/taxlists/tax0001.txt.**

**1799-1816. *Mason County, Kentucky Court Orders: An Every-Name Index* [Printed Book],** by T.L.C. Genealogy, Miami Beach, FL. These books index films (FHL film #3281832 & #281833) in the Family History Library. Published 1994, 2 vols., FHL book 976.9323 P22t.

**1799-1990.** See ***Kentucky Probate Records* [Online Database],** digitized and partially indexed at the Historic Record Collections of the FamilySearch.org. This is a digital collection and partial index of selected will records created in a few Kentucky county courts. The current index covers wills from Caldwell, Henry, Hickman, Russell, and Trimble counties, Kentucky. The date 1727 in the FamilySearch title is impossible – our date was placed at 1799, only because the earliest county formation of the five counties listed was Henry County, Kentucky in 1799. The other four were created between 1809 and 1837. It is possible that "1727" is a typo and should be "1837." But there is no way to search the database by date to know for sure. This database has 12,429 records. See **https://familysearch.org/search/collection/1875188.**

**1800.** ***Second Census of Kentucky: A Privately Compiled and Published Enumeration of Tax Payers Appearing in the 79 Manuscript Volumes Extant of Tax Lists of the 42 Counties of Kentucky in Existence in 1800*** **[Printed Book],** compiled by Garrett Glenn Clift, published by the Kentucky Historical Society, Frankford, KY, 1954, 333 pages. A good substitute for the lost 1800 federal census for Kentucky. FHL book 976.9 X2p and FHL film #390838.

**1800 Tax List, Breckinridge County, Kentucky [Online Database],** indexed at the USGenWeb site for Breckinridge Co KY. See **http://files.usgwarchives.net/ky/breckinridge/taxlists/taxs001a.txt.**

***1800 Tax List, Bullitt County, Kentucky*** **[Online Database],** indexed at the USGenWeb site for Bullitt Co KY. For the list of various indexes, see **http://files.usgwarchives.net/ky/bullitt/taxlists/.**

***1800 Tax List, Campbell County, Kentucky*** **[Online Database],** indexed at the RootsWeb site for Campbell Co KY. See **www.rootsweb.ancestry.com/~kycchgs/1800tax.htm.**

***1800-1809 Tax Lists, Knox County, Kentucky*** **[Online Database],** indexed at the comteck.com site. See **www.comteck.com/~jjackson/knox.html.**

***1800 Tax List, Nelson County, Kentucky*** **[Online Database],** indexed at the USGenWeb site for Nelson Co KY. See **http://files.usgwarchives.net/ky/nelson/taxlists/1800tax.txt.**

***1800 Tax List, Scott County, Kentucky*** **[Online Database],** indexed at the USGenWeb site for Scott Co KY. See **http://files.usgwarchives.net/ky/scott/taxlists/tax1800.txt.**

***1800 Tax List, Woodford County, Kentucky*** **[Online Database],** indexed at the RootsWeb site for Woodford Co KY.
- For part 1, A-L: see **www.rootsweb.ancestry.com/~kywoodfo/woodfordtx1800.html.**
- For part 2, M-Z, see **www.rootsweb.ancestry.com/~kywoodfo/woodfordtx1800_2.html.**

**1800-1829.** ***Register of Silas Baptist Church*** **[Online Database],** by Edna Talbott Whitley, published in the KY Historical Register, 1929. Indexed at the Bourbon Co KY Church Records website. See **http://bourboncoky.info/ChurchRecords.html.**

**1800-1920.** ***Kentucky Marriages: From the Register of the Kentucky Historical Society*** **[Online Database],** digitized from the original book published by the society, reprinted 1983, Genealogical Publishing Co., Baltimore. Digitized and indexed at the Ancestry.com website. This database has 1,030 pages. **https://search.ancestry.com/search/db.aspx?dbid=48035.**

**1801-1850.** ***Name Changes, Legitimations and Adoptions Found in the Kentucky Acts*** **[Printed Book],** compiled by Barbara Augspurger, Frankfort, KY, 1982, 25 pages, FHL book 976.9 A1No 304.

***1802 Adair County Tax List*** **[Online Database],** indexed at the KYkinfolk.com site. See **http://kykinfolk.com/adair/Census/1802adairtaxlist.htm.**

**1802-1850.** ***Kentucky Marriages*** **[Online Database],** indexed at the Ancestry.com website. This database was originally prepared by Jordan Dodd, with over 145,000 names. Each entry includes groom, bride, marriage date, and state of marriage. See **http://search.ancestry.com/search/db.aspx?dbid=2089.**

***1803 Tax List, Bullitt County, Kentucky*** **[Online Database],** indexed at the USGenWeb site for Bullitt Co KY. For the list of various indexes, see **http://files.usgwarchives.net/ky/bullitt/taxlists/.**

**1805 Tax Roll, Fleming County, Kentucky [Online Database],** this is the image of page 7 only (letter H), and a good example of how hard it is to read some of the old documents – get out your Magnabrite. Image at the USGenWeb site for Fleming Co KY. See **www.usgwarchives.net/ky/fleming/1805pg7.gif.**

***1805-1814 Court Abstracts, Order Book B, Pendleton County, Kentucky*** **[Online Database],** indexed at the USGenWeb site for Pendleton Co KY: **www.usgennet.org/usa/ky/state/counties/pendleton/taxrec/abstracts18051814.htm.**

**1806.** ***Lexington (Fayette County KY) Directory, Taken for Charles' Almanac, for 1806*** **[Online Database],** indexed at the RootsWeb site for Fayette Co KY. See
**www.rootsweb.ancestry.com/~kyfayett/1806directory.htm.**

**1806-1935 City Directories.** See ***Lexington (Kentucky) City Directories*** **[Microfiche/Microfilm],** from various publishers, filmed by Research Publications, Woodbridge, CT, 1980-1984. The FHL has the directories for 1806, 1818, 1838-1839, 1859-1860,1864-1865, 1867, 1873-1878, 1881-1882, 1898-1899, 1902-1907, 1909, 1911-1917, 1919, 1921, 1923, 1925, 1927-1928, and 1930-1935. 12 fiche/rolls, beginning with FHL fiche #6044043. For a complete list of fiche/roll numbers and the contents of each, see the online FHL catalog page for this title. See
**https://familysearch.org/search/catalog/530196.**

***1807 Tax List, Clay County, Kentucky*** **[Online Database],** indexed at the RootsWeb site for Clay Co KY. See
**http://homepages.rootsweb.ancestry.com/~twspence/tim/clay/tax/1807.html.**

***1807 Tax List, Hopkins County, Kentucky*** **[Online Database],** indexed at the KYkinfolk site for Hopkins Co KY. See
**http://kykinfolk.com/hopkins/tax/1807.html.**

**1807-1843**. ***Circuit Court Records*** **[Microfilm],** from the originals at the Kentucky Historical Society. Each volume is indexed. Filmed by the society, 1968, 33 rolls, beginning with FHL film #460538 (Court records, v A 1807). To access the digital images, see the online FHL catalog page:
**https://familysearch.org/search/catalog/139354.**

**1810.** ***Index to the Third Census of the United States, 1810, State of Kentucky*** **[Printed Book, Microfilm, & Digital Capture],** compiled 1936, LDS Church. Filmed by the Genealogical Society of Utah, 1956, 1 roll, FHL film #8657. To access the digital images, see the online FHL catalog page:
**www.familysearch.org/search/catalog/86289.**

**1810.** ***Kentucky 1810 Census*** **[Printed Index],** edited by Ronald Vern Jackson, published by Accelerated Indexing Systems, 1974, 220 pages, FHL book 976.9 X2jrv.

**1810.** ***Third Census of the United States, 1810, State of Kentucky*** **[Printed Index],** compiled by Annie W.B. Bell, published Washington, DC, 1933, 7 vols., FHL book 976.9 X28.

**1810.** ***Index to the 1810 Census of Kentucky*** **[Printed Index],** compiled by Ann T. Wagstaff, published by Genealogical Publishing Co, Baltimore, 1980, 230 pages, FHL book 976.9 X2w.

**1810.** ***An Index to the 1810 Federal Census of Kentucky*** **[Printed Index],** compiled by Lowell M. Volkel, Springfield, IL, 1971, 4 vols., FHL book 976.9 X2p.

**1810-1840.** ***Kentucky, 1810 Thru 1840 Federal Census: Population Schedules*** **[Microfilm & Digital Capture],** from originals at the National Archives, Washington, DC. The 1810, 1820, 1830, and 1840 census schedules for Kentucky were filmed together in one series. Filmed by the National Archives, 1938-1961, 29 rolls, beginning with FHL film #181350 (1810 census, Adair, Barren, Boone, Bourbon, Bracken, Breckinridge, Bullitt, and Butler counties). To access the digital images, see the online FHL catalog page:
**https://familysearch.org/search/catalog/745490.**

**1810-1890.** ***Kentucky, Compiled Census and Census Substitutes Index*** **[Online Database],** indexed at the Ancestry.com website. This collection contains the following indexes: 1810 Federal Census and Index; 1820 Federal Census Index; 1830 Federal Census Index; 1840 Federal Census Index; 1840 Pensioners List; 1850 Federal Census Index; 1850 Slave Schedules; 1860 Federal Census Index; 1870 Federal Census Index; 1890 Veterans Schedules; Early Census Index. Original data: Jackson, Ronald V., Accelerated Indexing Systems, see
**http://search.ancestry.com/search/db.aspx?dbid=3549.**

***1811 Tax List, Clay County, Kentucky*** **[Online Database],** indexed at the RootsWeb site for Clay Co KY. See
**http://homepages.rootsweb.ancestry.com/~twspence/tim/clay/tax/1811.html.**

***1811 Census of Greenup County, Kentucky*** **[Online Database],** indexed at the RootsWeb site for Greenup Co KY. See
**www.rootsweb.ancestry.com/~kygreen2/1811tax.html.**

**1811-1834**. *Court Order for Kentucky* **[Microfilm & Digital Capture]**, from the originals at the Kentucky Historical Society, Frankfort, KY. Filmed by the society, 1968, 6 rolls, beginning with FHL film #467314 (Court order, v. C-D, 1811-1816). To access the digital images, see the online FHL catalog page: **https://familysearch.org/search/catalog/139310.**

**1812-1917.** ***Index to Veterans of American Wars from Kentucky*** **[Microfilm & Digital Capture],** film of a manuscript at the Kentucky Historical Society. Includes veterans of War of 1812, War with Mexico, War with Spain, Civil (Confederate), Civil War (Union), and World War I. filmed 1966, 47 rolls, beginning with FHL film #471728. To access the digital images, see the online FHL catalog page: **https://familysearch.org/search/catalog/135459.**

***1814 & 1816 Delinquent Tax Lists, Pendleton County, Kentucky*** **[Online Database],** indexed at the USGenWeb site for Pendleton Co KY. See **www.usgennet.org/usa/ky/state/counties/pendleton/taxrec/dltax1814.html.**

**1815 Tax Roll, Fleming County, Kentucky [Online Database]**, this is an image ( page 19 only) at the USGenWeb site for Fleming Co KY. See **www.usgwarchives.net/ky/fleming/1815pg19.gif.**

**1816-1824.** ***Bracken County, KY Wills & Estate, Volume II (Book A)*** **[Online Database],** an index to the book by Jana Sloan Broglin, published by Ye Olde Genealogie Shoppe, Indianapolis. Like Volume I, this volume contains will abstracts and estate division for Bracken County, Kentucky from 1816-1824. Included in the database at Ancestry.com. See **www.ancestry.com/search/collections/48031.**

**1818-1995.** ***Kentucky Church Records*** **[Online Database],** digitized and indexed at FamilySearch.org, obtained from collections at the University of Louisville, Kentucky Historical Society, and Cythiniana Presbyterian Church. This database has 9,536 records, see **www.familysearch.org/search/collection/2790250.**

***1819 List of Males Transferred from Knox to Harlan County Tax Lists*** **[Online Database].** In 1819, Harlan County was formed from the eastern portion of Knox County. This is a list of all those males age 21 and over who were living in the section of Knox County that was set off to form Harlan. Indexed at the RootsWeb site for Harlan Co KY. See **www.rootsweb.ancestry.com/~seky/datafile/1819list.html.**

***1819 Tax List, Hart County, Kentucky*** **[Online Database],** indexed at: **https://web.archive.org/web/201908121140505/http://censusdiggins.com/1819hart.html**

**1820.** ***Index to the 1820 Census of Kentucky*** **[Printed Index],** compiled by Jeanne Robey Felldin and Gloria K V Inman, published by Genealogical Publishing Co, Baltimore, 1981, 318 pages, FHL book 976.9 X22f.

**1820.** ***An Index to the 1820 Federal Census of Kentucky*** **[Printed Index],** compiled by Lowell M. Volkel, published by Heritage House, Indianapolis, IN, 1974, 4 vols, FHL book 976.9 X29.

**1820.** ***Kentucky 1820 Census Index*** **[Printed Index],** edited by Ronald Vern Jackson, published by Accelerated Indexing Systems, Bountiful, UT, 168 pages, FHL book 976.9 X22ja.

**1820.** ***First Taxpayers of Grant County, Kentucky*** **[Online Database],** indexed at the RootsWeb site for Grant Co KY. See **www.rootsweb.ancestry.com/~kygrant/gtax.htm**

**1820.** ***Murray's City Directory of Louisville/ Jefferson County, Kentucky for the year 1820*** **[Printed Book],** compiled by Alan D. Murray, Gregath, Wyandotte, OK, 2007, 238 pages. The author constructed a directory of 1820 Louisville from a variety of original records from the time period. Includes cemetery inscriptions. Includes index. See FHL book 976.944/L1 E4m.

**1820-1829.** ***Tax Lists, Grant County, Kentucky*** **[Online Database],** indexed at the RootsWeb site for Grant Co KY. See **www.rootsweb.ancestry.com/~kygrant/tax.html.**

**1820-1839.** ***Index to Kentucky Court Order Books*** **[Microfilm & Digital Capture],** from the originals filmed by the University of Kentucky, Lexington, KY, 1958, 1 roll, FHL film #182302. To access the digital images, see the online FHL catalog page: **www.familysearch.org/search/catalog/422048.**

**1820-1899.** ***Pioneers of Trigg County,***

Western KY History site for Trigg Co KY. See **www.westernkyhistory.org/trigg/Pioneers.txt.**

***1820-1900 Land Grants West of the Tennessee River* [Microfilm & Digital Capture],** from the original records at the Kentucky Land Office, Frankfurt. Originally filmed by the Genealogical Society of Utah, 1962, 4 rolls, beginning with FHL film #272865 (Index to grants 1820-1858). To access the digital images, see the online FHL catalog page:
**www.familysearch.org/search/catalog/242482.**
- This entire database is online at the Kentucky Secretary of State's website, see
**https://www.sos.ky.gov/land/military/wtrpatents/Pages/default.aspx.**

*1820-1915.* See ***Index of Wills, Book A (1820)-Book M (1815), Todd County, Kentucky* [Online Database],** indexed at the USGenWeb site for Todd Co KY. See
**www.usgennet.org/usa/ky/county/todd/record/will.htm.**

**1822-1824. *Jackson Purchase Tax Lists* [Printed Book & Digital Version],** by Don Simmons, publ. 1974, Melber, KY, 62 pages, digitized by FamilySearch International, 2015. To access the digital version, see the online FHL catalog page: **www.familysearch.org/search/catalog/2547336.**

***1823 Tax List, Pike County, Kentucky* [Online Database],** indexed at the USGenWeb site for Pike Co KY. For part 1, see
**http://files.usgwarchives.net/ky/pike/taxes/1823tax.txt.**
- For part 2, see
**http://files.usgwarchives.net/ky/pike/taxes/1823-pt2.txt.**

***1824-1853 Tax Lists, Lawrence County,* Kentucky [Online Database],** links to each tax year at the RootsWeb site for Lawrence Co KY. See
**www.rootsweb.ancestry.com/~kylawren/tax.html.**

**1824-1995. *Kentucky, Church Marriages* [Online Database],** indexed at the FamilySearch.org website. Source: FamilySearch extractions from various KY churches. Each record includes Name, Event type, Event date, Event place, Gender, Marital status, Spouse's gender, and Spouse's gender. This database has 8,841 records. See
**www.familysearch.org/search/collection/2549562.**

***1825 Caldwell County, Kentucky Delinquent Tax List* [Online Database],** indexed at the USGenWeb site for Caldwell Co KY. See
**http://files.usgwarchives.net/ky/caldwell/taxlists/tax-001.txt.**

***1825 Tax List, Edmonson County, Kentucky* [Online Database],** surname index at the USGenWeb site for Edmonson Co KY. See
**www.kygenweb.org/edmonson/.**

**1827-1844.** See ***County Court Order Warrant Surveys, 1836-1844; Survey Warrants for Headright, 1827* [Microfilm & Digital Capture],** from the originals at the Kentucky State Land Office. Filmed by the Genealogical Society of Utah, 1962, 2 rolls, FHL film #272972 and #272973. To access the digital images, see the online FHL catalog page:
**www.familysearch.org/search/catalog/430335.**

***1830 Tax List, Monroe County, Kentucky* [Online Database],** indexed at **https://web.archive.org/web/20090730060508/**
**www.censusdiggins.com/18301.html.**

**1830. *Kentucky 1830 Census Index* [Printed Index],** compiled by Dora Wilson Smith, published by Heritage House, Thomson, IL, 1973, 6 vols, FHL book 976.9 X2p.

**1830. *Kentucky 1830 Census Index* [Printed Index],** edited by Ronald Vern Jackson, et al, published by Accelerated Indexing Systems, Bountiful, UT, 1976, 206 pages, FHL book 976.9 X2paa.

**1830-1854. *Index to Will Book #1, Clay County, Kentucky* [Online Database],** indexed at the RootsWeb site for Clay Co KY. See
**www.rootsweb.ancestry.com/~kyclay2/wills/bookone.html.**

**1833-1844. *Biographical Memoir of Daniel Boone: The First Settler of Kentucky; Interspersed with Incidents in the Early Annals of the Country* [Digitized Book],** by Timothy Flint, originally published 1933, published Cincinnati, 1944, digitized by the Genealogical Society of Utah, 2012. See the catalog page for this title for a link to the digital version. **https://familysearch.org/search/catalog/2015577.**

**1834-1885. *Tax Assessment Books, Louisville, Kentucky* [Microfilm & Digital Capture],** from the originals at the Jefferson County Courthouse, Louisville, KY. Each year is arranged alphabetically by first letter of surname. Filmed by the Genealogical Society of Utah, 1974, 54 rolls,

beginning with FHL film #959112. To access the digital images, see the online FHL catalog page:
**https://familysearch.org/search/catalog/136643**

**1835.** ***Kentucky Pension Roll of 1835*** **[Printed Book & Digital Version],** reprint of "Report from the Secretary of War," originally published by Congress (23rd, 1st Session: 1833:1834), Senate: Ex. Doc. 514. Reprint by Genealogical Publishing Co, Baltimore, MD, 1959, 152 pages, FHL book 976.9 M24. An abstracted version of the Kentucky name list is online at the USGenWeb Archives site. See
**http://files.usgwarchives.net/ky/state/military/kypen.txt.**

**1837** ***Tax Lists, Trimble County, Kentucky*** **[Online Database],** indexed at the ole.net site. See
**www.ole.net/~maggie/trimble/tax.htm.**

**1838-1839.** ***Directory of the City of Lexington and County of Fayette*** **[Online Database],** a complete facsimile reproduction is at the RootsWeb site for Fayette Co KY. See
**www.rootsweb.ancestry.com/~kyfayett/directory1838/1838_directory.htm**

***1839 Tax List, Carter County, Kentucky*** **[Online Database],** indexed at the USGenWeb site for Carter Co KY. See
**http://files.usgwarchives.net/ky/carter/taxlists/1839tax.txt.**

**1839-1960.** ***Kentucky Births and Christenings*** **[Online Database],** indexed at the FamilySearch.org website. This is a name index to birth, baptism and christening records from the state of Kentucky, based on data collected by the Genealogical Society of Utah, Salt Lake City. This database has 546,313 records. See
**https://familysearch.org/search/collection/1674843**.

**1840.** ***Kentucky 1840 Census Index*** **[Printed Index],** edited by Ronald Vern Jackson, et al, published by Accelerated Indexing Systems, Bountiful, UT, 1976, 250 pages, FHL book 976.9 X2paa.

***1840 Special Federal Census of Kentucky Pensioners of Revolutionary War or Military Service*** **[Printed Book],** compiled by Sharroll K. Minix, published by the Magoffin County Historical Society, 1983, 28 pages, FHL book 976.9 X2mi.

***1840 & 1845 Tax Lists, Todd County, Kentucky*** **[Online Database],** indexed at the USGenWeb site for Todd Co KY. See
**www.usgennet.org/usa/ky/county/todd/tax/index.htm.**

**1840-1988.** ***Kentucky, Louisville, Cemetery Index Cards*** **[Online Database],** digitized and indexed at FamilySearch.org. Includes Index and images of index cards recording burials in the Eastern, Schardein, and Greenwood cemeteries located in Louisville, Kentucky. This database has 38,119 records, see
**www.familysearch.org/search/collection/3019662.**

**1841-1901.** ***Miscellaneous Crittenden County, Kentucky Deeds*** **[Online Database],** abstracted at the Western KY History website. See
**http://westernkyhistory.org/crittenden/Crittdeeds.html.**

***1843 Tax List, Letcher County, Kentucky*** **[Online Database],** indexed at the RootsWeb site for Letcher Co KY. See
**www.rootsweb.ancestry.com/~kyletch/tax_lists/1843_tax.htm**

**1843-1970.** ***Kentucky Deaths and Burials*** **[Online Database],** indexed at the Historic Record Collections of the FamilySearch.org website. This is a name index to death and burial records collected by the Genealogical Society of Utah, Salt Lake City. This database has 627,320 records. See
**https://familysearch.org/search/collection/1674848.**

***1844 Tax List, Johnson County, Kentucky*** **[Online Database],** indexed at the USGenWeb site for Johnson Co KY. See
**http://files.usgwarchives.net/ky/johnson/taxlists/1844john.txt.**

***1844 Tax List, Letcher County, Kentucky*** **[Online Database],** indexed at the RootsWeb site for Letcher Co KY. See
**www.rootsweb.ancestry.com/~kyletch/tax_lists/1844_tax.htm**

**1847-1911.** See ***Kentucky, Birth Records*** **[Online Database],** indexed at the Ancestry.com website. Source: KY Dept of Libraries and Archives. Each record includes Name of child, Gender, Color or race, Birth date, Birthplace, Parents' name, Parents' birthplaces, and Parents' ages. This database has 1,216,505 records. See
**https://search.ancestry.com/search/db.aspx?dbid=1213.**

**1847–2000s.** ***Kentucky Collection Catalog at MyHeritage*** **[Online Database],** 22 collections with 17,427,495 records can be searched at the Kentucky, USA MyHeritage website. Databases include censuses, vital records, directories, family histories, town histories, military rosters, college/school year books, and more. This is a subscription site, but a free search can be done for a name, place, year, or keyword. See **www.myheritage.com/records/Kentucky/all-records.**

***1848 Tax List, Letcher County, Kentucky*** **[Online Database],** indexed at the RootsWeb site for Letcher Co KY. See
**www.rootsweb.ancestry.com/~kyletch/tax_lists/1848_tax.htm**

**1850.** ***Kentucky, 1850 Federal Census: Population Schedules*** **[Microfilm & Digital Capture],** from the originals at the National Archives, Washington, DC. Filmed by the National Archives, series M432, 1964, 39 rolls, beginning with FHL film #7843 (Kentucky: Adair, Allen, Anderson and Ballard counties). To access the digital images, see the online FHL catalog page:
**https://familysearch.org/search/catalog/744480.**

**1850.** ***Kentucky, 1850 Census Index*** **[Printed Index],** edited by Ronald Vern Jackson, published by Accelerated Indexing Systems, Bountiful, UT, 469 pages, FHL book 976.9 X2pj.

***1850 Census Index of Eastern Kentucky*** **[Printed Index],** compiled by Mrs. M. T. Parrish, Stamping Ground, KY, 1973. This index includes the counties of Breathitt, Carter, Clay, Floyd Harlan, Johnson, Knox, Laurel, Lawrence, Letcher, Morgan, Perry and Pike. See FHL book 976.9 X22p.

**1850.** ***1850 Census… [14 Kentucky Regions],*** **[Printed Index],** compiled by Barbara, Bryan, and Samuel Sistler, Nashville, TN, 1995, 14 vols., FHL book (subject class) 976.X28. For the title and FHL call number for each volume, see
**https://familysearch.org/search/catalog/759293.**

**1850-1880.** See ***Federal Mortality Census Schedules and Related Indexes: Kentucky; 1850; 1860; 1870; 1880*** **[Microfilm & Digital Capture],** from the original records in the custody of the Daughters of the American Revolution, Washington, DC. Each year includes an index. Filmed by the National Archives, 1962, series T655, 9 rolls, beginning with FHL film #422419 (1850, Pendleton-Woodford counties). To access the digital images, see the online FHL catalog page: **https://familysearch.org/search/catalog/783162.**

**1850-1895.** ***Marriage, Birth and Death Records of Families with Proved Lineages of American Revolution Ancestors: Who Emigrated from Virginia to Kentucky and from there to Texas, 1850-1895*** **[Printed Book],** by Lucy Bender, published Langley Field, VA, 1937, 94 pages, FHL book 976.4 V2b.

**1851-1900.** ***Kentucky (Marriages)*** **[CD-ROM],** by Broderbund, 1998 (Family Tree Archives No. 233), originally prepared by Liahona Research, Orem, Utah. Contains information on approximately 318,000 individuals who were married in sixty-two Kentucky counties between 1851-1900. FHL CD-ROM No. 9, pt. 233. This same database was added to the Ancestry.com website. See
**http://search.ancestry.com/search/db.aspx?dbid=4428.**

**1852-1914.** ***Kentucky, Birth Records*** **[Online Database],** digitized and indexed at the Ancestry.com website. Source: Kentucky Department for Libraries and Archives, Frankfort, KY. Each record includes Name, Age, Est. Birth Year, Birth Location, Residence, Spouse name, Spouse age, Spouse birth location, Spouse residence, Marriage date, Marriage location, and County of record. This database has 230,792 records. See
**https://search.ancestry.com/search/db.aspx?dbid=1117.**

**1852-1914.** ***Kentucky, Marriage Records*** **[Online Database],** digitized and indexed the Ancestry.com website. Original data: Kentucky Birth, Marriage and Death Records – Microfilm (1852-1910). Microfilm rolls #994027-994058. Kentucky Department for Libraries and Archives, Frankfort, Kentucky. See
**http://search.ancestry.com/search/db.aspx?dbid=1117.**

**1852-1965.** ***Kentucky, Death Records*** [Online Database], indexed at the Ancestry.com website. Source: KY Dept of Libraries & Archives. Death records extracted from KY Death Certificates, Mortuary records, death registers, and records of death from various KY locations. Each record may include a Name, Race, Age at time of death, Gender, Death date,

Death place, Birthplace, Residence, Parents' names, and Parents' birthplaces. Some records include added information, such as Occupation, or Cause of death. This database has 5,740,496 records. See **https://search.ancestry.com/search/db.aspx?dbid=1222.**

***1854 Tax Roll, Floyd County, Kentucky* [Online Database],** indexed at the RootsWeb site for Floyd Co KY. See **www.rootsweb.ancestry.com/~kyfloyd/Mis_files/1854tax.htm.**

**1859. *Kentucky Lawyers in 1859* [Online Database],** indexed for all counties at the USGenWeb site for Kentucky. See **http://files.usgwarchives.net/ky/state/history/lawyers.txt.**

***1859 City Directory, Louisville, Kentucky* [Online Database],** archived version available. See **http://web.archive.org/web/20070819065957/http://kentuckycitydirectory.com/Louisville/1859.**

***1859-1860 George W. Hawes's Kentucky State Gazetteer and Business Directory* [Microfilm]**, filmed by Research Publications, Woodbridge, CT, 1980, 1 roll, FHL film #6044020.

**1859-1860. *Lexington (Fayette County, Kentucky) Directory, City guide and Business Mirror* [Online Database],** indexed at the RootsWeb site for Fayette Co KY. See **www.rootsweb.ancestry.com/~kyfayett/directory1859/1859_directory.htm.**

**1860. *Kentucky, 1860 Federal Census: Population Schedules* [Microfilm & Digital Capture],** from the originals at the National Archives, Washington, DC. The 1860 census was filmed twice. The second film is listed first and is usually easier to read. Filmed by the National Archives, series M653, 64 rolls, beginning with FHL film #803353 (Kentucky: Adair, Allen, and Anderson counties). To access the digital images, see the online FHL catalog page: **https://familysearch.org/search/catalog/704819.**

**1860. *Kentucky 1860 East* [Printed Index]**, edited by Ronald Vern Jackson, published by Accelerated Indexing Systems, North Salt Lake, UT, 1988, 1,175 pages, FHL book 976.9 X22je.

**1860. *Kentucky 1860 West* [Printed Index]**, edited by Ronald Vern Jackson, published by Accelerated Indexing Systems, North Salt Lake, UT, 1988, 1,289 pages, FHL book 976.9 X22kw.

**1860. *Kentucky 1860 Mortality Schedule* [Printed Index],** edited by Ronald Vern Jackson, published by Accelerated Indexing Systems, Salt Lake City, UT, 162 pages, FHL book 976.9 X22k.

**1860. *Kentucky 1860 Agricultural Census* [Printed Book],** compiled by Linda L. Green, Woodbridge, VA, 2001, 3 vols., FHL book 976.9 X2

***1860 Boyd County Kentucky Tax List* [Online Database],** indexed at the USGenWeb site for Boyd Co KY. See **http://files.usgwarchives.net/ky/boyd/taxlists/1860tax.txt.**

***1860-1936 General Index to Court of Appeals* [Microfilm & Digital Capture],** from the originals at the Margaret I. King Library, University of Kentucky in Lexington, Kentucky. Filmed by the library, 1955, 5 rolls, beginning with FHL film #8661. To access the digital images, see the online FHL catalog page: **https://familysearch.org/search/catalog/430510.**

**1861 Boyd County Kentucky Tax List [Online Database],** indexed at the USGenWeb site for Boyd Co KY. See **http://files.usgwarchives.net/ky/boyd/taxlists/1861tax.txt.**

**1861-1865. *Index to Compiled Service Records of Confederate Soldiers Who Served in Organizations From the State of Kentucky* [Microfilm & Digital Capture],** from the original records at the National Archives, Washington, DC, series M319, 14 rolls, beginning with FHL film #881380 (Index, A-Bi 1861-1865). To access the digital images, see the online FHL catalog page: **https://familysearch.org/search/catalog/311984.**

**1861-1865. *Kentucky Civil War Service Records of Confederate Soldiers* [Online Database],** digitized documents and index at the FamilySearch.org website. Includes Confederate service records of soldiers who served in organizations from Kentucky. The records include a jacket-envelope for each soldier, labeled with his name, his rank, and the unit in which he served. The jacket-envelope typically contains card abstracts of entries relating to the soldier as found in original muster rolls, returns, rosters, payrolls, appointment books, hospital registers, Union prison registers and rolls, parole rolls, inspection reports; and the originals of any papers relating solely to the particular soldier. For each military unit the service records are arranged alphabetically by the soldier's surname. The Military Unit field may also display the surname range (A-G) as found on the microfilm. This collection is a part of RG 109, War Department Collection of Confederate Records and is National Archive Microfilm Publication M319. Index courtesy of Fold3. This database has 267,987 records. See **https://familysearch.org/search/collection/1932371.**

**1861-1865.** ***Index to Compiled Service Records of Volunteer Union Soldiers Who Served in Organizations From the State of Kentucky*** **[Microfilm & Digital Capture],** from the original records at the National Archives, Washington, DC, series M386, 30 rolls, beginning with FHL film #881492 (Index, A, 1861-1865). To access the digital images, see the online FHL catalog page: **https://familysearch.org/search/catalog/316094.**

**1861-1865.** ***Kentucky Civil War Service Records of Union Soldiers*** **[Online Database],** digitized documents and index at the Historic Record Collections of the FamilySearch.org website. Includes Union service records of soldiers who served in organizations from Kentucky. The records include a jacket-envelope for each soldier, labeled with his name, his rank, and the unit in which he served. The jacket-envelope typically contains card abstracts of entries relating to the soldier as found in original muster rolls, returns, rosters, payrolls, appointment books, hospital registers, prison registers and rolls, parole rolls, inspection reports; and the originals of any papers relating solely to the particular soldier. For each military unit the service records are arranged alphabetically by the soldier's surname. The Military Unit field may also display the surname range (A-G) as found on the microfilm. This collection is a part of RG 94, Records of the Adjutant General's Office, 1780's-1917 and is National Archive Microfilm Publication M397. Index courtesy of Fold3. This database has 1,256,188 records. See **https://familysearch.org/search/collection/1932398.**

**1861-1940 Louisville City Directories.** See ***Louisville (Kentucky) City Directories*** **[Microfilm],** by various publishers, filmed by Research Publications, Woodbridge, CT, 1980-1984. The FHL has 1861, 1864-1935, 1938, and 1940. 57 rolls, beginning with FHL film #1376990. For a complete list of roll numbers and the contents of each roll, see the online FHL catalog page for this title. See **https://familysearch.org/search/catalog/530821.**

***1862 Boyd County Kentucky Tax List*** **[Online Database],** indexed at the USGenWeb site for Boyd Co KY. See **http://files.usgwarchives.net/ky/boyd/taxlists/1862tax.txt.**

***1862-1866 Internal Revenue Assessment Lists for Kentucky*** **[Microfilm & Digital Capture],** from the originals at the National Archives, Washington, DC. Divisions are often not in order, but names are generally in alphabetical order. Some are arranged by division, county, and then the year. The FHL catalog page for this title has a list of the divisions and counties on each roll. Filmed by the National Archives, series M0768, 24 rolls, beginning with FHL film #1491176. To access the digital images, see the online FHL catalog page: **https://familysearch.org/search/catalog/209869.**

***1865 Tax List, Bath County, Kentucky*** **[Online Database]**, from the Internal Revenue Assessment Lists, indexed at the USGenWeb site for Bath Co KY. See **http://files.usgwarchives.net/ky/bath/taxes/1865.txt.**

***1865 Tax List, Fleming County, Kentucky*** **[Online Database],** indexed at the USGenWeb site for Fleming Co KY. See **http://files.usgwarchives.net/ky/fleming/taxes/1865tax.txt.**

***1865 Tax List, Mason County, Kentucky*** **[Online Database],** indexed at the USGenWeb site for Mason Co KY. See **http://files.usgwarchives.net/ky/mason/tax/tax001.txt.**

***1865 Tax List, Montgomery County, Kentucky*** **[Online Database]**, from the Internal Revenue Assessment Lists, indexed at the USGenWeb site for Montgomery Co KY. See **http://files.usgwarchives.net/ky/montgomery/taxes/1865 .txt.**

**1865-1872.** ***Kentucky, Freedman's Bureau Field Office Records*** **[Online Database],** digitized at the FamilySearch.org website. This is an image-only database. The Bureau of Refugees, Freedmen, and Abandoned Lands (often called the Freedmen's Bureau) was created in 1865 at the end of the American Civil War to supervise the relief efforts, including education, health care, food and clothing, refugee camps, legalization of marriages, employment, labor contracts; and securing back pay, bounty payments and pensions. These records include letters and endorsements sent and received, account books, applications for rations, applications for relief, court records, labor contracts, registers of bounty claimants, registers of complaints, registers of contracts, registers of disbursements, registers of freedmen issued rations, registers of patients, reports, rosters of officers and employees, special and general orders and circulars received, special orders and circulars issued, records relating to claims, court trials, property restoration, and homesteads. This database has 101,031 images. See **www.familysearch.org/search/collection/2333771**.

**1866-1870 Louisville City Directories.** See ***Edward's Annual Directory to the Inhabitants, Institutions. . .*** **[Microfilm],** from originals published by Edwards, Greenough & Daved, Louisville, KY, 1866-1870. The FHL has 1865-1866, 1866-1867, 1868, 1869, and 1870. Filmed by Louisville Microfilms, 5 rolls, beginning with FHL film #156937 (1865-1866). For a complete list of roll numbers and contents of each roll, see the online FHL catalog page for this title. See **https://familysearch.org/search/catalog/50394.**

***1869 Tax List, Elliott County, Kentucky*** **[Online Database],** indexed at the USGenWeb site for Elliott Co KY. An archived version is available. See **http://web.archive.org/web/20040415111609/http://home.zoomnet.net/~cbarker/ell69tl.htm.**

**1870.** ***Kentucky, 1870 Federal Census: Population Schedules*** **[Microfilm & Digital Capture],** from the originals at the National Archives, Washington, DC. The 1870 census was filmed twice. The second filming is listed first and is usually easier to read. Filmed by the National Archives, 1962-1968, series M593, 49 rolls, beginning with FHL film #545943 (Kentucky: Adams, Adair, Allen, and Anderson counties). To access the digital images, see the online FHL catalog page: **https://familysearch.org/search/catalog/698898.**

**1870.** ***Kentucky 1870 Census Index*** **[Printed Index],** edited by Raeone Christensen Steuart, published by Heritage Quest, North Salt Lake, UT, 2000, 3 vols., FHL book 976.9 X22ken.

**1870.** ***Federal Census Index, Kentucky West, 1870: With Addendum, Union County*** **[Printed Index],** edited by Ronald Vern Jackson, published by Accelerated Indexing Systems, Salt Lake City, UT, 1988, 876 pages, FHL book 976.9 X22kw.

**1870.** ***Kentucky 1870 Federal Census – East*** **[Printed Index],** edited by Ronald Vern Jackson, published by Accelerated Indexing Systems, 1988, 702 pages, FHL book 976.X22ke.

***1873-1924 Wills, Book C – Index, Livingston County, Kentucky*** **[Online Database],** indexed at the Western KY History site. See **www.westernkyhistory.org/livingston/willbookcindex.html.**

**1874.** ***History of Kentucky*** **[Printed Book & Online Database],** "by the late Lewis Collins, Judge of the Mason County Court…Revised, Enlarged four-fold, and brought down to the year 1874 by his son Richard H. Collins, A.M., LL.B.," 2 Vols., published by Collings & Co., Covington, KY, 1874. This is the definitive history of Kentucky, with name lists for the earliest settlers, early soldiers of the Revolutionary War and later, and much more. Reprinted by the Kentucky Historical Society, Frankfort, KY, 1966, 2 Vols, FHL book 976.9 H2c vo.1-2. A digital version of this book is available online at the Ancestry.com subscription website. And, for a link to a free digital version of this title, see the online FHL catalog page: **https://familysearch.org/search/catalog/1921656.**
- See also ***Personal and Family Name Index to the History of Kentucky*** **(Printed Book),** compiled by Albert S. Hunter, 1970, 50 pages. See FHL book 976.9H2c.

**1880.** ***Kentucky, 1880 Federal Census: Soundex and Population Schedules*** **[Microfilm & Digital Capture],** from the originals at the National Archives. After microfilming, the National Archives transferred the original 1880 manuscripts to the Kentucky Department of Archives & libraries. Filmed by the National Archives, ca1970, 139 rolls, beginning with FHL film #447040 (Soundex A000 thru A400). To access the digital images (Population Schedules), see the online FHL catalog page: **https://familysearch.org/search/catalog/673556.**

***1880 Industrial Census, Boone County, Kentucky*** **[Online Database],** extracted at the RootsWeb site for Boone Co KY. See **www.rootsweb.ancestry.com/~kyboone/1880industrialcensus.htm.**

**1880s–1911.** See ***Delayed Birth Records, Livingston, Kentucky*** **[Online Database],** indexed at the Western KY History site. See **www.westernkyhistory.org/livingston/livdelayedbths.html.**

**1880s–1920s.** ***Kentucky Index of Biographical Sketches in State, Regional and County Histories*** **[Printed Book],** by Michael L. Cook. This book indexes 65 various state, regional and county histories of Kentucky areas. Published by Cook Publications, Evansville, IN, 1986, 179 pages, FHL book 976.9 D32c.

**1884.** ***Bracken County 1884 Atlas*** **[Online Database],** images at the KYkinfolk site for Bracken Co KY. See **http://kykinfolk.com/bracken/1884.html.**

***1887 Tax List, Mason County, Kentucky*** **[Online Database],** indexed at the USGenWeb site for Mason Co KY. See **http://files.usgwarchives.net/ky/mason/tax/tax002.txt.**

**1887-1959.** ***Naturalization Records, Louisville, Kentucky*** **[Microfilm & Digital Capture],** from the originals at the National Archives, East Point, GA. Most volumes are individually indexed. Filmed by the Genealogical Society of Utah, 1987-1989, 11 rolls, beginning with FHL film #1510177. To access the digital images, see the online FHL catalog page: **www.familysearch.org/search/catalog/667667.**

***1888 Tax List, Harlan County, Kentucky*** **[Online Database],** indexed at the RootsWeb site for Harlan Co KY. See **www.rootsweb.ancestry.com/~kyharlan/1888HarlanTaxListA_F.htm.**

***1890 Property Tax List, Floyd County, Kentucky*** **[Online Database],** indexed at the RootsWeb site for Floyd Co KY. See **www.rootsweb.ancestry.com/~kyfloyd/Mis_files/part_of_the_1890_property_tax_li.htm.**

***1890 Kentucky Census Index of Civil War Veterans or Their Widows*** **[Printed Index],** compiled by Bryan Lee Dilts, Salt Lake City, UT, 1984, 135 pages, FHL book 976.9 X22d.

***1890 Kentucky Census Index, Special Schedule of the Eleventh Census (1890) Enumerating Union Veterans and Widows of Union Veterans of the Civil War*** **[Printed Index],** edited by Ronald Vern Jackson, published by Accelerated Indexing Systems, 1984, 266 pages, FHL book 976.9 X22j.

***1891 Tax List, Harlan County, Kentucky*** **[Online Database],** indexed at the RootsWeb site for Harlan Co KY. See **www.rootsweb.ancestry.com/~kyharlan/1891HarlanTaxListA_F.htm.**

***1894-1934 School Censuses, LaRue County, Kentucky*** **[Online Databases],** links to each school census at the KYkinfolk site for LaRue Co KY. See **http://kykinfolk.com/larue/larue4.htm.**

***1894 School Census, Simpson County, Kentucky*** **[Online Database[,** indexed at the Simpson Co Biz Land site. For the name lists and Index, See **http://simpsonco.bizland.com/SCHOOL_RECORDS.HTM**

**1895-1896.**. ***Kentucky Places and People: R. L. Polk & Co.'s Kentucky State Gazetteer and Business Directory for 1895-96*** **[Printed Book],** originally published, R.L. Polk & Co., 1895. Reprinted by McDowell Publications, Utica, KY, 1984, 323 pages. FHL book 976.9 E4k. For a link to a digital version of this title, see the online FHL catalog page. See **https://familysearch.org/search/catalog/5234.**

**1895-1896.** ***R.L. Polk's Kentucky State Gazetteer and Business Directory for Owen County, Kentucky*** **[Online Database],** indexed at the USGenWeb site for Owen Co KY. See **http://files.usgwarchives.net/ky/owen/misc/1895gaza.txt.**

***1895-1910 Delayed Birth Records, Lyon County, Kentucky*** **[Online Database],** indexed at the RootsWeb site for Lyon Co KY. See **www.rootsweb.ancestry.com/~kylyon/delayedbirthrecords.html.**

**1895-1964. Morganfield High School Alumni [Online Database],** a list of graduates for each year, with a batch of graduates with no known year. Morganfield is in Union County, Kentucky. For an archived database, see **https://web.archive.org/web/20130331041753/http://home.comcast.net/~unioncountyky/alumni.html.**

**1897-1928.** See ***School Census Records, Lee County, Kentucky, 1897, 1900-1901, & 1928*** **[Online Database],** indexed at the USGenWeb site for Lee Co KY. See **www.usgennet.org/usa/ky/county/lee/schcensus.html.**

**1900. *Kentucky, 1900 Federal Census: Soundex and Population Schedules*** **[Microfilm & Digital Capture],** from the original records held by the Bureau of the Census in the 1940s. After microfilming, Congress allowed the Census Bureau to destroy the originals to free up space for WWII-related files. Filmed on 250 rolls, beginning with FHL film #1244052 (Soundex: A000 Lily thru A216 John A). To access the digital images, see the online FHL catalog page: **https://familysearch.org/search/catalog/653092.**

**1906-1991. *Kentucky, Naturalization Records*** **[Online Database],** digitized and indexed at the Ancestry.com website. Source: Microfilmed Records of District Courts of the United States, Record Group 21. The National Archives at Atlanta, Georgia. This database has 67,206 records. See **http://search.ancestry.com/search/db.aspx?dbid=2501.**

**1910. *Kentucky, 1910 Federal Census: Soundex and Population Schedules*** **[Microfilm & Digital Capture],** from the original records held by the Bureau of the Census in the 1940s. After microfilming, Congress allowed the Census Bureau to destroy the originals to free up space for WWII-related files. Filmed on 239 rolls, beginning with FHL film #1370445 (Soundex: A000 thru A260 John). To access the digital images, see the online FHL catalog page: **https://familysearch.org/search/catalog/653187.**

***1911 Tax List, Morgan County, Kentucky*** **[Online Database],** indexed at the USGenWeb site for Morgan Co KY. See **http://files.usgwarchives.net/ky/morgan/taxes/1910tax.txt.**

***1911 Grand Jury List, Morgan County, Kentucky*** **[Online Database],** indexed at the USGenWeb site for Morgan Co KY. See **http://files.usgwarchives.net/ky/morgan/court/1911gj.txt.**

**1911-1930. *Crittenden County, Kentucky Births*** **[Online Database]**, indexed at the Western KY History site. See **http://westernkyhistory.org/crittenden/crittbths.html.**

**1911-1930**. See ***Births, 1911-1920 & 1921-1930, Livingston County, Kentucky*** **[Online Database],** indexed at the Western KY History site. See **www.westernkyhistory.org/livingston/bthrec.html.**

**1911-1995. *Kentucky Birth Indexes*** **[Microfiche],** from the Kentucky office of Vital Statistics, Frankfort, KY. Filmed by the KY Office of Vital Statistics, 1997, 1,038 fiche, beginning with FHL fiche #6118873 (Child: A-Very, Edson). For a complete list of fiche numbers and contents of each, see the online FHL catalog page for this title. See **https://familysearch.org/search/catalog/740438.**

**1911-1954. *Births and Deaths Index*** **[Microfilm & Digital Capture],** from the Kentucky Office of Vital Statistics, Frankfort, KY. Filmed by the Genealogical Society of Utah, 1960, 92 rolls, beginning with FHL film #209595 (Aa – Bur, v. 1911-1915). To access the digital images, see the online FHL catalog page: **https://familysearch.org/search/catalog/231754.**

**1911-1963. *Kentucky Death Records*** **[Online Database],** indexed at the FamilySearch.org website. Statewide death registration began in 1911. This database has 1,681,924 records. See **https://familysearch.org/search/collection/1417491.**

**1911-1999. *Kentucky Birth Index*** **[Online Database],** indexed at the Ancestry.com website. Original data: Kentucky Department for Libraries and Archives. Kentucky Birth, Marriage, and Death Databases: Births 1911-1999. Frankfort, Kentucky: Kentucky Department for Libraries and Archives. This database has 5,859,513 records. See **http://search.ancestry.com/search/db.aspx?dbid=8788.**

**1911-1999, *Kentucky Vital Records Indexes*** **[Online Database],** indexed at the FamilySearch.org website. Source: Indexes created by the KY Vital Statistic Office, now at the KY Dept for Libraries and Archives. Includes indexes of births, marriages, and deaths from January 1911 to July 1999. This database has 9,865,938 records. See **www.familysearch.org/search/collection/2531527**.

**1911-2000**. ***Kentucky Death Index*** **[Online Database],** indexed at the Ancestry.com website. Original data: Commonwealth of Kentucky, Health Data Branch, Kentucky Death Index, 1911-present. Kentucky Department of Information Systems. This database has 3,320,556 records. See
**http://search.ancestry.com/search/db.aspx?dbid=3077.**

**1912-1950.** ***Kentucky Confederate Pension Applications*** **[Online Database],** images at the FamilySearch.org website. Includes pension applications filed by surviving former Confederate soldiers or their widows who lived in Kentucky. The law providing for pensions was enacted in 1912 by the Kentucky General Assembly. This database has 29,959 records. See
**https://familysearch.org/search/collection/1916017.**
- This image-only database is also available at the Ancestry.com website See
**https://search.ancestry.com/search/db.aspx?dbid=60293.**

**1917-1918.** ***Kentucky, World War I Selective Service System Draft Registration Cards*** **[Microfilm & Digital Capture],** from the originals at the National Archives, filmed by the National Archives, 1987-1988, 92 rolls, beginning with FHL film #1643933. The card images are arranged in alphabetical order. To access the digital images, see the online FHL catalog page:
**www.familysearch.org/search/catalog/746979.**
- See also ***World War I Draft Registration Cards: Prisoners, Indians, Insane, In Hospitals & Late Registrants, Kansas & Kentucky*** [Printed Book & Digital Version]. To access the digital images, see the online FHL catalog page:
**www.familysearch.org/search/catalog/1368555.**

**1917-1920.** ***Certificates of Death Completed by Civil Authorities Outside the State of Kentucky for World War I Soldiers from the State of Kentucky*** **[Microfilm & Digital Capture],** from the originals at the KY Dept. of Libraries and Archives, 1 roll, FHL film #2241626. To access the digital images, see the online FHL catalog page:
**www.familysearch.org/search/catalog/1119118.**

**1920.** ***Kentucky, 1920 Federal Census: Soundex and Population Schedules*** **[Microfilm & Digital Capture],** from the original records held by the Bureau of the Census in the 1940s. After microfilming, Congress allowed the Census Bureau to destroy the originals to free up space for WWII-related files. Filmed on 226 rolls, beginning with FHL film #1825340 (Soundex: A000 thru A260 Myrtle). For a complete list of roll numbers and contents of each roll, see the online FHL catalog page for this title. See
**https://familysearch.org/search/catalog/570928.**

**1922 History.** See ***History of Kentucky*** **[Printed Book & Online Database],** edited by Charles Kerr, by William Elsey Connelley, published by the American Historical Society, Chicago, 1922, 5 vols., 976.9 H2k v. 1-5. A digital version of this title is available and indexed at the Ancestry.com website.
**http://search.ancestry.com/search/db.aspx?dbid=7675.**

**1930.** ***Kentucky, 1930 Federal Census: Soundex and Population Schedules*** **[Microfilm & Digital Capture],** from the original records held by the Bureau of the Census in the 1940s. After microfilming, Congress allowed the Census Bureau to destroy the originals to free up space for WWII-related files. Filmed on 75 rolls, beginning with FHL film #2338646 (Soundex: A123 thru B256). To access the digital images (Population Schedules), see the online FHL catalog page:
**https://familysearch.org/search/catalog/1036353.**

**1931-1932.** ***Polk's Danville (Kentucky) City Directory*** **[Online Database],** a PDF of the original directory is available at the RootsWeb site for Boyd Co KY. See the document index page:
**https://www.ancestry.com/search/collections/22750/**

**1931-1932.** ***Kentucky City Directories (Polk's Lexington)*** **[Online Database],** digitized and OCR indexed at the Ancestry.com website. This database has 840 pages. See
**https://search.ancestry.com/search/db.aspx?dbid=8982.**

**1933-1990.** ***Tennessee Valley Cemetery Relocation Files*** **[Online Database],** digitized and indexed at the Ancestry.com website. Source: Tennessee Valley Authority (TVA) at the National Archives, East Point, GA. Each record includes Name, Birth date, Death date, Death age, Grave number, and Reinternment place. This database has 172,537 records. See
**https://search.ancestry.com/search/db.aspx?dbid=60427.**

**1934-1954.** ***Master File Relocation Card Index for Grave and Cemetery Removal and Relocation*** **[Microfilm & Digital Capture],** from original records of the Tennessee Valley Authority (TVA) at the National Archives, East Point, GA. Lists cemetery name and number, name of the deceased, date of birth, date of death, age, type and condition of marker and inscription, nearest living relative or source of information, source's address and relationship to deceased. TVA Projects involved in the index are: Norris, Wheeler, Pickwick, Hiwassee, Chichamauga, Douglas, Cherokee, Watts Bar, Boone, Gallatin, Sevier Stone, Fontana, Nottely, Chatuge, Ft. Loudon, Nichajack, Wautauga, South Holston, Johnsonville Steam, Tims Ford, Tellico, Bear Creek, Watershed, Kentucky, Normandy, Land Between the Lakes Area, Brown Ferry Area. Cemeteries included from Tennessee, Alabama, Mississippi, North Carolina, Georgia, Kentucky, and Virginia. Filmed by the Genealogical Society of Utah, 1996, 58 rolls, beginning with FHL film #2050038 (Norris Project, 1934-1936). To access the digital images, see the online FHL catalog page:
**https://familysearch.org/search/catalog/778971.**

**1940.** ***Kentucky, 1940 Federal Census: Population Schedules*** **[Digital Capture],** from the original records held by the Bureau of the Census in the 1940s. After microfilming, Congress allowed the Census Bureau to destroy the originals to free up space for WWII-related files. Filmed on 101 rolls, beginning with FHL film #5460587 (Kentucky: Adair & Allen County). To access the digital images, see the online FHL catalog page: **https://familysearch.org/search/catalog/2057757**

***1940 Federal Census Finding Aids*** **[Online Database].** The National Archives prepared a special website online with a detailed description of the 1940 federal census. Included at the site are descriptions of location finding aids, such as Enumeration District maps, Geographic Descriptions of Census Enumeration Districts, and a list of 1940 City Directories available at the National Archives. The finding aids are all linked to other National Archives sites. The National Archives website also has a link to 1940 Search Engines using Stephen P. Morse's "One-Step" system for finding a 1940 E.D. or street address conversion. See
**www.archives.gov/research/census/1940/general-info.html#questions.**

**1940-1947.** ***Kentucky, World War II Draft Registration Cards*** **[Digital Capture],** digital images of originals held by the National Personnel Records Center, St. Louis, MO. The card images are arranged in alphabetical order. To access the digital images, see
**https://www.ancestry.com/search/collections/2238/**

**1942.** ***Kentucky, Military Records: World War II 4th Draft Registration Cards*** **[Digital Capture],** digital images of original records at the National Personnel Records Census, St. Louis, MO. These cards represent older men, ages 45 to 65 in April 1942, that were registered for the draft. They had birth dates between 28 Apr 1877 and 16 Feb 1892. Each card includes name of individual, date and place of birth, address, age, telephone number, employer's name and address, name and address of person who would know where the individual can be located, signature, and physical description. To access the digital images, see the online FHL catalog page:
**www.familysearch.org/search/catalog/2624877.**

**1942.** ***Polk's Danville (Boyle County, Kentucky) City Directory*** **[Online Database],** a PDF of the original directory is available at the Ancestry site for Boyd Co KY. See the document index page:
**https://www.ancestry.com/imageviewer/collections/2469/images/15291942?ssrc=&backlabel=Return**

**1945.** ***Polk's Danville (Boyle County, Kentucky) City Directory*** **[Online Database],** a PDF of the original directory is available at the Ancestry site for Boyd Co KY. See the document index page:
**https://www.ancestry.com/imageviewer/collections/2469/images/13879055?ssrc=&backlabel=Return**

**1948.** ***Polk's Danville (Boyle County, Kentucky) City Directory*** **[Online Database],** a PDF of the original directory is available at the Ancestry site for Boyd Co KY. See the document index page:
**https://www.ancestry.com/imageviewer/collections/2469/images/15383712?ssrc=&backlabel=Return**

**1950-1953.** ***Korean War – Missing Personnel (Report for Kentucky)*** **[Online Database],** a list of names from the Dept of Defense report. The database is used in an ongoing effort to identify remains and return them to families. The effort now entails collecting DNA from kin and using that in the identification process. Indexed at:
www.usgwarchives.net/ky/state
**www.usgwarchives.net/ky/state/korean.html.**

**1954.** ***Polk's Danville (Boyle County, Kentucky) City Directory*** **[Online Database],** a PDF of the original directory is available at the Ancestry site for Boyd Co KY. See the document index page: **https://www.ancestry.com/imageviewer/collections/2469/images/14429191?ssrc=&backlabel=Return**

**1962-2005** ***Kentucky, Divorce Records*** **[Online Database],** indexed at the Ancestry.com website. Source: Ancestry extractions from KY County Record Offices. Each record includes a Full name, Spouse's full name, Date of Divorce, and Place of divorce. This database has 515,731 records. See **https://search.ancestry.com/search/db.aspx?dbid=61049.**

**1964-1975.** ***U.S. Unaccounted for – From the Vietnam War (Report for Kentucky)*** **[Online Database],** a list of names from the Dept of Defense report. The database is used in an ongoing effort to identify remains and return them to families. The effort now entails collecting DNA from kin and using that in the identification process. Indexed at the USGenWeb Archives site for Kentucky. See **www.usgwarchives.net/ky/state/vietnam.html.**

**1973-1984.** ***Cumulative Index to "Bluegrass Roots"*** **[Printed Book & Digital Version],** by Brian D. Harney, publ. KY Gen. Soc., Frankfort KA, 1985, 204 pages. To access the digital version, see the online FHL catalog page: **www.familysearch.org/search/catalog/479320.**

**1973-1999.** ***Kentucky, Marriage Index*** **[Online Database],** indexed at the Ancestry.com website. Original data: Kentucky Department for Libraries and Archives. Kentucky Birth, Marriage, and Death Databases: Marriages 1973-1999. Frankfort, KY. See **http://search.ancestry.com/search/db.aspx?dbid=8787.**

**1974-1995.** ***Kentucky Divorce Indexes*** **[Microfiche],** from the Kentucky Office of Vital Statistics, Frankfort, KY, 82 fiche, FHL fiche #6118877 (husbands), and #6118878 (wives).

**1984-Current.** ***Kentucky Recent Newspaper Obituaries*** **[Online Database]**, digitized and indexed newspaper obituaries at the GenealogyBank website, including newspapers from Ashland, Barbourville, Bardstown, Bedford, Campbellsville, Carrollton, Columbia, Corbin, Covington, Cynthiana, Danville, Elizabethtown, Frankfort, Georgetown, Glasgow, Grayson, Olive Hill, Harlan, Harrodsburg, Hazard, Henderson, Hodgenville, LaGrange, Lancaster, Lawrenceburg, Lebanon, Leitchfield, Lexington, Liberty, Louisville, Madisonville, Maysville, Middlesboro, Monticello, Morehead, New Castle, Nicholasville, Owensboro, Owenton, Paris, Prestonsburg, Richmond, Russellville, Shelbyville, Somerset, Springfield, Stanford, Taylorsville, Washington, Union, Whitley City, Williamstown, and Winchester. See

**www.genealogybank.com/gbnk/obituaries/explore/USA/Kentucky.**

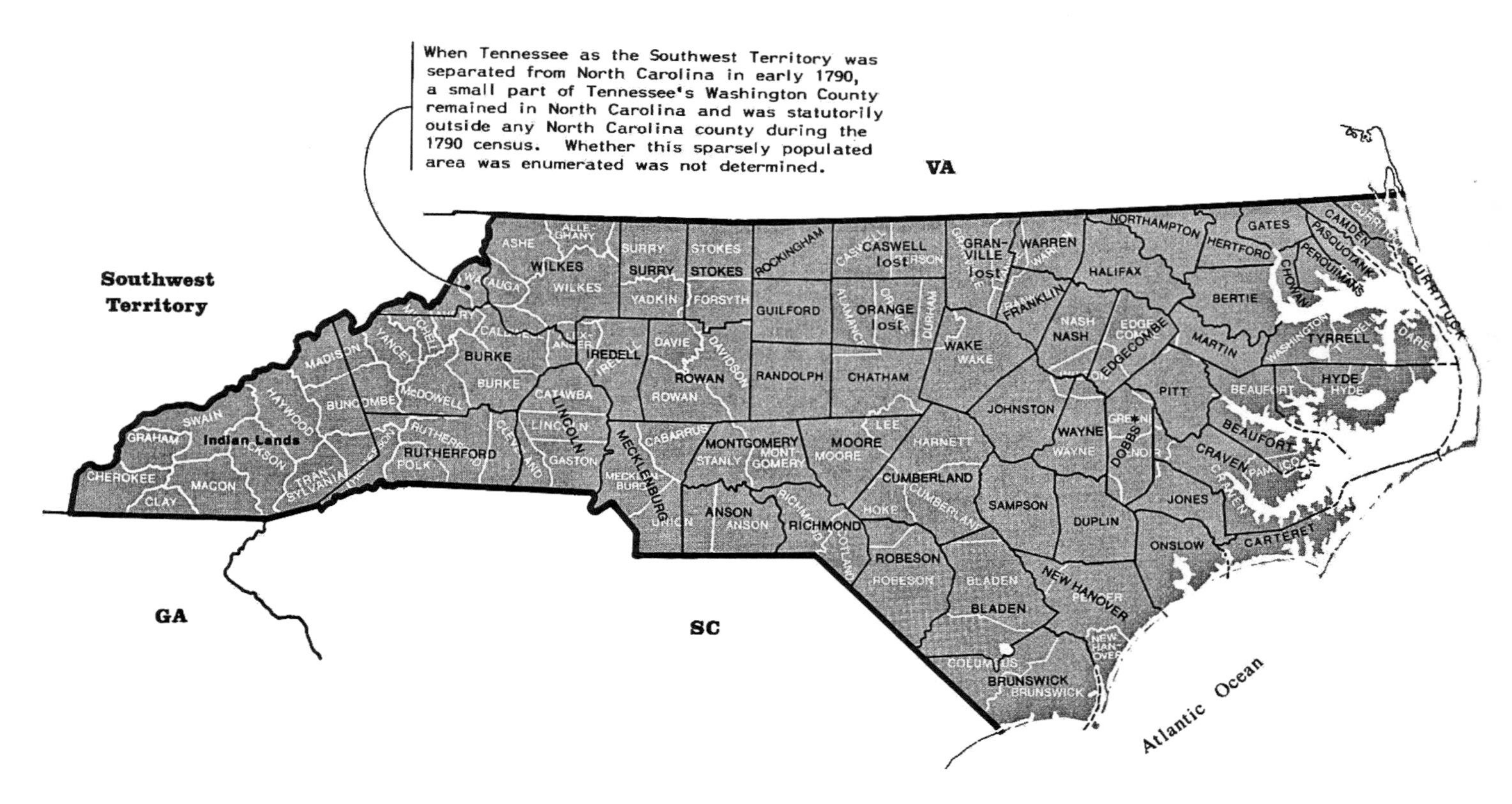


**North Carolina • Aug 1790.** The 53 counties of North Carolina at the time of the 1790 Federal Census are shown in black. The current 100 counties of North Carolina are shown in white. The federal census is extant for all counties except Caswell, Granville, and Orange, shown as "lost" on the map. Those three counties were reconstructed from tax lists in the Census Bureau's *1790 Heads of Families* publication. * **Note:** The name Dobbs was dropped when that county was split into Glasgow and Lenoir counties in 1791. Glasgow was then renamed Greene in 1799. **Map Source:** Page 228, *Map Guide to the U.S. Federal Censuses, 1790-1920*, by William Thorndale and William Dollarhide.

# North Carolina

## Censuses & Substitute Name Lists

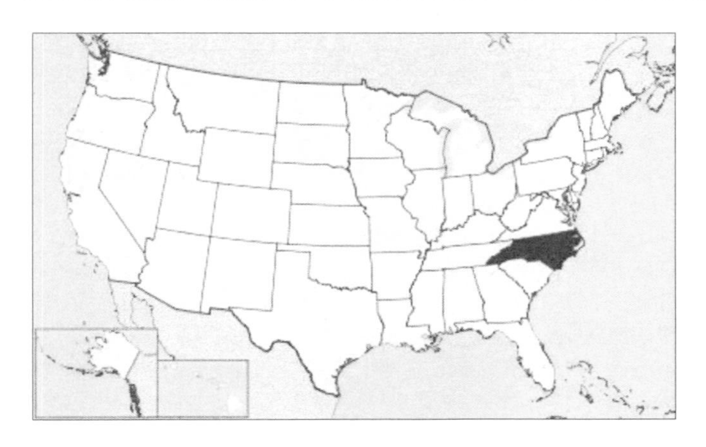

### Historical Timeline for North Carolina, 1497-1794

**1497-1498.** Italian sea captain Giovanni Caboto was commissioned by the English King Henry VII to explore America. He landed in 1497 on the island of Newfoundland. On his second trip in 1498, he visited the coasts of present New Jersey, Delaware, Maryland, Virginia, North Carolina, South Carolina, and Georgia. In honor of the event, the king anglicized his name to John Cabot.

**1558.** Elizabeth I became Queen of England. The early exploration of North America took place during her 45-year reign, the Elizabethan Era, or "Golden Age." When Elizabeth I was crowned, England was nearly bankrupt, but during her reign, the English Empire expanded and thrived, and English culture flourished in Literature, Theatre, Music, and Architecture.

**1584. Virginia.** Sir Walter Raleigh claimed and named Virginia for the "Virgin Queen," Elizabeth I, an area from present Chesapeake Bay to Florida, and everything below a northwestern line to the North Pole.

**1584-1590. Roanoke Colony.** In 1584, Queen Elizabeth I granted to Sir Walter Raleigh a charter for the colonization of the entire area of North America. In 1585, the first group of settlers led by Sir Richard Grenville, established a colony at the north end of Roanoke Island (present Dare County, North Carolina). The first group left Roanoke Island after a few months, returning to England with Sir Francis Drake. When a second group brought by Grenville in 1586 found the colony abandoned, the bulk of the second group returned to England as well. The final group, led by Governor John White, arrived in 1587. Soon after, he returned to England to plead for more supplies. White had left 90 men, 17 women, and 11 children, including his grand-daughter, Virginia Dare, the first English birth in America. It took White over three years to return to Roanoke due to several incidents with pirates, the Anglo-Spanish War, and the Spanish Armada. When he did return to Roanoke Island in August 1590, there was no trace of the colonists. There was no sign of a struggle or battle at the site or surrounding areas. To this day, no one is completely sure what happened to "The Lost Colony."

**1603. England.** James I became King of England, the first monarch to rule both England and Scotland. (He was James VI of Scotland since 1566). During his reign, the first permanent English colonies were established in Virginia and New England. James I was an advocate for the transportation of thousands of clan people living along the Scottish-English border to Ulster Province / Northern Ireland.

**1606.** Two joint stock companies were founded in 1606, both with royal charters issued by King James I for the purpose of establishing colonies in North America. The Virginia Company of London was given a land grant between Latitude 34° (Cape Fear) and Latitude 41° (Long Island Sound). The Virginia Company of Plymouth was founded with a similar land grant between Latitude 38° (Potomac River) and Latitude 45° (St. John River), which included a shared area with the London Company between Latitude 38° and Latitude 41°..

**1607. April 26. Virginia.** Three ships under the command of Capt. Christopher Newport sought shelter in Chesapeake Bay. The forced landing led to the founding of Jamestown on the James River, the-first permanent English settlement, consisting of 104 men and boys. The Jamestown colony was led by Capt. John Smith and his cousin, Bartholomew Gosnold. A year later, about 100 new settlers arrived, finding only 38 survivors from the first group. In 1610, recently appointed governor of Virginia, Thomas West (Lord De La Warr) arrived at Jamestown to find only 60 settlers alive.

**1623. Carolina.** The first charter for a colony in the area of the Carolinas was granted to Sir Robert Heath by King James I, but due to the political climate in England, the charter would never be used.

**1625. England.** Charles I became King of England, Scotland, and Ireland. Soon after taking office, Charles began to note a large number of non-conformists among his subjects. Along with his Archbishop, William Laud, the King began a campaign to purge his church of the largest group of non-conformists, the so-called "Puritans," a militant Calvinist religious group attempting to purify the Church of England.

**1629-1640.** As a result of the Charles I campaign to purge non-conformists from the Church of England, large groups of people were disenfranchised. Charles I disbanded Parliament and ruled England alone for eleven years. The Puritans referred to this era as "the eleven years of tyranny." It was during these eleven years that some 21,000 Puritan immigrants established the Massachusetts Bay Colony of North America.

**1633. Virginia.** The Middle Plantation of the Virginia Colony was founded. The first inland settlement after Jamestown, it later became Williamsburg.

**1641. Virginia.** Sir William Berkeley was appointed governor by Charles I. He served from 1642 to 1652 and again from 1660 to 1677. His brother Lord John Berkeley, was the first Proprietor of the East New Jersey colony, and both brothers were Lords Proprietors of the Province of Carolina. William Berkeley transformed the Virginia colony by emulating the culture of southwest England's plantation system.

**1642. English Civil War.** When Parliament was restored in 1640, it quickly became dominated by the same Puritans who King Charles I had removed from the Church of England. Beginning in 1642, Royalist supporters were forced to fight the armies of the Puritan Parliament in the English Civil War. The English Colonies took sides: the Virginia colony favored the Royalist/Cavalier side, while the New England colonies were in support of the Parliamentarian/Puritan side. The Province of Maryland had earlier allowed all religious persuasions to settle in Maryland. During the English Civil War, Maryland granted free land as refuge to any Puritans from Virginia to settle there.

**1645-1651. England.** After his defeat and capture in 1645, Charles I refused to accept his captors' demands for a constitutional monarchy, and briefly escaped captivity in 1647. While recaptured, his teenage son, Prince Charles, was able to marshal Scottish forces for the king. However, by 1648, Oliver Cromwell had consolidated the English opposition. King Charles I was tried, convicted, and beheaded for high treason in January 1649. The Civil War continued until 1651, when Oliver Cromwell, a Puritan, became Lord Protectorate, ruling the Commonwealth of England for the next seven years.

**1650. Virginia (present North Carolina).** The first settlements near Albemarle Sound were established by pioneers from tidewater Virginia.

**1658-1660. England.** After Oliver Cromwell died in 1658, his son, Richard, was too weak politically to remain in power. In 1660, a new Parliament offered a restored English throne to the exiled Scottish King, son of Charles I, who accepted to become King Charles II.

**1663. Carolina.** Charles II granted eight noblemen a charter to *Carolina*, from Latitude 31$^{O}$ (present FL/GA line) to Latitude 35$^{O}$ (present GA/TN line). This was a repayment for their loyalty and support during the English Civil War. The eight became known as the Lords Proprietors. In 1665, the charter was extended north to the present NC/VA line to include the Albemarle Sound settlements, The name Carolina came from "Carolus," Latin for Charles.

**1669-1670. Carolina.** In late 1669, three shiploads of colonists sailed from London, headed for Carolina. At Barbados, the ships were struck by a hurricane. The *Albemarle* was destroyed, and the *Port Royal* and *Carolina* were severely damaged. In March 1670, the *Carolina* arrived at Sewee Bay, and temporarily anchored at the north end of Bull's Island. In April, Charles Towne was founded as the capital of the Province of Carolina.

**1682. Carolina.** The first four counties of the Province of Carolina were created, named after Lords Proprietors Berkeley, Colleton, Craven, and Granville.

**1699. Virginia.** The colonial capital moved from Jamestown to the newly incorporated town of Williamsburg.

**1705.** Bath was the first town in present North Carolina.

**1707.** England and Scotland merged into the **United Kingdom of Great Britain.** The English Colonies now became the British Colonies.

**1712. North and South Carolina.** The territory of the Province of Carolina since 1665 ran from about Latitude 31$^{O}$ to the present NC/VA line (36$^{O}$30'), including the area of present Georgia. In 1712, the Proprietors divided Carolina into North Carolina and South Carolina (proprietary provinces) on nearly the same division line as today, but the line was not surveyed for several more years. Each province had its own colonial governor, under the authority of the eight Lords Proprietors.

**1717.** The arrival of the first Scots-Irish immigrants to the British Colonies was via Boston, New York City, Philadelphia, Alexandria, Norfolk, New Bern, and Charles Towne. The so-called Scots-Irish (or Ulster Scots) were former border clan people who had lived near the Scottish-English border for centuries. A good number of them had moved into areas of Northern Ireland in the early 1600s, and a mass migration to most of the British colonies of America began in about 1717.

**1721.** The **Province of South Carolina** became a Royal British Colony in 1721 (no longer a proprietary colony).

**1729-1777.** In 1729, the **Province of North Carolina** became a separate Royal British Colony after seven of the eight Lords Proprietors sold their interest back to the Crown. A large portion of original proprietor land was retained by Lord John Carteret. In 1744, Carteret inherited the title of Earl of Granville. Soon after, the former proprietor began selling land in his privately held **Granville District**, the northern half of present North Carolina & Tennessee. The first few years of land sales were well documented, providing good evidence of the earliest inhabitants of central and western North Carolina into the 1760s. Later records were incomplete due to cross-claim disputes. The Granville District operation dissolved in 1777.

**1768.** The **Regulators** were organized in the North Carolina back country. Mostly farmers, they were formed in protest of excessive taxes. Though they were the earliest rebels against the Royal government in North Carolina, they more resembled a vigilante mob rather than a Sons of Liberty organization.

**1771.** Gov. Tyron had seven Regulators executed after an uprising at Alamance.

**1776.** North Carolina was the first British Colony to vote for independence. The state's first American Revolution battle was fought at Moores Creek Bridge.

**1784. State of Franklin.** Feeling cut off from their government in New Bern, North Carolina, settlers living in present Northeastern Tennessee declared their area an independent state and named it Franklin. Jonesborough was their capital. Franklin functioned as a state for four years with the consent of the local population. But in 1788, Franklin's petition to Congress for official recognition was denied. The area was reclaimed by North Carolina where it remained until the Southwest Territory was formed in 1790.

**1789.** Nov 21. **North Carolina** became the 12$^{th}$ state in the Union, with the state capital at New Bern.

**1790.** North Carolina ceded to the U.S. Government the area that became the "Territory Southwest of the River Ohio." The Southwest Territory became the state of Tennessee in 1796.

**1794. North Carolina.** The capital of North Carolina was moved from New Bern to Raleigh.

---

## Online Resources at North Carolina State Websites

**North Carolina State Archives – Manuscript and Archives Reference System (MARS).** This is an extensive list of archival records, cataloging the contents of millions of documents and artifacts at the three branches of the North Carolina State Archives: 1) State Archives (Raleigh), 2) Outer Banks History Center (Mateo), and 3) Western Regional Archives (Asheville). Use the "Search Text" box (Basic Search) to locate a surname or Class/Collection/Series. To start a search at the Advanced Search webpage, see **http://mars.archives.ncdcr.gov/AdvancedSearch.aspx.**

**State Library of North Carolina – NC Digital Collections.** The collections contain over 90,000 historic and recent photographs, state government publications, manuscripts, and other resources on topics related to North Carolina. The Collections are free and full-text searchable and bring together content from the State Archives of North Carolina and the State Library of North Carolina. There are 38 separate databases. See **http://digital.ncdcr.gov.**

**North Carolina Family Records Online.** This is a project of the State Library and State Archives of North Carolina. Specific records are categorized into 1) Bible Records, 2) Marriage and Death Notices, 3) Books (Family histories, et al), and 4) Cemetery Records. For more information, see **https://digital.ncdcr.gov/digital/custom/family-records.**

**North Carolina Digital Heritage Center.** This is a statewide digitizing program sponsored by the University of North Carolina at Chapel Hill. Included are yearbooks, newspapers, images, memorabilia, city directories, and audiovisuals. For details, see **www.digitalnc.org.**

## Bibliography

### North Carolina Censuses & Substitutes

**NC State Censuses.** In 1784, an act of the North Carolina General Assembly asked each of the county courts for a "list of inhabitants," i.e., a census, which was completed for all counties, between 1785 and 1787. That enumeration made North Carolina one of 38 state census states. But, North Carolina has not taken a state-sponsored census since then. Land records, tax lists, and other name lists provide substitutes for the entire state.

**NC Federal Censuses.** The 1790 federal census for North Carolina is missing Caswell, Granville, and Orange counties. The *1790 Heads of Families* publication by the Census Bureau attempted to reconstruct those three counties with tax lists from the same time period. The 1800 through 1880 federal censuses for North Carolina are complete for all counties, the 1890 was lost (like all states), and the 1900 through 1940 are complete. The 1950 federal census name lists will open to the public in 2022.

**NC Census Substitutes.** In addition to the census name lists for North Carolina, there are many substitute name lists available. They include State & County Court Records, Directories, County Histories, State Military Lists, Tax Lists, Vital Records, and Voter Lists. A listing begins below:

♦ ♦ ♦ ♦ ♦

**1660-1790.** ***North Carolina Will Abstracts*** **[Online Database],** indexed at the Ancestry.com website. Source: Series of abstracts of wills from all North Carolina counties, compiled by J. Bryan Grimes, et al, Secretaries of State, *Original and Recorded Wills, 1910-*. Eight (8) separate databases contain about 2,000-3,000 entries with about 15,000-20,000 names each. Each will entry contains the person filing the will, county of filing, date of will and date of probate. Also provided is the entire text of the will abstract, often containing many family members including, but not limited to, spouse and children. The Ancestry databases are organized as follows:

- For 1663-1760, see **http://search.ancestry.com/search/db.aspx?dbid=48338.**
- For Supplement to above (1760-1800), see **http://search.ancestry.com/search/db.aspx?dbid=10164.**
- For 1666-1790, See **http://search.ancestry.com/search/db.aspx?dbid=4197.**
- For NC Wills (ca1700-), see **http://search.ancestry.com/search/db.aspx?dbid=10163.**
- For NC Wills (Index), see **http://search.ancestry.com/search/db.aspx?dbid=48337.**
- For NC Wills & Inventories (Index), see **http://search.ancestry.com/search/db.aspx?dbid=48340.**
- For NC Wills & Inventories, publ. 1912, see **http://search.ancestry.com/search/db.aspx?dbid=10164.**
- For NC Will Abstracts (by county, no dates), see **http://search.ancestry.com/search/db.aspx?dbid=48339.**

**1660-1959.** ***Land Records (North Carolina)*** **[Microfilm & Digital Capture],** from the original records at the NC State Archives, Raleigh. This is the major collection of land grants for all of North Carolina from its very beginnings to 1957. In North Carolina, land ownership was enjoyed by 90-95% of the adult white male population – a list of the names of land owners is often better than a census to confirm the residence place of a person. To give a sense of the importance of this series of land records, out of some 740 rolls of microfilm, six sets of name index cards fill the first 45 rolls of microfilm. One roll has the index cards for the extinct counties of Bath, Bute, Dobbs, Glasgow & Tryon; another roll has the index cards to

the land grants in the Granville District, ca1750-1763, which at one time extended from the Atlantic Ocean to the Mississippi River and included the top half of present North Carolina and Tennessee. 45 rolls of 35mm microfilm is the equivalent of over 80,000 3x5 index cards. The land documents themselves could number well over 500,000 pages. If you think your ancestor was in North Carolina to buy land, this is where you will find his name listed, along with the exact location of the purchased land. This major series was filmed by the NC archives, 1980-2007, 742 rolls, beginning with FHL film #1942649 (Western country [now Tennessee] land documents in alphabetical order). To access the digital images, see the online FHL catalog page:
**https://familysearch.org/search/catalog/695114.**

**1662-1790.** ***Index to the Colonial and State Records of North Carolina, Vols. 1-28*** **[Online Database],** indexed at the Ancestry.com website. An introduction and index to each volume, vol. 1 (1662-1712) through vol. 26 (1790 census), vol. 27 (Index A-L), and vol. 28 (Index M-R and S-Z and Historical Review of the Colonial and State Records of North Carolina). This database has 2,238 records (pages):
**http://search.ancestry.com/search/db.aspx?dbid=15793.**

**1663-1744.** ***North Carolina Headrights: A List of Names*** **[Printed Book],** compiled by Carolina B. Whitley; prepared for publication by Susan M. Trimble, published by the Division of Archives and History, NC Dept. of Cultural Resources, 2001, Raleigh, NC. 312 pages. Includes index. See FHL book 975.6 R2wc.

**1663-1760.** ***Abstract of North Carolina Wills, Compiled From Original and Recorded Wills in the Office of the Secretary of State*** **[Printed Book & Online Database],** compiled by J. Bryan Grimes, Reprint. Originally published: Raleigh, N. C., 1910. Reprinted Genealogical Publishing Co., Inc., Baltimore, 1967, 670 pages. Includes index. FHL book 975.6 P2gr, also on microfiche, FHL film #6046876. An online version of this book was digitized and indexed at Ancestry.com. See
**www.ancestry.com/search/collections/48338.**

**1663-1900. Index to North Carolina Wills [Printed Book & Digital Version],** compiled by William Perry Johnson, published by the author, 1965. Contents: Vol. 1: Alamance, Alexander, Alleghany, Anson, Ashe, Beaufort counties; Vol. 2: Bertie, Bladen, Brunswick, Buncombe, Burke counties; Vol. 3: Cabarrus, Caldwell, Camden, Carteret, Caswell, Catawba, Chatham, Cherokee counties; Vol. 4: Chowan, Clay, Cleveland, Columbus counties. FHL has bound volumes 1-4 into one volume, FHL book 975.6 P2j and FHL film #1036601. To access the digital version, see the online FHL catalog: See
**https://familysearch.org/search/catalog/182134.**

**1663-1979.** ***North Carolina Estate Files*** **[Online Database],** indexed at the FamilySearch.org website. Index and images of estate files from North Carolina counties. The originals were filmed at the North Carolina Department of Archives and History. The estate records contain loose papers relating to the settlement of estates including such matters as provision for heirs including minor children as well as distribution of funds, land, and property, including slaves. This project was indexed in partnership with the North Carolina Genealogical Society and Library. This database has 233,721 records. See
**https://familysearch.org/search/collection/1911121.**

**1665-1998.** ***North Carolina, Wills and Probate Records*** **[Online Database],** digitized and indexed at the Ancestry.com website. Source: County records, all counties of North Carolina. In most cases, the details found in probates include the names and residences of beneficiaries and their relationship to the decedent. An inventory of the estate assets may reveal personal details about the deceased's occupation and lifestyle. There may also be references to debts, deeds, and other documents related to the settling of the estate. This database has 1,145,137 records. See
**http://search.ancestry.com/search/db.aspx?dbid=9061.**

**1679-1790.** ***North Carolina Taxpayers (Vol. 1 & 2)*** **[Printed Book],** compiled by Clarence E. Ratcliff, published Genealogical Publishing Co., Inc., Baltimore, 1987-1989, vol. 1: 1701-1786; vol. 2: 1679-1790. FHL book 975.6 R4rc v.1-2.
- See also ***North Carolina Taxpayers (Vol. 1), 1701-1786*** **[Online Database],** indexed at the Ancestry.com website. Source: Clarence E. Ratcliff's *North Carolina Taxpayers, 1701-1786, Vol. 1*, publ. GPC, 2002. This database lists the names of taxpayers residing in about half of the North Carolina counties formed before 1786. Most of the data came from tax lists microfilmed at the North Carolina State Archives in Raleigh, and they are supplemented with names from the periodical *North Carolina Genealogy,* which includes persons owning headrights and landrights. The names of the taxpayers are listed alphabetically with the county of residence and date, and in some cases additional data is supplied.

In all there are about 28,000 names. See **http://search.ancestry.com/search/db.aspx?dbid=49054.** - See also **North Carolina Taxpayers, 1679-1790. Vol. 2 [Online Database],** indexed at the Ancestry.com website. Source: Clarence E. Ratcliff's *North Carolina Taxpayers, 1679-1900, Vol. 2,* publ. GPC, 2003. This volume has the names of about 29,000 taxpayers. See **http://search.ancestry.com/search/db.aspx?dbid=49269.**

**1680-1830. *Directory of Scots in the Carolinas* [Online Database],** indexed at the Ancestry.com website. Source: book, same title, by David Dobson, publ. Genealogical Pub. Co., 1986. Dobson explains that it was impossible to distinguish between Scots and Scots-Irish, but history tells us that there were many more lowland Scots (Scots-Irish) than highland Scots in the Old South. This database has 334 records (pages). See **http://search.ancestry.com/search/db.aspx?dbid=48518.**

**1700-1970. *North Carolina, Church Records* [Online Database],** digitized and indexed at FamilySearch.org. Includes records from various denominations, extracted from microfilm at the Family History Library, Salt Lake City. This database has 62,494 records, see **www.familysearch.org/search/collection/2790262.**

**1700s-1900s. *Early North Carolina Settlers* [CD-ROM],** by Broderbund, 2000, as Family Tree Maker's Family Archives: Genealogical Records, No. 524. Produced in collaboration with the Genealogical Publishing Co., Inc., Baltimore. See FHL CD-ROM No. 9, pt. 524. Contents:

- *Historical Sketches of North Carolina from 1584 to 1851: Compiled From Original Records, Official Documents and Traditional Statements With Biographical Sketches of her Distinguished Statesmen, Jurists, Lawyers, Soldiers, Divines, etc.,* by John Hill Wheeler (vols. I-II);
- *Sketches of Western North Carolina, Historical and Biographical,* by C.L. Hunter;
- *Marriage and Death Notices From Raleigh Register and North Carolina State Gazette, 1799-1825*, compiled by Carrie L. Broughton;
- *Marriage and Death Notices From Raleigh Register and North Carolina State Gazette, 1826-1845*, compiled by Carrie L. Broughton;
- *Marriage and Death Notices from Raleigh Register and North Carolina State Gazette, 1846-1867*, compiled by Carrie L. Broughton;
- *The North Carolina Historical and Genealogical Register*, J.R.B. Hathaway, editor (vols. I-III);
- *Reminiscences and Memoirs of North Carolina and Eminent North Carolinians,* by John H. Wheeler;
- *North Carolina Land grants in South Carolina,* by Brent H. Holcomb.

**1712-1970. *North Carolina, Civil Action Court Papers* [Online Database],** digitized at the FamilySearch.org website. Civil suits were generally brought to settle questions of land ownership, unpaid debts, unfulfilled contracts, and unperformed agreements. Suits concerning dower, breach of contract, and slander were frequent. Divorces were included. The legitimating of "bastard children" fell within the province of this court. The records also include some records of slave emancipation and of naturalization proceedings. Browse through the images, organized by county, and within each county, by date of the case. Any indexes as part of the record books are included. This database has 1,297,129 records. See **https://familysearch.org/search/collection/1930242.**

**1712-1970. *North Carolina, Civil Action Court Papers* [Online Database],** digitized at the Ancestry.com website. Source: FamilySearch, from county records on microfilm at the Family History Library, Salt Lake City, UT. Browse the images by county. No index yet. This database has 1,235,848 records (images). See **http://search.ancestry.com/search/db.aspx?dbid=60088.**

**1714-1769 Early North Carolina Censuses [Online Database],** indexed at the USGenWeb site for Onslow Co NC. See **http://web.archive.org/web/20160619024806/http://ncgenweb.us/nc/onslow/census-records/1741-1769-early-nc-census**

**1720-1764. *Tax Lists of Various Counties of North Carolina* [Microfilm & Digital Capture]** from the originals at the Secretary of State's Office, Raleigh, NC. Includes Anson County, 1763; Beaufort County, 1764; Bladen County, 1763; Brunswick County, 1769; Caswell County, 1777; Craven County, 1720 and 1769; Granville County, 1769; Onslow County, 1769 and 1770; Pasquotank County, 1754 and 1769; and Pitt County, 1762. Names are arranged alphabetically within the county. Filmed by the Genealogical Society of Utah, 1941, 1 roll, FHL film #18071. To access the digital images, see the online FHL catalog page: **www.familysearch.org/search/catalog/332552.**

**1735-1775. Colony of North Carolina, Abstracts of Land Patents [Printed Book],** by Margaret M. Hofmann, published by the author, Roanoke Rapids, NC, 1982-1984, vol. 1: 1735-1764; vol. 2, 1765-1775. FHL book 975.6 R2hm.

**1735-1970.** ***North Carolina Probate Records*** **[Online Database],** digitized at the FamilySearch.org website. Source: NC county records extracted from microfilm at the Family History Library, Salt Lake City, UT. Includes wills, guardianships, and estate records in bound volumes. Although the coverage dates include a larger span of years, most of the records in this collection are from 1800-1930. Browse through the images, organized by county, then type of record, date range, volume. This database has 1,147,259 records. See **https://familysearch.org/search/collection/1867501.**

**1741-1868.** ***An Index to Marriage Bonds Filed in the North Carolina State Archives*** **[Microfiche],** from the original records at the NC Div. of Archives and History, Raleigh. Marriage bonds were statements of intent documenting bonds taken out by the groom, usually from the county in which the bride resided. Index lists bride's and groom's names, date of bond, bondsmen's and witness' names, a code for the county where the bond was taken out and the volume and page of the abstracted marriage bond. Filmed by the archives, 88 microfiches, beginning with FHL film #6330241 (Bride list, Anonymous to Andrews, Julia C.). For a complete list of fiche numbers and contents of each, see the online FHL catalog page for this title. See **https://familysearch.org/search/catalog/18207.**

**1741-1868.** ***North Carolina, Index to Marriage Bonds*** **[Online Database],** indexed at the Ancestry.com website. Source: NC State Archives, an index prepared by the WPA. Most of the bonds contain the following information: groom's name, bride's name, date of bond, bondsmen, witnesses. Additional information may include parents' names, date of the marriage, person performing the ceremony, and other similar data. This database has 339,887 records. See
**http://search.ancestry.com/search/db.aspx?dbid=4802.**

**1741-2004.** ***North Carolina, Marriage Index,*** **[Online Database],** indexed at the Ancestry.com website. This is a combined index from the Liahona Research project, the NC State Archives index, and the NC Health Statistics office. Information provided in this index includes: Names of bride and groom, Genders, Birth dates, Ages at time of marriage, Race or color of bride and groom, Marriage date, Marriage place (usually a county), and Source information (compiler, microfilm number, location of county court, etc.). This database has 2,709,602 records. See
**http://search.ancestry.com/search/db.aspx?dbid=8909.**

**1741-2011.** ***North Carolina, Marriage Records*** **[Online Database],** digitized and indexed at the Ancestry.com website. Source: NC State Archives. This collection includes marriage bonds, licenses, certificates, and registers, as well as indexes and abstracts to the various records from 87 North Carolina counties. Each record may include groom's name, bride's name, bride and groom's current ages, or age at next birthday, marriage application date, marriage date, marriage county, places of residence, occupation, places of birth for the bride and groom, color and nationality, parents' names for the bride and groom (including mother's maiden name), location of the marriage, name of the officiant, and names of witnesses. This database has 10,884,574 records. See
**http://search.ancestry.com/search/db.aspx?dbid=60548.**

**1748-1763.** ***The Granville District of North Carolina: Abstracts of Land Grants*** **[Printed Book],** by Margaret M. Hofmann, published by Roanoke News, Weldon, NC, 1986, 5 vols., FHL book 975.6 R28h, v.1-5. See also, **The Granville District [Printed Book],** by W.N. Watt, 1992, includes index. Includes information about land ownership, tax records and public officials. FHL book 975.6 R2w.

**1759-1979.** ***North Carolina Marriages*** **[Online Database],** indexed at the FamilySearch.org website. Name index to marriage records from microfilm at the Family History Library, Salt Lake City, UT. This database has 2,128,230 records. See
**https://familysearch.org/search/collection/1675514.**

**1760-1800.** See ***Abstract of North Carolina Wills From About 1760 to About 1800, Prepared From the Originals and Other Data*** **[Microfilm & Digital Capture],** by Fred A. Olds, microfilm of typescript edition on file in the Library of Congress, Washington, DC, published by the Family History Library, FHL film #496782. To access the digital images, see the online FHL catalog page:
**www.familysearch.org/search/catalog/239949.**
- Indexed in ***Index to abstract of North Carolina Wills From about 1760 to about 1800*** [Printed Book & Microfilm], prepared by Fred A. Olds, compiled, and typed by the FHL, see FHL film #1033627.
- See also ***North Carolina, Will Abstracts, 1760-1800*** **[Online Database],** indexed at the Ancestry.com website. Source: Fred A. Olds, *Abstracts of Willis, 1925*. Each entry contains the year of filing and name of the person filing the will. Also provided are family

members mentioned in the will including, but not limited to, spouse and children. With over 10,000 entries, it contains nearly 50,000 names. See **http://search.ancestry.com/search/db.aspx?dbid=3945.**

**1762-1979.** ***North Carolina, County Marriages*** **[Online Database],** indexed at the FamilySearch.org website. Name index and images of marriage records from North Carolina county courthouses. These records include licenses, marriage applications, marriage bonds, marriage certificates, marriage packets and cohabitation registers. See the FamilySearch description for the counties included. This database has 1,840,781 records. See **https://familysearch.org/search/collection/1726957.**

**1763-1868.** ***North Carolina, Civil Marriages*** **[Online Database],** indexed at the FamilySearch.org website. Index to selected county marriage bonds and certificates. This database has 53,614 records. See **https://familysearch.org/search/collection/2524877.**

**1770s-2000s.** ***North Carolina GenWeb Archives*** **[Online Database].** The NCGenWeb site offers free genealogical databases with searchable statewide name lists and for all North Carolina counties, which may include Bibles, Biographies, Cemeteries, Censuses, Court, Death, Deeds, Directories, Histories, Marriages, Military, Newspapers, Obituaries, Photos, Schools, Tax Lists, Wills, and more. See **http://usgwarchives.net/nc/ncfiles.htm.**

**1770s-2000s.** ***Linkpendium – North Carolina: Family History & Genealogy, Census, Birth, Marriage, Death Vita Records & More*** **[Online Databases].** Linkpendium is a genealogical portal site, with links to state, county, town, and local databases. Currently listed are selected sites for North Carolina statewide resources (722), Independent Cities, Renamed Counties, Discontinued Counties (19), Alamance County (480), Alexander County (203), Alleghany County (199), Anson County (393), and 96 more North Carolina counties. See **www.linkpendium.com/nc-genealogy.**

**1875-1940. Mecklenburg County Directories [Online Database],** for the following years/places:

- 1875/1876 – Beasley & Emerson's Charlotte Directory
- 1903 – Walsh's Charlotte Directory
- 1905/1906 – Walsh's Charlotte Directory
- 1907 – Walsh's Charlotte Directory
- 1909 – Charlotte
- 1910 – Charlotte
- 1911 – Charlotte
- 1912 – Charlotte
- 1913 – Charlotte
- 1914 – Charlotte
- 1915 – Charlotte
- 1916 – Charlotte
- 1917 – Charlotte
- 1918 – Charlotte
- 1920 – Charlotte
- 1931 – Miller's Charlotte Directory
- 1932 – Hill's Charlotte Directory
- 1933 – Hill's Charlotte Directory
- 1934 – Hill's Charlotte Directory
- 1935 – Hill's Charlotte Directory
- 1938 – Hill's Charlotte Directory
- 1940 – Hill's Charlotte Directory

Indexed at the USGenWeb site for Mecklenburg Co NC. See **http://ncgenweb.us/nc/mecklenburg/mecklenburg-county-directories.**

**1775-1993.** ***North Carolina Newspaper Archives*** **[Online Databases],** digitized and indexed newspapers at the GenealogyBank website, from Charlotte, Edenton, Fayetteville, Greensboro, Halifax, Hillsborough, Lincolnton, Littleton, Milton, Murfreesboro, New Bern, Raleigh, Tarboro, Washington, Wilmington, and Winston-Salem. See **www.genealogybank.com/explore/newspapers/all/usa/north-carolina.**

**1776-1783.** ***Index to Compiled Service Records of Volunteer Soldiers Who Served During the Revolutionary War in Organizations From the State of North Carolina*** **[Microfilm & Digital Capture],** from the original records in the National Archives. This is an alphabetical card index to the compiled service records of volunteer soldiers of North Carolina containing names of soldiers to which references were found in the records used in compiling the service records. The cards give the name of the soldier, his rank, and the unit in which he served. There are cross-reference cards for soldiers' names that appeared in the records under more than one spelling. National Archives microfilm series M0257, 2 rolls, FHL film #821595 (Index, A-Q); #821596 (Index, R-Z). To access the digital images, see the online FHL catalog page: **www.familysearch.org/search/catalog/316413.**

**1776-1783.** ***North Carolina, Revolutionary War Soldiers*** **[Online Database],** digitized and indexed at the Ancestry.com website. From the years 1776 to

1783, approximately 36,000 men from North Carolina served in the American Revolution. This database is a roster of these individuals, which has been compiled by various sources, such as: the North Carolina Daughters of the American Revolution, U.S. War Department Report of Pensions, Pierce's Register, records of the 10 regiments, company rosters, Army accounts, and State records. This database has 43,293 records. See **http://search.ancestry.com/search/db.aspx?dbid=3185.**

**1776-1783.** ***Roster of Soldiers from North Carolina in the American Revolution*** **[Online Database],** indexed at the Ancestry.com website. Source: DAR, 1932. This database has 716 records (pages). See **http://search.ancestry.com/search/db.aspx?dbid=10162.**

**1776-1845.** ***Abstract of Pensions of North Carolina Soldiers of the Revolution, War of 1812 & Indian Wars*** **[Online Database],** indexed at the Ancestry.com website. Source: book, same title, by Annie Walker Burns, 1960. This database has 563 records (pages) See **http://search.ancestry.com/search/db.aspx?dbid=30057.**

***1778-1795 Index to North Carolina Land Entries*** **[Printed Book],** by A. B. Pruitt. Published by the author, Whitakers, NC, vol. 1: surnames A-F; vol. 2, surnames G-N; vol. 3, surnames O-Z. FHL book 975.6 R22pa v.1-3.

**1779-1782.** ***North Carolina Revolutionary Pay Vouchers*** **[Online Database],** digitized at FamilySearch.org, from originals at the NC State Archives in Raleigh. The collection is arranged alphabetically. This database has 97,668 images, see **www.familysearch.org/search/collection/1498361.**

**1784-1787.** ***State Census of North Carolina: From Records in the North Carolina Department of Archives and History*** **[Microfilm],** from the original transcribed and indexed by Alvaretta Kenan Register, Norfolk, VA, 1971, 240 pages. Includes index. Filmed by the Genealogical Society of Utah, 1972, FHL film #897274.

- See also, ***State Census of North Carolina, 1784-1787*** **[Printed Book],** by Alvaretta Kenan Register, reprinted by Genealogical Publishing Co., Baltimore, 1993, 233 pages. FHL book 975.6 X2r.
- See also, ***State Census of North Carolina, 1784-1787*** **[Online Database],** digitized and indexed at the Ancestry.com website. Source: *State Census of NC*, compiled by A. Register, Raleigh, 1979. This is a 244-page transcription of the original records on microfilm, with numerous corrections to hard-to-read names and includes a large typescript index. See **http://search.ancestry.com/search/db.aspx?dbid=10169.**
- See also, another version digitized from the Genealogical Publishing Co 2001 reformatted reprint: **http://search.ancestry.com/search/db.aspx?dbid=3005.**
- See also, ***1786 State Census, Granville County, North Carolina*** **[Microfilm],** from the originals. Filmed by the North Carolina Division of Archives and History, Raleigh, 1975, 1 roll, FHL film #1014833.

**1790.** ***North Carolina Heads of Families at the First Census of the United States Taken in the Year 1790*** **[Online Database],** indexed at the Ancestry.com website. Source: Heads of Families, publ. Census Bureau, 1908. The missing counties of Caswell, Granville, and Orange counties in the original manuscripts are included here with substitute name list compiled from local tax lists. Refer to the map on page 144. This database has 291 pages. See **http://search.ancestry.com/search/db.aspx?dbid=10170.**

**1790-1840. North Carolina, 1790 thru 1840 Federal Census: Population Schedules [Microfilm & Digital Capture],** filmed by the National Archives, 1938-1969, 34 rolls, beginning with FHL film #568147 (NC 1790). To access the digital images, see the online FHL catalog page: **www.familysearch.org/search/catalog/745501.**

**1790-1890.** ***North Carolina, Compiled Census and Census Substitute Index*** **[Online Database],** digitized and indexed at the Ancestry.com website. Originally edited by Ronald Jackson, Accelerated Indexing Systems, Salt Lake City. This collection contains the following indexes: 1790 Federal Census Index; 1800 Federal Census Index; 1810 Federal Census Index; 1812-14 Muster Rolls; 1820 Federal Census Index; 1830 Federal Census Index; 1840 Federal Census Index; 1840 Pensioners List; 1850 Federal Census Index; 1860 Federal Census Index; 1870 Federal Census Index; 1890 Veterans Schedule; Early Census Index. This database has 141,002 records. See **http://search.ancestry.com/search/db.aspx?dbid=3566.**

**1799-1825.** ***Index to Marriage and Death Notices in Raleigh Register and North Carolina State Gazette*** **[Printed Book & Digital Version],** published by Oakland Genealogy Library, FHL book 975.6 V2b and FHL film #824074, another filming: film #844969.

To access the digital version, see the online FHL catalog page:
**www.familysearch.org/search/catalog/46235.**

**1800-1909.** ***North Carolina, State Supreme Court Case Files*** **[Online Database],** digitized at FamilySearch.org. Source: NC State Archives. Images of original case files from the North Carolina State Supreme Court. This database has 876,445 records. See **https://familysearch.org/search/collection/1878751.**
- For the Ancestry.com version of this database, see **http://search.ancestry.com/search/db.aspx?dbid=60091.**

**1800-2000.** ***North Carolina, Department of Archives and History, Index to Vital Records*** **[Online Database],** digitized and indexed at FamilySearch.org. Index and images of vital record indexes, including births, delayed births, and deaths. This database has 7,906,030 records, see
**www.familysearch.org/search/collection/2848682.**

**1800-2000.** ***North Carolina Birth Index*** **[Online Database],** indexed at the FamilySearch.org website. An index to birth records at the NC State Archives, compiled by Ancestry.com. This database has 6,957,267 records. See
**https://familysearch.org/search/collection/1949336.**
- For the original Ancestry.com version of this database, see
**http://search.ancestry.com/search/db.aspx?dbid=8783.**

**1812-1814.** See ***Muster Rolls of the Soldiers of the War of 1812: Detached from the Militia of North Carolina in 1812 and 1814*** **[Online Database],** indexed at the Ancestry.com website. Source: C.C. Raboteau, Raleigh, NC, 1851. This database has 140 records (pages). See
**http://search.ancestry.com/search/db.aspx?dbid=10166.**

**1833-1970.** ***North Carolina, County Records*** **[Online Database],** digitized at the FamilySearch.org website. Collection of various county records including, wills, guardianships, estates, voter registration books, coroner's inquests, etc. Browse through the images, organized by county, then by type of record, date range, and volume. This database has 594,183 records. See **https://familysearch.org/search/collection/1916185.**

***1835 Poll Books, North Carolina: 12th Congressional District for the Counties of Burke, Haywood, Yancey, Macon, Rutherford, and Buncombe*** **[Printed Book],** edited by Charles David Biddix, published by Old Buncombe County Genealogical Society, Asheville, NC, 1988, 103 pages. FHL book 975.6 N4p.

**1835.** See ***Pension Roll of 1835 - Statewide North Carolina*** **[Online Database],** indexed at the USGenWeb Archives site for North Carolina.
- For surnames A-E, see
**http://files.usgwarchives.net/nc/statewide/military/1835pens.txt.**
- For surnames F-L, see
**http://files.usgwarchives.net/nc/statewide/military/1835pens2.txt.**
- For surnames M-R, see
**http://files.usgwarchives.net/nc/statewide/military/1835pens3.txt.**
- For surnames S-Z, see
**http://files.usgwarchives.net/nc/statewide/military/1835pens4.txt.**

***1840 Census of Pensioners Revolutionary or Military Service (North Carolina)*** **[Online Database],** with names, ages, and places of residence. These lists were returned by the marshals of the several judicial districts of the U.S. Indexed at the US-Roots.org site. See **www.us-roots.org/colonialamerica/census/1840/1840nc_a.html.**

**1850.** ***North Carolina, 1850 Federal Census: Population Schedules*** **[Microfilm & Digital Capture],** filmed by the National Archives, 1964, 38 rolls, beginning with FHL film #18105 (NC: Alamance, Alexander, and Anson Cos). To access the digital images, see the online FHL catalog page: **www.familysearch.org/search/catalog/744493.**

**1850-1880.** ***Nonpopulation Schedules for North Carolina, Mortality and Manufacturing/Industry*** **[Microfilm & Digital Capture],** filmed by the National Archives, 1997, 9 rolls, beginning with FHL film #2155598. To access the digital images, see the online FHL catalog page:
**www.familysearch.org/search/catalog/737954.**

**1852.** ***Rejected or Suspended Pension Applications – North Carolina*** **[Online Database],** indexed at the USGenWeb Archives site. See
**http://files.usgwarchives.net/nc/statewide/military/reject.txt.**

**1860.** ***North Carolina, 1860 Federal Census: Population Schedules*** **[Microfilm & Digital Capture],** filmed by the National Archives, 1950, 1967, 48 rolls, beginning with FHL film #803886. To access the digital images, see the online FHL catalog page: **www.familysearch.org/search/catalog/705512.**

**1860.** ***North Carolina 1860 Federal Census: Agricultural Schedules*** **[Digital Capture],** digitized by FamilySearch International, 2018, To access the digital version, see the online FHL catalog page:
**www.familysearch.org/search/catalog/3019390.**

**1860-1965.** ***North Carolina City Directories*** **[Online Database],** digitized at the DigitalNC website. Browse by City (list of 111 cities with directories), Browse by County, or Browse by Year. See
**www.digitalnc.org/collections/city-directories.**

**1861-1865.** ***Roster of North Carolina Troops in the War Between the States*** **[Online Database],** digitized and indexed at the Ancestry.com website. Source: Adjutant General's report, 1882. This database has 2,541 records. See
**http://search.ancestry.com/search/db.aspx?dbid=10165.**

**1861-1865.** ***North Carolina, Civil War Service Records of Confederate Soldiers*** **[Online Database],** indexed at the FamilySearch.org website. Source: National Archives microfilm series M270. The records include a jacket-envelope for each soldier, labeled with his name, his rank, and the unit in which he served. The jacket-envelope typically contains card abstracts of entries relating to the soldier as found in original muster rolls, returns, rosters, payrolls, appointment books, hospital registers, Union prison registers and rolls, parole rolls, and inspection reports. This database has 1,773,886 records. See
**https://familysearch.org/search/collection/1932376.**

**1861-1865.** ***North Carolina, Civil War Service Records of Union Soldiers*** **[Online Database],** indexed at the FamilySearch.org website. Source: National Archives microfilm series M401. Each jacket-envelope typically contains card abstracts of entries relating to the soldier as found in original muster rolls, returns, rosters, payrolls, appointment books, hospital registers, prison registers and rolls, parole rolls, inspection reports; and the originals of any papers relating solely to the particular soldier. This database has 58,417 records. See
**https://familysearch.org/search/collection/1932416.**

**1862-1870.** ***North Carolina, Freedmen's Bureau Assistant Commissioner Records*** **[Online Database],** indexed at the FamilySearch.org website. Source: National Archives microfilm series M843. These records include letters sent and received, account books, applications for rations, applications for relief, court records, labor contracts, registers of county claimants, registers of complaints, registers of contracts, registers of disbursements, registers of freedmen issued rations, registers of patients, reports, rosters of officers and employees, special and general orders and circulars received, special orders and circulars issued, records relating to claims, court trials, property restoration, and homesteads. This database has 127,316 records. See
**https://familysearch.org/search/collection/1803698.**

**1863-1872.** ***North Carolina, Freedmen's Bureau Field Office Records*** **[Online Database],** digitized at the FamilySearch.org website. Source: National Archives microfilm series M1909. These records include letters and endorsements sent and received, account books, applications for rations, applications for relief, court records, labor contracts, registers of bounty claimants, registers of complaints, registers of contracts, registers of disbursements, registers of freedmen issued rations, registers of patients, reports, rosters of officers and employees, special and general orders and circulars received, special orders and circulars issued, records relating to claims, court trials, property restoration, and homesteads. This database has 69,605 records. See
**https://familysearch.org/search/collection/2143119.**

***1864-1866 Internal Revenue Assessment List for North Carolina*** **[Microfilm & Digital Capture],** from the originals at the National Archives, Washington, DC. Contains information for the following districts: **District 1:** Beaufort, Bertie, Camden, Chowan, Currituck, Gates, Halifax, Hertford, Hyde, Martin, Northampton, Pasquotank, Perquimans, Tyrrell, and Washington. **District 2:** Carteret, Craven, Duplin, Edgecombe, Greene, Jones, Lenoir, New Hanover, Onslow, Pitt, Wayne, and Wilson. **District 3:** Anson, Bladen, Brunswick, Columbus, Cumberland, Harnett, Montgomery, Moore, Richmond, Robeson, Sampson, and Stanly. **District 4:** Chatham, Franklin, Granville, Johnston, Nash, Orange, Wake, and Warren. **District 5:** Alamance, Caswell, Davidson, Forsyth, Guilford, Person, Randolph, Rockingham, Stokes, and Surry. **District 6:** Alexander, Cabarrus, Catawba, Davie, Gaston, Iredell, Lincoln, Mecklenburg, Rowan, Union, Wilkes, and Yadkin, and **District 7:** Alleghany, Ashe, Buncombe, Burke, Caldwell, Cherokee, Clay, Cleveland, Haywood, Henderson, Jackson, Macon, Madison, McDowell, Mitchell, Polk, Rutherford, Transylvania, Watauga, and Yancey. For further information, see the note at the beginning of the first roll of film. Filmed by the Genealogical Society of Utah, 1988, 2 rolls, FHL #1578467 (District 1-2, 1864-1866); film #1578468 (District 3-7). To access the digital images, see the online FHL catalog page: **www.familysearch.org/search/catalog/577904.**

**1866-1964.** ***North Carolina Births and Christenings*** **[Online Database],** indexed at the FamilySearch.org website. Name index to birth, baptism, and christening records from microfilm at the Family History Library, Salt Lake City, UT. This database has 156,281 records. **https://familysearch.org/search/collection/1675484.**

**1867-2006.** ***North Carolina, Davidson County Vital Records*** **[Online Database],** digitized at the FamilySearch.org website. Source: NC State Archives. Images of death records and marriage licenses recorded in Davidson County, North Carolina. Some of the individual volumes include an index and there are comprehensive indexes to some of the records. Browse through Death records, Index to deaths, Indexed register of marriages, and Marriage licenses. This database has 155,502 records. See **https://familysearch.org/search/collection/1387049.**

**1868-1898.** ***North Carolina, Voter Registration Records*** **[Online Database],** digitized and indexed at FamilySearch.org. Includes Voting Registers for Orange, Beaufort, and Chatham Counties in North Carolina for years 1868-1898. From microfilm of original records at the North Carolina State Archives in Raleigh, NC. This database has 11,106 records, see **www.familysearch.org/search/collection/3326982.**

**1870.** ***North Carolina, 1870 Federal Census: Population Schedules*** **[Microfilm & Digital Capture],** filmed by the National Archives, 1962, 1968, 59 rolls, beginning with FHL film #552620. To access the digital images, see the online FHL catalog page: **www.familysearch.org/search/catalog/698914.**

**1872-1996.** ***North Carolina, Naturalization Records*** **[Online Database],** indexed at the Ancestry.com website. Source: National Archives microfilm of US District Court records. The records include petitions, declarations, and certificates of naturalization. This database has 72,850 records. See **http://search.ancestry.com/search/db.aspx?dbid=2503.**

**1880.** ***North Carolina, 1880 Federal Census: Soundex and Population Schedules*** **[Microfilm & Digital Capture],** filmed by the National Archives, c1970, 118 rolls, beginning with FHL film #1254050 (Pop Scheds Alamance, et al). To access the digital images (Population Schedules), see the online FHL catalog page: **www.familysearch.org/search/catalog/676501.**

**1885-1953.** ***North Carolina, Confederate Soldiers and Widows Pension Applications*** **[Online Database],** digitized at the FamilySearch.org website. Source: NC State Archives. In 1885, pensions were provided for Confederate veterans who were residents of North Carolina and who were incapacitated for manual labor while in the service of the Confederate States during the Civil War. Widows of soldiers who were killed in service were entitled to the same benefits as long as they did not remarry. In 1901, a new pension law was passed, in which, "Every person who has been for twelve months immediately preceding his or her application for pension bona fide resident of the State, and who is incapacitated for manual labor and was a soldier or a sailor in the service of the State of North Carolina or of the Confederate States of America, during the war between the States (provided, said widow was married to said soldier or sailor before the first day of April, 1865)" was entitled to a pension. This database has 189,158 records. Browse through the records, organized by 1885 law, 1901 law, general index to applications, and images of the applications in alphabetical order, interfiled for soldiers, sailors, and widows. See **https://familysearch.org/search/collection/1911763.**

- See also, ***North Carolina, Confederate Soldiers and Widows Pension Applications, 1885-1953*** **[Online Database],** indexed at the Ancestry.com website. Source: FamilySearch digitizing and indexing system. The records are divided into Applications 1885 to 1901, and Applications after 1901. The records are arranged alphabetically by the first letter of the last name within each record set. There are also indexes for the two collections. This database has 189,157 records. See **http://search.ancestry.com/search/db.aspx?dbid=60089.**

**1898-1899.** ***North Carolina Volunteers, Spanish American War*** **[Online Database],** digitized and indexed at the Ancestry.com website. Source: 1899 Adjutant General's report. Each record provides the soldier's name, unit, rank, post office of residence, and enrollment location. Provided as an aid to the researcher, the page number refers to the original state document. This database has 3,906 records. See **http://search.ancestry.com/search/db.aspx?dbid=4136.**

**1898-1994.** ***North Carolina Deaths and Burials*** **[Online Database],** indexed at the FamilySearch.org website. Name index to death and burial records from microfilm at the Family History Library, Salt Lake City, UT. This database has 109,511 records. See **https://familysearch.org/search/collection/1675510.**

**1900.** ***North Carolina, 1900 Federal Census: Soundex and Population Schedules*** **[Microfilm & Digital Capture],** filmed by the National Archives, c1970, 214 rolls, beginning with FHL film #1241180 (Pop. Sched: Alamance Co). To access the digital images, see the online FHL catalog page: **www.familysearch.org/search/catalog/639823.**

**1900-1909.** ***North Carolina, Wake County, Death Records*** **[Online Database],** Digitized and indexed at FamilySearch.org. Source: NC State Archives, Raleigh. This database has 3,216 records, see **www.familysearch.org/search/collection/1949206.**

**1906-1930.** ***North Carolina Deaths*** **[Online Database],** indexed at the FamilySearch.org website. Source: NC Vital Records Section. Name index and images of death certificates recorded in North Carolina from 1906-1930. This database has 615,657 records. See **https://familysearch.org/search/collection/1609799.**

**1906-1930.** ***North Carolina, Deaths*** **[Online Database],** digitized and indexed at the Ancestry.com website. Source: FamilySearch digitizing and indexing system, deaths extracted from county microfilm at the Family History Library, Salt Lake City. This database has 1,890,748 records. See **http://search.ancestry.com/search/db.aspx?dbid=60090.**

**1908-1958.** ***North Carolina, Wilmington and Morehead City Passenger and Crew Lists, 1908-1958*** **[Online Database],** indexed at the FamilySearch.org website. Source: National Archives microfilm series A3481. This collection contains passenger and crew lists for vessels arriving at Wilmington and Moorhead City, North Carolina from 1908-1958. This database has 88,345 records. See **https://familysearch.org/search/collection/2072744.**

**1908-2004.** ***North Carolina, Death Indexes*** **[Online Database],** digitized and indexed at the Ancestry.com website. Source: NC State Archives and Vital Statistics Office. This database includes images for part of the series, and indexes for the entire series. See the description for a list of counties with images, and a list of county codes to find the coded county listed on the death record index. Each record includes the name of the deceased, date of death, place of death, and several more items. A Social Security number from a death certificate may be included in the index (obscured if less than ten years old). This database has 4,134,003 records. See **http://search.ancestry.com/search/db.aspx?dbid=8908.**

**1909.** ***Asheville, North Carolina City Directory*** **[Online Database],** indexed at the Ancestry.com website. This database has 548 records (pages). See **http://search.ancestry.com/search/db.aspx?dbid=1001.**

**1909-1976.** ***North Carolina, Death Certificates*** **[Online Database],** digitized and indexed at the Ancestry.com website. Source: NC State Archives. Information contained in this database includes: Name of deceased, Certificate number, Death place, Death date, Residence, Gender, Race, Birth date, Birthplace, Age at time of death, Father's name, Mother's name, and Spouse's name. Additional information such as social security number, birth-places of parents, occupation, burial information (name and address of cemetery, and date buried), and cause of death may also be listed on the certificate and can be obtained by viewing the image. This database has 7,543,578 records. See **http://search.ancestry.com/search/db.aspx?dbid=1121.**

**1910.** ***North Carolina, 1910 Federal Census: Soundex and Population Schedules*** **[Microfilm & Digital Capture],** filmed by the National Archives, c1970, 221 rolls, beginning with FHL film #1375108 (Pop. Sched: Alamance Co). To access the digital images, see the online FHL catalog page: **www.familysearch.org/search/catalog/639064.**

***Pre-1914 Cemetery Inscription Card Index,*** **[Microfilm & Digital Capture],** from the originals in the North Carolina Department of Archives and History in Raleigh, North Carolina, prepared by the Historical Records Survey, Work Projects Administration. Surname index cards list county, name of cemetery, town, person, date of birth, death date, age, spouse or parents, location of grave, military information. Cemetery cards are organized alphabetically by county, alphabetically by town and then alphabetically by cemetery name. Filmed by the archives, 23 rolls, beginning with FHL film #882944 (Surnames Aa-At). To access the digital images, see the online FHL catalog page: **https://familysearch.org/search/catalog/176542.**

***Post-1914 Cemetery Inscription Card Index,*** **[Microfilm & Digital Capture],** from the originals at the NC State Archives. Prepared by the Historical

Records Survey, Works Progress Administration. The cards give county, name of cemetery, town, name of person, birth date, death date, age, spouse or parents, location of grave, and military information, if known. Filmed by the archives, 5 rolls, beginning with FHL film #882965 (Surnames A-C). To access the digital images, see the online FHL catalog page:
**https://familysearch.org/search/catalog/736359.**

**1917-1919.** ***North Carolina, World War I Service Cards*** **[Online Database],** digitized and indexed at FamilySearch.org. Includes Index and images of service cards for the Army, Marine Corps, Navy and Coast Guard. The collection is located at the North Carolina State Archives in Raleigh. This database has 92,649 records, see
**www.familysearch.org/search/collection/2568864.**

**1920.** ***North Carolina, 1920 Federal Census: Soundex and Population Schedules*** **[Microfilm & Digital Capture],** filmed by the National Archives, c1970, 226 rolls, beginning with FHL film #1821282 (Pop. Sched: Alamance Co). To access the digital images, see the online FHL catalog page:
**www.familysearch.org/search/catalog/534323.**

**1926-1975.** ***North Carolina, County Divorce Records*** **[Online Database],** digitized and indexed at FamilySearch.org. Source: NC State Archives, Raleigh. Includes an "index to former husbands and maiden names of divorced women." This database has 20,027 records, see
**www.familysearch.org/search/collection/2848500.**

**1930.** ***North Carolina, 1930 Federal Census: Soundex and Population Schedules*** **[Microfilm & Digital Capture],** filmed by the National Archives, c1970, 229 rolls, beginning with FHL film #2341405 (Pop. Sched: Alamance Co). To access the digital images, see the online FHL catalog page:
**www.familysearch.org/search/catalog/1037495.**

**1931-1994.** ***North Carolina Deaths*** **[Online Database],** indexed at the FamilySearch.org website. Source: NC Vital Records Section. Name index to deaths recorded in North Carolina, 1931-1994. Many entries include a name of a spouse, child, parents, and more. This database has 2,642,875 records. See
**https://familysearch.org/search/collection/1584959.**

**1933-1990.** ***Tennessee Valley Cemetery Relocation Files*** **[Online Database],** indexed at the Ancestry.com website. Source: National Archives. The Tennessee Valley Authority (TVA) was established in 1933 with the goals of alleviating flooding problems, generating affordable electricity, facilitating better river navigation, manufacturing fertilizer, and bolstering local economies. While there were many benefits, thousands of people, cemeteries, and other institutions had to be relocated from places that were to be flooded to make way for dams and hydroelectric power plants. This collection includes grave removal records from cemeteries that were in the path of projects. Included are grave removals near Chatuge, Fontana, Hiwassee, and Johnsonville, North Carolina. This database has 172,537 records. See
**http://search.ancestry.com/search/db.aspx?dbid=60427.**

***1934-1954 North Carolina Population Relocation Files, Tennessee Valley Authority*** **[Microfilm & Digital Capture],** from the originals housed in the National Archives Record Office, East Point, Georgia. Records of relocation of people due to the development of dams and reservoirs. Lists name, address, marital status, birthplace of parents, number of and ages of children, occupation, real estate, religion, for families in Cherokee and Swain counties. Filmed by the Genealogical Society of Utah, 1996, 3 rolls, beginning with FHL film #2033919 (Hiwassee project, Cherokee County, 1936-1944, 970 files). To access the digital images, see the online FHL catalog page:
**www.familysearch.org/search/catalog/647131.**

**1934-1953.** ***U.S., Tennessee Valley, Family Removal and Population Readjustment Case Files*** **[Online Database],** indexed at the Ancestry.com website. This collection includes case histories and surveys of those who were in the path of the TVA projects. Included is the communities near the Appalachia Reservoir, Fontana, and Hiwassee, North Carolina. This database has 81,862 records. See
**http://search.ancestry.com/search/db.aspx?dbid=4903.**

***1934-1954 Master File Relocation Card Index for Grave and Cemetery Removal and Relocation, Tennessee Valley Authority*** **[Microfilm & Digital Capture],** from the originals housed in the National Archives, East Point, Georgia. Records of relocation of burials due to the development of dams and reservoirs. Lists cemetery name and number, deceased, date of birth, date of death, age, type and condition of marker and inscription, nearest living relative or source of information, source's address, and relationship to deceased. Filmed by the Genealogical Society of Utah, 1996, North Carolina begins with FHL film #2050608 (North Carolina Grave Removal Master Card Index).

To access the digital images, see the online FHL catalog page:
**www.familysearch.org/search/catalog/778971.**

***1940 North Carolina Federal Census: Population Schedules* [Digital Capture],** from the original records held by the Bureau of the Census in the 1940s. After microfilming, Congress allowed the Census Bureau to destroy the originals to free up space for WWII-related files. The Family History Library (FHL) has the 1940 microfilm archived at their Granite Mountain Record Vault. They are not available for viewing but the entire digital collection is available online at several sites. To access the digital images, see the online FHL catalog page: **www.familysearch.org/search/catalog/2057776.**

***1940 Federal Census Finding Aids* [Online Database].** The National Archives prepared a special website online with a detailed description of the 1940 federal census. Included at the site are descriptions of location finding aids, such as Enumeration District maps, Geographic Descriptions of Census Enumeration Districts, and a list of 1940 City Directories available at the National Archives. The finding aids are all linked to other National Archives sites. The National Archives website also has a link to 1940 Search Engines using Stephen P. Morse's "One-Step" system for finding a 1940 E.D. or street address conversion. See
**www.archives.gov/research/census/1940/general-info.html#questions.**

**1940-1948.** See ***North Carolina, Discharge and Statement of Service Records* [Online Database],** digitized and indexed at FamilySearch.org. Includes index and images of discharges and Selective Service statement of service records for World War II, acquired from the North Carolina State Archives. The following counties are included in this collection: Alamance, Alexander, Alleghany, Anson, Ashe, Avery, Beaufort, Bertie, Bladen, Brunswick, Burke, Buncombe, Cabarrus, Caldwell, Camden, Carteret, Caswell, Catawba, Chatham, Cherokee, Chowan, Clay, Cleveland, Columbus, Craven, Cumberland, Currituck, Dare, Davidson, Davie, Duplin, Durham, Edgecombe, Franklin, Forsyth, Gaston, Gates, Granville, Greene, Guilford, Halifax, Harnett, Haywood, Henderson, Hertford, Hoke, Hyde, and Iredell. This collection is being published as images become available. This database has 196,206 records, see
**www.familysearch.org/search/collection/2053639.**

**1958-1963.** ***North Carolina, Passenger and Crew Lists* [Online Database],** indexed at the Ancestry.com website. Source: National Archives microfilm series A4110. This database consists of manifests from ships arriving in North Carolina, and include the name of the vessel and arrival date, ports of departure and arrival (as well as future destinations on a ship's itinerary), dates of departure and arrival, shipmaster, full name, age, gender, physical description, military rank (if any), occupation, birthplace, citizen of what country, and residence. For military transports, you may find the next of kin, relationships, and address listed as well. Later manifests may include visa or passport numbers. This database has 5,845 records. See
**http://search.ancestry.com/search/db.aspx?dbid=60981.**

**1958-2004.** ***North Carolina, Divorce Index* [Online Database],** indexed at the Ancestry.com website. Source: NC Health Statistics. The superior court in each county in North Carolina has granted divorce decrees since 1814. This database is an index to divorces that occurred in North Carolina between 1958 and 2004. Information available in this database includes: Names of husband and wife, Birth dates of husband and wife, Marriage date, Marriage state and county, Divorce date, and Divorce county, This database has 2,326,603 records. See
**http://search.ancestry.com/search/db.aspx?dbid=1115.**

**1988-Current.** ***North Carolina Recent Newspaper Obituaries)* [Online Database],** digitized and indexed newspaper obituaries at the GenealogyBank website, including newspapers from Ahoskie, Albemarle, Andrews, Apex, Asheboro, Belhaven, Blowing Rock, and 103 more North Carolina cities. See
**www.genealogybank.com/explore/obituaries/all/usa/north-carolina.**

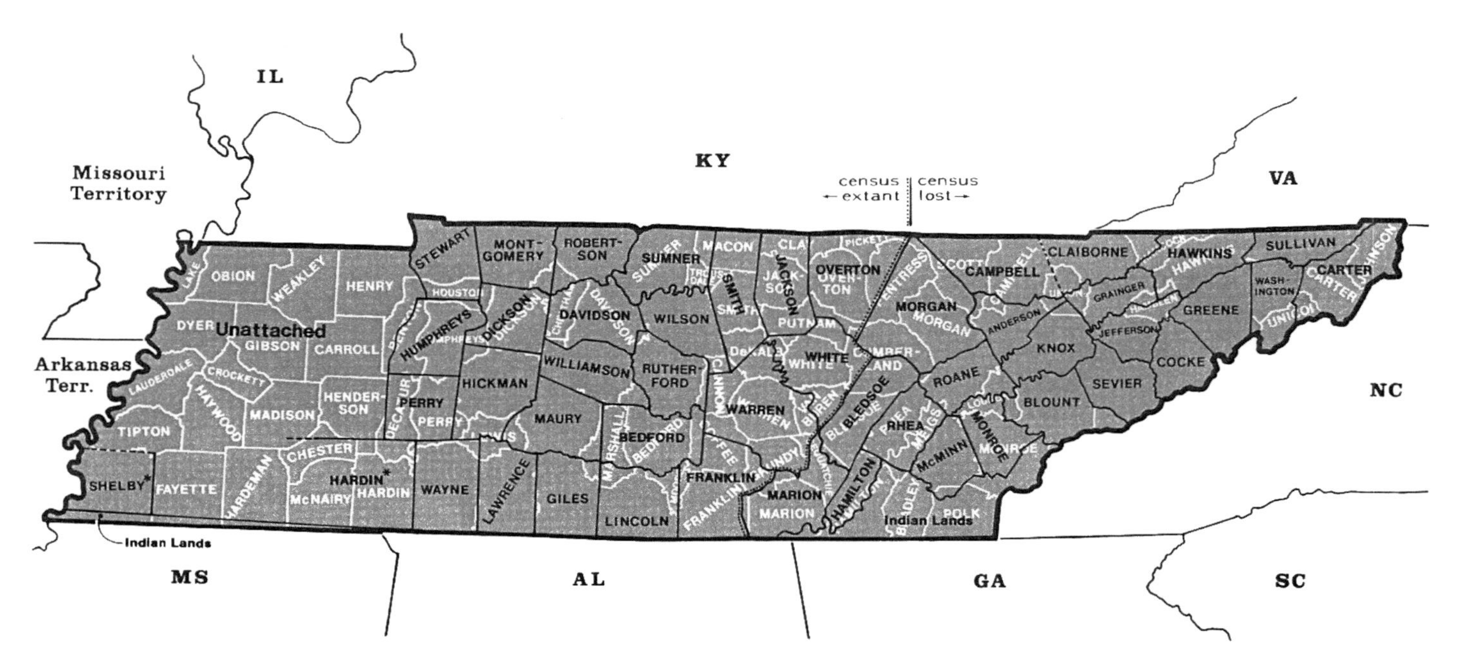


**Tennessee • Aug 1820.** The 48 counties of Tennessee at the time of the 1820 Federal Census are shown in black. The current 95 counties of Tennessee are shown in white. ***Notes:** 1) The large "Unattached" area of West Tennessee on this map was part of the Chickasaw Cession of 1818. See Cession No. 100, Map No. 54, "Tennessee and Portions of Bordering States," in ***Indian Land Cessions of the United States***, compiled by Charles C. Royce, publ. GPO, 1899. To view map 54, see **http://usgwarchives.net/maps/cessions/ilcmap54.htm.** 2) In 1819, Hardin County was created to run to the Mississippi, but eleven days later Shelby was created, its northern boundary defined by a General Assembly unsure about where the line should lie. The law stated that the eastern line of Shelby should extend "...as far north as necessary to include a constitutional county." About the lost counties of 1820: The 22 eastern counties indicated as "census lost" on this map were all included in Tennessee's eastern federal court district (Courthouse: Knoxville). The 26 western counties indicated as "census extant" were all included in the western federal court district (Courthouse: Nashville). As part of the 1830 Federal Census enabling act, the Clerks of the U.S. District Courts in all states were asked to transmit to Washington, all of their original census manuscripts, 1790 through 1830. The Clerk of the Court for the western district complied with that law by transmitting to Washington the originals for all counties in his district for 1820; while the Clerk of Court for the eastern district did not comply. **Map Source:** Page 317, *Map Guide to the U.S. Federal Censuses, 1790-1920*, by William Thorndale and William Dollarhide.

# Tennessee

## Censuses & Substitute Name Lists

### Historical Timeline for Tennessee, 1623-1812

**1623. Carolina.** The first charter for a colony in the area of the Carolinas was granted to Sir Robert Heath by King James I, but due to the political climate in England, the charter would never be used.

**1663. Carolina.** Charles II granted eight noblemen a charter to *Carolina*, "sea to sea," from Latitude 31$^{O}$ (present FL/GA line) to Latitude 35$^{O}$ (present GA/TN line). This was a repayment for their loyalty and support during the English Civil War. The eight became known as the Lords Proprietors. In 1665, the charter was extended north to the present NC/VA line to include the Albemarle Sound settlements, The name Carolina came from "Carolus," Latin for Charles.

**1682. Carolina.** The first four counties of the Province of Carolina were created, named after Lords Proprietors Berkeley, Colleton, Craven, and Granville.

**1712. North and South Carolina.** The territory of the Province of Carolina since 1665 ran from about Latitude 31$^{O}$ to the present NC/VA line (36$^{O}$30'), including the area of present Georgia. In 1712, the Lords Proprietors divided Carolina into North Carolina and South Carolina (proprietary provinces) on nearly the same division line as today, but the line was not surveyed for several more years. Each province had its own colonial governor, under the authority of the eight Lords Proprietors. The area of North Carolina included all of present Tennessee to the Mississippi River.

**1717.** The arrival of the first Scots-Irish immigrants to the British Colonies was via Boston, New York City, Philadelphia, Alexandria, New Bern, and Charles Towne. The so-called Scots-Irish (or Ulster Scots) were former border clan people who had lived near the Scottish-English border for centuries. A good number of them had moved into areas of Northern Ireland in the early 1600s, and a mass migration to most of the British colonies of America began in about 1717. By 1775, the Scots-Irish outnumbered (by three times) the total of the other British groups in colonial America (Puritans, Cavaliers, or Quakers). The Scots-Irish were the earliest settlers of western Virginia and North Carolina (aka Kentucky and Tennessee); as well as Georgia, Alabama, Mississippi, and Texas.

**1729-1777.** In 1729, the **Province of North Carolina** became a separate Royal British Colony after seven of the eight Lords Proprietors sold their interest back to the Crown. A large portion of original proprietor land was retained by Lord John Carteret. In 1744, Carteret inherited the title of Earl of Granville. Soon after, the former proprietor began selling land in his privately held **Granville District**, the northern half of present North Carolina and Tennessee. The first few years of land sales were well documented, providing good evidence of the earliest inhabitants of central and western North Carolina into the 1760s. Later records were incomplete due to cross-claim disputes. The Granville District operation dissolved in 1777. Surviving records of the land sales in the Granville District, including the first land sales in present Tennessee, are located today at the NC State Archives in Raleigh.

**1746. Pioneer's Road.** The first wagon road through the Blue Ridge Mountains of Virginia was constructed in 1746, allowing wagon traffic from Alexandria to Winchester, Virginia. The first travelers on the roadway were mostly Scots-Irish immigrants, who had changed their travel plans to arrive in Alexandria instead of Philadelphia. The trace of the old Pioneer's Road is now called US Hwy 50. At Winchester, the Great Valley Road / Shenandoah Valley of Western Virginia gave travelers a way to the southwestern end of Virginia – eventually the primary route used by the first settlers to migrate into East Tennessee.

**1763.** The **Treaty of Paris** ended the French and Indian War (in Europe and Canada: the Seven Years War). France ceded all of its North American claims east of the Mississippi to Britain. Soon after, King George III declared the "Proclamation Line of 1763," as a way of rewarding the Indians who had helped Britain against the French. The proclamation line established an Indian Reserve that stretched from the Appalachian Mountain Range to the Mississippi River.

**1768. Treaty of Fort Stanwix.** A new "Line of Property" was drawn, separating British Territory from Indian Territory. From Fort Stanwix (present Rome, NY), the division line ran to Fort Pitt (now Pittsburgh) and down the Ohio River to the Tennessee River. The Fort Stanwix treaty line effectively ceded all of present West Virginia and Kentucky to the British Colony of Virginia.

**1770-1775. East Tennessee.** The first migrations of people into present East Tennessee began between 1770 and 1775 with the Watauga settlements, evolving into the North Carolina communities of Elizabethton and Jonesborough. Most came by way of the Great Valley Road of Virginia, leading to the Clinch River Valley and into present Tennessee.

**1775-1783. The Transylvania Land Company.** In 1775, the Cherokee Indians sold North Carolina Judge Richard Henderson huge quantities of land between the Ohio, Kentucky, and Cumberland rivers for the Transylvania Land Company. Under Henderson's employ, Daniel Boone blazed and cleared the "Wilderness Trail" and established Fort Boonesborough. By 1783, some 60,000 settlers had used the Wilderness Trail to move into Kentucky. Plans for the Transylvania Company's proposed colony in present Tennessee were never fulfilled – the company was not recognized by either Virginia or North Carolina and was dissolved in 1783.

**1779. French Lick Settlements.** The first Cumberland River settlements of present Middle Tennessee were in the French Lick area, beginning with Fort Nashborough, the forerunner of the city of Nashville. Both the Tennessee and Cumberland Rivers provided access to the Middle Tennessee settlements.

**1784. State of Franklin.** Feeling abandoned by their government in New Bern, North Carolina, settlers living in present Northeastern Tennessee declared their area an independent state and named it Franklin. Jonesborough was their capital from 1784 to 1785; followed by Greenville, 1785-1788. Franklin functioned as a state for four years with the consent of the local population. But in 1788, Franklin's petition to Congress for official recognition was denied. The area was reclaimed by North Carolina where it remained until 1789.

**1785.** Nov. **Cherokee Land Cession.** After the demise of the Transylvania Company, the earliest recognized Indian Land Cession west of the Cumberland Mountains was part of a treaty between the U.S. Government and the "Cherokee Nation of Indians" in 1785. The treaty included an area of the Cumberland River region of Middle Tennessee. Although there were numerous squatters living in the area before 1785, no one could legally purchase land in the ceded area until after the Cherokee Indian Cession of 1785.

**1787-1795. Avery's Trace - Nashville Road.** To attract settlers into its newly opened western areas, the state of North Carolina financed the construction of a 200-mile wagon road from Knoxville west to the Cumberland River settlements around Fort Nashborough. However, no wagons could manage the trail when it was first opened in 1787. The road was first called Avery's Trace after the scout and woodsman who was hired to blaze the trail. The first trail was passable by single-file pack teams only. After many improvements, by 1795, fully loaded wagons could negotiate the roadway, and it became known as the Nashville Road. As a direct result of Avery's Trace-Nashville Road, land sales in the Middle Tennessee region surged.

**1789.** Dec. North Carolina ceded the area of present Tennessee to the federal government.

**1790.** May. The Territory South of the River Ohio (more commonly, the Southwest Territory) was created by Congress. The first capital was Knoxville.

**1791.** July. A tally of the residents of the Southwest Territory showed a population of 35,691 people.

**1796.** June 1. **Tennessee** became the 16th state in the Union, with Knoxville as the first state capital.

**1812. Nashville** became the state capital (for the first time); lost it to Murfreesboro, 1818-1826; but the capital returned to Nashville in 1826 (and thereafter).

## Online Resources at the Tennessee State Library & Archives

Visit the TSL&A webpage for Online Resources. See **http://sos.tn.gov/tsla.** A selection of their searchable databases include the following:

**Maps at the TN State Library & Archives.** The TSL&A has the largest and most significant collection of historical maps in the state and available for public use.

**Family Bible Records Project.** The TSL&A holds hundreds of family Bible records in several formats and within many collections. See **http://tnsos.net/TSLA/Bibleproject.**

**The Tennessee Electronic Library** is a collection of databases that provide access to over 400,000 magazine, journal, and newspaper articles, essays, podcasts, videos, and e-books. See **http://tntel.tnsos.org.**

**Tennessee Supreme Court Cases** represent an especially valuable resource for historical and genealogical research. See **http://supreme-court-cases.tennsos.org.**

**The Tennessee Virtual Archive** (TeVA) is a digital repository that provides a searchable array of historical records, photographs, documents, maps, postcards, film, audio, and other original materials of enduring value. Major databases included in the TeVA are the Confederate Pensions Applications; the Library Photographs Collections; Maps of the Tennessee State Library and Archives; Records of the Revolutionary War; and Records of the Civil War era. See **http://teva.contentdm.oclc.org.**

# Bibliography

## Tennessee Censuses & Substitutes

**State Censuses:** There are references to state censuses authorized in the state constitution of 1796 and again in 1834, but no evidence can be found that shows either were actually taken. There were no state-sponsored censuses in Tennessee until 1891. In that year, the state completed an enumeration of all males over the age of 21 years. It was the only known state census taken in Tennessee.

**1790 Federal Census:** The Northwest and Southwest Territories were specifically left out of the first census of 1790. But, Secretary of State Thomas Jefferson, perhaps as an afterthought, asked Governor William Blount if he would not mind taking a census in the Southwest Territory. Blount responded with a tally of the inhabitants (but no names) in each of the original seven counties, taken in July 1791. For that time period, tax lists and other names lists from the counties of Greene, Hawkins, Knox, and Washington cover the first areas of settlement in East Tennessee; while lists from the Middle Tennessee counties of Tennessee County (later replaced with Montgomery and Robertson), Davidson, and Sumner counties cover the rest of the population.

**1800-1830 Federal Censuses.** As part of the 1830 Federal Census enabling act, all states and territories were asked to transmit to Washington, all of their original census manuscripts, 1790 through 1830.

Thomas Jefferson, the Secretary of State in 1790, was the author of the instructions to the Assistant Marshals charged with conducting the federal census in every U.S. Circuit Court District. The original manuscripts of the federal censuses were to be "carefully preserved with the Clerk of the District Court"

The Clerk of the Court for the Western Tennessee District (Nashville) complied with that 1830 law by transmitting to Washington the originals for no counties for 1800; one county (Rutherford) in his district for 1810; all 26 counties in his district for 1820; and all counties in his district for 1830. The Clerk of the Court for the Eastern Tennessee District (Knoxville) was able to transmit the originals from his district for 1830 only.

Refer to the 1820 map on page 160 for the divisions between the eastern district counties and the western district counties.

**1820 Census Substitutes.** There are tax lists (census substitutes) available for the 22 lost counties of 1820, the East Tennessee counties of Anderson, Bledsoe, Blount, Campbell, Carter, Claiborne, Cocke, Grainger, Greene, Hamilton, Hawkins, Jefferson, Knox, McMinn, Marion, Monroe, Morgan, Rhea, Roane, Sevier, Sullivan, and Washington counties.

**1840-1940 Federal Censuses.** All of Tennessee's federal censuses are complete for all counties, with the exception of the 1890, lost in a fire in 1921 (like all states). A detailed list of available censuses & substitutes follows:

**1769-1800.** ***The Annals of Tennessee to the End of the Eighteenth Century: Comprising its Settlement, as the Watauga Association, From 1769 to 1777; a Part of North Carolina, from 1777 to 1784; the State of Franklin, From 1788 to 1790; the Territory of the US South of the Ohio, From 1790 to 1796; and the State of Tennessee, From 1796 to 1800*** **[Microfilm],** by James Gettys McGready Ramsey, reprint of original publ. Charleston: Walker and James, 1853. Filmed with ***Fain's Critical and Analytical Index and Genealogical Guide to Ramsey's Annals of Tennessee: Embracing All Proper Names as Well as Important Topical Subjects***, compiled by John Tyree Fain, original published: Nashville: Paul Hunter, 1920, 86 pages. *The Annals of Tennessee* and *Fain's Index* are together on FHL film #24525.

**1770-1842.** ***Early Tennessee Settlers, 1700's-1900's*** **[CD-ROM],** originally published by Broderbund in collaboration with Genealogical Publishing Co., Inc., Baltimore, 2002, Family Tree Maker's Family Archives, Genealogical Records No. 511. See FHL CD-ROM No. 9, Part 511. Contents:

- *Pioneers of Davidson County, Tennessee*, compiled by Edythe Rucker Whitley
- *Red River Settlers: Records of the Settlers of Northern Montgomery, Robertson, and Sumner counties, Tennessee*, by Edythe Rucker Whitley
- *Tennessee Genealogical records: Henry County "Old Time Stuff,"* researched, compiled and published by Edythe Rucker Whitley
- *Tennessee Genealogical Records: Records of Early Settlers From State and County Archives*, by Edythe Rucker Whitley
- *Overton County, Tennessee, Genealogical Records.* compiled by Edythe Rucker Whitley
- *1770-1790 Census of the Cumberland Settlements: Davidson, Sumner, and Tennessee counties (in what is now Tennessee),* compiled by Richard Carlton Fulcher
- *Index to the 1820 census of Tennessee*, compiled by Elizabeth Petty Bentley
- *Tennessee Records: Bible Records and Marriage Bonds,* compiled by Jeannette Tillotson Acklen
- *Sumner County, Tennessee: Abstract of Will Books 1 and 2, 1788-1842,* compiled by Edythe Rucker Whitley
- *Tennessee Records: Tombstone Inscriptions and Manuscripts: Historical and Biographical,* compiled by Jeannette Tillotson Acklen
- *Tennessee Soldiers in the Revolution*, by Penelope Johnson Allen
- *Some Tennessee Heroes of the Revolution:* Compiled from Pension Statements, by Zella Armstrong
- *Twenty-four Hundred Tennessee Pensioners; Revolution - War of 1812,* by Zella Armstrong
- *Record of Commissions of Officers in the Tennessee Militia, 1796-1815,* compiled by Mrs. John Trotwood Moore.

**1770-1931.** ***North Carolina and Tennessee, Early Land Records*** **[Online Database],** digitized and indexed at the Ancestry.com website. Source: TN State Library & Archives. The first land grants in present Tennessee were issued by North Carolina in the Watauga settlements as early as 1772. North Carolina grants continued with land warrants issued to Revolutionary War veterans from North Carolina militia units, the first military reserves were within the area of present Middle Tennessee. After North Carolina ceded the area to the federal government, the formation of the Southwest Territory was in 1790, and statehood came in 1796, This database has 200,458 records. See **http://search.ancestry.com/search/db.aspx?dbid=2882.**

**1775-1782.** ***The Wataugah Purchase, March 19, 1775 at Sycamore Shoals of Wataugah River: the Cherokee Indians to Charles Robertson, trustee for the Wataugah settlers, an index of the Wataugah Purchase, the North Carolina land grants and deeds through 1782*** **[Printed Book],** by Mary Hardin McCown and Irma Bowman Kitzmiller, publ. Overmountain Press, Johnson City, TN, 1976, 27 pages, FHL book 975.6 A1 No. 138.

**1776-1840.** ***Twenty-Four Hundred Tennessee Pensioners*** **[Online Database],** indexed at the Ancestry.com website. Source: Zella Armstrong's *Twenty-Four Hundred Tennessee Pensioners: Revolution & War of 1812*, publ. GPC, 1975. This database has 120 pages. See **http://search.ancestry.com/search/db.aspx?dbid=48298.**

***1778-1885 Tax Books, Washington County, Tennessee*** **[Microfilm & Digital Capture],** from the original records at the Trustee's Office, Washington County Courthouse, Jonesboro, TN. Filmed by the TN State Library & Archives, 1969, 4 rolls, as follows:

- Tax Books, 1778-1846, FHL film #825545.
- Tax Books, 1814-1850, FHL film #825546.
- Tax Books, 1851-1861, FHL film #825547.
- Tax Books, 1861-1865, FHL film #825548.

To access the digital images, see the online FHL catalog page: **www.familysearch.org/search/catalog/276758.**

- See Also, ***East Tennessee Tax Records Index (Washington County)*** **[Printed Book],** compiled by Geoffrey D. Rasmussen, publ., Heritage Books, Westminster, MD, 2005, 3 vols. From preface: "In 1935, the Works Progress Administration (WPA) oversaw the transcription of the original tax records.

The 1778-1827 portion of this index was compiled using these records. The remaining records were indexed from the originals, which were microfilmed by the TN State Library & Archives." Contents: Vol. 1: Washington County, 1778-1821; Vol. 2: Washington County, 1822-1839; Vol. 3: Washington County, 1840-1850. See FHL book 976.897 R42r.

**1778-1927.** ***Tennessee, Early Land Registers*** **[Online Database],** digitized and indexed at Ancestry.com. Source: Tennessee State Library & Archives, Nashville, TN. The area we now know as the state of Tennessee was at one time the western part of North Carolina. In 1784, North Carolina ceded those lands back to the United States, setting aside a military reserve to be given as land grants to North Carolina Revolutionary War veterans and other individuals who had been involved in surveying the area. This collection includes land records relating to the settlement of the areas of Tennessee outside of the Military Reserve, see **www.ancestry.com/search/collections/3658.**

**1779-2008.** ***Tennessee, Wills and Probate Records*** **[Online Database],** digitized and indexed at the Ancestry.com website. Source: TN county, district, and probate courts. In most cases, the details found in probates include the names and residences of beneficiaries and their relationship to the decedent. An inventory of the estate assets may reveal personal details about the deceased's occupation and lifestyle. There may also be references to debts, deeds, and other documents related to the settling of the estate. This database has 635,238 records. See **http://search.ancestry.com/search/db.aspx?dbid=9176.**

**1780-1790. Census of the Cumberland Settlements [Online Database],** indexed at the Ancestry.com website. Source: *1780-1790 Census of the Cumberland Settlements: Davidson, Sumner, and Tennessee Counties (In What is Now Tennessee),* by Richard C. Fulcher, publ. 1987. This database has 4,443 records: **http://search.ancestry.com/search/db.aspx?dbid=3006.**

**1780s-1800.** ***Tennessee Marriages, Early to 1800: A Research Tool*** **[Printed Book],** compiled, extracted, and transcribed by Liahona Research; edited by Jordan R. Dodd, published by Precision Indexing, div. of AGLL, Bountiful, UT, 1990, 69 pages. FHL book 976.8 V22t.

**1780-1825.** ***Tennessee, Compiled Marriages*** **[Online Database],** indexed at the Ancestry.com website. Source: Jordan Dodd, *Tennessee Marriages to 1825* extracted from county records on microfilm located at the Family History Library in Salt Lake City. This database has 48,666 records. See **http://search.ancestry.com/search/db.aspx?dbid=2099.**

**1780-1890.** ***Tennessee, Marriage and Bible Records*** **[Online Database],** indexed at the Ancestry.com website. Source: Robert Acklen's *Tennessee Records, Bible Records and Marriage Bonds,* publ. 1933. This database contains over 25,000 records for the state of Tennessee up to 1890. The information in this database, which includes marriages, births, deaths, and wills, etc., has been obtained from family bibles, church, court, and county records. See **http://search.ancestry.com/search/db.aspx?dbid=3186.**
- See also ***Tennessee Records: Tombstone Inscriptions and Manuscripts*** **[Online Database],** (no dates). This is a companion to *Marriages and Bible Records*, an exhaustive cemetery-by-cemetery listing of Tennessee mortuary inscriptions, with a separate section of over 100 pages devoted to biographical and historical sketches. Includes a comprehensive index of 12,500 entries. See **http://search.ancestry.com/search/db.aspx?dbid=48300.**

**1780-2000s.** ***Tennessee GenWeb Archives*** **[Online Database].** The TNGenWeb site offers free genealogical databases with searchable statewide name lists and for all Tennessee counties. Databases may include Bibles, Biographies, Cemeteries, Censuses, Court, Death, Deeds, Directories, Histories, Marriages, Military, Newspapers, Obituaries, Photos, Schools, Tax Lists, Wills, and more. See **http://usgwarchives.net/tn/tnfiles.htm.**

**1780-2000s.** ***Linkpendium-Tennessee: Family History & Genealogy, Census, Birth, Marriage, Death Vita Records & More*** **[Online Databases].** Linkpendium is a genealogical portal site, with links to state, county, town, and local databases. Currently listed are selected sites for Tennessee statewide resources (687), Independent Cities, Renamed Counties, Discontinued Counties (1), Anderson County (341), Bedford County (760), Benton County (244), Bledsoe County (201), Blount County (432), and 90 more Tennessee counties. See **www.linkpendium.com/tn-genealogy.**

**1780-2002.** ***Tennessee State Marriage Index*** **[Online Database],** indexed at the FamilySearch.org website. Source: TN State Library & Archives. This database has 3,331,399 records. See **https://familysearch.org/search/collection/1936414.**

**1780-2002.** ***Tennessee State Marriages*** **[Online Database],** digitized and indexed at the Ancestry.com website. Source: TN State Library & Archives. Information that may be found in this database for each entry includes: Groom's name, Bride's name, Marriage date (or date of record), and Marriage county. Additional information about the bride and groom may be listed on the actual record and can be found by viewing the corresponding image. This database has 6,844,269 records. See
**http://search.ancestry.com/search/db.aspx?dbid=1169.**

**1783-1843.** ***North Carolina and Tennessee, Revolutionary War Land Warrants*** **[Online Database],** indexed at the Ancestry.com website. Source: TN State Library & Archives. Following the Revolutionary War, North Carolina set aside land in upper Middle Tennessee as a military reservation. The land was being reserved for soldiers (or their heirs) who served in the North Carolina Continental Line during the Revolutionary War. In 1782 surveyors were sent out to the area, and they, along with others involved in the surveying process, were also eligible for grants in the area, as were settlers who had lived there since prior to 1 June 1780. This database has 6,181 records. See
**http://search.ancestry.com/search/db.aspx?dbid=2885.**

**1783-1895.** ***Tennessee, Early Tax List Records*** **[Online Database],** indexed at the Ancestry.com website. Source: TN State Library & Archives. This database contains early tax lists from 71 of the 95 counties in Tennessee. The database contains many tax lists for some counties, and just one or two tax lists for others. Use the Browse this Collection box to see what is available. Each tax list shows the names of white males over age 21 and will sometimes provide information about that person's land, slaves, and other property. They also include valuations of property. This database has 262,784 records. See
**http://search.ancestry.com/search/db.aspx?dbid=2883.**

***1784-1946 Land and Property Records, Davidson County, Tennessee*** **[Microfilm & Digital Capture],** from the original records of the office of the Register of Deeds, Davidson County Courthouse, Nashville, TN. Filmed by the TN State Library & Archives, 1965, 547 rolls, beginning with FHL film #392082 (Grantee Index A-K 1784-1871). To access the digital images, see the online FHL catalog page:
**https://familysearch.org/search/catalog/229234.**

***1786-1962 Deed Records, Montgomery County, Tennessee*** **[Microfilm & Digital Capture],** from original records at the TN State Library & Archives, Nashville, TN. Includes general index with some volumes individually indexed. Filmed by the TN State Library & Archives, 1963, 95 rolls, beginning with FHL film #320851 (Index, 1786-1869). To access the digital images, see the online FHL catalog page:
**https://familysearch.org/search/catalog/182323.**

**1787.** ***"The Lost State of Franklin" Petition of the Inhabitants of the Western Country*** **[Online Database],** full text and signers at the Tracers.Tripod.com website. See
**http://tracers.tripod.com/franklin.htm.**
For a list of names in alphabetical order, see
**http://tracers.tripod.com/alphabetic_petition.htm.**

**1787-1791.** ***Partial Census of 1787 to 1791 of Tennessee as Taken From the North Carolina Land Grants*** **[Microfilm & Digital Version],** from a typescript compiled by Lucy Kate McGhee, 3 vols., filmed by the Genealogical Society of Utah, 1990, 2 rolls, FHL film #1728882 (parts 1 &2); and FHL film #1683130 (part 3). To access the digital version, see the online FHL catalog page:
**www.familysearch.org/search/catalog/484757.**

***1787-1794 Tax Lists, Sumner County, Tennessee*** **[Microfilm & Digital Capture],** from a typescript prepared by the Historical Records Project (WPA), at the TN State Library & Archives in Nashville. Includes index. Filmed by the Genealogical Society of Utah, 1940, 1 roll, FHL film #24839. To access the digital images, see the online FHL catalog page:
**www.familysearch.org/search/catalog/240686.**

**1787-1872.** ***Tax Records and Other Early Lists, Sumner County, Tennessee*** **[Online Database],** indexed at the RootsWeb site for Sumner Co TN. See
**www.rootsweb.ancestry.com/~tnsumner/sumnlist.htm.**

**1787-1919.** ***Sketches of Tennessee's Pioneer Baptist Preachers*** **[Online Database],** an index and full text to over 200 biographies from the book by J.J. Burnett. Indexed at the Knoxcotn.org website. See
**http://knoxcotn.org/old_site/tnbaptists/index.html.**

**1787-1949.** ***Sumner County, Tennessee Deeds & Land Records*** **[Online Database],** index of Grantors (Direct Deed Index, 1787-1949) and index to Deed & Land Records-Transcription Project. Indexed at the RootsWeb site for Sumner Co TN. See
**www.rootsweb.ancestry.com/~tnsumner/deeds.htm.**

***1787-1967 Deed Records & Indexes, Sumner County, Tennessee* [Microfilm & Digital Capture],** from the originals at the TN State Library & Archives, Nashville. Filmed by the TNSL&A, 1966-1967, 161 rolls, beginning with FHL film #467510 (Direct Index to Deeds, A-D, 1787-1947). To access the digital images, see the online FHL catalog page:
**https://familysearch.org/search/catalog/291679.**

**1787-1975. *Tennessee, Relocated Cemeteries Index* [Online Database],** indexed at the Ancestry.com website. Source: TVA website. This database has 28,784 records. See
**http://search.ancestry.com/search/db.aspx?dbid=70713.**

***1790 List of Voters, Hawkins County (Now Tennessee)* [Online Database],** indexed at the RootsWeb site for Hawkins Co TN. See
**www.rootsweb.ancestry.com/~tnhawkin/1790.htm.**

***1790-1794 List of Taxables, Washington County (Now Tennessee)* [Online Database],** names listed in 4 groups:
- For group 1 (1790), see **http://files.usgwarchives.net/tn/washington/taxlists/washtx01.txt.**
- For group 2 (1790), see **http://files.usgwarchives.net/tn/washington/taxlists/washtx02.txt.**
- For group 3 (1792), see **http://files.usgwarchives.net/tn/washington/taxlists/washtx03.txt.**
- For group 4 (1794), see **http://files.usgwarchives.net/tn/washington/taxlists/washtx04.txt.**

**1790-1950. *Tennessee, County Marriages* [Online Database],** digitized and indexed at the FamilySearch.org website. Source: TN State Library & Archives. This collection contains searchable index data and images for marriage registers, marriage licenses, marriage bonds, and marriage certificates. This database has 4,599,297 records. See
**https://familysearch.org/search/collection/1619127.**

***1791-1966 Deed Records & Index, Knox County, Tennessee* [Microfilm & Digital Capture],** from the original records at the Knox County Courthouse, Knoxville, TN. Filmed by the TN State Library & Archives, 1966, 1,564 rolls, beginning with FHL film #464119 (Deed Index, A-C). To access the digital images, see the online FHL catalog page:
**https://familysearch.org/search/catalog/147206**.

**1793-1890. *Wills & Estate Records, Davidson County, Tennessee* [Online Database],** indexed at the USGenWeb archives site for Tennessee. See
**http://usgwarchives.net/tn/davidson/wills.html.**

**1793-1969. *Tennessee Newspaper Archives* [Online Databases],** digitized and indexed newspapers at the GenealogyBank website, for Carthage, Chattanooga, Clarksville, Jackson, Knoxville, Memphis, Murfreesboro, Nashville, Rogersville, and Shelbyville:
**www.genealogybank.com/explore/newspapers/all/usa/tennessee.**

**1795-1927. *Tennessee Probate Court Books* [Online Database],** digitized at the FamilySearch.org website. Source: FamilySearch extracts of county courthouse records on microfilm at the Family History Library, Salt Lake City, UT. This collection of probate court records/images is from all Tennessee counties. Browse the images, organized by county, then type of record book and year. Some of the original bound books were indexed at the back of the book. In the case of wills, there may be a separate bound book entitled, *Index to Wills*. This database has 628,641 records. See
**https://familysearch.org/search/collection/1909088.**

**1795-1955. *Tennessee Probate Court Files* [Online Database],** digitized at the FamilySearch.org website. Source: FamilySearch extracts of county courthouse records on microfilm at the Family History Library, Salt Lake City, UT. This collection of probate court records/images is from 21 Tennessee counties. These records were kept either as loose papers or in files, rather than bound volumes. Browse the images, organized by county, then type of record. This database has 1,021,998 records. See
**https://familysearch.org/search/collection/1909193.**

**1796-1875. *Tennessee* [CD-ROM].** Early Tennessee Court and Miscellaneous Records a series of records compiled by Carol Wells and others. A publication by Heritage Books, Bowie, MD, 2001, 3 CDs. edited by Carol Wells. Contents: Vol. 1: *Davidson County, Tennessee, County Court minutes, v. 1-3,* by Carol Wells; Vol. 2: *Robertson County, Tennessee, Court Minutes, 1796-1807*; *Williamson County, Tennessee, County Court minutes, 1806-1812*; *Williamson County, Tennessee, County Court minutes, 1812-1815*, compiled by Carol Wells; *Abstracts of Giles County, Tennessee, County Court minutes, 1813-1816, and Circuit Court minutes, 1810-1816*, by Carol Wells; *Rhea County, Tennessee, Circuit Court minutes, September 1815-March 1836,* by Carol Wells; Rhea County, *Tennessee, Tax lists, 1832-1834 & County*

*Court minutes, Volume D, 1829-1834,* by Carol Wells; *Dickson County, Tennessee County and Circuit Court minutes, 1816-1828 and witness docks,* by Carol Wells; *Notable men of Tennessee, from 1833 to 1875,* by Oliver P. Temple; compiled and arranged by his daughter, Mary B. Temple; Vol. 3: *Davidson County, Tennessee, Deed Books,* by Mary Sue Smith; *Historic Sumner County, Tennessee with genealogies of the Bledsoe, Cage and Douglas families,* by Jay Guy Cisco, indexed by Vera Meek Wimberly; *History of Sweetwater Valley, Tennessee,* by William Ballard Lenoir; *Historical sketches of the Holston valleys,* by Thomas Wilson Preston. These books are published in Adobe Acrobat PDF format. See FHL CD-ROM No. 678.

**1796-1950.** ***Tennessee Marriages*** **[Online Database],** indexed at the FamilySearch.org website. Source: FamilySearch. Name index to death and burial records from microfilm at the Family History Library, Salt Lake City, UT. This database has 1,667,895 records. See **https://familysearch.org/search/collection/1681022.**

***1796-1963 Deed Books; Index to Deeds, 1796-1965, Robertson County, Tennessee*** **[Microfilm & Digital Capture],** from the original records at the TN State Library & Archives, filmed by the Genealogical Society of Utah, 1965, 90 rolls, beginning with FHL film #422467 (Index to Deeds, 1796-1907); and FHL film #422468 (Reverse Index to Deeds, A-Z, 1900-1965). To access the digital images, see the online FHL catalog page:
**www.familysearch.org/search/catalog/234586.**
- See also ***1796-1838 General Index to Deeds, Robertson County, Tennessee*** **[Microfilm & Digital Capture],** from a typescript prepared by the Historical Records Survey (WPA) at the TN State Library & Archives, Nashville. Filmed by the Genealogical Society of Utah, 1941, 1 roll, FHL film #24802. To access the digital images, see the online FHL catalog page: **www.familysearch.org/search/catalog/214408.**

***1796-1864 County Court Minutes, Books 1-14, Robertson County, Tennessee*** **[Online Database],** indexed at the Genealogy Trails website for Robertson Co TN. See
**http://genealogytrails.com/tenn/robertson/court.html.**

***1798 Property Tax List and 1820 Census of Montgomery County, Tennessee*** **[Printed Book, Microfilm & Digital Version],** transcribed, indexed, and published by Ursula S. Beach and Ann E. Alley, Clarksville, TN, 1969, 43 pages. FHL book 976.845 X2p and FHL film #1033729. To access the digital version, see the online FHL catalog page:
**www.familysearch.org/search/catalog/324914.**
- See also, ***Montgomery County, Tennessee 1798 Tax List*** **[Printed Book & Microfilm],** compiled by James L. Douthat, published by Mountain Press, Signal Mountain, TN, 2000, 32 pages, FHL book 976.845 R4d and FHL film #6003699.
- See also, **1798-1802 Tax Lists of Montgomery County Tennessee [Online Database],** indexed at the TNGenWeb site for Montgomery Co TN.
- For 1798, see
**http://tngenweb.org/stewart/1798tax.htm.**
- For 1799, see
**http://tngenweb.org/stewart/1799tax.htm.**
- For 1800, see
**www.tngenweb.org/montgomery/taxlist1800.html.**
- For 1801, see
**http://tngenweb.org/stewart/1801tax.htm.**
- For 1802, see
**http://tngenweb.org/stewart/1802tax.htm.**

**1800-1965.** ***Tennessee Divorce and Other Records*** **[Online Database],** digitized and indexed at the Ancestry.com website. Source: TN State Library & Archives. This database contains divorce records and other court and probate records. The record types and years covered varies with each county. Counties: Anderson, Carroll, Cheatham, Dickson, Franklin, Haywood, Henderson, Obion, Tipton, and Williamson counties. This database has 35,246 records. See
**http://search.ancestry.com/search/db.aspx?dbid=1237.**

***1801-1825 Tennessee Marriages*** **[Printed Book],** compiled, extracted & transcribed by Liahona Research, Inc.; edited by Jordan R. Dodd, published by Heritage Quest, North Salt Lake, 2001, 270 pages, FHL book 976.8.

**1801-1974.** ***Tennessee, Jackson County Records*** **[Online Database],** digitized at FamilySearch.org. This collection includes digital images of marriage records, 1888-1974 and records of the Chancery and Circuit Courts, 1801-1962 from Jackson County, Tennessee. This collection is being published as images become available. This database has 13,799 records:
**www.familysearch.org/search/collection/1922414.**

***1806 Tax List, Knox County, Tennessee*** **[Printed Book],** author and publisher unknown, name list published in FHL book 976.885 R4ka and FHL film #1320525.

***1809-1812 Tax List, Hawkins County, Tennessee* [Printed Book],** author and publisher unknown, 13-page typescript at the FHL as FHL book 976.8 A1 No. 95.

***1809-1817 Tax Books, Greene County, Tennessee* [Microfilm & Digital Capture],** from a typescript prepared by the Historical Records Project (WPA), at the TN State Library & Archives, Nashville, TN. Includes index. Filmed by the Genealogical Society of Utah, 1939, 1 roll, FHL film #film 24667. To access the digital images, see the online FHL catalog page:
**www.familysearch.org/search/catalog/211122.**

**1809-1950. *Tennessee, Supreme Court Case Index* [Online Database],** indexed at the Ancestry.com website. Source: TN State Library & Archives. This is a 3rd party database, also available at the TN State Library & Archives website. This database has 69,130 records. See
**http://search.ancestry.com/search/db.aspx?dbid=9292.**

**1809-1975. *Tennessee, White County Records* [Online Database],** digitized at the FamilySearch.org website. Source: White County Archives, Sparta, TN. This is a collection of records from White County including marriages, 1836-1963; chancery court records 1825-1923, and circuit court records, 1809-1900. This database has 235,814 records. See
**https://familysearch.org/search/collection/1989162.**

**1810. *The Reconstructed 1810 Census of Tennessee: 33,000 Long-lost Records From Tax Lists, Court Minutes, Church Records, Wills, Deeds and Other Sources* [Printed Book],** by Charles A. Sherrill, published by the author, Mt. Juliet, TN, 2001, 576 pages. Names listed in alphabetical order. FHL book 976.8 X2s.

***1810-1840 Federal Censuses, Tennessee* [Microfilm & Digital Capture],** all East Tennessee counties for 1800, 1810, and 1820 were lost. This microfilm series includes the surviving Middle & West Tennessee counties for 1810 (1 county) and 1820 (26 counties), and the 1830 and 1840 (all TN counties). To access the digital images, see the online FHL catalog page:
**www.familysearch.org/search/catalog/745506.**

**1810-1891. *Tennessee, Compiled Census and Census Substitutes Index, 1810-1891* [Online Database],** indexed at the Ancestry.com website. Originally edited by Ronald Jackson, Accelerated Indexing Systems, Salt Lake City. This collection contains the following indexes: 1810 Federal Census Index; 1820 Federal Census Index; 1830 Federal Census Index; 1840 Federal Census Index; 1840 Pensioners List; 1850 Federal Census Index; 1860 Federal Census Index; 1860 Slave Schedule; 1890 Veterans Schedule; 1891 Voters List; Early Census Index. This database has 486,897 records. See
**http://search.ancestry.com/search/db.aspx?dbid=3574.**

**1810-1965. *Tennessee Church Marriages* [Online Database],** indexed at the FamilySearch.org website. Index and images of selected marriages. Source: TN State Library & Archives. Many of the records are for Bradley and Lincoln counties. This database has 1,533 records. See
**https://familysearch.org/search/collection/2556020.**

***1812 Davidson County, Tennessee, Tax List: Taken From the Microfilm Copy Found in the Tennessee State Archives* [Printed Book],** by James L. Douthat, published by Mountain Press, Signal Mountain, TN, 2000, 28 pages. FHL book 976.855 R4d and FHL film #6003700.

***1814-1819 Tax Lists, Washington County, Tennessee* [Microfilm & Digital Capture],** from a typescript prepared by the Historical Records Project (WPA) at the TN State Library & Archive, Nashville. Includes index. Filmed by the Genealogical Society of Utah, 1940, 1 roll, FHL film #24853. To access the digital images, see the online FHL catalog page:
**www.familysearch.org/search/catalog/233120.**

**1816-1995. *Tennessee, Church Records* [Online Database],** digitized and indexed at FamilySearch.org. This collection contains Church records from various denominations in Tennessee. The record content and time period varies by denomination and locality. This database has 3,909 records, see
**www.familysearch.org/search/collection/2790270.**

**1820. *Tennessee Census Reports for 1820* [Printed Book, Microfilm & Digital Version],** an extract of the 1820 federal census originals, with names of heads of household arranged by the first letter of their surname, typed and published by Martha Lou Houston, Washington, DC, 1933-1934. Filmed by the Genealogical Society of Utah, 1955-1981, 8 rolls, beginning with FHL film #1036796 (Bedford Co – Franklin Co). To access the digital images, see the online FHL catalog page:
**https://familysearch.org/search/catalog/270039.**

**1820s East Tennessee Taxpayers.** Four titles, substitutes for the lost 1820 federal census for 22 East Tennessee Counties:
- See **1)** ***Early East Tennessee Taxpayers: A Compiled List of Residents of the Area Covered in 22 East Tennessee Counties For Which There is No Census Record Prior to 1830*** **[Printed Book],** compiled by Mary Barnett Curtis, published by Arrow Point, Ft. Worth, TX, 1964, 93 pages. These lists are composed of names of those people who appear on tax lists or petitions for the early 1800's. Names are listed in alphabetical order within each tax list. FHL book 976.8 R4c.
- See **2)** ***Early East Tennessee Taxpayers*** **[Printed Book],** compiled by Pollyanna Creekmore, published by Southern Historical Press, Easley, SC, 1980, 277 pages. FHL book 976.8 R4 and FHL film #1486601.
- Indexed in **3)** ***Revised Index to Early East Tennessee Taxpayers*** **[Printed Book],** by S. Emmett Lucas, published by Southern Historical Press, Easley, SC, 1982, 36 pages. Index was revised because of an error made in pagination of original book. Includes names from footnotes, not originally indexed. FHL book 976.8 R4cp index.
- See also **4)** ***Index to Early Tennessee Tax Lists*** **[Printed Book],** transcribed and indexed by Byron and Barbara Sistler, published by the authors, Evanston, IL, 1977, 217 pages. FHL book 976.8 R4s and FHL film #1697905.

**1828-1939.** ***Tennessee Births and Christenings*** **[Online Database],** indexed at the FamilySearch.org website. Source: FamilySearch. Name index to birth, baptism, and christening records from microfilm at the Family History Library, Salt Lake City, UT. This database has 210,380 records. See **https://familysearch.org/search/collection/1681012.**

**1831-1870.** ***Tennessee Convicts: Early Records of the State Penitentiary*** **[Printed Book],** by Charles A. Sherrill and Tomye M. Sherrill, published by the authors, Mt. Juliet, TN, 1997-2002, 2 vols., includes index of places (vol. 1) and full-name indexes (vols. 1 & 2). FHL book 976.8 J6s v.1-2.

**1832-1850.** ***Chancery Court Records, Knox County, Tennessee, 1832-1849; Index, 1832-1850*** **[Microfilm],** from the original records at the TN State Library & Archives, Nashville, TN. Filmed by TNSL& A, 1965, 1 roll, FHL film #464119.

***1832-1874 Index & Circuit Count Minutes, Books A-G, Robertson County, Tennessee*** **[Online Database],** indexed at the Genealogy Trails website for Robertson Co TN. See **http://genealogytrails.com/tenn/robertson/court.html.**

**1835 Pension Roll – Tennessee [Online Database],** indexed at the USGenWeb archives site for Tennessee: **http://files.usgwarchives.net/tn/statewide/military/warof1812/pensions/pen1835.txt.**

***1836 Hamilton County, Tennessee, Civil Districts and Tax Lists*** **[Printed Book & Microfilm],** compiled by James L. Douthat, published by Mountain Press, Signal Mountain, TN, 1993, 41 pages, FHL book 976.882 R4d and FHL film #2055166.

***1836 Hawkins County, Tennessee Civil Districts and Tax Lists*** **[Printed Book & Microfilm],** compiled by James L. Douthat, published by Mountain Press, Signal Mountain, TN, 1994, 32 pages. FHL book 976.895 R4 and FHL film #2055166.

***1836 Robertson County, Tennessee, Civil Districts and Tax Lists*** **[Printed Book],** compiled by James L. Douthat, published by Mountain Press, Signal Mountain, TN, 1999, 49 pages. FHL book 976.8464 R4.

**1836-1839.** ***Indexes to Compiled Service Records of Volunteer Soldiers Who Served During the Cherokee Disturbances and Removal in Organizations From the State of Tennessee, and the Field and Staff of the Army of the Cherokee Nation*** **[Microfilm & Digital Capture],** filmed by the National Archives, series M0908, 1 roll, FHL film #1205384. To access the digital images, see the online FHL catalog page: **www.familysearch.org/search/catalog/302008.**

**1838-1888.** ***Tennessee Civil Marriages*** **[Online Database],** indexed at the FamilySearch.org website. Source: FamilySearch. Counties included in this collection are Crockett, Benton, Sevier, Davidson, and Lauderdale. Some information on slaves at the Hermitage (1845-1877) are also included. This database has 5,946 records. See **https://familysearch.org/search/collection/2559093**.

**1842-1955.** ***Tennessee, Putnam County Records*** **[Online Database],** digitized at the FamilySearch.org website. Source: TN State Library & Archives. This collection includes records from the circuit and chancery courts of Putnam County. The records include disputed property and estates, wills, divorces, and records of other civil proceedings. Browse the images, organized by record type, date range, and volume. This database has 158,825 records. See **https://familysearch.org/search/collection/2001083.**

**1843-1962.** ***Tennessee, Davidson County, Nashville City Cemetery Record*** **[Online Database],** Register of interments at the Nashville City Cemetery for years 1843-1962. This database has 3,558 records, see **www.familysearch.org/search/collection/3491876.**

**1848-1913.** ***Tennessee, Shelby County, Memphis, Board of Health Death Records*** **[Online Database],** digitized and index at FamilySearch.org, from microfilm at the TN State Library & Archives, Nashville. This database has 44,835 records, see **www.familysearch.org/search/collection/3460987.**

**1850.** ***Tennessee, 1850 Federal Census: Population Schedules*** **[Microfilm & Digital Capture],** filmed by the National Archives, 1964, 39 rolls, beginning with FHL film #24560 (Anderson and Bedford Cos.). To access the digital images, see the online FHL catalog page: **www.familysearch.org/search/catalog/744499.**

**1850-1880.** ***Federal Mortality Schedules and Related Indexes: Tennessee; 1850-1860, 1880*** **[Microfilm & Digital Capture],** filmed by the National Archives, 1962, series T0655, 5 rolls, beginning with FHL film #422433 (1850 schedules and indexes). To access the digital images, see the online FHL catalog page: **www.familysearch.org/search/catalog/783171.**

**1851-1900.** ***Tennessee Marriages*** **[CD-ROM],** a publication by Genealogy.com, 2000. (Family Tree Maker's Family Archive, Marriage Index, CD No. 235). Lists approximately 439,000 individuals from Tennessee who were married between 1851 and 1900. FHL CD-ROM No. 9 pt. 235.

**1851-1900.** ***Tennessee, Marriages*** **[Online Database],** indexed at the Ancestry.com website. Source: Jordan Dodd, Tennessee Marriages, 1851-1900, extracted from TN county microfilms at the Family History Library, Salt Lake City. This database has 292,425 records. See **http://search.ancestry.com/search/db.aspx?dbid=4125.**

**1853.** ***The Nashville, State of Tennessee, and General Commercial Directory*** **[Microfilm],** from the original published by American Book and Job Printing Office, Nashville, 5 vols., includes index. Filmed by the TN State Library & Archives, 1 roll, FHL film #570814.

**1860.** ***Tennessee, 1860 Federal Census: Population Schedules*** **[Microfilm & Digital Capture],** filmed by the National Archives, 1950, 1967, series M653, 57 rolls, beginning with FHL film #805239. To access the digital images, see the online FHL catalog page: **www.familysearch.org/search/catalog/706407.**

**1860-1861.** ***John L. Mitchell's Tennessee State Gazetteer, and Business Directory*** **[Microfilm],** from the originals, filmed by Research Publications, Woodbridge, CT, 1980-1984. FHL film #6044535.

**1860-1930.** ***Tennessee, Cocke County Records*** **[Online Database],** digitized at the FamilySearch.org website. Source: Cocke County Archives, Newport, TN. This collection includes marriage records, 1870-1929; wills, 1860-1929 and chancery court records, 1860-1930. Browse the images. This database has 95,979 records. See **https://familysearch.org/search/collection/2001053.**

**1861-1865.** ***Tennessee, Civil War Service Records of Confederate Soldiers*** **[Online Database],** indexed at the FamilySearch.org website. Source: National Archives microfilm series M268. The records include a jacket-envelope for each soldier, labeled with his name, his rank, and the unit in which he served. This database has 1,117,605 records. See **https://familysearch.org/search/collection/1932378.**

**1861-1865.** ***Tennessee, Civil War Service Records of Union Soldiers*** **[Online Database],** indexed at the FamilySearch.org website. Source: National Archives microfilm series M395. This database has 578,993 records. See **https://familysearch.org/search/collection/1932422.**

***1861-1865 Assessment Lists of the United States Direct Tax Commission for the District of Tennessee*** **[Microfilm & Digital Capture],** from the original records at the National Archives, Washington, DC. Filmed by the National Archives, series T0227, 6 rolls. To access the digital images, see the online FHL catalog page: **www.familysearch.org/search/catalog/573483.**

**1861-1865.** ***Index to Questionnaires of Civil War Veterans*** **[Printed Book, Microfilm & Digital Version],** compiled by the TN State Library &

Archives, 1962, Nashville, 33 pages. FHL book 976.8 M2ti and FHL film #982038. To access the digital version, see the online FHL catalog page:
**www.familysearch.org/search/catalog/172322.**

**1861-1866.** ***Report of the Adjutant General of the State of Tennessee: of the Military Forces of the State*** **[Online Database],** indexed at the Ancestry.com website. Includes rosters of men, organized by regiments. Includes Roll of Honor, lists of officers, and full index. This database has 707 records (pages). See
**http://search.ancestry.com/search/db.aspx?dbid=29992.**

**1861-1865 & 1894-1978.** ***Confederate Patriot Index*** **[Printed Book & Microfiche],** compiled by the Tennessee Division, United Daughters of the Confederacy, 1976-1978. Includes a name index to soldiers from Tennessee. Vol. 1: 1894-1924; Vol. 2: 1924-1978. FHL book 976.8 M2u and FHL fiche #6046695.

**1865-1872.** ***Tennessee, Freedmen's Bureau Field Office Records*** **[Online Database],** digitized at the FamilySearch.org website. Source: National Archives microfilm series M1911. These records include letters and endorsements sent and received, account books, applications for rations, applications for relief, court records, labor contracts, registers of bounty claimants, registers of complaints, registers of contracts, registers of disbursements, registers of freedmen issued rations, registers of patients, reports, rosters of officers and employees, special and general orders and circulars received, special orders and circulars issued, records relating to claims, court trials, property restoration, and homesteads. Browse the images, organized by title of officers, and field office locations. This database has 164,277 records. See
**https://familysearch.org/search/collection/2333777.**

**1869-1909.** ***Tennessee, Delayed Birth Records*** **[Online Database],** indexed at the Ancestry.com website. Source: TN State Library & Archives. The state began to issue delayed birth certificates starting in 1935 after a proof of birth was required to register for the newly created Social Security program. Delayed birth certificates provided documentation for those born before the 1909 state registration law. People applying for a delayed birth certificate were required to supply supporting documents that proved their birth information. Each record may have these details: place of birth, name, date of birth, sex, color, father's name/birthplace/ residence/ race/ age, and occupation, mother's name, birthplace, residence, race, age, occupation, number of other children, and supporting evidence. This database has 337,621 records. See
**http://search.ancestry.com/search/db.aspx?dbid=2282.**

**1870.** ***Tennessee, 1870 Federal Census: Population Schedules*** **[Microfilm & Digital Capture],** filmed by the National Archives, 1962, 1968, series M594, 76 rolls, beginning with FHL film #553012. To access the digital images, see the online FHL catalog page:
**www.familysearch.org/search/catalog/698920.**

**1872-1923.** ***Tennessee, City Death Records*** **[Online Database],** indexed at the Ancestry.com website. Source: TN State Library & Archives. This database contains a collection of death records from the cities of Nashville, Knoxville, and Chattanooga. Prior to 1914, registration was sometimes done on a county or city level. Information contained in this database includes: Name of deceased, Death place, Death date, Gender, Birth date, Birthplace, Age at time of death, Father's name, Mother's name, Father's birth place, and Mother's birth place. This database has 201,087 records. See
**http://search.ancestry.com/search/db.aspx?dbid=5076.**

**1874-1955.** ***Tennessee Deaths and Burials*** **[Online Database],** indexed at the FamilySearch.org website. Source: FamilySearch. Name index to death and burial records from microfilm at the Family History Library, Salt Lake City, UT. This database has 227,540 records. See
**https://familysearch.org/search/collection/1681020.**

**1874-1955.** ***Tennessee, Deaths and Burials Index*** **[Online Database],** indexed at the Ancestry.com website. Source: FamilySearch. Details may include: name, birth date, birthplace, age, occupation, race, marital status, gender, residence, street address, date of death, place of death, date of burial, place of burial, cemetery, father's name and birthplace, mother's name and birthplace, spouse, and FHL film number. This database has 1,478,997 records. See
**http://search.ancestry.com/search/db.aspx?dbid=2546.**

**1880.** ***Tennessee, 1880 Federal Census: Soundex and Population Schedules*** **[Microfilm & Digital Capture],** filmed by the National Archives, c1970, series T272, 130 rolls, beginning with FHL film #1255244 (Anderson Co, et al). To access the digital images (Population Schedules), see the online FHL catalog page:
**www.familysearch.org/search/catalog/676518.**

**1881-1915.** ***Tennessee, City Birth Records*** **[Online Database],** indexed at the Ancestry.com website. Source: TN State Library & Archives. This database contains a collection of birth records from the cities of Nashville, Knoxville, and Chattanooga. Most of the records are registers, which typically list the following details: name, birth date and place, gender, father's name, and mother's name. This database has 70,804 records. See
**http://search.ancestry.com/search/db.aspx?dbid=2491.**

**1885.** ***Norwood's Knoxville City Directory, 1885 Index*** **[Online Database],** indexed at the Knoxcotn.org website. See
**www.knoxcotn.org/old_site/directories/1885knoxville/index.html.**

**1888-1955.** ***Index to Naturalization Records of the U.S. District Court for the Eastern District of Tennessee at Chattanooga*** [Microfilm & Digital Capture], filmed by the Genealogical Society of Utah, 1989, 1 roll, FHL film #1452262. To access the digital images, see the online FHL catalog page:
**www.familysearch.org/search/catalog/455521.**

**1890-1891.** ***Memphis, Tennessee City Directories*** **[Online Database],** indexed at the Ancestry.com website. Includes *Dow's Memphis Directory, 1890* and *Dow's Memphis Directory, 1891.* This database has 59,808 records.
**http://search.ancestry.com/search/db.aspx?dbid=4416.**

**1890-1891.** ***Chattanooga, Tennessee Directories*** **[Online Database],** indexed at the Ancestry.com website. This database has 17,398 records. See
**http://search.ancestry.com/search/db.aspx?dbid=4978.**

**1891.** ***Enumeration of Male Inhabitants of Twenty-one Years of Age and Upward, Citizens of Tennessee, January 1, 1891, as Provided for by an Act of General Assembly of Tennessee, Passed January 15, 1891, and Approved January 22, 1891*** **[Printed Book & Digital Version],** abstracted and indexed by Sue S. Reed, published by the author, Houston, TX, 1989, 8 vols., each volume indexed. Contents: Vol. 1: Anderson, Blount, Knox, and Sevier counties; Vol. 2. Benton, Carroll, Henry, Houston, and Stewart counties; Vol. 3. Dyer, Gibson, Lake, Obion, and Weakley counties; Vol. 4. Shelby county; Vol. 5. Cumberland, Fentress, Jackson, Loudon, Morgan, Overton, Putnam, Roane, and Scott counties; Vol. 6. Campbell, Clay, Hancock, Macon, Pickett, Smith, and Trousdale counties; Vol. 7. Carter, Greene, Hawkins, Johnson, Sullivan, Unicoi, and Washington counties; Vol. 8. Cheatham, Dickson, Hickman, Humphreys, Lawrence, Lewis, Perry, Wayne, and Williamson counties. FHL book 976.8 X2r v. 1-8. A digital version of this title is available for certain volumes. See the online FHL catalog page for details. See
**https://familysearch.org/search/catalog/461479.**
- See also, ***Tennessee, Enumeration of Male Voters, 1891*** **[Online Database],** digitized and indexed at the Ancestry.com website. Source: TN State Library & Archives. The records list the name of the voter, county, and race. Missing counties: Bledsoe, Campbell, Perry, Sequatchie counties. This database has 391,186 records. See
**http://search.ancestry.com/search/db.aspx?dbid=2884.**

**1891-1965.** ***Tennessee, Confederate Pension Applications, Soldiers and Widows*** **[Online Database],** digitized at the FamilySearch.org website. Digital images of pension applications filed by Confederate veterans and their widows. Tennessee began granting pensions to resident Confederate veterans in 1891 and to their widows in 1905. This database has 379,476 records. See
**https://familysearch.org/search/collection/1874474.**

**1891-1965.** ***Tennessee, Civil War Confederate Pension Applications Index*** **[Online Database],** indexed at the Ancestry.com website. Source: Samuel Sistler's Index to Tennessee Confederate Pension Applications. This database is an index to approximately 28,000 individuals who applied for Civil War Confederate pensions in Tennessee. These pension applicants were either Confederate soldiers (from 1891) or the widows of deceased soldiers (from 1905). Information found in this index includes the applicant's name, county of residence at the time of application, whether soldier or widow, application number, name of soldier if not the applicant, state served in, and source information. This database has 38,423 records. See
**http://search.ancestry.com/search/db.aspx?dbid=7875.**

**1895.** ***Clarksville, Tennessee Directory*** **[Online Database],** indexed at the Ancestry.com website. Source: *Zion's 1895 Directory of Clarksville*. This database has 5,470 records. See
**http://search.ancestry.com/search/db.aspx?dbid=3848.**

**1900.** ***Tennessee, 1900 Federal Census: Soundex and Population Schedules*** **[Microfilm & Digital Capture],** filmed by the National Archives, c1970, series T1072 (Soundex) and T623 (Population), 238

rolls, beginning with FHL film #1241557 (Anderson & Benton Cos). To access the digital images, see the online FHL catalog page:
**www.familysearch.org/search/catalog/650826.**

**1904-2001.** ***Tennessee Funeral Home Records Index*** **[Microfilm & Digital Capture],** microfilm of original records at the Henry County Archives in Paris, Tennessee. The indexes are kept in the Gordon Browning Museum in McKenzie, Tennessee. Lists name of funeral home, name of individual, death date, book, and page number. Filmed by the Genealogical Society of Utah, 2006. To access the digital images, see the online FHL catalog page:
**www.familysearch.org/search/catalog/1339707?.**

**1907-1991.** ***Tennessee, Naturalization Records*** **[Online Database],** indexed at the Ancestry.com website. Source: National Archives, Records of the District Courts of the United States. Includes petitions, declarations, and certificates. This database has 50,349 records. See
**http://search.ancestry.com/search/db.aspx?dbid=2505.**

**1908-1912.** ***Tennessee, Birth Records (ER Series)*** **[Online Database],** digitized at FamilySearch.org. images of birth records from the "Enumerator Record Series" in the Tennessee Division of Vital Records. These births were reported yearly by the Board of School Directors in each county; the enumeration was not taken in 1913. This database has 212,545 records, see **www.familysearch.org/search/collection/2515873.**

**1908-1958.** ***Tennessee, Death Records*** **[Online Database],** digitized and indexed at the Ancestry.com website. Source: TN State Library & Archives. This database contains death certificates, as well as indexes to those certificates for the state of Tennessee from 1908 to 1958. Includes: Name of the Deceased, Age at time of death, Death place, Death date, Gender, Birth date, Birthplace, Parents' names, and Parents' birthplace. Additional information, such as occupation, cause of death, and date and place of burial, may be available on the original record and can be obtained by viewing the image. This database has 1,471,796 records. See
**http://search.ancestry.com/search/db.aspx?dbid=2376.**

**1909.** ***R. L. Polk & Co.'s 1909 Memphis City Directory*** **[Online Database],** indexed at the Ancestry.com website. This database has 2,154 records (pages). See
**http://search.ancestry.com/search/db.aspx?dbid=24760.**

**1910.** ***Tennessee, 1910 Federal Census: Soundex and Population Schedules*** **[Microfilm & Digital Capture],** filmed by the National Archives, c1970, series T1276 (Soundex) and T624 (Population), 179 rolls, beginning with FHL film #1275503 (Anderson, Bedford, Benton, and Bledsoe Co). To access the digital images, see the online FHL catalog page:
**www.familysearch.org/search/catalog/646859.**

**1914-1955.** ***Tennessee Death Records*** **[Online Database],** digitized and indexed at the FamilySearch.org website. Source: TN State Library & Archives. Name index and images of Tennessee death certificates. Statewide death registration began in 1914. This database has 1,851,299 records. See
**https://familysearch.org/search/collection/1417505.**

**1920.** ***Tennessee, 1920 Federal Census: Soundex and Population Schedules*** **[Microfilm & Digital Capture],** filmed by the National Archives, c1970, series M1588 (Soundex) and T625 (Population), 206 rolls, beginning with FHL film #1821728 (Anderson, Bedford, and Benton Co). To access the digital images, see the online FHL catalog page:
**www.familysearch.org/search/catalog/558323.**

**1926.** ***Knoxville City Directory*** **[Online Database],** indexed at the Ancestry.com website. This database has 1,755 records (pages). See
**http://search.ancestry.com/search/db.aspx?dbid=25363.**

**1930.** ***Tennessee, 1930 Federal Census: Soundex and Population Schedules*** **[Microfilm & Digital Capture],** filmed by the National Archives, c1970, series M2058 (Soundex) and T626 (Population), 223 rolls, beginning with FHL film #2341967 (Anderson, Bedford, and Benton Co). To access the digital images, see the online FHL catalog page:
**www.familysearch.org/search/catalog/1037515.**

**1930-1961.** ***Tennessee, Putnam County Marriages*** **[Online Database],** digitized at the FamilySearch.org website. Source: Putnam County Archives, Cookeville, TN. This collection includes digital images marriage records from Putnam County. Browse the records by year. No index yet. This database has 3,620 records:
**https://familysearch.org/search/collection/1877098.**

**1933-1990.** ***Tennessee Valley Cemetery Relocation Files*** **[Online Database],** indexed at the Ancestry.com website. This collection includes grave removal records from cemeteries that were in the path of TVA projects. Details may include the original location of

the grave, name of the deceased, date and cause of death, name, and address of the nearest relative, location where the remains were reburied, condition of the remains, and date of reburial. Included are grave removals near the communities of Bear Creek, Boone, Bull Run, Cherokee, Chickamauga, Douglas, Ford Loudon, Gallatin, Nickajack, Normandy, Norris, Pickwick, South Holston, Tellico, Tims Ford, Watauga, Wats Bar, and Wheeler, Tennessee. This database has 172,537 records. See
**http://search.ancestry.com/search/db.aspx?dbid=60427.**

**1934-1953.** ***Tennessee Valley, Family Removal and Population Readjustment Case Files*** **[Online Database],** indexed at the Ancestry.com website. Source: National Archives ARC ID:656701. This collection includes case histories and surveys of those who were in the path of the TVA projects. Included is the communities near Boone, Cherokee, Chickamauga, Fort Loudon, Fort Patrick Henry, John Sevier Steam Plant (Rogersville), Norris, Pickwick, South Holston, Watauga, and Watts Bar, Tennessee. This database has 81,862 records. See
**http://search.ancestry.com/search/db.aspx?dbid=4903.**

**1940.** ***Tennessee, 1940 Federal Census: Population Schedules*** **[Digital Capture],** digitized for the National Archives, 2012, from the original records held by the Bureau of the Census in the 1940s. After microfilming, Congress allowed the Census Bureau to destroy the originals to free up space for WWII-related files. The Family History Library (FHL) has the 1940 microfilm archived at their Granite Mountain Record Vault. To access the digital images, see the online FHL catalog page:
**www.familysearch.org/search/catalog/2057790.**

***1940 Federal Census Finding Aids*** **[Online Database].** The National Archives prepared a special website online with a detailed description of the 1940 federal census. Included at the site are descriptions of location finding aids, such as Enumeration District maps, Geographic Descriptions of Census Enumeration Districts, and a list of 1940 City Directories available at the National Archives. The finding aids are all linked to other National Archives sites. The National Archives website also has a link to 1940 Search Engines using Stephen P. Morse's "One-Step" system for finding a 1940 E.D. or street address conversion. See
**www.archives.gov/research/census/1940/general-info.html#questions.**

**1958-1961.** ***Passenger and Crew Manifest of Airplanes Arriving at Memphis*** **[Online Database],** indexed at the Ancestry.com website. Source: National Archives microfilm series A3785.
This database has 1,599 records. See
**http://search.ancestry.com/search/db.aspx?dbid=9272.**

**1990-Current.** ***Tennessee Recent Newspaper Obituaries*** **[Online Database],** digitized and indexed newspaper obituaries at the GenealogyBank website, including newspapers from Athens, Chattanooga, Cleveland, Columbia, Cookeville, and 28 more Tennessee cities. See
**www.genealogybank.com/explore/obituaries/all/usa/tennessee.**

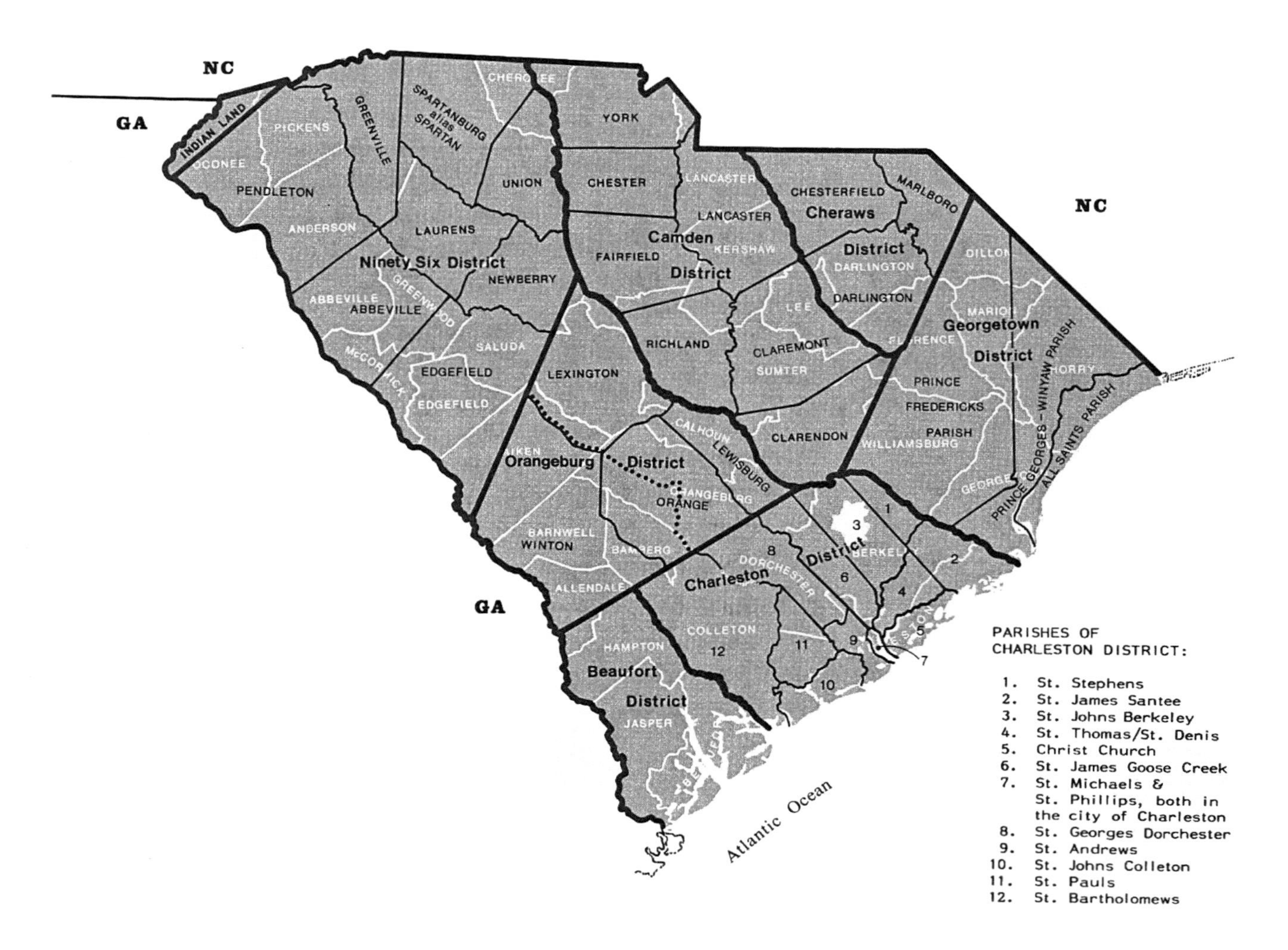


**South Carolina • 1790.** This map shows the districts, counties, and parishes used by the 1790 federal census-takers. The 46 current counties of South Carolina are shown in white. The 1790 federal census employed the seven districts then existing, shown as bold lines on the map. Within the districts were differing census subdivisions, shown as lighter black lines: 1) Camden, Cheraws, and Ninety-Six Districts used their county subdivisions. 2) Charleston and Georgetown Districts employed their parish bounds. Their counties of 1790 never functioned and are not shown on the map. 3) Beaufort District was not enumerated by subdivisions in 1790. Its counties of 1790 never functioned and are not shown on the map. 4) Orangeburg District had four active counties, but the census-takers ignored them. Orangeburg for this one census was divided into North and South, shown as a dotted line on the map. This division was the road in the forks of the Edisto River from Edgefield County to the town of Orangeburg and then down the North Edisto and Edisto rivers to the Charleston District line. **Map source:** Page 297, *Map Guide to the U.S. Federal Censuses, 1790-1920*, by William Thorndale and William Dollarhide.

# South Carolina

## Censuses & Substitute Name Lists

### Historical Timeline for South Carolina, 1497-1788

**1497-1498.** Italian sea captain Giovanni Caboto was commissioned by the English King Henry VII to explore North America. He landed in 1497 on the island of Newfoundland. On his second trip in 1498, he visited the coasts of present New Jersey, Delaware, Maryland, Virginia, North Carolina, South Carolina, and Georgia. In honor of the event, the king changed his name to John Cabot.

**1521-1526.** Spaniard Francisco Gordillo was probably the first European to land on the shore of present South Carolina. He was followed in 1526 by another Spaniard, Lucas Vazquez de Ayllon, who founded the first European settlement on land now in the United States. The settlement was named San Miguel de Gualdape, had 600 settlers, but was abandoned after three months.

**1558.** Elizabeth I became Queen of England. The early explorations of North America took place during her 45-year reign, the Elizabethan Era, or "Golden Age." When Elizabeth I was crowned, England was nearly bankrupt, but during her reign, the English Empire expanded and thrived, and English culture flourished in Literature, Theatre, Music, and Architecture.

**1584. Virginia.** Sir Walter Raleigh claimed and named Virginia for the "Virgin Queen," Elizabeth I, an area from present Chesapeake Bay to Florida, and everything below a northwestern line to the North Pole.

**1584-1590. Roanoke Colony.** In 1584, Queen Elizabeth I granted to Sir Walter Raleigh a charter for the colonization of the entire area of North America. In 1585, the first group of settlers led by Sir Richard Grenville, established a colony at the north end of Roanoke Island (present Dare County, North Carolina). When new Governor White finally returned to Roanoke Island in August 1590, there was no trace of the colonists.

**1603. England.** James I became King of England, the first monarch to rule both England and Scotland. (He was James VI of Scotland since 1566). During his reign the first permanent English colonies were established in Virginia and New England. James I was an advocate for the transportation of thousands of clan people living along the Scottish-English border to Ulster Province / Northern Ireland.

**1606.** Two joint stock companies were founded in 1606, both with royal charters issued by King James I for the purpose of establishing colonies in North America. The Virginia Company of London was given a land grant between Latitude 34° (Cape Fear) and Latitude 41° (Long Island Sound). The Virginia Company of Plymouth was founded with a similar land grant between Latitude 38° (Potomac River) and Latitude 45° (St. John River), which included a shared area with the London Company between Latitude 38° and Latitude 41°..

**1607.** April 26. **Virginia.** Three ships under the command of Capt. Christopher Newport sought shelter in Chesapeake Bay. The forced landing led to the founding of Jamestown on the James River, the first permanent English settlement, consisting of 104 men and boys. The Jamestown colony was led by Capt. John Smith and his cousin, Bartholomew Gosnold. A year later, about 100 new settlers arrived, finding only 38 survivors from the first group. In 1610, recently appointed governor of Virginia, Thomas West (Lord De La Warr) arrived at Jamestown to find only 60 settlers alive.

**1623. Carolina.** The first charter for a colony in the area of the Carolinas was granted by King James I to Sir Robert Heath. But due to the political climate in England, the charter would never be used.

**1625. England.** Charles I became King of England, Scotland, and Ireland. Soon after taking office, Charles began to note a large number of non-conformists among his subjects. Along with his Archbishop, William Laud, the King began a campaign to purge his church of the largest group of non-conformists, the so-called "Puritans," a militant Calvinist religious group attempting to purify the Church of England.

**1629-1640.** As a result of the Charles I campaign to purge non-conformists from the Church of England, large groups of people were disenfranchised. Charles I disbanded Parliament and ruled England alone for eleven years. The Puritans referred to this era as "the eleven years of tyranny." It was during these eleven years that some 21,000 Puritan immigrants established the Massachusetts Bay Colony of North America.

**1641. Virginia.** Sir William Berkeley was appointed governor by Charles I. He served from 1642 to 1652 and again from 1660 to 1677. His brother Lord John Berkeley, was the first Proprietor of the East New Jersey colony, and both brothers were Lords Proprietors of the Province of Carolina. William Berkeley transformed the Virginia colony by emulating the culture of southwest England's plantation system.

**1642. English Civil War.** When Parliament was restored in 1640, it quickly became dominated by the same Puritans who King Charles I had removed from the Church of England. Beginning in 1642, Royalist supporters were forced to fight the armies of the Puritan Parliament in the English Civil War. The English Colonies took sides: the Virginia colony favored the Royalist/Cavalier side, while the New England colonies were in support of the Parliamentarian/Puritan side. The Province of Maryland had earlier allowed all religious persuasions to settle in Maryland. During the English Civil War, Maryland granted free land as refuge to any Puritans from Virginia to settle there.

**1645-1651. England.** After his defeat and capture in 1645, Charles I refused to accept his captors' demands for a constitutional monarchy, and briefly escaped captivity in 1647. While recaptured, his teenage son, Prince Charles, was able to marshal Scottish forces for the king. However, by 1648, Oliver Cromwell had consolidated the English opposition. King Charles I was tried, convicted, and beheaded for high treason in January 1649. The Civil War continued until 1651, when Oliver Cromwell, a Puritan, became Lord Protectorate, ruling the Commonwealth of England for the next seven years.

**1650. Virginia (present North Carolina).** The first settlements near Albemarle Sound were established by pioneers from tidewater Virginia.

**1658-1660. England.** After Oliver Cromwell died in 1658, his son, Richard, was too weak politically to remain in power. In 1660, a new Parliament offered a restored English throne to the exiled Scottish King, son of Charles I, who accepted to become King Charles II.

**1663. Carolina.** Charles II granted eight noblemen a charter to *Carolina*, from Latitude 31° (present FL/GA line) to Latitude 35° (present GA/TN line). This was a repayment for their loyalty and support during the English Civil War. The eight became known as the Lords Proprietors. In 1665, the charter was extended north to the present NC/VA line to include the Albemarle Sound settlements, The name Carolina came from "Carolus," Latin for Charles.

**1669-1670. Carolina (present South Caroline).** In late 1669, three shiploads of colonists sailed from London, headed for Carolina. At Barbados, the ships were struck by a hurricane. The *Albemarle* was destroyed, and the *Port Royal* and *Carolina* were severely damaged. In March 1670, the *Carolina* arrived at Sewee Bay, and temporarily anchored at the north end of Bull's Island. In April, Charles Towne was founded as the capital of the Province of Carolina.

**1682. Carolina.** The first four counties of the Province of Carolina were created, named after Lords Proprietors Berkeley, Colleton, Craven, and Granville.

**1707.** England and Scotland merged into the **United Kingdom of Great Britain.** The English Colonies now became the British Colonies.

**1712. North and South Carolina.** The territory of the Province of Carolina since 1665 ran from about Latitude 31$^{O}$ to the present NC/VA line (36$^{O}$30'), including the area of present Georgia. In 1712, the Lords Proprietors divided Carolina into North Carolina and South Carolina (proprietary provinces) on nearly the same division line as today, but the line was not surveyed for several more years. Each province had its own colonial governor, under the authority of the eight Lords Proprietors.

**1717.** The arrival of the first Scots-Irish immigrants to the British Colonies was via Boston, New York City, Philadelphia, Alexandria, Norfolk, New Bern, and Charles Towne. The so-called Scots-Irish (or Ulster Scots) were former border clan people who had lived near the Scottish-English border for centuries. A good number of them had moved into areas of Northern Ireland in the early 1600s, and a mass migration to most of the British colonies of America began in about 1717. By 1775, the Scots-Irish would outnumber all other British groups (Puritans, Cavaliers, or Quakers), by about 3 to 1.

**1721-1733.** The **Province of South Carolina** became a Royal British Colony in 1721 (no longer a proprietary colony). The king appointed Sir Francis Nicholson as the Royal Governor. In 1733, a new royal charter for the Colony of Georgia was taken from the area of South Carolina, created from lands south of the Savannah River. Even with its remaining western claims, more than half of South Carolina's area was lost to the Georgia colony.

**1783-1786. South Carolina.** Charles Towne was renamed Charleston in 1783. In 1786, the capital was moved from Charleston to Columbia.

**1788.** Mar 23. **South Carolina** became the 8$^{th}$ state in the Union, with the state capital at Columbia.

## Online Resources at South Carolina State Websites

**SC State Archives - Online Records Index:** Databases of records from SC Archives holdings are indexed by topics, including: Will Transcripts (1782-1855); Records of Confederate Veterans (1909-1973); Plats for State Land Grants (1784-1868); Legislative Papers (1782-1866); Criminal Court Records (1769-1891); School Insurance Photographs (1935-1952); and National Register Properties. See **www.archivesindex.sc.gov.**

**South Carolina Digital Library:** This consortium website provides free access to historic materials, such as photographs, manuscripts, journals, books, oral histories, objects, etc. illustrating the history and culture of South Carolina from over 40 cultural heritage institutions across the state. Over 200,000 items have been added so far. Browse Geography (By SC Counties), Browse Institutions, Browse Media Types, and Browse Time Periods. See **http://scmemory.org.**

**University of South Carolina – Digital Collections – Browse by Topic: Genealogy:** Peruse through city directory listings, family Bible records, family papers, church records, maps, memoirs, and much more. See **http://library.sc.edu/p/Collections/Digital/Browse?tag=17.**

# Bibliography

## South Carolina Censuses & Substitutes

**SC State Censuses**. Several state censuses were taken in South Carolina, but few of the census manuscripts exist today. The surviving state census schedules are all located today at the South Carolina Department of Archives and History in Columbia. Surviving state census schedules include:

- **1829:** Fairfield and Laurens districts only.
- **1839:** Beaufort, Chesterfield, Kershaw, and Lexington Districts only
- **1869:** Entire state. All South Carolina counties filmed, Abbeville to York.
- **1875:** Name lists exist for Clarendon, Newberry, and Marlboro counties. There are partial listings for Abbeville, Beaufort, Fairfield, Lancaster, and Sumter counties.

There were no state censuses taken after 1875.

**SC Federal Censuses.** The 1790 federal census taken in South Carolina was enumerated by districts, counties within districts, parishes within districts, and a couple of extra jurisdictions invented by the census takers. (See the 1790 map on page 176 for details). By 1800, a few districts still had subordinate counties, but by 1810, all South Carolina districts functioned the same as a single county unit as in other states. In 1869, all South Carolina districts were converted into counties. The 1870 and later federal censuses were all enumerated using a county as the basic jurisdictional unit.

**Census Losses.** South Carolina's federal censuses are complete for all districts/counties except the 1800 is missing Richland District, and the entire SC 1890 was lost (like all states) in a 1921 fire in the Commerce Building in Washington, DC.

A detailed list of censuses and substitutes available follows:

♦ ♦ ♦ ♦ ♦

**1670-1930.** ***History of Charleston County, South Carolina: Narrative and Biographical*** **[Printed Book],** by Thomas Petigru Lesesne, publ. Cawston, Charleston, SC, 1931, 369 pages, FHL book 975.7915 D3L. For a digital version of this book, see the online FHL catalog page for this title. See **https://familysearch.org/search/catalog/53420.**

**1670-1980.** ***South Carolina, Wills and Probate Records*** **[Online Database],** indexed at the Ancestry.com website. Source: SC county, district, and probate courts. In most cases, the details found in probates include the names and residences of beneficiaries and their relationship to the decedent. An inventory of the estate assets may reveal personal details about the deceased's occupation and lifestyle. There may also be references to debts, deeds, and other documents related to the settling of the estate. This database has 229,958 records. See **http://search.ancestry.com/search/db.aspx?dbid=9080.**

**1670-1985.** ***Dictionary of South Carolina Biography*** **[Printed Book],** edited by Richard N. Cote and Patricia H. Williams. This is a major finding aid to thousands of bibliographies, autobiographies, and biographical sketches of South Carolinians found in hundreds of volumes of individual and collective biographies, local, state, church, and family histories and periodicals. This book is self-indexing for the subjects, and lists the name, birth, and death years, primary residences, primary occupations and full source references for more than 10,000 sketches of 17th through 20th century South Carolinians. Separate indexes to occupation and place of residence are provided. Publ. Southern Historical Press, Easley, SC, 1985, FHL 975.7

**1670-1990s.** ***South Carolina Genealogical Society Surname Index*** **[Printed Book],** publ. by the society. Includes names of members who submitted surnames of interest, publ. 1999, 371 pages, FHL book 975.7 D22s.

**1670 – 2000s.** ***South Carolina GenWeb Archives*** **[Online Database].** The SCGenWeb site offers free genealogical databases with searchable statewide name lists and for all South Carolina counties, which may include Bibles, Biographies, Cemeteries, Censuses, Court, Death, Deeds, Directories, Histories, Marriages, Military, Newspapers, Obituaries, Photos, Schools, Tax Lists, Wills, and more. See **http://usgwarchives.net/sc/scfiles.htm.**

**1670-2000s.** ***Linkpendium – South Carolina: Family History & Genealogy, Census, Birth, Marriage, Death Vita Records & More*** **[Online Databases].** Linkpendium is a genealogical portal site, with links to state, county, town, and local databases. Currently listed are selected sites for South Carolina statewide resources (573), Independent Cities, Renamed Counties, Discontinued Counties (4), Abbeville County (407), Aiken County (238), Allendale County (107), Anderson County (428), and 42 more South Carolina counties. See **www.linkpendium.com/sc-genealogy.**

**1671-1868.** ***Index to Wills of Charleston County, South Carolina*** **[Printed Book],** this book completes the series of indexes to the WPA transcripts of South Carolina wills prepared by the University of South Carolina Library in 1939 under the title, *Indexes to the County Wills of South Carolina.* This book publ. Charleston, SC, 1950, 324 pages, FHL book 975.791 S2L. To see a digital version of this book, see the online FHL catalog page. **https://familysearch.org/search/catalog/203386**.

**1671-1977.** ***South Carolina Probate Records, Bound Volumes*** **[Online Database],** digitized at the FamilySearch.org website. Source: SC State Archives. This collection includes wills, records of estates and guardianships recorded by the counties of South Carolina. Browse through the records, organized by county, then by type of record book, including any index books. No complete index yet. This database has 222,656 records. See **https://familysearch.org/search/collection/1919417.**

**1672-1679.** ***Warrants for Land in South Carolina*** **[Online Database],** indexed at the Ancestry.com website. This is a digital version of the book, same title, edited by A. S. Salley, Jr., Secretary of the Historical Commission of South Carolina, publ. 1910. This database has 222 records (pages). See
**http://search.ancestry.com/search/db.aspx?dbid=48302.**

**1675-1965.** ***South Carolina, Compiled Marriage Index*** **[Online Database],** indexed at the Ancestry.com website. Original data came from the Hunting for Bears index, notorious for transcription errors and poorly edited data. For example, the date of 1641 in the title should be 1741, but that is not the earliest marriage. Use this database with caution and compare the information with other marriage lists available. This database has 69,131 records. See
**http://search.ancestry.com/search/db.aspx?dbid=7840.**

**1680-1692.** ***Warrants for Land in South Carolina*** **[Online Database],** indexed at the Ancestry.com website. This is a digital version of the book, same title, edited by A. S. Salley, Jr., Secretary of the Historical Commission of South Carolina, publ. 1911. This database has 224 records (pages) . See
**http://search.ancestry.com/search/db.aspx?dbid=48303.**

**1680-1830.** ***Directory of Scots in the Carolinas*** **[Online Database],** indexed at the Ancestry.com website. Source: book, same title, by David Dobson, publ. Genealogical Pub. Co., 1986. Dobson explains that it was impossible to distinguish between Scots and Scots-Irish, but history tells us that there were many more lowland Scots (Scots-Irish) than highland Scots in the Old South. This database has 334 records (pages). See
**http://search.ancestry.com/search/db.aspx?dbid=48518.**

**1681-1935.** ***South Carolina Births and Christenings*** **[Online Database],** indexed at the FamilySearch.org website. Name index to birth, baptism and christening records from microfilm at the Family History Library, Salt Lake City, UT. This database has 14,805 records:
**https://familysearch.org/search/collection/1675535.**

**1685-1925.** ***St. James Santee Plantation Parish*** **(South Carolina):** History & Records, 1685-1925 [Printed Book], by Anna Baker Leland Bridges and Roy Williams. The old parish existed in today's Charleston & Berkeley counties. Church records for St. James Santee, 1758-1788 (Church of England), and previously unpublished records, 1846-1921 (assumed to be Episcopalian) are available, plus cemetery records for the church. Includes lists of French & Swiss refugees & inhabitants. Includes index. Publ. Reprint Co., Spartanburg, SC, 1997, 541 pages, FHL book 975.79 H2b.

**1688-1799.** ***South Carolina Marriages*** **[Online Database],** indexed at the Ancestry.com website. Source: Brent H. Holcomb's *South Carolina Marriages, 1688-1799.* This database has 355 records (pages). See
**http://search.ancestry.com/search/db.aspx?dbid=49056.**

**1692-1711.** ***Warrants for Land in South Carolina*** **[Online Database],** indexed at the Ancestry.com website. Source: Book, same title, by A.S. Salley, publ. 1915. This database has 263 records (pages). See
**http://search.ancestry.com/search/db.aspx?dbid=48304.**

**1695-1925.** ***Combined Alphabetical Index: Consolidated Index & Spindex*** **[Microfilm & Digital Capture],** from the original manuscript at the SC State Archives. From intro: The combined Alphabetical Index is a computer-generated microfilm finding aid to thirty early record series held either in the original or on microfilm by the South Carolina Department of Archives and History. Filmed by the archives, 1999, 19 rolls, beginning with FHL film #1690457 (Consolidated Index, A.C. Tuxberry Land & Timber Co – Berkeley County). To access the digital images, see the online FHL catalog page:
**https://familysearch.org/search/catalog/485140.**

**1700-1900s.** ***South Carolina Name Index to Genealogical Records Collected by South Carolina Daughters of the American Revolution (DAR)*** **[Microfiche],** records compiled from genealogy indexes, vital records, church records, cemeteries, military records, probate records, land and property records, taxation records, court records, and censuses. Filmed by the Genealogical Society of Utah, 1988, 102 fiche. See FHL fiche #6052835

**1709-1913.** ***South Carolina Marriages*** **[Online Database],** indexed at the FamilySearch.org website. Name index to marriage records from microfilm at the Family History Library, Salt Lake City. This database has 4,154 records. See
**https://familysearch.org/search/collection/1675541.**

***1716-1783 Residents, Colony of South Carolina* [Online Database],** indexed at the USGenWeb site for South Carolina. This webpage has a good introductory history to the colony of Carolina, discussing the eight Lords Proprietors, and identifying the various name lists taken. The lists identify Loyalists, Petitioners, Residents, District, Last name, and First name. See **http://files.usgwarchives.net/sc/colonial/sccolony.txt.**

**"1732 Tax Return, Edisto Island" [Printed Article],** in *South Carolina Magazine of Ancestral Research,* Vol. 18, No. 4 (Fall 1990).

**1732-1775. *Death Notices in the South Carolina Gazette* [Online Database],** indexed at the FamilySearch.org website. Source: A.S. Salley's *Death Notices in the South Carolina Gazette*, 1917. This database has 48 pages. See **http://search.ancestry.com/search/db.aspx?dbid=27040.**

**1732-1775. *Index of Surnames, South Carolina Gazette* [Printed Book],** by John H. Wilson and Gary S. Wilson. 2 vols., 1732-1751, vol. 1 & 1752-1775, vol. 2. Publ. ESCN Database Reports, Mt. Pleasant, SC, 1996-2002, FHL book 975.7 D225w 1732-1751 & 975.7 D225w 1752-1775.

**1732-1801. *South Carolina, Newspaper Marriage Notices* [Online Database],** indexed at the Ancestry.com website. Source: *Marriage Notices in the South Carolina Gazette,* 1902. This database has 919 records (pages). See **http://search.ancestry.com/search/db.aspx?dbid=4665.**

**1732-1844. *South Carolina, Charleston District, Estate Inventories* [Online Database],** digitized and indexed at FamilySearch.org. This collection contains inventory and appraisement books as well as inventories of estates from Charleston, South Carolina between 1732 and 1872. These records are a good resource for finding slave ancestors. Because slaves were treated as property at the time, when an estate was appraised for probate or tax purposes, slaves were listed and appraised along with other items belonging to the estate. In some cases, slaves did not have surnames and may need to be located using the name of the slave owner. In other cases, records may include the slave's American and African names. Additionally, there are records of free African Americans, which provides a glimpse into their lifestyles and possessions. This collection is part of a joint project with the South Carolina Department of Archives and History, Family Search, and the Lowcountry Africana group. This database has 398,496 records, see **www.familysearch.org/search/collection/3460989.**

**1732-1964. *South Carolina Probate Records, Files and Loose Papers* [Online Database],** digitized at the FamilySearch.org website. Source: county records at the county courthouses and SC State Archives. This collection includes wills, records of estates and guardianships recorded by the counties of South Carolina. Most of the records fall between the mid-1800s through 1930. Browse through the records, organized by county, then by type of record book, including any index books. No complete index yet. This database has 654,824 records. See **https://familysearch.org/search/collection/1911928.**

**1733-1742. *South Carolina Tax List* [Printed Book],** compiled by Tony Draine and John Skinner, publ. Congaree Publications, Columbia, SC, 1986, 103 pages, FHL book 975.7 R48d.

**1735-2001. *South Carolina Newspaper Archives* [Online Databases],** digitized and indexed newspapers at the GenealogyBank website, for Beaufort, Camden, Charleston, Columbia, Edgefield, Georgetown, and Pendleton. See **www.genealogybank.com/explore/newspapers/all/usa/south-carolina.**

**1752-1920. *South Carolina, State and City Census Records* [Digital Capture],** digitized by FamilySearch International, 2018, from images held by SC Dept. of Archives & History, Columbia. The digital file numbers and contents of each are listed in this order:
- **Contents, DGS #101621250:** State Censuses 1829-1875, 1839 South Carolina State Census Beaufort, Chesterfield, Kershaw, and Lexington.
- **Contents, DGS #101621251:** 1829 SC State Census, Fairfield District.
- **Contents, DGS #101621252:** 1875 SC State Census Newberry and Sumter Counties.
- **Contents, DGS #101621253:** 1868, City of Aiken.
- **Contents, DGS #101621254:** 1869 SC State Census, Newberry and Sumter Counties.
- **Contents, DGS #101621255:** 1869 SC State Census, Union County.
- **Contents, DGS #101621256:** 1869 SC State Census, Horry-Marlboro Counties.
- **Contents, DGS #101621257:** 1869 Census Union County.

**- Contents, DGS #101621258:** 1875 SC State Census, Abbeville-Marlboro Counties.
**- Contents, DGS #101621259:** 1920 City of Georgetown Census.
**- Contents, DGS #101621247:** 1869 SC State Census, Abbeville-Beaufort counties.
**- Contents, DGS #101621248:** 1869 SC State Census, Charleston-Clarendon counties.
**- Contents, DGS #101621249:** 1869 SC State Census, Colleton-Greenville counties.
To access the digital images, see the online FHL catalog page:
**www.familysearch.org/search/catalog/2841555.**

**1762-1979.** ***Heritage Book Archives, South Carolina*** **[CD-ROM],** also known as *The Annals of Newberry in Two Parts: A Sketch of the History of South Carolina to the Close of the Proprietary Government by the Revolution of 1719,* by Brent H. Holcomb, Publ. Heritage Books, Bowie, MD, 1999, 2 CDs ISBN 0788411640 v.1 & 0788414178 v. 2. Contents:

- *Early records of Fishing Creek Presbyterian Church, Chester County, South Carolina, 1799-1859: with appendices of the visitation list of Rev. John Simpson, 1774-1776, and the cemetery roster, 1762-1979,* by Brent H. Holcomb.
- *History of Spartanburg County : embracing an account of many important events and biographical sketches of statesmen, divines and other public men and the names of many others worthy of record in the history of their county,* by J.B.O. Landrum.
- *Kershaw County, South Carolina minutes of the county court, 1791-1799,* by Brent H. Holcomb.
- *Marriage and death notices from the Charleston Observer, 1827-1845,* by Brent H. Holcomb.
- *The People's journal : Pickens, South Carolina, 1894-1903, historical and genealogical abstracts,* by Peggy Burton Rich.
- *The Pickens sentinel, favorite newspaper of Pickens County: Pickens Court House, South Carolina 1872-1893, historical and genealogical abstracts,* by Peggy Burton Rich.
- *Winton (Barnwell) County, South Carolina minutes of county court and will book 1, 1785-1791,* by Brent H. Holcomb.

**1763-1773.** ***A Compilation of the Original Lists of Protestant Immigrants to South Carolina*** **[Online Database],** indexed at the Ancestry.com website. Source: Janie Revill's *A Compilation of the Original Lists of Protestant Immigrants to South Carolina, 1763-1773*, publ. Genealogical Publishing Co, 1968-1981. This database has 163 records (pages). See **http://search.ancestry.com/search/db.aspx?dbid=48270.**

**1764-1772.** ***North Carolina Land Grants in South Carolina*** **[Online Database],** indexed at the Ancestry.com website. Source: Brent H. Holcomb's *North Carolina Land Grants in South Carolina,* publ. 1980. This database has 190 records (pages). See **http://search.ancestry.com/search/db.aspx?dbid=48259.**

**1766-1901.** ***South Carolina, Delayed Birth Records, 1766-1900 and City of Charleston, South Carolina, Birth Records, 1877-1901*** **[Online Database],** indexed at the Ancestry.com website. Source: SC State Archives. This database contains approximately 25,000 birth records (returns) for the city of Charleston, South Carolina from the years 1877-1901. Charleston began keeping birth records in 1877. It also contains approximately 55,000 delayed birth records (applications for birth certificates) from throughout the state, covering the years 1766-1900. Information available in this database includes: Child's name, birth date, Birthplace, and Parents' names. Additional information, such as the child's gender and race, birth town, parents' birthplaces and father's occupation, may also be listed and can be found by viewing the image of the birth record. This database has 261,465 records. See **http://search.ancestry.com/search/db.aspx?dbid=1239.**

**1769-1789.** ***Tryon County, North Carolina, Index to Land Surveys*** **[Printed Book],** by Miles S. Philbeck. From the intro: "Although usually considered to have been formed in 1769 and to have been abolished in 1779 in favor of Rutherford and Lincoln Counties, Tryon County land grants begin in 1768 and continued into 1784 with one being granted as late as 1789… Old Tryon County encompassed present day Burke, Cleveland, Gaston, Henderson, Lincoln, McDowell, and Rutherford counties in North Carolina and Greenville, Spartanburg, Cherokee, York, Laurens, Union and Chester counties in South Carolina." Publ. M.S. Philbeck, 1987, Chapel Hill, NC, 1987, 82 pages, FHL book 975.682 R22p.

**1770-1820.** ***Patent Land Survey (Index of Land Acquisitions, 1770-1820): Located in Greenville County, Laurens County, Newberry County, and Parts of the Old Ninety-Six District*** **[Printed Book],** by Alma Spires Smith and Jean Smith Owens, publ. A Press, Greenville, SC, 1978, 178 pages, FHL book 975.7 R2as.

***1770-1858 Indexes to the County Wills of South Carolina*** **[Online Database],** indexed at the Ancestry.com website. This is a digital version of the book, same title, compiled by Martha Lou Houston, publ. Genealogical Publishing Co., 1975. The title page has this note: "This volume contains a separate index compiled from the W.P.A. copies of each of the County Will Books, except those of Charleston County Will Books, in the South Carolina Collection of the University of South Carolina Library." Browse by county and date range. This database has 249 records (pages). See
**http://search.ancestry.com/search/db.aspx?dbid=48254.**

**1772. *Scotch-Irish Migration to South Carolina* [Online Database],** indexed at the Ancestry.com website. Source: *Scotch-Irish Migration to South Carolina, 1772: Rev. William Martin And His Five Shiploads of Settlers*, by Jean Stephenson, 1971. This database has 138 records (pages). See
**http://search.ancestry.com/search/db.aspx?dbid=48628.**

**1774-1872. *South Carolina, Charleston District, Bill of Sales of Negro Slaves* [Online Database],** digitized and indexed at FamilySearch.org. This collection contains bills of sales of Negro slaves from 1774-1872. Because slaves were considered property, a bill of sale was filled out when they were sold, making this collection an excellent resource for finding slave ancestors. who were considered property at that time. In some cases, slaves did not have surnames and may need to be located using the name of the slave owner. In other cases, records may include the slave's American and African names. Additionally, there are records of free African Americans, which provides a glimpse into their lifestyles and possessions. This collection is part of a joint project with the South Carolina Department of Archives and History, Family Search, and the Lowcountry Africana group. This database has 245,755 records, see
**www.familysearch.org/search/collection/3463015.**

**1776-1783. *Accounts Audited of Claims Growing out of the Revolution in South Carolina: Alphabetical Name Index* [Printed Book & Digital Version],** by Helen Craig Carson, publ. SC State Archives, microcopy No. 8, digitized by the Genealogical Society of Utah, 2015. To view the digital version, see the online FHL catalog page for this title. See
**https://familysearch.org/search/catalog/2516593.**

**1776-1783. *Roster of South Carolina Patriots in the American Revolution* [Online Database],** indexed at the Ancestry.com website. This database identifies the more than 20,000 rank and file South Carolina soldiers who made up the battle lines in an untold number of skirmishes with the British and the Tories. The information was taken from pension records, bounty land warrants, annuitants' claims, audited accounts, muster rolls, pay lists, and published sources. See
**http://search.ancestry.com/search/db.aspx?dbid=49323.**

**1778-1779. *The Jury Lists of South Carolina* [Online Database],** indexed at the Ancestry.com website. Source: *The Jury Lists of South Carolina, 1778-1779,* compiled by Geelee Corley Hendrix and Morn McKoy Lindsay, publ. Genealogical Pub. Co., 1980. This database has 139 records (pages). See
**http://search.ancestry.com/search/db.aspx?dbid=48258.**

***1779 Census, Ninety-Six District, South Carolina*** **[Online Database],** indexed at the USGenWeb site for South Carolina. Old 96 District of SC was created in 1769, abolished in 1798. At one time, the area included the modern counties of Abbeville, Edgefield, Laurens, Newberry, Spartanburg, and Union counties, South Carolina. See
**http://files.usgwarchives.net/sc/districts/census/1779_96d.txt.**

***1781 South Carolina Residents (County Unknown)*** **[Online Database],** indexed at the USGenWeb site for South Carolina. See
**http://files.usgwarchives.net/sc/districts/census/1781_unk.txt.**

***1782-1934 City Directories, Charleston, South Carolina*** **[Microfiche],** from various publishers. FHL has directories for 1782, 1785, 1794, 1806, 1807, 1809, 1824, 1836, 1856, and 1860. Beginning with 1866, the directories are complete for every year published (every two years, most every year), 1866/1867 through 1934. Filmed by Research Publications, Woodbridge, CT, 1980-1984, beginning with FHL fiche #6052954 (1782 South Carolina and Georgia Almanac). For a complete list of fiche numbers and contents of each, see the online FHL catalog page for this title. See
**https://familysearch.org/search/catalog/533591.**

**"1783 Tax List, St. Bartholomew Parish, Charleston District, South Carolina" [Printed Article],** in *South Carolina Magazine of Ancestral Research,* Vol. 2, No. 4 (Fall 1974); and Vol. 3, No. 3 (Summer 1975).

**1783-1850.** See ***South Carolina Naturalizations* [Online Database],** indexed at the Ancestry.com website. Source: Brent H. Holcomb's *South Carolina Naturalizations 1783-1850.* This database has 261 records (pages). See
**http://search.ancestry.com/search/db.aspx?dbid=48272.**

**1785-1865. *Richland District, South Carolina Land Records* [Printed Book],** by Tony Draine and John Skinner, publ. Congaree Publications, Columbia, SC, 1986, 124 pages, FHL book 975.771 R28d.

**1785-1911. *Spartanburg County Marriages Implied in Spartanburg County, South Carolina Probate Records* [Printed Book],** by Barbara R. Langdon. From intro: "This collection of 4,007 marriage references and relationships is the result of the searching of Spartanburg County, SC original Loose Probate Papers, Boxes 1 through 75 and Oversize Flat Folios 1 through 13." Names are in alphabetical order by men, then women. Includes sub-index of other individuals. Publ. 1992, 317 pages, FHL book 975.729 V2L.

**"1786 Tax Returns, St. Paul's Parish, Charleston District, South Carolina" [Printed Article],** in *South Carolina Magazine of Ancestral Research,* Vol. 9, No. 2 (Spring 1981).

**"1786 Tax Returns, St. Bartholomew's Parish, Charleston District, South Carolina" [Printed Article],** in *South Carolina Magazine of Ancestral Research,* Vol. 9, No. 2 (Spring 1981); through Vol. 10, No. 3 (Summer 1982).

**1786-1913.** See ***Deeds, 1786-1865; Index to Deeds, 1786-1913, Greenville County, South Carolina* [Microfilm & Digital Capture],** filmed by the Genealogical Society of Utah, 1950, 16 rolls, beginning with FHL film #24009 (Index to Grantees, A-D 1786-1913). To access the digital images, see the online FHL catalog page:
**www.familysearch.org/search/catalog/472237.**
- See also ***Greenville County, South Carolina Deed Books Index 1787-1802* [Printed Book & Digital Version],** by Robertalee Lent, publ. Bridgeport, WA, 1966, 104 pages, FHL book US SC Greenville R 2L. To access a digital version of this book, see the online FHL catalog page:
**https://familysearch.org/search/catalog/2044452**.
- See also ***Abstracts of Deeds, Greenville County, S.C.* [Printed Book],** by A. B. Pruitt, 6 vols, as follows: Vol. 1: Books A, B & C, 1787-1795; Vol. 2: Books D & E, 1795-1798; Vol. 3: Books F & G, 1800-1807; and Vol. 4: Books H & I, 1807-1817; Vol. 5: Books K thru M, 1817-1823; and Vol. 6: Books N, O & P, 1823-1828, Books Q & R, 1828-1835, Books S & T, 1835-1842, Books U & V, 1842-1850, and Books Y & Z, 1856-1865. Publ. by the author, 1997-2012.
- See also ***Index to Greenville County, SC Deed Books A-Z* [Printed Book],** by A. B. Pruitt. Contents: Part 1: People, A-McKelyea; and Part 2: People, McKenny-Yount and places. Publ. by the author, 2014, 2 vols., FHL book 975.727 R22p pt. 1 & pt. 2.

**"1787 Tax List, Barnwell District, South Carolina" [Printed Article],** in *Georgia Genealogical Magazine,* Vol. 49 (Summer 1973).

**"1787 Winton County, Barnwell District" [Printed Article],** in *Carolina Genealogist,* Vol. 11 (Summer 1972).

**1787-1853.** See ***Greenville County, South Carolina, Will Abstracts* [Printed Book],** by Brent H. Holcomb, publ. SCMAR, 2012, 222 pages, FHL book 975.727 P2h.

**1790-1840. *South Carolina, 1790 thru 1840 Federal Census: Population Schedules* [Microfilm & Digital Capture],** filmed by the National Archives, 1938-1969, 21 rolls, beginning with FHL film #568151 (1790, entire state). To access the digital images, see the online FHL catalog page:
**www.familysearch.org/search/catalog/745505.**

**1790-1890. *South Carolina, Compiled Census and Census Substitutes Index, 1790-1890* [Online Database],** indexed at the Ancestry.com website. Originally edited by Ronald Jackson, Accelerated Indexing Systems, Salt Lake City. This collection contains the following indexes: 1790 Federal Census Index; 1800 Federal Census Index; 1810 Federal Census Index; 1820 Federal Census Index; 1830 Federal Census Index; 1840 Federal Census Index; 1840 Pensioners List; 1850 Federal Census Index; 1850 Slave Schedule; 1860 Federal Census Index; 1860 Slave Schedule; 1890 Veterans Schedule; Colonial Probate Index; Early Census Index. This database has 57,762 records. See
**http://search.ancestry.com/search/db.aspx?dbid=3572.**

**1794.** See **"Early Residents of South Carolina – Among the Better Know Citizens of Charleston, South Carolina, who were residents of that city in January 1794" [Printed Article],** in *Genealogy,* Vol. 1, No. 19 (May 1912). To view a digital version of this article, see the online FHL catalog page for this title. See **https://familysearch.org/search/catalog/2212489.**

**1796-1905.** ***Dowers, Citizenship Petitions, Etc., Charleston County, South Carolina*** **[Microfilm & Digital Capture],** from the originals at the Charleston County Courthouse, Charleston, SC. Filmed by the Genealogical Society of Utah, 1953, 1 roll, FHL film #23657. To access the digital images, see the online FHL catalog page:
**www.familysearch.org/search/catalog/387457.**

**1798-1928.** ***South Carolina, Darlington County Records*** **[Online Database],** digitized at the FamilySearch.org website. Includes digital images of probate, naturalization, coroner and other court records captured at the Darlington County Historical Commission in Darlington, South Carolina. Browse the images, organized by Court of Common Pleas, Probate Records, and Vital Records. Some index books included in the image sets. This database has 331,447 records. See
**https://familysearch.org/search/collection/2144005.**

**1799-1930.** ***A History of Richland County*** **[Printed Book],** by Edwin L. Green, publ. 1932, reprint 1974, FHL book 975.771 H2gel. See also ***Index to A History of Richland County (South Carolina)*** **[Printed Book],** by James McKain, FHL book 975.771 H22m.

**1800-1820. South Carolina Marriages [Online Database],** indexed at the Ancestry.com website. Source: Brent H. Holcomb's *South Carolina Marriages, 1800-1820.* This database has 178 records (pages). See
**http://search.ancestry.com/search/db.aspx?dbid=49331.**

**1820-1829.** ***Passenger Arrivals at the Port of Charleston*** **[Online Database],** indexed at the Ancestry.com website. Source: *Passenger Arrivals at the Port of Charleston, 1820-1829,* transcribed by Brent H. Holcomb, publ. 1994. This database has 184 records (pages). See
**http://search.ancestry.com/search/db.aspx?dbid=48269.**

**1821-1965.** ***South Carolina, Death Records*** **[Online Database],** indexed at the Ancestry.com website. Source: SC State Archives. This database contains the following South Carolina death records: Statewide death certificates, 1915-1960; Charleston City death records, 1821-1914; Spartanburg City death records, 1895-1897 and 1903-1914; and Union City death records, 1900 and 1913-1914. Death records can consist of certificates, registers, returns of interment, returns of death, transportation for burial forms, and physician's certificates, among other documents. These records may provide information such as: Name of deceased, Death date, Death place, Age at time of death, Gender, Race or color, and Death certificate number. This database has 3,535,808 records. See
**http://search.ancestry.com/search/db.aspx?dbid=8741.**

***1824 Individual Tax Returns (South Carolina)*** **[Microfilm & Digital Capture],** from the originals at the SC State Archives. Lists statewide taxpayers with amounts paid on taxable property. Filmed by the Genealogical Society of Utah, 2005, 4 rolls, beginning with FHL film #1784639 (Tax returns no. 1-10161). To access the digital images, see the online FHL catalog page: **https://familysearch.org/search/catalog/1326567.**

**1826-1854.** ***Some South Carolina Marriages and Obituaries and Miscellaneous Information, Abstracted From Early Newspapers: The Greenville Republican, the Greenville Mountaineer, the Laurensville Herald*** **[Printed Book],** compiled by Robert F. Simpson and Mrs. Charles R. Barham,. The *Greenville Republican* (the name was changed to the *Greenville Mountaineer* in 1829) was abstracted for the years 1826 to Dec. 1849. The *Laurensville Herald* was abstracted for the years 1845-1846 and 1853- 1854. Publ. 1978, 209 pages, FHL book 975.7 B338s.

**"1829 Census of Laurens District" [Printed Article],** in *South Carolina Magazine of Ancestral Research,* Vol. 4, No. 2 (Spring 1976); and Vol. 4, No. 3 (Summer 1976).

***1835 Federal Pension Report – South Carolina* [Online Database],** indexed at the USGenWeb archives site for South Carolina. See
**http://files.usgwarchives.net/sc/military/pensions/1835report.txt.**

**1835-1865.** ***South Carolina Baptist Marriages and Deaths* [Online Database],** indexed at the Ancestry.com website. Source: Brent H. Holcomb's *Marriages and Death Notices from Baptist Newspapers of South Carolina.* This database was incorporated into an updated version. See
**http://search.ancestry.com/search/db.aspx?dbid=3322.**

**1837-2008.** ***South Carolina, Wofford College Library Obituary Index* [Online Database],** indexed at the Ancestry.com website. To learn more about the records, this 3rd party database can be accessed via the Ancestry site. This database has 58,118 records. See
**http://search.ancestry.com/search/db.aspx?dbid=9154.**

***1839 South Carolina State Census* [Microfilm],** from the originals at the SC State Archives. Contains the census (white population only) for Beaufort, Chesterfield, Kershaw, and Lexington Districts. Filmed by the SC Archives, 2002, 1 roll, FHL film #2453283.

**"1839 South Carolina State Census, Lexington District" [Printed Article]**, in *South Carolina Magazine of Ancestral Research*, Vol. 25, No. 3 (Summer 1997).

**"1839 South Carolina State Census, Chesterfield District" [Printed Article]**, in *Darlington Flag*, "A-E," in Vol. 7, No. 2 (Spring 1995); "G-M" in Vol. 7, No. 3 (Summer 1995); and "M-S" in Vol. 7, No. 4 (Fall 1995).

**1843-1863.** ***Reformed Presbyterian Marriages and Deaths* [Online Database],** indexed at the Ancestry.com website. Source: Lowry Ware's *Reformed Presbyterian Death and Marriage Notices.* This database has 1,899 records (pages). An extract from the discontinued Ancestry database is at
**http://images.rootseekers.org/kaufman-county-families/I/Irwin_140726.pdf.**

**1846-1848.** ***An Annotated Roster of the Palmetto Regiment of South Carolina in the Mexican War* [Printed Book],** compiled by Jack Allen Meyer, publ. Greenbrier Press, 1994, 92 pages, FHL book 975.7 M2mj.

- See also, ***South Carolina in the Mexican War: A Regiment of Volunteers, 1846-1917* [Printed Book]**, by Jack Allen Meyer, includes index, publ. SC State Archives 1996, 310 pages, FHL book 975.7 M2mje. Also on microfilm, FHL film #1598463.

**1850.** ***South Carolina, 1850 Federal Census: Population Schedules* [Microfilm & Digital Capture],** filmed by the National Archives,1964, 21 rolls, beginning with FHL film #22528 (Abbeville and Anderson Cos). To access the digital images, see the online FHL catalog page:
**www.familysearch.org/search/catalog/744498.**

**1850-1880.** ***Agriculture, Industry, Social Statistics and Mortality Schedules for South Carolina, 1850-1880* [Microfilm & Digital Capture],** filmed by the SC Dept. of Archives & History, c1975, 22 rolls, beginning with FHL film #1294270.To access the digital images (Mortality only), see the online FHL catalog page:
**www.familysearch.org/search/catalog/144150.**

**1860.** ***South Carolina, 1860 Federal Census: Population Schedules* [Microfilm & Digital Capture],** filmed by the National Archives, 1950, 1967, 31 rolls, beginning with FHL film #805212 (Abbeville and Anderson districts). To access the digital images, see the online FHL catalog page:
**www.familysearch.org/search/catalog/706378.**

**1861-1865.** ***South Carolina Civil War Service Records of Confederate Soldiers* [Online Database],** indexed at the FamilySearch.org website. Source: National Archives microfilm series M267. The jacket-envelope typically contains card abstracts of entries relating to the soldier as found in original muster rolls, returns, rosters, payrolls, appointment books, hospital registers, Union prison registers and rolls, parole rolls, inspection reports; and the originals of any papers relating solely to the particular soldier. This database has 1,195,302 records. See
**https://familysearch.org/search/collection/1849624.**

**1864-1866.** ***Internal Revenue Assessment Lists for South Carolina* [Microfilm & Digital Capture],** from the originals at the National Archives, Washington, DC. Includes index that references counties to districts and indicates whether the county is represented on

reel 1, reel 2, or, both reels. This index is found at the beginning of each reel of film. Film by the National Archives, series M789, 2 rolls, FHL film 1578451 (Districts 1-2, 1865-1866); and FHL film #1578452 (District 2-3, 1864-1866). To access the digital images, see the online FHL catalog page:
**www.familysearch.org/search/catalog/577887.**

**"1865 Darlington Tax Returns" [Printed Article],** in *Darlington Flag,* Vol. 7, No. 2 (Spring 1995); and Vol. 7, No. 3 (Summer 1995

**1865-1872.** ***South Carolina, Freedmen's Bureau Field Office Records*** **[Online Database],** digitized at the FamilySearch.org website. Source: National Archives microfilm series M1910. These records include letters and endorsements sent and received, account books, applications for rations, applications for relief, court records, labor contracts, registers of bounty claimants, registers of complaints, registers of contracts, registers of disbursements, registers of freedmen issued rations, registers of patients, reports, rosters of officers and employees, and circulars issued, records relating to claims, court trials, property restoration, and homesteads. Browse the images, organized by field office location, then record types. No index yet. This database has 118,737 records. See
**https://familysearch.org/search/collection/2127881.**

**1866-1887.** ***South Carolina, Baptist Deaths and Marriages*** **[Online Database],** indexed at the Ancestry.com website. Source: Brent H. Holcomb's *Marriages and Death Notices from Baptist Newspapers of South Carolina.* This database has 3,288 records. See
**http://search.ancestry.com/search/db.aspx?dbid=3322.**

**1866-1888.** ***Reformed Presbyterian Marriages and Deaths*** **[Online Database],** indexed at the Ancestry.com website. Source: Lowry Ware's *Reformed Presbyterian Death and Marriage Notices.* This database has 2,197 records (pages). An extract from the discontinued Ancestry database is at
**http://images.rootseekers.org/kaufman-county-families/G/Gentry_140726.pdf.**

**1868-1820.** ***Supplement to South Carolina Marriages*** **[Online Database],** indexed at the Ancestry.com website. Source: Brent H. Holcomb's Supplement to South Carolina Marriages, 1688-1820. This database has over 1,000 entries. See
**http://search.ancestry.com/search/db.aspx?dbid=49370.**

**1868-1991.** ***South Carolina, Naturalization Records*** **[Online Database],** indexed at the Ancestry.com website. Source: National Archives, *Records of the District Courts of the United States.* Records include petitions, declarations, and certificates. This database has 79,588 records. See
**http://search.ancestry.com/search/db.aspx?dbid=2504.**

**1869.** ***South Carolina State Population Census Schedules*** **[Microfilm & Digital Capture],** from the originals at the SC State Archives. The 1869 state census was the only year taken that has surviving manuscripts for all SC counties. Filmed by the SC Archives, 1994, 6 rolls, as follows:

- Abbeville - Beaufort Co., FHL film #2453275.
- Charleston – Clarendon Co., FHL film #2453276
- Colleton – Greenville Co., FHL film #453277.
- Horry – Marlboro Co., FHL film #2453278.
- Newberry – Sumter Co., FHL film #2453279.
- Union – York Co., FHL film #2453280.

To access the digital images, see the online FHL catalog page:
**www.familysearch.org/search/catalog/2047647.**

**"1869 South Carolina State Census, Lexington County" [Printed Article],** in *Dutch Fork Digest,* Vol. 14, No. 3 through Vol. 17, No. 4.

**"1869 South Carolina State Census, Lexington & Newberry Districts" [Printed Article],** in *Dutch Fork Digest,* Vol. 14, No. 2 (Apr 1999); through Vol. 16, No. 1 (Jan 2001).

**"1869 South Carolina State Census, Blacks in York County" [Printed Article],** in *Family Records Today,* Vol. 6, No. 1 (Jan 1985).

**1870.** ***South Carolina, 1870 Federal Census: Population Schedules*** **[Microfilm & Digital Capture],** filmed by the National Archives, 1962, 1968, 41 rolls, beginning with FHL film #552980 (Abbeville Co). To access the digital images, see the online FHL catalog page:
**www.familysearch.org/search/catalog/698919.**

**"1875 South Carolina State Census, Agricultural, York County" [Printed Article],** in *Broad River Notebook*, (Sep 1997).

**1880.** ***South Carolina, 1880 Federal Census: Soundex and Population Schedules*** **[Microfilm & Digital Capture],** filmed by the National Archives, c1970, 83 rolls, beginning with FHL roll #1255217 (Abbeville

Co). To access the digital images (Population Schedules), see the online FHL catalog page:
**www.familysearch.org/search/catalog/676515.**

**1894-1944.** ***South Carolina, Clemson University Student Military Service Records*** **[Online Database],** indexed at the Ancestry.com website. From 1893 until 1955, Clemson was an all-male military institution that taught agricultural and mechanical disciplines. These records were kept of the students' service in the military either after graduating or in the middle of their time at Clemson. The majority of the records are from World War I, but there are some training program records from World War II. Most index lists have at least a name and class year for either cadet enrollment, officer training, or registration lists. Some also contain regiment, rank, or home address. This database has 8,413 records. See
**http://search.ancestry.com/search/db.aspx?dbid=1951.**

***1896 Pensioners on the List, South Carolina*** **[Online Database],** indexed at the Military /GenealogyTrails website. See
**www.genealogytrails.com/scar/1896_pensioners.htm.**

**1900.** ***South Carolina, 1900 Federal Census: Soundex and Population Schedules*** **[Microfilm & Digital Capture],** filmed by the National Archives, 156 rolls, beginning with FHL film #1241514 (Abbeville Co). To access the digital images (Population Schedules), see the online FHL catalog page:
**www.familysearch.org/search/catalog/642368.**

**1906-1962.** ***South Carolina, Passenger Lists*** **[Online Database],** indexed at the Ancestry.com website. Source: National Archives microfilm, *South Carolina, Passenger Lists.* This database contains passenger and crew lists from vessels and aircraft arriving in Florida and South Carolina. Most of the planes departed from the British West Indies, Cuba, and Puerto Rico and arrived at Key West Naval Air Station, Florida, or at Charleston, South Carolina. The records typically include the crew member's or passenger's name, age, gender, and citizenship. This database has 140,501 records. See
**http://search.ancestry.com/search/db.aspx?dbid=2996.**

**1907-2000.** ***South Carolina, County Marriage Records*** **[Online Database],** digitized and indexed at Ancestry.com. Source: SC Dept of Archives & History, Columbia, SC. This database contains selected county marriage licenses, certificates, and registers for South Carolina from the years 1907-2000. Information available in this database includes: Marriage date, Groom's name, Groom's birthdate and birthplace, Groom's race, Bride's name, Bride's birthdate and birthplace, and Bride's race. This database has 568,806 records, see
**www.ancestry.com/search/collections/61450.**

**1909-1958.** ***South Carolina, Confederate Home Records*** **[Online Database],** digitized and indexed at the FamilySearch.org website. Source: SC State Archives. Includes images of application folders of Confederate veterans who were inmates of the SC Confederate Home in Columbia. This database has 1,295 records. See
**https://familysearch.org/search/collection/2126716.**

**1910.** ***South Carolina, 1910 Federal Census: Soundex and Population Schedules*** **[Microfilm & Digital Capture],** filmed by the National Archives, 122 rolls, beginning with FHL film #1375459 (Abbeville & Calhoun Co). To access the digital images (Population Schedules), see the online FHL catalog page:
**www.familysearch.org/search/catalog/646852.**

**1911-1951.** ***South Carolina, Chesterfield County, Original Marriage Licenses*** **[Online Database],** indexed at FamilySearch.org. Source: SC Dept of Archives & History, Columbia, SC. This database has 47,526 records, see
**www.familysearch.org/search/collection/2790464.**

**1911-1951.** ***South Carolina, Colleton County Marriage Licenses*** **[Online Database],** digitized and indexed at FamilySearch.org. This collection contains marriage licenses from the county of Colleton in South Carolina, 1911-1951. Colleton County is located between Beaufort and Charleston. Included in the collection is a jacket envelope, affidavit to obtain a marriage license, marriage certificate, and marriage license for each couple. Licenses are arranged by license number in loose chronological order.
This database has 26,920 records, see
**www.familysearch.org/search/collection/3161369.**

**1911-1952.** ***Richland County, South Carolina Registers, 1911-1952, Marriage Licenses, 1911-1922*** **[Microfilm & Digital Capture],** from the originals at the SC Dept of Archives, Columbia, SC. Filmed by the Genealogical Society of Utah, 2004, 19 rolls, beginning with FHL film #2224259 (Marriage registers, brides, alpha. order, 1911-1929). To access the digital images (Licenses only), see the online FHL catalog page: **https://familysearch.org/search/catalog/1238187**.

**1915-1944.** ***Death Certificate Indexes*** **[Microfiche & Online Database],** from the original records of the State Board of Health, now at the SC State Archives, Columbia. Index cards include name, vol. no., certificate no., county, date of death, and age. 53 microfiche, in alphabetical order, are divided chronologically: 1915-1924, 1925-1934, and 1935-1944, beginning with FHL fiche #6334927 (Aanes, Bennett to Murray, Potter, 1915-1924). To access the online database, see the online FHL catalog page: **https://familysearch.org/search/catalog/719584.**

**1915-1965.** ***South Carolina Deaths*** **[Online Database],** digitized and indexed at the FamilySearch.org website. Source: SC Dept of Health & SC State Archives. Name index and images of South Carolina death records. This database has 1,025,342 records. See **https://familysearch.org/search/collection/1417492.**

**1919-1948.** ***South Carolina, Charleston U.S. Citizens Passenger Lists*** **[Online Database],** digitized at the FamilySearch.org website. Source: National Archives microfilm series A3647. This collection contains passenger lists of U.S. citizens arriving at Charleston, South Carolina, November 1919-December 1948. The records may contain the ports and dates of departure and arrival, name, age, gender, marital status, date and place of birth, date and court of naturalization (if naturalized), and residence. Browse the images. No index yet. This database has 775 records. See **https://familysearch.org/search/collection/2443352.**

**1920.** ***South Carolina, 1920 Federal Census: Soundex and Population Schedules*** **[Microfilm & Digital Capture],** filmed by the National Archives, 144 rolls, beginning with FHL film #1821682 (Abbeville Co). To access the digital images (Population Schedules), see the online FHL catalog page: **www.familysearch.org/search/catalog/555231.**

**1921.** ***Who's Who in South Carolina: A Dictionary of Contemporaries Containing Biographical Notices of Eminent Men of South Carolina*** **[Printed Book],** edited by Geddings Hardy Crawford, publ. Columbia, SC, McCaw, 1921, 220 pages, FHL book D36c. 975.7 D3w. Also on microfilm, FHL film #873788. See also ***Index to Who's Who in South Carolina, Edited by Geddings Hardy Crawford [Printed Book],*** indexed and typed by LDS volunteers, 1979, FHL book 975.7 D3w index.

**1923-1939. South Carolina, Georgetown, Passenger Lists [Online Database],** indexed at the FamilySearch.org website. Source: National Archives microfilm series M1842. This collection contains passenger lists of vessels arriving at Georgetown, South Carolina (1923-1939), and at several small Florida ports (1904-1942). The records may include full name, age, gender, marital status, citizenship, last permanent residence, birthplace, and final destination. This database has 943 records. See **https://familysearch.org/search/collection/2297290.**

**1930.** ***South Carolina, 1930 Federal Census: Soundex and Population Schedules*** **[Microfilm & Digital Capture],** filmed by the National Archives, 142 rolls, beginning with FHL film #2341918 (Abbeville Co). To access the digital images (Population Schedules), see the online FHL catalog page: **www.familysearch.org/search/catalog/1037512.**

**1940.** ***South Carolina, 1940 Federal Census: Population Schedules*** **[Digital Capture],** digitized for the National Archives, 2012, from the original records held by the Bureau of the Census in the 1940s. After microfilming, Congress allowed the Census Bureau to destroy the originals to free up space for WWII-related files. The Family History Library (FHL) has the 1940 microfilm archived at their Granite Mountain Record Vault. They are not available for viewing but the entire digital collection is available online at several sites. To access the digital images, see the online FHL catalog page: **www.familysearch.org/search/catalog/2057788.**

***1940 Federal Census Finding Aids*** **[Online Database].** The National Archives prepared a special website online with a detailed description of the 1940 federal census. Included at the site are descriptions of location finding aids, such as Enumeration District maps, Geographic Descriptions of Census Enumeration Districts, and a list of 1940 City Directories available at the National Archives. The finding aids are all linked to other National Archives sites. The National Archives website also has a link to 1940 Search Engines using

Stephen P. Morse's "One-Step" system for finding a 1940 E.D. or street address conversion. See **www.archives.gov/research/census/1940/general-info.html#questions.**

**1944-1945.** ***Florida and South Carolina, Airplane Arrival Manifests*** **[Online Database],** digitized at the FamilySearch.org website. Source: National Archives microfilm series A4234. This collection contains Arrival Manifests of Airplanes Arriving at Boca Chica, Fort Lauderdale, Jacksonville, Key West, Miami, Orlando, Pensacola, and Tampa, Florida, and at Charleston, South Carolina. The records may include full name, age, gender, marital status, citizenship, last permanent residence, birthplace, and final destination. Browse the images. No index yet. This database has 127 records (pages). See **https://familysearch.org/search/collection/2443942.**

**1950-1952.** ***South Carolina Death Index*** **[Online Database],** indexed at the Ancestry.com website. Source: SC Health Statistics. Includes the deceased's full name, sex, race, age, date of death, county of death, and death certificate number. This database has 55,423 records. See **http://search.ancestry.com/search/db.aspx?dbid=7591.**

**1987-Current.** ***South Carolina Recent Newspaper Obituaries*** **[Online Database],** digitized and indexed newspaper obituaries at the GenealogyBank website, including newspapers from Aiken, Anderson, Barnwell, Beaufort, Belton, Bluffton, Charleston, Cheraw, Chester, Clemson, Columbia, Conway, County, Easley, Edgefield, Florence, Fort Mill, Gaffney, Georgetown, Goose Creek, Greenwood, Greer, Hampton, Hardeeville, Hartsville, Hemingway, Hilton Head, Kingstree, Lake City, Lake Wylie, Lancaster, Moncks Corner, Mt. Pleasant, Mullins, Murrells Inlet, Myrtle Beach, Newberry, North Augusta, Orangeburg, Pageland, Pawleys Island, Pickens, Easley, Ridgeland, Rock Hill, Seneca, Spartanburg, St. George, Summerville, Union, Walterboro, Williamston, Winnsboro, and York. See **www.genealogybank.com/explore/obituaries/all/usa/south-carolina.**

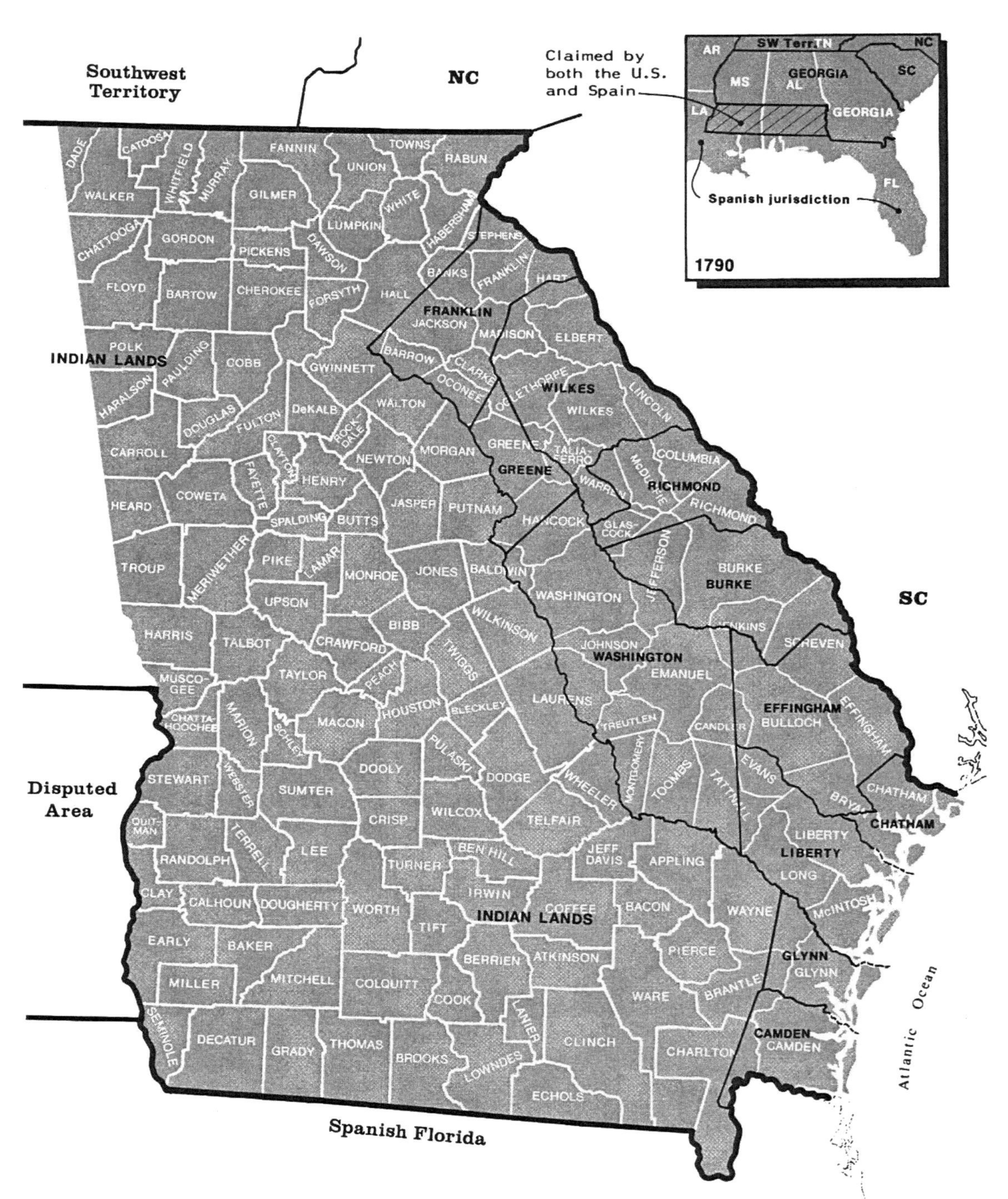


**Georgia in 1790.** The eleven counties of Georgia at the time of the August 1790 Federal Census are shown in black. The current 159 counties of Georgia are shown in white. In August 1790, virtually all of the land west of the first eleven counties was still under control of the Creeks or Cherokees. Nine of the 1790 counties reflect the same area of the original Royal Grant of Georgia of 1732, i.e., " . . lands between the Savannah and Altamaha Rivers." The Disputed Area west of the Chattahoochee River was claimed by both the U.S. and Spain until the U.S. purchased the area in 1796. In 1798, Congress created Mississippi Territory in the purchased area. In 1802, Georgia ceded its western lands to the U.S. and Congress then added those lands to Mississippi Territory in 1803. **Map source:** Page 79, ***Map Guide to the U.S. Federal Censuses, 1790-1920,*** by William Thorndale and William Dollarhide. **NOTE:** For a detailed map showing all Indian Cessions in Georgia, see ***Indian Land Cessions of the United States,*** by Charles C. Royce, publ. GPO, 1899. To view map 15 (Georgia), see **http://usgwarchives.net/maps/cessions/ilcmap15.htm.**

# Georgia

## Censuses & Substitute Name Lists

### Historical Timeline for Georgia, 1497 - 1803

**1497-1498.** Italian explorer Giovanni Caboto (John Cabot), sailing under the commission of Henry VII of England, landed in 1497 on the island of Terra Nova, now called Newfoundland. In 1498, Cabot's second trip to North America may have included visits along the coast of present North Carolina, South Carolina, and Georgia. However, the historian who made this discovery, Dr. Alwyn Ruddock, died in 2005 after instructions to destroy all of her notes relating to Cabot's voyages. Since 2009, the *Cabot Project* is an international and collaborative project to investigate the Bristol discovery voyages, and to reaffirm the revelations made by Dr. Ruddock.

**1526**. The first European attempt to establish a settlement in what is now the continental United States, was by a party of six ships and some 600 men led by Spaniard Lucas Vazques de Ayllon. The San Miguel de Guadalpe colony, believed to have been located on Georgia's Sapelo Island, lasted less than three months. The Spanish were later more successful with colonies in Florida but continued to hold their claims to the coastal areas of present Georgia.

**1539-1542.** Spaniard Hernando DeSoto, on a quest to find gold and a route to China, landed on Florida's West Coast in 1539, somewhere between present Cape Coral and Bradenton. He traveled on land towards Tampa Bay and then further north to present-day Tallahassee. In 1540, DeSoto led his party of some 620 men, 400 horses, numerous beef cattle, and over 200 pigs north into Georgia, where he was met unfavorably by the Creek Indians. DeSoto was the first European to travel into the interior of present Georgia, South Carolina, North Carolina, Kentucky, Tennessee, Alabama, Mississippi, and Arkansas.

**1629-1641.** In 1629, English King Charles I granted a patent to Sir Robert Heath for lands between Latitude 31° and 36°, sea to sea, named "Carolana," which including the entire area of present Georgia. However, Heath never established a settlement there. He may have been dissuaded by a Spanish declaration that the area in question was part of La Florida and for the British to stay away or there would be war. But a more likely reason was that the British interest in the Carolina area had faded during the era of the Civil War in England. In 1629, the preferred destination of the purged Puritans so disliked by Charles I was to Massachusetts Bay, not Albemarle Sound.

**1660-1663.** After the Cromwell era and the restoration of the throne in 1660, Charles II renewed England's interest in establishing colonies in America, which he did over the next twenty years in Carolina, New York, and Pennsylvania. His first action on colonies was to transfer the original 1629 Carolina grant to eight prominent loyalists in 1663, who became the real founders and Lords Proprietors of Carolina. The Carolina grant included all of present-day Georgia.

**1665-1670.** Beginning in 1665, the Spanish started building coastal missions north of St. Augustine well into present Georgia and South Carolina. The 1670 Treaty of Madrid between Spain and England attempted to divide up the eastern half of North America. Spain asserted that the actual possession of land should determine ownership. The boundary created by this treaty was at latitude 32°30', a bit north of where the present-day boundary between Georgia and South Carolina begins (mouth of the Savannah River).

**1673.** The Spanish built a presidio at Santa Catalina (now St. Catherines Island, Georgia). The fort was attacked by the British in 1680, and the Spanish abandoned it in 1681, moving the garrison to Sapelo Island.

**1686.** Sir Francis Drake attacked and burned the Spanish presidio at St. Augustine. The Spanish rebuilt the fort and continued to assert their claims to La Florida as their land by possession, including areas well north of present Savannah, Georgia.

**1707.** England and Scotland merged into the United Kingdom of Great Britain. The English Colonies now became the British Colonies.

**1721.** The British built Fort King George at the mouth of the Altamaha River, the southernmost outpost of the British Empire in North America. The fort was built to reinforce the British claims to the region and stop the Spanish from advancing any further north.

**1730.** The Earl of Egmont (James Edward Oglethorpe), and 19 associates petitioned King George II for a royal charter to establish a colony southwest of the Carolinas.

**1732. Royal Charter of Georgia.** George II granted the Oglethorpe group a royal charter, specifying that the new colony should be named after himself, and that the land area should be ". . between the Savannah and Altamaha Rivers from the Atlantic coast to the headwaters of these streams and thence to the South Seas." Oglethorpe had argued to the King that there was a need for a British colony between Spanish Florida and South Carolina as a military buffer. Not only did the King agree, he donated a grant of £5,000 to the cause.

As a well-known prison reformer and philanthropist, Oglethorpe also acquired financial support from some of England's leading reformers. Oglethorpe's original plan was to provide a place to salvage Britain's destitute poor, particularly those in debtor's prisons, an endeavor he and many of his associates had been involved in as members of Parliament in England. The Georgia colony was set up as a Corporate Trust, with Trustees running the business of the colony from London.

Oglethorpe was the leader of the colony, but his titles were military rather than civilian. He arrived in Charleston, South Carolina in late 1732 on the ship "Anne" with a party of about 120 passengers, and settled near the present site of Savannah, Georgia in February 1733. Although he never got many debtors-prisoners to Georgia, he did encourage many of the "worthy poor" to come. In a more practical plan, English and Scottish tradesmen, artisans, and religious refugees from Switzerland, France, and Germany were welcomed. The Royal Charter provided for acceptance of all religions except Roman Catholicism and Judaism. But when a group of refugee Jews showed up in Savannah, Oglethorpe let them stay. Oglethorpe also set a tone for the new colony's moral and cultural beginnings. While he was the leader for ten years, there was no slavery, no legal sale of rum, and no lawyers allowed.

**1736.** James Oglethorpe went back to England to convince the King to send troops to ward off the Spanish incursions into Georgia. He returned to Georgia with 600 soldiers and more colonists. Now a Colonel in the British Army, he established a settlement on St. Simons Island, called Fort Frederica. Meanwhile, William Stephens of Savannah was named the Secretary of the colony by the Trustees.

**1741.** Convinced that the city and town court systems were not working, the Georgia Trustees established two counties, dividing the colony into Savannah County and Frederica County. But, Frederica was revoked in 1743, leaving the colony with one county.

**1743-1749.** James Oglethorpe returned to England for the last time in 1743 (as a General), and the Georgia ban on Slavery was not lifted until 1749. After Oglethorpe's departure, Trustee Georgia's government consisted of a body of associates who essentially ran the business of the colony as a committee, with William Stephens (now President) in charge in Savannah.

**1752.** The 1732 grant to the Oglethorpe party had a life of 21 years. A year before its expiration, the trustees of the colony of Georgia relinquished their charter to the British government and became a Royal Colony. Until a royal governor could be appointed and installed in the colony, Patrick Graham was appointed as President.

**1754.** John Reynolds was named the first royal governor of Georgia. A Royal Navy man, he brought joy to the colonists because they believed Georgia's economy needed more industry, slavery, and trade, which Reynolds promised to deliver. But Reynolds quit after two years, replaced by Henry Ellis.

**1755.** As Trustee Georgia, the colony could only recommend laws for passage by Parliament in London. Becoming a Royal Colony meant some self-government and the right to issue their own laws, but still under the control of the English monarch. In 1755, Georgia's first General Assembly met at Savannah. The first law dealt with the punishment for anyone questioning the decisions of the Assembly.

**1758.** As a royal colony, Georgia was required to adopt the Church of England as the established church of Georgia. By an act of the Georgia General Assembly, this was formally done in 1758. Several districts and divisions of the province were divided into eight parishes. The parish system used in England was installed in which the Church of England worship divisions and activities were administered under a parish vestry. A vestry was empowered to assess rates (taxes) for the repair of churches, the relief of the poor, and other parochial services. The original eight parishes replaced the single county, Savannah, and were all between the Savannah and Altamaha Rivers, the area of the original Royal Grant. The complete text of the *1758 Act Dividing Georgia into Parishes* is online at the Georgia-Info website and includes detailed descriptions of the 1758 bounds of the eight parishes. See **http://georgiainfo.galileo.usg.edu/parishes.htm.**

**1760.** Georgia's third and final Royal Governor, James Wright, was appointed by the King in 1760. Soon after taking office, a proclamation by Governor Wright increased the coastal land area of the colony from the Altamaha River to the St. Marys River.

- Also in 1760, King George III began a reign that would last over 60 years. He was the British monarch who lost the American colonies.

**1763.** When George III took the throne, the British were still at war with France. In colonial American it was called the French and Indian War and ended with the Treaty of Paris in 1763. To deal with the lands east of the Mississippi River acquired from France in that treaty, by declaration, George III redefined the royal charters of Virginia, North Carolina, South Carolina, and Georgia, all to end at the Mississippi River. He then issued the Proclamation Line of 1763, in which Indian Reserves were established west of the Appalachian Mountains, limiting western migrations by all of the British colonies.

**1763-1764 British Florida.** In the 1763 treaty negotiations concluding the French and Indian War (In Europe: Seven Years' War), France ceded to Britain the areas east of the Mississippi River. In exchange for lands west of the Mississippi, Britain acquired all of Florida from Spain. The British immediately divided the area into East Florida, with a capital at St. Augustine and West Florida, with a capital at Pensacola, both areas with a northern border at Latitude 31°.

- In 1764, the British extended the boundaries of West Florida to include all lands north of Latitude 31° to the mouth of the Yazoo River on the Mississippi (at about Latitude 32° 30'), and running on that line to the Chattahoochee River, the current boundary between Georgia and Alabama. That extended area was to become a matter of dispute when the new U.S. met with Britain, France, and Spain at the Treaty of Paris in 1783.

**1764.** The Sugar Act was passed by the British Parliament to raise revenues from the colonies. Georgia was one of the leading sugar producers of the thirteen colonies and was heavily impacted by the new tax. The sugar tax was one of the first serious disputes between the colonies and Great Britain.

**1765.** The Stamp Act was passed by the British Parliament, credited as the start of the American rebellion, and the cry of "no taxation without representation."

**1776.** The Declaration of Independence included Georgia as one of the original thirteen colonies in rebellion.

**1777.** As part of the Constitution of 1777, Georgia converted all parishes into eight counties: Burke, Camden, Chatham, Effingham, Glynn, Liberty, Richmond, and Wilkes.

**1780-1783.** During the Revolutionary War, the British hold on West Florida and East Florida came to an end. With the Spanish as allies of the French, the British lost West Florida to Spanish forces, who captured Mobile in 1780 and Pensacola in 1781.

Soon after the British loss of West Florida, Georgia reasserted its claim to all land west of the Altamaha and St. Marys Rivers to the Mississippi River; from the Florida line (Latitude 31°) up to the North Carolina/Tennessee line (Latitude 35°). This was Georgia's original Royal Charter plus the 1763 declaration in which King George III had expanded Georgia's Royal Charter to the Mississippi River. Georgia determined that the western lands were all up for grabs after the Spanish defeat of the British, and the loss of Florida to Spain. There were some flamboyant land speculations in the western areas during the 1780s, but no new settlements by Georgia were ever established, as most of the region was still under treaty with the five civilized tribes.

Early in 1783, the British returned East Florida to Spain, causing many American loyalists from Georgia who had fled the Revolutionary War to St. Augustine to flee again, this time heading for the Bahamas or West Indies.

The treaty of Paris in 1783 ended the Revolutionary War with Britain, and the United States of America became an independent nation. Although the U.S. recognized Georgia's claim to the area from Latitude 31° to 35°, the language of the treaty left out of the U.S. the area from 31° to 32° 30'. The U.S. claimed the area based on Georgia's claim (and because of Britain's inclusion of the area in 1763). Spain claimed the area because they felt that Britain had extended their claim in West Florida illegally back in 1763. Now claimed by both the U.S. and Spain, that area was left out of the U.S. at the Treaty of 1783, requiring both the Spanish and Americans to survey the land and come up with a plan separate from the main treaty. As a result, the area remained in dispute, belonging to no one until 1796.

**1788.** January 2. Georgia ratified the U.S. Constitution to become the 4th state in the Union.

**1789-1803.** Georgia's claim to huge tracts of western land, extending across both present-day Alabama and Mississippi to the Mississippi River, was to be the scene of some extraordinary and flamboyant land trading schemes. Two notorious land scandals emerged during this period: 1) From 1789 to 1796, three Governors of Georgia made gifts of land covering more than three times as much land as Georgia contained. Mostly centered in Montgomery County, Georgia, the *Pine Barrens Speculation* was the basis for a landmark U.S. Supreme Court decision in 1810, the first time the Supreme Court ruled a state law unconstitutional.[1] 2) The 1794-1803 *Yazoo Land Scandal* involved the Governor and other Georgia state officials accepting bribes in return for land sales to speculators in the region of present-day Mississippi's Yazoo River area, land that was later ceded by Georgia to the U.S. Public Domain.[2]

**1795-1798.** In the October 1795 Treaty of San Lorenzo (also called Pinckney's Treaty), the U.S. settled the Spanish-U.S. Disputed Area, which was ratified by Congress in August 1796. The lands above West Florida (Latitude 31° up to 32°30') became U.S. territory. In April 1798, Congress created Mississippi Territory in the area, the first Public Domain land south of the Ohio River. The same Mississippi Territory act signed by President John Adams also authorized him to begin negotiations with Georgia over the cession of their western lands.

**1798-1803.** After the notorious Yazoo Land Scandal, and the Pine Barrens Speculation, and after losing its claim to the U.S./Spanish Disputed Area, Georgia was now being asked to cede its remaining western lands to the U.S. Public Domain. President Adams had received authorization from Congress to negotiate with Georgia for the western lands, and he had hoped that Georgia would cede the land without further demands. All other landed states had ceded their western lands by 1790, and without compensation. But, Georgia held out, and refused to give the land away until the U.S. Government paid them for it. An amount of 1.25 million dollars was finally negotiated in 1802. The area of land ceded by Georgia ran from its present western boundary to the Mississippi River, and north from Latitude 32° 30" to 35°. In 1803, Georgia's ceded area was added to Mississippi Territory. After the cession of its western lands, Georgia's boundaries have not changed since.

---

## Georgia's Colonial & Statewide Name Lists

**1733-1776 – British Colonial Era:** No census lists from the colonial era have survived. But, there are some good compilations of the earliest settlers in Georgia, taken from histories, headright land grants, and miscellaneous court records.

**Headright Grants.** Beginning in 1733, Georgia distributed its land through the headright land system. Land was available to individuals based on the number of persons/heads in their household. Men were eligible for 200 acres in their own right, plus an additional 50 acres for each dependent, up to 1,000 acres total.[3] The land areas of Georgia surveyed and distributed under the headright system are the same as the eleven eastern and coastal counties shown on the 1790 GA map on page 192. The early land surveys in Georgia under the headright system were recorded using metes and bounds surveys, land described by the lay of the land, often using natural features as markers.

**1776-1787 – Revolutionary War Era:** During and immediately after the Revolutionary War, Georgia's surviving name lists are mostly tax lists from the counties. In Georgia, the term "tax digest" was used by the General Assembly as a description of lists of taxpayers required from each of the counties. The words today may refer to recompilations from original, longer records – but in early Georgia, the term was simply the same as "tax list."

**1788-Present – State of Georgia Era:** In 1787, the U.S. had created a new Rectangular Survey System, which used square blocks/sections of land, and was first surveyed in the earliest public land surveys in the Northwest Territory, Mississippi Territory, and all 30 public land states thereafter. Most of the 20 state land states retained the metes and bounds surveys, because the areas of the state land states were mostly already surveyed fully. But, two of the state land states with large areas of unsurveyed land (Georgia and Texas), went to a rectangular survey system of their own design.

**Land Lotteries.** In 1805, Georgia installed a new system for land surveying and distribution after a couple of land frauds had rocked the new state. Georgia's new surveying system was much like the U.S. Public Land Rectangular System. But rather than a Section, the Georgia base unit was called a Land Lot. A few hundred Land Lots made up a Land District, and multiple Land Districts made up an Original County. After the new land surveying system was in place, Georgia then did something different than most other states – Georgia began distributing land randomly, through the use of Land Lotteries.

Eight times between 1805 and 1833 Georgia held lotteries to distribute land, the largest held in the United States. The lotteries followed a simple pattern:

1. The General Assembly passed an act that authorized the lottery and spelled out who would be eligible to participate and the grant fees that would apply.
2. Eligible citizens registered their names in their county of residence and paid a small fee. The names were sent to the governor's office at the state capital. Beginning with the second lottery the names were copied onto slips of paper called "tickets" and placed in a large drum called a "wheel."
3. The land to be distributed was surveyed and laid out in districts and lots. The surveyors sent the district and lot numbers to the governor's office. These were placed in a separate wheel.
4. Commissioners appointed by the governor drew a name ticket from one wheel and a district/lot ticket from the other wheel. If the district/lot ticket was blank, the person received nothing. If the ticket contained a district/lot number, the person received a prize of that parcel of land. A ticket that contained a number was called a "Fortunate Draw."
5. Anyone who received a Fortunate Draw could take out a grant for the lot he drew, after paying the grant fee. If he did not take out a grant, the lot reverted back to the state to be sold to the highest bidder.[4]

Lotteries were used to fairly distribute land grants in Georgia's western lands after Creek and Cherokee Indian cessions made the land available for purchase. Participants in the lottery paid a small fee to enter, and those with a "fortunate draw" paid a grant fee to obtain title to the land. Other states had used land lotteries – but no other state used lotteries to distribute land on the scale as was done in Georgia. In most of the lotteries, unmarried men were given one draw, while married men were given two draws, and both had to be residents of Georgia for at least three years to qualify. All of the Georgia Land Lotteries provide the names of a large portion of Georgia's adult, male population, and thus, they are good census substitutes. Georgia's eight Land Lotteries from 1805 to 1833 were as follows:

1. **1805 Land Lottery.** This encompassed Creek Indian lands just west of the Oconee River ceded to the state in 1802 and a small strip of land in the southeast section of the state.
2. **1807 Land Lottery.** Included additional Creek lands.
3. **1820 Land Lottery.** After the Creek War (1814), President Jackson demanded from the Creeks an immense area of land which would become the southern third of the entire state of Georgia. A second section of land in northeast Georgia was included. This other, smaller section defined the eastern end of the Cherokee Nation for 12 years.
4. **1821 Land Lottery.** Further Creek cessions which included the future site of Atlanta.
5. **1827 Land Lottery.** Signaled the end of the Creek Indians in Georgia.
6. **1832 Land Lottery.** This lottery, along with the 1832 Gold Lottery, gave the Cherokee Nation to Georgia settlers. Sparked the "Trail of Tears."
7. **1832 Gold Lottery.** By the time of the gold lottery the Georgia Gold Rush was already beginning to wind down. The state did not guarantee that gold existed on the lots given away.
8. **1833 Fractions Lottery.** The State of Georgia held one final land lottery in December 1833, to distribute fractions from the Cherokee territory and other remaining lots not drawn in previous lotteries.[5]

### End Notes
(Land Scandals & Land Lotteries)

1. *Pine Barrens Speculation*, an article published by Wikipedia, The Free Encyclopedia, last revised 6 Sep 2011.
**http://en.wikipedia.org/w/index.php?title=Pine_Barrens_speculation&oldid=448793030.**

2. *Yazoo Land Scandal*, an article published by Wikipedia, The Free Encyclopedia, last revised 1 Feb 2012.
**http://en.wikipedia.org/w/index.php?title=Yazoo_land_scandal&oldid=474413611.**

3. Paul K. Graham, *Georgia Land Lottery Research*, (Georgia Genealogical Society, Atlanta, GA), 2010, page 1.

4. *Land Lottery*, an article published by the Georgia Archives, under Secretary of State Brian P. Kemp: **http://www.georgiaarchives.org/**

5. *Georgia Land Lotteries*, an article published by Wikipedia, The Free Encyclopedia, last revised 2 Oct 2011.
**http://en.wikipedia.org/wiki/Georgia_Land_Lotteries.**

---

## Georgia's Virtual Vault

**1733–Present.** See **Georgia's Virtual Vault, Digital Treasures from the Georgia Archives [Online Database],** see **http://vault.georgiaarchives.org/**. this is an official portal to some of Georgia's most important historical documents, from 1733 to the present, including manuscripts, photographs, maps, and government records housed in the state archives. There are several search options to see the scanned images or indexed databases. The collections are organized as follows:

### Archives Collections with Images

**Ad Hoc Collection.** After being used for any random use, such as various projects, exhibits, or class presentations, the images are placed here for access by the public.

**Carnegie Family Collection.** Photograph albums compiled by the family of Lucy Coleman Carnegie, who owned most of Cumberland Island, Georgia, from 1881 to 1972.

**Chatham County Deed Books.** 1785-1806 deed books showing property transactions of Chatham County, Georgia.

**Colonial Will Books.** 1754-1779 wills recorded in the Royal Colony of Georgia.

**Colonial Wills.** 1733-1778 wills probated in the Colony of Georgia.

**Confederate Enlistment Oaths and Discharges.** 1861-1864 documents, including enlistment oaths, oaths of allegiance, discharges, and pay records, from troops recruited by the State of Georgia, either before the units were turned over to Confederate service outside of Georgia, or for units intended for service only with the state.

**Confederate Pension Applications.** 1879-1960 Applications, supporting documentation, and correspondence for indigent or maimed Confederate veterans or indigent widows of Confederate soldiers.

**Confederate Pension Application Supplements.** 1879-1960 applications, supporting documentations, and correspondence for indigent or maimed Confederate veterans or indigent widows of Confederate soldiers.

**County Maps.** The county map file consists of maps of Georgia's 161 (now 159) counties collected by the Office of Surveyor General.

**County Tax Digests.** These are records scanned from microfilm in the Georgia Archives. The digital collection currently includes eighteenth century tax records.

**District Plats of Survey.** Original surveys of land districts in counties made prior to distribution of land by lottery, 1805-1833, plus resurveys or renewed surveys of districts.

**District Survey Field Notebooks.** Before each of Georgia's land lotteries of 1805-1833, land surveyors measured the districts to be distributed and created plat maps. These are the field notes from the original surveys.

**Georgia Death Certificates.** 1919-1927 death certificates represent the bulk of the records, but there are also a number of certificates from 1914-1918.

**Georgia Non-Indexed Death Certificates,** 1928-1930. These death certificates can be searched at the archives site until the records are added to the Death Certificate Search System. The steps to search the 1928-1930 records are included here.

**Georgia Power Photograph Collection.** Includes photos from various Georgia power installations and construction projects.

**Governors' Letterbooks.** Outgoing correspondence from eight Georgia Governors.

**Headright and Bounty Plats of Survey.** 1783-1909 original plats of survey for headright and bounty land plats in the area of Georgia before land lotteries (within the Royal Grant between the Altamaha and Savannah Rivers.

**Historic Postcard Collection.** 1,666 postcards, dating from the early 1900s through the 1970s, come from a variety of sources in the collections of the Georgia Archives. They depict many historical buildings and landmarks throughout the state. Of particular interest are postcards collected in the 1920s by the Georgia Chapter of the Daughters of the American Revolution of historical markers erected in Georgia by the DAR.

**Lamar Q. Ball Photograph Collection:** World War II in Georgia. The photographs date from 1934 to 1945.

**Marriage Records from Microfilm.** Most of these scanned marriages records are still held by the counties, with microfilm at the Georgia Archives.

**Militia Enrollment Lists, 1864.** Enrollment lists of all free white males between sixteen and sixty not serving in Confederate or State Service, required for re-organizing the Georgia Militia.

**Small Print Collection.** This collection consists of photographs and visual images roughly 8x10 or smaller collected by the Georgia Archives. The images relate to Georgia and include street scenes, buildings, industrial and commercial sites, aerial views, and portraits of politicians and other individuals.

**Spanish-American War Service Summary Cards.** Georgia raised three militia regiments for service in the Spanish-American War (April-December 1898).

**Touring Georgia.** This is a collection of 50,000 slides produced by Georgia's tourist departments to promote the state. They are high quality scenes of every part of Georgia.

**Vanishing Georgia.** This is a collection of almost 18,000 images from a project begun in the mid-1970s to locate and copy historically significant photographs held by individuals throughout Georgia.

**Virtual Georgia.** This collection is intended to document the lives of Georgians from all walks of life: their religious and social celebrations, homes, art, architecture, dress, and customs.

**Trademark Registrations, 1894-1959.** These records are the recorded copy of official trademarks and union labels of goods sold or distributed in Georgia.

### Archives Collections Without Images

**County Records Microfilm Index.** The card catalog index compiled by the Georgia Archives staff of county records available on microfilm at the archives was scanned and saved in PDF format, one PDF for the cards for each county.

**General Name File.** This is a scanned card index compiled by Georgia Archives staff of personal names in state, local and personal records housed in the archives.

**Georgia Colonial and Headright Plat Index Collection, 1735-1866.** The original Colonial and Headright Plat Indices were compiled between 1856 and 1859 in four manuscript volumes. Separate volumes cover all names beginning with the letters A through F, G through M, N through S, and T through Z. The index lists the name of the person for whom the land was surveyed, the number of acres, watercourses if any, the year of the survey, the plat volume and page number in which the plat is recorded. Although land continued to be granted under the headright system until 1909, there is only one plat recorded in this index after 1858, dated 1866. Colonial and Headright Plat Books are available on microfilm at the Georgia Archives. A database at the FamilySearch.org website is ***Georgia, Headright and Bounty Land Records, 1783-1909***. See the entry in the bibliography.

# Bibliography
## Georgia Censuses & Substitutes

**State Censuses.** For the purpose of apportionment of the General Assembly, Georgia's Constitution of 1798 provided that a state census be taken in 1810 and every seven years thereafter. Accordingly, over the years, the state's General Assembly authorized censuses to be taken in the years 1810, 1817, 1824, 1831, 1838, 1845, 1852, and 1859. Legislative journals confirm that all of these censuses were actually taken through reference to resolutions for compensation of enumerators, reports from governors, etc., yet in 1941, the Public Archives of Georgia had only one package containing fragments from the censuses of 1824 and 1831.

Since then, a few partial lists were found in various Georgia county courthouses for county copies of state censuses for the 1838, 1845, 1852, and 1859 state censuses, but still represent just a fraction of the totals taken for those years. Census name lists discovered for 1827 (1 county) and 1834 (7 counties), appear to be school or county censuses separate from the state censuses. Most of the original county lists were transferred to the state archives. The census of 1859 was probably the last state census taken in Georgia. No state census legislation has been seen after the act of 1858, and the Constitution of 1877 provided that reapportionment would be based on the results of the decennial national censuses.

During the Civil War, an extraordinary military census was conducted, called the *1864 Census for Re-organizing the Georgia Militia*, and identified males between the ages of 16 and 60, those who were not at the time in military service.

**Federal Censuses.** Except for 1800 Oglethorpe County, the first three federal censuses (1790, 1800, and 1810) for all of Georgia were lost. The old Georgia Department of Archives & History website explained that the earliest censuses were probably lost when British troops burned Washington during the War of 1812 – but no census originals from any state were ever sent to Washington until an 1830 federal law asked for them – so the early Georgia census losses should probably be blamed on the Clerk of the U.S. District Court for Georgia, not the British Army. Statewide tax lists and indexes to the early Georgia Land Lotteries for a few years can be used as substitutes to the lost 1790-1810 censuses. Since 1820, all federal censuses for Georgia are complete for all counties (except the 1890, lost for all states).

Federal censuses 1790-1940 are identified in detail in the Nationwide Chapter (Vol. 5). The five main websites where all federal censuses are digitized and indexed are FamilySearch, Ancestry, MyHeritage, FindMyPast, and HeritageQuest. However, Georgia's federal censuses were all digitized again by FamilySearch International and their later images may be of a higher quality, thus easier to read. For that reason, all surviving Georgia federal censuses are included in this bibliography with details on the microfilm and online FHL catalog page location.

In addition to the State and Federal Censuses taken in Georgia, there were many other valuable name lists compiled. The most useful resources are listed in chronological order and annotated below:

**1732-1805. *The Colonial Records of the State of Georgia* [Printed Books & Digital Versions],** early vols. publ. at Atlanta, Franklin-Turner Co; later vols. publ. at Athens, University of Georgia Press. **Contents:** v. 1-2. 1732-1752; v. 3. Accounts, monies, & effects, 1732 to 1751; v. 4. and suppl. Stephen's journal, 1737-1740; v. 5. Journal of the Earl of Egmont, first president of the Board of Trustees from June 14, 1738 to May 25, 1744; v. 6. Proceedings of the President and assistants from October 12, 1741 to October 30, 1754; v. 7-12. Proceedings and minutes of the Governor and Council from October 30, 1754 to February 13, 1782; v. 13-15. Journal of the Commons House of Assembly, January 7, 1755 to June 16, 1782; v. 16-17. Journal of the Upper House of Assembly, January 7, 1755 to March 12, 1774; v. 18. Statutes enacted by the Royal Legislature of Georgia from its first session in 1754 to 1768; v. 19, pts. 1-2. Statutes, colonial and revolutionary, 1768 to 1805; v. 20 Original papers, correspondence to the trustees, James Oglethorpe, and others, 1732-1735; v. 21-25. Original papers: correspondence, trustees, General Oglethorpe and others, 1735-1752; v. 26. Original papers: trustees, president and assistants and others, 1750-1752; v. 27 Original papers of Governor John Reynolds, 1754-1756; v. 28:1. Original papers of Governors Reynolds, Ellis, Wright, and others, 1757-1763; v. 28:2. Original papers of Governor Wright, President Habersham, and others, 1764-1782; v. 29. Trustees' letter book, 1732-1738; v. 30. Trustees' letter book, 1738-1745; v. 31. Trustees' letter book, 1745-1752. To access the digital versions (vol. 1-26), see the online FHL catalog page: **www.familysearch.org/search/catalog/2052310.**

**1733-1755.** ***Entry of Claims for Georgia Landholders*** **[Printed Book & Digital Version],** compiled by Pat Bryant, publ. State Printing Office, Atlanta, 1975. Includes index. To access the digital version, see the online FHL catalog page:
**www.familysearch.org/search/catalog/76882.**

**1733-Current.** ***Georgia USGenWeb Archives*** **[Online Databases].** For statewide resources, or genealogical resources specific to Georgia cities, towns, and virtually every county, thousands of separate databases have been posted online. The statewide databases include Bibles, Bibliographies, Census Records, Cemeteries, Churches, Court Records, Histories, Maps, Place Names, Land Records, Military Records, Newspapers, Obituaries, Photos, Vital Records, or Wills. See **www.usgwarchives.net/ga/gafiles.htm.**

**1733-Current.** ***Linkpendium – Georgia: Family History & Genealogy, Census, Birth, Marriage, Death Vita Records & More*** **[Online Databases].** Linkpendium is a genealogical portal site with links to state, county, town, and local databases. Currently listed are selected sites for Georgia statewide resources (610), Independent Cities, Renamed Counties, Discontinued Counties (5), Appling County (152), Atkinson County (90), Bacon County (90), Baker County (152), Baldwin County (264), Banks County (141), Barrow County (103), Bartow County (258), Ben Hill County (96), and 150 more Georgia counties. See **www.linkpendium.com/ga-genealogy.**

***1733-1819. Early Georgia*** **[Printed Book],** Ronald Vern Jackson, editor, extracted from registers of vital records from several Georgia counties, the names lists may help locate people in Georgia. Published by Accelerated Indexing, Bountiful, UT, 1981, 561 pages, FHL book 973 D2.

**1733-1776.** See ***A List of the Early Settlers of Georgia*** **[Microfilm & Digital Version],** from the 1949 book by E. Merton Coulter and Albert B. Saye, originally published, University of Georgia Press, Athens, GA, 1949, 111 pages. The revised edition in 1967 includes the list of the first settlers to Georgia aboard the ship "Anne" carrying founder James Oglethorpe and about 120 others. See FHL book 975.8 W2L 1967. - The 1967 edition was filmed with ***An Every-Name Index: A List of the Early Settlers of Georgia***, by Karen Buss. Filmed by the Genealogical Society of Utah, 1968, 1 roll, FHL film #1421844. To access the digital version, see the online FHL catalog page: **www.familysearch.org/search/catalog/271620**.

**1733-1778.** ***Index to Probate Records of Colonial Georgia*** [Printed Book], from the Colonial Records Series No. 4, published by R.J. Taylor, Jr. Foundation, 1983, 106 pages, FHL book 975.8 P2i.

**1733 & 1772.** ***Emigrants from Great Britain to the Georgia Colony*** **[Microfilm],** from a manuscript by Jeannette H. Austin. An alphabetical listing of the names of the people who emigrated from Great Britain on the ship "Britannica" to Georgia in 1772 and those who emigrated beginning in 1733. Original manuscript, Atlanta, GA, 1970, 27 pages. Filmed by the Genealogical Society of Utah, 1990, 1 roll, FHL film #1597743. To see if this microfilm has been digitized yet, see the FHL catalog page:
**www.familysearch.org/search/catalog/576249.**

**1733-1783.** ***The Germans of Colonial Georgia*** **[Printed Book & Online Database],** by George F. Jones, published by Genealogical Publishing Co., Baltimore, MD, 1986, 129 pages, FHL book 975.8 F2j. An online version of this book was digitized, and OCR indexed at the Ancestry.com website. See
**http://search.ancestry.com/search/db.aspx?dbid=48469.**

**1733-1900s.** ***Georgia Bible Records*** **[Online Database],** digitally captured and OCR indexed at the Ancestry.com website. Original data: Austin, Jeannette Holland. *Georgia Bible Records.* Baltimore, MD, Genealogical Publishing Co., 2002. This collection contains an itemized list of the births, marriages, and deaths found in approximately 1,000 family Bibles. Included are Bible records of some of Georgia's first settlers and prominent figures, as well as records of ordinary individuals. The collection spans a period stretching from the early 1700s to the 1900s, In all, some 20,000 persons are named in these records which often span several generations in a family. This database has 557 pages. See
**https://search.ancestry.com/search/db.aspx?dbid=49169.**

**1739-1889.** ***Early Miscellaneous Georgia Records*** **[Printed Book],** compiled by Christine Adridge. Includes the following: Confederate soldiers in Georgia; Whitfield County, muster roll; Company B, 44th Georgia Regiment Confederate volunteers, Jasper County; Randolph County, disabled soldiers and widows; burials in Warren County; soldiers and their widows' drawers in the 1827, land lottery--Muscogee County; Carroll County, Georgia Rangers, 1836; Miscellaneous divorces 1793-1833; Southern Masonic Female College, 1855, Covington; Quaker settlement; invalid pensioners report from the "House Executive Documents" March 1849; minutes of the Savanna, Executive Council, October 2, 1784; unclaimed letters, Fayette County, September 20, 1828; persons banished from the British Dominan, May 4, 1782; Bethesda Orphanage, 1739-1746; Lee County, Newspaper records; poor school fund, Washington County; depredations committed by Indians since 1786, Washington County; Sparta Female Model School, 1835, Hancock County; Lee County, slave owners in the 1860, census; poor school Jones County, 1828-1830; miscellaneous estate records of Lee County; Shady Dale Academy, 1837, Jasper County and Milford Lodge #181, 1870-1889. Published by Partin Publications, Nacogdoches, TX, 1994, 93 pages, FHL book 975.8 H29a.

**1739-1944. Georgia Marriages [Online Database],** indexed at the Ancestry.com website. The marriage information in this series was taken from the original Hunting for Bears database, with marriages extracted from various Georgia counties. Presumably, all of the marriages were extracted from FHL microfilm. The title dates of this series is "1699-1944," based on one marriage dated 1699 from Warren County. That date is rather suspect, because the colony of Georgia began in 1733, and Warren County was created in 1793. The next earliest marriage was for 1739 from Liberty County, one of Georgia's first eight counties converted from parishes at the Constitution of 1777, and there is a chance that a 1739 marriage from one of the parishes that was later Liberty county was retained in the Liberty county courthouse. For that reason, the marriage dates shown here begin in the year 1739. This database does not include images of the documents from which the index was compiled. Therefore, the index is a secondary source, and all of the dates and other information for the marriages in this database are prone to error. (Hunting for Bears databases are notorious for transcription errors, incorrect dates, misspellings, etc.). As with any secondary source, the original microfilmed record from the courthouse should be viewed to confirm the information. See **http://search.ancestry.com/search/db.aspx?dbid=7839.**
- For the Ancestry version of this database with 216,770 records, see **https://search.ancestry.com/search/db.aspx?dbid=7839.**

**1739-1850.** ***Georgia Marriages to 1850*** **[Online Database],** indexed at the Ancestry.com website. The marriage information in this series was taken from the original Liahona Research database, from extractions of marriages at Georgia counties on microfilm at the FHL in Salt Lake City. The database contains 165,000 names. Each entry includes groom, bride, marriage date, and county. There is no reference to the source of the information except the county of Georgia where the original record resides today. To get a copy of a marriage record, one must access the online FHL catalog at www.familysearch.org, then a Place search for Georgia, followed by a search for a county in Georgia. The list of categories for each county will have "Vital Records," which is where any marriage records on microfilm will be shown. See **http://search.ancestry.com/search/db.aspx?dbid=2085.**

**1740-1935.** ***Georgia Obituaries*** **[Printed Book],** compiled by Jeannette Holland Austin, published by J.H. Austin, Rayetteville, GA, 1993, 241 pages, FHL book 975.8 V4a.

**1742-1990.** ***Georgia, Probate Records*** **[Online Database],** digitized at the FamilySearch.org website. This image-only database is a collection of records of probate proceedings from Georgia counties. The records include estate files, inventories, wills, administrations, minutes, guardianships, and other records related to probate. This database has 2,280,204 images. Browse through the images, organized by County, Record Type, Date Range, and Volume. See **https://familysearch.org/search/collection/1999178.**

**1742-1992.** ***Georgia, Wills and Probate Records*** **[Online Database],** digitized and indexed at the Ancestry.com website. Original data: Georgia County, District and Probate Courts. The records include Wills, Letters of Administration, Inventories, Distributions and Accounting, Bonds, and Guardianships. Each index record may include: Name, Gender, and Relationship. This database has 450,915 records. See **https://search.ancestry.com/search/db.aspx?dbid=8635.**

**1748-1773.** ***Headright Surveys, Book C*** **[Microfilm],** from the original records at the GDAH, Atlanta, GA. The Secretary of State found a book containing 664 plats which he copied and the Surveyor-General examined and certified to be accurately copied from the original. They were given to the Surveyor-General's office by an act of February 2, 1798. Includes index. Filmed by the GDAH, 1960, 1 roll, FHL film #465059. To see if this microfilm has been digitized yet, see the FHL catalog page:
**www.familysearch.org/search/catalog/570070.**

**1748-1783.** ***Colonial Georgia Genealogical Data*** **[Printed Book],** by William H. Dumont. Contains marriage agreements, administrations of colonial estates, guardianships, grants, genealogical data, supplement to genealogical data from deed books, and stock owners. Published by the National Genealogical Society, Special Publications No. 36, Washington, DC, 1971, 77 pages, FHL book 975.8 D2dw.

**1750-1829.** ***Colonial Records of Georgia*** **[Microfilm & Digital Capture],** from the original (Governor's) manuscript at the Georgia State Archives, Atlanta, GA. Includes index. Records include conveyances, mortgages, bills of sale, deeds of gift, powers of attorney, fiats for grants, entry of claims, proclamations, and miscellaneous records. Filmed by the Genealogical Society of Utah, 1957, 25 rolls, beginning with FHL film #158965 (C1-C2 Conveyances, 1750-1766). For a complete list of roll numbers and contents of each roll, see the online FHL page for this title:
**www.familysearch.org/search/catalog/309455.**

**1750-1761.** ***Abstracts of Georgia Colonial Conveyance Book, C*** **[Printed Book],** compiled by Frances Howell Beckemeyer. Includes index. Published by R.J. Taylor, Jr., Foundation, Atlanta, GA, 1975, 429 pages, FHL book 975.8 R2b.

**1752-2005.** ***The Georgia Frontier*** **[Printed Book],** by Jeannette Holland Austin, published by Clearfield, Baltimore, MD, 2005, 3 vols., 1,616 pages, FHL book 975.8 D2agf v.1-3. Vol. 1: Colonial Families to the Revolutionary War Period. Vol. 2: Revolutionary War Families to Mid-1800s. Vol. 3: Descendants of Virginia, North Carolina, and South Carolina families. Following James Oglethorpe's initial settling of Europeans from England, Scotland, and the Palatine to the Georgia Colony and the dissolution of the Georgia trustees' charter, the British Crown offered substantial land grants to entice other colonists to settle and work the Georgia countryside. As early as 1752, colonists from New England, Virginia, and the Carolinas poured into Georgia, bringing with them their families, servants, and sometimes entire religious communities. By 1775, these "frontier" settlements had established extensive coastal cotton and rice plantations. After the Revolution, Patriot veterans established homesteads by taking up land grants for their war services. During the early 1800s, Georgia employed a series of land lotteries to attract even more settlers. Once the federal government had "removed" Georgia's Cherokee and Creek populations during the late 1820s, the stage was set for a climactic state lottery of middle and western Georgia lands in 1832. A detailed list of the family names identified in these volumes can be found at the publisher's page for the book. See
**https://library.genealogical.com/printpurchase/3D92v.**

**1754-1850.** ***Georgia, Compiled Marriages*** **[Online Database],** indexed at the Ancestry.com website. Source: Jordan Dodd, *Georgia Marriages to 1850.* Each entry includes groom, bride, marriage date, county, and state. Every name is indexed so you can search for one name, or two names that are linked. This database has 167,492 records. See
**https://search.ancestry.com/search/db.aspx?dbid=2085.**

**1754-1960.** ***Georgia Births and Christenings*** **[Online Database],** digitized and indexed at the FamilySearch.org website. This database is a name index to birth, baptism and christening records from the state of Georgia taken from microfilm copies at the Family History Library in Salt Lake City. This database has 25,161 records. See
**https://familysearch.org/search/collection/1674802.**
- Another version of this database is at the Ancestry.com website. See
**https://search.ancestry.com/search/db.aspx?dbid=60264.**

**1754-1960.** ***Georgia Church Marriages*** **[Online Database],** indexed at the FamilySearch.org website. Source: FamilySearch extractions from various churches in Georgia. This database is an index and images of selected church marriages. Many of the records are from Bibb, Chatham, Liberty, and Richmond counties. This database has 1,535 records. See **www.familysearch.org/search/collection/2549568.**

**1755-1758.** ***Georgia, Entry of Land Claims*** **[Microfilm & Digital Capture],** from a manuscript at the Georgia State Archives. Includes index. Filmed by the Georgia Department of Archives and history, 1951,

1951, 1 roll, FHL film #488183. To access the digital images, see the online FHL catalog page: **www.familysearch.org/search/catalog/21009.**

**1755-1775.** ***First Settlers in Georgia: Abstracts of the English Crown Grants in Georgia*** **[Printed Book],** compiled by Marion R. Hemperley and Pat Bryant from records of the Georgia Surveyor General Department, Atlanta, GA. Abstracts arranged alphabetically by surname within each volume. Contents: vol. 1: St. Paul Parish (Columbia, Glascock, Jefferson, McDuffie, Richmond, Warren counties); vol. 2: St. George Parish (Burke, Glascock, Jefferson, Jenkins, Screven counties); vol. 3: St. Matthew Parish (Effingham, Screven counties); vol. 4: St. Philip Parish (Bryan, Bullock, Candler, Chatham, Effingham, Jenkins counties); vol. 5: Christ Church Parish (Chatham County), vol. 6: St. John Parish (Bullock, Candler, Evans, Liberty, Long, Tattnall counties); vol. 7: St. Andrew Parish (Evans, Liberty, Long, McIntosh, Tattnall counties); vol. 8: St. David, St. Mary, St. Patrick and St. Thomas Parishes (Brantley, Camden, Charlton, Glynn, Wayne counties); vol. 9: Islands of Georgia (St. Simons, Skidway, Tybee, Sea Island, and others). Published by Boyd Pub. Co., Milledgeville, GA, 1998, FHL book 975.8 R28f v.1-9.

**1755-1793.** ***Colonial Records of Georgia; Marks and Brands, Vol. K*** **[Microfilm],** from the original manuscript at the Georgia State Archives, Atlanta, GA. Includes index. Filmed by the Genealogical Society of Utah, 1957, 1 roll, FHL film #158972.

**1756-1939.** ***Headrights and Land Grants of Georgia*** **[Microfilm & Digital Capture],** from originals at the Georgia State Archives, Atlanta, GA. Includes general index and indexes at the front of each volume. Filmed by the GDAH, 1953-1954, 61 rolls, beginning with FHL film #465072 (Index to Grants and Headrights). For a complete list of roll numbers and contents of each roll, see the online catalog page for this title. **www.familysearch.org/search/catalog/46190.**

**1758-1946.** ***Church Histories and Assorted Papers*** **[Microfilm],** from the original manuscripts compiled by the Episcopal Diocese of Georgia, Savannah, originals now located at the Georgia State Archives, Atlanta, GA. The manuscripts, beginning with vestry records from the first eight parishes in Georgia, were filmed by the Genealogical Society of Utah in 1958, 1 roll, FHL film #177520. To see if this microfilm has been digitized yet, see the FHL catalog page: **www.familysearch.org/search/catalog/204368.**

**1763-2003.** ***Georgia Newspaper Archives*** **[Online Database],** digitized and indexed at the GenealogyBank.com website. One search screen for names and keywords in city newspapers from Athens, Atlanta, Augusta, Brunswick, Columbus, Darien, Griffin, Louisville, Macon, Marietta, Milledgeville, Mt. Zion, New Town, Savannah, Sparta, Thomson, and Washington. See **www.genealogybank.com/gbnk/newspapers/explore/USA/Georgia/.**

**1767-1908.** ***Land Office Records Index*** **[Microfilm & Digital Capture],** from originals at the Georgia Department of State. Filmed by the Department of State, 19--, 12 rolls, beginning with FHL film #465173 (land Office Records Index 1767-1908 Al – An). To access the digital images, see the online FHL catalog page: **www.familysearch.org/search/catalog/315610.**

**1770-1832.** ***Georgia Lands*** **[Microfilm],** from an original manuscript compiled by Leonardo Andrea, records of land lotteries in Georgia from 1770-1832. Filmed by the Genealogical Society of Utah, 1974, 1 roll, FHL film #954249. To see if this microfilm has been digitized yet, see the FHL catalog page: **www.familysearch.org/search/catalog/322453.**

**1773-1999.** ***Atlanta, Georgia, Oakland Cemetery Records*** **[Online Database],** indexed at the Ancestry.com website. Source: R. L. Grizzle, compiler for this Ancestry.com database. This database is a transcription of headstone inscriptions from the cemetery. Each record provides the name of individual, date of birth and date of death. This database has 42,551 records. See **https://search.ancestry.com/search/db.aspx?dbid=4105.**

**1775-1865.** ***Some Early Tax Digests of Georgia*** **[Online Database],** digitized and OCR indexed at the Ancestry.com website. Source: Book, same title, by Ruth Blair, 1926. Includes tabulated county lists of names of taxpayers. This database has 318 pages. See **https://search.ancestry.com/search/db.aspx?dbid=25650.**

**1776-1783.** ***Roster of Revolutionary Soldiers in Georgia, Vols 1-3*** **[Online Database],** digital capture and OCR index at the Ancestry.com website. Original data: McCall, Mrs. Howard H. *Roster of Revolutionary Soldiers in Georgia. Vol. I-3.* Baltimore, MD, Genealogical Publishing Co., 2004. Volume I of this

cumulative work contains the records of hundreds of Revolutionary War soldiers and officers of Georgia, with genealogies of their families, and lists of soldiers buried in Georgia whose graves have been located. The arrangement of Volume II is similar; however, it contains records of officers and soldiers not only from Georgia but from other states, many of whose descendants later came to Georgia because of liberal land grants. Volume III, the longest of the work, is similar in scope to Volume II except that the majority of the entries are for Georgia officers and soldiers, with only some material relating to other states. The three volumes, each of which is indexed, refer to as many as 20,000 persons overall. This database has 986 pages. Index to vol. 1, see:
**https://search.ancestry.com/search/db.aspx?dbid=49320.**
- For the index to Vol. 2, see:
**https://search.ancestry.com/search/db.aspx?dbid=49321.**
- For the index to Vol. 3, see:
**https://search.ancestry.com/search/db.aspx?dbid=49322.**

**1779-1785.** ***Abstracts of Georgia Land Plat Books A & B*** **[Printed Book],** by Nathan & Kaydee Mathews. Includes index. Published by Wolfe Pub., Roswell, GA, 1995, 292 pages, FHL book 975.8 R28m.

***1780 Tax List, Greene Co., Georgia*** **[Printed Book],** compiled by MariLee Beatty Hageness, Anniston, AL, MLH Research, 1998, 13 pages. Tax list is abstracted in alphabetical order by name of tax payer. FHL book 975.8 A1 no. 147.

**1780s-1990s.** ***30,638 Burials in Georgia*** **[Printed Book & Digital Version],** compiled by Jeannette Holland Austin, this is a list of burials from 600 cemeteries in 100 counties in the state of Georgia. Published by Genealogical Publishing Co., Baltimore, MD, 1995, 708 pages, FHL book 975.8 V3a. A digitized version of this book is at the Ancestry.com website. See
**https://search.ancestry.com/search/db.aspx?dbid=49007.**

**1785-1895. Liberty County, Georgia Marriages [Online Database],** indexed at the Ancestry.com website. Source: Clint Owen, compiler. This database is a collection of marriage records from the county between 1785 and 1895. With over 1,000 records and nearly 2,100 names, this database provides the names of each spouse, date of marriage license, marriage date, and, for some, other notes. This database has 1,063 records. See
**https://search.ancestry.com/search/db.aspx?dbid=3487.**

**1783-1794.** ***Early Settlers of Georgia: A List of File Headings of the Loose Headright and Bounty Land Grant Files in the Georgia Department of Archives and History*** **[Printed book],** edited by Robert Scott Davis. Names listed alphabetical by surname. This books lists names of people from the files of loose headright and bounty land grant papers housed at the Georgia Department of Archives and History in Atlanta. The files are primarily from 1783-1794 when Georgia's population was expanding. The files include military land certificates given to Georgia's Revolutionary War soldiers, including those recruited from the Carolinas and Virginia. This list may be helpful as a substitute for Georgia's lost 1790 and 1800 censuses, since so many Georgians applied for headright or bounty land grants. Published by Boyd Pub. Co., Milledgeville, GA, 1997, 202 pages, FHL book 975.8 R2dr.

**1783-1909.** ***Georgia Headright and Bounty Land Records*** **[Online Database],** digitized at the FamilySearch.org website. This image-only database is a collection of individual documents from Georgia's original land grant system, the headright and bounty system, 1783-1909. Bounty lands were awarded for service in the Revolutionary War. Headright law provided an individual with a grant of land based on the number of heads in a family. This database has 157,959 records. See
**https://familysearch.org/search/collection/1914217.**

**1785-1895. Liberty County, Georgia Marriages [Online Database],** indexed at the Ancestry.com website. See
**http://search.ancestry.com/search/db.aspx?dbid=3487.**

**1785-1950.** ***Georgia, County Marriages*** **[Online Database],** indexed and digitized at the FamilySearch.org website. Source: FamilySearch extractions from various county courthouses. Includes images of marriages recorded in Georgia counties. This database has 779,774 records. See
**https://familysearch.org/search/collection/1927197.**

**1787-1899.** ***Index to Tax Digests*** **[Microfilm],** from the original records at the GA Archives, Atlanta, GA. Filmed by the Genealogical Society of Utah, 1947, 1 roll, FHL film #7023. Part of this microfilm was digitized and indexed at the Ancestry.com website. See
**http://search.ancestry.com/search/db.aspx?dbid=3467.**

**1787-1962.** ***Georgia, Church Marriages*** **[Online Database],** indexed at the FamilySearch.org website. Index to selected church marriage records from throughout the state of Georgia. Many of the records are for the county of Camden. This database has 182 records. See
**www.familysearch.org/search/collection/2543297.**

***1788 and 1789 Voters, Camden County, Georgia*** **[Online Database],** indexed at the RootsWeb site for Camden Co GA. See
**www.rootsweb.ancestry.com/~gacamden/Voters.htm.**

***1789 Petition of Inhabitants, Burke County, Georgia*** **[Online Database],** indexed at the USGenWeb site for Burke Co GA. See
**http://files.usgwarchives.net/ga/burke/history/letters/ms138petition.txt.**

***1789 Tax List, Greene County, Georgia*** **[Printed Book],** compiled by MariLee Beatty Hageness, Anniston, AL,MLH Research, 1998, 13 pages. FHL book 975.8612 R4.

**1789-1817.** ***An Index to Georgia Tax Digests*** **[Printed Book],** 5 vols., published for the R. J. Taylor Foundation; Spartanburg, SC: Reprint Co., 1986. FHL book 975.8 R42i.

**1789-1799.** ***Georgia Tax Index*** **[Online Database],** indexed at the Ancestry.com website. Each index record includes: Name, County, Year, District, and Page. This database has 11,509 records. See
**https://search.ancestry.com/search/db.aspx?dbid=3467.**

**1789-1870.** See ***General Index Books, 1789-1928; Minute Boks and Bench Dockets, 1789-1870 (U.S. District Court, Georgia: Southern District)*** **[Microfilm & Digital Capture],** housed in the Atlanta Regional Branch of the National Archives, East Point, Georgia. Includes index. Contains civil, criminal, bankruptcy, and admiralty cases. Also includes naturalization oaths, admission of attorneys to practice before the court, names of persons summoned to serve as jurors, etc. Admiralty bench dockets are for 1817, 1820-1832, 1834-1859, and 1867-1868. Filmed by the National Archives, series M1172, 3 rolls, beginning with FHL film #1405184. To access the digital images, see the online FHL catalog page:
**www.familysearch.org/search/catalog/396265.**

**1790.** ***The Reconstructed 1790 Census of Georgia: Substitutes for Georgia's Lost 1790 Census*** **[Printed Book & Online Database],** compiled by Marie DeLamar and Elizabeth Rothstein. From intro: "Wills, deeds, tax digests, court minutes, voter lists, and newspapers were searched to compile this list." Published by Genealogical Publishing Co., Baltimore, MD, 1989, 180 pages, FHL book 975.8 X2L. An online digital capture and OCR index of this book is available at the Ancestry.com website. See
**http://search.ancestry.com/search/db.aspx?dbid=48008.**

***1790 Tax Return, Glynn County, Georgia*** **[Online Database],** indexed at the GlynnGen.com:
**www.glynngen.com/census/taxreturns/1790.htm.**

**1790s.** ***Index to Some Early Tax Digests of Georgia*** **[Printed Book],** compiled by Earldene Rice, 68 pages, 1971. FHL book 975.8 R4g.

**1790-1818.** ***Some Early Tax Digests of Georgia*** **[Printed Book],** edited by Ruth Blair, State Historian, 2 vols., 174 pages. (Atlanta: Georgia Archives, 1926). FHL book 975.8 R4. This book was digitized and indexed at the Ancestry.com website. See
**http://search.ancestry.com/search/db.aspx?dbid=25650.**

**1790-1850.** ***Early Georgia Wills*** **[Printed Book],** compiled and published by American Heritage Research, Salt Lake City, UT, 1976, FHL book 975.8 S2a v. 1.

**1790-1860.** ***Savannah, Georgia, Southeast Coastwise Inward and Outward Slave Manifests*** **[Online Database],** indexed at the Ancestry.com website. This is a database of manifests for slaves arriving in Savannah, Georgia from 1811-1860. The Act of 1807, signed into law by President Thomas Jefferson, made the international slave trade illegal. The domestic slave trade (transportation between states) was still legal and because of this distinction the slave manifest records became more detailed. Before 1808, the information on slaves on board these ships was less informational and sometimes was solely the number of slaves onboard. Post-1808, personal information for each slave was included and the owner had to affirm the slave had been imported prior to 1808. The manifests include, Name of ship, Master, Port of departure, Port of destination, and List of slaves on board. The slave information includes, First name, Sex, Age, Stature, Name of shipper/owner, and Shipper/owner's place of residence. This database has 22,049 records. See
**http://search.ancestry.com/search/db.aspx?dbid=1714.**

**1790-1860.** See ***Minutes of the U.S. Circuit Court for the District of Georgia, 1790-1842; and Index to Plaintiffs and Defendants in the Circuit Court, 1790-1860*** **[Microfilm & Digital Capture],** housed in the Federal Archives and Records Center, Atlanta, Georgia. Includes index. Shows dates of sessions, names of presiding judges, and, usually judgments and orders of the court arising out of the litigation of all cases before it, original and appellate, civil and criminal. The minutes also record some naturalization proceedings, the admission of attorneys to practice before the court, names of persons summoned to serve as grand and petit jurors, fines imposed upon defaulting jurors, findings and verdicts of juries, settlement of cases by agreement, and more. Filmed by the National Archives, 1981, series M1184, 3 rolls, beginning with FHL film #1405275 (Minutes, 1790-1816). To access the digital images, see the online FHL catalog page: **www.familysearch.org/search/catalog/256308.**

**1790-1890.** ***Georgia, Compiled Census and Census Substitutes Index*** **[Online Database],** Indexes originally edited by Ronald V. Jackson, Accelerated Indexing, Salt Lake City, UT. Electronic files were acquired by Ancestry, Inc. which has these Georgia lists indexed at their website. This database has 99,830 records. A combined index contains the following:

- 1790 Tax Substitute Index
- 1792-1819 Tax Lists Index
- 1800 Oglethorpe County Census Index
- 1820-1930 Federal Census Index
- 1838 State Census
- 1840 Pensioners List
- 1845 State Census Index
- 1850-1860 Slave Schedules
- 1850-1880 Mortality Schedules & Index
- 1890 Veterans Schedule

See **http://search.ancestry.com/search/db.aspx?dbid=3542.**

**1790-1910.** ***Savannah, Georgia, Naturalization Records*** **[Online Database],** digitized and indexed at Ancestry.com. Source: Municipal Archives, Savannah, GA. Includes Petitions, Declarations, and Naturalization Certificates. This database has 5,646 records, see **www.ancestry.com/search/collections/2767/.**

***1790-1940 Naturalization Records*** **[Microfilm & Digital Capture],** from the original records at the U.S. Courthouse, Savannah, GA. Filmed by the Genealogical Society of Utah, 1990, 7 rolls, beginning with FHL film #1651295 (Declarations of Intention, 1908-1921). For a complete list of roll numbers and contents of each roll, see the online FHL catalog page for this title: **www.familysearch.org/search/catalog/367105.**

**1790-1950.** ***Index to Georgia's Federal Naturalization Records to 1950 (Excluding Military Petitions)*** **[Printed Book & Digital Version],** compiled by Linda Woodward Geiger and Meyer L. Frankel, publ. Georgia Genealogical Society, Atlanta, 1966, 221 pages. FHL book 975.8P42. To access the digital version, see the online FHL catalog page: **www.familysearch.org/search/catalog/760980.**

**1790s-2000s.** ***Georgia – Collection Catalog at MyHeritage*** **[Online Database],** over 31 collections with 226,063 records can be searched at the MyHeritage website. Databases may include censuses, directories, family histories, town histories, military rosters, college year books, and more. A search can be done for a name, place, year, or keyword. See **www.myheritage.com/records/Georgia/all-records.**

**1790-2002.** ***Georgia, Ebert County Records*** **[Online Database],** digitized at the FamilySearch.org, from a collection of marriages, court records, land records, school records, and other records from Elbert County. This is an image-only database with 63,290 images. Browse through the records, organized by categories: Cemetery records, Court records, Land and property records, Military records, Public records, School records, Slave records, and Vital records. The categories are organized by Record type, Volume, and Date. See **https://familysearch.org/search/collection/2071974.**

***1793-1806 Tax Lists, Elbert County, Georgia*** **[Online Database],** indexed at the USGenWeb site for Elbert Co GA. See **http://files.usgwarchives.net/ga/elbert/taxlists/mccurrys.txt.**

**1793-1858.** See ***Index to Land Plats, 1793-1831; and Index to Plats of Colonial and Headright Grants, 1837-1858*** **[Microfilm],** from originals at the GDAH, Atlanta, GA. Filmed by the GDAH, 1953, 2 rolls, FHL film #465069 (Index Plats Headrights); and FHL film #465070 (Index Plats Headrights).

**1793-1892. Georgia, Property Tax Digests [Online Database],** indexed at the Ancestry.com website. Source: Georgia Archives, Property Tax Digests, 140 volumes. This database contains tax digest books for 137 Georgia counties from 1793-1892. The books list names of taxpayers and assessments of value for various types of property and assets, as well as indicating who owed the poll tax. As such, the records should include all men 21 and over and women who owned property. Another important feature of the digests is their inclusion of African-American freemen by name. Digests were compiled by militia districts within a county. Index records may include: Name, Number of polls, Taxable profession, Number of employees, Acres owned (and location), Value of land, Value of city or town property, Shares held in banks and corporations, Stocks, and securities. Investments in cotton, foundries, shipping, mining, and Personal possessions (jewelry, agricultural products, animals, tools, etc.). This database has 4,820,413 records. See **https://search.ancestry.com/search/db.aspx?dbid=1729.**

***1794 Grand Jury List, Camden County, Georgia* [Online Database],** indexed at the RootsWeb site for Camden Co GA. See **www.rootsweb.ancestry.com/~gacamden/Jury.htm.**

***1794 Tax Return, Glynn County, Georgia* [Online Database],** indexed at the GlynnGen.com site. See **www.glynngen.com/census/taxreturns/1794.htm.**

***1794 Militia List, Effingham County, Georgia* [Online Database],** indexed at the RootsWeb site for Effingham Co GA. See **www.rootsweb.ancestry.com/~gaeffing/milit.html.**

**1796-1875. *Marriage Records of Bulloch County, Georgia* [Online Database],** indexed at the Ancestry.com website. See **http://search.ancestry.com/search/db.aspx?dbid=29467**.

***1796 Tax List, Oglethorpe County, Georgia: With Statistical Information Added* [Printed Book],** name list compiled by Joseph T. Maddox, 1980, 40 pages. FHL book 975.8175 R4m.

**1796. *Oglethorpe County, Georgia Tax List for the Year 1796 in the Office of the Clerk of the Superior Court* [Printed Book],** compiled by Mrs. Edgar Lamar Smith, 1958. FHL book 975.8175 R4s.

***1797-1802 Tax Digest, Jackson County, Georgia* [Printed Book],** compiled by Belinda E. Savadge. Published by B.E. Savadge, Jefferson, GA, 2000, 369 pages. Includes index. See FHL book 975.8145 R4s.

**1798-1839. *Franklin County, Georgia Tax Digests* [Printed Book],** compiled by Martha Walters Acker. Birmingham, AL, 1980, 4 vols., Each volume includes three indexes. Contents: vol. 1: 1798-1807; vol. 2: 1808-1818; vol.. 3: 1819-1823" vol. 4: 1825-1839. FHL book 975.8135 R4f v.1-4.

***1798-1839 Tax Lists, Oglethorpe County, Georgia* [Online Database],** indexed at the USGenWeb site for Oglethorpe Co GA. See **http://usgwarchives.net/ga/oglethorpe/taxlists.html.**

***1799 Tax List of Oglethorpe County, Georgia* [Printed Book],** compiled by MariLee Beatty Hageness, Anniston, AL, 1995, 26 pages. FHL book 975.8175 R4h.

**1799-1839. *Lincoln County, Georgia Tax Digests* [Microfilm],** original name lists filmed by Heritage Papers, Danielsville, GA, 1985. See FHL film #1276564. To see if this microfilm has been digitized yet, see the FHL catalog page: **www.familysearch.org/search/catalog/21326.**

***1800 (Federal) Census of Oglethorpe County, Georgia: the Only Extant Census of 1800 for the State of Georgia* [Printed Book],** transcribed from the originals at the GA Archives and indexed by Mary Bondurant Warren, Athens, GA, 1965, 53 pages. Includes index. FHL book 975.8175 X2p 1800.

**1800-1810. *Franklin County, Georgia Tax Book, 1800, and Tax Digest, 1810* [Microfilm],** filmed by Heritage Papers, Danielsville, GA, 1985. FHL film #1276565 Item 2.

**1800-Present. *North-Central Georgia Cemeteries* [Online Database],** indexed at the Ancestry.com website. Original data: Grizzle, R. L., and S. R. Criner, *Select Georgia Cemeteries.* Located east and north of Atlanta, Georgia, the three counties of Hall, Walton, and Rockdale are now home to over 200,000 people. This collection of headstone inscriptions includes records from 14 cemeteries, each listed at the Ancestry website. This database has 8,693 records. See **https://search.ancestry.com/search/db.aspx?dbid=3472.**

**1800-1856. *Names Changed Legally in Georgia: From the Acts and Resolutions of the General Assembly of the State of Georgia* [Printed Book & Digital Version],** by Arthur Ray Rowland, originally published National Genealogical Society, 1967, reprinted RR Books, North Augusta, SC, 2008. To access the digital version, see the online FHL catalog page: **www.familysearch.org/search/catalog/1452760.**

**1803-1966. *Savannah, Georgia Vital Records* [Online Database],** indexed at the Ancestry.com website. Original data: City of Savannah, Georgia Records - Health Department, Vital Statistics Registers. Documents in this database include birth, marriage, and death records for Savannah for the following years: **Births, 1889-1919:** includes date of birth, gender, race, father's name and nationality, mother's name

and nationality, and residence/address. **Marriages: 1898-1911:** includes name, spouse, age, birthplace, residence, race, and occupation. **Deaths: 1803-1966:** includes name, age, occupation, country/place of birth, cause of death, gender, place of death, place of burial, marital status, nativity, name of undertaker, street, and ward. This database has 178,865 records. See
**https://search.ancestry.com/search/db.aspx?dbid=2209.**

***1805 Georgia Land Lottery* [Printed Book],** name list of lottery ticket holders transcribed and indexed by Virginia S. Wood and Ralph V. Woods, published by Greenwood Press, Cambridge, MA, 1964, 393 pages. FHL book 975.8 R2wv 1805.

**1805-1806. *List of Lottery Names, 1805-1806 Index; 1805 Land Lottery for Baldwin, Wilkinson, and Wayne Counties* [Microfilm & Digital Capture],** from the originals at the State Archives in Atlanta, GA. Includes partial index. Filmed by the GDAH, 1959, 1 roll, FHL film #194353. To access the digital images, see the online FHL catalog page:
**www.familysearch.org/search/catalog/285452.**
- Another filming, FHL film #514007. To access the digital images, see the online FHL catalog page:
**www.familysearch.org/search/catalog/74234.**
- See also, ***Index to People Entitled to Participate in Land Lotteries from the Various Georgia Counties, 1805-1806* [Microfilm & Digital Capture],** GDAH, 1967, 1 roll, FHL film #519001. To access the digital images, see the online FHL catalog page:
**www.familysearch.org/search/catalog/74203.**

***1805 Georgia Land Lottery, Fortunate Drawers and Grantees* [Printed Book],** compiled by Paul K. Graham. From page i: "The Act of 11 May 1803 established the general process by which the land lottery would operate. The law outlined the creation of three counties and thirteen districts: five districts in Baldwin County, three districts in Wayne County, and five districts in Wilkinson County. Each district was to be surveyed into lots, containing 202.5 acres each in Baldwin and Wilkinson counties and 490 acres each in Wayne County. In the end, 4,580 land lots were surveyed. All square (or whole) lots, as well as all islands containing more than 100 acres, were included in the land lottery drawing. All fractions were held out and sold at public auction in 1806." Published by Genealogy Co., Decatur, GA, 2004, 278 pages, FHL book 975.8 R2gp.

***1805-1806 Tax Lists, Columbia County, Georgia* [Online Database],** indexed at the USGenWeb site for Columbia Co GA. See
**http://files.usgwarchives.net/ga/columbia/taxlists/.**

**1805-1914. *The Georgia Land Lottery Papers: Genealogical Data From the Loose Papers Filed in the Georgia Surveyor General Office Concerning the Lots Won in the State Land Lotteries and the People Who Won Them* [Printed Book],** compiled by Robert S. Davis, Jr. and Rev. Silas Emmett Lucas, Jr.. Includes index prepared by Jim Herman. Published by Southern Historical Press, Easley, SC, 1979, 323 pages, FHL book 975.8 R2d.

***1806 Tax List, Columbia County, Georgia* [Online Database],** indexed at the Genealogy Wise site under Columbia Co GA. See
**www.genealogywise.com/group/georgiarootdiggers/forum/topics/columbia-co-ga.**

**1807. *Index to 1807 Land Lottery of Georgia,* [Typescript],** from the originals at the Georgia Surveyor General's Office. Lists name of lottery participant, county, military district, county in which the person drew land. Lottery participants are listed alphabetically by surname. Typescript index filmed by the Genealogical Society of Utah, 1957, FHL film #159018.

**1807. *The Second or 1807 land lottery of Georgia* [Printed Book],** compiled by Silas Emmett Lucas, published by Southern Historical Press, Easley, SC, 1986, 168 pages, map, index. FHL book 975.8 R2Ls.

***1807 Georgia Land Lottery* [Online Database],** an index to the 10,150 "Fortunate Drawers" from the drawing of 1807. Indexed at the RootsWeb site for Georgia. See
**www.rootsweb.ancestry.com/~gatroup2/georgia_1807landlottery.htm.**

***1807 Tax List, Baldwin County, Georgia* [Online Database],** indexed at the USGenWeb site for Baldwin Co GA. See
**http://files.usgwarchives.net/ga/baldwin/tax/baldwintax1807.txt.**

**1807-1995. *Savannah, Georgia, Cemetery Burial Lot Cards* [Online Database],** indexed at the Ancestry.com website. Original data: Cemeteries Dept.

Burial and Lot Owner Cards from Bonaventure and Laurel Grove Cemeteries, through 1994. Microfilm. City of Savannah, Savannah, Georgia. Burial cards list each individual in the cemetery and are searchable. They can include the following details: name, residence, date of death, age, gender, place of death, undertaker's name, date of burial, and grave location. This database has 39,068 records. See
**https://search.ancestry.com/search/db.aspx?dbid=9024.**

**1808-1967.** ***Georgia Marriages*** **[Online Database],** indexed at the FamilySearch.org website. From FHL sources, this database has 991,456 records. See
**https://familysearch.org/search/collection/1674807.**

***1809 Tax Digest, Jackson County, Georgia*** **[Online Database],** indexed at the RootsWeb site for Jackson Co GA. See
**www.rootsweb.ancestry.com/~gajackso/1809taxdigest.htm**

***1809 Grand Jurors, Pulaski County, Georgia*** **[Online Database],** indexed at the USGenWeb site for Pulaski Co GA. See
**http://files.usgwarchives.net/ga/pulaski/history/other/gms73grandjur.txt.**

***1809-1910 Tax Lists, Morgan County, Georgia*** **[Online Database],** indexed at the USGenWeb site for Morgan Co GA. See
**www.usgwarchives.net/ga/morgan/taxlists.html.**

***1810 Tax Digest, Lincoln County, Georgia*** **[Online Database],** indexed at the USGenWeb site for Lincoln Co GA. See
**http://files.usgwarchives.net/ga/lincoln/taxlists/1810indx.txt.**

**1811-1819. Jones County, Georgia Tax Digest [Microfilm & Digital Capture],** copied by the Georgia State College and James B. Deireaux. Typescript at the GDAH, filmed by the Genealogical Society of Utah, 1946, FHL film #7139. To access the digital images, see the online FHL catalog page:
**www.familysearch.org/search/catalog/111412.**
- See also. Tax lists for each year are indexed online at the Jones Co GA USGenWeb site. See
**www.usgwarchives.net/ga/jones/taxlists.html.**

**1811-1820.** ***Georgia Marriages: Prepared From Extant Legal Records, and Published Sources*** **[Printed Book],** edited by Mary Bondurant Warren. Includes brides and grooms' indexes. Published by Heritage Papers, Danielsville, GA, 1988, 411 pages, FHL book 975.8 V2g.

**1813.** ***Baldwin County, Georgia, 1813 Tax List*** **[Printed Book],** compiled by Frances Ingmire, Signal Mountain, TN, Mountain Press, 1999, 20 pages. FHL book 975.8573 R4if.

***1813 Tax List, Putnam County, Georgia*** **[Online Database],** indexed at the USGenWeb site for Putnam Co GA. See
**http://files.usgwarchives.net/ga/putnam/taxlists/1813taxd.txt.**

**1815-1847.** See ***Reverted Lottery Land Records, 1815-1872, Register of Grants, 1834-1847*** **[Microfilm & Digital Capture],** from original records at the GDAH, Atlanta, GA. Filmed by the GDAH, 1967, 9 rolls, beginning with FHL film #511996 (Wilkinson and Baldwin counties, Book A 1815-1818). To access the digital images, see the online FHL catalog page:
**www.familysearch.org/search/catalog/74218.**

**1817-1976.** ***Georgia, Central Register of Convicts*** **[Online Database],** digitized and indexed at the Ancestry.com website. Source: Georgia Archives, Morrow, GA. This collection contains a list of convicts in the Georgia prison system. Included are name, file number, received date, sentence, crime, gender, age, release date, and county of conviction. Some registers even have columns for date of escape and recapture. Browse the images by date or view the document image for more information. This database has 293,155 records. See
**https://search.ancestry.com/search/db.aspx?dbid=3056.**

***1818-1853 Tax Digests, Twiggs County, Georgia*** **[Online Database],** indexed at the USGenWeb site for Twiggs Co GA. See
**http://files.usgwarchives.net/ga/twiggs/taxlists/twiggtax.txt.**

**1820.** ***Index to 1820 Land Lottery of Georgia*** **[Printed Book],** from originals of the Georgia Surveyor General's Office. Contains list of participants in the 1820 land lottery. Contents: v. 1. A-M -- v. 2. M-Z. See FHL book 975.8 R2iL 1820 v.1 and 975.8 R2iL 1820 v.2.

**1820.** ***The Third or 1820 Land Lottery of Georgia*** **[Printed Book],** compiled by the Rev. Silas Emmett

Lucas, Jr., published by Southern Historical Press, 1986, 374 pages, map, index. FHL book 975.8 R2La.

***1820 Land Lottery, Twiggs County, Georgia* [Online Database],** indexed at the RootsWeb site for Twiggs Co GA. See **www.rootsweb.ancestry.com/~gatwiggs/deedland/1820_landlottery.htm.**

**✓ 1820, 1827, 1832 NOTE:** Beginning with the third land lottery (1820), veterans of the Revolutionary War were given a preference of two additional draws, thus a married veteran would receive four draws. The soldier had to live in Georgia but could have served from any state/unit of the Revolutionary War. The preference for Rev War soldiers was repeated for the Fifth (1827) and Sixth (1832) Land Lotteries.

**1820, 1827, 1832. *Authentic List of All Land Lottery Grants Made to Veterans of the Revolutionary War by the State of Georgia* [Printed Book & Online Database],** compiled by Alex M. Hitz, former officer in charge, Surveyor-General Department, by authority of Ben W. Fortson, Jr., Secretary of State. This list includes 2,069 veterans in the Third (1820), Fifth (1827), and Sixth (1832) Land Lotteries. Published by the Georgia Secretary of State, 1966, 78 pages, FHL book 975.8 R2ha. Also on microfilm, filmed by the Genealogical Society of Utah, 1974, 1 roll, FHL film #924606. Note: A PDF version of this typescript is at the online FHL catalog page for this item. See **www.familysearch.org/search/catalog/2568128.**
- The typescript was also digitized, and OCR indexed at the Ancestry.com website, with the title, ***Land Grants to Georgia Revolutionary War Veterans.*** See **http://search.ancestry.com/search/db.aspx?dbid=7186.**

***1820, 1830 & 1840 Georgia Federal Censuses: Population Schedules* [Microfilm & Digital Capture],** from originals at the National Archives, Washington, DC. Filmed by the National Archives, 1938-1960, as a series of census years 1820-1840, 18 rolls total, beginning with FHL film #175765 (GA 1820: Appling, Baldwin, Emanuel, Habersham, Hall, Irwin, and Jasper Cos.). To access the digital images, see the online FHL catalog page: **www.familysearch.org/search/catalog/745486.**

**1820. *Index to United States Census of Georgia for 1820* [Printed Index & Online Database],** compiled by members of the Georgia Genealogical Society, Savannah, GA, published by Genealogical Publishing Co., Baltimore, MD, 1969, 167 pages, FHL book 975.8 X2p 1820 index. An online digital capture and OCR indexed version of this book is available at the Ancestry.com website. See **http://search.ancestry.com/search/db.aspx?dbid=48000.**

***1820 Georgia Census Index* [Printed Index],** edited by Ronald Vern Jackson, et al, published by Accelerated Indexing Systems, Bountiful, UT 1976, 76 pages, FHL book 975.8 Xp 1820.

***1820 Census, Rabun Co, Georgia (Reconstructed)* [Online Database],** one of the lost counties of the 1820 census for Georgia, a reconstructed name list can be found on the Internet at **http://freepages.genealogy.rootsweb.ancestry.com/~booleygirl/garabun/1820/1820.html.**

**1821. *Index to 1821 Land Lottery of Georgia* [Microfilm & Digital Capture],** from a typescript at the GA State Archives, filmed by the Genealogical Society of Utah, 1957, 1 roll, FHL film 159020. To access the digital images, see the online FHL catalog page: **www.familysearch.org/search/catalog/157539.**

**1821. *The Fourth or 1821 Land Lottery of Georgia* [Printed Book],** compiled by the Rev. Silas Emmett Lucas, Jr. Arranged alphabetically. From intro: "The fourth, or 1821 land Lottery opened the portion of Georgia between the Ocmulgee and Flint Rivers for settlement. This area, comprised of original Fayette, Henry, Monroe, Houston and Dolly counties, extended from today's Roswell on the north to Ashburn on the South. The tract was ceded to the United States by the Creek Nation of Indians on January 8, 1821 at the Treaty of Indian Springs. Approximately four months later, by Act of May 15, 1821, the drawing of the lottery was held at Milledgeville, the State Capital." Published by Southern Historical Press, Easley, SC, 1986, 2653 pages, FHL book 975.8 R2Lb.

***1821 Georgia Land Lottery for DeKalb County* [Online Database],** indexed at the DeKalb History Center, see **https://dekalbhistory.org.**

**1821-1827. *Indexes of the Various Counties to Land Grants and Lotteries* [Microfilm & Digital Capture],** from the originals at the Georgia State Archives, Atlanta, GA. Includes indexes to grants for the following counties: Irwin, Lee, Coweta, Hall, Gwinnett, Walton, Rabun, Habersham, Troup, Carroll,

and Muscogee; Baldwin, Wilkinson, and Wayne counties 1805; Carroll, Coweta 1827; Fayette, Henry, Monroe, Gwinnett, Habersham, Hall, Rabun, Walton County, Houston, and Irwin. Filmed by the GDAH, 1967, 3 rolls, beginning with FHL film #514007 (Index to grants, Irwin, Lee, Coweta, Hall, Gwinnett, Walton, Rabun, Habersham, Troup, Carroll, and Muscogee Counties. To access the digital images, see the online FHL catalog page:
**www.familysearch.org/search/catalog/74234**.

***1821-1903 Land Records, DeKalb County, Georgia* [Online Database],** District/Land Lots, Grantor Index, and Grantee Index, at the DeKalb History Center website (under construction). See
**www.dekalbhistory.org/dekalb_history_center_archives_online-resources.htm.**

**1823-1834. *First Tax Digests of Fayette County, Georgia* [Printed Book],** published by Ancestors Unlimited, Jonesboro, GA, 1988, 246 pages. Includes tax digest for the years 1823, 1824, 1827, 1829, 1831, 1832, 1833, and 1834. Includes index. FHL book 975.8426 R4f.

***1824 Tax List, Decatur County, Georgia* [Online Database],** indexed at the USGenWeb site for Decatur Co GA. See
**http://files.usgwarchives.net/ga/decatur/taxlists/1824tax.txt.**

**1824-1896. *Savannah, Georgia, Select Board of Health and Health Records, 1824-1864, 1887-1896* [Online Database],** digitized and indexed at the Ancestry.com website. Source: Research Library & Municipal Archives, Savannah, GA. Each index record includes: Name, Age, Birth year, Birth place, Death date, Burial date, and Burial place. The document image may have more information. This database has 28,803 records. See
**https://search.ancestry.com/search/db.aspx?dbid=9208.**

***1825 Tax Digest, Pike County, Georgia* [Online Database],** indexed at the AncestrallyChallenged.com site. See
**www.ancestrallychallenged.com/~gapike/1825TD-Daniel.htm.**

**1825. *Washington County, Georgia, 1825 Tax Digest* [Printed Book],** edited by Elizabeth Pritchard Newsom, Sandersville, GA, 1968, 168 pages, includes index, FHL book 975.867 R4n.

***1825 Tax List, Upson County, Georgia* [Online Database],** indexed at the USGenWeb site for Upson Co GA. See
**http://files.usgwarchives.net/ga/upson/taxlists/1825tax.txt.**

***1825 Tax Digest, Watkinsville, Oconee County, Georgia* [Online Database],** indexed at the USGenWeb site for Oconee Co GA. See
**http://files.usgwarchives.net/ga/oconee/newspapers/watkinsv2025nw.txt.**

***1825 Military Indian Wars, "Macon Volunteers," Bibb County, Georgia* [Online Database],** indexed at the USGenWeb site for Bibb Co GA. See
**http://files.usgwarchives.net/ga/bibb/military/indian/roster/maconvol.txt.**

**1826-1852. *Houston, Muscogee, and Talbot Counties, Georgia Marriages, 1826-1852* [Online Database],** indexed at the Ancestry.com website. This database has 2,999 records. See
**http://search.ancestry.com/search/db.aspx?dbid=3687.**

***1826-1917 Court Records, 1831-1858 Jury Lists, Rabun County, Georgia* [Online Database],** indexed at the USGenWeb site for Rabun Co GA. See
**www.usgwarchives.net/ga/rabun/court.html.**

**1827. *Reprint of Official Register of Land Lottery of Georgia, 1827* [Printed Book],** compiled and published by Martha Lou Houston, 1929, Walton-Forbes, Columbus, GA, original printed in 1927 by Grantland & Orme, Milledgeville, GA, 298 pages, map, index. See FHL book 975.8 R2h.

**1827. *Georgia Land Lottery, 1827* [Online Database],** indexed at the Ancestry.com website. Original data: State of Georgia. Recorder Office. Official Register of the Land Lottery of 1827. The 1827 lottery dispensed lots in Carroll, Coweta, Lee, Muscogee and Troup counties. This database is a list of the 26,332 "Fortunate Drawers." See
**http://search.ancestry.com/search/db.aspx?dbid=2072.**

***1827 Land Lottery Winners, Clay County, Georgia* [Online Database],** indexed names from the original Lee County list at the USGenWeb site for Clay Co GA:
**www.thegagenweb.com/gaclay/landlot/land_lottery_winners7th.htm.**

***1827 Georgia Land Lottery, Jasper County* [Online Database],** indexed at the RootsWeb site for Jasper Co GA. See
**www.rootsweb.ancestry.com/~gajasper/willsestatesetc/1827lottery.htm.**

***1827 Georgia Land Lottery, Montgomery County Residents, by Date of Drawing* [Online Database],** indexed at the USGenWeb site for Montgomery Co GA. See
**http://files.usgwarchives.net/ga/montgomery/deeds/1827lot.txt.**

***1827 Georgia Land Lottery, Putnam County Residents, Sorted by Last Name* [Online Database],** indexed at the USGenWeb site for Putnam Co GA:
**http://files.usgwarchives.net/ga/putnam/deeds/1827lot1.txt.**

***1827 Georgia Land Lottery, Upson County Residents, Sorted by Last Name* [Online Database],** indexed at the USGenWeb site for Upson Co GA. See
**http://files.usgwarchives.net/ga/upson/deeds/1827alpha.txt.**

***1827 Land Lottery, Twiggs County, Georgia* [Online Database],** indexed at the USGenWeb site for Twiggs Co GA. See
**http://files.usgwarchives.net/ga/twiggs/deeds/1827name.txt.**

***1827 Land Lottery, Lee County in Districts Which Became Randolph County* [Online Database],** indexed at the USGenWeb site for Randolph Co GA:
**http://files.usgwarchives.net/ga/randolph/deeds/1827surname.txt.**

**1827 & 1800. *State Census Reports at the Georgia Archives* [Microfilm].** These two years are indicated as state censuses, but are actually the 1827 Taliaferro County school census, and a county copy of the 1800 federal census for Oglethorpe County. Both of these county name lists were published in printed indexes. For the online page, ***State Census Reports at the Georgia Archives,*** see
**www.georgiaarchives.org/research/census_records.**

**1827, 1838 & 1845.** See ***Censuses for Georgia Counties: Taliaferro 1827, Lumpkin 1838, Chatham 1845* [Printed Index],** compiled and published by R. J. Taylor, Jr. Foundation, 1979, 57 pages, FHL book 975.8 X2c.

**1827-1955. *Georgia, Fulton County Records from the Atlanta History Center* [Online Database],** digitized at the FamilySearch.org website. Includes Atlanta city censuses and voter registrations and a necrology with transcribed obituaries, death records, and cemetery records from Fulton County. This database has 73,393 records. See
**https://familysearch.org/search/collection/2125026.**

**1827-1969. *Troup County, Georgia, Miscellaneous Papers* [Online Database],** digitized at the Ancestry.com website. Source: Georgia Archives, Morrow, GA. This is an image-only database containing 128 miscellaneous record books from Troup County, Georgia, They include: deeds and homestead records, registers of medical practitioners, court records, city directories, war records, bond books, and other types of records. The records vary widely in the types of details they contain, but they are typically good sources for names and dates. Use the *Browse the Collection* feature for the categories, most of the record books have an index at the beginning. See
**https://search.ancestry.com/search/db.aspx?dbid=2264.**

**1828 & 1836. *Washington County, Georgia, Index to 1828 Tax Digest, Index to 1836 Tax Digest, With Genealogical Gleanings* [Printed Book],** compiled by William R. Henry for the Central Georgia Genealogical Society, Warner Robins, GA, 1987, 55 pages, FHL book 975.8672 R4h index.

**1828-1978. *Georgia, Marriage Records from Select Counties* [Online Database],** indexed at the Ancestry.com website. Original data: County Marriage Records, 1828–1978. The Georgia Archives, Morrow, Georgia. This database contains marriages records from 45 Georgia counties. The list of included counties is available at the *Browse this Collection* menu. Marriage records were kept on a county level and required by law to be recorded beginning in 1805 (though compliance was not always the order of the day). Each index record includes: Name, Spouse, Bride's maiden name, Marriage date, and county. This database has 2,322,348 records. See
**https://search.ancestry.com/search/db.aspx?dbid=4766.**

**1828-1991. *Georgia, Church Vital Records* [Online Database],** digitized and indexed at FamilySearch.org. Includes records from Georgia locations (Brunswick, Savannah, Macon, and Richmond Co GA). To access the online database images, see the online FHL catalog page: **www.familysearch.org/search/catalog/2790246.**

**1830.** ***Index to the 1830 Census of Georgia*** **[Printed Index & Online Database],** compiled by Alvaretta Kenan Register, published by Genealogical Publishing Co., Baltimore, MD, 1974, 520 pages, FHL book 975.8 X2p 1830 index. An online digital capture and OCR indexed version of this book is online at the Ancestry.com website. See
**http://search.ancestry.com/search/db.aspx?dbid=48001.**

***1830 Georgia Census Index*** **[Printed Index],** edited by Ronald Vern Jackson, et al, published by Accelerated Indexing Systems, Bountiful, UT 1976, 127 pages, FHL book 975.8 X2p 1830.

**1830.** ***Index to Heads of Families 1830 Census of Georgia*** **[Printed Index[,** compiled and published by Delwyn Associates, Albany, GA, 1974, 323 pages, FHL book 975.8 Xp 1830 index.

**1832.** ***State of Georgia, Sixth or 1832 Land Lottery: Lists of Persons Eligible to Draw*** **[Printed Book],** compiled by Joel Dixon Wells; indexed by Mrs. Fred H. Hodges, Armchair Publications, Hampton, GA, 1983, 62 pages, index. See FHL book 975.86 R2w.

**1832.** ***The Cherokee Land Lottery of Georgia: Containing a Numerical List of the Names of the Fortunate Drawers in Said Lottery; With and Engraved Map of Each District*** **[Printed Book & Online Database],** by James F. Smith, a reprint of the original published by Harper & Bros., New York, 1838. Includes surname index. Reprinted by Southern Historical Press, 1998, 464 pages, FHL book 975.8 R2s. A digital capture and index of this database is at the Ancestry.com website and includes a listing of persons allotted land in 1832 from what was ceded Cherokee Land located in the northeastern part of the state. Over 18,500 parcels were distributed by lottery in that year. Each record of this collection contains the individual's name, residence, and county. Additionally, it provides the district and section number of the parcel of land. See
**https://search.ancestry.com/search/db.aspx?dbid=4242.**

**1832.** ***Georgia Cherokee Land Lottery, 1832*** **[Online Database],** indexed at the Ancestry.com website. Data was extracted from the original Harper & Bros. 1838 publication. This database has 18,505 records. See
**http://search.ancestry.com/search/db.aspx?dbid=4242.**

***1832 Fortunate Drawers of the 1832 Land Lottery, Putnam County, Georgia Residents*** **[Online Database],** indexed at the USGenWeb site for Putnam Co GA. See
**http://files.usgwarchives.net/ga/putnam/deeds/lott1832.txt.**

***1832 Georgia Land Lottery, Randolph County, Georgia*** **[Online Database],** indexed at the RootsWeb site for Randolph Co GA. See
**www.rootsweb.ancestry.com/~gatroup2/1832randolphgrants.htm.**

**1832.** ***Index, Cherokee "Gold" Land Lotter, 1832 (6th)*** [Printed Book, Microfilm & Digital Capture],4 vols: v. 1: A-D; v. 2: D-I; v. 3: I-P; and v. 4: P-Z. To access the digital images, see the online FHL catalog page:
**www.familysearch.org/search/catalog/176817.**

**1832.** ***The 1832 Gold Lottery of Georgia: Containing a List of the Fortunate Drawers in Said Lottery*** **[Printed Book],** compiled by S. Emmett Lucas, Jr., published by Southern Historical Press, 1988, 588 pages, FHL book 975.8 R2L.

***1832 Cherokee County Georgia Land Lottery aka Georgia 1832 Gold Land Lottery*** **[Online Database],** indexed at the RootsWeb site for Georgia:
**www.rootsweb.ancestry.com/~gatroup2/georgia_1832goldlottery.htm.**

***1832 Election, Cherokee County, Georgia*** **[Online Database],** indexed at the RootsWeb site for Cherokee Co GA. See
**www.rootsweb.ancestry.com/~gacherok/1832election.htm.**

**1832-2015.** ***Georgia, Houston County, Marriage Records*** **[Online Database],** digitized and indexed at the FamilySearch.org website. Source: Probate Judge, Houston, County, Georgia. Includes index and images of marriage records held at the Houston County Probate Court. This database has 119,277 records. See
**www.familysearch.org/search/collection/2748952.**

**1833.** ***The 1833 Land Lottery of Georgia: And Other Missing Names of Winners in the Georgia Land Lotteries*** **[Printed Book],** by Robert S. Davis, Jr. Includes name index. Published by Southern Historical Press, Greenville, SC, 1991, 51 pages, FHL book 975.8 A1 No. 96.

**1833-2012.** ***Floyd County, Georgia, Myrtle Hill Cemetery Index*** **[Online Database],** a database provided by the Myrtle Hill Cemetery, indexed at the

Ancestry.com website. Each index record includes: Name, Death date, Burial date, Burial place, Cemetery, and a link to the Myrtle Hill Cemetery website. This database has 6,484 records.
**https://search.ancestry.com/search/db.aspx?dbid=9261.**

***1834 Georgia State Census Reports at the University of Georgia* [Printed Articles].** There were state censuses authorized for the years 1831 and 1838, but there is no legislative record of a census authorized for 1834. However, since there are extant name lists for several counties, it seems the authorization issue is mute. A number of county name lists exist for 1834 which are often called state censuses but could actually be county censuses. Scattered census returns for the following years and counties are available at the Hargrett Library, Special Collections, University of Georgia. These records are from County Files, Telamon Cuyler Collection, and abstracted in various periodicals.

- **1834 Cass County [Printed Article].** 1834 name list in *Georgia Genealogical Magazine*, No. 90 (Fall 1983).
- **1834 Cobb County [Printed Article].** 1834 name lists published in *Alabama-Georgia Queries*, Vol. 5, No. 3 (May 1996); *Georgia Genealogical Magazine,* No. 89 (Summer 1983); and *Family Tree Newsletter*, No. 62 (Jul 1984).
- **1834 Lumpkin County [Printed Book].** See *1834 Census of Lumpkin County, Georgia,* compiled by Frances T. Ingmire, St. Louis, MO, 198?, 8 pages. An alphabetical listing of all heads of household from 1834 Lumpkin County, GA State Census. FHL book 975.8 A1 no. 80.
- **1834 Lumpkin County [Printed Article].** 1834 name list published in *Georgia Genealogical Magazine*, No. 87 (Winter 1983); and in *Georgia Genealogist*, No. 31 (Summer 1977).
- **1834 Cass/Bartow County [Printed Book].** See *1834 State census, Cass/Bartow Counties, Georgia*, name list compiled by MariLee Beatty Hageness, Anniston, AL, MLH Research, 1994. Bartow County was called Cass County from 1831-1961. See FHL book 975.8365 X2.
- **1834 Cherokee County [Printed Book].** See *1834 State Census Cherokee County, Georgia,* name list compiled by MariLee Beatty Hageness, Anniston, AL, MLH Research, 1995, 6 pages. FHL book 975.8253 X2h.
- **1834 Cass, Cherokee, Cobb, Forsyth, Gilmer, Lumpkin, Murray, and Union [Article],** county-wide 1834 name lists published in *Northwest Georgia Historical and Genealogical Society Quarterly,* Vol. 12, No. 2 - 4.

For the online page, ***State Census Reports at the Georgia Archives,*** see
**www.georgiaarchives.org/research/census_records.**

***1834 Cobb County Georgia Census* [Online Database],** indexed at the USGenWeb site for Cobb Co GA. See
**http://files.usgwarchives.net/ga/cobb/census/1834census.txt.**

***1834 Forsyth County Census* [Online Database],** originally indexed at the Donna Parrish site. For an archived database, see
**https://web.archive.org/web/20080705053051/http://donnaparrish.com/forsyth/census/1834/**

***1834 Lumpkin County Georgia Census* [Online Database],** indexed at the RootsWeb site for Lumpkin Co GA. See
**www.rootsweb.ancestry.com/~galumpki/census/1834Census.txt.**

***1834 Murray County Georgia Census* [Online Database],** indexed at the RootsWeb site for Murray Co GA. See **www.rootsweb.ancestry.com/~gamurray/.**

***1834 Union County Georgia Census* [Online Database],** indexed at the USGenWeb site for Union Co GA. See
**http://files.usgwarchives.net/ga/union/census/1830/1834cens.txt.**

***1834-1844 Tax Digests, Monroe County, Georgia* [Online Database],** indexed at the USGenWeb site for Monroe Co GA. See
**http://files.usgwarchives.net/ga/monroe/taxlists/monrotax.txt.**

***1835-1939 Vital Records, Randolph County, Georgia* [Online Database],** index to births, 1875-1877; marriages, 1835-1861; and deaths 1919-1930, at the USGenWeb site for Randolph Co GA. See
**www.usgwarchives.net/ga/randolph/vitals.html.**

**1835 Georgia Pension Roll [Online Database],** indexed at the USGenWeb site for Georgia. See
**http://files.usgwarchives.net/ga/military/revwar/pensions/1835pens.txt.**

***1836 Tax Digest, Rabun County, Georgia* [Online Database],** indexed at the USGenWeb site for Rabun Co GA. See
**http://files.usgwarchives.net/ga/rabun/taxlists/1836.txt.**

***1836-1843 Superior Court Records, DeKalb County* [Online Database],** indexed at the DeKalb History Center website (under construction). See
**www.dekalbhistory.org/dekalb_history_center_archives_online-resources.htm.**

**1837-2012.** ***Floyd County, Georgia, Eastview and Oakland Cemetery Index*** **[Online Database]**, a database provided by the Eastview and Oakland Cemetery, Rome, GA, with a shared index at the Ancestry.com website. Each index record includes name Death date, Burial date, Burial place, Cemetery, and a link to the Eastview and Oakland Cemetery website. This database has 17,700 records:
**https://search.ancestry.com/search/db.aspx?dbid=9262.**

***1838-1859 Georgia State Census Records*** **[Microfilm & Digital Capture].** Under this title, some of the county name lists of the GA 1838, 1845, 1852, and 1859 State Censuses were filmed by the Genealogical Society of Utah, 1957, 1961, 2 rolls, including:

- 1838 Laurens County, Film #7010 Item 4.
- 1838 Newton County, Film #7010 Item 5.
- 1838 Tattnall County, Film #7010 Item 6.
- 1845 Chatham County, Film #7010 Items 1-2.
- 1845 Forsyth County, Film #7010 Item 3.
- 1845 Warren County, Film #7010 Items 7-8.
- 1845 Dooly County, Film #7010 Item 9.
- 1852 Jasper County, Film #7010 Item 10.
- 1859 state census & 1879 tax list, Columbia County, Film #234619 (This roll not digitized yet).

To access the digital images, see the online FHL catalog page:
**www.familysearch.org/search/catalog/195750.**

***1838 Tax Digest for Macon County, Georgia*** **[Printed Book],** by Davine V. Campbell, published by McDowell Publications for the Central Georgia Genealogical Society, Warner Robins, GA, 1993, 51 pages. Includes index. FHL book 975.8513 R4c.

**"1838 State Census of Lumpkin County, Georgia" [Printed Article],** name list published in *Armchair Researcher*, Vol. 4, No. 1 (Summer 1983); and in *Georgia Genealogist,* No. 31 (Summer 1977), and No. 32 (Fall 1977).

**"1838 Georgia State Census, Paulding County" [Printed Article],** name list published in *Northwest Georgia Historical and Genealogical Society Quarterly,* Vol. 12, No. 4; and in *Georgia Genealogical Magazine,* No. 86 (Fall 1982).

**"1838 Georgia State Census, Murray County" [Printed Article],** name list published in *Georgia Genealogical Magazine,* No. 91 (Winter 1984).

**1838-1845.** ***Indexes to Seven State Census Reports for Counties in Georgia*** **[Printed Index],** compiled by Brigid S. Townsend. This book includes 1838 (Laurens, Lumpkin, Newton, Tattnall counties) and 1845 (Dooly, Forsyth, and Warren counties). published by R. J. Taylor, Jr., Foundation, Atlanta, GA, 1975, 152 pages, FHL book 975.8 X2pt.

**1840.** See ***Citizens of Georgia, 1840*** **[Printed Index],** compiled by Frances T. Ingmire, a name list extracted from the 1840 federal census schedules for Georgia, published by F. Ingmire, St. Louis, MO, c1985, 342 pages, FHL book 975.8 X2i 1840.

***1840 Index to Georgia Census*** **[Printed Index],** compiled by Barbara Woods and Eileen Sheffield, published by B. Wood & E. Sheffield, 1969, 380 pages, FHL book 975.8 X2w 1840 index.

***1840 Georgia Census Index*** **[Printed Index],** edited by Ronald Vern Jackson, et al, published by Accelerated Indexing Systems, Bountiful, UT 1977, 175 pages, FHL book 975.8 X22j 1840.

***1840-1845, 1858 Tax Digest, Crawford County, Georgia*** **[Microfilm & Digital Capture],** originals at the Court of Ordinary, filmed by the Genealogical Society of Utah, 1965. FHL film #415203. To access the digital images, see the online FHL catalog page:
**www.familysearch.org/search/catalog/234703.**

**1840-1908.** ***DeKalb County, Georgia, Marriage Index*** **[Online Database],** indexed at the Ancestry.com website. Source: DeKalb History Center, Decatur, GA. Each index record includes: Groom's name, Bride's name (including maiden name), Marriage date, and book and page number, used to locate original record. This database has 11,708 records. See
**https://search.ancestry.com/search/db.aspx?dbid=60549.**

***1842 Tax Digest, Carroll County, Georgia*** **[Online Database],** indexed at the RootsWeb site for Carroll Co GA. See
**www.rootsweb.ancestry.com/~gacarrol/1842.htm.**

***1844 Tax Digest, Sumter County, Georgia*** **[Online Database],** indexed at the USGenWeb site for Sumter Co GA. See
**http://files.usgwarchives.net/ga/sumter/taxlists/sumtax01.txt.**

***1844-1846 Poor School Records, Upson County, Georgia* [Online Database],** indexed at the USGenWeb Site for Upson Co GA. For 1844, see:
**http://files.usgwarchives.net/ga/upson/history/1844lista.txt.**
- For 1845, see:
**http://files.usgwarchives.net/ga/upson/history/schools/1845.txt.**
- For 1846, see:
**http://files.usgwarchives.net/ga/upson/history/schools/1846.txt.**

***1844-1883 Tax Digests, Schley County, Georgia* [Online Database],** indexed at the RootsWeb site for Schley Co GA. See
**www.rootsweb.ancestry.com/~gaschley/.**

***1845 Tax Digest, Baker County, Georgia* [Online Database],** indexed at the USGenWeb site for Baker Co GA. See
**http://files.usgwarchives.net/ga/baker/taxlists/1845tax.txt.**

***1845 Tax Roll, Forsyth County, Georgia* [Online Database],** indexed at the USGenWeb site for Forsyth Co GA. See
**http://files.usgwarchives.net/ga/forsyth/taxlists/1845tax.txt.**

***1845-1912 Tax Digests, Lumpkin County,* Georgia [Online Database],** indexed at the RootsWeb site for Lumpkin Co GA. See
**www.rootsweb.ancestry.com/~galumpki/taxes/.**

***1845 Revolutionary War Soldiers, Bibb County, Georgia* [Online Database],** indexed at the USGenWeb site for Bibb Co GA. See
**http://files.usgwarchives.net/ga/bibb/newspapers/gnw3georgiar.txt.**

**1847-1865. *Georgia, Civil War Correspondence* [Online Database],** digitized and indexed at Ancestry.com. Source: GA State Archives. This database contains correspondence received by Governor Joseph E. Brown, who served as governor of Georgia from 6 November 1857 to 17 June 1865, as well as some correspondence to his predecessors going back to 1847. This database has 8,735 records, see **www.ancestry.com/search/collections/1730.**

**1850. *Georgia, 1850 Federal Census: Population Schedules* [Microfilm & Digital Capture],** from the originals at the National Archives, Washington, DC. Filmed by the National Archives, 1964, 35 rolls, beginning with FHL film #7057 (Georgia: Appling, Baker, Baldwin, and Bibb Cos.). To access the digital images, see the online FHL catalog page:
**www.familysearch.org/search/catalog/744476.**

***1850 Georgia Census Index* [Printed Index],** edited by Ronald Vern Jackson, et al, published by Accelerated Indexing Systems, 1976, Bountiful, UT, 298 pages, FHL book 975.8 X2p 1850 index.

***1850 Georgia Census of Georgia Slave Owners* [Printed Index],** compiled by Jack F. Cox, names extracted from the 1850 Georgia Federal Census, (Slave Schedules), published by Genealogical Publishing Co., Baltimore, MD, 1999, 2001, 348 pages, FHL book 975.8 X2cj 1850.

***1850 Mortality Schedules, Georgia* [Printed Index],** edited by Ronald Vern Jackson, et al, published by Accelerated Indexing Systems, Bountiful, UT, 58 pages, FHL book 975.8X22m 1850.

***1850 Georgia Mortality Schedules* [Printed Index],** compiled by Aurora C. Shaw, published by A. Shaw, Jacksonville, FL , 1971, 43 pages, FHL book 975.8 X2sa 1850.

**1850-1870. *Federal Mortality Census Schedules and Related Indexes: Georgia: 1850; 1860; 1870; 1880* [Microfilm & Digital Capture],** filmed by the National Archives, 1962, 6 rolls, beginning with FHL film #422413 (1850 schedules and indexes, Appling-Wilkinson Cos.). To access the digital images, see the online FHL catalog page:
**www.familysearch.org/search/catalog/783149.**
- NOTE: The DAR Library in Washington, DC once held these records, but they were later returned to the National Archives. While in their custody, a name index was prepared to several census years, and the indexes were included in the National Archives filming.
- The indexes were also published separately, see ***Index, Georgia Mortality Records for the Years Ending June 1, 1850, 1860, 1870* [Printed Book],** compiler and publisher not noted, published 1949-1950 (perhaps by the DAR), FHL book 975.8 V23d. Also on microfilm, filmed by the Genealogical Society of Utah, 1972, 1 roll, FHL film #873729.

**1850-1880.** ***Non-population Census Schedules of Georgia*** **[Microfilm],** from the originals at the Duke University Library, Durham, NC. This series includes Georgia Agricultural Schedules, 1860, 1870, and 1880; Manufactures Schedules, 1880; and Social Status Schedules, 1860, 1870, and 1880. Before the originals were donated to the Duke University Library, they were microfilmed by the National Archives, Series T1137, 1988, 27 rolls, beginning with FHL film #1602477 (GA Agricultural Schedules, Appling – Crawford Cos.). For a complete list of roll numbers and contents of each roll, see the online FHL catalog page, this title: **www.familysearch.org/search/catalog/589484.**

**1850-1999.** ***Oakland Cemetery, Atlanta, Georgia*** **[Online Database],** indexed at the Ancestry.com website. This database contains over 50,000 burials. See **http://search.ancestry.com/search/db.aspx?dbid=4105.**

***1850 Georgia Commercial Tax Digest and Directory*** **[Microfiche],** from the original business directory book, publisher unnamed. Filmed by Research Publications, Woodbridge, CT, 1980-1984, 2 fiche, FHL fiche #6043926.

***1851 Tax List, Coweta County, Georgia*** **[Online Database].** indexed at the RootsWeb site for Coweta Co GA. For 1st District, see
**www.rootsweb.ancestry.com/~gacoweta/1851tax1.htm.**
-For 2nd District, see
**www.rootsweb.ancestry.com/~gacoweta/1851tax2.htm.**
- For 3rd District, see
**www.rootsweb.ancestry.com/~gacoweta/1851tax3.htm.**

**1851-1861.** ***A Decade of Georgia Information: Abstracts of Genealogical and Historical Interest From Selected Acts of the Georgia General Assembly*** **[Printed Book/Index].** Contents: Changing boundary lines; commissioners of incorporated towns; changes in election precincts, miscellaneous city and county acts, school and church trust records, lodges and societies, business records, estate executors, administrators, guardians; name changes, adoptions, heirs-at-law, marriages and divorces. Compiled and published by the Coweta County Genealogical Society, Newman, GA, 1999, 101 pages, FHL book 975.8 H2cc.

**1851-1900.** ***Georgia Marriages*** **[Online Database],** indexed at the Ancestry.com website. The marriage information in this series was taken from the original Liahona Research database, rom extractions of marriages at Georgia counties on microfilm at the FHL in Salt Lake City. Each entry includes groom, bride, marriage date, and county. An update to the 1739-1850 series, this database adds records from Meriwether, to those in the earlier series for Berrien, Catoosa, Coweta, Dodge, Dougherty, Early, Ebert, Fannin, Fayette, Gilmer, Henry, Houston, Irwin, Macon, Mitchell, Pierce, Pulaski, Schley, Telfair, Terrell, Thomas, Towns, Troup, Wayne, and Worth counties. See **http://search.ancestry.com/search/db.aspx?dbid=4453.**

***1852 Tax Digest for Macon County, Georgia*** **[Printed Book],** by Davine V. Campbell, published by McDowell Publications for the Central Georgia Genealogical Society, Warner Robins, GA, 1989, 55 pages. Includes index. FHL book 975.8513 R4c.

**1852.** ***Georgia Residents in the 1852 California State Census*** **[Printed Book],** compiled by MariLee Beatty Hageness, Anniston, AL, MLH Research, 1998, 63 pages. The 1852 CA State Census had a question, "Residence before coming to California," which identified most of the gold rush people from other states. See FHL book 975.8 X2h 1852.

***1852 Tax Digest, Taylor County, Georgia*** **[Online Database],** indexed at the USGenWeb site for Taylor Co GA. See
**http://files.usgwarchives.net/ga/taylor/taxlists/1852.txt.**

***1852-1866 Court Records, Taylor County, Georgia*** **[Online Database],** some deeds, estates, homestead exemptions/applications, and Court of Ordinary Minutes. Indexed at the RootsWeb site for Taylor Co Ga. See
**www.rootsweb.ancestry.com/~gataylo2/court/court.htm.**

**1852-1939.** ***Savannah, Georgia, Cemetery and Burial Records*** **[Online Database],** indexed at the Ancestry.com website. Original data: Research Library & Municipal Archives, City of Savannah, Georgia. Most interments are separated by cemetery or register type and year range. These records contain name, age, gender, date of death, cause of death, residence, and place of birth. This database has 50,369 records. See **https://search.ancestry.com/search/db.aspx?dbid=2770.**

**1852-1942.** ***Georgia, Chatham, Savannah, Laurel Grove Cemetery Record Keeper's Book (Colored)*** **[Online Database],** digitized and index at FamilySearch.org. This database has 16,516 records, see **www.familysearch.org/search/collection/3479704.**

***1853 Tax Digest, Carroll County, Georgia*** **[Online Database],** indexed at the RootsWeb site for Carroll Co GA. See
**www.rootsweb.ancestry.com/~gacarrol/1853.htm.**

***1853 Registered Voters, Carroll County, Georgia*** **[Online Database],** indexed at the USGenWeb site for Carroll Co GA. See
**http://files.usgwarchives.net/ga/carroll/history/voters/1853/register706gms.txt.**

***1853 Tax Lists, Spalding County, Georgia*** **[Online Database],** indexed at the USGenWeb site for Spaulding Co GA. See
**www.usgwarchives.net/ga/spalding/taxlists.html.**

**1854-1877.** ***Tax Digests and Compilation*** **[Microfilm & Digital Capture],** from the manuscript at the GDAH, Atlanta, GA. Filmed by the Genealogical Society of Utah, 1957, 13 rolls, beginning with FHL film #159195 (Appling, 1877; Burke, 1863; Berrien, 1867; Baldwin, 1871; Bryan, 1871; Bibb, 1871; Dade, 1864, 1871; Effingham, 1866, 1870-1872). To access the digital images, see the online FHL catalog page:
**www.familysearch.org/search/catalog/297323.**

**1855-1960.** ***Declarations of Intentions, Naturalizations, and Petitions*** **[Microfilm & Digital Capture],** from the originals at the National Archives, East Point, GA. The records are from the U.S. District Court (Alabama: Southern District, with jurisdiction over the states of Alabama, Florida, Georgia, Kentucky, Mississippi, North Carolina, South Carolina, and Tennessee. Most volumes are individually indexed. Filmed by the Genealogical Society of Utah, 1987-1997, 9 rolls, beginning with FHL film #1481392 (Declarations of Intention, 1890-1906). To access the digital images, see the online FHL catalog page:
**www.familysearch.org/search/catalog/393102.**

**1856-1917.** ***Savannah, Georgia, Voter Records, 1856-1896, 1901-1919*** **[Online Database],** indexed at the FamilySearch.org website. Original data: Voter Records. Savannah, Georgia, Research Library & Municipal Archives. This database contains voter registers, 1856-1896; and bond election records, 1901-197; for citizens of the city of Savannah, Georgia. Books are divided by year, district, and often by race. Information found in these records typically includes name, age, occupation, street address, race, and an original signature. This database has 73,646 records: **https://search.ancestry.com/search/db.aspx?dbid=2766.**

***1857 Tax List, Irwin/Telfair Counties, Georgia*** **[Online database],** indexed at the USGenWeb site for Irwin Co GA. See
**http://files.usgwarchives.net/ga/irwin/taxlists/gms47irwincou.txt.**

***1859 State Census, Heads of household, Columbia County, Georgia*** **[Printed Book],** compiled by the Gwinnett Historical Society, Lawrenceville, GA, published by MariLee Beatty Hageness, 1995, 127 pages. FHL book 975.8635 X2h.

**"1859 State Census of Columbia County, Georgia" [Printed Article],** Name list published in *Georgia Genealogical Society Quarterly,* Vol. 13, No. 4 (Winter 1977).

***1859 City Directory, Augusta, Georgia*** **[Online Database],** indexed at the RootsWeb site for Augusta, GA. Site no longer available. An original copy of the directory is at the Augusta Genealogical Society. See
**http://augustagensociety.org/.**

**1860.** See ***Georgia, 1860 Federal Census: Population Schedules*** **[Microfilm & Digital Capture],** from the originals (federal copies) at the National Archives, Washington, DC. Filmed twice by the National Archives, 1950 & 1967, 51 rolls total, beginning with FHL film #803111 (2nd filming, Appling, Baker, Baldwin, Banks, Berrien, and Bibb Counties). To access the digital images, see the online FHL catalog page: **www.familysearch.org/search/catalog/704739**.

***1860 Georgia Federal Census, Franklin, Irwin, and Terrell County (State Copy)*** **[Microfilm],** from the originals (state copies) at the Georgia State Archives. Contains population and slave schedules for three counties only. Filmed by the Genealogical Society of Utah, 1946, 2 rolls, FHL film #7016 (Franklin and

Irwin counties), and FHL film #7021 (Terrell County). To see if this microfilm has been digitized yet, see the FHL catalog page:
**www.familysearch.org/search/catalog/196782.**

**1860.** ***An Index for the 1860 Federal Census of Georgia*** **[Printed Index],** compiled by Aris Acord, Martha S. Anderson, & others, published by Family Tree, LaGrange, GA, 19986, 1,024 pages, FHL book 975.8 X22ac 1860.

***1860 Georgia Census Index*** **[Printed Index],** edited by Ronald Vern Jackson, et al, published by Accelerated Indexing Systems, 1986, North Salt Lake, UT, 298 pages, FHL book 975.8 X2p 1850 index.

***1860 Mortality Schedules, Georgia*** **[Printed Index],** edited by Ronald Vern Jackson, et al, published by Accelerated Indexing Systems, North Salt Lake, UT, 1986, 70 pages, FHL book 975.8X2ja 1860.

***1860 Tax Digest, Taylor County, Georgia*** **[Online Database],** indexed at the USGenWeb site for Taylor Co GA. See
**http://files.usgwarchives.net/ga/taylor/taxlists/1860.txt.**

**1860-1864.** ***Georgia, Civil War Muster Rolls*** **[Online Database],** indexed at the Ancestry.com website. Original data: *Muster Rolls—Men Subject to Military Duty from 1860–1864*. Georgia Archives, Morrow, GA. In answer to Georgia's governor's call for troops to defend both Georgia and the Confederate States of America, men formed companies, battalions, and other military units in counties throughout the state. This database includes muster rolls for these units, lists of men subject to militia duty (men ages 18–45), lists of men over 45, correspondence regarding these lists, and other miscellaneous records related to military enrollment. Most were created on a county level. Some documents list only a name, county, and possibly a unit. Others may provide rank, enlistment date, age, marital status, even height. This database has 56,912 records:
**https://search.ancestry.com/search/db.aspx?dbid=2371.**

***1861 Tax List, Rabun County, Georgia*** **[Online Database],** indexed at the USGenWeb site for Rabun Co GA. See
**http://files.usgwarchives.net/ga/rabun/taxlists/1861.txt.**

***1861 City Directory, Augusta, Georgia*** **[Online Database],** indexed at the USGenWeb site for Richmond Co GA. See
**http://files.usgwarchives.net/ga/richmond/directories/business/1861/1861augu591gms.txt.**

**1861-1865.** ***Index to Compiled Service Records of Confederate Soldiers Who Served in Organizations from the State of Georgia*** **[Microfilm & Digital Capture],** from the originals at the National Archives, Washington, DC. Filmed by the National Archives, 1955, Series M226, 67 rolls, beginning with FHL film #821700 (A – All). To access the digital images, see the online FHL catalog page:
**www.familysearch.org/search/catalog/311091.**

**1861-1865.** ***Georgia Civil War Service Records of Confederate Soldiers*** **[Online Database],** digitized and indexed at the FamilySearch.org website. The records include a jacket-envelope for each soldier, labeled with his name, rank, and unit in which he served. The jacket typically contains card abstracts of entries relating to the soldier as found in original muster rolls, returns, rosters, payrolls, appointment books, hospital registers, Union prison registers and rolls, parole rolls, inspection reports; and the originals of any papers relating solely to the particular soldier. Each military unit is arranged alphabetically by the soldier's surname. Taken from the National Archives microfilm, series M266. Index courtesy of Fold3. This database has 1,776,643 records. See
**https://familysearch.org/search/collection/1932370.**

**1861-1865.** ***Index to Compiled Service Records of Volunteer Union Soldiers Who Served in Organizations from the State of Georgia*** **[Microfilm],** from the originals at the National Archives, Washington, DC. Filmed by the National Archives, 1955, Series M385, 1 rolls, FHL film #881394.

**1861-1865.** ***Index to Georgia Civil War Confederate Pension Files*** **[Printed Index],** compiled by Virgil D. White, published by National Historical, Waynesboro, TN, 1996, 1,063 pages, FHL book 975.8 M22w.

**1861-1865.** ***Index to Roster of Confederate Soldiers of Georgia, 1861-1865*** **[Printed Index],** an 80,000-name index to Roster of the Confederate Soldiers of Georgia, 1861-1865, six volumes, by Lillian Henderson, published by Longino & Porter, Hapeville, GA, 1959-1964, 6 vols., FHL book 975.8 M22h v.1-v.6. The index was compiled for the Lake Blackshear Regional Library, Americus, GA, by Juanita S. Brightwell, Eunice S. Lee, Elsie C. Fulghum. Originally published

By the Lake Blackshear Regional Library, 1964. Reprinted 1982 by the Reprint Co., Spartanburg, SC, 513 pages, FHL book 975.8 M22h 1982 index.

**1861-1865.** ***Georgia, Civil War Service Records of Union Soldiers*** **[Online Database],** digitized and indexed at the FamilySearch.org website. This is a collection of Union service records of soldiers who served in the First Battalion of Georgia Infantry. The records include a jacket-envelope for each soldier, labeled with his name, his rank, and the unit in which he served. The jacket-envelope typically contains card abstracts of entries relating to the soldier as found in original muster rolls, returns, rosters, payrolls, appointment books, hospital registers, prison registers and rolls, parole rolls, inspection reports; and the originals of any papers relating solely to the particular soldier. For each military unit the service records are arranged alphabetically by the soldier's surname. The Military Unit field may also display the surname range (A-G) as found on the microfilm. This collection is a part of RG 94, Records of the Adjutant General's Office, 1780's-1917 and is National Archive Microfilm Publication M403. Index courtesy of Fold3.This database has 1,613 records. See
**https://familysearch.org/search/collection/1932397.**

**1861-1865.** ***Georgia, Civil War Correspondence*** **[Online Database],** digitized and indexed at Ancestry.com. Source: GA State Archives. This database contains incoming and outgoing correspondence from the Adjutant General of Georgia's office. This database has 4,719 records, see
**www.ancestry.com/search/collections/2051.**

***1861-1945 Military Records, Taylor County, Georgia*** **[Online Database],** Civil War, Spanish American War, World War I, and World War II soldiers from Taylor County. Indexed at the RootsWeb site for Taylor Co GA. See
**www.rootsweb.ancestry.com/~gataylo2/war/war.htm.**

***1861-1933 Military Records, Troup County, Georgia*** **[Online Database],** indexed at the USGenWeb site for Troup Co GA. See
**www.usgwarchives.net/ga/troup/military.html**.

**1862-1865.** ***Georgia, Andersonville Prison Records*** **[Online Database],** digitized at the FamilySearch.org website. Source: National Archives microfilm M1303.. Includes images of records of Federal (Union) prisoners of war confined at Andersonville prison 1864-1865. The collection consists of prison hospital admissions, death and burial records, registers of prison departures, prisoner claims for reimbursements, and consolidated monthly reports. This database has 4,184 images. Browse through the images, organized by document type: Claims and reports, Deaths and burials, Departures, and Hospital. See
**https://familysearch.org/search/collection/2019835.**

**1864-1940.** ***Militia Enrollment Lists; Re-Organizing the Militia, ca 1864; Pension Enrollments Lists*** **[Microfilm & Digital Capture],** from the originals at the GDAH, Atlanta, GA. Militia lists arranged alphabetically by county. Included with the county lists are typed copies of the enrollment lists prepared by the Georgia Pensions and Records Department between 1920 and 1940. Filmed by the Genealogical Society of Utah, 1963, 7 rolls, beginning with FHL film #351787 (Appling – Carlton Co.). To access the digital images, see the online FHL catalog page:
**www.familysearch.org/search/catalog/231660.**

***1864 Census For Re-Organizing the Georgia Militia*** **[Printed Book & Online Database],** compiled by Nancy J. Cornell, published by Genealogical Publishing Co. Inc., Baltimore, 2000, 843 pages. From preface: "From originals at GDAH, this is an extraction and index of a special statewide census during the Civil War of all white males between the ages of 16 and 60 who were not at the time in the service of the Confederate States of America, it is a list of some 42,000 men; name, age, occupation, place of birth, and reason (if any) for his exemption from service. See FHL book 975.8 X22. An online version of this book was digitized and indexed at the Ancestry.com site. See
**http://search.ancestry.com/search/db.aspx?dbid=3007**.

**1865-1866.** ***Internal Revenue Assessment Lists for Georgia*** **[Microfilm & Digital Capture],** from the originals at the National Archives, Central Plains, Kansas City, MO. Contents: DISTRICT 1 contains Appling, Berrien, Brooks, Bryan, Bulloch, Camden, Charlton, Chatham, Clinch, Coffee, Colquitt, Echols, Effingham, Emanuel, Glynn, Irwin, Johnson, Laurens, Liberty, Lowndes, McIntosh, Montgomery, Pierce, Tattnall, Telfair, Thomas, Ware, Wayne, and Wilcox counties. DISTRICT 2 contains Baker, Bibb, Butts, Calhoun, Chattahoochee, Clay, Crawford, Decatur,

Dooly, Dougherty, Early, Harris, Houston, Lee, Macon, Marion, Miller, Mitchell, Monroe, Muscogee, Pike, Pulaski, Quitman, Randolph, Schley [sic], Spalding, Stewart, Sumter, Talbot, Taylor, Terrell, Upson, Webster, and Worth counties. DISTRICT 3 contains Baldwin, Burke, Columbia, Elbert, Glascock, Greene, Hancock, Jasper, Jefferson, Jones, Lincoln, Morgan, Newton, Oglethorpe, Putnam, Richmond, Screven, Taliaferro, Twiggs, Warren, Washington, Wilkes, and Wilkinson counties. DISTRICT 4 contains Banks, Campbell, Carroll, Cass, Catoosa, Chattooga, Cherokee, Clarke, Clayton, Cobb, Coweta, Dade, Dawson, De Kalb, Fannin, Fayette, Floyd, Forsyth, Franklin, Fulton, Gilmer, Gordon, Gwinnett, Habersham, Hall, Haralson, Hart, heard, Henry, Jackson, Lumpkin, Madison, Meriwether, Milton, Murray, Paulding, Pickens, Polk, Rabun, Towns, Troup, Union, Walker Walton, White, Whitfield. Filmed by the National Archives, 1988, Series M762, 8 rolls, beginning with FHL film #1578459 (District 1: Annual lists 1865-1866, et al). To access the digital images, see the online FHL catalog page: **www.familysearch.org/search/catalog/577895.**

**1865-1872.** ***Georgia, Freedmen's Bureau Field Office Records*** **[Online Database],** indexed at the FamilySearch.org website. Source: National Archives microfilm M1903. This is an image-only database. The Bureau of Refugees, Freedmen, and Abandoned Lands (often called the Freedmen's Bureau) was created in 1865 at the end of the American Civil War to supervise relief efforts including education, health care, food and clothing, refugee camps, legalization of marriages, employment, labor contracts, and securing back pay, bounty payments and pensions. These records include letters and endorsements sent and received, account books, applications for rations, applications for relief, court records, labor contracts, registers of bounty claimants, registers of complaints, registers of contracts, registers of disbursements, registers of freedmen issued rations, registers of patients, reports, rosters of officers and employees, special and general orders and circulars received, special orders and circulars issued, records relating to claims, court trials, property restoration, and homesteads. This database has 108,788 images. Browse through the images, organized by Bureau office, Field office, and Contents of each roll of film. See **www.familysearch.org/search/collection/2331267.**

**1866-2000.** ***Georgia, Columbus, Linwood and Porterdale Colored Cemeteries, Interment Records*** **[Online Database].** Digitized and indexed at FamilySearch.org. The Porterdale, also known as Old Porterdale, O.P., or West Porterdale is a historically black cemetery dating back to the early 1800s. East Porterdale appears to have been used beginning in 1946 and is also historically black. This database has 21,489 records, see **www.familysearch.org/search/collection/3491475.**

**1866-2010.** ***Marrietta National Cemetery, Marietta, Georgia*** **[Online Database],** digitized and indexed at the Ancestry.com website. The database contains digital images of over 15,000 gravestones: **http://search.ancestry.com/search/db.aspx?dbid=2305.**

**1866-1867.** ***Barnwell's Atlanta City Directory*** **[Online Database],** digitized and OCR indexed at the Ancestry.com website. Includes City officials, Strangers (hotel guests) Firemen, Church lists, Masonic lists, and Odd-fellows lists. This database has 285 pages. See **https://search.ancestry.com/search/db.aspx?dbid=22721.**

**1867.** ***Berrien County, Georgia, 1867 Tax Digest*** **[Printed Book],** compiled by Myrtie Lou Griffin, et al, published by the Huxford Genealogical Society, Homerville, GA, 19??. FHL book 975.8862 R4b.

***1867 Voter Registration List, Franklin District, Heard County, Georgia*** **[Online Database],** indexed at the USGenWeb site for Heard Co GA. See **http://files.usgwarchives.net/ga/heard/history/1867voters.txt.**

***1867 City Directory, Augusta, Georgia*** **[Online Database],** indexed at the USGenWeb site for Richmond Co GA. See **http://files.usgwarchives.net/ga/richmond/directories/business/1867/1867augu592gms.txt.**

**1867-1868.** ***Reconstruction Registration Oath Book*** **[Microfilm & Digital Capture],** from the originals at the GDAH, Atlanta, GA. Filmed by the GDAH, 1991, 23 rolls, beginning with FHL film #1843848 (Oath Books, Bryan Co - Chatham Co). To access the digital images, see the online FHL catalog page: **www.familysearch.org/search/catalog/76983.**

- For an online version of this database, see ***Georgia, Reconstruction Registration Oath Books, 1867-1868*** **[Online Database],** indexed at the FamilySearch.org website. This collection consists of Registration Oath Books created by U.S. military officials stationed in Georgia following the Civil War. Registers typically contain each voters name, county of residence, date of registration, race, and an oath of allegiance to the United States. The oath of allegiance was required in order to register. Registered voters would then elect delegates to the state's constitutional convention. The oath books are located at the Georgia Archives. This database has 174,149 records. See
**www.familysearch.org/search/collection/2739725.**

**1867-1869. *Georgia, Returns of Qualified Voters and Reconstruction Oath Books* [Online Database],** digitized and indexed at the Ancestry.com website. Source: Georgia Archives, Morrow, GA. The Reconstruction Acts of 1867 required Southern states to ratify the 14th Amendment, draft new state constitutions, and register voters, both black and white. In order to vote, men had to swear an oath of allegiance to the United States, and some were disqualified for their participation in Confederate government posts. This database contains books recording those oaths of allegiance and returns listing qualified voters registered in Georgia in 1867. It includes both black and white citizens. The returns provide: date of registration, name, number and page number of the county's registration oath book with the voter's oath of allegiance, race, time of residence in state, county, and precinct within a year, nativity by state or county, and remarks. The document image may have more information. This database has 390,373 records. See
**https://search.ancestry.com/search/db.aspx?dbid=1857.**

**1867-1868. Index to Georgia's 1867-1868 Returns of Qualified Voters and Registration Oath Books, White [Printed Index],** compiled by John David Brandenburg and Rita Brinkley Worthy, published by J.D. Brandenburg, Atlanta, GA, 1995, 532 pages, FHL book 975.8 N42

***1869 Georgia Military Roster Index*** **[Microfilm & Digital Capture],** from originals at the GDAH, filmed 1965, 1 roll, FHL film #465190. To access the digital images, see the online FHL catalog page:
**www.familysearch.org/search/catalog/237671.**

***1869-1874 Tax Digests, City of Americus, Sumter County, Georgia*** **[Online Database],** indexed at the SumterCountyHistory.com website. See
**www.sumtercountyhistory.com/tax/1869_1874taxdigest.htm.**

**1870. *Georgia, 1870 Federal Census: Population Schedules* [Microfilm & Digital Capture],** from the originals (federal copies) at the National Archives, Washington, DC. Filmed twice by the National Archives, 1962 & 1968, 66 rolls total, beginning with FHL film #545633 (2nd filming, Appling, Baker, Baldwin, and Banks Counties). To access the digital images, see the online FHL catalog page:
**www.familysearch.org/search/catalog/698893.**

**1870. *Census Returns of the Federal 1870 Census for Georgia* [Microfilm],** from the originals (state copies) at the Georgia State Archives. Contains population and Mortality schedules for 48 counties (less than half the total counties in 1870). Filmed by the Genealogical Society of Utah, 1946, 12 rolls, beginning with FHL film #7016 (Cherokee, Clarke, Clay, Clayton counties). To see if this microfilm has been digitized yet, see the FHL catalog page:
**www.familysearch.org/search/catalog/196782.**

**1870. *Georgia 1870 Census Index* [Printed Index],** edited by Bradley W. Steuart, published by Precision Indexing, Bountiful, UT, 1991, 3 vols., FHL book 975.8 X22g 1870, v.1: A-F, v.2: G-M, v.3: N-Z.

**1870-1960. *Georgia, County Delayed Birth and Death Records* [Online Database],** digitized and indexed at FamilySearch.org, for several Georgia counties. This database has 101,857 records, see
**www.familysearch.org/search/collection/3438747.**

**1871-1880. *Tax Digest of Dodge County, Georgia* [Microfilm & Digital Capture],** from originals at the Court of Ordinary, Dodge County, Georgia. Filmed by the Genealogical Society of Utah, 1966. FHL film #470171. To access the digital images, see the online FHL catalog page:
**www.familysearch.org/search/catalog/230302.**

***1875 Tax Digest, Douglas County, Georgia*** **[Online Database],** indexed at the RootsWeb site for Douglas Co GA. See
**www.rootsweb.ancestry.com/~gadougla/Douglas_Tax_1875.htm.**

**1875-1915.** ***Oconee Court, Georgia Probate Court Birth Certificates*** **[Online Database],** indexed at the Ancestry.com website. Depending on the form, birth records may include a name, sex, date of birth, place of birth, length of pregnancy; mother's name, race, birthplace, address, age a time of birth, birth date, marital status, and occupation; number of other children born to mother, father's name, race, birthplace, age at time of birth, birthdate, occupation; complications related to birth or pregnancy. This database has 11,894 records. See **http://search.ancestry.com/search/db.aspx?dbid=2156.**

**1875-2010.** ***Oconee Court, Georgia Probate Marriage Records*** **[Online Database],** indexed at the Ancestry.com website. Each record contains the bride's name, groom's name, license date, marriage date, marriage place, race, official. This database has 24,669 records. See **http://search.ancestry.com/search/db.aspx?dbid=2463.**

**1879-1920.** ***Confederate Pension Rolls (Georgia)*** **[Microfilm & Digital Capture],** from the original records at the GDAH in Atlanta, GA. Confederate soldiers received pensions for military service beginning in 1879. The law establishing pension payment was changed in 1891 to include widows of soldiers. There are cards in this record for the witnesses of these soldiers and widows attesting to the service of each soldier. The arrangement is alphabetical by the name of the pensioner and included on the card are notations concerning the county of residence, unit designation, and husband's name in the case of widow cards. Filmed by the GDAH, 1963, 634 rolls, beginning with FHL film #315678 (Appling County, Abbott, J. H. – Johnson, Obadiah). To access the digital images, see the online FHL catalog page: **www.familysearch.org/search/catalog/283808.**

**1879-1960.** ***Georgia, Confederate Pension Applications*** **[Online Database],** digitized and indexed at the Ancestry.com website. An index contains the name of applicant (soldier or widow), the year of application, and the type of application (indigent soldier, indigent widow, indigent colored, widow, soldier, or colored). The index items are linked to the actual application image where there will be additional information. The images are arranged by county of application, then by surname of the pensioner. See **http://search.ancestry.com/search/db.aspx?dbid=1560.**

**1880.** ***Georgia, Federal Census: Soundex and Population Schedules*** **[Microfilm & Digital Capture],** from the originals (federal copies) at the National Archives, Washington, DC. After microfilming the National Archives transferred the original 1880 population schedules to local repositories. The 1880 was the only census handled in this way. Georgia's original 1880 population schedules, contained in 26 bound volumes, were donated to the Georgia Department of Archives and History (GDAH) in Atlanta, GA. Filmed by the National Archives, 126 rolls, beginning with FHL film #445553 (Soundex: A000-A352); and FHL film #1254133 (Population Schedules: Appling, Baker, Baldwin, Banks, and Bartow counties). To access the digital images, see the online FHL catalog page: **www.familysearch.org/search/catalog/670387.**

***1880 Short Form, Georgia Federal Census, Crawford and Franklin Counties*** **[Microfilm],** from the originals (county copies) at the Georgia State Archives. FHL catalog title: *Lists of Persons Enumerated in the 1880 Federal Census for Georgia.* Contains 1880 Short Forms for two counties (Crawford and Franklin) only. For the 1880 census year only, the Census Bureau asked each county to make a copy of their population schedules in the form of an alphabetized list, showing just a person's name, age, sex, and color. The lists became known as "Short Forms," and were retained at the county courthouse for public inspection. The original full-size schedules were sent to the Census Office in Washington DC. Filmed by the Genealogical Society of Utah, 1946, 2 rolls, FHL film #7013 (Crawford County); and FHL film #7016 (Franklin County). To see if this microfilm has been digitized yet, see the FHL catalog page: **www.familysearch.org/search/catalog/196827.**

***1880 Mortality Schedule and Index of Georgia*** **[Microfilm],** from a typescript compiled by Robert Ellington Torbert, published by R.E. Torbert, Lakewood, CO, 1987, 260 pages. Filmed by the Genealogical Society of Utah, 1987, 2 rolls, FHL film #1528064 (part 1), and FHL film #1689598 (Part 2). To see if this microfilm has been digitized yet, see the FHL catalog page: **www.familysearch.org/search/catalog/9398.**

**1880.** ***List of Prisoners in Penitentiary, Convict Camps, Chain Gangs and Jails in Georgia: Including a List of Guards, Jailers, Sheriffs and Others, from***

***1880 Federal Census Records* [Printed Book & Digital Version],** compiled by Arthur Ray Rowland, published by RR Books, North Augusta, GA, 2007, 42 pages, FHL book 975.8 X22r 1880. To access the digital version, see the online FHL catalog page: **www.familysearch.org/search/catalog/1452769.**

**1880-1922. *Atlanta, Georgia, U.S. Penitentiary, Prisoner Index* [Online Database],** indexed at the Ancestry.com website. This data collection is an index to case files of inmates held at the Atlanta U.S. Federal Penitentiary from approximately 1902 to 1922. The Atlanta penitentiary opened in 1902. However, the case files include documentation of prisoners incarcerated at other federal prisons as early as 1880. The purpose of the case files was to document an inmate's time in prison. The files were compiled between 1902 and 1921 and include information such as: Name of inmate (full name and other aliases), Inmate number, Age at time of sentencing, Race, Date incarcerated, Release dates, Place of conviction, Crime, Sentence and fine amounts, Dispensation (i.e. "served full sentence," "pardoned," "paroled," "deceased," etc.), Physical description, Birthplace, Level of education, Citizenship status, Info related to the inmate's time in prison (i.e. violations, medical treatments, copies of letters sent or received, work assignments, etc.). Many case files also include a fingerprint card and a mug shot. See
**http://search.ancestry.com/search/db.aspx?dbid=1632.**

***1882-1883 City Directory of Barnesville, Lamar County, Georgia* [Online Database],** indexed at the USGenWeb site for Lamar Co GA. See
**http://files.usgwarchives.net/ga/lamar/history/citydir.txt.**

***1883 Military Pensions* [Online Database],** indexed by county at various USGenWeb sites. To see the statewide files available or see the resources available for one of Georgia's 159 counties, visit the Georgia USGenWeb Archives Project. See
**www.usgwarchives.net/ga/gafiles.htm.**

**1885. *Berrien County, Georgia, 1885 Tax Digest* [Printed Book],** publication information unknown, 150 pages. FHL book 975.8862 R49b.

**1888-1891. *Savannah, Georgia Directories* [Online Database],** indexed at the Ancestry.com website. This database is a transcription of city directories originally published from 1888-1891. In addition to providing the residents' names, it provides their addresses and occupational information. The database includes more than 72,200 names, mostly heads of household. See
**http://search.ancestry.com/search/db.aspx?dbid=4487.**

**1889-1890. *Atlanta, Georgia Directories* [Online Database],** indexed at the Ancestry.com website. This database is a transcription of two city directories originally published in 1889 and 1890. Includes a name, address, and occupation. This database has 53,239 names, mostly heads of households. See
**http://search.ancestry.com/search/db.aspx?dbid=4527.**

**1889-1897. *Clinch County, Georgia, Tax Digest* [Printed Book],** published by the Huxford Genealogical Society, Homerville, GA, 19??, 3 vols. Contents: Vol. 1. Wild land or unimproved land -- v. 2. Real estate and personal estate – v. 3. Real estate and personal estate. FHL book 975.8812 R4c v.1-3.

**1890. *Gwinnett County, Georgia 1890 Tax Digest with Land Lots: Substitute For Lost 1890 Federal Census* [Printed Book],** compiled by Terry Edward Pyatt Manning, published by the Gwinnett Historical Society, Lawrenceville, GA, 127 pages. FHL book 975.8223.

***1890 Tax Digest of Coweta County, Georgia: A Partial 1890 Census Substitute* [Printed Book],** compiled by Mrs. Artie May Jones Storey and Elizabeth Faith Storey for Coweta County Genealogical Society, Inc., Newnan, Ga., 1992. Includes index. 141 pages. FHL book 975.8423 R4.

***1890 City Directory, Brunswick, Georgia* [Online Database],** originally indexed at the distant cousin.com site. For an archived database, see
**https://web.archive.org/web/20160325193620/http://distantcousin.com/Directories/GA/Brunswick/1890/.**

**1890. *Census Returns of Washington County Taken by the County, 1890* [Microfilm & Digital Capture].** The 1962 film crew were a bit mistaken with the title – this census name list is actually the official "Short Form" of the 1890 federal census population schedules. (Confirmation: *Bureau of the Census* was printed on the forms that were used). A Short Form copy was offered to any county in the U.S. if they would pay the cost to make the copy. Only two counties in the U.S. had a copy made (Washington Co GA and Ascension

Parish LA). They are called Short Forms because the information was much less than the full schedules: Name, Race, Age, Sex, and Place of Residence. The full schedules for Washington Co GA (and all other counties of the U.S.) were mostly destroyed by fire in 1921. The Short Form originals are still located at the Washington County Courthouse, Sandersville, GA. They are on 3 rolls of microfilm, FHL film #295947-295949. To access the digital images, see the online FHL catalog page:
**www.familysearch.org/search/catalog/287607.**

***1890 Federal Census, Court of Ordinary, Washington County, Georgia: Population Schedule* [Printed Book],** compiled by William R. Henry, published by the Central Georgia Genealogical Society, Warner Robins, GA, 1994, 262 pages. FHL book 975.8672 X28h.

***1890 United States Federal Census Fragment* [Online Database],** indexed at the Ancestry.com website. Source: National Archives microfilm M407. These records were extracted from the remaining population schedules for the 1890 Federal Census, which was mostly destroyed by a fire at the Commerce Department in Washington, DC on 10 January 1921. The surviving fragments consists of 1,233 pages or pieces, including enumerations for Alabama, the District of Columbia, Georgia, Illinois, Minnesota, New Jersey, New York, North Carolina, Ohio, South Dakota, and Texas. The records of only 6,160 of the 62,979,766 people enumerated survived the fire. The only Georgia pages that survived came from Columbus, Muscogee County. The original 1890 census enumerated people differently than ever before that time. Each family was enumerated on a separate sheet of paper. 1890 was the only year this was done. This database has 6,304 records. See
**https://search.ancestry.com/search/db.aspx?dbid=5445.**

***1892 List of Registered Voters, Wayne County, Georgia* [Online Database],** indexed at the USGenWeb site for Wayne Co GA. See
**http://files.usgwarchives.net/ga/wayne/history/voter1892.txt.**

***1892-1895 Tax Digests, Haralson County, Georgia* [Online Database],** indexed at the USGenWeb site for Haralson Co GA. See
**www.usgwarchives.net/ga/haralson/taxlists.html.**

***1893-1901 Citizens of Antioch Community, Troup County, Georgia* [Online Database],** indexed at the RootsWeb site for Troup Co GA. See
**www.rootsweb.ancestry.com/~gatroup/antioch.html.**

**1893-1991. Georgia, Naturalization Records [Online Database],** indexed at the Ancestry.com website. National Archives, records of the U.S. District Courts. Records include Petitions, Declarations, and Certificates. Each index record may include: Name, Age, Record Type, Birth date, Birth place, Petition date, Petition place, and Petition number. View the image documents for more information. This database has 166,400 records. See
**https://search.ancestry.com/search/db.aspx?dbid=2500.**

**1896. *Georgia, Atlanta City Census* [Online Database],** records from the Atlanta History Center, digitized and indexed at FamilySearch.org. Includes index and images of census returns from 1896 for Wards 1 through 6. Records compiled alphabetically by Ward. This database has 80,935 records, see
**www.familysearch.org/search/collection/2765183.**

**1898. *Spanish-American War Service Summary Cards* [Online Database],** from the original scanned images at the Georgia Archives Virtual Vault. See
**http://cdm.georgiaarchives.org:2011/cdm/.**

**1898. *A Roster of Spanish American War Soldiers from Georgia* [Printed Book],** edited and arranged by Carlton J. Thaxton, Donna B. Thaxton, Stan Thaxton, published by Thaxton Co., Americus, GA, 1984, 139 pages, FHL book 975.8 M2th.

**1898-1900s. *Georgia Veterans: & Their Widows Who Applied for Government Pensions in Alabama* [Printed Book],** compiled by F.W. Weatherbee, Jr., published by Pioneer Pub. Co., Carrolton, MS, 1991, 206 pages, FHL book 975.8 M2wf.

**1900. *Georgia, 1900 Federal Census: Soundex and Population Schedules* [Microfilm & Digital Capture],** from the original records held by the Bureau of the Census in the 1940s. After microfilming, Congress allowed the Census Bureau to destroy the originals to free up space for WWII-related files. Filmed on 267 rolls, beginning with FHL film #1242699 (Soundex, A000-A250), and FHL film #1240180 (Population schedules, Appling, Baker, and

Baldwin counties). To access the digital images, see the online FHL catalog page:
**www.familysearch.org/search/catalog/648480.**

**1900.** ***Houston County, Georgia Census, 1900*** **[Online Database],** indexed at the Ancestry.com website. This database has 22,501 records. See
**http://search.ancestry.com/search/db.aspx?dbid=4168.**

**1900.** ***Irwin County, Georgia Census, 1900*** **[Online Database],** indexed at the Ancestry.com website. This database has 13,007 records. See
**http://search.ancestry.com/search/db.aspx?dbid=4319.**

***1900-1901 Tax Lists, Quitman County, Georgia*** **[Online Database],** indexed at the USGenWeb site for Quitman Co GA. See
**www.usgwarchives.net/ga/quitman/taxlists.html.**

**1901.** ***Berrien County, Georgia, 1901 Tax Digest*** **[Printed Book],** published by the Huxford Genealogical Society, Homerville, GA, 19??, 104 pages. FHL book 975.8862 R4b 1901.

**1901-1930.** ***Georgia Confederate Home Records*** **[Online Database],** digitized and indexed at the FamilySearch.org website. Source: Georgia Archives. This database includes an index and images of registers of Confederate veterans who were inmates of the home in Atlanta. Volume contents includes name, occupation, county of residence, date of birth, date and place entered military service, rank, company, regiment, when and where wounded, when and where taken prisoner of war, when and where put on specific detail, when and where separated from service, commanding officers, rank, branch of service, age upon admission to home, date entered home, relatives, date of death or discharge, date and place of burial. This database has 1,091 records. See
**www.familysearch.org/search/collection/2126718.**

**1904-1939.** ***Georgia, Brunswick Passenger Lists*** **[Online Database],** indexed at the FamilySearch.org website. Source: National Archives microfilm A3641. This collection contains Passenger Lists of Vessels Arriving at Brunswick, Georgia, November 1904-November 1939. The records usually include full name, age, gender, marital status, occupation, citizenship, race, last permanent residence, birthplace, and final destination. This database has 776 records. See
**www.familysearch.org/search/collection/2442694.**

**1904-1962.** ***Georgia, Passenger and Crew Lists*** **[Online Database],** indexed at the Ancestry.com website. Source: National Archives microfilm A3638, A3639, A3674, A3908 (Savannah); and A3641, A3642 (Brunswick). Each index record may include name, Arrival date, Arrival place, Nationality, and Name of vessel. The image document may have more information. This database has 10,194 records. See
**https://search.ancestry.com/search/db.aspx?dbid=60517.**

**1905-1910.** ***Georgia Obituaries*** **[Printed Book],** compiled by Jeannette Holland Austin. Obituaries abstracted from "The Atlanta Georgian" and "The Atlanta Constitution" newspapers. Names in alphabetical order. Published by J. H. Austin, 198?, 431 pages, FHL book 975.8 V4a.

***1905 Tax List Catoosa County, Georgia*** **[Printed Book],** compiled by MariLee Beatty Hageness, Anniston, AOL, MLH Research, 2001, 52 pages. FHL book 975.8326 R4h.

***1906 List of Ex-Confederated Soldiers, Towns County, Georgia*** **[Online Database],** indexed at the USGenWeb site for Towns Co GA. See
**http://files.usgwarchives.net/ga/towns/military/civilwar/other/mt314listofex.txt.**

**1906-1934.** ***Naturalization Records, Atlanta, Georgia*** **[Microfilm],** from the original records at the National Archives, East Point, GA. Filmed by the Genealogical Society of Utah, 1989, 15 rolls, beginning with FHL film #1491876 (Declarations of Intention, 1906-1918). For a complete list of roll numbers and contents of each roll, see the online FHL catalog page for this item:
**www.familysearch.org/search/catalog/667664.**

**1906-1989.** ***Index to Aliens Admitted to Citizenship*** **[Microfilm & Digital Capture],** from originals at the U.S. District Court house, Savannah, GA. Filmed by the Genealogical Society of Utah, 1989, 2 rolls, FHL film #1643605 and #1643606. To access the digital images, see the online FHL catalog page:
**www.familysearch.org/search/catalog/366195.**

**1907-1928.** ***Naturalization Records (Athens, Georgia)*** **[Microfilm & Digital Capture],** from the original records at the National Archives, East Point, GA. Filmed by the Genealogical Society of Utah, 1989, 2 rolls, FHL film #1491873 (Declarations of Intentions 1907-1928; Petitions and Records 1910-1925); and

FHL film #1605318 (Naturalization Certificate stubs, 1910-1926). To access the digital images, see the online FHL catalog page:
**www.familysearch.org/search/catalog/667571.**

*1909 Road Tax Record, Rabun County, Georgia* **[Online Database],** indexed at the USGenWeb site for Rabun Co GA. See
**http://files.usgwarchives.net/ga/rabun/taxlists/1909road.txt.**

**1909-1910.** ***Young & Co.'s Business and Professional Directory of the Cities and Towns of Georgia*** **[Online Database],** digitized and indexed at FamilySearch.org. See **www.familysearch.org/search/catalog/2478979.**

*1909-1910 Business Directory, Decatur County, Georgia* **[Online Database],** indexed at the USGenWeb site. See
**http://files.usgwarchives.net/ga/decatur/history/direct01.txt.**

*1909-1910 Business and Professional Directory, Worth County, Georgia* **[Online Database],** originally indexed at the USGenWeb site for Worth Co GA. For an archived database, see
**https://web.archive.org/web/20120913041849/www.thegagenweb.com/gaworth/business/busdir190910.html.**

**1910.** ***Georgia, 1910 Federal Census: Soundex and Population Schedules*** **[Microfilm & Digital Capture],** from the original records held by the Bureau of the Census in the 1940s. After microfilming, Congress allowed the Census Bureau to destroy the originals to free up space for WWII-related files. Filmed on 225 rolls, beginning with FHL film #1369636 (Soundex: A000-A325 – Entire state, except the cities of Atlanta, Augusta, Macon, and Savannah); and FHL film #1369784 (Soundex: A000-B220 – cities of Atlanta, Augusta, Macon, and Savannah only); and FHL film #1374183 (Population Schedules, Appling, Butts, Baker, and Baldwin counties). To access the digital images, see the online FHL catalog page:
**www.familysearch.org/search/catalog/648013.**

**1910.** ***Georgia 1910 Census Index*** **[Printed Index],** compiled and published by HeritageQuest, North Salt Lake, UT, 2003, 5 vols., FHL book 975.8 X22gc 1910 v.1: A-CP, v.2: CR-HEN, v.3: HEO-MCL, v.4: MCM-SI, & v.5: SJ-Z.

*1911 Roster of Confederate Veterans, Tattnall County* **[Online Database],** indexed at the USGenWeb site for Tattnall Co GA. See
**http://files.usgwarchives.net/ga/tattnall/military/civilwar/wadehamp.txt.**

**1914-1927.** ***Georgia Deaths*** **[Online Database],** digitized and indexed at the FamilySearch.org website. From FHL microfilm of deaths from the Georgia Department of Health and Vital Statistics, Atlanta, GA. This database has 305,880 records. See
**https://familysearch.org/search/collection/1320969.**

**1914-1940.** ***Georgia Deaths*** **[Online Database],** indexed at the Ancestry.com website. Original data: "Georgia Deaths, 1914–1927." Index. FamilySearch, Salt Lake City, Utah, 2007. "Georgia Deaths, 1914–1927" and "Georgia Deaths, 1930," images, FamilySearch. Georgia Department of Health and Vital Statistics, Atlanta, Georgia. Details listed in the index will vary depending on form type and how completely the form was filled out, but information may include: Name, Gender, Birth date, Birthplace, Marital status, Spouse, Race/ethnicity, Age, Place of death, Date of death, Place of burial, Date of burial, Father, Mother, and FHL film number. This database has 2,132,228 records. See
**https://search.ancestry.com/search/db.aspx?dbid=2562.**

*1917 Tax List, Banks County, Georgia* **[Online Database],** indexed at the USGenWeb site for Banks Co GA. See
**http://files.usgwarchives.net/ga/banks/taxlists/.**

**1917-1918.** ***Georgia, World War I Selective Service System Draft Registrations Cards*** **[Microfilm & Digital Capture],** from originals at the National Archives, East Point, GA. Filmed by the National Archives,1987-1988, Series 1509, 100 rolls, beginning with FHL film #1556940 (Appling Co, A-Z; Atlanta City, No. 1, A-G). To access the digital images, see the online FHL catalog page:
**www.familysearch.org/search/catalog/746973.**

*1917-1918 WWI Service Records, Banks County, Georgia* **[Online Database],** indexed at the USGenWeb site for Banks Co GA. See
**http://files.usgwarchives.net/ga/banks/military/ww1/records.txt.**

*1917-1918 WWI Rosters, Clayton County, Georgia* **[Online Database],** indexed at the USGenWeb site for Clayton Co GA. See
**http://files.usgwarchives.net/ga/clayton/military/ww1/rosters/wwi.txt.**

*1917-1918 WWI Enlisted Men, Taylor County, Georgia* **[Online Database],** indexed at the USGenWeb site for Taylor Co GA. See
**http://files.usgwarchives.net/ga/taylor/military/ww1/taylormen.txt.**

**1917-1919.** ***Georgia, World War I Service Cards*** **[Online Database],** indexed at the Ancestry.com website. Source: Georgia Adjutant General's records at the Georgia Archives. The cards include the following details: Name, Serial/service number, Race, Place and date of enlistment or induction, Place of birth, Age or date of birth, Service organization(s) with assignment dates and transfers, Rank (grade) with date of appointment, Engagements, Whether wounded in action, degree and date, Overseas service dates, Discharge/separation date, and Degree of disability at discharge. This database has 110,665 records. See
**https://search.ancestry.com/search/db.aspx?dbid=3129.**

**1917-1919.** ***Georgia, World War I American Expeditionary Forces, Deaths*** **[Digital Capture],** digitized by FamilySearch International, 2018. To access the digital images, see the online FHL catalog page: **www.familysearch.org/search/catalog/3023921.**

**1919-1998.** ***Georgia Deaths*** **[Online Database],** indexed at the Ancestry.com website, from Georgia Health Dept., Office of Vital Statistics. The index includes the name of the deceased, the volume of the certificate number, the death date, the race of the deceased, the deceased's gender, the county of death, the death certificate number, the date the certificate was file, and the deceased age. This database has 3,166,686 records:
**http://search.ancestry.com/search/db.aspx?dbid=5426.**

**1919-1999.** ***Georgia Death Index*** **[Microfiche],** from records at the Georgia Dept. of Health and Vital Statistics, Atlanta, GA. Index is by year, then county, then alphabetical for the surname of the deceased. The index line refers to a county with a code number. Filmed by the GA Health Department, 1999. 442 microfiche, beginning with FHL fiche #6334629 (Death Index 1919 A.M. Aaron – Pauline Zuker). For a complete list of fiche numbers and contents of each, see the online FHL catalog page for this title:
**www.familysearch.org/search/catalog/750864.**

**1920.** ***Georgia, 1920 Federal Census: Soundex and Population Schedules*** **[Microfilm & Digital Capture],** from the original records held by the Bureau of the Census in the 1940s. After microfilming, Congress allowed the Census Bureau to destroy the originals to free up space for WWII-related files. Filmed on 254 rolls, beginning with FHL film #1824057 (Soundex: A000-A136); and FHL film #1820233 (Population schedules: Appling, Atkinson, Baker, Bacon, and Baldwin counties). To access the digital images, see the online FHL catalog page:
**www.familysearch.org/search/catalog/567711.**

**1920.** ***Worth County, Georgia Census*** **[Online Database],** indexed at the Ancestry.com website. This database has over 25,092 records. See
**http://search.ancestry.com/search/db.aspx?dbid=3886.**

**1920-1929.** ***Georgia World War I Statement of Service Summary Card Files*** **[Microfilm & Digital Capture],** from the originals at the GDAH, Atlanta, GA. Contents: Each card contains the following information: 1) Full name, 2) Service or serial number, 3) Race (Army only), 4) Full address, 5) Place of enlistment or induction, 6) Place of birth, 7) Age (in years and fractions of years), 8) Service organization, 9) Grades, 10) Engagements, 11) Wounds, 12) Overseas service, 13) Date of honorable discharge, and 14) Report of disability and percentage thereof, if applicable. Filmed by the Genealogical Society of Utah, 2001-2007, 121 rolls, beginning with FHL film #2259222 (Aaron, Burgress A – Albritton, Callan T.). To access the digital images, see the online FHL catalog page:
**www.familysearch.org/search/catalog/1013317.**

*1920-1939 Civil War Pensioners, Dodge County, Georgia* **[Online Database],** indexed at the USGenWeb site. See.
**http://files.usgwarchives.net/ga/dodge/military/civilwar/csapension.txt.**

*1925 Business Tax List, Lamar County, Georgia* **[Online Database],** indexed at the USGenWeb site for Lamar Co GA. See
**http://files.usgwarchives.net/ga/lamar/taxlists/1925.txt.**

**1927-1979.** ***Georgia, (Troup County) Deed Indexes*** **[Online Database],** indexed at the Ancestry.com website. Original data: Troup County, Georgia Grantor/Grantee Deed Indexes. LaGrange, Georgia, publ. Troup Co Historical Society. These indexes include names of grantors and grantees, as well as the date the deed was filed. They also provide a brief description of the property as well as the volume and page number where the transfer of the deed was officially recorded. This database has 313,096 records: **https://search.ancestry.com/search/db.aspx?dbid=3164.**

**1927-2010.** ***Oconee County, Georgia, Probate Death Certificates*** **[Online Database],** indexed at the Ancestry.com website. Original data: Vital Records; Marriage Licenses. Watkinsville, Georgia: Oconee County Probate Court. Each index record includes name, residence/address, sex, color or race, birth date, age, birthplace, occupation, marital status, spouse's name, father's name and birthplace, mother's name and birthplace, date of death, cause of death, place of burial, undertaker/funeral director, and informant's name and address. This database has 25,388 records. See **https://search.ancestry.com/search/db.aspx?dbid=2480.**

**1928-1942.** ***Georgia Deaths*** **[Online Database],** digitized and indexed at the FamilySearch.org website. From FHL microfilm of the Department of Health and Vital Statistics, Atlanta, GA. This database has 462,877 records. See
**https://familysearch.org/search/collection/1385727**.

**1930.** ***Georgia, 1930 Federal Census: Soundex and Population Schedules*** **[Microfilm & Digital Capture],** from the original records held by the Bureau of the Census in the 1940s. After microfilming, Congress allowed the Census Bureau to destroy the originals to free up space for WWII-related files. Filmed on 319 rolls, beginning with FHL film #2338393 (Soundex: A000-A240); and FHL film #2340071 (Population schedules: Appling, Atkinson, Bacon, Baker and Baldwin counties). To access the digital images, see the online FHL catalog page:
**www.familysearch.org/search/catalog/1035335.**

***1932 Confederate Veterans/Pensioners, Walker County, Georgia*** **[Online Database],** indexed at the USGenWeb site for Walker Co GA. See
**www.usgwarchives.net/ga/walker/military.html.**

**1933-1990.** ***Tennessee Valley Cemetery Relocation Files*** **[Online Database],** indexed at the Ancestry.com website. The Tennessee Valley Authority (TVA) was established in 1933 with the goals of alleviating flooding problems, generating affordable electricity, and more. This collection includes grave removal records from cemeteries that were in the path of projects. Included are grave removals near Nottely, Georgia. See
**https://search.ancestry.com/search/db.aspx?dbid=60427**.

- See also ***Tennessee Valley, Family Removal and Population Readjustment Case Files, 1934-1953*** **[Online Database],** indexed at the Ancestry.com website. Included are relocations near Chatuge and Nottely, Georgia. This database has records. See
**https://search.ancestry.com/search/db.aspx?dbid=4903.**

**1933-1998.** ***Georgia, Death Index*** **[Online Database],** indexed at the FamilySearch.org website. From the Georgia Department of Health and Vital Statistics, Atlanta, GA. This database has 2,701,430 records. See
**https://familysearch.org/search/collection/1937238**.

***1940 Georgia Federal Census: Population Schedules*** **[Digital Capture],** digitized images and every-name index taken from the microfilm of original records held by the Bureau of the Census in the 1940s. After microfilming, Congress allowed the Census Bureau to destroy the originals to free up space for WWII-related files. Digitizing of the 1940 census schedules microfilm images was done for the National Archives and made public on April 2, 2012. No microfilm copies were distributed. To access the digital images, see the online FHL catalog page:
**www.familysearch.org/search/catalog/2057749.**

***1940 Federal Census Finding Aids*** **[Online Database].** Well before the release of the 1940 census to the public, the National Archives created a special website online with a detailed description of the 1940 federal census. Included at the site are descriptions of location finding aids, such as Enumeration District Maps, Geographic Descriptions of Census Enumeration Districts, and a list of 1940 City Directories available at the National Archives. The finding aids are all linked to other National Archives sites. This National Archives website also has a link to 1940 Search Engines using Stephen P. Morse's "One-Step" system for finding a 1940 E.D. or for a street address conversion. See
**www.archives.gov/research/census/1940/general-info.html#questions.**

**1940-1942** ***Georgia World War II Draft Registration Cards*** **[Online Database],** digitized at the FamilySearch.org website. Draft registration cards arranged numerically by local board number then alphabetically by surname of registrant. This database has 839,636 records. See
**https://familysearch.org/search/collection/1880573.**

***1941-1945 WWII Army Enlistments*** **[Online Database],** indexed by county at the various USGenWeb sites, for the following counties:
- Appling Co GA. See
**http://files.usgwarchives.net/ga/appling/military/ww2/.**
- Atkinson Co GA. See
**http://files.usgwarchives.net/ga/atkinson/military/ww2.**
Bacon Co GA. See
**http://files.usgwarchives.net/ga/bacon/military/ww2/.**
- Baker Co GA. See
**http://files.usgwarchives.net/ga/baker/military/ww2/.**
- Baldwin Co GA. See
**http://files.usgwarchives.net/ga/baldwin/military/ww2/.**
- Banks Co GA. See
**http://files.usgwarchives.net/ga/banks/military/ww2/.**
- Barrow Co GA. See
**http://files.usgwarchives.net/ga/barrow/military/ww2/.**

***1941-1945 WWII Service Men, Taylor County, Georgia*** **[Online Database],** indexed at the USGenWeb site for Taylor Co GA. See
**http://files.usgwarchives.net/ga/taylor/military/ww2/taylormenii.txt.**

**1947-1949.** ***Georgia Obituaries, June 1947-June 1949*** **[Printed Book],** compiled by Wade H. Joyce; copied by Hilda J. Hambleton. 7 vols, contents: Vol. : A-B, Vol. 2: C-E, Vol. 3: F-I, Vol. 4: J-L, Vol. 5: M-P, Vol. 6: R-S, and Vol. 7: T-Z. Published 1954-1955, FHL book 975.8 V23j v.1-7.

**1950-2005.** ***Georgia, Hall County Marriages*** **[Online Database],** indexed at the FamilySearch.org website. Source: Hall County Probate Court, Gainesville, GA. This is an image-only database of marriages records. This database has 28,533 images. Browse through the images, organized by Record Type, Year Range, and Volume Number/Letter. See
**www.familysearch.org/search/collection/2373860.**

**1964-1992.** ***Marriage Register Index*** **[Microfiche],** from the originals at the Georgia Dept. of Health and Vital Statistics, Atlanta, GA. The year 1972 is missing. Filmed by the Genealogical Society of Utah, 1995, 341 microfiche, beginning with FHL fiche #6334704 (Marriage Register Index, 1964, Mary A. Aalto – Chester J. Zysko). For a complete list fiche numbers and contents of each, see the online FHL catalog page for this title:
**www.familysearch.org/search/catalog/750962.**

**1965-1992.** ***Divorce Register Index*** **[Microfiche],** from the originals at the Georgia Dept. of Health and Vital Statistics, Atlanta, GA. The year 1972 is missing. Filmed by the Genealogical Society of Utah, 1995, 149 microfiche, beginning with FHL fiche #6334732 (Divorce Index, 1965, James W. Aaron – John W. Zvoncheck). For a complete list fiche numbers and contents of each, see the online FHL catalog page for this title:
**www.familysearch.org/search/catalog/750963.**

**1985–Current.** ***Georgia Newspaper Obituaries*** **[Online Database].** Digitized and indexed at the GenealogyBank.com website. One search screen for obituaries published in over 70 city newspapers:
**www.genealogybank.com/gbnk/obituaries/explore/USA/Georgia/.**

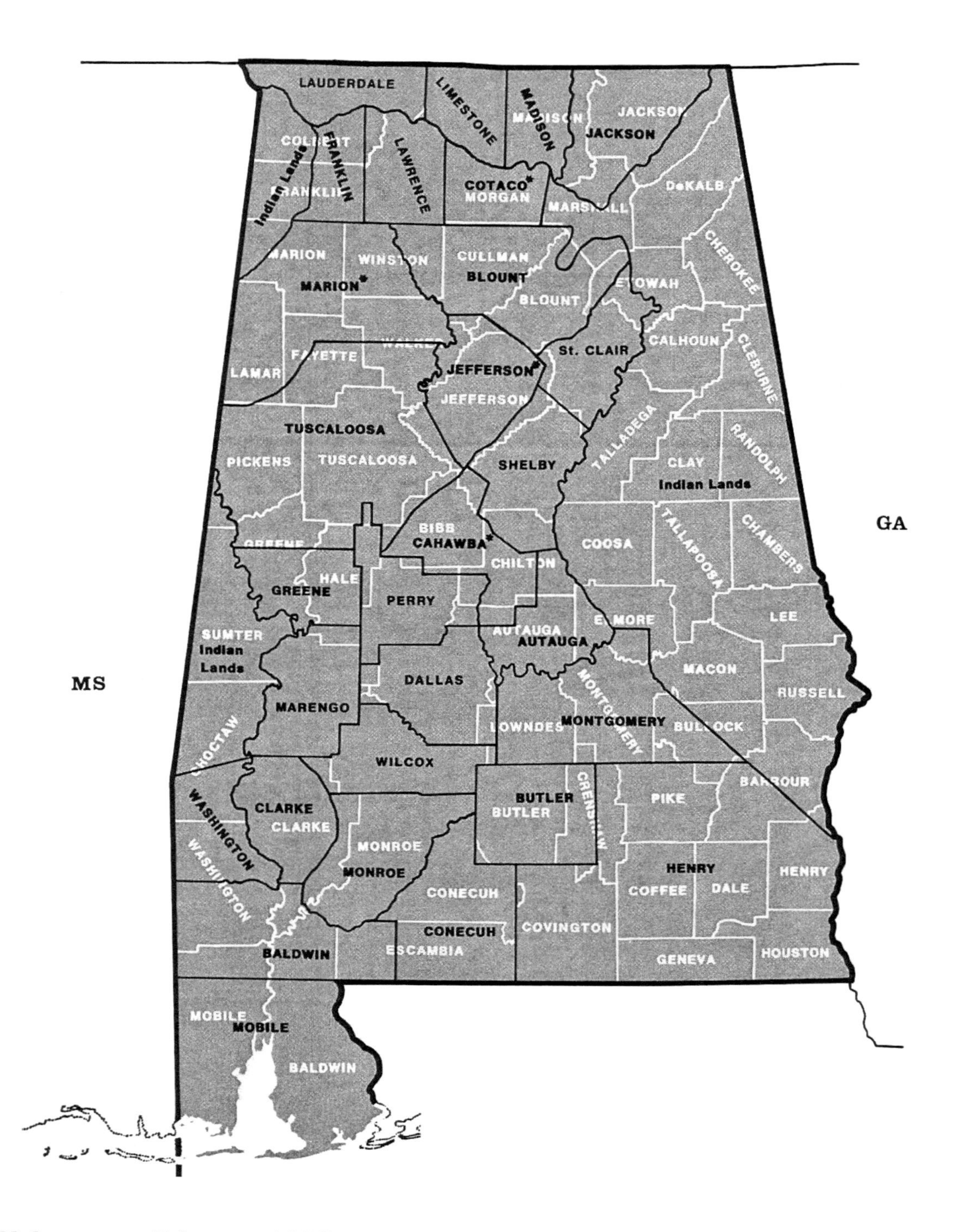


**Alabama • 7 August 1820.** Shown in black are the 30 counties of Alabama at the time of the 1820 Federal Census. The current 67 counties of Alabama are shown in white. An 1820 Alabama State Census was taken a few weeks after the federal enumeration. The federal census schedules were lost for all counties; while the 1820 AL state census originals exist for eight (8) counties only: Baldwin, Conecuh, Dallas, Franklin, Limestone, St. Clair, Shelby & Wilcox. Asterisks (*) next to certain counties on the map refer to the following notes: *Cahawba was renamed Bibb in December 1820. *Cotaco was renamed Morgan in 1821.*Jefferson and Marion are not on the federal government's population list. **Map Source:** Page 13, *Map Guide to the U.S. Federal Censuses, 1790-1920,* by William Thorndale and William Dollarhide.

# Alabama

## Censuses & Substitute Name Lists

### Historical Timeline of Alabama, 1519-1820

**1519.** The Spanish believed there must be a sea lane from the Gulf of Mexico to China. From the Florida keys, Alvarez de Pineda followed the shoreline of the Gulf of Mexico from present Florida to Texas to find that sea lane. At one point he entered a large bay with a sizable native settlement on one shore. He sailed upriver for eighteen miles and observed as many as forty villages on the bank. It has long been assumed that Alvarez de Pineda had discovered the Mississippi River, but based on his recorded observations, many historians now believe he was describing Mobile Bay and the Alabama River.

**1682.** French explorer René-Robert Cavelier (Sieur de la Salle) erected a cross near the confluence of the Mississippi River and the Gulf of Mexico, after floating down rivers from the Great Lakes area. He claimed the entire Mississippi Basin for Louis XIV of France, for whom Louisiana was named. All of the rivers and streams flowing into the Mississippi were part of the Mississippi Basin and included in the Louisiana claim.

**1698.** Pensacola was founded by the Spanish as the Presidio Santa Maria de Galve. They claimed the entire Florida Panhandle, including the area in present Alabama, which they did not recognize as part of French Louisiana.

**1699.** The French established the first settlement on Biloxi Bay, now Ocean Springs. (Biloxi, founded in 1719, was the capital of French Louisiana until 1722, replaced by New Orleans).

**1702.** Mobile was founded by the French as **Fort Louis de la Louisianne**. They were in an area also claimed by the Spanish.

**1719.** The French captured Pensacola, and now occupied all gulf ports plus New Orleans. But, as a result of an alliance with Spain against England, the French soon returned all of the gulf ports back to Spain.

**1755.** Resulting from the war between France and England, France ceded to Britain its claim to a portion of Lower Louisiana east of the Mississippi.

**1763.** Until this year, many cross-claims to territory in North America existed between the French, English and Spanish, and it took a war to settle the issue of land ownership. In Europe and Canada it was called the Seven Years War, but in colonial America it was called the French and Indian War. France was the big loser, and at the 1763 Treaty of Paris ending the war, the British retained or gained undisputed title to Nova Scotia, Quebec, Newfoundland, Labrador, the Great Lakes and Hudson Bay regions, their Atlantic colonies, and all other lands east of the Mississippi River. Before the 1763 treaty, the British had grandiose western claims based on Royal Charters of its Atlantic colonies using the words "sea to sea." In the 1763 treaty, the British modified their western claims to end at the Mississippi River. In 1762, the French had secretly transferred Louisiana west of the Mississippi to Spain, and in 1763, they transferred all of remaining Louisiana east of the Mississippi to Britain. Also in 1763, by separate treaty, the Spanish ransomed Florida to the British in exchange for Cuba. The British immediately divided the territory into East Florida and West Florida with the Apalachicola – Chattahoochee River as the dividing line. The area of West Florida included the portion of present-day Alabama south of Latitude 31 degrees.

**1780-1783.** During the Revolutionary War, the British hold on East and West Florida came to an end. With the Spanish as allies of the French, the British lost West Florida to Spanish forces, who had captured Mobile in 1780 and Pensacola in 1781. The British then returned East Florida to Spain in 1783, causing many American loyalists who had fled the Revolutionary War to St. Augustine to flee again, this time heading for the Bahamas or West Indies.

The Treaty of Paris of 1783 first recognized the United States as an independent nation. Its borders were described generally from the Atlantic Ocean to the Mississippi River, and from Maine to Georgia. However, the northern third of Maine was not included; nor was East Florida or West Florida south of Latitude 31 degrees. Spain continued its claim to East and West Florida after the 1783 Treaty of Paris. Spain also claimed the area south of Latitude 32° 30' of present-day Mississippi and Alabama.

**1800.** Georgia's 1800 federal census jurisdiction included its western Indian lands to the Mississippi, but no whites were enumerated there. The entire Georgia 1800 census was lost. Washington County, Mississippi Territory was enumerated in the 1800 census, including areas of present-day Alabama, but that census was also lost.

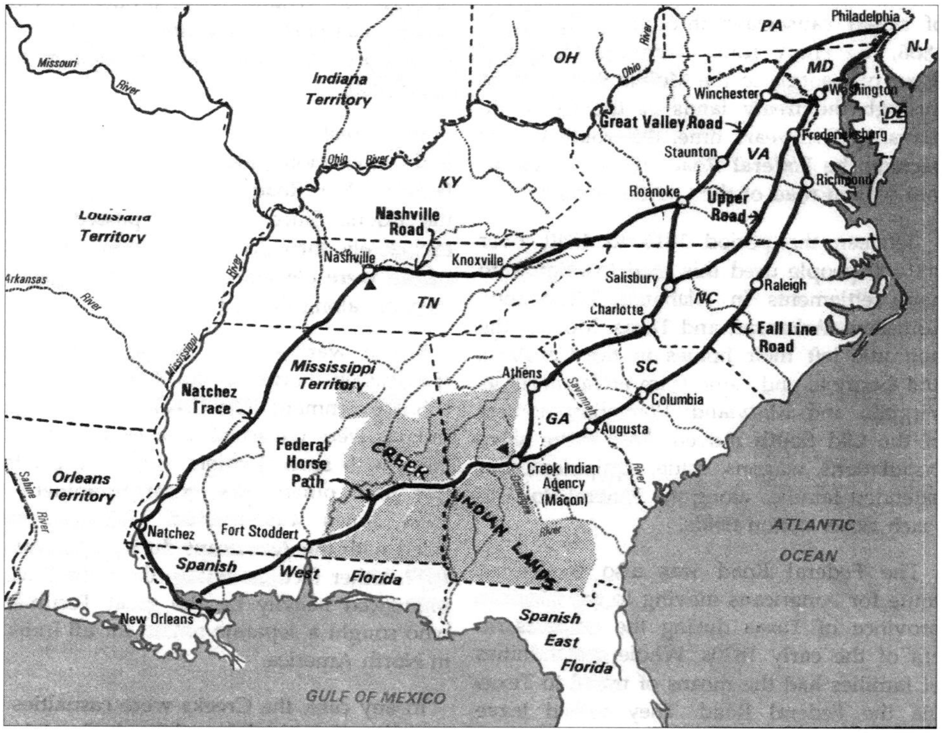

**Roads from Philadelphia to New Orleans by 1806.**

**1790.** The present-day area of Alabama and Mississippi was part of Georgia, part of the disputed area, and part of Spanish West Florida at the time of the 1790 federal census. Although there were American settlements near Natchez and Mobile, no federal census was taken there.

**1796.** The U.S. resolved the Spanish-U.S. disputed area by purchasing the area from Spain. The lands above West Florida (Latitude 31° up to 32°30'), became U.S. territory. The purchase did not include East Florida or West Florida.

**1798.** Congress created **Mississippi Territory** within the purchased lands. This area is now in both Alabama and Mississippi, from Latitude 31° to Latitude 32°30'. West Florida, including Mobile, was still under control of the Spanish.

**1802.** In this year, the portion of present-day Alabama and Mississippi above Latitude 32° 30' was ceded by Georgia to the U.S. federal government's "public domain." In 1803 Congress added the ceded lands to Mississippi Territory, tripling its size.

**1802.** France acquired title to Louisiana again, resulting from Napoleon's defeat of the Spanish in battle, and an exchange of lands in Europe.

**1803. The Louisiana Purchase**. The U.S. purchased the huge tract from France, doubling the size of the United States. The purchase of Louisiana immediately created a dispute with Spain about the ownership of land east of the Mississippi River. The legal description of the Louisiana Purchase in 1803 was the "drainage of the Mississippi and Missouri Rivers." Spain disagreed that it included lands east of the Mississippi.

**1804.** Congress divided the Louisiana Purchase area into two new legal jurisdictions: **Louisiana District** and **Orleans Territory**. The latter had north and south Bounds, the same as the present state of Louisiana, but did not include land east of the Mississippi River, and its northwestern corner extended west into Spanish Texas. For a year, Louisiana District was attached to Indiana Territory for judicial administration, but in 1805, Louisiana District became **Louisiana Territory**, with its own governor.

**1806. The Federal Horse Path.** (Refer to the map, *Roads from Philadelphia to New Orleans by 1806,* opposite). The time it took for mail via express riders between Philadelphia and New Orleans was cut in half, from six weeks to three weeks, after the opening of the Federal Horse Path. A treaty with the Creek Nation, which encompassed a large area of present-day Georgia and Alabama was necessary to clear the pathway, beginning at the Creek Indian Agency (now Macon) and through Mississippi Territory and Spanish West Florida to New Orleans. With federal funds, the same route was continually improved and became known as the *Federal Road,* the primary route for thousands of Scots-Irish families migrating into the Old South.

**1810.** September. Americans overcame the Spanish garrison at Baton Rouge and unfurled the new flag of the Republic of West Florida.

**1810.** October. In a proclamation by President James Madison, the U.S. arbitrarily annexed Spain's West Florida from the Mississippi River to the Perdido River. The area included Baton Rouge, Biloxi, and Mobile, but was not organized, and was not included in the 1810 census. Spain did not recognize the annexation, and continued their claim to West Florida in dispute with the U.S.

**1812.** Congress added to Mississippi Territory the portion of the West Florida annexation from the Perdido River to the Pearl River, an area which included Mobile and Biloxi; and the portion from the Pearl River to the Mississippi River was added to Orleans Territory (an area that included Baton Rouge). Soon after, Orleans Territory became the State of Louisiana.

**1817. Alabama Territory** was created on March 3rd, taken from Mississippi Territory, with nearly the same boundaries as the current state bounds.

**1819. Adams-Onis Treaty.** After years of refusing to negotiate with the U.S. over the ownership of Florida, Spain finally relented with the 1819 Adams-Onis treaty, also called the Purchase of Florida. Spain's problems with colonial rebellions in Central and South America saw a change in their attitudes. By 1818, Spain had effectively abandoned Florida and was unwilling to support any more colonists or garrisons. The treaty involved Spain's cession of Florida to the U.S. in exchange for the U.S. paying any legal claims of American citizens against Spain, up to 5 million dollars. But, the treaty also set the boundary between the U.S. and New Spain (now Mexico), from Louisiana to the Oregon Country. The treaty finally confirmed the Sabine River border with Spanish Texas, and

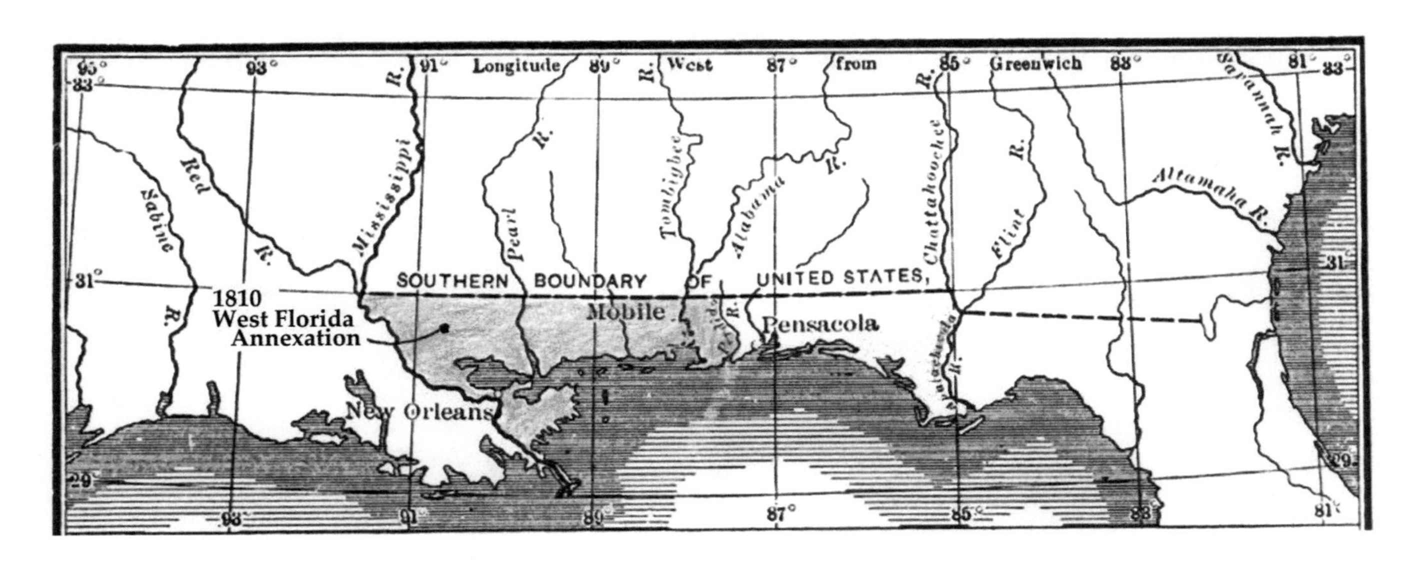


**1810 West Florida Annexation**

recognized (for the first time), the American claim to the Oregon Country. The treaty was named after John Quincy Adams, U.S. Secretary of State, and Luis de Onis, the Spanish Foreign Minister, the parties who signed the treaty at Washington on February 22, 1819. John Quincy Adams was given credit for a brilliant piece of diplomacy by adding the western boundary settlements with Spain to the Florida Purchase. It was considered his crowning achievement, before, during, or after his presidency. Although Baton Rouge, Biloxi, and Mobile were annexed to the U.S. in 1810, then organized in 1812; they did not become U.S. territory free of dispute until the Adams-Onis Treaty of 1819.

**1819. Alabama** became the 22nd state on December 14th, with nearly the same boundaries as today.

**1820.** The federal census for Alabama was lost, but the State of Alabama took its own census in 1820 and several counties survive. In July 1820, the Alabama-Mississippi boundary line was resurveyed, and it was discovered that a tract of Alabama land lying along the east side of the Tombigbee River was really in Mississippi.

---

## Alabama's Colonial, Territorial, and Statewide Censuses

**1702-1797 Colonial Censuses:** The gulf port city of Mobile was established by the French in 1702, as Fort Louis de la Louisianne. Soon after, the French military cadre conducted a census of the fort's inhabitants and its surroundings. The French were very fond of censuses, which they did every other year or so in all of their colonies, mainly as a means of identifying people who were subject to taxation. However, only a few of the French census name lists exist today. Within the area of the gulf, the French censuses of 1702, 1706, 1721, and 1725 have survived. Censuses and tax lists were also taken by the English landlords (from 1764), and by the Spanish (from 1785), during the colonial period.

**1800-1818 Mississippi and Alabama Territorial Censuses:** U.S. federal censuses taken in the area of present Alabama began with the Mississippi Territory 1800 federal census. In that year, a portion of old Washington County, Mississippi Territory, was in present Alabama, but that federal census year was lost. In 1810 the federal census for Mississippi Territory included parts of present Alabama in Baldwin, Madison, and Washington counties, but again, that census was lost. Mississippi took its own 1810 territorial census, and Washington County survives in that census. In 1816, the Mississippi Territory census included areas of present Alabama, and the surviving name lists from that census have been published. After becoming Alabama Territory in 1817, a census was taken a year later, but only one county (Montgomery) survives the 1818 Alabama territorial census.

**1820-1940 Alabama Federal Censuses:** Alabama's first federal census taken in its own name was the 1820, a year after statehood, but that year was lost. (There exists an 1820 census taken by the state of Alabama separate from the federal, and several county name lists have survived). Alabama's federal censuses taken from 1830 through 1880; and 1900 through 1940, are complete for all counties. The 1890 federal census for all states was almost completely destroyed due to a fire at the Commerce Building in Washington, DC, in 1921. A handful of names from Alabama's Perry County survived the fire and are now on microfilm and available to the public. The name lists from the 1940 federal census for Alabama opened to the public on April 2, 2012. The 1950 opens on April 1, 2022.

**1818-1866 Alabama State Censuses:** Alabama's periodic constitutions and acts of the General Assembly authorized several state censuses taken separately from the federal censuses. They began in the year 1818 (Territory of Alabama). After statehood in 1819, the legislature also authorized state censuses to be taken in 1820, 1821, 1823, 1832, 1838, 1844, 1850, 1855, and 1866, all of which were known to be taken, but not all of them survive. In 2009, the extant portions of the 1820, 1850, 1855, and 1866 AL state censuses were digitized and indexed and made available online at the Ancestry.com subscription website.

The Alabama Department of Archives & History (ADAH) website briefly describes the content of the original AL state censuses, 1820-1866, all head of household listings, and all on microfilm. The microfilm was used for digitizing the images, and provided the means of indexing the names, all undertaken by Ancestry, Inc. The Ancestry.com website indicates the counties represented for AL1820-1866 are presented as one database. All of the Alabama state censuses were microfilmed by the Genealogical Society of Utah for the Family History Library in Salt Lake City, with the possible exception of the AL 1850 state census, which may have been microfilmed by the ADAH in Montgomery (since no AL 1850 state census film is at the FHL, but Ancestry.com cites the microfilm numbers for all AL state censuses, including the 1850 AL state census). An 1875 Alabama State Census was authorized but never taken. The 1875 Constitution of Alabama dictated that beginning with the 1880 federal census, apportionment of representatives would be determined by federal census population figures rather than state censuses. As a result, the 1866 state census was the last statewide census taken by the state of Alabama. Most of the surviving non-federal censuses have been published on microfilm and are available on interlibrary loan, mostly located at the ADAH in Montgomery or the Family History Library (FHL) in Salt Lake City.

**National Census Substitutes:** There are several national name lists for the entire U.S. that may include Alabama residents. These national lists are not shown here in the Alabama chapter, so a researcher should check the final chapter in Vol. 5, *Nationwide Censuses & Substitutes*. Examples of national name lists include Military Rosters; Army, Navy, and Widow's Pensions, Find a Grave, and the Social Security Death Index. In addition to the colonial, territorial, and state censuses taken in Alabama, there were numerous and valuable substitute name lists. Some of them at the ADAH website are listed below:

## Online Resources
### at the Alabama Department of Archives & History (ADAH)

Online guides, indexes and records available at the ADAH are described here with a link to an ADAH webpage for more information:

***Local Government/County Records on Microfilm Index* [Online Database].** This searchable database contains records from local, county and municipal offices, such as the probate office, tax assessor, and orphan's court. Most of the original records remain in the originating office. Other sources for local records include Alabama Loose Papers Index; Addresses of County Probate Offices; Secretary of State Land Records, Microfilm purchase procedures; and Alabama Counties. See
**www.archives.alabama.gov/localrecords/search.cfm.**

***Alabama Newspapers on Microfilm Index* [Online Database].** This searchable database includes newspapers that are available on microfilm. The microfilm is available for use in the ADAH reference room. The microfilm may be ordered on interlibrary loan from your local library, and some reels are available for purchase. For the search screen, see
**www.archives.alabama.gov/newsmicro/search.cfm.**

***Hardbound Newspapers Index* [Online Database].** This searchable database includes original newspapers available at the ADAH. Most have been bound in large, oversize volumes. These newspapers have not been microfilmed, and it is not always possible to have scanned copies made of certain articles. For the search screen, see
**www.archives.alabama.gov/newshard/search.cfm.**

***Map Index* [Online Database].** This searchable database contains descriptive information about maps at the ADAH, and links to images of some of the maps scanned and viewable via the website of the Cartographic Research Laboratory, which operates under the auspices of the College of Arts and Sciences at the University of Alabama. For the search screen, see
**www.archives.alabama.gov/mapbase/mapbase.cfm.**

***Alabama Church and Synagogue Records Collection Index* [Online Database].** This is an index to the records of several denominations within Alabama, including Baptist, Catholic, Church of Christ, Episcopal, Jewish, Methodist and Presbyterian. The records document the church activities through minutes, registers, financial records, correspondence, reports, programs, and scrapbooks. Search screen:
**www.archives.alabama.gov/AlChurchRecs/search.cfm.**

***Alabama Civil War Service Database* [Online Database].** This is a searchable database available online at the ADAH website. Sources include muster rolls, governors' correspondence, veterans' censuses, manuscript collections, newspapers, and pension records. See
**https://archives.alabama.gov/civilwar/search.cfm.**
- This database is also available at FamilySearch.org, listed in the chronological bibliography as *1861-1865 Alabama Civil War Service Database*.

***1867 Alabama Voter Registration Lists*** **[Original Documents/Online Index],** originals for all Alabama counties at the ADAH. There is no microfilm. The volumes are arranged alphabetically by county, then chronologically by date of registration. The archives has 131 original volumes, of which the books for Dallas; Franklin; Lauderdale; Limestone; Lowndes; Monroe; Randolph; and Washington counties were severely damaged due to age and mold. No book is available for Clarke County. The ADAH recently completed an index to the 1867 Voter Registrations. This is a searchable database available online at the ADAH website, see
**https://archives.alabama.gov/voterreg/search.cfm.**
- This database is also available at Ancestry.com, listed in the chronological bibliography as *1867 Alabama Voter Registration Lists*

***ADAH Digital Collections*** **[Online Database].** The ADAH Digital Collections consist of digitized photographs, documents, audio, and video material drawn from the vast holdings of the ADAH. Included are the following:

- Alabama Photographs and Pictures. Over 15,000 images from the ADAH holdings.
- Alabama Textual Materials Collection. Letters, diaries, minutes, fliers, clippings, and excerpts from books.
- Alabama Audio-Visual Collection. Oral history interviews and recordings from the Alabama Folklife Festival.
- History of Alabama and Dictionary of Alabama Biography.
- Alabama Official and Statistical Register.
- The Alabama Historical Quarterly.

For a complete description of all collections, see
**http://digital.archives.alabama.gov/.**

***World War I Gold Star Database, 1917-1918*** **[Online Database],** a list of Alabama people who died in service during WWI. This is a searchable database available online at the ADAH website. The name "Gold Star" was derived from the gold stars awarded to mothers of service people who lost their lives, see
**https://archives.alabama.gov/goldstar/search.cfm.**
- This database is also available at Ancestry.com, listed in the chronological bibliography as *1917-1918 World War I Gold Star Database*.

***Alabamians at War – ADAH Military Records*** **[Online Database].** The collection contains records which document the participation of Alabamians in the following wars: the Revolutionary War; the War of 1812 and 1st Creek War; the 2nd Creek War; the Texas War for Independence; the Mexican War; the Spanish-American War; World War I; World War II; the Korean War; and the Vietnam War. Most of the information is about people and events associated with the various wars. Compiled information on the Civil War is found in a separate file, Civil War and Reconstruction - ADAH Public Information Subject Files. For a general information page and a link to "Instructions on how to submit an online research request," see
**www.archives.alabama.gov/referenc/military.html**.

***Alabama City Directories, 1837-2006*** **[Online PDF File].** This 22-page finding aid has an alphabetical listing of places in Alabama with an indication of city directories available at the ADAH. For example, the list starts with Box 1, Albertville-Boaz, dates: 1959, 1961, 1966, 1967, 1969, 1971, 1973, 1974, and 1975; and ends with Box 236, Wetumpka, dates: 1990. For the downloadable PDF, see
**www.archives.alabama.gov/findaids/v10153.pdf.**

## Bibliography

## Alabama Censuses & Substitutes

**1702-1813.** ***Creole Mobile: A Compendium of the Colonial Families of the Central Gulf Coast*** **[Printed Book],** by Johnnie Andrews, Jr. and William David Higgins. Includes index. Typescript published by the Bienville Historical Society, Prichard, AL, 1974, 126 pages. FHL book 976.122 V2.

**1702-1981.** ***Alabama, Surname Files Expanded*** **[Online Database],** digitized and indexed at Ancestry.com. Staff members at the Alabama Department of Archives and History (ADAH) started compiling these records on Alabamians in 1901. They include a variety of items and record types arranged by surname: newspaper clippings, obituaries, local and family histories, donated family research and records, extracts from censuses, research requests made to the archives, and other items. names of people included can predate 1901. See
**www.ancestry.com/search/collections/61266.**

**1706. "Census at Fort Louis de la Louisianne" [Printed Article],** settlements in and around Mobile. Name list published in *Deep South Genealogical Quarterly*, Vol. 1, No. 1 (Aug 1963), p. 30.

**1710-1795.** ***Mobile Land Grants*** **[Printed Book,** by Johnnie Andrews, Jr., and William David Higgins, published By the Bienville Historical Society, Prichard, AL, 1973, 28 pages. FHL book 976.1 A1. Also on microfilm, FHL film #908670.

**1721. "Fort Louis, Mobile" [Printed Article],** settlements in or near Mobile. Name list published in *Deep South Genealogical Quarterly*, Vol. 1, No. 2 Mar 1964), pp. 136-139; and in *New Orleans Genesis*, Vol. 27, No. 107 (Jul 1988).

**1725. "Colonial French Census" [Printed Article],** settlements in or near Mobile. Name list published in *Deep South Genealogical Quarterly*, Vol. 1, No.2 (Dec 1963), p. 86.

**1750-1784.** ***Spanish and British Land Grants in Mississippi Territory*** **[Online Database],** indexed at the Ancestry.com website. Source: Book, same title, by Clifford Neal Smith, 151 pages, see
**http://search.ancestry.com/search/db.aspx?dbid=49216.**

**1753-1999.** ***Alabama, Wills and Probate Records*** **[Online Database],** digitized and indexed at the Ancestry.com website. Source: Ancestry.com extractions from Alabama county, district and probate courts. The contents of a probate file can vary from case to case, but certain details are found in most probates, most importantly, the names and residences of beneficiaries and their relationship to the decedent. An inventory of the estate assets can reveal personal details about the deceased's occupation and lifestyle. There may also be references to debts, deeds, and other documents related to the settling of the estate. Note: Some of the records in this collection are organized in packets. Ancestry has included a table of contents to help navigate the types of documents. This database has 332,894 records. See
**http://search.ancestry.com/search/db.aspx?dbid=8799**

**1763-1813.** ***Mobile Colonials*** **[Printed Article],** by Johnnie Andrews, Jr., microfilm of original book published by Bienville Historical Society, Prichard Museum, Prichard, AL, 1969, 29 pages. Filmed by the Genealogical Society of Utah, 1978, 1 roll, FHL film #1031515.

**1764. "Mobile Residents Who Took the Oath of Allegiance" [Printed Article],** published in *Deep South Genealogical Quarterly*, Vol. 13, No. 2 (May 1976).

**1775-1783.** ***Revolutionary Soldiers in Alabama*** **[Printed Book & Digital Version],** compiled by Thomas M. Owen, publ. Brown Print. Co., 1911, 131 pages, FHL book 976.1 M23. To access the digital version, see the online FHL catalog page:
**www.familysearch.org/search/catalog/147268.**
- See also, ***Alabama Revolutionary War Soldiers [Online Database],*** digitized and indexed at Ancestry.com. see
**www.ancestry.com/search/collections/4237.**

**1781-1795.** ***Anglo-Americans in Spanish Archives: Lists of Anglo-American Settlers in the Spanish Colonies of America; A Finding Aid*** **[Printed Book],** by Lawrence H. Feldman, publ. Genealogical Publishing Co., Baltimore, 1991. Included in this book are lists of heads of household for Mobile and Tombecbe now St. Stephens, Washington County, for the years 1781, 1785, 1786, 1791, and 1795. See FHL book 973 X2.

**1782-1816.** ***Spanish West Florida, Archives of the Spanish Government*** **[Online Database],** indexed at the Ancestry.com website. Source: National Archives microfilm series T1116: Records of the Adjutant General's Office, 1780's-1917. The West Florida region today encompasses the panhandle of the state of Florida, the southernmost parts of the states of Mississippi and Alabama, and the Florida Parishes of the state of Louisiana (the area east of the Mississippi River). This collection consists of transcribed and translated records of the Spanish Empire related to the Spanish province of West Florida. Included records related to property sales, mortgages, inventories and assessments, money lending and debt settlements, wills and probates, inquests, and records related to slavery. This database has 9,202 records. See
**http://search.ancestry.com/search/db.aspx?dbid=2454.**

**1784-1920.** ***Alabama, Marriages, Deaths, Wills, Court, and Other Records*** **[Online Database],** indexed at the Ancestry.com website. Source: ADAH Public Information Subject Files: A Card Index of Personal and Corporate Names and of Subjects. The cards include references to births, marriages, deaths and burials, wills, court records, occupation, land ownership, sureties, registered voters, petitions, interments, plaintiffs and defendants, and other pertinent biographical and family information.
This database has 99,354 records. See
**http://search.ancestry.com/search/db.aspx?dbid=1898.**

**1785. "Some Anglo-Americans in the Deep South" [Printed Article],** includes a census of the town of Tensas, east of Mobile, an article by Winston DeVille, published in *Everton's Genealogical Helper*. (Sept-Oct. 1982): pp5-6.

**1786-1805.** ***Spanish Census Reports at Mobile*** **[Printed Book & Digital Capture],** by Johnnie Andrews, Jr., and William David Higgins, published by Bienville Historical Society, 1973. Included are the years 1786, 1787, 1789, and 1805. To view the digital images, see the FHL catalog page:
**https://familysearch.org/search/catalog/186411.**

**1786. "Colonial Spanish Census, Mobile" [Printed Article],** published in *Deep South Genealogical Quarterly,* Vol. 19, No. 1 (Feb 1982).

**1787.** ***Spanish Census of the Tensaw District*** **[Online Database],** compiled by Sherry Hicks. The list of names is in a table showing name, age married (y/n) and age of spouse. See
**www.trackingyourroots.com/data/1787cen.htm.**

**1788-1798.** ***Original Spanish, French and English Documents (Probate Court, Mobile County, Alabama)*** **[Microfilm & Digital Capture].** Documents deal with land and property matters, criminal and civil matters, bills of sales, slavery matters, military items and vital information. Many records are from the city of Mobile. Filmed by the Probate Court of Mobile Co, 2000, 2 rolls, FHL film #2200097-8. To access the digital images, see the online FHL catalog page:
**www.familysearch.org/search/catalog/976666.**

**1789.** ***Spanish Census for Tombikbee District*** **[Online Database],** compiled by Sherry Hicks. The list of name is in a table showing name, age marriage data, and spouses age. See
**www.trackingyourroots.com/data/1789cen.htm.**

**1796. "Colonial Spanish Census, Mobile Families" [Printed Article],** published in *Everton's Genealogical Helper,* Vol. 37, No. 6 (Nov 1983).

**1796-1907.** ***Alabama, Homestead and Cash Entry Patents, Pre-1908*** **[Online Database],** indexed at the Ancestry.com website. Source: Bureau of Land Management, General Land Office (GLO) Automated Records Project. By 1800, the only GLOs in Alabama areas were at Huntsville, St. Stephens, and Washington, Mississippi Territory. In 1820, the GLOs were at Cahaba, Conecuh Court House, Huntsville, St. Stephens, and Tuscaloosa, Alabama, the only places where federal public land could be purchased. The records are virtually complete, and if your ancestor bought land in Alabama, there will be a record of that purchase in this database. Ancestry's version of this BLM database has the means of searching by GLO, then surname. Information recorded in a Patent (first deed) may include: Name, GLO, Sequence, Document number, Total acres, Signature, Canceled document, Issue date, Mineral rights reserved, Metes and bounds (if applicable), Statutory reference, Multiple warrantee and patentee names, Act or treaty, Entry classification, and Land description. This database has 256,621 records. See
**http://search.ancestry.com/search/db.aspx?dbid=2069.**

**1796-1999.** ***Linkpendium – Alabama: Family History & Genealogy, Census, Birth, Marriage, Death Vita Records & More*** **[Online Databases].** Linkpendium is a genealogical portal site, with links to state, county, town, and local databases. Currently listed are selected sites for Alabama statewide resources (520), and all 67 AL counties, Autauga County (297) to Winston County (17), see **www.linkpendium.com/al-genealogy.**

**1798-2000s.** ***Alabama GenWeb Archives*** **[Online Databases].** The ALGenWeb site offers free genealogical databases with searchable name lists for all Alabama counties, which may include Bibles, Biographies, Cemeteries, Censuses, Court, Death, Deeds, Directories, Histories, Marriages, Military, Newspapers, Obituaries, Photos, Schools, Tax Lists, Wills, and more, see
**http://usgwarchives.net/al/alfiles.htm.**

**1800s – 1946.** ***Alabama Cemetery Records*** **[Online Database],** digitized and indexed at Ancestry.com, from a typescript compiled by the LDS Church's Southern States Mission in 1946. Cemeteries from every county of Alabama are included in this 6 vol.,1,368-page listing. Use the Browse this Collection feature to see the contents of each Volume. See **www.ancestry.com/search/collections/26317.**

**1800-1969.** ***Alabama, Marriage Index*** **[Online Database],** indexed at the Ancestry.com website. Source: Hunting for Bears database & Jordan Dodd's Early America Marriages: Alabama to 1825. This database has 2,404,099 records. See
**http://search.ancestry.com/search/db.aspx?dbid=7838.**

**1801, 1808, 1810. "Washington County, Mississippi Territory (now Alabama) Census," [Printed Article],** published in *The Alabama Genealogical Register,* Vol. 9, No. 3 (September 1967), pp 123-26.

**1802.** ***List of Taxable Property: Madison County, Mississippi Territory*** **[Online Database],** compiled by Lisa R. Franklin. See
**www.trackingyourroots.com/data/1802madison.htm.**

**1802-1825.** ***Alabama, Compiled Marriages*** **[Online Database],** indexed at the Ancestry.com website. Source: Jordan Dodd's Early American Marriages: Alabama to 1825. Each entry includes groom, bride, marriage date, county, and state. This database has 12,255 records. See
**http://search.ancestry.com/search/db.aspx?dbid=2080.**

**1803-1816.** ***Washington County, Mississippi Territory Tax Rolls*** **[Printed Book],** compiled by Ben and Jean Strickland, published by the authors, Milton, FL, 1980, 117 pages. Washington County, Mississippi Territory later became Wayne, Greene, Jones, Perry, George and Jackson Counties, Mississippi; and Washington, Baldwin, Monroe, Clarke and Mobile Counties, Alabama. Includes index. See FHL book 976 R4s.

**1805.** ***Taxable Property: Washington County, Mississippi Territory*** **[Online Database],** compiled by Lisa R. Franklin. The list includes male inhabitants over 21 possessing taxable property. Identifies house lots, lands, real estate, with number of houses, number of slaves, horses, and cattle. See
**www.trackingyourroots.com/data/1805tax.htm.**

**1805-1967.** ***Alabama, County Marriages*** **[Online Database]**, indexed at the Ancestry.com website. Source: FamilySearch extractions from microfilm of original records at the Family History Library, Salt Lake City, UT. Each index record includes, Name, Age at marriage, Marriage date, Marriage place, and Parents' names. This database has 5,117,756 records, see **http://search.ancestry.com/search/db.aspx?dbid=61365.**

**1808-1870.** ***Index to Alabama Wills*** [Online Database], indexed at the Ancestry.com website. Source: Book, same title, compiled by the AL Society, DAR, 190 pages, see
**http://search.ancestry.com/search/db.aspx?dbid=48006.**

**1809.** ***Mississippi Territory Census*** [Printed Book]. Includes present-day Alabama area. A name list was published as part of Vol. 5: *The Territory of Mississippi, 1798-1817;* in *The Territorial Papers of the United States,* compiled and edited by Clarence Edwin Carter, United States Department of State. The series is no longer listed in the FHL catalog, but may be available at Amazon, Google Books, et al. For a catalog entry at the HathiTrust Digital Library, see
**https://catalog.hathitrust.org/Record/000495370.**

**1809. "Madison County (Now Alabama) 1809 Census," [Printed Article],** name list published in *The Alabama Genealogical Register*, Vol. 10, No. 4 (December 1968): pp175-82.

**1809-1920.** ***Alabama, Compiled Marriages From Selected Counties*** **[Online Database],** indexed at the Ancestry.com website. Source: Jordan Dodd's Early American Marriages: Alabama, 1800-1920. Visit the webpage for a list of counties and years of coverage. This database has 298,298 records. See
**http://search.ancestry.com/search/db.aspx?dbid=4192.**

**1809-1950.** ***Alabama, County Marriages*** **[Online Database],** digitized and indexed at the FamilySearch.org website. This collection of marriage records for Alabama counties includes, 1) indexed records with images, 2) indexed records without images, and 3) images which can be browsed but do not have searchable indexes. This database currently has 2,050,570 records, see
**https://familysearch.org/search/collection/1743384.**

**1809-1959.** ***County Records Online for Madison County, Alabama*** **[Online Database].** The following databases are available online at the Madison County Records Center website: Confederate Pensions, 1898-1907; Confederate Pensions, 1908-1914; Cotton Mill Affidavits for Child Laborers, 1908-1915; Delinquent Tax Docket, 1890; Estray, 1902-1918; Justice of the Peace Bond (and other bonds), 1847-1853; Madison County Minute Book, 1811-1819; Marriage Record Indexes, 1809-1973; Miscellaneous Court Records; Naturalization Certificates, 1847-1906; Naturalization Records, 1818-1846; Pensions Warrant Delivery Book 2; Probate Record Indexes, 1809-1965; Unofficial Register of Births, 1881-1912; and more. See
**http://mcrc.madisoncountyal.gov/mcrc.**

**1809-1985.** ***Alabama Probate Records*** **[Online Database],** digitized at the FamilySearch.org website. This collection includes digital images of various probate records created in the county courts in Alabama. It includes wills, administrations, guardianships, estate inventories, bonds and other records. This database has 322,058 images, see
**https://familysearch.org/search/collection/1925446.**

**1810.** ***Washington Co., Mississippi Territorial Census*** **[Online Database],** a typescript name list in alphabetical order. See
**www.trackingyourroots.com/data/wshngt10.htm.**

**1810.** ***Census of Baldwin County, Mississippi Territory*** **[Online Database],** compiled by Lisa R. Franklin.
**www.trackingyourroots.com/data/1810bald.htm**

**1810.** ***List of Taxable Property in Madison County, MS Territory*** **[Online Database],** compiled by Lisa R. Franklin. See
**www.trackingyourroots.com/data/1810madison.htm.**

**1810-1890.** ***Alabama, Compiled Census and Census Substitutes Index*** **[Online Database],** indexed at the Ancestry.com website. This database was originally edited by Ronald Jackson of Accelerated Indexing Systems, Salt Lake City UT and acquired by Ancestry in 1999. This collection contains the following indexes: 1810 Census Index; 1810-1819 Tax Lists Index; 1820 Federal Census Index; 1830 Federal Census Index; 1830-1839 Early Records; 1840 Federal Census Index; 1840 Pensioners Index; 1850 Federal Census Index; 1855 State Census Index; 1860 Federal Census Index; 1860 Mortality Schedules; 1860 Slave Schedules; 1870 Federal census Index; 1890 Pensioners Index; Alabama Early Census, Vol. 1 and Vol. 2. See
**http://search.ancestry.com/search/db.aspx?dbid=3531.**

**1811-1819.** ***Decennary Census Index*** **[Printed Index],** by Ronald Vern Jackson, published by Accelerated Indexing, Salt Lake City UT, 1983,. Although the title has impossible dates for Alabama, it appears that the name lists were extracted from areas of present Alabama (Mississippi Territory, 1811-1816; Alabama Territory, 1817-18; and the state of Alabama, 1819. See FHL book 976.1 X22j 1811-1819.

**1812.** ***Soldiers in Franklin County, AL War of 1812*** **[Online Database],** compiled by Patricia Cooper, Russelville, AL. See
**www.trackingyourroots.com/data/1812.htm**

**1813.** ***Baldwin County, Alabama Voters*** **[Online Database],** compiled by Lisa R. Franklin. See
**www.trackingyourroots.com/data/1813bald.htm**

**1813.** ***Taxable Property of Clarke County for the Year 1813*** **[Online Database],** compiled by Lisa R. Franklin. See
**www.trackingyourroots.com/data/1813clrk.htm**

**1813.** ***Petition of Inhabitants of Mobile County*** **[Online Database],** compiled by Lisa R. Franklin. See
**www.trackingyourroots.com/data/1813mobi.htm**

**1813.** ***Petition by the Inhabitants on Chickesawhay River, Washington County*** [Online Database], compiled by Lisa R. Franklin. See
**www.trackingyourroots.com/data/1813wash.htm**

**1814-1935.** ***Alabama, Marriage Indexes*** **[Online Database],** indexed at the Ancestry.com website. Source: WPA indexes, by county, at the ADAH, Montgomery, AL. Each index record may contain, Full name, Spouse's full name, Marriage date, and Marriage county. This database has 521,550 records:
**http://search.ancestry.com/search/db.aspx?dbid=60922**

**1816.** ***Inhabitants of Alabama in 1816*** **[Printed Book & Digital Version],** published by the Broken Arrow Chapter, DAR, Pell City, AL, 1955, 100 pages. FHL book 976.1 X3i. To view the digital version, see the FHL catalog page:
**https://familysearch.org/search/catalog/215867**

**1816. "Mississippi Territory Census" [Printed Article].** Census name list published in the *Alabama Historical Quarterly*, Vol. 24, No. 1 (Spring 1962).

**1816. "Clarke County, Mississippi Territory (now AL)" [Printed Article],** name list published in *American Monthly Magazine*, Vol. 83, No. 5 (May 1949).

**1816. Madison County, AL Census [Online Database],** compiled by Lisa R. Franklin. See
**www.trackingyourroots.com/data/1816madison.htm**

**1816. "Monroe County, Mississippi Territory (now AL)" [Printed Articles],** name list published in *American Monthly Magazine*, Vol. 83, No. 4 (April 1949) and in *Roots & Branches,* Vol. 19, No. 2 (April 1998), and in *Clarke County Historical Society Quarterly*, Vol. 10, No. 1 (Summer 1985).

**1816.** ***List of Taxable Property Baldwin County, MS Territory*** **[Online Database],** compiled by Lisa R. Franklin. See
**www.trackingyourroots.com/data/1816baldwin.htm**

**1816.** ***List of Taxable Property of Washington County, MS Territory*** **[Online Database],** compiled by Lisa R. Franklin. See
**www.trackingyourroots.com/data/1816washington.htm**

**1816.** ***List of the Taxable Property of Monroe County for the year 1816*** **[Online Database],** compiled by Lisa R. Franklin. See
**www.trackingyourroots.com/data/1816mnro.htm**

**1816.** ***List of Taxable Property of Mobile County for the Year 1816*** **[Online Database],** compiled by Lisa R. Franklin. See
**www.trackingyourroots.com/data/1816tax.htm**

**1816-1847.** ***Alabama Divorce Cases (U.S. Chancery Court, Alabama 1st District Southern Division)*** **[Microfilm & Digital Capture],** from the originals at the University of South Alabama, Mobile, AL. Filmed by the Genealogical Society of Utah, 1994, 1 roll, FHL film #1940655. To access the digital images, see the online FHL catalog page:
**www.familysearch.org/search/catalog/696422.**

**1816-1942.** ***Alabama, Select Marriages*** **[Online Database],** indexed at the Ancestry.com website. Source: FamilySearch extractions. This database has 2,858,848 records, see
**http://search.ancestry.com/search/db.aspx?dbid=60000**

**1816-1957.** ***Alabama Marriages*** **[Online Database],** digitized and indexed at the FamilySearch.org website. This is a name index to marriage records from the state of Alabama, extracted from the microfilmed records at the Family History Library in Salt Lake City, UT. This database has 1,338,311 records, see
**https://familysearch.org/search/collection/1674672**

**1816-1974.** ***Alabama – Collection Catalog*** **[Online Databases],** digitized and indexed databases at the MyHeritage website: 12 collections with 9,319,560 records. This is a subscription site, but index searching is free. Incudes the following Alabama database titles: 1) *Alabama, Deaths, 1908-1974*; 2) *Alabama, Marriages, 1816-1957*; 3) *Land Patents – Alabama*; 4) *1866 Alabama State Census*; 5) *1855 Alabama State Census*; 6) *Birmingham Southern College, 1914-1922* (Yearbooks); 7) *Hand-Book of Alabama, a Complete Index To the State, With Map, 1892*; 8) *Alabama A&M College, General Catalog of Sigma Alpha Epsilon, 1918* (Yearbooks); 9) *A History of Methodism in Alabama*; 10) *History of Alabama and Dictionary of Alabama Biography* (1921); 11) Alabama: Her History, Resources, War Records, and Public Men, 1540-1872; and 12) *Early Settlers of Alabama*. See
**www.myheritage.com/records/Alabama/all-records.**

**1816-1992.** ***Alabama Newspaper Archives*** **[Online Database],** digitized and indexed at the GenealogyBank.com website, newspapers from the following Alabama cities are available: Birmingham, Blakeley, Cahawba, Claiborne, Cullman, Grove Hill, Huntsville, Marion, Mobile, Montgomery, Notasulga, Selma, St. Stephens, Tuscaloosa, and Tuscumbia. Go to the search screen for Alabama Newspaper Archives:
**www.genealogybank.com/gbnk/newspapers/explore/USA/Alabama**

**1817.** ***List of Voters in Baldwin County for 1817*** **[Online Database],** compiled by Lisa R. Franklin. See
**www.trackingyourroots.com/data/1817bald.htm.**

**1817.** ***List of Taxable Property of Mobile County, Alabama for the Year 1817*** **[Online Database],** compiled by Lisa R. Franklin. See
**www.trackingyourroots.com/data/1817mobile.htm**

**1818. "Montgomery County 1818 Alabama Territory Census" [Printed Article].** name list published in *Alabama Historical Quarterly*, Vol. 18, No. 1 (Spring 1956). Note: The Montgomery County name list from the 1818 AL Territorial census appears to be the only surviving county.

**1818-1936.** ***Alabama County Marriages*** **[Online Database],** digitized and indexed at the FamilySearch.org website. Source: FamilySearch extractions from microfilm at the Family History Library, Salt Lake City, UT. Each index record includes the names of the bride and groom, year of marriage, and reference number. This database has 80,469 records, see
**https://familysearch.org/search/collection/2534485**

**1818-1939.** ***Alabama, Civil Appointments*** **[Online Database],** indexed at the Ancestry.com website. Source: Card Index to the Commissions and Civil Appointments Register of the Secretary of State (ADAH, Montgomery, AL). This collection consists of a card index to officials who were appointed, commissioned, or elected in Alabama between 1818 and 1939. The cards are in alphabetical order by surname, and details for each person may include: Name, County, Precinct, Office Held, Date of

Appointment, Date of Commission, Date of Election, And Source. This database has 96,659 records. See **http://search.ancestry.com/search/db.aspx?dbid=60923**

**1818-1937.** ***County Divorce Reports (Alabama Bureau of Vital Statistic)*** **[Microfilm & Digital Capture],** from the originals at the ADAH, Montgomery, AL. Divorces once required an act of the legislature. From 1818-1864, the divorces were compiled by the ADAH from the Acts of Alabama. Includes names, complainant, respondent, year of act, and page number from acts. Some include the county of residence. For later years, the various courts reported divorces to the Bureau of Vital Statistics. An index is included for 1908-1937. Filmed by the Genealogical Society of Utah, 1988-1990, 11 rolls, beginning with FHL film #1653551 (2 compilations, 1818-1864). To access the digital images, see the online FHL catalog page: **www.familysearch.org/search/catalog/631927.**

**1818-1948.** ***Lawrence County, Alabama, Marriage Index*** **[Online Database],** indexed at the Ancestry.com website. This database is also accessible at the Lawrence County Archives website. For details, see the link at Ancestry's webpage. This database has 68,548 records, see **http://search.ancestry.com/search/db.aspx?dbid=70735**

**1819-2006.** ***Alabama, Huntsville-Madison County Public Library Obituary Index*** **[Online Database],** indexed at the Ancestry.com website. This database is also accessible at the Huntsville-Madison County Public Library website. For details, see the link at Ancestry's webpage. This database has 62,322 records: **http://search.ancestry.com/search/db.aspx?dbid=70696**

**1820.** ***Alabama (State) Census Returns 1820 and An Abstract of Federal Census of Alabama 1830*** **[Printed Book & Digital Capture],** by Marie Bankhead Owen, published by Genealogical Publishing Co., Inc., 1967, FHL book 976.1 X2o. The AL 1820 state census was taken separately from the 1820 federal census. Includes name of head of household; free white males and females in age categories; number of slaves and free persons of color in age categories. To access the digital images of this book, see the online FHL catalog page: **www.familysearch.org/search/catalog/42466.**

**1820.** ***State Census for the Year 1820*** **[Microfilm & Digital Capture],** from the originals at the ADAH, Montgomery, AL, filmed by the Genealogical Society of Utah, 1988, 2 rolls, FHL film #1533830 (Baldwin, Conecuh, Dallas, Franklin, Limestone, St. Clair, Shelby, and Wilcox counties); and FHL film #1533833 (Lawrence Co). To access the digital images, see the online FHL catalog page: **www.familysearch.org/search/catalog/632428.**

**1820.** ***Alabama Census Returns, 1820*** [Online Database], indexed at the Ancestry.com website, see **http://search.ancestry.com/search/db.aspx?dbid=48536**

**"1820 (State Census) Dallas County, Alabama"** [Printed Article] name list was published in *American Monthly Magazine,* Vol. 78, No. 3 (March 1944).

***1820 State Census of Lawrence County, Alabama*** **[Printed Book & Digital Version],** compiled and published by the Tennessee Valley Genealogical Society, Huntsville, AL, 1977, 41 pages, FHL book 976.1 A1. To access the digital version, see the online FHL catalog page: **www.familysearch.org/search/catalog/134941.**

**1820-1863.** ***Alabama, Register of Officers*** **[Online Database],** digitized and indexed at Ancestry.com. Source: Records of the Adjutant General Office of Alabama, ADAH, Montgomery, AL. The Adjutant General is appointed by the governor to supervise all the activities of the militia and all military property held by the state. This series of five volumes from the Adjutant General's Office of Alabama documents officers who served in the Alabama militia and Alabama military units from the beginning of statehood until the middle of the Civil War. Information included in the registers consists of the name of the officer, rank, the date of commission, date of resignation, remarks, and the name of the unit in which the officer served. Volume 5, which covers the years 1861 to 1863, also includes the date elected and residence place for each officer. This database has 26,094 records, see **www.ancestry.com/search/collections/60924.**

**1820-1866.** ***Alabama State Censuses*** **[Online Database],** digitized and indexed at the Ancestry.com website. Source: ADAH, Montgomery AL. This database contains state censuses from Alabama for the years 1820, 1850, 1855, and 1866. Each of these

censuses recorded the names of the head of households and the number of other household inhabitants according to gender and age categories. Some years also included race categories and distinguished between individuals who were free and slave. Unfortunately, records do not exist for every county that existed at the time. Below is a list showing what counties are available for each year. **1820:** Baldwin, Conecuh, Dallas, Franklin, Limestone, St. Clair, and Wilcox. **1850:** Autauga, Baldwin, Barbour, Benton, Blount, Butler, Chambers, Cherokee, Choctaw, Clarke, Coffee, Conecuh, Coosa, Covington, Dale, Dallas, De Kalb, Franklin, Greene, Henry, Jefferson, Lawrence, Macon, Madison, Marion, Marshall, Mobile, Monroe, Montgomery, Morgan, Perry, Pike, Randolph, Sumter, Tuscaloosa, Washington, and Wilcox. **1855:** Autauga, Baldwin, Blount, Coffee, Franklin, Henry, Lowndes, Macon, Mobile, Montgomery, Pickens, Tallapoosa, and Tuscaloosa. **1866:** Autauga, Baldwin, Barbour, Bibb, Blount, Butler, Calhoun, Chambers, Cherokee, Choctaw, Clarke, Coffee, Conecuh, Coosa, Covington, Dale, Dallas, De Kalb, Fayette, Franklin, Greene, Henry, Jackson, Jefferson, Lauderdale, Lawrence, Limestone, Lowndes, Macon, Marengo, Marion, Marshall, Mobile, Monroe, Montgomery, Morgan, Perry, Pickens, Pike, Randolph, Russell, Shelby, St Clair, Sumter, Talladega, Tallapoosa, Tuscaloosa, Walker, Washington, Wilcox, and Winston, see
**http://search.ancestry.com/search/db.aspx?dbid=1576**

**1820-1900.** ***Alabama Records*** **[Microfilm &Digital Capture],** compiled by Kathleen Paul Jones and Pauline Jones Gandrud, published by Huntsville Democrat, Huntsville, AL, 1939-, 235 vols. At least one volume for each Alabama county, this major compilation includes probate, vital (births, deaths, marriages), cemetery, Bible, census lists, (including AL 1850 state census), military, land, and court records. Also includes extracts from newspapers, family history information, and other miscellaneous materials of genealogical value. Filmed by the Genealogical Society of Utah, 1939-1983, 42 rolls, To access the digital images, see the online FHL catalog page: **https://familysearch.org/search/catalog/366715**

**1821-1829.** ***Alabama Decennary Census Index*** **[Printed Book],** edited by Ronald Vern Jackson, published Accelerated Indexing, Salt Lake City UT, FHL book 976.1 X22j 1821-1829.

**1824-2013.** ***Huntsville, Alabama, Cemetery Index*** **[Online Database],** indexed at the FamilySearch.org website. This database is also accessible at the City of Huntsville website. For details, see the link at Ancestry's webpage. This database has 33,642 records:
**http://search.ancestry.com/search/db.aspx?dbid=9263**

**1829-1968.** ***Alabama, Madison County Chancery and Circuit Court Records*** **[Online database]**, digitized at the FamilySearch.org website. Source: FamilySearch extractions from microfilm of the original records at the Madison County Record Center, Huntsville, AL. Information may differ between court files and may include any of the following: Name of interested parties, Associated event dates such as marriage, divorce, death, or probate; Names of relatives and heirs such as spouse, minor children, and dependents; Names of witnesses; Name of court; Type of event; Date of court hearing; Residences; Occupations; Lists or property disputed; and Document and recording dates. Browse through the images, organized by Court Record Type, and Year. This database has 442,506 images, see
**https://familysearch.org/search/collection/1978142**

**1830-1840.** See ***Alabama, 1830 and 1840 Federal Census: Population Schedules*** **[Microfilm & Digital Capture],** filmed by the National Archives, 1938, 1949, 1950, 8 rolls, beginning with FHL film #2328 (AL 1830: Blount Franklin, Jackson, Lauderdale, and Lawrence counties). To access the digital images, see the online FHL catalog page:
**www.familysearch.org/search/catalog/745480.**

**1830-1976.** ***Alabama Estate Files*** **[Online Database],** digitized and partially indexed at the FamilySearch.org website. Incudes images of estate files created by the probate courts of various Alabama counties. Probates were generally recorded in the county of residence. This collection covers probate records created 1830-1976. This database has 2,197,466 images, see
**https://familysearch.org/search/collection/1978117**

**1830-1996.** ***Birmingham, Alabama, Obituary Index*** **[Online Database],** indexed at the Ancestry.com website. This database is also accessible at the Birmingham Public Library website. For details, see the link at Ancestry's webpage. This database has 233,459 records. See
**http://search.ancestry.com/search/db.aspx?dbid=70021**

**1831-1839.** ***Decennary Census Index (Alabama)*** **[Printed Index],** by Ronald Vern Jackson, published Accelerated Indexing, Salt Lake city UT, FHL book 976.1 X22j 1821-1829).

**1832-1972.** ***Alabama, Episcopal Church Registers Index*** **[Online Database],** indexed at the Ancestry.com website. This database is also accessible at the Birmingham Public Library website. Source: Alabama Episcopal Church Registers, Birmingham Public Library. For details, see Ancestry's link to the Birmingham Public Library. This database has 14,276 records. See
**http://search.ancestry.com/search/db.aspx?dbid=70662**

**1834-1861.** ***Voters Lists, Sumter County, Alabama*** **[Printed Book],** compiled by James T. Dawson, published by the Lauderdale County Department of Archives and History, Inc., Meridian, MS, 1988. 2 volumes. See FHL books 976.141 N4d (vol. 1) and 976.141 N4d (vol. 2).

**1835-2014.** ***Lawrence County, AL, Burial Index*** **[Online Database],** indexed at the Ancestry.com website. This database is also accessible at the Lawrence County Archives website. For details, see the link at Ancestry's webpage. This database has 35,245 records. See
**http://search.ancestry.com/search/db.aspx?dbid=70732**

**1836-1995.** ***Alabama, Mobile Magnolia Cemetery Interment Cards*** **[Online Database],** digitized and indexed at the FamilySearch.org website. Source: Friends of Magnolia Cemetery Inc., Mobile, AL. Each index record includes Name of deceased, Birth year, and Death date. This database has 32,735 records, see
**https://familysearch.org/search/collection/2286030**

**1840-1950.** ***Alabama, Sumter County Circuit Court Files*** **[Online Database],** digitized at the FamilySearch.org website. Circuit court case files from the courthouse in Livingston. This collection is being published as images become available. This database currently has 73,069 images, see
**https://familysearch.org/search/collection/1939212**

**1843-1951.** ***Alabama Death Record of State Convicts*** **[Online Database],** from ADAH databases, digitized and indexed at the Ancestry.com website. Death records for Alabama state convicts who died while either a prisoner in custody or on parole are in this database. The records are ordered chronologically and in the 1908-1951 records chronologically and then alphabetically. This database has 3,867 records. See
**http://search.ancestry.com/search/db.aspx?dbid=1710**

**1850.** ***Alabama State Census*** **[Original Manuscripts & Online Database].** This state census was taken separately from the 1850 federal census. Originals at ADAH, but little information about the extent of the surviving schedules is provided by the ADAH, except the following: "no index, includes name of head of household; free white males and females in age categories; number of slaves and free persons of color in age categories." The 1850 AL state census (37 counties) was digitized and indexed online as part of Ancestry's *1820-1866 Alabama State Censuses* database, see
**http://search.ancestry.com/search/db.aspx?dbid=1576**

**1850.** ***Alabama, 1850 Federal Census: Population Schedules*** **[Microfilm & Digital Capture],** filmed by the National Archives, 1964, 24 rolls, beginning with FHL film #2343 (Autauga, Baldwin, Barbour and Benton counties). To access the digital images, see the online FHL catalog page:
**www.familysearch.org/search/catalog/744404.**

**1850.** ***United States Census (Mortality Schedules), Alabama, 1850: Autauga thru Wilcox Counties*** **[Microfilm & Digital Capture].** This database is the state's copy of the 1850 Mortality Schedules (Schedule 3), now located at the ADAH in Montgomery. Filmed by the Genealogical Society of Utah, 1988, 1 roll, FHL film #1533724. To access the digital images, see the online FHL catalog page:
**www.familysearch.org/search/catalog/632401.**

**1850.** ***Alabama 1850 Agricultural and Manufacturing Census*** **[Printed Book],** transcribed by Linda L. Green, published Woodbridge, VA, 1999, 2 vols. Includes surname index for each volume. Contents: Vol. 1: Dale, Dallas, De Kalb, Fayette, Franklin, Greene, Hancock and Henry counties. Vol. 2. Jackson, Jefferson, Lawrence, Limestone, Lowndes,
Macon, Madison and Marengo counties. FHL book 976.1 X2g v.1-2.

**1852. "Alabama People Listed in 1852 California State Census," [Printed Article],** in *Alabama Family History and Genealogy News,* Vol. 18, No. 3 (Jul 1997). NOTE: Lost your Alabama ancestor? Maybe he got the California gold rush fever. Buckminster Fuller once said, "The world is flat and tilted – anything loose eventually rolls to California."

**1855.** ***Alabama State Census*** **[Original Manuscripts & Online Database].** 14 counties extant: Autauga, Baldwin, Blount, Coffee, Franklin, Henry, Lowndes, Macon, Mobile, Montgomery (on film, but not included in the index), Pickens, Sumter (not on microfilm and not included in the Index), Tallapoosa, Tuscaloosa. Includes name of head of household; number of free white males and females in age categories; number of slaves and free persons of color in age categories. Note: the 1855 AL state census was digitized and indexed online as part of Ancestry's *1820-1866 Alabama State Censuses database,* see
**http://search.ancestry.com/search/db.aspx?dbid=1576**

**1855.** ***Alabama State Census*** **[Online Database],** indexed at the FamilySearch.org website. This index was obtained from the ADAH, Montgomery, AL. Each index record is limited to a Name, Event place, Event date, and Page. This database has 34,978 records, see
**https://familysearch.org/search/collection/1915984**

**1860.** ***Alabama, 1860 Federal Census: Population Schedules*** **[Microfilm & Digital Capture],** filmed by the National Archives, 1950,1967, 43 rolls, beginning with FHL film #803001 (Autauga, Baldwin and Barbour counties). To access the digital images, see the online FHL catalog page:
**www.familysearch.org/search/catalog/703854.**

***1860 Mortality Schedules for Alabama: Autauga thru Winston Counties*** **[Microfilm & Digital Capture],** from the originals at the ADAH, Montgomery, AL. This record is the state's copy of the 1860 Mortality Schedule, providing statistical information on persons who died during the year ending 30 June 1860, such as name, age, sex, race, free or slave, married or widowed, state or nation of births, month of death, occupation, cause of death and number of days ill. Filmed by the Genealogical Society of Utah, 1988, 2 rolls, FHL film #1533724 (Autauga thru Madison counties) & #153330 (Marengo thru Winston counties). To access the digital images, see the online FHL catalog page:
**www.familysearch.org/search/catalog/632406.**

**1860-1861.** ***County Directory, Marengo County, Alabama*** **[Online Database],** indexed at the USGenWeb site for Marengo Co AL. See
**http://files.usgwarchives.net/al/marengo/history/1860dir.txt.**

**1860-1865.** ***Alabama, Civil War Soldiers*** **[Online Database],** indexed at Ancestry.com. This database was created from an 8 x 5 card file maintained by the Alabama Department of Archives and History from the early 1900s until 1982. As staff came across information related to Alabama individuals during the American Civil War, a card was created. Information on individuals exempted from military service, or who served in the militia or home guard, is included. Soldiers from other states that have some connection to Alabama are also included. Sources include muster rolls, governors' correspondence, veterans' censuses, manuscript collections, newspapers, and pension records. This database has 238,288 records, see
**www.ancestry.com/search/collections/61017.**

**1861.** ***Roster of the Conecuh Guards, CSA, Conecuh County, Alabama*** **[Online Database],** index at the USGenWeb site for Conecuh Co AL. See
**http://files.usgwarchives.net/al/conecuh/military/civilwar/rosters/conecuhguards.txt**

**1861-1865.** ***Alabama Civil War Service Records of Confederate Soldiers*** **[Online Database],** digitized and indexed at the FamilySearch.org website. The records include a jacket/envelope for each soldier, labeled with his name, his rank, and the unit in which he served. Each record typically contains card abstracts of entries relating to the soldier as found in original muster rolls, returns, rosters, payrolls, appointment books, hospital registers, Union prison registers and rolls, parole rolls, inspection reports; and the originals of any papers relating solely to the particular soldier. Index courtesy of Fold3. This database has 1,213,534 records, see
**https://familysearch.org/search/collection/1932139**

**1861-1865.** ***Alabama Civil War Service Records of Union Soldiers*** **[Online Database],** digitized and indexed at the FamilySearch.org website. Includes Union service records of soldiers who served in the First Regiment of Alabama Cavalry. The records include a jacket / envelope for each soldier, labeled with his name, his rank, and the unit in which he served. National Archive Microfilm series M276. Index courtesy of Fold3. This database has 31,582 records, see
**https://familysearch.org/search/collection/1932389**

**1861-1865.** ***Alabama Civil War Muster Rolls*** **[Online Database],** from ADAH databases, digitized and indexed at the Ancestry.com website. The rolls are for Confederate units formed in Alabama, though many operated outside of the state over the course of the war. The records include rolls for infantry, cavalry, artillery,

reserves, navy, marines, and even out-of-state regiments. Muster rolls provide a "roll call" for a military unit at a specified place and time.
This database has 254,355 records, see
**http://search.ancestry.com/search/db.aspx?dbid=1736**

**1861-1865.** ***Index to Soldiers and Sailors of the Civil War*** **[Online Database],** a searchable name index to 6.3 million Civil War soldiers, Union and Confederate, is available online at the National Park Service website. A search can be done by surname, first name, state, or unit. Alabama has 200,269 indexed entries of soldiers (197,427 Confederate, 2,842 Union). To search for one, see
**www.nps.gov/civilwar/soldiers-and-sailors-database.htm.**

**1862-1863.** ***Roll of the Clintonsville Grays, Coffee County, Alabama*** **[Online Database],** indexed at the USGenWeb site for Coffee Co AL. See
**http://files.usgwarchives.net/al/coffee/military/civilwar/clintons.txt**

**1862-1868.** ***Probate Fee Books, Choctaw County, Alabama*** **[Online Database],** index at the ALGenWeb site for Choctaw Co AL. See
**www.algw.org/choctaw/Feebook.htm**

**1862-1947.** ***Alabama Confederate Pensions and Service Records*** **[Online Database],** from ADAH databases, digitized and indexed at the Ancestry.com website. This collection contains records that relate to Confederate veterans' pensions in Alabama. During the 35 years after the Civil War until 1900, only disabled soldiers were receiving a pension from the state of Alabama for their service. In 1899, the state legislature authorized pensions for Confederate veterans who weren't disabled and resided in Alabama or for their widows. The warrants for these payments were drawn up by the state auditor and include a name, number, occupation, where wounded, date of wound, whether a widow or veteran, company, regiment, and branch of service. Other records have applications for relief of veterans or their widows, correspondence, affidavits, widow applications for reclassification, and other related materials. These records may add the name of a spouse to a veteran. This database has 1,929,298 records, see
**http://search.ancestry.com/search/db.aspx?dbid=1593**

**1864. Militia List, Coffee County, Alabama [Online Database],** indexed at the USGenWeb site for Coffee Co AL. See
**http://files.usgwarchives.net/al/coffee/military/civilwar/cofemili.txt**

**1865-1866.** ***Internal Revenue Assessment Lists of Alabama*** **[Microfilm & Digital Capture],** from originals at the National Archives in Washington, DC. Names of taxpayers (both personal and property) are arranged within three districts, subdivided by division, and then by year/month of assessment. District 1: Baldwin, Barbour, Butler, Choctaw, Clarke, Coffee, Conecuh, Covington, Dale, Henry, Marengo, Mobile, Monroe, Pike, Washington, and Wilcox counties. District 2: Autauga, Bibb, Chambers, Coosa, Dallas, Greene, Lowndes, Macon, Montgomery, Perry, Pickens, Randolph, Russell, Shelby, Sumter, Talladega, Tallapoosa, and Tuscaloosa. District 3: Blount, Calhoun, Cherokee, DeKalb, Fayette, Franklin, Jackson, Jefferson, Lauderdale, Lawrence, Limestone, Madison, Marion, Marshall, Morgan, St. Clair, Walker, and Winston counties. Filmed by the National Archives, series M0754, 6 rolls, as follows:

- District 1 (1865-1866), FHL film #1578453.
- District 1 (1866), FHL film #1578454.
- District 2 (1865-1866), FHL film #1578455.
- District 2 (1866), FHL film #1578456.
- District 3 (1865-1866), FHL film #1578457.
- District 3 (1866), FHL film #1578458.

To access the digital images, see the online FHL catalog page:
**www.familysearch.org/search/catalog/577891.**

**1865-1872.** ***Alabama, Freedmen's Bureau Field Office Records*** **[Online Database],** digitized at the FamilySearch.org website. The Freedmen's Bureau was created in 1865 at the end of the American Civil War to supervise relief efforts including education, health care, food and clothing, refugee camps, legalization of marriages, employment, labor contracts, and securing back pay, bounty payments and pensions. These records include letters and endorsements sent and received, account books, applications for rations, rosters of officers and employees, special and general orders and circulars received, special orders and circulars issued, records relating to claims, court trials, property restoration, and homesteads. This database has 61,984 images, see
**https://familysearch.org/search/collection/2333780**

SCHEDULE NO. 3. **WHITE POPULATION** 13

Of Township No. 1, Range 9 E, in Conecuh County, Alabama,
Census of 1866.

EXPLANATION.—Where there is a fractional Township, the fact should be stated. Care should be taken to give the Number of the Township, and the Range, "East" or "West" as the case may be. It would be advisable to attach together, in book form, the blank sheets used for the Township Census in each County.

| NAMES. | MALES. Under 10 Years. | 10 to 20 | Over 20 | No. of Males. | FEMALES. Under 10 Years. | 10 to 20 | Over 20 | No. of Females. | Total of Township. |
|---|---|---|---|---|---|---|---|---|---|
| William T. Godwin | | 1 | | 1 | | 1 | | 1 | 2 |
| John N Gasky | | | 1 | 1 | | | | | 1 |
| William Moore | | | 1 | 1 | | 1 | | 1 | 2 |
| Peter Skamban | | | 1 | 1 | | | | | 1 |
| Caroline Grisham | | | | | 1 | 1 | 1 | 3 | 3 |
| Elizabeth Hammack | 1 | 1 | | 2 | | 2 | 1 | 3 | 5 |
| Mary J. Anthony | | | | | 1 | | 1 | 2 | 2 |
| Ambrose M. Meadows | | | 1 | 1 | 1 | 1 | 1 | 3 | 4 |
| Sarah Steele | | | | | | | 1 | 1 | 1 |
| James Stewart | | | 1 | 1 | | | | | 1 |
| William Jarnegan | 2 | | 1 | 3 | 3 | 2 | 1 | 6 | 9 |
| William B. Stanton | 2 | 2 | 1 | 5 | | 2 | 1 | 3 | 8 |
| Sabra Brenton | | 1 | 1 | 2 | | 2 | 1 | 3 | 5 |
| Betsy P. Coleman | 2 | | | 2 | 1 | | 1 | 2 | 4 |
| Feriby C. Powell | 3 | 1 | | 4 | 1 | | 1 | 2 | 6 |

**1866.** ***State Census for the State of Alabama in the Year 1866*** **[Microfilm & Digital Capture],** from originals at the ADAH, Montgomery, AL. Includes separate schedules for "white" and "colored" persons. This census lists the head of household and has statistical information about the makeup of the household. In some counties, the records indicate whether there were soldiers in the household who were killed, disabled, or died of sickness. Filmed by the Genealogical Society of Utah, 1988, 8 rolls, beginning with FHL film #1533830 (Autauga Co). To access the digital images, see the online FHL catalog page: **www.familysearch.org/search/catalog/632558.**

- See also, ***1866 Alabama State Census Index*** **[Online Database],** indexed at the FamilySearch.org website. Compiled from the microfilm of the original schedules held by the ADAH, Montgomery, AL, This database has 243,781 records, see https://familysearch.org/search/collection/1915987.

- See also, **1866.** ***Alabama State Census*** **[Original Manuscripts & Online Database].** Originals at ADAH, microfilm at ADAH and FHL. 46 counties extant. Lists the heads of households and gives the number of persons in the various age ranges. It also indicates the number of deceased or disabled Confederate soldiers who were members of that family. Note: the 1866 AL state census was digitized and indexed online as part of Ancestry's *1820-1866 Alabama State Censuses* database, see http://search.ancestry.com/search/db.aspx?dbid=1576

**1867.** ***Alabama, Voter Registrations*** **[Online Database],** digitized and indexed at the Ancestry.com website. Source: ADAH, Montgomery AL. The ADAH describes these voter registration records as follows: "The Alabama 1867 voter registration records were created as a direct result of a Reconstruction Act passed by the United States Congress on March 23, 1867. The act required the commanding officer in each military district to hold, before September 1, 1867, a registration of all male

citizens, 21 years and older, in each county who were also qualified to vote and who had taken the loyalty oath. Each registrant visited the local registration office, took the oath, and was listed in the Voter Registration record. The volumes are significant genealogical records as this is one of the first statewide government documents that record African-American males living in Alabama. Each volume has columns for the following information: Name, Race, County of residence, Precinct, Length of residence (in state, in county, in precinct), Book and page where the individual's Loyalty Oath is recorded, Native country or state, and other remarks. Several Alabama counties were not yet established at the time of the 1867 voter registration: Chilton, Cullman, Escambia, Geneva, and Houston. There is no voter registration book available for Clarke County. The books for the following counties were severely damaged from mold: Dallas, Franklin, Lauderdale, Limestone, Lowndes, Monroe, Randolph, and Washington. Some information may be missing due to the extent of the mold damage." See
**http://search.ancestry.com/search/db.aspx?dbid=60968**

**1869.** ***List of Registered Voters, Shelby County, Alabama*** **[Online Database],** indexed at the RootsWeb site for Shelby Co AL. See
**www.rootsweb.ancestry.com/~alshelby/voters1869.html**

**1870.** ***Alabama, 1870 Federal Census: Population Schedules*** **[Microfilm/Digital Capture],** filmed by the National Archives, 1962, 1968, 57 rolls, beginning with FHL film #545500 (Autauga Baker, and Baldwin counties). To access the digital images, see the online FHL catalog page:
**https://familysearch.org/search/catalog/696888.**
- NOTE: This set is the federal copy of the 1870 federal census, which was not the original set. The original set remained in the office of the Secretary of State of Alabama and is described below.

**1870.** ***Census Index to Selected Alabama Counties*** **[Microfilm & Digital Capture],** from original index cards at the Alabama Department of Archives and History (ADAH) in Montgomery, AL. This card file is believed to be a WPA project that was never completed. It does not index the federal copy of the 1870 census (which was microfilmed by the National Archives). Instead, it is an index to the Alabama Secretary of State duplicate original copy held by the ADAH (not on microfilm). The original (state copy) census schedules are missing for the counties of Cherokee, Cleburne, Coffee, Covington, Fayette, Franklin, Lamar (Sanford in 1870), Limestone, Marion, Morgan, and Winston. The Alabama Department of Archives holds 1870 census records for all other counties (25 more), but they are not all indexed in this card file. The key to census schedules that this card file indexes is as follows: Autauga, DeKalb, Baker, Elmore, Baldwin, Escambia, Barbour, Etowah, Bibb, Geneva, Blount, Green, Bullock, Hale, Calhoun, Henry, Chambers, Houston (See Henry County) Chilton (See Baker County) Jackson, Clarke, Jefferson, Colbert, Lauderdale, Conecuh, Lowndes, Coosa, Macon, Crenshaw, Dale, and Dallas. Card index filmed by the Genealogical Society of Utah, 1989, 14 rolls, beginning with FHL film #1556985 (Aaron, Adeline – Bizzle, Ned). To access the digital images, see the online FHL catalog page:
**https://familysearch.org/search/catalog/410510.**

**1870.** ***Alabama Death Census, Autauga-Winston Counties*** **[Microfilm & Digital Capture],** from originals at the ADAH, Montgomery, AL. This record is the state's copy of the 1870 Mortality Schedule, providing statistical information on persons who died during the year ending 30 June 1870, such as name, age, sex, race, free or slave, married or widowed, state or nation of births, month of death, occupation, cause of death and number of days ill. Filmed by the Genealogical Society of Utah, 1981, 1 roll, FHL film #1405189. (Another filming, film #1421105). To access the digital images, see the online FHL catalog page: **www.familysearch.org/search/catalog/306345.**

**1870-1916.** ***Alabama, Jefferson County Circuit Court Papers*** **[Online Database],** digitized and indexed at FamilySearch.org. These records are loose papers pertaining to disputed estates and property. This database has 71,159 records, see
**https://familysearch.org/search/collection/1548510**

**1871-1880.** ***Alabama, Southern Claims Commission Approved Claims*** **[Online Database].** Source: National Archives microfilm series M2062. This is an index and images of approved claims from civilians seeking compensation for lost or destroyed property as a result of the Civil War. It contains 828 approved applications arranged by county and then alphabetical by name. This database has 5,248 records, see
**www.familysearch.org/search/collection/2180391.**

**1873-2009.** ***Birmingham, Alabama, Oak Hill Cemetery Index*** **[Online Database],** indexed at the Ancestry.com website. This database is also accessible

at the Birmingham Public Library website. See the link at Ancestry's webpage for details. This database has 9,228 records, see
**www.ancestry.com/search/collections/70660.**

**1873-2009.** ***Birmingham, Alabama, Red Mountain Cemetery Index*** **[Online Database],** indexed at the Ancestry.com website. This database is also accessible at the Birmingham Public Library website. See the link at Ancestry's webpage for details. This database has 4,684 records, see
**http://search.ancestry.com/search/db.aspx?dbid=70661**

**1876.** ***Registration Book of Voters, Barbour County, Alabama*** **[Microfilm].** Originals housed in the Barbour County Courthouse in Clayton, Alabama. Microfilmed by the Genealogical Society of Utah, 1988. See FHL film #2317867. To see if this microfilm has been digitized yet, see the FHL catalog page: **www.familysearch.org/search/catalog/663207.**

**1880.** ***Alabama, 1880 Federal Census: Soundex and Population Schedules*** **[Microfilm & Digital Capture],** filmed by the National Archives, c1970, 109 rolls, beginning with FHL film #1254001 (Population: Autauga, Baldwin, and Bibb counties). To access the digital images, see the online FHL catalog page: **www.familysearch.org/search/catalog/668058.**

***1880 Alabama Death Schedules*** **[Microfilm & Digital Capture].** This is the state's copy of the 1880 Mortality Schedule, providing statistical information on persons who died during the year ending 30 June 1880, such as name, age, sex, race, free or slave, married or widowed, state or nation of births, month of death, occupation, cause of death and number of days ill. Filmed by the ADAH, Montgomery, AL, 2 rolls, FHL film #1405190-1. To access the digital images, see the online FHL catalog page:
**www.familysearch.org/search/catalog/372488.**

**1880-1895.** ***Montgomery, Alabama Directories*** **[Online Database],** indexed at the Ancestry.com website. This database includes directories from various publishers for the years 1880-1881, 1883-1884, 1887, 1891, 1893, and 1895. This database has 43,249 records. See
**http://search.ancestry.com/search/db.aspx?dbid=4639**

**1880-1930s.** ***Alabama, Confederate Pension Applications*** **[Online Database],** digitized and indexed at FamilySearch.org, from records at the ADAH, Montgomery, AL. This database has 69,601 records, see
**www.familysearch.org/search/collection/3029256.**

**1881-1930.** ***Alabama Births and Christenings*** **[Online Database].** Indexed at the FamilySearch.org website. This is a name index to birth, baptism and christening records from the state of Alabama, extracted from the microfilmed records at the Family History Library in Salt Lake City UT. This database has 6,836 records:
**https://familysearch.org/search/collection/1661470**

**1881-1930.** ***Alabama, County Birth Registers*** **[Online Database],** digitized and indexed at FamilySearch.org. This database has 290,695 records, see
**www.familysearch.org/search/collection/3335352.**

**1881-1952.** ***Alabama Deaths and Burials*** **[Online Database],** indexed at the FamilySearch.org website. This a name index to death and burial records from the state of Alabama, extracted from the microfilmed records at the Family History Library in Salt Lake City UT. This database has 105,683 records, see
**https://familysearch.org/search/collection/1674670**

**1881-1974.** ***Alabama, Deaths and Burials*** [Online Database], indexed at the Ancestry.com website. Source: FamilySearch extractions. Index entries may include: Name, Gender, Race, Birth date, Birthplace, Occupation, Residence, Street address, Marital status, Spouse, Date of death, Place of burial, Date of burial, Cemetery name, Father's name and birthplace, Mother's name and birthplace, and FHL film number. This database has 1,962,795 records. See
**http://search.ancestry.com/search/db.aspx?dbid=2543**

**1882.** ***Jurors List, Sumter County, Alabama*** [**Online Database],** indexed at the ALGenWeb site for Sumter Co AL. See
**http://theusgenweb.org/al/sumter/jurorsin1882.html**

**1884-1951.** ***Deaths of State Convicts and Deaths of County Convicts*** [Microfilm & Digital Capture], from the originals at the ADAH, Montgomery, AL. Filmed by the Genealogical Society of Utah, 1989, 1 roll, FHL film #1605680. To access the digital images, see the online FHL catalog page:
**www.familysearch.org/search/catalog/410567.**

**1886-1952.** ***Alabama Convict Records*** **[Online Database],** from ADAH databases, digitized and indexed at the Ancestry.com website. The collection includes two series of records created by government boards responsible for oversight and care of prisoners

during that period. One set was created as convicts were admitted into a state prison; the other monitored county convicts who were admitted into the state prison system. The collection includes both indexes and the records themselves. A record may have a name, alias, serial number, race, gender, age, county where convicted, sentence details, information on escapes or parole, discharges, date, cause, and place of death. This database has 115,408 records, see
**http://search.ancestry.com/search/db.aspx?dbid=1742**

**1887.** ***Poll of Persons Living Near Choctaw Corner, Clarke County, Alabama*** **[Online Database],** indexed at the USGenWeb site for Clarke Co AL. See
**http://files.usgwarchives.net/al/clarke/history/1887clpol.txt.**

**1888-1890.** ***Birmingham, Alabama Directories*** **[Online Database],** indexed at the Ancestry.com website. This database includes R.L. Polk and Co directories for 1888, 1889, and 1890. This database has 42,718 records. See
**http://search.ancestry.com/search/db.aspx?dbid=4667**

**1888-1991.** ***Alabama, Naturalization Records*** **[Online Database],** indexed at the Ancestry.com website. Source: National Archives: Records of the District Courts of the U.S. Records include Petitions for becoming a citizen, certificates, and associated papers related to the naturalization process. This database has 91,671 records. See
**http://search.ancestry.com/search/db.aspx?dbid=2512**

**1888-1910.** ***Register of Deaths, Winston County, Alabama*** **[Online Database],** with annotations from Winston County cemeteries, indexed at the Free State of Winston.org website. See
**www.freestateofwinston.org/deathregister.htm**

**1889-1895.** ***Reconstructed Census of Marshall County, Alabama*** **[Printed Book],** compiled by Margene Hemrick Black and Betty Jean Taylor, Past and Present Publications, Guntersville, AL, c1995, 80 pages. See FHL book 976.194 X2bm 1889-1895.

**1890.** ***Alabama Federal Census (Fragments)*** **[Printed Index & Online Database].** Alabama was one of eight states that had fragments survive from the fire and water damaged census schedules. Surviving the 1890 census were these fragments in Alabama: Perry County (Perryville Beat No. 11 and Severe Beat No. 8). An index to the 6,160 names from all surviving fragments was published by the Family History Library and others, see FHL book 973 X2. The entire set of surviving fragments were digitized and indexed, see
**http://search.ancestry.com/search/db.aspx?dbid=5445**
- See also, ***United States Census, 1890*** **[Online Database],** database search, with images by FamilySearch, index by Ancestry. See
**https://familysearch.org/search/collection/1610551.**

**1890.** ***Tax List of Crenshaw County, Alabama*** **[Printed Book],** compiled by Betty Holley and Wayne Rogers, Crenshaw County Historical Society, Luverne, AL, 1993, 23 pages. Includes index. See FHL book 976.136 R48h.

**1890-1892.** ***Mobile, Alabama City Directories*** **[Online Database],** indexed at the Ancestry.com website. Source: Mobile City Directory, 1890, 1891, & 1892, publ. by George Matzenger. This database has 36,005 records. See
**http://search.ancestry.com/search/db.aspx?dbid=4473**

**1890-1924.** ***Index to Passenger Lists of Vessels Arriving at Ports in Alabama, Florida, Georgia, and South Carolina*** **[Microfilm & Digital Capture],** a combined index for all of the ports, filmed by the National Archives, 1957, 26 rolls, beginning with FHL film #1324938 (Aabott, Leanoard – Anderson, Julia F.). To access the digital images, see the online FHL catalog page:
**www.familysearch.org/search/catalog/341257.**

**1891.** ***Registered Voters, Russell's Beat, Fayette County, Alabama*** **[Online Database],** indexed at the RootsWeb site for Fayette Co AL. See
**www.rootsweb.ancestry.com/~alfayett/1891Voters_Russells.html**

**1894.** ***Voter Census, Autauga County, Alabama*** **[Printed Book],** compiled by MariLee Beatty Hageness, published by MLH Research, Anniston, AL, 2000, 76 pages. See FHL book 976.1463 N4h.

**1897-1924.** ***Cards, Alabama, National Guard Index*** **[Online Database],** indexed at the Ancestry.com website. Source: ADAH, Montgomery, AL. The ADAH extracted details about soldiers in the Alabama National Guard, from muster rolls, oaths of office, petitions, special orders, reports, rosters, pay rolls, and other sources. Each card may include, Soldier's name, Date of muster-in, Occupation/Specialty, Unit, Date of enlistment, appointment, discharge, or retirement, Age, Rank, Physical description, and Source of information on the card. This database has 147,786 records. See **http://search.ancestry.com/search/db.aspx?dbid=2219**

**1898.** ***Alabama Spanish-American War Service*** **[Microfilm & Digital Capture],** from originals at the ADAH, Montgomery, AL. This is a card file listing persons involved in the war. Information was compiled by ADAH staff from various sources. Filmed by the Genealogical Society of Utah, 1986, 2 rolls, FHL film #1462790 (Cards A-L); and #1462791 (Cards, M-Z). To access the digital images, see the online FHL catalog page:
**www.familysearch.org/search/catalog/632754.**

**1898-1938.** ***Alabama, Coal Mine Fatalities*** **[Online Database],** indexed at the Ancestry.com website. This database is also accessible at the Birmingham Public Library website. See the link at the Ancestry.com webpage for details. This database has 2,204 records:
**http://search.ancestry.com/search/db.aspx?dbid=70253**

**1899-1931.** ***Confederate Pension Records, Tuscaloosa County, Alabama*** **[Microfilm & Digital Capture],** from original records (place where records are stored today was not given in FHL catalog, and the FHL title, "1928-1921" is incorrect). Filmed by the Genealogical Society of Utah, 1998, 4 rolls, FHL film #2114620 (1899), #2110836 (1925-1931), #2114653 (1899-1900), and #2114654 (1902-1903). To access the digital images, see the online FHL catalog page:
**www.familysearch.org/search/catalog/733899.**

**1900.** ***Alabama, 1900 Federal Census: Soundex and Population Schedules*** **[Microfilm & Digital Capture],** filmed by the National Archives, c1970, 221 rolls, beginning with FHL film #1240001 (Population: Autauga, Baldwin, and Barbour counties). To access the digital images, see the online FHL catalog page:
**www.familysearch.org/search/catalog/646298.**

**1901-1914.** ***Voters, Lawrence County Alabama*** **[Printed Book],** compiled by MariLee Beatty Hageness, published by MLH Research, Anniston, AL, 2000. See FHL book 976.192 N4h.

**1901-2005.** ***Alabama Surname Files*** **[Online Database],** from ADAH databases, digitized and indexed at the Ancestry.com website. This database contains various records providing biographical information on individuals who lived in Alabama. Staff members at the ADAH compiled these files, newspaper clippings, obituaries, local and family histories, donated family research and records, extracts from censuses, research requests made to the archives, and other items. This database has 6,256 records, see
**http://search.ancestry.com/search/db.aspx?dbid=1770.**

**1901-1932.** ***Voters List, Washington County, Alabama*** **[Microfilm & Digital Capture],** originals housed in the Washington County courthouse, Chatom, Alabama. Microfilmed by the Genealogical Society of Utah, 1991, 1995. See FHL film #1987691 Item 1 (1901) and #1752977 Item 2 (1902-1932). To access the digital images (1901 only), see the online FHL catalog page:
**www.familysearch.org/search/catalog/461950.**

**1902-1934.** ***Voter Lists, Butler County, Alabama*** **[Printed Book],** registered voters from probate court originals housed in the Butler County Courthouse in Greenville, Alabama. Microfilmed by the Genealogical Society of Utah, 1989. Names are listed alphabetically. See FHL film #1630451.

**1903-1927.** ***Alabama, Madison County, Census and Pension Rolls of Confederate Soldiers*** [Digital Capture], from the Alabama Pension Commission records at the Madison County Courthouse, Huntsville AL. Digitized by FamilySearch International, 2010. To access the digital images, see the online FHL catalog page:
**www.familysearch.org/search/catalog/1921170.**

**1904-1962.** ***Alabama, Passenger Lists*** **[Online Database],** indexed at the Ancestry.com website. Source: National Archives, Selected Passenger and Crew Lists and Manifests. These passenger and crew lists from both ships and aircraft were recorded on a variety of forms that were then turned over to the Immigration and Naturalization Service. Details requested on the forms varied, but they typically include the name of the vessel and arrival date, ports of departure and arrival (as well as future destinations on a ship's itinerary), dates of departure and arrival, shipmaster, full name, age, gender, physical description, military rank (if any), occupation, birthplace, citizen of what country, and residence. For military transports, you may find the next of kin, as well

as relationships, and an address. Later manifests may include visa or passport numbers. This database has 62,254 records. See
**http://search.ancestry.com/search/db.aspx?dbid=9119**

**1906-1930.** ***Register of Voters (Male), Calhoun County, Alabama*** **[Microfilm & Digital Capture],** originals housed at the Calhoun Probate Court in Anniston, AL. Microfilmed by the Genealogical Society of Utah, 1992. See FHL film #1845117. To access the digital images, see the online FHL catalog page: **www.familysearch.org/search/catalog/573437.**

**1907.** ***Alabama Census of Confederate Soldiers*** **[Printed Book].** The originals and microfilm are at the ADAH, Montgomery, AL. This is an abstract published in five volumes by Gregath, Cullman, AL, 1982. The volumes are alphabetical by county. This census gives the soldier's name, full birth date, city and state of birth, when and where enlisted, unit, and mustering-out date. See FHL book 976.1 X22c 1907. An index was prepared in a separate volume: ***Master Index to 1907 Census of Alabama Confederate Soldiers*** **[Printed Book],** compiled by the ADAH, published by Gregath, Cullman, AL, 1982, 100+ pages. See FHL book 976.1 X22c 1907 index.

**1907. "Census of Confederate soldiers," [Printed Article],** in *Alabama Genealogical Society Magazine,* Vol. 6, No. 2 (Apr 1972) to Vol. 8, No. 3 (Jul 1974).

**1907-1921.** ***Alabama Census of Confederate Soldiers*** **[Online Database],** from ADAH databases, digitized and indexed at the Ancestry.com website. This is a collection of two censuses of Confederate Soldiers residing in Alabama in the early 1900s. Both were carried out more for pension purposes than for numbering purposes, but the census counted any Confederate veterans residing in Alabama, not just those who served for a regiment or company from Alabama. This database has 15,754 records, see
**http://search.ancestry.com/search/db.aspx?dbid=1998**

**1907, 1921, 1927.** ***Alabama Confederate Soldiers*** **[Microfilm & Digital Capture],** at ADAH. The films for 1907 are first, followed by 1921 and 1927. The 1907 Series includes each person's name, place of residence, date and place of birth, rank, date of entry into military service, date and place of discharge or separation, and name of military unit. The 1921 Series provides each veteran's name, place and date of birth, place of residence, length of Alabama residence occupation, wife's age and place of birth, marriage date and place, names of living children, occupation, and post office box. The forms also contain the veteran's rank, company, regiment, captain and colonel's name, battles, wounds, captures, imprisonments, and transfers. The 1927 Series, contains the veteran's name, his widow's name, her age and birth date, and their marriage date. The records are arranged by county, then alphabetically by the name of the soldier or widow. Filmed by the Genealogical Society of Utah, 1988, on 10 FHL films beginning with #1533727. To access the digital images, see the online FHL catalog page:
**https://familysearch.org/search/catalog/631231**

**1907-1927.** ***Alabama, Census of Confederate Veterans, 1907, 1921, 1927*** **[Online Database]** [Online Database], digitized at the FamilySearch.org website. This FamilySearch database adds the census year 1927. Any indexes were digitized along with the records. This database has 13,710 images, see
**https://familysearch.org/search/collection/2487274**

**1908-1959.** ***Alabama, Death Index*** **[Online Database],** indexed at the Ancestry.com website. Source: Dept. of Health, Montgomery, AL. The index includes name of the deceased, county of death, date of death, and the state certificate number (volume and page). This database has 1,363,539 records. See
**http://search.ancestry.com/search/db.aspx?dbid=5188**

**1908-1974.** ***Alabama Deaths*** **[Online Database],** digitized and indexed at the FamilySearch.org website. This is an index to death certificates from the state of Alabama (Dept. of Health, Montgomery, AL). This database has 1,858,819 records, see
**https://familysearch.org/search/collection/1307888**

**1908-1926.** ***Alphabetical Registration of Voters in Elmore County, Alabama*** **[Microfilm & Digital Capture],** from the originals at the Elmore County courthouse, Wetumpka, AL, filmed by the Genealogical Society of Utah, 1991. See FHL film #1750445. To access the digital images, see the online FHL catalog page:
**www.familysearch.org/search/catalog/457203.**

**1908-1926.** ***Voter Lists, Monroe County, Alabama*** **[Microfilm],** from the originals in the Monroe County courthouse, Monroeville, AL. Some years are missing. Microfilmed by the Genealogical Society of Utah, 1988. See FHL film #1547983. To see if this microfilm has been digitized yet, see the FHL catalog page: **www.familysearch.org/search/catalog/663365.**

**1910.** ***Alabama, 1910 Federal Census: Soundex and Population Schedules*** **[Microfilm & Digital Capture],** filmed by the National Archives, c1970, 177 rolls, beginning with FHL film #1374014 (Population: Autauga, Baldwin, and Barbour counties). To access the digital images, see the online FHL catalog page: **www.familysearch.org/search/catalog/646368.**

**1910-1912.** ***Registration Book of Voters, Barbour County, Alabama*** **[Microfilm],** from the originals at the Barbour County Courthouse, Clayton, AL. Microfilmed by the Genealogical Society of Utah, 2002. See FHL film #1547514 Item 1 (1910-1911) and #1547514 Item 2 (1912). To see if this microfilm has been digitized yet, see the FHL catalog page: **www.familysearch.org/search/catalog/663207.**

**1910-1923.** ***Voter Lists, Bullock County, Alabama*** **[Microfilm],** a registration book of voters, originals at the Bullock County courthouse, Union Springs, AL, filmed by the Genealogical Society of Utah, 1991. See FHL film #1536091. To see if this microfilm has been digitized yet, see the FHL catalog page: **www.familysearch.org/search/catalog/654685.**

**1911-1965.** ***Alabama, Friends of Magnolia Cemetery, Funeral Books*** **[Online Database],** index and images of original records compiled by Friends of Magnolia Cemetery, Inc. in Mobile, Alabama. This database has 23,094 records, see **www.familysearch.org/search/collection/3264362.**

**1912.** ***Voter List, Chambers County, Alabama*** **[Microfilm],** voter register, originals housed at the Chambers County Courthouse, LaFayette, AL, filmed by the Genealogical Society of Utah, 1992. See FHL film #1854807. To see if this microfilm has been digitized yet, see the FHL catalog page: **www.familysearch.org/search/catalog/618410.**

**1917-1918.** ***Alabama, Military Card Files*** **[Online Database],** indexed at the Ancestry.com website. Source: Card file created by the ADAH from WWI draft records for all AL counties. The file contains the names of prospective draftees and those actually drafted. Details may include Name, Address/town, Occupation, Date, Camp/Station, and Serial number. This database has 119,500 records. See **http://search.ancestry.com/search/db.aspx?dbid=2236**

**1917-1918.** ***Alabama, WWI Gold Star Index*** **[Online Database],** indexed at the FamilySearch.org website. ADAH database. This database has 1,874 records, see **http://search.ancestry.com/search/db.aspx?dbid=61021**

**1917-1919.** ***Index to Birth and Death Certificates*** **[Microfilm & Digital Capture],** from the originals at the ADAH, Montgomery, AL. This index is to both birth and death certificates. It contains a name, reporting county, date, volume and page number. The birth index frequently gives the child's parents rather that the child's name. The letter "P" next to the name indicates parent. Many dates are incomplete. Certificate volumes are held by the State Health Department, Bureau of Vital Statistics. Filmed by the Genealogical Society of Utah, 1991, 2 rolls, FHL film #1787423-4. To access the digital images, see the online FHL catalog page: **www.familysearch.org/search/catalog/487299.**

**1917-1919.** ***Alabama, World War I Service Cards*** **[Online Database],** digitized and indexed at FamilySearch.org. Index to a card roster of Alabamians who served in the United States Army, Navy, Coast Guard, or Marines during World War I from 1917 to 1919. Each soldier has one or two cards giving information on his/her military service, such as name, serial number, residence, place and date of birth, military organizations he/she served in, rank, engagements participated in, wounds or injuries received, dates serving overseas, discharge date, percentage disabled, and additional remarks. See **www.familysearch.org/search/collection/2865018.**

**1920.** ***Alabama, 1920 Federal Census: Soundex and Population Schedules*** **[Microfilm & Digital Capture],** filmed by the National Archives, c1970, 204 rolls, beginning with FHL film #1820001 (Population: Autauga, Bibb, and Chambers counties). To access the digital images, see the online FHL catalog page: **www.familysearch.org/search/catalog/534257.**

**1920-1942.** ***Register of Voters (Females), Calhoun County, Alabama*** **[Microfilm & Digital Capture],** originals housed at the Calhoun Probate Court, Anniston, AL. Microfilmed by the Genealogical Society of Utah, 1992. See FHL film #1845117. To access the digital images, see the online FHL catalog page: **www.familysearch.org/search/catalog/573437.**

**1927.** ***Alabama, Questionnaires of Widows of Confederate Soldiers*** **[Online Database],** indexed at the Ancestry.com website. Source: ADAH, Birmingham, AL. The documents can include a wide variety of details on both the widow and the veteran, including the following: Name of widow, Residence/address, Age, Birth date, Birthplace, Father's name, Father's place of death (if deceased) Name of veteran, Marriage details, Veteran's death details, Veteran's military service, Personal property, Former pension roll information, Former residences (states), and Children (names, addresses, occupations). This database has 483 records, see
**http://search.ancestry.com/search/db.aspx?dbid=2716**

**1930.** ***Alabama, 1930 Federal Census: Soundex and Population Schedules*** **[Microfilm & Digital Capture],** filmed by the National Archives, c1970, 249 rolls, beginning with FHL film #233976 (Population: Autauga and Barbour counties). To access the digital images, see the online FHL catalog page:
**www.familysearch.org/search/catalog/1034446.**

**1930-1996.** ***Birmingham, Alabama, Obituary Index*** **[Online Database],** indexed at the Ancestry.com website. This database is also accessible at the Birmingham Public Library website. For details, see the link at Ancestry's webpage. This database has 233,459 records. See
**http://search.ancestry.com/search/db.aspx?dbid=70021**

**1933-1990.** ***Tennessee Valley Cemetery Relocation Files*** **[Online Database],** indexed at the Ancestry.com website. Source: Tennessee Valley Authority files, National Archives, Atlanta, GA. Thousands of people, cemeteries, and other institutions had to be relocated from places that were to be flooded to make way for dams and hydroelectric power plants. Includes grave removal records from Alabama locations. This database has 172,537 records:
**http://search.ancestry.com/search/db.aspx?dbid=60427**
- See also, ***Master File Relocation Card Index for Grave and Cemetery Removal and Relocation, 1934-1954 (Tennessee Valley Authority)*** **[Microfilm & Digital Capture],** filmed by the Genealogical Society of Utah, 1996, 58 rolls, with 3 rolls having Alabama grave removal records from the Pickwick Project, 1935-1937, see FHL film #2050546, 2050094, and 2050608. To access the digital images on these rolls, see the online FHL catalog page:
**www.familysearch.org/search/catalog/778971.**
- See also, ***Alabama, Tennessee, Mississippi, Georgia, North Carolina, Virginia, Kentucky Mixed Relocation Files (Records of the Tennessee Valley Authority), 1937-1954*** **[Microfilm & Digital Capture],** filmed by the Genealogical Society of Utah, 1996, 12 rolls, with several rolls related to Alabama people. To access the digital images, see the online FHL catalog page:
**www.familysearch.org/search/catalog/647043.**

**1938-1992.** ***Alabama Divorces, 1938-1992; Index, 1950-1959 & 1958-1992*** **[Microfilm & Digital Capture],** Includes indexes with some volumes individually indexed. Filmed by the Genealogical Society of Utah, 337 rolls, beginning with FHL film #1908984 (Divorce Index, 1950-1959). To access the digital images, see the online FHL catalog page:
**www.familysearch.org/search/catalog/690132.**

***1940 Alabama Federal Census: Population Schedules*** **[Digital Capture],** digitized images taken from the microfilm of original records held by the Bureau of the Census in the 1940s. After microfilming, Congress allowed the Census Bureau to destroy the originals to free up space for WWII-related files. Digitizing of the 1940 census schedules microfilm images was done for the National Archives and made public on April 2, 2012. No microfilm copies were distributed. To access the digital images, see the online FHL catalog page:
**www.familysearch.org/search/catalog/2034309.**

***1940 Federal Census Finding Aids*** **[Online Database].** Well before the release of the 1940 census to the public, the National Archives created a special website online with a detailed description of the 1940 federal census. Included at the site are descriptions of location finding aids, such as Enumeration District Maps, Geographic Descriptions of Census Enumeration Districts, and a list of 1940 City Directories available at the National Archives. The finding aids are all linked to other National Archives sites. This National Archives website also has a link to 1940 Search Engines using Stephen P. Morse's "One-Step" system for finding a 1940 E.D. or for a street address conversion. See
**www.archives.gov/research/census/1940/general-info.html#questions.**

**1940-1947.** ***Alabama, World War II Draft Registration Cards*** **[Digital Capture],** digital images of originals held by the National Personnel Center in St. Louis, MO. Digitized by FamilySearch Int'l, 2016. To access the digital images, see the online FHL catalog page:
**www.familysearch.org/search/collection/2865018.**

**1944-1946.** ***Alabama WWII Military Dead and Wounded*** **[Online Database],** from ADAH databases, digitized and indexed at the Ancestry.com website. This database contains index cards created by the ADAH that list facts about wounded, captured, and deceased soldiers from Alabama. Information on the cards varies somewhat but typically includes a name, rank, service, next of kin, condition (wounded, deceased, captured, etc.), source, and date for the information. Details may also include cause and place of death. This database has 20,704 records, see
**http://search.ancestry.com/search/db.aspx?dbid=1763.**

**1950-1952.** ***Alabama Soldiers in the Korean War*** **[Online Database],** from ADAH databases, digitized and indexed at the Ancestry.com website. Staff members from the ADAH created these index cards to document the military service of Alabamans during the Korean War. Cards can include details such as a name, branch of military service, rank, residence address, event dates (wounded, missing in action, rotation returnee, etc.), sources, source dates, and names of family members/next of kin. This database has 5,277 records, see
**http://search.ancestry.com/search/db.aspx?dbid=1764.**

**1950-1959.** ***Alabama Divorce Index*** **[Online Database],** indexed at the Ancestry.com website. Source: AL Dept. of Health, Montgomery, AL. Index may include, Husband's name, Wife's name, Divorce date, and Divorce county. This database has 211,120 records. See
**http://search.ancestry.com/search/db.aspx?dbid=8976.**

**1992-current.** ***Alabama Newspaper Obituaries*** **[Online Database].** Digitized and indexed at the GenealogyBank.com website including obituaries from the following Alabama newspapers: Alabaster, Albertville, Alexander City, Andalusia, Anniston, Athens, Atmore, Birmingham, Brewton, Clanton, Columbiana, Cullman, Dadeville, Decatur, Demopolis, Dothan, Eclectic, Enterprise, Eufaula, Florence, Fort Deposit, Fort Payne, Gadsden, Gardendale, Greenville, Guntersville, Hartselle, Heflin, Huntsville, Jasper, LaFayette, Lanett, Leeds, Luverne, Madison, Mobile, Moulton, Opelika, Pelham, Pell City, Piedmont, Rainsville, Russellville, Scottsboro, Selma, Talladega, Tallassee, Troy, Tuscaloosa, and Wetumpka, see
**www.genealogybank.com/gbnk/obituaries/explore/USA/Alabama.**

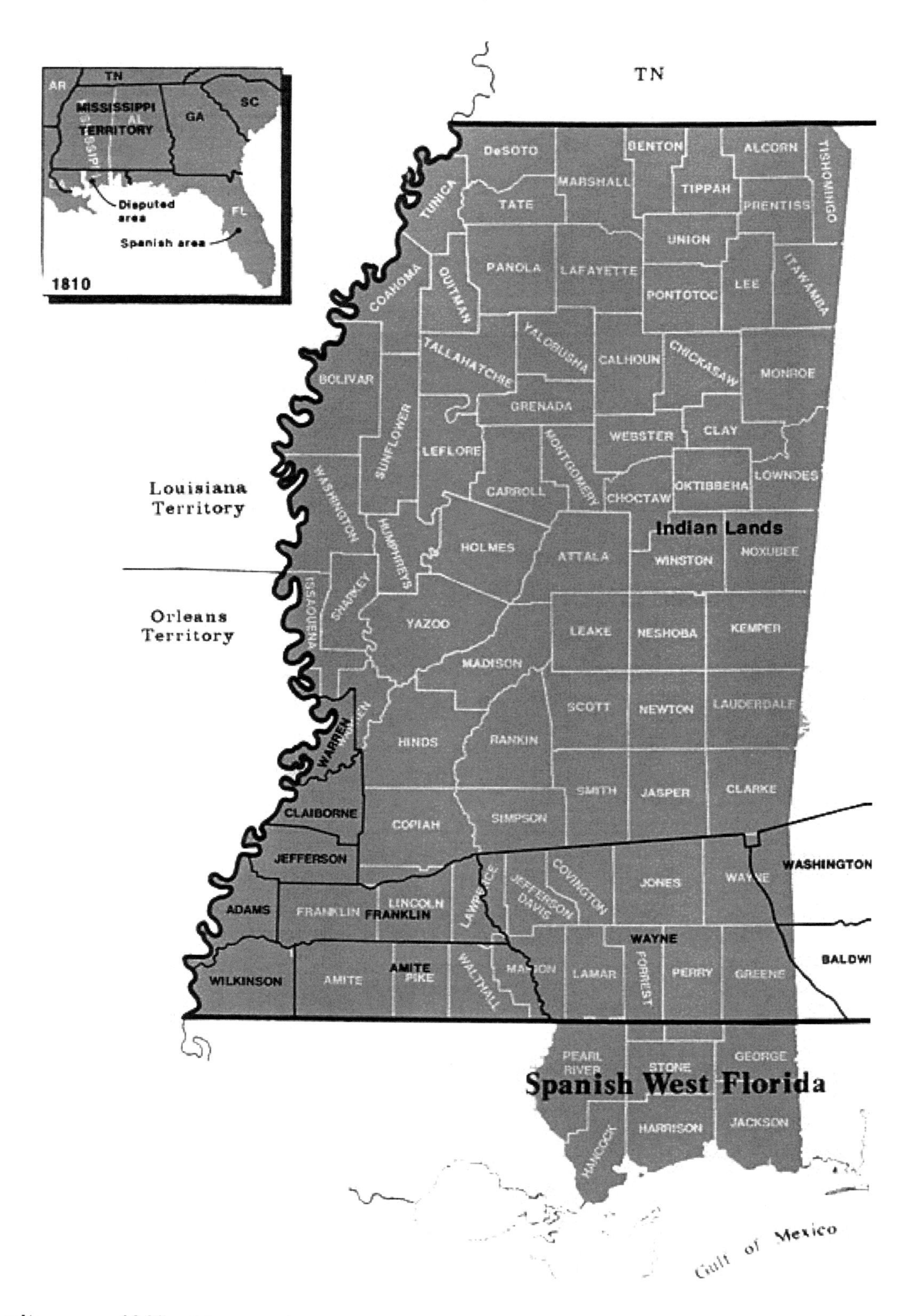


**Mississippi Territory • 1810**. Lines and names in white are for the modern counties; those in black are for the 1810 counties. The inset map shows the extent of Mississippi Territory, which included present Alabama in 1810. Washington and Baldwin are now Alabama counties. The 1810 federal census was lost for all counties; but, an 1810 Mississippi Territory census is extant for Amite, Claiborne (including Warren), Franklin, Jefferson, and Washington counties. For a detailed map showing the Indian Land Cessions of Mississippi, see **http://usgwarchives.net/maps/cessions/ilcmap36.htm.**

# Mississippi
## Censuses & Substitute Name Lists

### Historical Timeline for Mississippi, 1673-1820

**1673. Mississippi River.** French explorers Jacques Jolliet and Louis Marquette left their base at Ste. Sault Marie, and made their way to the Illinois River, which they descended to become the first Europeans to discover the Mississippi River. They floated down the Mississippi as far south as the mouth of the Arkansas River before returning to the Great Lakes area.

**1682. Mississippi River.** Following the same route as Jolliet and Marquette, René-Robert Cavelier (Sieur de LaSalle) floated down the Mississippi River, continuing all the way to its mouth at the Gulf of Mexico. He then claimed the entire Mississippi Basin for Louis XIV of France, for whom Louisiana was named.

**1699. Mississippi.** The French established the first settlement on Biloxi Bay at Old Biloxi (now Ocean Springs). New Biloxi, founded in 1719, was the capital of French Louisiana until 1722, when New Orleans replaced it.

**1702.** Mobile was founded by the French as Fort Louis de la Louisianne. They were in an area also claimed by the Spanish.

**1716. Mississippi.** Natchez, founded by the French, is the oldest city on the Mississippi River.

**1718.** New Orleans was founded by the French.

**1763 Treaty of Paris.** Until this year, many cross-claims to territory in North America existed between the French, British and Spanish, and it took a war to settle the issue of land ownership. In Europe it was called the Seven Years War, but in colonial America it was called the French and Indian War. France was divested of virtually all of its large North American claims. The British gained undisputed title to Acadia/Nova Scotia, Newfoundland, Labrador, and Quebec; as well as a new official recognition of their Atlantic colonies from present Maine to Georgia, plus all lands between the Appalachian Mountains and the Mississippi River. Spanish lands were recognized as those former French Louisiana lands west of the Mississippi. As part of the 1763 Treaty of Paris, the Spanish ransomed Florida to the British in exchange for Cuba. The British immediately divided the area into West Florida with a capital at Pensacola, and East Florida, with a capital at St. Augustine. The dividing line was the Apalachicola - Chattahoochee Rivers.

**1783.** The treaty of Paris of 1783 first recognized the United States as an independent nation. Its borders were described generally from the Atlantic Ocean to the Mississippi River, and from present Maine to Georgia. The British also returned West Florida and East Florida back to Spain at the 1783 Treaty of Paris.

**1783-1796.** Spain and the U.S. both claimed the area between Latitude 31° and Latitude 32° 30' of present-day Mississippi and Alabama. This disputed area was left out of the U.S. in the Treaty of 1783 and remained in dispute with Spain until 1796.

**1789-1803.** Georgia's claim to huge tracts of western land, extending across both present-day Alabama and Mississippi to the Mississippi River, was to be the scene of some extraordinary and flamboyant land trading schemes. Two notorious land scandals emerged during this period:

1) From 1789 to 1796, three Governors of Georgia made gifts of land covering more than three times as much land as Georgia contained.

Mostly centered in Montgomery County, Georgia, the **Pine Barrens Speculation** was the basis for a landmark U.S. Supreme Court decision in 1810, the first time the Supreme Court ruled a state law unconstitutional.

2) The **1794-1803 Yazoo Land Scandal** involved the Governor and other Georgia state officials accepting bribes in return for land sales to speculators in the region of present-day Mississippi's Yazoo River area, land that was later ceded by Georgia to the U.S. Public Domain.

**1790. Federal Census.** The present-day area of Alabama and Mississippi was part of Georgia, part of the disputed area, and part of Spanish West Florida at the time of the 1790 federal census. Although there were American settlements at Natchez and north of Mobile, no federal census was taken there. Georgia's 1790 federal census was lost.

**1796.** In the 1796 Treaty of San Lorenzo (also called Pinckney's Treaty), the U.S. resolved the Spanish-U.S. disputed area by purchasing the area from Spain. The lands above West Florida (Latitude 31° up to 32°30') became U.S. territory. The purchase did not include East Florida or West Florida.

**1798. Mississippi Territory** was created within the lands purchased in the 1796 Treaty of San Lorenzo. Natchez was the territorial capital.

**1800. Federal Census.** Georgia's 1800 federal census jurisdiction included Indian lands in present-day Alabama and Mississippi, but no whites were enumerated there. The entire GA 1800 census was lost. Washington County, Mississippi Territory was enumerated in the 1800 census, but that census was also lost.

**1802. Georgia Land Cession.** In this year, the portion of present-day Alabama and Mississippi above Latitude 32° 30' was ceded by Georgia to the U.S. federal government's "public domain." An amount of 1.25 million dollars was finally negotiated in 1802. The area of land ceded by Georgia ran from its present western boundary west to the Mississippi River, and north from Latitude 32° 30" to 35°. Later, Georgia's ceded area was added to Mississippi Territory. After the cession of its western lands, Georgia's boundaries have not changed since.

**1804. Mississippi Territory.** Congress officially added the 1802 Georgia land cession to Mississippi Territory, more than doubling its size, from Latitude 31° to Latitude 35°.

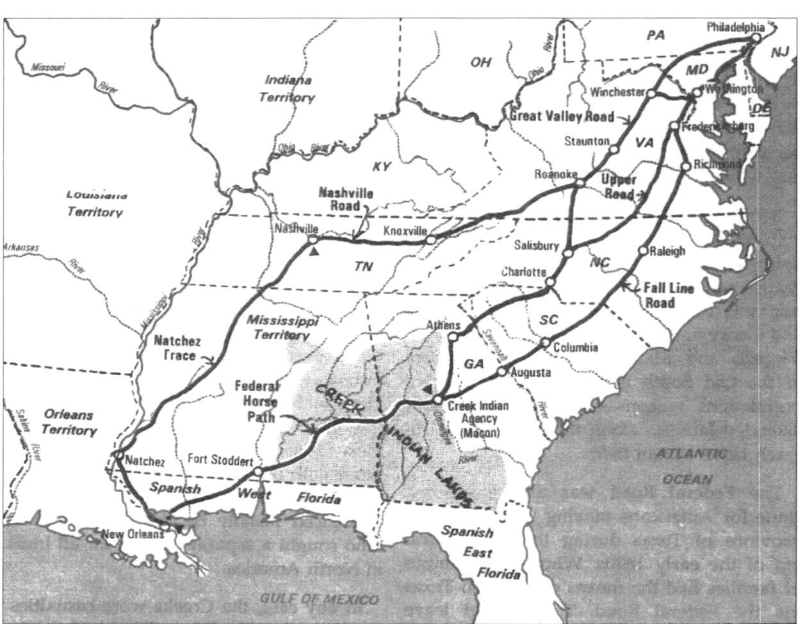


**1806. The Federal Horse Path.** The time it took for mail via express riders between Philadelphia and New Orleans was cut in half, from six weeks to three weeks, after the opening of the Federal Horse Path. A treaty with the Creek Nation, which encompassed a large area of present-day Georgia and Alabama was necessary to clear the pathway, beginning at the Creek Indian Agency (now Macon) and through Mississippi Territory and Spanish West Florida to New Orleans. With federal funds, the same route was continually improved and became known as the Federal Road, the primary route for thousands of Scots-Irish families migrating into the Deep South.

**1810.** The Federal Census was taken in Georgia and Mississippi Territory, but none of the original manuscripts have survived.

**1810. West Florida Annexation.** In September 1810, a group of rebel Americans overcame the Spanish garrison at Baton Rouge and unfurled the new flag of the Republic of West Florida. In October 1810, in a proclamation by President James Madison, the U.S. annexed part of Spain's West Florida, an area from the Perdido River to the Mississippi River, including Mobile, Biloxi, and Baton Rouge. The area was not officially organized for another two years. Spain did not recognize the annexation, and continued their claim to West Florida in dispute with the U.S.

**1812. Mississippi Territory and Orleans Territory.** The portion of the West Florida Annexation from the Perdido River to the Pearl River was recognized by Congress and officially added to Mississippi Territory. The portion from the Pearl River to the Mississippi River was added to Orleans Territory.

**1817.** March 3rd. **Alabama Territory** was created, taken from Mississippi Territory with nearly the same boundaries as the current state bounds. St. Stephens was the first territorial capital.

**1817.** Dec 10th. **Mississippi** became the 20th state in the Union with nearly the same boundaries as today. Washington was the first state capital, replaced by Jackson in 1822.

**1819-1821 Adams-Onis Treaty.** By 1818, Spain had effectively abandoned Florida and was unwilling to support any more colonists or garrisons. In 1819, the Adams-Onis Treaty formalized Spain's cession of East Florida and West Florida to the U.S. in exchange for the U.S. paying any legal claims of American citizens against Spain, up to 5 million dollars. But, the treaty also set the boundary between the U.S. and New Spain (now Mexico), from Louisiana to the Oregon Country. Although Baton Rouge, Biloxi, and Mobile were annexed to the U.S. in 1810, then organized in 1812; they did not become U.S. territory free of dispute until the Adams-Onis Treaty was ratified by Congress in 1821.

**1820.** June. A Federal Census was taken in the state of Mississippi. The population was 75,448 people. The 1820 was the first federal census year for which the population schedules have survived for all counties.

**1820.** July. The Alabama-Mississippi boundary line was resurveyed, and it was discovered that a tract of land lying along the east side of the Tombigbee River which had been attached to Alabama was really in Mississippi.

## Mississippi Department of Archives & History

The MDAH in Jackson, MS is the premier genealogical resource center for all of Mississippi. There is an abundance of genealogical materials at this facility, but except for a particularly good Online Catalog, there are no online databases available to the public. The MDAH has chosen, instead, to allow many of its microfilm collections to be digitized and indexed at other sites, such as Ancestry.com or FamilySearch.com. At the MDAH Genealogy webpage, there are descriptions of their most commonly used genealogical resources, including Birth and Death Records, Census Records, County Records, Court Cases, Dawes Rolls, Enumeration of Educable Children, Freedmen's Bureau Labor Contracts, Marriage Records, and Military Resources. For the MDAH Genealogy Page, see **http://www.mdah.ms.gov/new/research/genealogy.**

# Bibliography

## Mississippi Censuses & Substitutes

Mississippi's Colonial, Territorial, State, and Federal Censuses can be associated with the historic jurisdictional eras of Mississippi:

**Colonial French Era, 1682-1763:** French censuses exist for areas near Biloxi and Mobile in 1706, 1721, and 1725.

**Colonial British Era, 1763-1783:** British censuses taken in West Florida exist for 1763, 1771, 1776 and 1779.

**Colonial Spanish Era, 1783-1819:** A Spanish census for the Natchez District exists for 1792.

**Mississippi Territory Era, 1798-1817:** Censuses taken by the Territory of Mississippi exist for 1805, 1808, 1810, 1813, and 1815-1817.

**State of Mississippi Era, 1817-Present:** State censuses exit for 1818, 1820, 1822, 1822-1823, 1823, 1824, 1825, 1830, 1837, 1840, 1841, 1845, 1850, 1853, 1860, and 1866.

**Federal Censuses, 1800-1940:** Mississippi's federal censuses were lost for 1800 & 1810, complete for 1820 through 1880; lost for 1890, and complete for 1900 through 1940. Bibliographic details about Mississippi's censuses and substitutes begins below in chronological order:

**Census Substitutes, 1700s-2000s:** Mississippi may have more territorial/state censuses than any other state, but there are many more census substitutes available than there are actual censuses available. An identification of the substitutes begin with following:

**1719-1720.** ***The Ste. Catherine Colonists: Early Settlers of Natchez and Pointe Coupee in the French Province of Louisiana*** **[Printed Book],** by Winston De Ville, publ. Smith Books, Ville Platte, LA, 1991, 53 pages, FHL book 976.3 H2dw.

**1770s-2000s.** ***Mississippi GenWeb Archives*** **[Online Databases].** The MSGenWeb site offers free genealogical databases with searchable name lists for all Mississippi counties, which may include Bibles, Biographies, Cemeteries, Censuses, Court, Death, Deeds, Directories, Histories, Marriages, Military, Newspapers, Obituaries, Photos, Schools, Tax Lists, Wills, and more. See
**http://usgwarchives.net/ms/msfiles.htm.**

**1770s-2000s.** ***Linkpendium – Mississippi: Family History & Genealogy, Census, Birth, Marriage, Death Vita Records & More*** **[Online Databases].** Linkpendium is a genealogical portal site, with links to state, county, town, and local databases. Currently listed are selected sites for Mississippi statewide resources (449), Adams County (398), Alcorn County (161), and 80 more counties. See
**www.linkpendium.com/ms-genealogy.**

**1776-1816.** ***Early Inhabitants of the Natchez District*** **[Printed Book],** by Norman Gillis, published by the author, Baton Rouge, LA, 1963, 152 pages, FHL book 976.2 X2p.

**1776-1935.** ***Mississippi, Compiled Marriage Index*** **[Online Database],** indexed at the Ancestry.com website. This Hunting for Bears collection consists of marriages extracted from county records at the Family History Library in Salt Lake City, UT. For a list of the 89 counties included in this database, with the inclusive dates of marriages for each, visit the webpage. This database has 684,772 records. See
**http://search.ancestry.com/search/db.aspx?dbid=7842.**

**1780-1982.** ***Mississippi, Wills and Probate Records*** **[Online Database]** digitized and indexed at the Ancestry.com website. This database was extracted from over 75 county courthouses in Mississippi. Probate records relate to the disposition of an estate for a person who died with a will (testate) or without a will (intestate). Certain details are found in most probates, i.e., the names and residences of beneficiaries and their relationship to the decedent. An inventory of the estate assets can reveal personal details about the deceased's occupation and lifestyle. There may also be references to debts, deeds, and other documents related to the settling of the estate. This database has 256,168 records. See
**http://search.ancestry.com/search/db.aspx?dbid=8995.**

**1781-1797.** ***Anglo-Americans in Spanish Archives: Lists of Anglo-American Settlers in the Spanish Colonies of America; a finding Aid*** **[Printed Book],** by Lawrence H. Feldman, published by Genealogical Publishing Co., Inc., Baltimore, 1991, 349 pages. Includes original census documents and genealogical data about individuals and families who settled in the French territories of Louisiana and the Floridas after they came under Spanish rule in 1766 (the areas settled correspond to the present-day states of Florida, Alabama, Mississippi, Louisiana, and Missouri. Includes an index of personal names. See FHL book 973 X2fe.

**1781-1930.** ***Mississippi Probate Records*** **[Online Database],** digitized at the FamilySearch.org website. This collection includes probate records filed in Mississippi county courts. A few records may go beyond 1930, but most records in this collection were created between the 1850 and 1930. The records include wills, administrations, inventories, court minutes, guardianships, and other records of estates; plus miscellaneous court records, voter registrations, and more. Browse the images. No index yet. This database has 4,302,124 records. See
**https://familysearch.org/search/collection/2036959.**

**1782-1816.** ***Spanish West Florida, Archives of the Spanish Government*** **[Online Database],** indexed at the FamilySearch.org website. **Source:** National Archives microfilm series T1116: Records of the Adjutant General's Office, 1780's-1917. **About West Florida:** The area of the West Florida region today encompasses the panhandle of the state of Florida, the southernmost parts of the states of Mississippi and Alabama, and the Florida Parishes of the state of Louisiana. The treaty that officially brought West Florida into the U.S. was ratified in 1821. **Contents:** This collection consists of transcribed and translated records of the Spanish Empire related to the Spanish province of West Florida. Included are a wide variety of documents, such as records related to property sales, mortgages, inventories and assessments, money lending and debt settlements, wills and probates, inquests, and records related to slavery in Spanish West Florida. For best search results, search by name and date range. This database has 9,202 records. See
**http://search.ancestry.com/search/db.aspx?dbid=2454.**

**1789-1809.** ***First Settlers of the Mississippi Territory*** **[Online Database],** digitized book, same title (w/sub-title: "..Grants Taken from the American State Papers, Class VIII, Public Lands, Vol. 1, 1789-1809," publ. Ericson Books, Nacogdoches, TX, 1982. See
**www.ancestry.com/search/collections/26397.**

**1790.** ***List of Tobacco Growers in 1790, Spanish Natchez District*** **[Online Database],** indexed at the Natchezbelle.org website. See
**www.natchezbelle.org/sw/tobaccogrowers1790.htm.**

**1790-1791.** ***The Natchez Ledgers: A Finding-Aid for Anglo-Americans in Pre-Territorial Mississippi*** **[Printed Book],** compiled by Winston De Ville, publ. Ville Platte, LA, 1994, 89 pages. FHL book 976.2 R49d.

***1792 Spanish Census of the Natchez District*** **[Online Database],** indexed at the Natchezbelle.org website. See **www.natchezbelle.org/sw/1792cs.htm.**

**1792-1866.** ***Mississippi, State and Territorial Census Collection*** **[Online Database],** digitized and indexed at the Ancestry.com website. Source: MDAH, Jackson, MS. Most of the censuses only enumerate the heads of households by name. Other members of the household are counted in categories such as race, gender, age, and whether free or slave. **Years and counties included: 1792:** Natchez. **1805:** Jefferson, Wilkinson. **1808:** Jefferson, Washington, **1810:** Amite, Claiborne, Jefferson, Baldwin, Franklin, Washington. **1813:** Wilkinson. **1815-1817:** Monroe. **1816:** Adams, Baldwin, Clarke, Greene, Marion, Wayne, Amite, Claiborne, Franklin, Jefferson, Warren, Wilkinson. **1818:** Adams, Lawrence. **1820:** Amite, Marion, Wayne, Franklin, Pike, Wilkinson. **1822:** Claiborne, Wilkinson. **1822-1823:** Perry. **1823:** Bainbridge, Claiborne, Lawrence, Wilkinson. **1824:** Hinds, Lawrence, Simpson. **1825:** Jackson, Wilkinson. **1830:** Adams. **1837:** Chickasaw, Itawamba, Kemper, Oktibbeha, Pontotoc, Tishomingo, Choctaw, Jones, Lowndes, Panola, Simpson, Winston. **1840:** Hancock. **1841:** Adams, Coahoma, Itawamba, Madison, Neshoba, Simpson, Tunica, Attala, Copiah, Jones, Marion, Oktibbeha, Smith, Washington, Bolivar, Covington, Lawrence, Marshall, Panola, Tallahatchie, Wayne, Chickasaw, Franklin, Leake, Monroe, Scott, Tippah, Yazoo. **1845:** Amite, Noxubee, Pontotoc, Smith, Tishomingo, Wilkinson, Neshoba, Panola, Rankin, Sunflower, Warren, Yalobusha, Newton, Perry, Scott, Tippah, Wayne. **1850:** Hinds. **1853:** Adams, Copiah, Itawamba, Lauderdale, Panola, Wayne, Amite, Greene, Jefferson, Leake, Perry, Winston, Clarke, Hancock, Jones, Noxubee, Rankin. **1860:** Choctaw, Itawamba. **1866:** Bolivar, Holmes, Jasper, Leake, Simpson, Wayne, Claiborne, Issaquena, Jefferson, Marion, Smith. This database has 87,415 records. See
**http://search.ancestry.com/search/db.aspx?dbid=1125.**
- See Also, ***1792-1866 Mississippi State Census Records*** **[Microfilm & Digital Capture],** from originals located at the MDAH, Jackson, MS. Filmed by the MDAH, copies at the FHL in Salt Lake City, under the title, *State Census Records, 1792-1866, Mississippi Secretary of State.* This series of 3 rolls of microfilm begins with abstracts of census statistics, 1801-1845; plus the Spanish census of 1792 for Natchez District, beginning on FHL film #899868; followed by territory and state census records by county and year, To access the digital images, see the online FHL catalog page:
**www.familysearch.org/search/catalog/256479.**
**Roll Contents: Roll 1:** Adams - Holmes Counties, 1810-1866; **Roll 2:** Issaquena - Simpson Counties 1805-1866; and **Roll 3:** Smith - Yazoo Counties 1805-1866. **Note:** Census dates indicated below with an asterisk (*) are copies of census statistics only, and do not include a name list.

**Contents, Roll 1, FHL film #899868:**
- Natchez District, Spanish Census of 1792
- Adams County 1816, 1818, 1823*, 1830 (Natchez only), 1841 & 1853
- Amite County: 1810, 1816, 1820, 1824*, 1833*, 1845 & 1853
- Attala County: 1841
- Bainbridge County: 1823
- Baldwin County: (now Alabama) 1810 & 1816
- Bolivar County: 1841, 1866
- Chickasaw County: 1837 & 1841
- Choctaw County: 1837, 1840*, 1860, & 1837
- Claiborne County: 1810, 1816, 1822*, 1823* & 1825
- Clarke County: 1816, 1841* & 1853
- Coahoma County: 1841
- Copiah County: 1822*, 1824*, 1825*, 1841 & 1853
- Covington County: 1825* & 1841
- DeSoto County: 1841*
- Franklin County: 1810, 1816, 1820, 1833* & 1841
- Greene County: 1816, 1825*, 1841* & 1853
- Hancock County: 1823*, 1825*, 1830*, 1840 & 1853
- Hinds County: 1824* & 1850
- Holmes County: 1866

**Contents, Roll 2, FHL film #899869**
- Issaquena County: 1866
- Itawamba County: 1837, 1841, 1853 & 1860
- Jackson County: 1825 & 1841*
- Jasper County: 1866
- Jefferson County: 1805, 1808, 1810, 1816, 1823*, 1825*, 1841*, 1853 & 1866
- Jones County: 1837, 1841 & 1853
- Kemper County: 1837 & 1841*
- Lauderdale County: 1841* & 1853
- Lawrence County: 1818, 1823, 1824*, 1824*, 1825*, 1830*, 1841 & Census, date unknown
- Leake County: 1841, 1853 & 1866
- Lowndes County: 1837
- Madison County: 1841, ca. 1830-1840
- Marion County: 1816, 1820, 1823*, 1824*, 1825*, 1841, 1866
- Marshall County: 1841
- Monroe County: 1815-1817, 1841, 1845, ca. 1841-45

- Noxubee County: 1841*, 1845 & 1853
- Oktibbeha County: 1837, 1841 & 1845
- Panola County: 1837, 1841, 1845 & 1853
- Perry County: 1822-3*, 1825*, 1841*, 1845 & 1853
- Pike County: 1816, 1820, 1825*, 1830*, 1841* & 1845*
- Pontotoc County: 1837 & 1845
- Rankin County: 1845 & 1853
- Scott County: 1841& 1845
- Simpson County: 1824*, 1825*, 1837, 1841, 1845* & 1866

**Contents, Roll 3, FHL film #899870**

- Smith County: 1841, 1845, 1866
- Sunflower County: 1845
- Tallahatchie County: 1841, 1845*
- Tippah County: 1841 & 1845
- Tishomingo County: 1837, 1841* & 1845
- Tunica County: 1841 & 1845*
- Warren County: 1816, 1825* & 1845
- Washington County: (now Alabama) 1808 & 1810
- Washington County: (created 1827) 1841 & 1845*
- Wayne County: 1816, 1820, 1841, 1845, 1853 & 1866
- Wilkinson County: 1805, 1813, 1816, 1820, 1822*, 1823*, 1825 & 1845
- Winston County: 1837, 1845* 1853
- Yalobusha County: 1845
- Yazoo County: 1824*, 1825*, 1841 & 1845

- See also the entry, ***Mississippi State Census Returns: RG28, 1818-188,*** for certain state census years not included in the above listing.

**1797-1817.** ***Residents of Mississippi Territory*** **[Printed Book],** by Jean Strickland and Patricia N. Edwards, published Moss Point, MS, 1995, 3 vols. Contains miscellaneous records such as court records, land and property, census, maps, passports, tax rolls, etc. FHL book 976.2 X2s v1-3.

**1797-1817.** ***Residents of Southeastern Mississippi Territory*** **[Printed Book],** by Jean Strickland and Patricia N. Edwards, published Moss Point, MS, 1995-96, 7 vols. Includes censuses, tax rolls and petitions; James Leander Cathart journal; Journey from Georgia to Louisiana, 1812; John Landreth Journal; Washington and Baldwin Counties, Alabama Wills, Deeds and Superior Court minutes; Records of Spanish West Florida, 1782-1806; and Records of Spanish West Florida, 1806. FHL book 976.21 H29s v.1-7.

**1798-1818.** ***Early Pioneers and Settlers, Southwest Mississippi Territory*** **[Online Database],** indexed at the Natchezbelle.org website. Index is for the pioneers and settlers of Amite, Adams, Claiborne, Franklin, Jefferson, and Wilkinson counties, Mississippi. See **www.natchezbelle.org/sw/pioneerdb.htm.**

**1798-1906.** ***Index to Naturalization & Declaration Records, Adams County, Mississippi, 1798-1906*** **[Online Database],** indexed at the NatchezBelle.org website. This was originally prepared as a project of the WPA in 1942. The indexed names are linked to an image of the printed page of the book. See **www.natchezbelle.org/adams-ind/naturalization.htm.**

**1799-1801.** ***Transcription of County Archives of Mississippi (Adams County, MS)*** **[Online Database],** digitized and indexed at the Ancestry.com website. Source: WPA Historical Records Survey, 1942. Includes Minutes of the Court of General Quarter Sessions of the Peace, 1799-1801, the first set of court records for Adams Co MS. Includes index to names and subjects. See **http://search.ancestry.com/search/db.aspx?dbid=23047.**

**1799-1835.** ***Mississippi Court Records*** **[Online Database],** digitized and indexed at Ancestry.com. Source: Book, same title, by J. Estelle Stewart King, publ. Beverly Hills, CA,1936. See **www.ancestry.com/search/collections/48047.**

**"1800 Tax List, Adams County, Mississippi" [Printed Article],** in *Southern Genealogists Exchange Quarterly,* Vol. 14, No. 66 (Summer 1973).

**"1800, 1810 & 1816 Mississippi Territory Censuses (Western Part)" [Printed Article],** in *Alabama Historical Quarterly*, Vol. 24, No. 1 (Spring 1962).

**1800-1819.** See **"Pre 1820 Mississippi Tax rolls" [Printed Article],** in *Deep South Genealogical Quarterly*, Vol. 29, No. 2 (May 1992 ).

**1800-1911.** ***Mississippi Marriages*** **[Online Database],** indexed at the FamilySearch.org website. This an index to marriage records from the state of Mississippi, taken from microfilm county records at the Family History Library in Salt Lake City, UT. This database has 411,408 records. See **https://familysearch.org/search/collection/1680835.**

**1800-1825.** ***Mississippi, Compiled Marriages*** **[Online Database],** indexed at the Ancestry.com website. This database has 9,029 records. See **http://search.ancestry.com/search/db.aspx?dbid=2093.**

**1800s-1908.** ***Mississippi, Homestead and Cash Entry Patents, Pre-1908*** **[Online Database],** digitized and indexed at the Ancestry.com website. A land patent is the first-title deed and the true beginning of private ownership of the land. Information recorded in these records includes: Name, Land Office, Sequence, Document number, Total acres, Signature, Canceled document, Issue date, Mineral rights reserved, Rectangular survey descriptions (or Metes and bounds descriptions), Statutory reference, Multiple warrantee and patentee names, Act or treaty, and Entry classification. If nothing else, the value of learning of a person's land patent puts a person in a certain place at a certain time – that information is needed to search other records specific to a place, such as those in a courthouse. This database has 161,676 records. See **http://search.ancestry.com/search/db.aspx?dbid=3052.**

**"1801 Mississippi Territory Census, Jefferson County, Mississippi" [Printed Article],** in *Vicksburg Genealogical Society Newsletter,* Vol. 5, No. 1 (Sep 1988).

**"1801 Mississippi Territory Census, Washington County, Mississippi" [Printed Article],** in *Mississippi Records,* Vol. 2, No. 3 (Jul 1990).

**1801-1816.** ***Mississippi Territorial Census RG2, Series 497*** **[Original Records & Digital Capture],** at the MDAH, Jackson, MS. These are the state censuses digitized by the Genealogical Society of Utah on site at the MDAH in Jackson, MS in 2011, with the intent of including the images (and future indexes) online with the FamilySearch online series, *Mississippi, State Archives, Various Records, 1820-1951*. These original state census records were never microfilmed and were not included in the first-generation digitized set. Includes State Census returns, beginning with FHL/DGS #4822294 (Box 17014, 1816: Amite, Clarke, Franklin, Marion, Warren, and Wilkinson counties). To access the digital images, see the online FHL catalog page:
**https://familysearch.org/search/catalog/1927065.**

**1802-1964.** ***Mississippi Newspaper Archives*** **[Online Database],** digitized and indexed at the GenealogyBank.com website. One search screen for names and keywords in city newspapers from Aberdeen, Biloxi, Brandon, Gulfport, Handsboro, Jackson, Mound Bayou, Natchez, Port Gibson, Vicksburg, and Washington, MS. See
**http://genealogybank.com/explore/newspapers/all/usa/mississippi.**

***1803-1816 Tax Rolls, Washington County, Mississippi Territory*** **[Printed Book],** compiled by Ben and Jean Strickland, publ. Milton, FL, 1980, 117 pages. Washington County, Mississippi Territory later became Wayne, Greene, Jones, Perry, George and Jackson Counties, Mississippi and Washington, Baldwin, Monroe, Clarke and Mobile Counties, Alabama. Includes index. FHL book 976 R4s.

**"1805 Mississippi State Census, Wilkinson County, Mississippi" [Printed Article],** in *Journal of Mississippi History,* Vol. 11, No. 2 (Apr 1949).

**1805-1890.** ***Mississippi, Compiled Census and Census Substitutes Index*** **[Online Database],** indexed at the Ancestry.com website. This database was originally edited by Ronald Jackson of Accelerated Indexing Systems, Salt Lake City UT and acquired by Ancestry in 1999. This collection contains the following indexes: 1805 Jefferson and Wilkinson Counties; 1810 Territorial Census Index; 1818 State Census Index; 1820 State Census Index; 1822 State Census Index; 1823 State Census Index; 1824 State Census Index; 1825 State Census Index; 1830 State Census Index; 1837 State Census Index; 1840 Federal Census Index; 1840 State Census Index; 1840 Pensioners List; 1841 State Census Index; 1845 State Census Index; 1850 Federal Census Index; 1850 Slave Schedules; 1853 State Census Index; 1860 Federal Census Index; 1860 Slave Schedule; 1866 State Census Index; 1870 Federal Census Index; 1890 Veterans Schedules; Early Census Index. This database has 288,741 records. See
**http://search.ancestry.com/search/db.aspx?dbid=3556.**

**1809.** ***Mississippi Territory Census*** [Printed Book]. A name list was published as part of Vol. 5: *The Territory of Mississippi, 1798-1817;* in *The Territorial Papers of the United States,* compiled and edited by Clarence Edwin Carter, United States Department of State. The series is no longer listed in the FHL catalog, but may be available at Amazon, Google Books, et al. For a catalog entry at the HathiTrust Digital Library:
**https://catalog.hathitrust.org/Record/000495370.**

***1809 Squatters Census, Mississippi Territory*** **[Printed Book],** author/publisher not noted. This is a census of squatters/heads of household in alphabetical order. A squatter was someone who moved into and settled an area of the U.S. Public Domain land before the land was surveyed and available for sale by the Federal Government. Congress passed several acts relating to "preemption," where squatters were given an opportunity to prove title to their land based on their early occupation – but only if they could show that they actually lived on the property and crops had been planted. See FHL 976.2 X28s.

**1810 Mississippi Territory Censuses.** The federal census was taken for all Mississippi Territory counties (as shown on the map on page 258) and all were lost. But, Mississippi Territory took its own census in 1810 and name lists survive for Amite, Claiborne, Jefferson, Baldwin, Franklin, and Washington counties. A portion of old Washington County was in the present-day area of Alabama, see **"Washington County (now) Alabama 1801, 1808 and 1810 Census,"** in *The Alabama Genealogical Register,* Vol. 9, No. 3 (September 1967), pp 123-26.

***1810 Territorial Census of Amite County, Mississippi* [Online Database],** indexed at the USGenWeb site for Amite Co MS. See **http://files.usgwarchives.net/ms/amite/census/state/amit1810.txt**.

**1810-1919. *Mississippi, Church Records* [Online Database],** digitized and indexed at FamilySearch.org. This collection contains Church records from various denominations in Mississippi, 1910-1919. The record content and time period varies by denomination and locality. This database has 2,869 records, see **www.familysearch.org/search/collection/2790273.**

**1811-1812.** See ***Tax Lists 1811 & 1812, Madison County, Mississippi: & A Few Alabama Land Entries* [Online Database],** indexed at the Ancestry.com website. Source: Book, same title, by Blair Jones. Full text digital page images, with an OCR index. This database has records. See **http://search.ancestry.com/search/db.aspx?dbid=26591.**

**1812-1815. *Mississippi, Compiled Service Records of Volunteer Soldiers* [Online Database],** digitized and indexed at the Ancestry.com website. Source: National Archives microfilm series M678 (add to title: ".. *who served during the war of 1812*"). Compiled service records consist of cards that record information extracted by the Adjutant General's office about a soldier from muster rolls, payrolls, receipts rolls, returns, and other lists. This database has 5,557 records: **http://search.ancestry.com/search/db.aspx?dbid=2126.**

**"1815 (Territorial) Census, Monroe County, Mississippi" [Printed Article],** in *Northeast Mississippi Historical & Genealogical Society Quarterly*, Vol. 6, No. 3 (Spring 1986).

**"1816 State Census, Adams County, Mississippi" [Printed Article],** in *National Genealogical Society Quarterly,* Vol. 37, No. 4 (Dec 1949) thru Vol. 38, No. 3 (Sep 1950).

**"1816 State Census, Amite County, Mississippi" [Printed Article],** in *National Genealogical Society Quarterly,* Vol. 33, No. 4 (Dec 1945) thru Vol. 34, No. 2 (Jun 1946).

**1816.** See ***Inhabitants of Mississippi in 1816 – Amite County* [Online Database],** indexed at the MSGenWeb site for Amite Co MS. See **http://msgw.org/amite/amit1816.htm**.

**"1816 State Census, Clarke County, Mississippi" [Printed Article],** in *Deep South Genealogical Quarterly*, Vol. 16, No. 1 (Feb 1979); and *Mississippi Memories,* Vol. 10, No. 1 (2000).

**"1816 State Census, Greene County, Mississippi" [Printed Article],** in *Success,* Vol. 7, No. 3 (Jul 1977); and in *American Monthly Magazine*, Vol. 83, No. 3 (Mar 1949); and also in *Deep South Genealogical Quarterly*, Vol. 14, No. 4 (Nov 1977).

**"1816 State Census, Jefferson County, Mississippi" [Printed Article],** in *Mississippi Memories*, Vol. 6, No. 1 (1996).

**1818 Tax Rolls, Adams County, Mississippi [Online Database],** indexed at the NatchezBelle.org website. See **www.natchezbelle.org/adams-ind/tax.htm**.

**1818-1880. *Mississippi State Census Returns: RG28* [Original Records & Digital Capture],** at the MDAH, Jackson, MS. These are the state censuses digitized by the Genealogical Society of Utah on site at the MDAH in Jackson, MS in 2011, with the intent of including the images (and future indexes) online with the FamilySearch online series, *Mississippi, State Archives, Various Records, 1820-1951*. These original state census records were never microfilmed and were not included in the first-generation digitized set. Includes State Census returns beginning with FHL/DGS #4822293 (Box 2466, 1818 Lawrence); 1837 (Kemper, Lowndes, Tishomingo counties); 1841 (Adams Attala, Coahoma, Copiah, Covington, Itawamba, Jones, Lawrence, Leake, Madison, Marion, Marshall, Monroe, Oktibbeha counties). To access the digital images, see the online FHL catalog page: **https://familysearch.org/search/catalog/1927064.**

**1820-1825.** See ***Mississippi 1820-1825:* [Printed Index],** edited by Ronald Vern Jackson, et al, Accelerated Indexing, North Salt Lake, UT, 1986, 119 pages. Covers MS state censuses of 1820, 1822, 1823, 1824 &1825. See FHL book 976.2 X22j.

**1820-1840.** ***Mississippi, 1820 thru 1840 Federal Census: Population Schedules*** **[Microfilm & Digital Capture],** filmed by the National Archives, 1938-1960, 7 rolls, beginning with FHL film #181359 (1820: Adams, Amite, Franklin, Greene, Lawrence, Marion, Perry, and Wayne counties). To access the digital images, see the online FHL catalog page:
**www.familysearch.org/search/catalog/745496.**

**1820-1965.** ***Mississippi, State Archives, Various Records*** **[Online Database],** digitized and indexed at the FamilySearch.org website. This database includes narratives from former slaves, land records from the Office of the Secretary of State, lists of military veterans, military grave registrations, and naturalization records. This database has 42,673 records. See
**https://familysearch.org/search/collection/1919687.**

**1823-1859.** ***Yazoo County, Mississippi Pioneers*** **[Printed Book],** by Betty Couch Wiltshire, publ. Heritage Books, Bowie, MD, 1992, 263 pages. From the back cover: "Included in this book are: tax lists for 1823, 1825, 1834, 1843; wills 1829-1870; Probate Court minutes, 1834-1849, which include letters of administration for estates, guardianship appointments, and petitions for allotment of dowers; marriage records 1845-1859; information about Yazoo County's involvement in the Mexican War including a list of volunteers in Company A, First Mississippi Regiment; and brief genealogies of families living in Yazoo County in the 1800s ... information for the family histories from county records. U.S. census records, cemetery records and Yazoo County histories, as well as a few contributions from individuals with ancestors in Yazoo County." See FHL book 976.249 D2w.

**"1825 State Census, Wilkinson County, Mississippi" [Printed Article],** in *Mississippi Genealogical Exchange,* Vol. 32, No. 4 (Winter 1986).

**"1825 State Census, Jackson County, Mississippi" [Printed Article],** in *Jackson County Genealogical Society Journal,* Vol. 2, No. 2 (Spring 1985) and repeated in Vol. 17, No. 1-4 (Dec 2000).

**"1825 Mississippi State Census, Wilkinson County, Mississippi" [Printed Article],** in *Mississippi Genealogical Exchange*, Vol. 32, No. 4 (Winter 1986).

**1826-1850.** ***Mississippi, Compiled Marriages*** **[Online Database],** digitized and indexed at the Ancestry.com website. Originally compiled by Jordan Dodd from county marriage records on microfilm at the Family History Library in Salt Lake City, UT. Includes the name of the groom, bride, and the date and place of marriage. This database has 11,154 records. See
**http://search.ancestry.com/search/db.aspx?dbid=3739.**
- See Also, ***Mississippi, Compiled Marriages, 1826-1900*** **[Online Database],** digitized and indexed at the Ancestry.com website. The database was originally compiled by Jordan Dodd of Provo, UT. This database has just been updated to include more records for Itawamba, Pontotoc, and Marshall counties, in addition to the records previously posted for these counties and Carroll, Claiborne, Jefferson, Lafayette, Leake, Lowndes, Marion, Noxubee, Rankin, Tippah, Winston, Yalobusha, and Yazoo counties. Each record provides spouses' names, marriage date, and county of residence. This database has 60,557 records. See
**http://search.ancestry.com/search/db.aspx?dbid=4585.**

**1826-1906.** ***Orena V. Grant Genealogical Collection (Marriages and Cemetery Records)*** **[Online Database],** digitized and indexed at the Ancestry.com website. Source: Orena V. Grant Collection, publ. Salt Lake City, UT, 1964. Records are from several states, including the Mississippi counties of Forrest (ca 1906), Jasper, ca 1833) and Jones County, MS (ca 1826). This database has 409 pages. See
**http://search.ancestry.com/search/db.aspx?dbid=26523**.

**1827-1840s.** ***Early Mississippi Records, Issaquena County & Washington County*** **[Printed Book],** compiled by Katherine Branton & Alice Wade, published by Pioneer, Carrollton, MS, 1983-2000. Earlier title: *Early Mississippi Records, Washington County, Mississippi.* It should be noted that Washington County, Mississippi Territory (now Alabama) was created in 1800. The current Washington County, Mississippi was created in 1827; Issaquena was formed from Washington in 1844. Both lie adjoining the Mississippi River. These county records include court documents, will and probate records, cemetery records, census records, deaths, marriage records, licenses, and an index to apprentice records. See FHL book 976.24P28v.1-4.

**1828-1833.** ***Madison County, Mississippi Personal Tax Rolls*** **[Microfilm & Digital Capture],** from the originals at the Madison County Courthouse, Canton,

MS. Tax roll years are 1828, 1829, 1830 & 1833. Filmed by the Genealogical Society of Utah, 2002, 1 roll, FHL film #2342432. To access the digital images, see the online FHL catalog page:
**www.familysearch.org/search/catalog/1152533.**

**1828-1865.** A ***History of Rankin County, Mississippi*** **[Printed Book],** compiled and publ. Rankin Co Historical Society, 1984-1988, 2 vols. Includes bibliographical notes throughout. Includes index. Contents: Vol. 1: Rankin County tax rolls, 1828, 1830 and 1840 census records; Vol. 2: Lists of Civil War soldiers. See FHL book 976.259 H2h v.1-2. Also on microfiche, FHL fiche #6087272 & #60872763.

***1830-1837 Mississippi Censuses*** **[Printed Index].** edited by Ronald Vern Jackson, et al, Accelerated Indexing Systems, North Salt Lake, UT, 1986, 63 pages. FHL book 976.2 X2jac.

**"1833 State Census, Simpson County, Mississippi" [Printed Article],** *in Frameworks*, No. 2 (Summer 2000).

**"1834 Tax list, Carroll County, Mississippi" [Printed Article],** in *Mississippi Genealogy and Local History,* Vol. 5, No. 2 (Jun 1976).

**1834-1894.** ***History of Newton County, Mississippi: From 1834 to 1894*** **[Online Database],** digitized and indexed at the Ancestry.com website. Source: Book, same title, by A. J. Brown, publ. Clarion-Ledger Co., Jackson, MS, 1894. Full text page images with an OCR index. This database has 474 pages. See
**http://search.ancestry.com/search/db.aspx?dbid=22989.**

***1835 Federal Pension List, Mississippi*** **[Online Database],** indexed at the Rosters.Tripod website. See
**http://rosters.tripod.com/index-45.html.**

**1835-1905.** ***Mississippi, Adams County, Natchez Death Index*** **[Online Database],** digitized and indexed at FamilySearch.org, from the originals at the Adams County Circuit Court, Natchez, MS. This is a typed index of deaths. The records may contain information on slaves and former slaves. If a slave is mentioned, the owner's name was given in the comments column. There may be some additional information included from local newspapers. This database has 21,926 records, see
**www.familysearch.org/search/collection/3460904.**

**1836-1923.** ***Mississippi, Tippah County Records*** **[Online Database],** digitized at FamilySearch.org. This collection includes digital images of deeds and probate case files recorded in Tippah County, Mississippi. This collection is being published as images become available. This database has 115,097 images, see
**www.familysearch.org/search/collection/1911456.**
- See also ***Mississippi, Tippah County Family Histories*** **[Online Database],** digital images of various family history books housed at the Tippah County Development Foundation, Ripley, MS. Browse through 3,860 images. See
**www.familysearch.org/search/collection/1921135.**

**"1837 State Census, Chickasaw County, Mississippi" [Printed Article],** in *Northeast Mississippi Historical & Genealogical Society Quarterly,* Vol. 7, No. 1 (Fall 1986); and in Chickasaw Times Past, Vol. 9, No. 4 (Jan 1991).

**"1837 State Census, Jones County, Mississippi" [Printed Article],** in *Mississippi Genealogical Exchange,* Vol. 16, No. 2 (Summer 1970) and Vol. 16, No. 3 (Fall 1970).

**"1837 State Census, Kemper County, Mississippi" [Printed Article],** in *Mississippi Genealogical Exchange,* Vol. 18, No. 1 (Spring 1972); Vol. 18, No. 2 (Summer 1972), and Vol. 18, No. 4 (Winter 1972).

**"1837 State Census, Itawamba County, Mississippi" [Printed Article],** published in *Northeast Mississippi Historical & Genealogical Society Quarterly,* Vol. 6, No. 4 (1986).

**"1837 State Census, Panola County, Mississippi" [Printed Article],** in *Mississippi Genealogical Exchange,* Vol. 19, No. 1 (Spring 1973) thru Vol. 19, No. 3 (Fall 1973).

**"1837 State Census, Pontotoc County, Mississippi" [Printed Article],** in *Mississippi Records*, Vol. 1, No. 4 (Oct 1989); and in *Mississippi Genealogical Exchange*, Vol. 25, No. 1 (Spring 1979); and also in *Northeast Mississippi Historical & Genealogical Society Quarterly*, Vol. 6, No. 4 (1986).

**"1837 State Census, Simpson County, Mississippi" [Printed Article],** in *Mississippi Records*, Vol. 2, No. 1 (Jan 1990).

**"1837 State Census, Tishomingo County, Mississippi" [Printed Article],** in *Cross City Connections,* Vol. 8, No. 2 (Dec 1999); and in *Mississippi Genealogical Exchange,* Vol. 17, No. 1 (Spring 1971) thru Vol. 17, No. 2 (Summer 1971).

***1840-1841 Mississippi Censuses* [Printed Index],** edited by Ronald Vern Jackson, et al, Accelerated Indexing, North Salt Lake, UT, 1986. FHL book 976.X22mi.

**"1841 State Census, Attala County, Mississippi" [Printed Article],** in *Mississippi Records*, Vol. 1, No. 1 (Jan 1989).

***1841 State Census, Attala County, Mississippi* [Online Database],** indexed at the Attala-county-history-genealogy.org website. See **http://attala-county-history-genealogy.org/1841statecensusindex-attala.html**.

"**1841 State Census, Chickasaw County, Mississippi" [Printed Article],** in Mississippi Memories, Vol. 6, No. 3 (1996).

**"1841 State Census, Itawamba County, Mississippi" [Printed Article],** in *Northeast Mississippi Historical & Genealogical Society Quarterly,* Vol. 6, No. 4 (1986).

**"1841 State Census, Madison County, Mississippi" [Printed Article],** in *Mississippi Records,* Vol. 3, No. 1 (Jan 1991).

**"1841 State Census, Newton County, Mississippi" [Printed Article],** in *Mississippi Records,* Vol. 1, No. 3 (Jul 1989).

**"1841 State Census, Scott County, Mississippi" [Printed Article],** published in *Mississippi Records*, Vol. 3, No. 3 (Jul 1991).

**"1841 State Census, Tippah County, Mississippi" [Printed Article],** in *Northeast Mississippi Historical & Genealogical Society Quarterly,* Vol. 6, No. 4 (1986) and Vol. 7, No. 1 (Fall 1986).

**"1841 State Census, Tunica County, Mississippi" [Printed Article],** in *Mississippi Genealogical Exchange,* Vol. 16, No. 1 (Spring 1970); and in *Tate Trails,* Vol. 6, No. 2 (Jun 1982).

***1845 Mississippi State Census* [Printed Index],** edited by Ronald Vern Jackson, et al, Accelerated Indexing, North Salt Lake, UT, 1986, 169 pages. FHL book 976.2 X2j.

**"1845 State Census, Attala County, Mississippi" [Printed Article],** in *Frameworks*, Vol. 9, No. 1 (Spring 2000).

**"1845 State Census, Newton County, Mississippi" [Printed Article],** in *Mississippi Genealogical Exchange*, Vol. 26, No. 1 (Spring 1980) and in *Mississippi Records,* Vol. 2, No. 4 (Oct 1990).

**"1845 State Census, Noxubee County, Mississippi" [Printed Article],** in *Mississippi Records*, Vol. 1, No. 2 (Apr 1989).

**"1845 State Census, Pontotoc County, Mississippi" [Printed Article],** in *Northeast Mississippi Historical & Genealogical Society Quarterly*, Vol. 20, No. 3 (March 2000 ).

**"1845 State Census, Sunflower County, Mississippi" [Printed Article],** in *Mississippi Memories,* Vol. 2, No. 3 (1992); and in *Mississippi Genealogical Exchange*, Vol. 24, NO. 2 (Summer 1978).

**"1845 State Census, Tishomingo County, Mississippi" [Printed Article],** in *Northeast Mississippi Historical & Genealogical Society Quarterly*, Vol. 7, No. 2 (Dec 1986).

**1845-1951.** See ***Record of Marriages (DeSoto County, Mississippi), 1845-1860, 1865-1951* [Microfilm & Digital Capture],** from the originals a the DeSoto County Courthouse, Hernando, MS. Includes index books. Filmed by the Genealogical Society of Utah, 50 rolls, 1972, 2006, beginning with FHL film #2413617 (General Index to marriages, white, Vol. 1, A-S, Oct 1938-Sept 1942). To access the digital images, see the online FHL catalog page: **www.familysearch.org/search/catalog/248812.**

**1850. *Mississippi, 1850 Federal Census: Population Schedules* [Microfilm & Digital Capture],** filmed by the National Archives, 1964, 23 rolls, beginning with FHL film #14847 (Adams, Amite, Attala, and Bolivar counties). To access the digital images, see the online FHL catalog page: **www.familysearch.org/search/catalog/744487.**

**1850-1957.** See ***Mississippi Enumeration of Educable Children, 1850-1892; 1908-1957*** **[Online Database],** digitized and indexed at the FamilySearch.org website. These records are lists of students prepared by the counties and school districts. They include the names of both black and white students. The early records include the names of students and the school attended. Recent records include the age of the child and a name of a parent or guardian. This database has 7,141,738 records. Browse through 211,757images. See **https://familysearch.org/search/collection/1856425.**

**1850-1880.** ***Mississippi Mortality Schedules for 1850, 1860, 1870 and 1880*** **[Microfilm & Digital Capture],** filmed by the National Archives, c1965, 3 rolls, FHL film #1550803-1550805.To access the digital images, see the online FHL catalog page: **www.familysearch.org/search/catalog/422723.**

**1853.** ***Mississippi 1853 State Census Index*** **[Printed Index],** edited by Ronald Vern Jackson, et al, Accelerated Indexing Systems, North Salt Lake, UT 1988, 251 pages. FHL Book 976.2 X2jr.

**"1853 Mississippi State Census, Hancock County" [Printed Article],** names for 1840 and 1853 censuses listed in *Florida Parishes Genealogical Newsletter*, Vol. 16, No. 2 (May 1994).

**"1855 Tax list, Bolivar County, Mississippi" [Printed Article],** in *Mississippi Genealogy and Local History,* Vol. 5, No. 2 (Jun 1976).

**1858-1861.** ***Adams County, Mississippi, Slave Certificates*** **[Online Database],** digitized and indexed at the Ancestry.com website. Source: MDAH microfilm, Jackson, MS. This small collection contains records of slave certificates from 1858-1871 and is part of a book labeled "Record Book Adams County" that was found in the basement of the Adams County Courthouse in Natchez, Mississippi in 1999. These certificates where required by law for all the slaves that were brought to Mississippi from any other state for the purpose of being sold and cover the period from 1858 through 1861. It was to certify that no slave was guilty of any felony or crime and that they were lawfully possessed by the person offering them for sale. The information for the slaves is minimal and can include the Name, Gender, Color, Age and Weight. It can also contains the names of the slave trader, state, and county in which the oath is being made, name of the justice receiving the oath, witnesses, and the date it was received. This database has 1,591 records. See **http://search.ancestry.com/search/db.aspx?dbid=1787.**

**1858-1979. Mississippi, Tippah County Marriages [Online Database],** indexed at the FamilySearch.org website. Source: FamilySearch extractions from records on microfilm at the Family History Library, Salt Lake City, UT. This database includes digital images and index of marriages recorded from Tippah County, Mississippi, 1858-1950. The records were filmed at the county courthouse in Ripley, Mississippi. Each index record includes: Name, Event type, Event date, Event place, Gender, Spouse's name, Spouse's gender, and Page number. The digitized license and/or certificate may have much more information about a person. This database has 19,583 records. See **https://familysearch.org/search/collection/1916277.**

**1860.** ***Mississippi, 1860 Federal Census: Population Schedules*** **[Microfilm & Digital Capture],** filmed by the National Archives, 1950, 1967, 32 rolls, beginning with FHL film #803577 (Adams, Amite, and Attala counties). To access the digital images, see the online FHL catalog page: **www.familysearch.org/search/catalog/705426.**

**1861-1865.** ***Mississippi, Civil War Service Records of Confederate Soldiers*** **[Online Database],** digitized and indexed at the FamilySearchy.org website. Confederate service records of soldiers who served in organizations from Mississippi. The records include a jacket-envelope for each soldier, labeled with his name, his rank, and the unit in which he served. The jacket-envelope typically contains card abstracts of entries relating to the soldier as found in original muster rolls, returns, rosters, payrolls, appointment books, hospital registers, Union prison registers and rolls, parole rolls, inspection reports; and the originals of any papers relating solely to the particular soldier. This database has 1,269,794 records. See **https://familysearch.org/search/collection/1932375.**

**1861-1865.** ***Mississippi, Civil War Service Records of Union Soldiers*** **[Online Database],** digitized and indexed at the FamilySearch.org website. This database has 9,701 records. See **https://familysearch.org/search/collection/1932409.**

**1863-1866.** ***Mississippi, Freedmen's Department (Pre-Bureau Records)*** **[Online Database],** digitized at the FamilySearch.org website. These documents pre-date the creation of the Freedmen's Bureau, but were

acquired by the Bureau after its creation in 1865. Browse the images. No index yet. This database has 4,286 records. See
**https://familysearch.org/search/collection/2442776.**

***1865-1866 Internal Revenue Lists for Mississippi, U.S. Bureau of Internal Revenue* [Microfilm & Digital Capture],** from the originals at the National Archives, Washington, D.C, filmed 1988. Name lists for all of Mississippi, organized by districts. 3 rolls, FHL film #1578481-1578483. To access the digital images, see the online FHL catalog page:
**www.familysearch.org/search/catalog/577938.**

**1865-1872. Mississippi, Freedmen's Bureau Field Office Records [Online Database],** digitized at the FamilySearch.org website. The Bureau of Refugees, Freedmen, and Abandoned Lands (often called the Freedmen's Bureau) was created in 1865 at the end of the American Civil War to supervise relief efforts including education, health care, food and clothing, refugee camps, legalization of marriages, employment, labor contracts, and securing back pay, bounty payments and pensions. These records include letters and endorsements sent and received, account books, applications for rations, applications for relief, court records, labor contracts, registers of bounty claimants, registers of complaints, registers of contracts, registers of disbursements, registers of freedmen issued rations, registers of patients, reports, rosters of officers and employees, special and general orders and circulars received, special orders and circulars issued, records relating to claims, court trials, property restoration, and homesteads. Browse the images. No index yet. This database has 66,894 records. See
**https://familysearch.org/search/collection/2333768.**

**1866. *Mississippi 1866 State Census Index* [Printed Index],** edited by Ronald Vern Jackson, et al, Accelerated Indexing Systems, North Salt Lake, UT, 1988, 158 pages. FHL book 976.2 X22m.

**"1866 Mississippi State Census, Tippah County, Mississippi" [Printed Article],** in *News and Journal,* Vol. 8, No. 3 (1982) thru Vol. 12, No. 2 (Summer 1986).

**1866-2010. *Vicksburg, Mississippi, Vicksburg National Cemetery* [Online Database],** indexed at the Ancestry.com website. This database contains the photographic images of gravestones from the Vicksburg National Cemetery. Each index record includes: Name Origin state, Cemetery: Burial location, Section, and Suggested photos. Information on the grave markers varies. Some may contain only a number of initials; others may include facts such as name, birth date, death date, age, rank, and state of origin. This database has 4,703 records. See
**http://search.ancestry.com/search/db.aspx?dbid=2314.**

**1866-2010. *Corinth, Mississippi, Corinth National Cemetery* [Online Database],** indexed at the Ancestry.com website. This database contains the photographic images of gravestones from the Corinth National Cemetery. Each index record includes: Name Origin state, Cemetery: Burial location, Section, and Suggested photos. Information on the grave markers varies. Some may contain only a number of initials; others may include facts such as name, birth date, death date, age, rank, and state of origin. This database has 3,470 records. See
**http://search.ancestry.com/search/db.aspx?dbid=2295.**

**1867-1906. *Voter Registration Books and Poll Books, Lafayette County, Mississippi* [Microfilm & Digital Capture],** from the original records at the Skipwith Historical & Genealogical Society in the Karin Coffey Magdovitz Room of the Lafayette-Oxford Public Library, Oxford, MS. Lists name, race, residence, occupation, name of employer, signature of voter, and date registered. Filmed by the Genealogical Society of Utah, 2004, 4 rolls, beginning with FHL film #2312183 (Voters Registration Book, 1876-1906). To access the digital images, see the online FHL catalog page:
**www.familysearch.org/search/catalog/1192968.**

**1867-2008. *Mississippi, Naturalization Records* [Online Database],** digitized and indexed at the Ancestry.com website. Naturalization records for individuals may include a Declaration of Intention (first papers), Petitions (to become a citizen), Oaths (of Allegiance), and Certificates (of Naturalization). This database has 39,729 records. See
**http://search.ancestry.com/search/db.aspx?dbid=2502.**

**1870. *Mississippi, 1870 Federal Census: Population Schedules* [Microfilm & Digital Capture],** filmed by the National Archives, 1962, 1968, 46 rolls, beginning with FHL film #552219 (Adams and Alcorn counties). To access the digital images, see the online FHL catalog page:
**www.familysearch.org/search/catalog/698905.**

**1871-1900. *Personal Roll Assessment Tax Book, Lafayette County, Mississippi* [Microfilm & Digital Capture],** original records in the Skipwith Historical

& Genealogical Society located in the Karin Coffey Magdovitz Room in the Lafayette-Oxford Public Library in Oxford, Mississippi. To access the digital images, see the online FHL catalog page: **www.familysearch.org/search/catalog/1189004.**

**1871-1929.** ***Guardian Bonds, Rankin County, Mississippi*** **[Microfilm & Digital Capture],** filmed by the Genealogical Society of Utah, 2004, 2 rolls, FHL film #2180031-2). To access the digital images, see the online FHL catalog page:
**www.familysearch.org/search/catalog/1193630.**

**1875-1909.** ***State Tax on Lands; Adams County, Mississippi*** **[Microfilm & Digital Capture],** from the original records at the Adams County Courthouse, Natchez, MS. Filmed by the Genealogical Society of Utah, 1972, 1 roll, FHL film #886342. To access the digital images, see the online FHL catalog page:
**www.familysearch.org/search/catalog/237211.**

**1878-1940.** ***Hinds County Voter Registrations Poll Books*** **[Microfilm & Digital Capture],** from the originals at the City of Jackson Record Management Division, Jackson, MS. Filmed by the Genealogical Society of Utah, 1991, 2001, 3 rolls, beginning with FHL film #2314390 (Hinds Co Poll Books, Bk 1-30, 1878-1899). To access the digital images, see the online FHL catalog page:
**www.familysearch.org/search/catalog/1033707.**

**1880.** ***Mississippi, 1880 Federal Census: Soundex and Population Schedules*** **[Microfilm & Digital Capture],** filmed by the National Archives, c1970, 102 rolls, beginning with FHL film #1254639 (Population: Adams Co). To access the digital images, see the online FHL catalog page:
**www.familysearch.org/search/catalog/676477.**

***1880 Federal Census (Short Form), Harrison County, Mississippi*** **[Microfilm & Digital Capture],** from the county's original volumes of the 1880 name list, located at the Harrison County Courthouse in Biloxi, MS. Of the 74 Mississippi counties in place at the time of the 1880 federal census, only Harrison County's 1880 Short Form survives. Filmed by the Genealogical Society of Utah, 2001, 1 roll, FHL film #2230573. To access the digital images, see the online FHL catalog page: **www.familysearch.org/search/catalog/1014305.**

**✓ 1880 NOTE.** The 1880 "Short Form" was a county copy of the 1880 federal census. In every county of the U.S., the full schedules were transferred from a county directly to the Census Office in Washington, DC. Finding any extant manuscripts of the county copies today is rare. The Short Form name list is not by family, but as an index to the full schedules with all names arranged by the first letter of their surname. By law, the Short Form was to remain at a county courthouse for one month after the 1880 census was taken, allowing for public inspection of the name lists. The data was brief, including just a person's name, color, age, and sex. Only in 1880 did the Census Office ask for a county copy to be made that was different than the full schedules.

**1880-1889.** ***Assessment Rolls and Consolidated Tax Books, Rankin County, Mississippi*** **[Microfilm],** from the originals at the Rankin County Chancery Court Building, Brandon, MS. Includes owner's name, description and location of property, number of acres taxable, value of land and improvements, amount of state tax, and remarks. Filmed by the Genealogical Society of Utah, 2004, 2 rolls, FHL film #2180032-#2180033. To see if this microfilm has been digitized yet, see the FHL catalog page:
**www.familysearch.org/search/catalog/1193786.**

**1889-1942.** ***Mississippi, Confederate Records*** **[Online Database],** digitized at the FamilySearch.org website. This collection includes records of state pensions paid to Confederate veterans and to widows of Confederate veterans living in Mississippi. County pension reports, 1900-1933 and Confederate pension rolls, 1889-1935 are also included. There are also two censuses, an enumeration of veterans and widows dated 1907-1933 and an enumeration of indigent and disabled soldiers and dependents, 1863-1868. Browse the images. No index yet. This database has 34,022 records. See
**https://familysearch.org/search/collection/1979942.**
- See Also, ***Mississippi, Confederate Records, 1889-1942*** **[Online Database],** digitized at the Ancestry.com website. See
**http://search.ancestry.com/search/db.aspx?dbid=60049.**

**"1890 Tax List, Alcorn County, Mississippi" [Printed Article],** in *Northeast Mississippi Historical & Genealogical Society Quarterly*, Vol. 3, No. 2 (Dec 1982).

**1891-1967.** See ***Mississippi, Jackson County, Voting Registrations, 1891-1967*** **[Microfilm],** from the originals at the Jackson County Archives, Pascagoula, MS. Filmed by the Genealogical Society of Utah, 1999, 2 rolls, FHL film # 2184750 (Voting register, 1891, 1892, and 1895); and FHL film #2184751 (Voting registers, 1901-1967).

***1892 Natchez City Directory, Published Oct 1, 1892 by the Banner Publishing Company* [Online Database],** includes a name index and scanned images of the directory. See
**www.natchezbelle.org/adams-ind/1892directory.htm**.

**1892-1963.** See ***Harrison County Voter Registration Records, ca. 1892-1963* [Microfilm & Digital Capture],** from the originals at the Harrison County Courthouse in Biloxi, MS. Each book is arranged in loose alphabetical order by the first letter of a surname. Filmed by the Genealogical Society of Utah, 2001, 3 rolls, beginning with FHL film #2230767 (Harrison County voter registration books for the following precincts: Long Beach, dist. #2, 1892-1916; Stonewall dist. #2, 1892-1916; Pass Christian dist. #3, 1892-1916; Crescent, dist. #3, 1892-1915; Gulf Port, dist. #2, 1893-1903; Wolftown, 1892-1898; Stonewall, dist. #2, 1915-1926; Howison, 1915-1926; White Plains, 1915-1926; Beauvior, 1915-1926; Peace, 1916-1925; Lyman, 1915-1926; Howard Creek, 1915-1926; Handsboro, 1915-1926; Vidalia, 1916-1925; Seymour, 1926-1935; D'Iberville, 1935-1959; Lyman, 1926-1963; Long Beach, 1926-1950; West Gulfport, 1926-1942; Howard Creek, 1926-1962; Gulfport 1A, 1926-1958; Handsboro, 1926-1961; East Biloxi, vol #2, 1938-1950; Ladnier, 1926-1959). To access the digital images, see the online FHL catalog page:
**www.familysearch.org/search/catalog/1014325.**

**1896 *Scranton Town Census* [Microfilm & Digital Capture],** from the originals at the Jackson County Archives, Pascagoula, MS. Includes the 1896 census of the Town of Scranton, Jackson County, Mississippi. Taken July 1896, filed Aug 1896, by Town Clerk. Names are recorded in alphabetical order. Today's downtown Pascagoula used to be the town of Scranton, Mississippi (incorporated 1870) until the two towns merged in 1912. Filmed by the Genealogical Society of Utah, 1999, 1 rolls, FHL film #2148435. To access the digital images, see the online FHL catalog page:
**www.familysearch.org/search/catalog/959091.**

***1898 Tax Assessment, Alcorn County, Mississippi* [Online Database],** indexed by surname and page number at the MSGenWeb site for Alcorn Co MS. See
**www.msgw.org/alcorn/1898tax.html.**

**1900. *Mississippi, 1900 Federal Census: Soundex and Population Schedules* [Microfilm & Digital Capture],** filmed by the National Archives, c1970, 193 rolls, beginning with FHL film #1240799 (Adams and Amite counties). To access the digital images, see the online FHL catalog page:
**www.familysearch.org/search/catalog/636815.**

**1903-1964. *Passenger Lists of Vessels Arriving at Mississippi* [Online Database],** digitized and indexed at the Ancestry.com website. These passenger and crew lists typically include the name of the vessel and arrival date, ports of departure and arrival (as well as future destinations on a ship's itinerary), dates of departure and arrival, shipmaster, full name, age, gender, physical description, military rank (if any), occupation, birthplace, citizen of what country, and residence. For military transports, you may find the next of kin, relationships, and address listed as well. This database has 3,699 records. See
**http://search.ancestry.com/search/db.aspx?dbid=9124**

**1900-1974. *Mississippi, Confederate Veterans and Widows Pension Applications* [Online Database],** digitized at the FamilySearch.org website. This collection includes applications for state pensions filed by Confederate veterans and by widows of Confederate veterans living in Mississippi. Browse the images. No index yet. This database has 117,637 records. See
**https://familysearch.org/search/collection/1936413.**
- For the Ancestry version of this database, see
**http://search.ancestry.com/search/db.aspx?dbid=60050.**

**1907-2008. Mississippi, Naturalization Records [Online Database],** indexed at the Ancestry.com website. Source: National Archives microfilm: Records of the District Courts of the United States. This database contains Declarations of Intention to become a citizen of the U.S.; Oaths of Allegiance; and other Naturalizations documents. Each index record includes: Name, Petition age, Record type, Birth date, Birthplace, Petition date, Spouse, Court district, and Petition number. The digitized image will have more information about a person. This database has 48,723 records. See
**http://search.ancestry.com/search/db.aspx?dbid=2502**.

**1910. *Mississippi, 1910 Federal Census: Soundex and Population Schedules* [Microfilm & Digital Capture],** filmed by the National Archives, c1970, 153 rolls, beginning with FHL film #1374744 (Population: Adams, Alcorn, and Benton counties). To access the digital images, see the online FHL catalog page:
**www.familysearch.org/search/catalog/638141.**

***1910-1921 Birth Returns, City of Natchez, Adams County, Mississippi* [Online Database],** indexed at the NatchezBelle.org website. Names are sorted by father's surname. See
**www.natchezbelle.org/adams-ind/bth_idx.htm**.

**1910-1921 Death Certificates, Adams County, Mississippi [Online Database],** indexed at the NatchezBelle.org website. Information to be found on (most) records, in order of appearance: Name, Age, Sex, Color, Residence, Marital Status, Cause of Death, Occupation, Birthplace, Place of Death, Date of Death, Date Certificate Returned, Reported By, Date Reported, and Comments. See
**www.natchezbelle.org/adams-ind/1910-a.htm**.

**1911-1958.** ***Naturalization Records, Jackson, Mississippi*** **[Microfilm & Digital Capture],** from the original records of the U.S. District Courts, located at the National Archives, East Point, GA. Includes Declarations of Intention, Petitions, and Naturalization Certificates. Filmed by the Genealogical Society of Utah, 3 rolls, 1987-1989, beginning with FHL film #1514023 Declarations of Intention Vol. 1-3 1911-1958, Petitions and records, Vol. 1 1911-1919). To access the digital images, see the online FHL catalog page: **www.familysearch.org/search/catalog/667673.**

**1917-1918.** ***World War I Draft Registrants-Mississippi*** **[Online Database].** Indexed by county at the USGenWeb Mississippi Archives website. See
**http://usgwarchives.net/ms/ww1reg.htm.**

**1917-1918.** ***Mississippi, World War I Army Veterans, Master Alphabetical Index*** **[Online Database],** digitized and indexed at FamilySearch.org. Includes index and images of original typescript at the State Archives in Jackson, Mississippi. Records lists name of veteran, race, serial no., address, and county. This database has 54,610 records, see
**www.familysearch.org/search/collection/3010079.**

**1917-1919.** ***Mississippi, World War I Service Cards*** **[Online Database],** digitized and indexed at FamilySearch.org. This is an Index Card roster of Mississippians who served in the United States Army, Navy, Coast Guard, or Marines during World War I from 1917 to 1919. Each soldier has one or two cards giving information on military service, such as name, serial number, residence, place, and date of birth, military organizations served in, rank, engagements participated in, wounds or injuries received, dates serving overseas, discharge date, percentage disabled, and additional remarks. This database has 58,047 records, see
**www.familysearch.org/search/collection/2968243.**

**1920.** ***Mississippi, 1920 Federal Census: Soundex and Population Schedules*** **[Microfilm & Digital Capture],** filmed by the National Archives, c1970, 157 rolls, beginning with FHL film #1820868 (Adams and Alcorn counties). To access the digital images, see the online FHL catalog page:
**www.familysearch.org/search/catalog/574724.**

**1930.** ***Mississippi, 1930 Federal Census: Soundex and Population Schedules*** **[Microfilm & Digital Capture],** filmed by the National Archives, c1970, 195 rolls, beginning with FHL film #2340872 (Adams and Amite counties). To access the digital images, see the online FHL catalog page:
**www.familysearch.org/search/catalog/1037434.**

**1938-1977.** ***Delta Democrat Times (Greenville, Mississippi)*** **[Online Database],** indexed at the Ancestry.com website. The newspapers can be browsed or searched using an OCR computer-generated index. The accuracy of the index varies according to the quality of the original images. The images for this newspaper can be browsed sequentially, or via links to specific images, which may be obtained through the search results. This database has 180,083 records. See
**http://search.ancestry.com/search/db.aspx?dbid=51319.**

**1940.** ***Mississippi, 1940 Federal Census: Population Schedules*** **[Digital Capture],** digitized for the National Archives, 2012, from the original records held by the Bureau of the Census in the 1940s. After microfilming, Congress allowed the Census Bureau to destroy the originals to free up space for WWII-related files. The Family History Library (FHL) has the 1940 microfilm archived at their Granite Mountain Record Vault. They are not available for viewing but the entire digital collection is available online at several sites. To access the digital images, see the online FHL catalog page: **www.familysearch.org/search/catalog/2057766.**

***1940 Federal Census Finding Aids*** **[Online Database].** The National Archives prepared a special website online with a detailed description of the 1940 federal census. Included at the site are descriptions of location finding aids, such as Enumeration District maps, Geographic Descriptions of Census Enumeration Districts, and a list of 1940 City Directories available at the National Archives. The finding aids are all linked to other National Archives sites. The National Archives website also has a link to 1940 Search Engines using Stephen P. Morse's "One-Step" system for finding a 1940 E.D. or street address conversion. See **www.archives.gov/research/census/1940/general-info.html#questions.**

**1994–Current. Mississippi Newspaper Obituaries [Online Database].** Digitized and indexed at the GenealogyBank.com website. There are obituaries published in newspapers from Batesville, Biloxi, Booneville, Brookhaven, Charleston, Clarksdale, Cleveland, Columbia. Columbus, Corinth County, Eupora, Forest, Greenville, Greenwood, Hattiesburg, Indianola, Jackson, Kosciusko, Laurel, Louisville, Magee, McComb, Meridian, Natchez, New Albany, Oxford, Pascagoula, Picayune, Prentiss, Quitman, Starkville, Union, Vicksburg, West Point, Winona, and Yazoo City. See **http://genealogybank.com/explore/obituaries/all/usa/mississippi.**

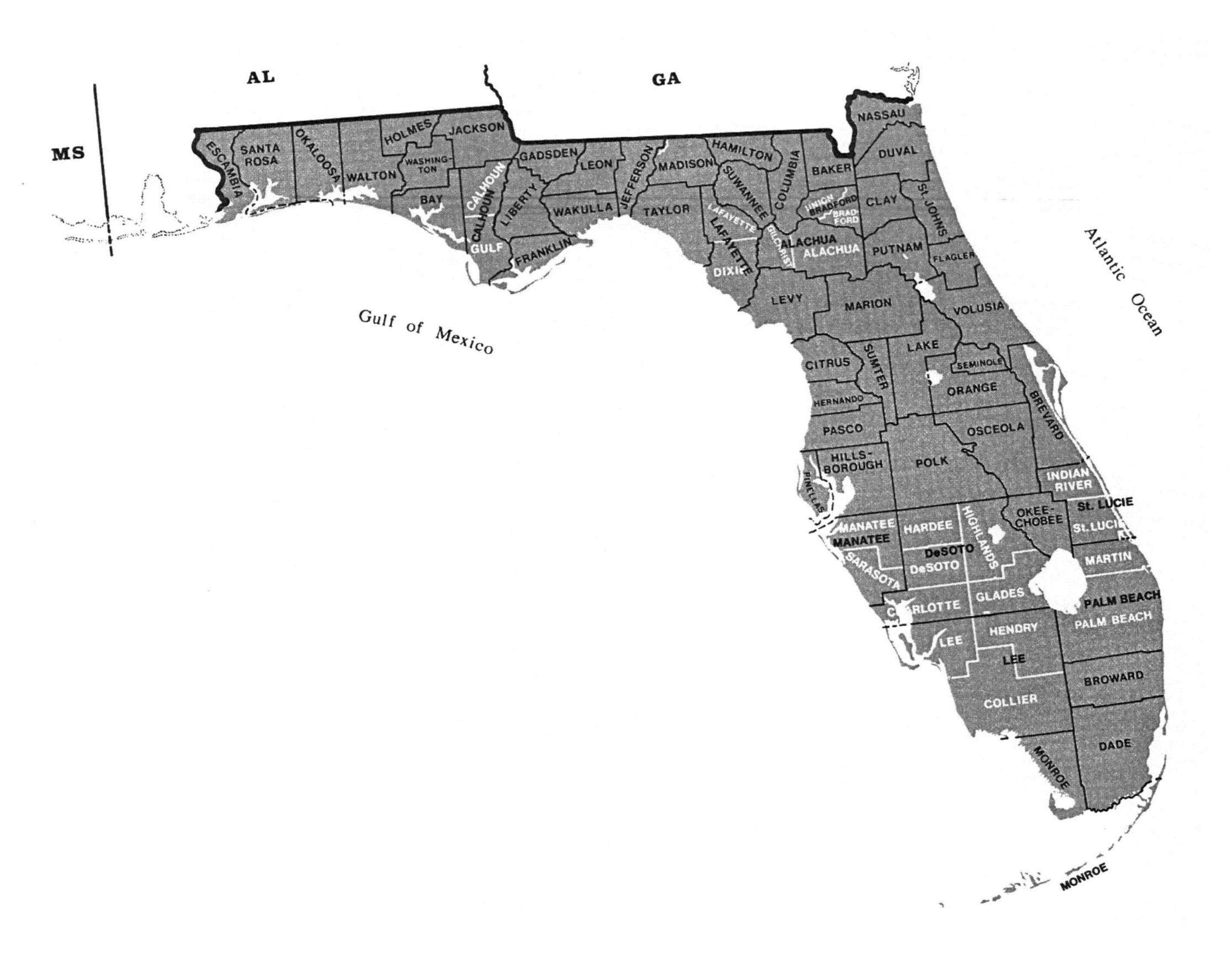


**Florida as of 1 June 1920.** This map shows in black, the 54 counties of Florida at the time of the 1920 Federal Census. Between the 1920 and 1930 censuses, Florida had a population increase from 968,470 to 1,468,211 people and created 13 more counties (shown in white): Charlotte, Dixie, Glades, Hardee, Highlands, Sarasota, and Union in 1921; Collier and Hendry in 1923; and Gilchrist, Gulf, Indian River, and Martin in 1925. Since 1925, there have been no significant changes to Florida's 67 counties, except that in 1968, the city of Jacksonville and Duval County consolidated into one government. And, in 1997, Dade County voters renamed themselves *Miami-Dade County*. After merging many county and city services, they are now managed by an elected Mayor of Miami-Dade County. **Map source:** Page 78, **Map Guide to the U.S. Federal Censuses, 1790-1920,** by William Thorndale and William Dollarhide.

# Florida

## Censuses & Substitute Name Lists

### Historical Timeline for Florida, 1513-1945

**1513.** Spaniard Juan Ponce de Leon, Governor of Puerto Rico, explored and named Florida (Pascua La Florida, after the Feast of Flowers). The fountain of youth he was looking for did not happen until Disney World arrived 458 years later.

**1539.** Spaniard Hernando DeSoto, Governor of Cuba, on a quest to find gold and a route to China, landed on Florida's West Coast, somewhere between present Cape Coral and Bradenton, traveled on land towards Tampa Bay and then further north to present-day Tallahassee. DeSoto was known to visit the Bay of Ochuse, now Pensacola Bay. Looking for gold, he left La Florida disappointed, but he became the first European to travel into present Georgia, South Carolina, North Carolina, Kentucky, Tennessee, Alabama, Mississippi, and Arkansas.

**1565.** The first colony at St. Augustine Bay was founded by the Spanish. Although the fort was sacked, burned, pillaged, and generally not treated well by the French or English, St. Augustine survived and is now acknowledged as the first permanent settlement in North America by Europeans.

**1586.** British seafarer, Sir Francis Drake, raided and burned St. Augustine, but the fort was rebuilt again by the Spanish soon after, along with several more missions in Florida over the next century.

**1682.** French explorer René-Robert Cavelier (Sieur de la Salle) erected a cross near the confluence of the Mississippi River and the Gulf of Mexico, after floating down rivers from the Great Lakes. He claimed the entire Mississippi basin for Louis XIV of France, for whom Louisiana was named. The French believed that Louisiana included the present areas of Biloxi, Mobile, and Pensacola.

**1698.** Pensacola was founded by the Spanish, as the Presidio Santa Maria de Galve.

**1719.** The French captured Pensacola and about the same time occupied all of the gulf ports to New Orleans, but as a result of an alliance with Spain against England, the French soon returned Pensacola to Spain.

**1754.** The Spanish built the Presidio San Miguel de Panzacola, within what is now downtown Pensacola's historical district.

**1763. Treaty of Paris.** Until this year, many cross-claims to territory in North America existed between the French, English and Spanish, and it took a war to settle the issue of land ownership. In Europe it was called the Seven Years War, but in colonial America it was called the French and Indian War. France was the loser, and at the 1763 Treaty of Paris ending the war, the English gained undisputed title to Nova Scotia, Labrador, Quebec, their Atlantic colonies from present Maine to Georgia, and all other lands east of the Mississippi River. Spanish lands were recognized as those west of the Mississippi. France was divested of its large North American claims. In a separate part of the treaty in 1763, the Spanish ransomed Florida to the British in exchange for Cuba. The British immediately divided the area into West Florida with a capital at Pensacola, and East Florida, with a capital at St. Augustine. The dividing line was the Apalachicola - Chattahoochee Rivers.

**1780-1783.** During the Revolutionary War, the British hold on East and West Florida came to an end. With the Spanish as allies of the French, the British lost West

Florida to Spanish forces, who captured Mobile in 1780 and Pensacola in 1781. The British then returned East Florida to Spain in 1783, causing many American loyalists who had fled the Revolutionary War to St. Augustine to flee again, this time heading for the Bahamas or West Indies.

**1783. The United States of America.** The treaty of Paris of 1783 first recognized the United States as an independent nation. Its borders were described generally from the Atlantic Ocean to the Mississippi River, and from present Maine to Georgia. Spain continued to possess East and West Florida after the 1783 Treaty of Paris. However, Spain and the U.S. both claimed the area between Latitude 31° and Latitude 32° 30' of present-day Mississippi and Alabama. This disputed area was left out of the U.S. in the Treaty of 1783 and remained in dispute with Spain until 1796.

**1790.** The present-day area of Alabama and Mississippi was part of Georgia, part of the disputed area, and part of Spanish West Florida at the time of the 1790 federal census. Although there were American settlements around Mobile and Natchez, no census was taken there.

**1796-1798.** In the 1796 Treaty of San Lorenzo (also called Pinckney's Treaty), the U.S. resolved the Spanish-U.S. disputed area by purchasing the area from Spain. The lands above West Florida (Latitude 31° up to 32°30') became U.S. territory. The purchase did not include East Florida or West Florida. In 1798, Congress created Mississippi Territory in the purchased area.

**1800. Louisiana.** Napoleon acquired title of Louisiana from Spain. At the Third Treaty of San Ildefonso, the Spanish acknowledged that it was too costly to explore the country and could not see the rewards being worth the investment. Spain retroceded Louisiana to France in exchange for the Grand Duchy of Tuscany (now part of Italy).

**1803. Louisiana Purchase.** The United States purchased Louisiana from France. Sent by President Jefferson to attempt the purchase of New Orleans, the American negotiators (James Madison and Robert Livingston) were surprised when Napoleon offered the entire tract to them. The Louisiana Purchase was officially described as the "drainage of the Mississippi and Missouri River basins." Adding the area doubled the size of the United States.

**1810. West Florida Annexation.** In September 1810, a group of rebel Americans overcame the Spanish garrison at Baton Rouge and unfurled the new flag of the Republic of West Florida. In October 1810, in a proclamation by President James Madison, the U.S. arbitrarily annexed Spain's West Florida from the Mississippi River to the Perdido River. The area included Baton Rouge, Biloxi, and Mobile, but was not organized, and was not included in the 1810 census. Spain did not recognize the annexation, and continued their claim to West Florida in dispute with the U.S.

**1812.** Congress added to Mississippi Territory the portion of the West Florida annexation from the Perdido River to the Pearl River, an area which included Mobile and Biloxi; and the portion from the Pearl River to the Mississippi River was added to Orleans Territory, an area that included Baton Rouge. Soon after, Orleans Territory became the State of Louisiana.

**1819-1821. Adams-Onis Treaty/Purchase of Florida.** After years of refusing to negotiate with the U.S. over the ownership of Florida, Spain finally relented with the 1819 Adams-Onis treaty, also called the Purchase of Florida. Spain's problems with colonial rebellions in Central and South America saw a change in their attitudes. By 1818, Spain had effectively abandoned Florida and was unwilling to support any more colonists or garrisons. The treaty involved Spain's cession of Florida to the U.S. in exchange for the U.S. paying any legal claims of American citizens against Spain, up to 5 million dollars. But, the treaty also set the boundary between the U.S. and New Spain/Mexico, from Louisiana to the Oregon Country. The treaty finally confirmed the Sabine River border with Spanish Texas; and recognized (for the first time), the American claim to the Oregon Country. Although Baton Rouge, Biloxi, and Mobile were annexed to the U.S. in 1810, then organized in 1812; they did not become U.S. territory free of dispute until the Adams-Onis Treaty was ratified by Congress in 1821.

**1820.** At the time of the 1820 federal census, Florida was left out of the enumeration since the Purchase of Florida was not ratified by Congress until 1821.

**1822. Florida Territory** was created by Congress, with bounds the same as the present state. The two main population centers in Florida in 1822 were Pensacola and St. Augustine, both wanting to be the new territorial capital. But, the travel time between the two cities was measured in weeks. It was decided to find a point about half-way between the two cities to locate the new territorial capital. Tallahassee was selected, at the time, an abandoned Indian village.

**1845.** March 3. Florida was admitted to the Union as the 27th state.

## Florida Memory – Online Records

**www.FloridaMemory.com** is a website sponsored by the Florida Division of Library & Information Services – an online collection of photographs, videos, audios, and historical documents, taken from both the State Archives of Florida and the State Library of Florida collections. The areas of most interest to genealogists are categorized under Collections and Guides, as follows:

**The Florida Folklife Collection** includes approximately 150 cubic feet of paper records (including field notes and administrative files) and thousands of audio and video recordings, which date from the 1930s through 2001. Created by Florida folklorists, the Collection consists of 88 individual series that document the performances by, interviews with, and fieldwork surveys of folk musicians, artisans, storytellers, folklife interpreters, and other Florida peoples and their traditions.

Search this database for descriptions of photographs and audio recordings from the Florida Folklife Collection available at the State Archives of Florida. About 46,000 photographic images and about 5,000 audio recordings are cataloged. See **www.floridamemory.com/collections/folklife.**

**Spanish Land Grants** were land claims filed by settlers in Florida after the transfer of the territory from Spain to the United States in 1821 in order to prove land ownership. In the Adams-Onis Treaty of 1819, Spain had ceded Florida to the United States, with the provision that the U.S. pay any legal claim against Spain.

As early as 1790, Spain had offered land grants to encourage settlement to the sparsely populated and vulnerable Florida colony. When the United States assumed control of Florida, it agreed to honor any valid land grants. Yet residents had to prove that validity through documentation and testimonials. Therefore, these records were the dossiers filed by grantees to the U.S. government. They were either confirmed (found to be valid) or unconfirmed (found invalid) by the US government through land commissions, federal courts, or by the U.S. Congress. Grantees had to provide the following information: description of land granted; date of grant; size of grant; property boundaries; and proof of residency and cultivation. Therefore the records contain surveys and plats, copies of royal grants, testimonials; correspondence, deeds, wills, and translations of Spanish documents. To browse all records or search for a specific person, see **www.floridamemory.com/collections/spanishlandgrants.**

**World War I Service Cards.** Since April 1917, millions of American men and women served their nation in the Great War, including over 42,000 Floridians, of which 35,829 served in the U.S. Army, 5,963 in the U.S. Navy and Coast Guard, and 283 in the U.S. Marine Corps. Both the Navy and the Marine Corps were strictly segregated and did not accept black enlistees or officers. Into segregated units, the Army took 13,024 black enlistees and 7 officers.

These service records originated with the Florida Adjutant General, the same officer now located at the St. Francis Barracks in St. Augustine, Florida. For each person, the cards provide a name; age; serial number; race; place of birth; and residence at time of entering service. Some cards also provide the organizations/ships served (with dates of beginning and transfer); engagements; wounds/injuries sustained in action; time served overseas; discharge notations; and general remarks. The Navy cards note the sailor's rate as well as rank. The digitized images of the WWI Service Cards can be browsed at this site, and an every-name index can be searched for a specific person. See **www.floridamemory.com/collections/wwi.**

**Confederate Pensions Application Files.** The first Confederate pensions in Florida were authorized in 1885 and granted to veterans the sum of $5.00 per month. The next three decades saw a new Confederate pension bill introduced at nearly every session of the Legislature. Residency requirements were added and adjusted, militia members and widows were declared eligible, various financial qualifications were added and changed, and the amount and method of distribution were changed many times.

The pension application files include both veterans' and widows' applications interfiled, approved and denied claims are filed separately. The veteran's application generally includes his full name, date and place of birth, unit of service, date and place of enlistment, date and place of discharge, brief description of service and/or wounds, proof of service, place and length of residence in Florida, as well as other miscellaneous documentation.

The widow's application is filed with that of her husband and includes her full name, date and place of marriage, date and place of her husband's death, her place and length of residence in Florida, and proof of her husband's service. Some early applications also include the widows' date and place of birth. Confederate pensions were awarded to residents of Florida regardless of the state in which their service was rendered. To browse all records or search the index for a specific person, see **www.floridamemory.com/collections/pensionfiles.**

**WPA Church Records.** This collection of Works Progress Administration (WPA) church records is from the State Library of Florida's collections. One of the most significant undertakings of the Historical Records Survey of the late 1930s and early 1940s was a nationwide survey of churches and church records, known as the Church Archives Inventory.

Each state created a list of known churches and synagogues to be surveyed and organized by county. Survey workers then ventured out into the field to document church histories and record holdings by interviewing clergy and congregation members. This collection contains the documents created by the state of Florida. The form used by field workers for the Church Archives Inventory, titled "Form 20HR," included fields for church name (or names), address, name of the pastor, architectural and building details, race and size of the congregation, location of church records, and additional information deemed relevant.

Browse all WPA Church Records, or an online search of the records can be done by the name of a pastor, church, or denomination, year of incorporation, county, or predominant race/ethnicity (of the congregation). See **www.floridamemory.com/collections/churchrecords.**

## Online Guides to Florida Memory Records

***A Guide to Civil War Records.*** The purpose of this guide is to identify and describe the state, federal, and private records pertaining to Florida's Civil War era (1860-1865) housed at the State Archives of Florida.

***The Black Experience: A Guide to African American Resources in the State Library and Archives of Florida.*** This resource guide is intended to present an overview of the resources that are available for the study of African American history.

***Collections Pertaining to Women's History and Women's Issues.*** This guide to collections relevant to women's issues and women's history was compiled from the State Archives of Florida's holdings of over 40,000 cubic feet of state and local government records and historical manuscripts.

***A Guide to New Deal Records.*** The purpose of this guide is to identify and describe those public records pertaining to Florida's New Deal era (1933-1942) housed at the State Archives of Florida.

***Filming Florida: Images of the Sunshine State.*** The State Archives of Florida's film and video collection contains approximately 2,500 movies and video tapes.

## Genealogical Collection at the State Archives of Florida

The collection consists of a 10,000-volume library of sourcebooks, including family, state, county, and local histories; immigration lists; church, cemetery, and military records; genealogy journals and reference books; and a wide variety of other published sources. A large selection of microfilmed federal census records and city directories supplement the printed records. The Reference staff also maintains a Family Name File of unpublished materials relating to specific families, and a Surname Exchange File. See the Genealogy webpage for more information. See **http://dos.myflorida.com/library-archives/research/explore-our-resources/genealogy.**

**Military Records:**

| Conflict | Available Records |
|---|---|
| Seminole Wars | - Compiled service records |
| Indian Wars and Disturbances | - Consolidated index to all soldiers |
| Revolutionary War | - Pension and bounty-land Warrant application files |
| Mexican War, 1846-1848 | - Muster rolls of Florida companies |
| Civil War | - Compiled service records, Union and Confederate armies from Florida |
| Civil War | - Original pension applications for soldiers living in Florida |
| Spanish-American War | - Compiled service records for Florida soldiers |

| | |
|---|---|
| World War I | - Induction records |
| World War I | - Card listing of all Floridians who served in Army, Navy, Marines, & Coast Guard |
| Other Records | - Listing of burial locations of FL military veterans |
| Other Records | - Registers of enlistments in US Army, 1798-1914 |
| Other Records | - Variety of Florida militia and National Guard records from 19th and 20th centuries |

**County Records.** Some of the most useful records in genealogy research are the deed, marriage, and probate records that were microfilmed in county courthouses throughout Florida. The records generally date from the creation of the county to the mid-1920s, although many courthouses burned or have lost records during their existence. Tax rolls and election returns are also useful in locating an elusive ancestor. County tax collectors and elections officials were required by law to compile and submit their tax rolls and election returns (which included the names of men who voted) to the state. Both groups of records are arranged by county and year and, while not indexed, are fairly easy to search, but there are gaps in the records. Generally, their usefulness spans the period from the 1820s to the 1870s.

**Census Records.** The Archives has a growing collection of U.S. Census and Soundex records currently numbering over 10,000 rolls of microfilm, as well as a collection of the Florida state censuses of 1885, 1935, and 1945 which, with a few exceptions, are complete enumerations of the state's residents. There are also 150 rolls of microfilm covering various Native American censuses and enrollment cards.

**Florida Pioneer Certificate Files.** These files contain applications and supporting genealogical data for individuals who received a Florida State Pioneer Descendant Certificate or Florida County Pioneer Descendant Certificate issued by the Florida State Genealogical Society. These files trace the genealogy of those living in a county at the time of its creation or living in Florida prior to statehood.

**Genealogy Book Collection.** Over 10,000 publications includes books on surname origins, family histories, genealogy sources, heraldry, cemetery records, bible records, county histories, census indexes, military rosters, published deeds, probate and marriage information, periodicals and journals from genealogy societies around the United States.

**Genealogical Resources on CD-ROM.** The Genealogy Collection includes a number of resources on CD-ROM, including the Genealogical Research System from Automated Archives, Inc. and the FamilySearch Files from the Church of Jesus Christ of Latter-day Saints. These resources are comprised of hundreds of compact discs containing millions of names from sources such as social security death benefit records, marriage records, and census indexes.

**Other Collections.** Resources regularly used by genealogy researchers include Spanish land grants application files, plat maps, homestead applications, tract books, prison registers, Supreme Court case files, and the Florida Photographic Collection.

# Bibliography

## Florida Censuses & Substitutes

Florida's Colonial, Territorial, State, and Federal Censuses can be associated with the historic jurisdictional eras of Florida:

**1565-1763. First Spanish Era:** During this period of some two hundred years, only one colonial Spanish census exists, a 1759 name list for an area near St. Augustine, Florida.

**1763-1783. British East & West Florida Era:** Colonial British censuses and name lists exist for 1763, 1771, 1776 and 1779.

**1783-1819. Second Spanish Era:** Colonial Spanish censuses & name lists exist for 1783, 1785, 1786, 1791, 1795, and 1814.

**1822-1844. Florida Territory Era:** Censuses of the Territory of Florida were taken in 1825 and 1838. Only a few county name lists have survived.

**1845 – Present. State of Florida Era.** Florida state censuses were conducted in 1845, 1855, 1867, 1875, 1885, 1895. 1905. 1915, 1925, 1935, and 1945. The mostly extant 1845 state census was referred to as "Statehood Election Returns," and was used to determine the population of the new state for apportionment of its first state legislature. A few county name lists survive for the 1855, 1867, 1875, and 1895 state censuses, but no original manuscripts from the 1905, 1915, or 1925 censuses have been located. It appears that the substantially complete state census enumerations that have survived for Florida are the 1845, 1885, 1935, and 1945 state censuses. In 1949, Florida abolished state censuses and began using federal census population figures for apportionment of its state legislature in 1950.

In addition to the federal and state censuses taken in Florida, there were numerous valuable substitute name lists, all listed below in chronological order:

**"1759 Colonial Spanish Census, Fort Mose" [Printed Article],** (now St. Johns County). Name list published in *Ancient City Genealogist* (St. Augustine Genealogical Society),Vol. 4, No. 4 (Dec 1993).

**1763-1771.** ***A List of Inhabitants of East Florida at the Beginning of the English Period When the Land was Ceded to England in 1763 by the Treaty of Paris.*** **[Copy of Manuscript],** extracted by Charles Mack Wills, Jr. From subtitle: "This List is Extracted from D. Braham's Report of the General Survey in the Southern District of North America Which He Presented to King George III, it Lists the Inhabitants of East Florida, Their Employ, Business and Qualifications in Science from 1763-1771," 8 pages, FHL book 975.9 X2w.

**1763-1821.** ***Spanish Land Grants in Florida: Briefed Translations From the Archives of the Board of Commissioners for Ascertaining Claims and Titles to Land in the Territory of Florida*** **[Printed Book & Digital Capture],** from the 5-volumes prepared by the Historical Records Survey, Division of Professional and Service Projects, Works Progress Administration, publ. by the FL State Library Board, 1940-1941. FHL book 975.9 R2hs v.1-5. To access digital versions of each of the five volumes, see the online FHL catalog page for this title:
**www.familysearch.org/search/catalog/143451.**

**1763-1821.** ***Florida, Spanish Land Grants*** **[Online Database],** digitized and indexed at the FamilySearch.org website. Source: Florida Memory, State Library & Archives of Florida. Includes Confirmed and Unconfirmed land grants. This database has 932 records. See
**www.familysearch.org/search/collection/2761954.**

**1766-1930.** ***Chronological Document Files*** **[Microfilm & Digital Capture],** from the original records at the Historical Society Library, St. Augustine, FL. Text in English and Spanish. Includes land records, probate records, census records, letters and other records. Filmed by the Genealogical Society of Utah, 1977, 8 rolls, beginning with FHL film #1019970 (1766-1779). To access the digital images, see the online FHL catalog page:
**www.familysearch.org/search/catalog/38350.**

**1776.** See **"Inhabitants, 1776, East Florida," [Printed Article].** See in *Jacksonville Genealogical Society Quarterly,* Vol./No. not cited. Publ. 1990.

**1779.** See **"Inhabitants of English Pensacola, 1779" [Printed Article]** in *West Florida Footprints* (West Florida Genealogical Society, Pensacola, FL), Vol. ?, No. 1. (Spring 1984).

**1780s-1820.** ***Florida's First Families: Translated Abstracts of Pre-1821 Spanish Censuses*** **[Printed Book],** compiled by Donna Rachal Mills, published by Mills Historical Press, Tuscaloosa, AL, 1992, 201 pages. Includes index. FHL book 975.9 X2f.

**1780s-Current.** ***Florida USGenWeb Archives*** **[Online Database],** includes databases for all counties of Florida. **Record categories:** Birth Records, Biographies, Cemeteries, Census and Tax Lists, Church Records, City Directories, Court Records, Death Records, Deeds and Real Estate Records, Divorce Records, Historical Records, Marriage Records, Military Records, Newspaper Articles, Obituaries, Photographs, Publications, and Schools. See **http://usgwarchives.net/fl/flfiles.htm.**

**1780s-Current.** ***Linkpendium – Florida: Family History & Genealogy, Census, Birth, Marriage, Death Vital Records & More*** **[Online Database],** Linkpendium is a portal to websites with genealogical information. The Florida section is organized by Location (Number of Sites), as follows: Statewide Resources Selected sites (433), Independent Cities, Renamed Counties, Discontinued Counties (6), Alachua County (333), Baker County (134), Bay County (209), Bradford County (176), Brevard County (268), Broward County (310), County (178), and 61 more Florida counties. See
**www.linkpendium.com/fl-genealogy.**

**1781-1797.** ***Anglo-Americans in Spanish Archives: Lists of Anglo-American Settlers in the Spanish Colonies of America; a Finding Tool*** **{Printed book],** by Lawrence H. Feldman. From source materials available in some of the major Spanish archives, the author abstracted from the original census documents genealogical data about individuals and families who settled in the French territories of Louisiana and the Floridas after they came under Spanish rule. Published by Genealogical Publishing Co., Baltimore, MD, 1991, 349 pages, FHL book 973.X2fe.

**1782-1816.** ***Spanish West Florida, Archives of the Spanish Government*** **[Online Database],** indexed at the Ancestry.com website. Source: National Archives microfilm T1116. This collection consists of transcribed and translated records of the Spanish Empire related to the Spanish province of West Florida. Today, this region encompasses the panhandle of the state of Florida, the southernmost parts of the states of Mississippi and Alabama, and the Florida Parishes of the state of Louisiana. Included are a wide variety of documents, such as records related to property sales, mortgages, inventories and assessments, money lending and debt settlements, wills and probates, inquests, and records related to slavery in Spanish West Florida. This database has 9,202 records. See
**https://search.ancestry.com/search/db.aspx?dbid=2454.**

**"1783-1793 Colonial Spanish Censuses" [Printed Article].** see *Early American Series,* vol. 2, 1783-1793.
- See also **"Spanish Census Listing, 1784-85," [Printed Article],** published in *Southern Genealogists Exchange Quarterly,* Vol. 11, No. 55 (Fall 1970).
- Also published as ***Early Florida Census*** **[Printed Book],** edited by Ronald Vern Jackson, published by Accelerated Indexing, 1984. See FHL book 973 D2jef.

**1783-1796.** ***Genealogical Papers*** **[Microfilm & Digital Capture],** by Winifred Shepard. Includes excerpts of the 1783 and 1793 Spanish Censuses of Florida; Father Hassett's Census of St. Augustine and Vicinity, 1786; and censuses of the Mosquito Territory including San Pablo Beach, Talbot, Shell and Amelia Islands, Tiger Isle, St. Mary's River, St. John's River, Nassau River, and Fernandina. Includes an index. Filmed by the Genealogical Society of Utah, 1977, 1 roll, FHL film #1014120. To access the digital images, see the online FHL catalog:
**www.familysearch.org/search/catalog/134297.**

***1783-1819 Spanish Land Grants in Florida*** **[Online Database].** The Florida Memory website has an online index to names of persons granted land by the Spanish prior to the transfer of Florida from Spain to the U.S. in 1819. The holders of Spanish land grants were required to submit evidence to U.S. courts to obtain U.S. title to the land. See
**www.floridamemory.com/Collections/SpanishLandGrants.**

**"1783 Colonial Spanish Census" [Printed Article],** published in *Georgia Genealogical Magazine,* No. 39-42. (1971).

***1783 Spanish Census of East Florida*** **[Online Database],** indexed at the USGenWeb website for Florida. See
**http://files.usgwarchives.net/fl/statewide/census/1783.txt.**

**1784.** See ***The Last Days of British Saint Augustine, 1784-1785: a Spanish Census of the English Colony of East Florida*** **[Printed Book],** by Lawrence H. Feldman. (Genealogical Publishing Co., Inc., Baltimore, 1998). Lists the English residents of East Florida in 1784 when it changed from British to Spanish rule. Includes index. See FHL book 975.918/S1 X2f.

**1784-1990.** ***Florida Probate Records*** **[Online Database],** digitized at the FamilySearch.org website. Includes case files, wills, and other documents created by the probate courts of various Florida counties. This is an image-only database with 662,980 images. Browse the images, organized by County, Volume Title, and Date Range:
**https://familysearch.org/search/collection/2046765.**

***1785 Residents of Pensacola*** **[Online Database],** indexed at the USGenWeb site for Escambia Co FL:
**http://files.usgwarchives.net/fl/escambia/history/1785resi.txt.**

**1790-1844.** ***Spanish Land Grant Archives*** **[Microfilm & Digital Capture],** from the originals at the Florida State Archives, Tallahassee, FL. From FHL catalog: "Some bundles have their own index. Text in Spanish and English. Includes memorials, concessions, lot descriptions, new settlers and citizens, 1790-1791 (with index), miscellaneous land grants, deeds, wills, bills of sale, etc. 1804-1844." Filmed by the Genealogical Society of Utah, 1977, 9 rolls, beginning with FHL film #1020288 (Memorials and Concessions, v. B-L 1790-1822). To access the digital images, see the online FHL catalog page:
**www.familysearch.org/search/catalog/293032.**

***1790-1844 Spanish Land Grants*** **[Online Database],** digitized and indexed at the Florida Memory collections of the Florida State Archives website. From FL archives description: "The Spanish Land Grants were land claims filed by settlers in Florida after the transfer of the territory from Spain to the United States in 1821 in order to prove land ownership. Starting in

1790, Spain offered land grants to encourage settlement to the sparsely populated and vulnerable Florida colony. When the United States assumed control of Florida, it agreed to honor any valid land grants. Yet residents had to prove that validity through documentation and testimonials. Therefore, these records were the dossiers filed by grantees to the U.S. government. A search/browse screen allows a search in confirmed claims, unconfirmed claims, or both, and fully digitized images of the papers from each claim are downloadable for free online. See **http://floridamemory.com/collections/spanishlandgrants**

**1798-1999.** ***Florida Collection Catalog at MyHeritage.com*** **[Online Database],** 17 collections with 15,652,136 records for Florida. Current databases include: Marriages & Divorces, 1970-1999; 1845 State Census, 1935 State Census, Land Patents, College Yearbooks, City Directories, Cemeteries, and Histories. This is subscription website, but a free search can be done for a name, place, year, or keyword. See **www.myheritage.com/records/Florida/all-records.**

**1800s-2000s.** ***A Florida Biographical Index: Being a Listing of Biographies of Notable Floridians Contained in Various Publications as Listed on the Source Documents List*** **[Printed Book & Digital** Version], by Charles Mack Wills, Jr. , publ. 2009, 131 pages. To access the digital version, see the online FHL catalog page: **www.familysearch.org/search/catalog/1621716.**

**1810-1974.** ***Florida, Wills and Probate Records*** **[Online Database],** digitized and indexed at the Ancestry.com website. Source: FL County, District, and Probate Courts. Probate records include Wills, Letters of Administration, Inventories, Distributions and Accounting, Bonds, and Guardianships. Each index record includes: Name, Probate place, Inferred death place, and Item description. The document image may have much more information. Case files with multiple pages have a Table of Contents showing the categories of papers and number of images. This database has 78,688 records. See **https://search.ancestry.com/search/db.aspx?dbid=8993.**

***1814 Colonial Spanish Censuses*** **[Microfilm & Digital Capture].** See ***Genealogical Papers***, by Winifred Shepard. Includes excerpts of the 1814 Spanish Censuses of Florida; Filmed by the Genealogical Society of Utah, 1977, 1 roll, FHL film #1014120. To access the digital images of this roll, see the online FHL catalog page for this title: **www.familysearch.org/search/catalog/134297.**

**1820-1890** See ***Florida, Compiled Census and Census Substitutes Index*** **[Online Database].** Originally edited by Ronald V. Jackson, Accelerated Indexing, Salt Lake City, UT. Electronic files were acquired by Ancestry, Inc. in 1999. This Florida combined index contains the following:

- 1820 Index, Pensacola & Escambia River
- 1825 Leon County Index
- 1830 Federal Census Index
- 1840 Federal Census Index
- 1840 Pensioners List
- 1850 Federal Census Index
- 1850 Slave Schedule
- 1860 Federal Census Index
- 1860 Slave Schedule
- 1870 Federal Census Index
- 1890 Veterans Schedule
- 1890 Naval Veterans Schedule

See **http://search.ancestry.com/search/db.aspx?dbid=3541.**

**1820-2013.** ***Alachua County Florida, Cemetery Index*** **[Online Database],** indexed at the FamilySearch.org website. Original data: Alachua County Virtual Cemetery Project. Each index record includes: Name, Death date, Cemetery, Section, General notes, and a link to the Alachua Co Virtual Cemetery Project website. This database has 18,322 records. See **https://search.ancestry.com/search/db.aspx?dbid=70763.**

**1821. "West Florida's Citizens" [Printed Article],** a selected name list from various sources, published in *Pensacola History Illustrated*, Vol. 5, No. 3 (Summer 1999).

**1821-2009.** ***A Florida Biographical Index: Being a Listing of Biographies of Notable Floridians Contained in Various Publications as Listed on the Source Documents Lists*** **[Printed Book & Digital Capture],** by Charles Mack Wills, Jr., publ. 2009, FHL book 975.9 D32w. To access the digital images, see the online FHL catalog page: **www.familysearch.org/search/catalog/1621716.**

**1822-1950.** ***Florida, Compiled Marriages*** **[Online Database],** indexed at the Ancestry.com website. Source: Jordan Dodd, compiler. Each index record includes: Name, Spouse, Marriage date, County, and State. This database has 5,659 records. **https://search.ancestry.com/search/db.aspx?dbid=4019.**

**1822-2001.** ***Florida, Marriage Indexes, 1822-1875 and 1927-2001*** **[Online Database],** digitized and indexed at the Ancestry.com website. The 1822-1875 marriages were taken from county sources and originally indexed by Jordan Dodd, Liahona Research (no images); the 1927-2001 marriages were taken from the Florida Marriage Index by the FL Dept. of Health-Vital Statistics, Jacksonville, FL. The marriage records from 1927-1969 were indexed by Ancestry.com and include digitized images of the records. Each index record includes: Name, Event type, Event date, Event place, Gender, Race, Volume, and Certificate number. This database has 11,718,373 records. See **http://search.ancestry.com/search/db.aspx?dbid=8784.** This database is also available at the FamilySearch.org website. See **https://familysearch.org/search/collection/1949340.**

***1823-1959 Florida Newspaper Archives*** **[Online Database],** digitized and indexed at the GenealogyBank.com website. One search screen for names and keywords in the following city newspapers: Apalachicola, Arcadia, Bradenton, Chipley, Crawfordville, Daytona Beach, De Land, Fernandina, Fort Pierce, Gainesville, Jacksonville, Key West, Live Oak, Madison, Miami, Ocala, Palatka, Panama City, Pensacola, Punta Gorda, Saint Joseph, St. Augustine, Starke, Tallahassee, Tampa, Titusville, West Tampa, and Ybor City See **www.genealogybank.com/gbnk/newspapers/explore/USA/Florida.**

**1823-1982.** ***Florida, County Marriages*** **[Online Database],** digitized and indexed at the Ancestry.com website. Source: FL State Archives and various county courthouses. Each index record includes: Name, Gender, Marriage date, Marriage place, Spouse, and Film number. This database has 3,512,403 records. See **https://search.ancestry.com/search/db.aspx?dbid=61369.**

***1824 Petition, Jackson County, Florida*** **[Online Database],** indexed at the RootsWeb site for Jackson Co FL. See **www.rootsweb.ancestry.com/~fljackso/Petition1824.htm.**

**"1825 Florida Territory Census, Jackson County" [Printed Article],** name list published in the *Florida Genealogist,* Vol. 16, No. 2 (Spring 1993); and in the *Huxford Genealogical Society Magazine,* Vol. 5, No. 1 (Mar 1978).

***1825 Petition, Jackson and Walton Counties, Florida*** **[Online Database],** indexed at the RootsWeb site for Jackson Co FL. See **www.rootsweb.ancestry.com/~fljackso/Petition1825.htm.**

**"1825 Florida Territory Census, Leon County" [Printed Article],** name list published in the *Southern Genealogists Exchange Quarterly,* Vol. 14, No. 68 (Winter 1973); and in the *A.I.S.I. Journal of Genealogy,* Vol. 1, No. 3 (Jul 1988); *Keystone Kin,* Vol. 2, No. 4 (Oct 1988); and *Florida Genealogist,* Vol. 24, No. 2 (Summer 2000).

**1825 Florida Territorial Census, Leon County [Online Database],** indexed at the Florida GenWeb site. See **https://sites.google.com/a/flgenweb.net/leon/census/1825-census.**

**1826-1865.** ***Florida Territorial and State Election Records*** **[Microfilm & Digital Capture],** from the originals of the Florida Division of Elections now located at the Florida State Archives, Tallahassee, FL. Election records arranged alphabetically by county, then chronologically (by date of election) within each county. Includes returns of elections for county, state and national offices, amnesty oaths, poll books, lists of registered voters, original ballots, etc. Filmed by the Genealogical Society of Utah, 1990, 9 rolls, beginning with FHL film #1673224. To access the digital images, see the online FHL catalog page: **www.familysearch.org/search/catalog/542643.**

**1826-1907.** ***Florida, Homestead and Cash Entry Patents, Pre-1908*** **[Online Database],** indexed at the Ancestry.com website. Source: Bureau of Land Management, Government Land Office Automated Records Project. Each index record includes: Name, Land office, Sequence, Document number, Total acres, Signature (Y/N), Canceled document (Y/N), Issue date, Mineral rights reserved (Y/N), Metes and Bounds (Y/N), Survey date, Statutory reference, Multiple warrantee names (Y/N), Act or treaty, Multiple patentee names (Y/N), Entry classification, and Land description. This database has 51,739 records. See **https://search.ancestry.com/search/db.aspx?dbid=2071.**

***1827 Jurors List, Pensacola, Escambia County, Florida*** [Online Database], indexed at the RootsWeb site for Escambia Co FL. See **www.rootsweb.ancestry.com/~flwfgs/escambiacountyfl/people/jurors.htm.**

**1827-1855.** ***Plat Book, Santa Rosa County, Florida*** **[Microfilm & Digital Capture],** from the originals at the Santa Rosa County Courthouse, Milton, FL. Includes land plats with names of landowners arranged by township and range for land in Santa Rosa Co FL, 1827-1855. Filmed by the Genealogical Society of Utah, 1973, 1 roll, FHL film #929704. For access to the digital images of this roll, see the online FHL catalog page for this title.
**www.familysearch.org/search/catalog/78949.**

**1828-1830.** ***Private Land Claims in East Florida*** **[Printed Book],** Includes index. Includes claims, reports from the Secretary of the Treasury, list of cases and list of claims, 1828-1830. Compiled and published by the Institute of Historic Research, Signal Mountain, TN, c1990, 174 pages, FHL book 975.9 R2p.

**1828-1886.** ***Admiralty Final Records of the U.S. District Court for the Southern District of Florida*** **[Microfilm & Digital Capture],** filmed by the National Archives, 1984, 12 rolls, beginning with FHL film #1605413 ( May 1828-May 1837). U.S. admiralty law is concerned with prize, ransom, and salvage cases; and a great variety of maritime contracts. Includes indexes at beginning of each volume. To access the digital images, see the online FHL catalog page:
**www.familysearch.org/search/catalog/573385.**

**1830-1840.** ***Florida, 1830 and 1840 Federal Census: Population Schedules*** **[Microfilm & Digital Capture],** from the originals at the National Archives, Washington, DC. Filmed by the National Archives, 1950, 2 rolls. FHL film #6711 (1830) and #6712 (1840). To access the digital images, see the online FHL catalog page:
**www.familysearch.org/search/catalog/745485.**

***1830 Florida U.S. Census*** **[Printed Index],** compiled by Aurora C Shaw, published by the Southern Genealogist's Exchange Quarterly, Jacksonville, FL, c1968, 38 pages, FHL book 975.9 X2p 1830.

**1830.** ***Florida 1830 Census Index*** **[Printed Index],** edited by Ronald Vern Jackson, et al, published by Accelerated Indexing Systems, Bountiful, UT, 1976, 62 pages, FHL book 975.9 X22f 1830.

**1830-1957.** ***Florida, County Marriages*** **[Online Database],** digitized and indexed at the FamilySearch.org website. Source: FL State Archives and Clerk of Courts, various counties. Each index record includes: Name, Event type, Event date, Event place, Gender, Marital status, Spouse's name, and Spouse's gender. The document image may have more information. This database has 480,849 records:
**www.familysearch.org/search/collection/2397260.**

**1830-1993.** ***Florida Marriages*** **[Online Database],** digitized and indexed at the FamilySearch.org website. Source: Clerk of Courts, various FL counties. This database has 1,699,231 records. See
**https://familysearch.org/search/collection/1803936.**

**1830s-1941.** ***Register of Deceased Veterans, Florida*** **[Microfilm & Digital Capture],** from a project of the Work Progress Administration, 1940-1941, 67 volumes. Includes an index to veteran's names. Dates (1830s-1941) are for the assumed earliest burial dates through the last year of the project. Not all Florida counties participated in the project, but for those included, the register has veteran burials from virtually every known cemetery in that county. Counties included in the project: Alachua, Baker, Bay, Bradford, Brevard, Broward, Calhoun, Charlotte, Citrus, Clay, Collier, Dade, DeSoto, Dixie, Duval, Flagler, Glades, Gulf, Hamilton, Hardee, Hernando, Hillsborough, Holmes, Indian River, Jackson, Lafayette, martin, Monroe, Nassau, Okaloosa, Okeechobee, Orange, Osceola, Palm Beach, Pasco, Polk, St. Lucie, Santa Rosa, Sarasota, Seminole, Sumter, Suwannee, Taylor, Union, Volusia, Wakulla, and Washington county. Filmed by the Genealogical Society of Utah, 1953,1 roll, FHL film #6716). To access the digital images, see the online FHL catalog page:
**www.familysearch.org/search/catalog/466837.**

**1834-1997.** ***Florida, Church Records*** **[Online Database],** digitized and indexed at FamilySearch.org. Church vital records from different denominations located in several counties of Florida.
See **www.familysearch.org/search/collection/2790244.**

**1835.** ***Federal Pension List of 1835, Territory of Florida*** **[Online Database],** indexed at the Rosters.Tripod.com site. See
**http://rosters.tripod.com/index-39.html.**

**1835-1858.** ***Florida, Compiled Service Records, Florida Indian Wars*** **[Online Database],** digitized and indexed at the Ancestry.com website. Source: National Archives microfilm M1086. Each index record includes: Name, Residence date, Enlistment date,

Enlistment place, Military unit, Rank, and War. The document image may have more information. This database has 23,159 records. See
**https://search.ancestry.com/search/db.aspx?dbid=2246.**

**1835-1898.** ***Soldiers of Florida in the Seminole Indian, Civil, and Spanish-American Wars*** **[Printed Book & Digital Capture],** includes rosters of Florida soldiers of the Seminole Indian Wars, 1835-1842 & 1855-1858; Civil War, 1861-1865; and Spanish-American War, 1898, compiled and published by the Board of State Institutions, Tallahassee, FL, 1903, 368 pages, FHL book 975.9 M2s. Also on microfilm, FHL film #6887. To access the digital images, see the online FHL catalog page:
**www.familysearch.org/search/catalog/139933.**
- See also, ***Soldiers of Florida in the Seminole Indian, Civil and Spanish-American Wars*** **[Printed Book],** a computerized index by Mack Wills, 2011, 202 pages, FHL book 975.9 M2wc.

**1836-1842** ***Florida War Death List*** **[Online Database],** indexed at the Ancestry.com website. Taken from a book by Sandra Sanford Gage, *Florida War Death List, 1836-1842.* See
**http://search.ancestry.com/search/db.aspx?dbid=5760.**

**1837-1974.** ***Florida Marriages*** **[Online Database],** indexed at the FamilySearch.org website. Taken from indexes, digital copies of original records, and compiled records at the FHL in Salt Lake City, this database has about 390,140 records. See
**https://familysearch.org/search/collection/1674804.**

**1839-1891.** ***Tax Rolls of Florida Counties, Some are Incomplete*** **[Microfilm & Digital Capture],** from the originals at the Florida State Archives, Includes name lists of Florida residents for most counties. Some missing counties. Filmed by the Genealogical Society of Utah, 1956, 66 rolls, beginning with FHL film #6888 (Alachua County, 1846-1869). For a complete list of roll numbers, roll contents, and the digital images of each roll, see the online FHL catalog page for this title:
**www.familysearch.org/search/catalog/298085.**

***1840 Florida U.S. Census*** **[Printed Index],** compiled by Aurora C Shaw, published by the Southern Genealogist's Exchange Quarterly, Jacksonville, FL, 1968, 44 pages, FHL book 975.9 X2p 1840.

***1840 Index to Florida Census*** **[Printed Index],** compiled by Lucille Simms Mallon, published by Beverly M. Taylor, c1977, FHL book 975.9 A1 No. 15.

**1840.** ***Florida 1840 Census Index*** **[Printed Index],** edited by Ronald Vern Jackson, et al, published by Accelerated Indexing Systems, Bountiful, UT, 1976, 12 pages, FHL book 975.9 X22pa 1840.

***1840 Florida Military Census*** **[Online Database],** indexed at the RootsWeb site for St. Augustine, FL:
**www.rootsweb.ancestry.com/~flsags/1840flarmycensus.htm.**

***1840 Jury List, Jackson County, Florida*** **[Online Database],** indexed at the USGenWeb site for Jackson Co FL. See
**http://files.usgwarchives.net/fl/jackson/history/1840jury.txt.**

***1842 Voters Registration, Santa Rosa County, Florida*** **[Online Database],** indexed at the USGenWeb site for Santa Rosa Co FL. See
**http://files.usgwarchives.net/fl/santarosa/history/1842votr.txt.**

**1842-1843.** ***Armed Occupation Act Settlers Records*** **[Microfilm & Digital Capture],** from the original records at the FL State Archives. The Florida armed occupation act granted 160 acres to settlers willing to claim, populate and hold by force, if necessary, undeveloped lands in east Florida. Permits are arranged somewhat alphabetically. Includes index of settlers. Filmed by the Genealogical Society of Utah, 1990, 3 rolls, beginning with FHL film #1671508 (Index to names of settlers on permit land). To access the digital images, see the online FHL catalog page:
**www.familysearch.org/search/catalog/540006.**

***1843 Voters List, Hernando County, Florida*** **[Online Database],** indexed at the Fivay.org site. See
**www.fivay.org/1843_voters.html.**

**1845.** ***Statehood Election Returns*** **[Microfilm & Digital Capture],** originals of the Florida Division of Elections, now located at Florida State Archives, Tallahassee, FL. This name list is Florida's "first state census - 1845." From the introduction: "Includes lists of electors or voters from Alachua, Baker, Benton, Calhoun, Columbia, Dade, Duval, Escambia, Franklin, Gadsden, Hamilton, Hillsborough, Jackson, Jefferson, Leon, Madison, Marion, Monroe, Mosquito, Nassau, St. Johns, St. Lucia, Santa Rosa, Wakulla, Walton, Washington counties." Filmed by the Genealogical Society of Utah, 1990, 1 roll, FHL film #1672587. To access the digital images, see the online FHL catalog page: **www.familysearch.org/search/catalog/538089.**

**1845.** ***Florida Voters in Their First Statewide Election, May 26, 1845*** **[Printed Book].** This is a printed extraction and index to the "Florida Statehood

Election Returns" shown above. Voter name lists by county, compiled by Brian Michaels, published by the Florida State Genealogical Society, Tallahassee, FL, 1987, 128 pages. See FHL book 975.9 N4.

**1845.** ***Alachua County Voters in First Florida Election, 1845*** **[Online Database],** indexed at the USGenWeb site for Alachua Co FL. See **http://files.usgwarchives.net/fl/alachua/history/1845votr.txt.**

**1845.** ***Benton (Now Hernando] County Voters in First Florida Election, 1845*** **[Online Database],** indexed at the USGenWeb site for Hernando Co FL. See **http://files.usgwarchives.net/fl/benton/history/1845votr.txt.**

***1845 Voters Registration, Columbia County, Florida*** **[Online Database],** indexed at the RootsWeb site for Baker Co FL. See **www.rootsweb.ancestry.com/~flbakehs/1845Election.html.**

***1845 Voters List, Escambia County, Florida*** **[Online Database],** indexed at the RootsWeb site for Escambia Co FL. See **www.rootsweb.ancestry.com/~flwfgs/escambiacountyfl/people/voters1845.htm.**

***1845 Voters List, Franklin County, Florida*** **[Online Database],** indexed at the RootsWeb site for Franklin Co FL. See **http://myweb.fsu.edu/rthompson2/franklin/frank-vote.html.**

***1845 Voters List, Gadsden County, Florida*** **[Online Database],** indexed at the USGenWeb site for Gadsden Co FL. See **http://files.usgwarchives.net/fl/gadsden/history/1845votr.txt.**

***1845 Voters List, Hamilton County, Florida*** **[Online Database],** indexed at the USGenWeb site for Hamilton Co FL. See **http://files.usgwarchives.net/fl/hamilton/history/1845votr.txt.**

**1845.** ***Jackson County Voters in First Florida Election, 1845*** **[Online Database],** indexed at the USGenWeb site for Jackson Co FL. See **http://files.usgwarchives.net/fl/jackson/history/1845votr.txt.**

**1845.** ***Jefferson County Voters in First Florida Election, 1845*** **[Online Database],** indexed at the USGenWeb site for Jefferson Co FL. See **http://files.usgwarchives.net/fl/jefferson/history/1845votr.txt.**

***1845 Lee County, Florida Census*** **[Online Database],** indexed at the RootsWeb site for Lee Co FL. See **www.rootsweb.ancestry.com/~flswphs/records/1945.html.**

**1845.** ***Madison County Voters in First Florida Election, 1845*** **[Online Database],** indexed at the USGenWeb site for Madison Co FL. See **http://files.usgwarchives.net/fl/madison/history/1845votr.txt.**

**1845.** ***Santa Rosa County Voters in First Florida Election, 1845*** **[Online Database],** indexed at the USGenWeb site for Santa Rosa Co FL. See **http://files.usgwarchives.net/fl/santarosa/history/1845votr.txt.**

**1845.** ***Walton County Voters in First Florida Election, 1845*** **[Online Database],** indexed at the USGenWeb site for Walton Co FL. See **http://files.usgwarchives.net/fl/walton/history/1845votr.txt.**

***1845 Census Index, Washington County, Florida*** **[Online Database],** indexed at the USGenWeb site for Washington Co FL. See **http://files.usgwarchives.net/fl/washington/census/1845indx.txt.**

**1845.** ***Washington County Voters in First Florida Election*** **[Online Database],** indexed at the USGenWeb site for Washington Co FL. See **http://files.usgwarchives.net/fl/washington/history/1845votr.txt.**

***1846 Jury List, Levy and Alachua Counties, Florida*** **[Online Database],** indexed at the Levy Co FL. See **http://files.usgwarchives.net/fl/levy/history/1846grju.txt.**

**1846-1848.** ***Too Late for Blood: Florida Volunteers in the Mexican War*** **[Printed Book],** by Russell D. James. Includes muster rolls and lists of deaths, discharges, pensions, and bounty land warrants; a historical summary of the five volunteer companies raised in Florida for service in the war with Mexico, 1846-1848; bibliographical references, and index. Published by Heritage Books, Westminster, MD, 2005, 130 pages, FHL book 975.9 M2j.

***1847 Jury List, Jefferson County, Florida*** **[Online Database],** indexed at the USGenWeb site for Jefferson Co FL. See **http://files.usgwarchives.net/fl/jefferson/history/1847jury.txt.**

**1847-1995.** ***Florida, Naturalization Records*** **[Online Database],** digitized and indexed at the Ancestry.com website. Source: Records of the District Courts of the U.S., National Archives, Atlanta, GA. Naturalization

records include Declarations, Petitions, and Certificates. Each index record includes: Name, Petition age, Record type, Birth date, Birth place, Marriage date, Marriage place, Arrival date, Arrival place, Petition date, Petition place, Spouse, Petition number, Origin, and Volume number. The document image may have more information. This database has 931,539 records. See
**https://search.ancestry.com/search/db.aspx?dbid=1850.**

**1850.** ***Florida, 1850 Federal Census: Population Schedules*** **[Microfilm & Digital Capture],** from the originals at the National Archives, Washington, DC. Filmed by the National Archives, 1964, 3 rolls, beginning with FHL film #6714 (Florida: Alachua, Benton, Calhoun, Columbia, Dade, Duval, Escambia, Franklin, Gadsden, Hamilton, Hillsborough, Holmes, and Jackson counties). To access the digital images, see the online FHL catalog page:
**www.familysearch.org/search/catalog/744475.**

**1850.** ***Index to 1850 Florida Census*** **[Printed Index],** compiled and published by members of the Southern Genealogist's Exchange Society, Jacksonville, FL, 1976, 131 pages, FHL book 975.9 X22s 1850.

**1850.** ***Florida 1850 Census Index*** **[Printed Index],** edited by Ronald Vern Jackson, et al, published by Accelerated Indexing Systems, Bountiful, UT, 1978, 36 pages, FHL book 975.9 X2pa 1850.

**1850.** ***Florida 1850 Mortality Schedule*** **[Printed Index],** edited by Ronald Vern Jackson, et al, published by Accelerated Indexing Systems, Salt Lake City, UT, 1982, 38 pages, FHL book 975.9 X22f 1850.

**1850.** ***Benton (now Hernando) County, Florida Revenue for 1850*** **[Online Database],** indexed at the USGenWeb site for Hernando Co FL:
**http://files.usgwarchives.net/fl/benton/history/tax1850u.txt.**

**1851-2009.** ***Florida, Jacksonville Area Obituary Collection*** **[Online Database],** indexed at the Ancestry.com website. From a collection compiled by the Southern Genealogist's Exchange Society of Jacksonville, FL. Minimum information for each record includes the given name and surname of the deceased, the publication with the obituary, date of publication; and many records may include a name of spouse, death date, birth date, age, names of surviving relatives, photo of the deceased, death location, burial location, funeral service date and location, religious affiliation, and names of parents. This database has over 105,000 records. See
**http://search.ancestry.com/search/db.aspx?dbid=2120.**

***1855 Florida State Census, Marion County*** **[Microfilm],** from the originals at the Florida State Archives. From the Details Page: "This series contains returns from the second state census conducted in 1855. Returns for Marion County are the only existing state census records for 1855 at the FL State Archives. The information recorded in the book includes the name of the head of the family, the number of white males over and under 21, the number of white females over and under 18, the number of children between 5 and 18, the number of children in schools, the number of male and female slaves, the value of the slaves, the number of male and female free persons of color, the number of acres of and value of land, and the value of buildings, furniture, and plantation livestock." Filmed by the FL State Archives, 1 roll, Record Group 001021, Series/Collection No. S1374. There is no copy of this film at the FHL in Salt Lake City, UT. See the Genealogy webpage (State Censuses) for more information. See **http://dos.myflorida.com/library-archives/research/explore-our-resources/genealogy.**

**"1855 Florida State Census, Marion County" [Printed Article].** Name list published in the *Florida Genealogist* (Florida State Genealogical Society, Maitland, FL), Vol. 11, No. 4 (Summer 1988).

**"1855 Florida State Census, Orange County" [Printed Article].** Name list published in *Buried Treasures* (Central Florida Genealogical Society, Orlando, FL), Vol. 30, No.3 (July 1998 ).

**"1855 Florida State Census, Putnam County" [Printed Article].** Name list and index in *Putnam County Genealogical Society Quarterly Journal,* Vol. 3, No. 4 (Winter 1986).

***1855 Tax List, St. Augustine, Florida*** **[Online Database],** indexed at the RootsWeb site for St. Augustine, FL. See
**www.rootsweb.ancestry.com/~flsags/1855staugustinetaxlist.htm.**

**1860.** ***Florida, 1860 Federal Census: Population Schedules*** **[Microfilm & Digital Capture],** from the originals at the National Archives, Washington, DC. Filmed twice by the National Archives, 6 rolls total, 1950, 1967, beginning with FHL film #803106 (2nd

filming, Alachua, Brevard, Calhoun, Clay, Columbia, Dade, Duval, Escambia, Franklin, and Gadsden Counties). To access the digital images, see the online FHL catalog page:
**www.familysearch.org/search/catalog/704736.**

***1860 Florida Census Index: Heads of Households and Other Surnames in Households Index* [Printed Index],** compiled by Bryan Lee Dilts, published by Index Publishing, Salt Lake City, UT, 1984, 93 pages, FHL book 975.9 X22d 1860. Also on microfiche, FHL fiche #6331477 (1 fiche).

**1860. *Florida 1860 Census Index* [Printed Index],** edited by Ronald Vern Jackson, et al, published by Accelerated Indexing Systems, Bountiful, UT, 1984, 283 pages, FHL book 975.9 X22j 1860.

**1860. *Florida 1860 Mortality Schedule* [Printed Index],** edited by Ronald Vern Jackson, et al, published by Accelerated Indexing Systems, Bountiful, UT, 1983, 48 pages, FHL book 975.9 X22f 1860.

**1860. *Florida 1860 Agricultural Census* [Printed index],** compiled by Linda L. Green. Includes index. Includes name of owner, acres of improved land, acres of unimproved land, cash value of the farm, value of farm implement and machinery, and value of livestock. Published by Southern Cross Publications, Chapel Hill, NC, 2002, 179 pages, FHL book 975.9 X2g 1860.

***1860 Non-Population Census Schedules (Mortality, Agriculture, and Industry) for 15 Southern States* [Microfilm],** from originals at the National Archives, Washington,, DC. Filmed by the National Archives, 1963, 1 roll, FHL film #1550796 (Includes Florida). To see if this microfilm has been digitized yet, see the FHL catalog page:
**www.familysearch.org/search/catalog/422729.**

***1860 Tax Roll, Hernando County, Florida* [Online Database],** indexed at the Fivay.org site. See **www.fivay.org/tax.html.**

**1861-1865. *Index of Floridians Serving in War Between the States* [Microfilm & Digital Capture],** from the original typescript at the Florida State Archives Tallahassee, FL. Indexes the Civil War section of Soldiers of Florida in the Seminole Indian, Civil, and Spanish American Wars. Filmed by the Genealogical Society of Utah, 1956, 1 roll, FHL film #6887. To access the digital images, see the online FHL catalog page:
**www.familysearch.org/search/catalog/479862.**

**1861-1865. *Index to Compiled Service Records of Volunteer Union Soldiers Who Served in Organizations From the State of Florida* [Microfilm],** from the original records at the National Archives, Washington, DC. Filmed by the National Archives, 1958, series M264, 1 roll, FHL film #821767. To see if this microfilm has been digitized yet, see the FHL catalog page:
**www.familysearch.org/search/catalog/318939.**

**1861-1865. *Compiled Service Records of Volunteer Union Soldiers Who Served in Organizations From the State of Florida* [Microfilm],** from the original records at the National Archives, Washington, DC. Includes index. Includes soldier's name, rank, unit served in, card abstracts of muster rolls, returns, hospital rolls, descriptive books, list of deserters, and originals of any papers relating solely to the particular soldier. Filmed by the National Archives, Series M400, 11 rolls, beginning with FHL film #1299987 (First Cavalry, A-C). To see if this microfilm has been digitized yet, see the FHL catalog page:
**www.familysearch.org/search/catalog/36050.**

**1861-1865. *Florida Civil War Service Records of Union Soldiers* [Online Database],** digitized and indexed at the FamilySearch.org website. Source: National Archives microfilm M251. Union service records of soldiers who served in organizations from Florida. The records include a jacket-envelope for each soldier, labeled with his name, his rank, and the unit in which he served. The jacket-envelope typically contains card abstracts of entries relating to the soldier as found in original muster rolls, returns, rosters, payrolls, appointment books, hospital registers, Union prison registers and rolls, parole rolls, inspection reports; and the originals of any papers relating solely to the particular soldier. For each military unit the service records are arranged alphabetically by the soldier's surname. This database has 25,416 records. See **https://familysearch.org/search/collection/1932395.**

**1861-1865. *Index to Compiled Service Records of Confederate Soldiers Who Served in Organizations from the State of Florida* [Microfilm],** from the original records at the National Archives. Filmed by the National Archives, 1955, 9 rolls, beginning with FHL film #191679 ( Index, A-Bru). To see if this microfilm has been digitized yet, see the FHL catalog: **www.familysearch.org/search/catalog/623348.**

**1861-1865. *Florida Civil War Service Records of Confederate Soldiers* [Online Database],** digitized and indexed at the FamilySearch.org website. Source: National Archives microfilm M251. Confederate service records of soldiers who served in organizations from Florida. The records include a jacket-envelope for each soldier, labeled with his name, his rank, and the unit in which he served. The jacket-envelope typically contains card abstracts of entries relating to the soldier as found in original muster rolls, returns, rosters, payrolls, appointment books, hospital registers, Union prison registers and rolls, parole rolls, inspection reports; and the originals of any papers relating solely to the particular soldier. For each military unit the service records are arranged alphabetically by the soldier's surname. This database has 285,975 records: **https://familysearch.org/search/collection/1932369.**

**1861-1865. *Confederate Service Record, Out of State, Florida* [Microfilm & Digital Capture],** from the originals at the Alabama Department of Archives and History, Montgomery, AL. Includes records for soldiers serving in Alabama units who reported their home as Florida. Filmed by the Genealogical Society of Utah, 1987, 1 roll, FHL film #1411532, item 2). To access the digital images, see the online FHL catalog page: **www.familysearch.org/search/catalog/633047.**

**1861-1865. *Biographical Rosters of Florida's Confederate and Union Soldiers* [Printed Book],** compiled by David W. Hartman, et al. From Preface: "Compiled from service records, pension records, diaries, family and local histories, descendants' letters, wartime newspapers and diaries, etc. to create a biographical record for as many Confederate and Union soldiers as possible who have been identified as having served in Florida units." Contents: Vol. 1: Histories of Florida Infantry Regiments: First (old and new), companies A-K; Second, companies A-M; Third-Fourth, companies A-K; Vol. 2: Histories of Florida Infantry Regiments: Fifth-Eighth, companies A-K; Vol. 3: Histories of Florida Infantry Regiments: Ninth-Tenth, companies A-K; Eleventh, companies A-L; Second Florida Battalion, companies A-F; History of the First Florida Reserve Regiment, companies A-L; Vol. 4: Histories of the First and Second Florida Cavalry Regiment; the Third Battalion Florida Cavalry; the Fifth Florida Cavalry Battalion; the Fifteenth Confederate Cavalry Regiment; First East Florida (US) Cavalry; and the First Florida (US) Cavalry; Vol. 5: 2nd Florida Cavalry (US), and Home Guard and miscellaneous units; and Vol. 6: Miscellaneous, bibliography, footnotes, index. Includes staff members for each company. Published by Broadfoot Publishing Co., Wilmington, NC, 1995, 6 vols., 2,380 pages, FHL book 975.9 M28h v.1-6.

**1864. *Department for the South, November 1864, for Jacksonville, Fernandina and St. Augustine, Florida, Ordered by the Department of the South, Hilton Head, South Carolina* [Printed Book],** extracted by members of the Florida State Genealogical Society, Tallahassee, FL, published by Heritage Books, Bowie, MD, 2002, 280 pages. Includes index. From the forward: "One of the forgotten legacies... was a special census of eastern Florida conducted on the orders of Federal military authorities. Its motivation is to this day unclear, but it seems likely to have been part of the work done to help register voters under Lincoln's "10%" reconstruction plan. African-Americans living in the region were also enumerated despite the fact that they did not yet have the legal right to vote." Includes name, height, color of eyes, complexion, age, where born or contraband [slave], last residence, where registered for draft or name of owner, date moved into the south, oath of allegiance, and remarks. See FHL book 975.91 X2f.

**"1864 Florida Military Census, Fernandina County" [Printed Article],** name list published serially in the *Nassau County Genealogist,* Vol. 1, No. 1 (Winter 1994), thru Vol. 2, No. 1 (Fall 1994).

***1865 Voters List, Hernando County, Florida* [Online Database],** indexed at the Fivay.org site. See **www.fivay.org/1865_voters.html.**

**1865-1866. *Internal Revenue Assessment Lists for Florida* [Microfilm & Digital Capture],** from the originals at the National Archives, Washington, DC. Filmed by the National Archives, 1968, series M761, 1 roll, FHL film #1578499. To access the digital images, see the online FHL catalog page: **www.familysearch.org/search/catalog/577972.**

***1867 Florida State Census* [Microfilm],** from the original records at the Florida State Archives. The Civil War disrupted the Florida provision for state censuses to be taken exactly every ten years, beginning with the "Statehood Election Returns" enumeration in 1845, followed by the second state census in 1855. This series contains returns from the third state census conducted in 1867. Although incomplete, the records include books of enumeration from Hernando, Madison, Orange, and Santa Rosa Counties, total tabulations for the State, and miscellaneous fragments, such as a page listing the enumeration for Franklin County. The books of enumeration have separate listings for colored and white inhabitants. Both include the name of the head of the family, the number of males over and under 21, the number of females over and under 18, the total number of inhabitants, and the number of males between 18 and 45. The tabulations list population totals by county for colored and white populations. Filmed by the FL State Archives, 1 roll, Record Group No. 001021, Series/Collections Number S1375. There is no copy of this film at the FHL in Salt Lake City, UT. See the Genealogy webpage (State Censuses) for more information. See ***http://dos.myflorida.com/library-archives/research/explore-our-resources/genealogy.***

**1867-1945.** ***Florida State Censuses, 1867-1945*** **[Online Database],** digitized and indexed at the Ancestry.com website. Original state census records residing at the FL State Archives are included in one searchable database:

- **1867** – Hernando, Madison, Orange, and Santa Rosa counties only.
- **1875** – Alachua county only.
- **1885** – All 1885 counties except Alachua, Clay, Columbia, and Nassau.
- **1935** – All FL counties.
- **1945** – All FL counties.

The 1867 enumeration was a head of household census, with other members of a family in age categories. The 1875 through 1945 enumerations were listings for every member of a family. This database has 4,131,297 records. See **http://search.ancestry.com/search/db.aspx?dbid=1506.**

**"1867 Florida Voter Registration List, Madison County" [Printed Article],** published serially in *Tallahassee Genealogical Society Newsletter,* beginning with Vol. 15, No. 3 (Spring 1996).

***1867-1968 Florida Voter Registration Lists*** **[Printed Book],** compiled by members of the Tallahassee Genealogical Society, Published Tallahassee, FL, 1992, 400 pages. Compiled from original documents at the Florida State Archives. Includes index. Includes county voter lists of Hernando, Leon, Levy, Liberty, Madison, Marion, Nassau, Orange, Polk, Putnam, St. Johns, Santa Rosa, Sumter, Suwannee, Taylor, Volusia, Wakulla, Walton, and Washington counties. Includes voter's name, race, length of residence in the state, where born and date of registration, as provided by the voter himself. From forward: "A qualified voter had to be at least twenty-one years old, a resident of his county... For the first time in southern history, race was not a qualifying factor in registering to vote. See FHL book 975.9.

***1867-1868 Voters List, Orange County, Florida*** **[Online Database],** indexed at the USGenWeb site for Orange Co FL. See **http://files.usgwarchives.net/fl/orange/history/1867votr.txt.**

***1867-1868 Voters List, Polk County, Florida*** **[Online Database],** indexed at the USGenWeb site for Polk Co FL. See **http://fl-genweb.org/decole/Polk/voters/index.html.**

**1867-1905.** ***Florida Voter Registration Rolls*** **[Microfilm & Digital Capture],** from originals of the Florida Secretary of State, now located at the Florida State Archives, Tallahassee, FL. From the introduction: "Congress passed an act on March 23, 1867 calling for a registration of qualified voters. These voters would then elect delegates to a convention for the purpose of establishing a constitution and civil government. A qualified voter had to be male, twenty-one years of age, a resident of the county, and had to take an oath of allegiance to the United States government. A Board of Registration composed of three loyal officers or persons was set up to make, complete, and witness the registration. This was the first time that Blacks were allowed to register to vote… most volumes list voter's name, race, time of residence in county and state, native (of what state), naturalization (where, when, and how) and date of registration." Filmed by the Genealogical Society of Utah, 1990, 2 rolls, FHL film #1672578 and #1672579. To access the digital images, see the online FHL catalog page: **www.familysearch.org/search/catalog/537206.**

**1870.** ***Florida, 1870 Federal Census: Population Schedules*** **[Microfilm & Digital Capture],** from the originals at the National Archives, Washington, DC. Filmed twice by the National Archives, 9 rolls total, 1962, 1968, beginning with FHL film #545627 (2nd filming, Alachua, Baker, Bradford, Brevard, Calhoun, Clay, and Columbia Counties). To access the digital images, see the online FHL catalog page: **www.familysearch.org/search/catalog/698892.**

***1870 Florida Census Index: An Every-Name Index*** **[Printed Index],** compiled by Bryan Lee Dilts, published by Index Publishing, Salt Lake City, UT, 1984, 662 pages, FHL book 975.9 X22d 1870.

**1870.** ***Florida 1870 Census Index*** **[Printed Index],** edited by Ronald Vern Jackson, et al, published by Accelerated Indexing Systems, North Salt Lake, UT, 1985, 221 pages, FHL book 975.9 X22j 1870.

**1870.** ***Florida 1870 Census Index, A-Z*** **[Printed Index],** edited by Raeone Christensen Steuart, published by Heritage Quest, Bountiful, UT, 2000, 352 pages, FHL book 975.9 X22s 1870.

**1870.** ***Florida 1870 Mortality Schedule*** **[Printed Index],** edited by Ronald Vern Jackson, et al, published by Accelerated Indexing Systems, Bountiful, UT, 1983, 60 pages, FHL book 975.9 X22f 1870.

***1870-1908 Wills Index, Nassau County, Florida*** **[Online Database],** indexed at the USGenWeb site for Nassau Co FL. See
**http://files.usgwarchives.net/fl/nassau/wills/18701908.txt.**

**1870s-1930s.** ***Delayed Birth Certificates, Book 1, Suwannee County, Florida*** **[Online Database],** indexed at the USGenWeb site for Suwannee Co FL:
**http://files.usgwarchives.net/fl/suwannee/vitals/births/delay1.txt.**

**1874-1898.** ***Florida Land Sold for Taxes, 1874-1898*** **[Microfilm & Digital Capture],** from the originals at the FL State Archives. Land was liable for sale if taxes were not paid before April 1 of any year. Contains county and year, certificate number, name of owner, description of land and total number of acres, expenses, total of taxes and expenses, by whom redeemed, date of redemption, and amount paid for redemption of land. Includes index. Filmed by the Genealogical Society of Utah, 1990, 1 roll, FHL film #1672937. To access the digital images, see the online FHL catalog page:
**www.familysearch.org/search/catalog/542036.**

**1875.** ***State Census Book for 1875 Alachua County, Florida,*** **[Microfilm & Digital Capture],** from the originals at the Florida State Archives. This series contains the only extant returns of the fourth state census of Florida conducted in 1875, containing only the records of Alachua County. The information recorded in the returns includes the name, age at last birthday, sex, and race of all those persons listed. For some entries, other information is provided including occupation, the value of real estate, the value of personal property, the number of acres planted in cotton, the number of acres planted in cane, and the number of orange trees. This was the only Florida State Census filmed by the Genealogical Society of Utah, 1956. FHL film #6962. For access to the digital images of this roll, see the online FHL catalog page:
**www.familysearch.org/search/catalog/19502.**

**1875-1900.** ***Florida Prison Records*** **[Printed Book],** compiled by Carol Cox Bouknecht, Transcribed from records at the State of Florida Division of Correction's prison records at the Florida State Archives. Includes prisoner's name, sex, race, age, birth state, county where sentenced, crime, length of sentence, date sentenced, date of release, and notes on whether the prisoner escaped (date of escape and date of capture, if any); and prison identification number and manner of termination of residence (end of sentence, pardon, or death). Published by C.C. Bouknecht, Tallahassee, FL, 1993, 152 pages, FHL book 975.9 J6b. Also on microfilm, FHL film #1698049.

**1876-1877.** ***Titusville, Oil City, Franklin, Warren, Bradford, etc. Directory, 1876-77…*** **[Online Database],** digitized and OCR indexed at the Ancestry.com website. This database has 224 pages:
**https://search.ancestry.com/search/db.aspx?dbid=23519.**

**1877 Taxpayers for Baker County, Florida [Online Database],** indexed at the RootsWeb site for Baker Co FL. See
**www.rootsweb.ancestry.com/~flbakehs/bakerTaxpayers1877.html.**

**1877-1939.** ***Florida Death Certificates*** **[Microfilm & Digital Capture],** from the original records at the Florida Dept. of Health – Vital Statistics, Jacksonville, FL Arranged in numerical order of certificate generally by year of death. An index to these records is in a separate title, shown below. Filmed by the Genealogical Society of Utah, 1998-1999, 185 rolls, beginning with FHL film #2116913 (Death certificates, Vol. 1-6, Aug 1877-1895). For a complete list of roll numbers, roll contents, and the digital images of each roll, see the online FHL catalog page for this title. See
**www.familysearch.org/search/catalog/816256.**

**1877-1939.** ***Florida Deaths*** **[Online Database],** digitized index at the FamilySearch.org website. This is a name index of Florida death records created by the Florida Dept. of Health and Vital Statistics in Jacksonville, Florida. This database has 471,800 records. See **https://familysearch.org/search/collection/1595003.**

**1877-1969.** ***Florida Combined Death Index*** **[Microfiche],** from the original records at the Florida Dept. of Health-Vital Statistics, Jacksonville, FL. Includes a name, place of death, volume, number, and year of death. Codes for counties, and codes for other information was used in later volumes. Filmed by the Genealogical Society of Utah, 1992, 305 microfiche, beginning with FHL fiche #6081769 (1877-1916 10 fiches). For a complete list of fiche numbers and contents of each, see the online FHL catalog page for this title. See **www.familysearch.org/search/catalog/513869.**

**1877-1998.** ***Florida Death Index*** **[Online Database],** indexed at the Ancesty.com website. Taken from the *Florida Death Index, 1877-1998* by the FL Dept. of Health-Vital Statistics, Jacksonville, FL. This index contains over 5 million deaths. Each record usually has the following. 1) Name of deceased, 2) Death place (city and/or county), 3) Death date, 4) Race, 5) Birth date, 6) Gender, and 7) Certificate and/or volume number. See **http://search.ancestry.com/search/db.aspx?dbid=7338.**

**1877-1998.** ***Florida Death Index*** **[Online Database],** digitized and indexed at the FamilySearch.org website. This database has 5,187,074 records. Index provided by Ancestry, Inc.: **https://familysearch.org/search/collection/1946805.**

**1880.** ***Florida, 1880 Federal Census: Soundex and Population Schedules*** **[Microfilm & Digital Capture],** from the originals at the National Archives, Washington, DC. After microfilming the National Archives transferred the original 1880 census population schedules to local repositories. The 1880 was the only census handled in this way. Florida's original 1880 population schedules, contained in five bound volumes, was donated to Florida State University in Tallahassee, FL. Filmed by the National Archives, c1970, 24 rolls, beginning with FHL film #445537 (Soundex: A100-B400), and FHL film #1254125 (Population schedules, Alachua and Baker Co). To access the digital images, see the online FHL catalog page: **www.familysearch.org/search/catalog/670384.**

***1880 Florida Federal Census, Mortality and Manufactures Schedules*** **[Microfilm],** from originals at the National Archives. Filmed by the National Archives, 1963, 1 roll, FHL film #1550797. To see if this microfilm has been digitized yet, see the FHL catalog page: **www.familysearch.org/search/catalog/467521.**

**1880.** ***Florida's Unfortunates, the 1880 Federal Census, Defective, Dependent and Delinquent Classes*** **[Printed Book],** compiled by Donna Rachal Mills, comprised of seven schedules enumerating members of social classes considered "social dysfunctional: insane inhabitants (sufferers of either permanent or temporary insanity); idiots, blind (either totally or partially); homeless children; inhabitants of prison; and paupers and indigents (inhabitants of institutions, poorhouse or asylums, or those boarded at public expense in private homes). Published by Mills Historical Press, Tuscaloosa, AL, 1993, 103 pages, FHL book 975.9 X28m.

**1880-1935.** ***Florida Births and Christenings*** **[Online Database],** indexed at the FamilySearch.org website. Data from various FamilySearch and Family History Library sources. Each index record includes: Name, Gender, Birth date, Birthplace, Name notes, Race, Father's name, Father's birthplace, Mother's name, and Mother's birthplace. This database has 20,227 records. See **https://familysearch.org/search/collection/1674799.**

**1881-1905.** ***Homestead Application Files*** **[Microfilm & Digital Capture],** from the original application forms submitted by Florida settlers. These are arranged by homestead application number, which identifies both the applicant and the year the application was made. Filmed by the Genealogical Society of Utah, 1990, 6 rolls, beginning with FHL film #1672580. To access the digital images, see the online FHL catalog page: **www.familysearch.org/search/catalog/537438.**

**1883.** ***Titusville, Oil City, Franklin and Warren Directory for 1883…*** **[Online Database],** digitized and OCR indexed at the Ancestry.com website. This database has 319 pages. See **https://search.ancestry.com/search/db.aspx?dbid=23518.**

**1884-1885.** ***Census of Apalachicola, Franklin Co., Florida*** **[Microfilm & Digital Capture],** compiled by Rose Marie Lovett, Includes index. From intro: "Patrick J. Lovett (marshal of Apalachicola, Florida) took this census, 1 January 1884-31 May 1885. The census was taken on blank pages in an account ledger; it does not appear to be part of the 1885 state census." Filmed by the Genealogical Society of Utah, 1976, 1 roll, FHL film #988192. To access the digital images, see the online FHL catalog page: **www.familysearch.org/search/catalog/98743.**

✓ **1885 NOTE:** In 1885, the US Census Office offered federal assistance (up to half the cost) to any state or territory wanting to take a census in 1885. Only five states or territories took up the government's offer: Colorado, Dakota Territory, Florida, Nebraska, and New Mexico Territory. Each state/territory was to supply the federal government with a duplicate original (federal) copy of the census schedules for all counties and retain a duplicate (state) copy. The Florida State Archives has no record of the state's copy, and presumably, their own copy was lost, unless it is buried in some unknown Florida repository.

**1885.** ***Schedules of the Florida State Census of 1885*** **[Microfilm & Digital Capture],** from originals at the National Archives, Washington, DC. Missing from the federal copy of the 1885 Florida state census are Alachua, Clay, Columbia, and Nassau counties. The National Archives microfilmed their copy as series M845, 13 rolls, beginning with FHL film #888962 (Baker, Bradford, Brevard, Calhoun, Dade counties). To access the digital images, see the online FHL catalog page:
**www.familysearch.org/search/catalog/82520.**
- See also ***Florida State Census, 1885*** **[Online Database],** indexed at the FamilySearch.org website. Source: National Archives microfilm M845. All counties of Florida are represented except Alachua, Clay, Columbia, and Nassau. Taken from the federal copy of the 1885 census originally filmed by the National Archives. The FL 1885 census is comprised of four schedules: Population, Agriculture, Manufacturers, and Mortality. The Population schedules are available for all counties represented, but the other schedules are not complete for all counties. This database base has 309,323 records. See
**https://familysearch.org/search/collection/1457854.**
- See also ***Florida State Census, 1885*** **[Online Database],** indexed at the Ancestry.com website. This database was an earlier version of the one included with Ancestry's 1867-1945 FL State Census series. This database has 291,261 records, population schedules only. See
**http://search.ancestry.com/search/db.aspx?dbid=7605.**
- See also ***1885 Florida State Census, Countywide Extractions*** **[Printed Articles],** available for the following Florida counties:

- "Census, 1885, Dade County, Florida," in *Southern Genealogists Exchange Quarterly,* Vol. 21, No. 96 (Winter 1980): and in *Heritage,* Vol. 17, No. 3 (Jul 1990).
- "Census, 1885, Duval County, Florida," in *Southern Genealogists Exchange Quarterly,* Vol. 22, No. 97 (Spring 1981).
- Jackson County. 1885 name list serially published in *Southern Genealogists Exchange Quarterly,* beginning with Vol. 18, No. 83 (Fall 1977).
- Liberty County. 1885 name list published in *Southern Genealogists Exchange Quarterly,* Vol. 25, No. 109 (March 1984).
- Orange County. 1885 name list published in *Buried Treasures,* beginning with Vol. 24, No. 2 (Apr 1992) through Vol. 29, No. 2 (April 1997).
- Putnam County. 1885 name list published in *Putnam County Genealogical Society Quarterly Journal,* beginning with No. 20 (Apr 1994).
- Wakulla County. 1885 name list in *Southern Genealogists Exchange Quarterly,* Vol. 21, No. 94 (Summer 1980).
- Washington County. 1885 name list in *Florida Genealogist,* Vol. 16, No. 4 (Fall 1993).

- See also, ***Addendum to the 1885 Florida State Census Index*** **[Printed Index & Digital Capture].** An every-name index to 312,551 entries in the 1885 Florida State Census was compiled and published by William T. Martin and Patricia Martin of Miami, FL in 1991. There is no copy of this index at the Family History Library (a copy is known to be at the Jacksonville Public Library and may be in several other Florida libraries as well). This *Addendum* edition allows a conversion of page numbers due to differences in the originals. Digitized by the Genealogical Society of Utah, 2012. For access to the digital version, see the online FHL catalog page:
**www.familysearch.org/search/catalog/2709503.**

***1885-1886 Pensacola City Directory*** **[Online Database],** indexed at the RootsWeb site for Escambia Co FL. See
**www.rootsweb.ancestry.com/~flwfgs/escambiacountyfl/directories/1885directory/directindex1885.htm.**

**1885-1954.** ***Confederate Pension Application Index: Dade County, Florida; Monroe County, Florida; Broward County, Florida*** **[Printed Index],** compiled by Harriet Stiger Liles; typed by Deborah Bond Baker. Lists name and file number. Published by the Genealogical Society of Greater Miami, Miami, FL, 1999, 5 pages, FHL book 975.9 M22L.

**1885-1955.** See ***Pension Claims of Confederate Veterans and Their Widows Beginning 1885-1955*** **[Microfilm & Digital Capture],** from the originals records at the Florida State Archives, Tallahassee, FL. Includes index. Filmed by the Genealogical Society of Utah, 1955, 169 rolls, beginning with FHL film #6717

(Index of Pensioners, Widows of pensioners and denied pension claims). For a complete list of roll numbers, roll contents, and the digital images of each roll, see the online FHL catalog page for this title:
**www.familysearch.org/search/catalog/294522.**

**1885-1955.** ***Florida Confederate Pension Application Files*** **[Online Database],** digitized and indexed by name and application number at the Florida Memory collections of the Florida State Archives website. A printable list is available, or a search/browse screen for one person:
**http://floridamemory.com/collections/pensionfiles.**

**1885-1955.** ***Florida Confederate Veterans and Widows Pension Applications*** **[Online Database],** digitized at the FamilySearch.org website. This is an image-only database of applications for pensions filed by Confederate veterans and widows living in Florida. Taken from the Florida State Comptroller's Office files, now located at the Florida State Archives and microfilmed for the FHL library in Salt Lake City, UT. This database has 101,513 images. See
**https://familysearch.org/search/collection/1913411.**
- This image-only database is also available at Ancestry.com. See
**https://search.ancestry.com/search/db.aspx?dbid=60262.**

**1885-1955.** ***Register of Florida CSA Pension Applications*** **[Printed Index],** transcribed by Virgil D. White, published by National Historical Pub. Co., Waynesboro, TN, 1989, 278 pages, FHL book 975.9 M2w.

**1885-1970 Florida City Directories,** as part of ***U.S. City Directories, 1822-1995*** **[Online Database],** digitized and OCR indexed at the Ancestry.com website. See each directory title page image for the full title and publication information. This collection is one of the largest single databases on the Internet. All states are represented (except Alaska) with a total of 1.56 billion names, all indexed from scanned images of the city directory book pages. Florida directories are listed here for a Florida City (No. of years), and Date-Range: **Arcadia** (5) 1915-1926, **Bartow** (6) 1925-1960, **Boca Raton** (5) 1956-1960, **Bradenton** (16) 1921-1960, **Brooksville** (1) 1926, **Clearwater** (18) 1920-1960, **Daytona Beach** (10) 1914-1957, **Fort Lauderdale** (13) 1936-1960, **DeLand** (16) 1924-1960, **Delray Beach** (6) 1948-1959, **Eustis** (5) 1924-1960, **Fort Myers** (18) 1915-1960, **Fort Pierce** (18) 1916-1960, **Gainesville** (17) 1915-1960, **Hollywood** (10) 1942-1960, **Homestead** (1) 1927, **Jacksonville** (65) 1885-1960, **Key West** (8) 1887-1927, **Lake Worth** (2) 1944-1946, **Lakeland** (26) 1915-1960, **Miami** (44) 1904-1960, **Miami Beach** (5) 1955-1960, **New Port Richey** (2) 1957-1959, **New Smyrna** (1) 1926), **New Smyrna Beach** (8) 1947-1960, **Ocala** (20) 1908-1960, **Orlando** (37) 1915-1960, **Palatka** (10) 1915-1960, **Panama City** (9) 1935-1960, **Pensacola** (34) 1885-1960, **Perry** (2) 1956-1960, **Plant City** (4) 1956-1959, **Pompano Beach** (1955-1970), **Punta Gorda** (2) 1958-1959, **Sanford** (13) 1909-1960), **Sarasota** (17) 1926-1960, **St. Augustine** (20) 1911-1960, **St. Petersburg** (37) 1914-1957, **Tallahassee** (8) 1904-1936, **Tampa** (32) 1899-1936, **West Palm Beach** (28) 1915-1953, and Winter Park (1) 1937. Use Ancestry's *Browse this Collection* feature to choose a state, choose a city, and choose a directory year available for that city.
**https://search.ancestry.com/search/db.aspx?dbid=2469.**

**1885-1955.** ***Confederate Pension Applications Files Index, Florida Counties*** **[Online Database],** indexed at various USGenWeb sites for Florida counties. At the FL state home page, click on a county to access the databases, then click on "Military." See "Military-Civil War" for access to an index to Pension Applications for that county. See
**http://usgwarchives.net/fl/flfiles.htm#counties.**

***1887-1892 General Index to Land Grants, DeSoto County, Florida*** **[Online Database],** indexed at the USGenWeb site for DeSoto Co FL. See
**http://files.usgwarchives.net/fl/desoto/land/landgrnt.txt.**

***1887-1945 Delayed Birth Certificates, DeSoto County, Florida*** **[Online Database],** extracted at the USGenWeb site for DeSoto Co FL. See **www.fl-genweb.org/decole/desoto/New%20Down/delaybirth.html.**

**1888-1893.** ***Jacksonville, Florida Directories*** **[Online Database],** indexed at the Ancestry.com website. Source: Wanton S. Webb Directories, 1888-1893. Each index record includes Name, Location 1, City, State, Occupation, Year, Business name, and Location 2. This database has 48,246 records. See
**https://search.ancestry.com/search/db.aspx?dbid=4863.**

***1888-1893 Births, Volusia County, Florida*** **[Online Database],** indexed at the Volusia Genealogy site. See
**www.volusiagenealogy.net/old_births.htm.**

**1888-1938.** ***Florida, Old Confederate Soldiers and Sailors Home Records*** **[Online Database],** indexed at the FamilySearch.org website. Index includes name of soldier, city and county of residence, and military unit of each soldier. Index provided by the State Archives of Florida. This database has 164 records. See
**www.familysearch.org/search/collection/2761956**.

***1890 List of Registered Voters, Hillsborough County, Florida* [Online Database],** indexed at the USGenWeb site for Hillsborough Co FL. See **http://files.usgwarchives.net/fl/hillsborough/history.**

**1890-1914. *Adoptions, Apprenticeships and Indentures, Lake County, Florida* [Microfilm],** from the original records at the Lake County Courthouse, Tavares, FL. Filmed by the Genealogical Society of Utah, 1993, 1 roll, FHL film #1871107. To see if this microfilm has been digitized yet, see the FHL catalog page: **www.familysearch.org/search/catalog/632301.**

**1890-1924. *Index to Passenger Lists of Vessels Arriving at Miscellaneous Ports in Alabama, Florida, Georgia, and South Carolina* [Microfilm & Digital Capture],** from the original records at the National Archives, Washington, DC. This database is a combined index to passenger arrivals in four states. Filmed by the Immigration and Naturalization Service, 1957, National Archives series T517, 26 rolls, beginning with FHL film #1324938 (Index: Aabott, Leonard - Anderson, Julia F.). To access the digital images, see the online FHL catalog page: **www.familysearch.org/search/catalog/341257.**

***1891-1902 Guardian's Bonds, Book A, DeSoto County, Florida [Online Database],*** indexed at the USGenWeb site for DeSoto Co FL. See **http://files.usgwarchives.net/fl/desoto/history/gbonds.txt.**

***1892 School Census, St. Augustine, Florida* [Online Database],** indexed at the RootsWeb site for St. Augustine, FL. See **www.rootsweb.ancestry.com/~flsags/1893stjohnscountyschoolcensus.htm.**

***1893-1894 Pensacola City Directory* [Online Database],** indexed at the RootsWeb site for Escambia Co FL. See **www.rootsweb.ancestry.com/~flwfgs/escambiacountyfl/directories/1893directory/directindex1893.htm.**

***1895 State Census, Nassau County, Florida* [Printed Index],** compiled by the Jacksonville Genealogical Society, 1976, 236 pages. Includes index. See FHL book 975.911 X2j.

***1895 State Census, Nassau County, Florida* [Online Database],** originally indexed at the Amelia Island Genealogical Society website. For an archived database, see **https://web.archive.org/web/20141020203859/www.aigensoc.org/1895.asp.**

**1895. *Fernandina, Nassau County, Florida Census 1895* [Printed Book & Digital Version],** from a typescript of the original census entries taken by the enumerator John M. Thompson. Census information is listed in columns by dwellings he visited, includes surname, age, marital status, occupation and birthplace, 217 pages, FHL book 975.911 X2tjmTo access the digital version, see the online FHL catalog page: **https://www.familysearch.org/search/catalog/2524517.**

**1895-1945. *Vital Records Card File for North Florida and South Georgia* [Microfilm],** from records at the Jacksonville Branch Genealogical Library, Jacksonville, FL. Contains birth, death, and marriage records from newspapers and cemeteries. Filmed by the Genealogical Society of Utah, 1977, 1980, 17 rolls, beginning with FHL film #1204579 (A – Bigelow, Mary). To see if this microfilm has been digitized yet, see the FHL catalog page: **www.familysearch.org/search/catalog/307648.**

**1896-1924. *Census of School Age Youth (6-12 years of age), 1896-1924* [Microfilm & Digital Capture],** from the original records at the Florida State Archives, Tallahassee, FL. Bound volumes listing school age children in Baker, Dade, Duval, Escambia, Palm Beach, Pasco, Polk, St. Lucie, and Volusia counties. From guide: "Generally included is the name of the student, school district, age, sex, level of reading skills, degree of literacy, and physical disabilities." Filmed by the Genealogical Society of Utah, 2 rolls, beginning with FHL film #1672587. To access the digital images, see the online FHL catalog page: **www.familysearch.org/search/catalog/538091.**

***1897-1918 Voter Lists, Lee County, Florida* [Online Database],** indexed at the USGenWeb site for Lee Co FL. See **http://files.usgwarchives.net/fl/lee/history/voters.**

**1898. *Compiled Service Records of Volunteer Soldiers Who Served in the Florida Infantry During the War with Spain* [Microfilm],** from the original records at the National Archives, Washington, DC. From Intro: "Includes card abstracts of entries relating to the soldiers as found primarily in original muster rolls and regimental returns, and occasionally in such other records as medical and assignment cards, and originals of any papers relating solely to individual soldiers, such as enlistment, discharge, requests for leaves of absence and furloughs, etc. The compiled

service records are arranged alphabetically by surname of soldier. Preceding the jacket-envelopes for individual soldiers are envelopes containing record-of-events cards for the field and staff offices and for each company. These cards are abstracts of information found on muster rolls and regimental returns, which indicate the stations, movements, and activities of the regiment from the time of its organization to its disbandment. Card abstracts for an individual soldier show his rank; the company in which he served; when, where, and how long he served; and any payment due him, either as salary or compensation. In addition, abstracts of descriptive lists give the soldier's age, physical description, date and place of birth, residence, occupation, marital status, and name of next of kin. Medical card abstracts show any type of illness incurred, length of illness, where the soldier recuperated or was transferred to, and the date of return to active duty." Filmed by the National Archives, 1979, Series M1087, 13 rolls, beginning with FHL film #1314126 (Record of event service records, A-Bo). To see if this microfilm has been digitized yet, see the FHL catalog page:
**www.familysearch.org/search/catalog/36143.**

**1898.** ***Florida, Spanish American War Compiled Service Records*** **[Online Database],** digitized and indexed at the Ancestry.com website. Source: National Archive microfilm M1087. Each index record includes: Name, Age, Birth year, Birth place, Enlistment date, Enlistment place, Company, and Regiment. The document image may have more information. This database has 1,401 records. See
**https://search.ancestry.com/search/db.aspx?dbid=2135.**

**1898-1945.** ***Florida, Key West Passenger Lists*** **[Online Database],** digitized and indexed at the FamilySearch.org website. Source: National Archives microfilm T940. Includes passenger lists of those arriving at Key West, FL. Each index record includes: Name, Event type, Event date, Event place, Gender, Age, Birth year, and Ship name. The document image may have more information. This database has 223,879 records. See
**https://familysearch.org/search/collection/1916042.**

**1898-1945.** ***Florida, Tampa, Passenger Lists*** **[Online Database],** digitized and indexed at the FamilySearch.org website. Source: National Archives microfilm M1844. This is a name index and images of passenger lists for those arriving in Tampa, November 2, 1898-December 30, 1945 (with some gaps in years). Each index record includes: Name, Event type, Event date, Event place, Gender, Age, Birth year, and Ship name. The document image may have more information. This database has 92,575 records:
**https://familysearch.org/search/collection/1916082.**

**1898-1963.** ***Florida, Passenger Lists*** **[Online Database],** digitized and indexed at the Ancestry.com website. This database is an index to passenger lists of ships and airplanes arriving from foreign ports at various Florida ports. The index includes the following ports: Tampa, St. Petersburg, Pensacola, Knights Key, Port Everglades, Key West, Jacksonville, Miami, Panama City, West Palm Beach, and Apalachicola-Boynton-Boca Grande-Carrabelle- Fernandina-Fort Pierce-Hobe Sound-Lake Worth- Mayport-Millville-Port Inglis-Port St. Joe-St. Andrews, and Stuart, Florida. The names found in the index are linked to actual images of the passenger lists, from the National Archives microfilm. Information in this index varies according to the type of form used. Generally, the following information is included: 1) Given name and surname of passenger. 2) Age, 3) Sex, 4) Ethnicity or nationality, 5) Birthplace, 6) Last residence, 7) Name of friend or relative, 8) Final destination, 9) Port of departure, 10) Port of arrival, 11) Date of arrival (or departure). This database has 8,390,606 records. See
**http://search.ancestry.com/search/db.aspx?dbid=8842.**

***1899-1907 Lunacy Book 1, DeSoto County, Florida*** **[Online Database],** indexed at the USGenWeb site for DeSoto Co FL. See
**http://files.usgwarchives.net/fl/desoto/history/lunacy.txt.**

**1900.** ***Florida, 1900 Federal Census: Soundex and Population Schedules*** **[Microfilm & Digital Capture],** from the original records held by the Bureau of the Census in the 1940s. After microfilming, Congress allowed the Census Bureau to destroy the originals to free up space for WWII-related files. Filmed on 75 rolls, beginning with FHL film #1242637 (Soundex, A000-A436), and FHL film #1240165 (Population schedules, Alachua Co). For a complete list of roll numbers, roll contents, and the digital images of each roll (mostly population schedules), see the online FHL catalog page:
**www.familysearch.org/search/catalog/648022.**

***1900-1908 Marriages, Levy County, Florida*** **[Online Database],** indexed at the USGenWeb site for Levy Co FL. See
**http://files.usgwarchives.net/fl/levy/vitals/marriages/1900-08.txt.**

**1900-1921.** ***Florida Deaths and Burials*** **[Online Database],** indexed at the FamilySearch.org website. Source: Data from various FamilySearch and Family History Library sources. Each index record includes: Name, Gender, Burial date, Burial place, Death date, Death place, Age, Birth date, Birthplace, Occupation, Race, Marital status, Spouse's name, Father's name, Father's birthplace, Mother's name, Mother's birthplace, and FHL film number. This database has 24,800 records. See
**https://familysearch.org/search/collection/1674803.**

**1900-1945.** ***Florida, Pensacola, Passenger Lists*** **[Online Database],** indexed at the FamilySearch.org website. Source: National Archives microfilm A3666. This is an image-only database. The records usually include full name, age, gender, marital status, occupation, citizenship, race, last permanent residence, birthplace, and final destination. This database has 1,937 images. Browse the images, organized by Roll Number and Date Range. See
**www.familysearch.org/search/collection/2442761.**

***1908 Voter List, Escambia County, Florida*** **[Online Database],** indexed at the RootsWeb site for Escambia Co FL. See
**www.rootsweb.ancestry.com/~flwfgs/escambiacountyfl/people/voters1908.htm.**

**1908-1912.** ***Florida, Knights Keys Passenger Lists*** **[Online Database],** digitized and indexed at the FamilySearch.org website. Source: National Archives microfilm A3371: *Passenger Lists of Vessels Arriving at Knights Key, Florida, February 1908-January 1912.* Each index record includes: Name, Event type, Event date, Event place, Gender, Age, Birth year, Birth Country, and Ship name. The document image may have more information. This database has 4,010 records. See
**www.familysearch.org/search/collection/2421846.**

***1908-1945 Homestead & Exemption Record, Book 1, DeSoto County, Florida*** **[Online Database],** indexed at the USGenWeb site for DeSoto Co FL. See
**http://files.usgwarchives.net/fl/desoto/land/homestd.txt.**

**1910.** ***Florida, 1910 Federal Census: Soundex and Population Schedules*** **[Microfilm & Digital Capture],** from the original records held by the Bureau of the Census in the 1940s. After microfilming, Congress allowed the Census Bureau to destroy the originals to free up space for WWII- related files. Filmed on 98 rolls, beginning with FHL film #1369552 (Soundex: A000-A425), and FHL film #1374171 (Population schedules: Clay, Dade, Columbia, Desoto, Franklin, and Duval Co). For a complete list of roll numbers, roll contents, and the digital image of each roll (mostly population schedules), see the online FHL catalog page for this title. See
**www.familysearch.org/search/catalog/647830.**

***1910 Florida Federal Census Index*** **[Printed Index],** compiled by William T. Martin and Patricia Thomas Martin. Lists name of resident and page number of census. Contents: Vol. 1: Duval Co, Vol. 2: Clay and Dade Counties, Vol. 3. Columbia, DeSoto, and Franklin Cos, Vol. 4. Brevard Co, Vol. 5. Baker Co. Published by W.T. Martin, Miami, FL, 1989, FHL book 975.9 X22m 1910. V.1-5.

**1910.** ***Florida 1910 Census Index*** **[Printed Index],** compiled and published by Heritage Quest, North Salt Lake, UT, 2002, 2 vols., FHL book 975.9 X22f 1910.

**1911.** ***Founding Citizens of Ft. Lauderdale – 1911*** **/Online Database],** indexed at the USGenWeb site for Broward Co FL. See
**http://files.usgwarchives.net/fl/broward/history/1911ftla.txt.**

**1913-1946.** ***Naturalization Records, Miami, Florida*** **[Microfilm & Digital Capture],** from the originals at the National Archives. Filmed by the Genealogical Society of Utah, 1987-1998, 16 rolls, beginning with FHL film #1481412 (Declarations, 1913-1916). For a complete list of roll numbers, roll contents, and the digital images of all rolls, see the online FHL catalog page for this title:
**www.familysearch.org/search/catalog/667563.**

***1913-1991 Florida, Petitions for Naturalization*** **[Online Database],** indexed at the Ancestry.com website. This database is from the U.S. District Court for the Miami Division of the Southern District of Florida. Information may include a name, age, date of birth, nationality, residence/address, marital status, gender, physical description, occupation, spouse's name, marriage date and place, spouse's birth date and birthplace, number of children, children's names, gender, and date and place of birth; date admitted to the U.S., name change information, alien registration number, ship name or mode of arrival, port or place of arrival, date of arrival, event date, date of residence in the U.S., dates departed and returned to the U.S. during the residency requirement period, and names of witnesses. This database has 296,838 records. See
**http://search.ancestry.com/search/db.aspx?dbid=1850.**

**1915-1971.** ***Death Reports, Death Certificates and Inquests, Lake County, Florida*** **[Microfilm & Digital Capture],** from the originals at the Lake County Courthouse, Tavares, FL. Filmed by the Genealogical Society of Utah, 1993, 5 rolls, beginning with FHL film #1870904 (Index, A-Z 1915-1974). To access the digital images, see the online FHL catalog:
**www.familysearch.org/search/catalog/632025.**

**1917-1918.** ***Florida, World War I Service Cards*** **[Online Database],** digitized and indexed at the Florida Memory collections of the Florida State Archives website. Over 42,000 Floridians served (35,829 U.S. Army; 5,963 U.S. Navy; and 238 U.S. Marine Corps). These records consist of cards showing for each person, a name, age, serial number, race; place of birth; and residence at the time of entering service, and other comments. A digital copy of the records can be downloaded from this site for no charge. A certified copy of the record is available for a fee from the FL State Archives. A search/browse screen is available online. See
**http://floridamemory.com/collections/wwi/.**
- This database is also available at the Family-Search.org website, see
**www.familysearch.org/search/collection/2761957.**

**1917-1918.** ***Florida, World War I Selective Service System Draft Registration Cards*** **[Microfilm & Digital Capture],** from the original records at the National Archives, East Point, GA. Filmed by the National Archives, 1987-1988, 40 rolls, beginning with FHL film #1556849 (Florida: Alachua County, A-Taylor, William Aaron). For a complete list of roll numbers, roll contents, and the digital images of each roll, see the online FHL catalog page for this title. See
**www.familysearch.org/search/catalog/751204.**

***1917-1918 WWI Civilian Draft Registration, Florida Counties*** **[Online Database],** indexed at the USGenWeb site for Florida. Click on a county to access the databases, then click on "Military" to access the Civilian Draft Registrations indexed for that county:
**http://usgwarchives.net/fl/flfiles.htm#counties.**

**1917-1919.** ***Florida, World War I American Expeditionary Forces, Deaths, 1917-1919*** **[Microfilm & Digital Capture],** digitized by FamilySearch International, 2018. To access the digital images, see the online FHL catalog page:
**www.familysearch.org/search/catalog/3023920.**

**1917-1920.** ***Florida, World War I Navy Card Roster*** **[Online Database],** digitized and indexed at FamilySearch.org. Index and images of a card roster of Floridians that served in the United States Navy during the First World War. This database has 5,950 records, see **www.familysearch.org/search/collection/3010015.**

**1919-1939.** ***Soldiers and Sailors Discharge Records, Lake County, Florida, 1919-1939*** **[Microfilm],** from the originals at the Lake County Courthouse, Tavares, FL. Filmed by the Genealogical Society of Utah, 1993, 1 roll, FHL film #1871107.

**1920.** ***Florida, 1920 Federal Census: Soundex and Population Schedules*** **[Microfilm & Digital Capture],** from the original records held by the Bureau of the Census in the 1940s. After microfilming, Congress allowed the Census Bureau to destroy the originals to free up space for WWII-related files. Filmed on 93 rolls, beginning with FHL film #1823983 (Soundex: A100-A131), and FHL film #1820214 (Alachua, Bradford, and Calhoun Co). For a complete list of roll numbers, roll contents, and the digital images of each roll (population schedules), see the online FHL catalog page for this title. See
**www.familysearch.org/search/catalog/567664.**

**1923-1930.** ***Births, Deaths, Marriages, Etc. From Hernando County, Florida Newspapers*** **[Online Index].** Indexed at the USGenWeb site for Hernando Co FL. See
**http://files.usgwarchives.net/fl/hernando/vitals/deaths.**

***1923-1933 & 1940 Poll Tax/Voter Lists, Indian River County, Florida*** **[Online Database],** indexed at the USGenWeb site for Indian River Co FL. See
**http://files.usgwarchives.net/fl/indianriver/history.**

**1924-1949 Florida City Directories,** as part of ***Ohio and Florida, City Directories*** **[Online Database],** digitized and indexed at the Ancestry.com website. This is a collection of city directories from 1902-1960 hat cover different cities and states in the U.S. The directories include private residents and their profession, as well as places of business. At this time, the collection includes directories for 1) the State of Florida, Jacksonville, and St. Augustine, and 2) the State of Ohio, Lorain County, including Ohio state farm directories. The directories are searchable by name, year and location and the index contains: City, Name, Other locations, Occupation, and Business

name. Additional information from the images may include: Personal street address, Rent or own home, Marital status, Business address, and a Spousal reference. This database has 4.912,472 records. See
**https://search.ancestry.com/search/db.aspx?dbid=1988.**

**1927-1950.** ***Report of Divorces Granted and Report of Marriages Annulled*** **[Microfilm & Digital Capture],** images of the originals at the Florida Dept. of Health, Vital Statistics, Jacksonville, FL. Arranged by year and number as filed by a Circuit Court Clerk, arranged alphabetically by county within each year, but some dates are out of order, or range of dates are approximate. Filmed by the FL Vital Statistic Office, c1990, 141 rolls, beginning with FHL film #1913900 (Vol. 1-5, 1927-1928). To access the digital images, see the online FHL catalog page:
**www.familysearch.org/search/catalog/655313.**
- See also, ***Florida Combined Divorce and Annulment Index, 1927-1969*** [Microfiche], from the original records at the Florida Dept. of Health, Vital Statistics, Jacksonville, FL. Includes name, volume, certificate number, county, and date. Filmed by the Genealogical Society of Utah, 1991, 143 microfiche, beginning FHL fiche #6081683 (1927, 2 fiche).

**1927-1960.** ***Naturalization Records, Tampa, Florida*** **[Microfilm & Digital Capture],** from the originals at the National Archives. Filmed by the Genealogical Society of Utah, 1987-1989, 14 rolls, beginning with FHL film #1491858 (Declarations, 1909-1912). To access the digital images, see the online FHL catalog:
**www.familysearch.org/search/catalog/667566.**

**1927-1969.** ***Florida Combined Marriage Index*** **[Microfiche],** from the original records at the Florida Dept. of Health-Vital Statistics, Jacksonville, FL. Includes name of bride and groom, place of marriage, volume, number, and year of marriage. Filmed by the Genealogical Society of Utah, 1991, 471 microfiche, beginning with FHL fiche #6081726 (1927 – 6 fiches). For a complete list of fiche numbers and contents of each, see the online FHL catalog page for this title.
**www.familysearch.org/search/catalog/497719.**

**1927-2001.** ***Florida Divorce Index*** **[Online Database],** digitized and indexed at the FamilySearch.org website. This database has 3,012,178 records. See
**https://familysearch.org/search/collection/1967745.**
- for the Ancestry.com version, see
**http://search.ancestry.com/search/db.aspx?dbid=8837.**

***1928 Potential Jurors for Baker County, Florida*** **[Online Database],** indexed at the RootsWeb site for Baker Co FL. See
**www.rootsweb.ancestry.com/~flbakehs/1928JurorList.html.**

***1928, 1934, 1940 Voter/Jury Lists, Hendry County, Florida*** **[Online Database],** indexed at the USGenWeb site for Hendry Co FL. See
**http://files.usgwarchives.net/fl/hendry/history.**

**1928-1950.** ***Marriage Licenses and Certificates of Florida*** **[Microfilm & Digital Capture],** from the original records at the Dept. of Health – Vital Statistics, Jacksonville, FL. An index to these records is in a separate title, shown above. Filmed by the Dept. of Health-Vital Statistics Office, 1985-1986, 148 rolls, beginning with FHL film #2115679 (Delayed marriage certificates, 1928-1946). For a complete list of roll numbers, roll contents, and the digital images of each roll, see the online FHL catalog page for this title. See
**www.familysearch.org/search/catalog/824455.**

**1930.** ***Florida, 1930 Federal Census: Soundex and Population Schedules*** **[Microfilm & Digital Capture],** from the original records held by the Bureau of the Census in the 1940s. After microfilming, Congress allowed the Census Bureau to destroy the originals to free up space for WWII-related files. Filmed on 128 rolls, beginning with FHL film #2338295 (Soundex: A-000-A-415), and FHL film #2340041 (Alachua, Baker, and Bay Cos.). To access the digital images, see the online FHL catalog:
**www.familysearch.org/search/catalog/1035334.**

***1930-1942 Index to Alien Arrivals by Airplane at Miami, Florida*** **[Online Database],** indexed at the Ancestry.com website. The index cards to air passenger manifests of alien arrivals at Miami, Florida, that make up this database are Form 548, "Manifest or Report of Inspection," used by the Immigration Service. According to the National Archives, "At many ports, the Immigration and Naturalization Service (INS) normally used this card as a complete record of all the information about an alien's arrival. In this instance, the INS used it as an index card containing most, if not all, of the information on related airplane passenger lists." The cards ask more than two dozen questions and will generally contain a person's name, age, sex, marital status, place of birth, physical description, occupation, citizenship (nationality), race, ability to read and write and in what language, place of last permanent residence, port and date of arrival, final destination, and purpose for entering the U.S. They can also include the

name and address of a friend or relative the alien intended to meet up with, people who were accompanying the traveler, and the name and address of the aliens nearest relative or friend in the country from which he or she came. On the back of the card is a medical certificate where any medical concerns an inspector had might be noted, as well as other remarks and endorsements. Records can be searched by date of arrival, name, estimated birth year, gender, country of birth, and race, or they can be browsed by surname. This database has 51,624 records. See
**http://search.ancestry.com/search/db.aspx?dbid=1959.**

**1930-1997.** ***Lee County, Florida, Obituary Index*** **[Online Database],** indexed at the Ancestry.com website. Original data: *Lee County Deaths.* Lee County Genealogical Society. Each index record includes: Name, Death date, Publication title, Publication or record date, Publication or record place, and a link to the Lee Co GS website. This database has 72,956 records. See
**https://search.ancestry.com/search/db.aspx?dbid=70654.**

**1932-1951.** ***Florida, Port Everglades Passenger Lists*** **[Online Database],** digitized and indexed at the FamilySearch.org website. Source: National Archives microfilm A3394: Passenger Lists of Vessels and Airplanes Arriving at Port Everglades, Florida, February 1932-May 1951. Each index record includes: Name, Event type, Event date, Event place, Gender, Age, Birth year, and Birthplace. The document image may have more information. This database has 24,375 records:
**www.familysearch.org/search/collection/2421845.**

***1935 Florida State Census*** **[Microfilm & Digital Capture],** from the originals at the Florida State Archives, Tallahassee, FL. The name lists include a name, address, inside or outside of city limits, age, sex, race, relation to family, place of birth (state or country), degree of education, own or rent home, and occupation. Filmed by the Florida State Archives, 1986-1987, 30 rolls, beginning with FHL film #2425147 (Alachua Co). To access the digital images, see the online FHL catalog page:
**www.familysearch.org/search/catalog/1417054.**
- See also, ***Florida State Census, 1935*** **[Online Database],** digitized and indexed at the FamilySearch.org website. The records are organized alphabetically by county, then election precinct. All Florida counties are represented, although there are a few missing election precincts. This database has 1,599,085 records. See
**https://familysearch.org/search/collection/1457856.**

**1939-1945.** ***Florida, Fort Lauderdale Crew Lists*** **[Online Database],** digitized at the FamilySearch.org website. Source: National Archives microfilm A4233: *Crew Lists of Vessels Arriving at Fort Lauderdale, Florida, December 1939-December 1945.* This is an image-only database. The records usually include the name of the vessel, ports and dates of departure and each crew member's full name, position in ship's company, age, gender, race, nationality This database has 10,103 images. Browse the images, organized by roll number and date range:
**www.familysearch.org/search/collection/2432943.**

**1939-1945.** ***World War II Honor List of Dead and Missing, State of Florida*** **[Microfilm & Digital Capture],** from a manuscript at the Florida State Archives, Tallahassee, FL. Filmed by the Genealogical Society of Utah, 1976, 1 roll, FHL film #988193. To access the digital images, see the online FHL catalog page: **www.familysearch.org/search/catalog/79519.**

**1940.** ***Florida, 1940 Federal Census: Population Schedules*** **[Digital Capture],** digitized images from the microfilm of original records held by the Bureau of the Census in the 1940s. After microfilming, Congress allowed the Census Bureau to destroy the originals to free up space for WWII-related files. Digitizing of the 1940 census schedules was done for the National Archives and made public in 2012. To access the digital images, see the online FHL catalog:
**www.familysearch.org/search/catalog/2057748.**

***1940 Federal Census Finding Aids*** **[Online Database].** As a guide to the release of the 1940 census to the public, the National Archives created a special website online with a detailed description of the 1940 federal census. Included at the site are descriptions of location-finding aids, such as Enumeration District (ED) Maps, Geographic Descriptions of Census EDs, and a list of 1940 City Directories available at the National Archives. This National Archives website also has a link to Search Engines using Stephen P. Morse's "One-Step" system for finding a 1940 E.D., or for a street address conversion. See
**www.archives.gov/research/census/1940/general-info.html#questions.**

**1940-1947.** ***Florida, World War II Draft Registration Cards*** **[Digital Capture],** from the original cards at the National Personnel Records Center, St. Louis, MO. Microfilm no longer available, all 508 rolls were

digitized by the Genealogical Society of Utah, 2016. The cards contain detailed vital information about the person. To access the digital images, see the online FHL catalog page:
**www.familysearch.org/search/catalog/2695955.**
- See also, ***Florida, World War II Draft Registration Cards [Online Database],*** digitized and indexed at FamilySearch.org. Draft registration cards of men who registered during World War II, with the exception of the fourth registration. Images courtesy of Ancestry. The event place is the residence of the registrant. This database has 536,621 records, see
**www.familysearch.org/search/collection/2695955.**

**1941. *Guide to Public Vital Statistics Records in Florida* [Online Database],** indexed at the Ancestry.com website. Source: Works Progress Administration (WPA) Survey, publ. Jacksonville, FL, 1941. This WPA guide is an invaluable reference tool, listing the availability of birth, marriage, and death records for Florida at the state level and for each county, as of 1941. Original vital records books are identified for each county by the volume number and date range. This database has 74 pages.. See
**https://search.ancestry.com/search/db.aspx?dbid=29834.**

***1941-1945 WWII Army Enlistments* [Online Database],** indexed at the various USGenWeb sites for the Florida counties: Click on a county to access the databases, then click on "Military" to access the WWII Army Enlistments indexed for that county. See
**http://usgwarchives.net/fl/flfiles.htm#counties.**

**1944-1945. *Florida and South Carolina, Airplane Arrival Manifests* [Online Database],** indexed at the FamilySearch.org website. Source: National Archives microfilm A4234: *Arrival Manifests of Airplanes Arriving at Boca Chica, Fort Lauderdale, Jacksonville, Key West, Miami, Orlando, Pensacola, and Tampa, Florida, and at Charleston, South Carolina.* The date range spans from 17 April 1944 to 27 December 1945. This is an image-only database. The records may include full name, age, gender, marital status, citizenship, last permanent residence, birthplace, and final destination. This database has 127 images. Browse the images, organized by roll number and date range. See
**www.familysearch.org/search/collection/2443942.**

***1945 Florida State Census* [Microfilm & Digital Capture],** from the originals at the Florida State Archives, Tallahassee, FL. The name lists include a name, address, inside or outside of city limits, age, sex, race, relation to family, place of birth (state or country), degree of education, own or rent home, and occupation. Filmed by the Florida State Archives, 1986-1987, 43 rolls, beginning with FHL film #2425176 (Alachua Co). To access the digital images, see the online FHL catalog page:
**www.familysearch.org/search/catalog/1417055.**
- See also, ***Florida State Census, 1945* [Online Database],** digitized and indexed at the FamilySearch.org website. The records are organized alphabetically by county, then election precinct. All Florida counties are represented, although there are a few missing election precincts. This database has 2,249,138 records. See
**https://familysearch.org/search/collection/1457855.**

**1950-1957. *Florida U.S. Military Personnel Who Died From Hostile Action in the Korean War, 1950-1957 (Including Missing and Captured)* [Digital Capture],** from a Journal Article, covers Alachua County to Charlotte County, to be continued in next issue (not included). To access a digital version of this article, see the online FHL catalog page:
**www.familysearch.org/search/catalog/1842624.**

**1982-Current. *Florida Newspaper Obituaries* [Online Database],** digitized and indexed at the GenealogyBank.com website. One search screen for obituaries published in over 65 city newspapers: Apalachicola Carrabelle, Arcadia, Aventura, et al, to West Palm Beach, Williston, Winter Garden, and Winter Haven, Florida. See
**www.genealogybank.com/gbnk/obituaries/explore/USA/Florida.**